THE CAMBRIDGE HISTORY OF
MODERN EUROPEAN THOUGHT

*

VOLUME II:
The Twentieth Century

This second volume of *The Cambridge History of Modern European Thought* surveys twentieth-century European intellectual history, conceived as a crisis in modernity. Comprised of twenty-one chapters, it focuses on figures such as Freud, Heidegger, Adorno, and Arendt, surveys major schools of thought including Phenomenology, Existentialism, and Conservatism, and discusses critical movements such as Postcolonialism, Structuralism, and Poststructuralism. Renouncing a single "master narrative" of European thought across the period, Peter E. Gordon and Warren Breckman establish a formidable new multi-faceted vision of European intellectual history for the global modern age.

PETER E. GORDON is Amabel B. James Professor of History at Harvard University. He is a resident faculty member at Harvard's Minda de Gunzburg Center for European Studies, and has held fellowships from the Princeton Society of Fellows and the Davis Center at Princeton University. He is the award-winning author of *Rosenzweig and Heidegger: Between Judaism and German Philosophy* (2003), *Continental Divide: Heidegger, Cassirer, Davos* (2010), and *Adorno and Existence* (2016) and co-editor of several books, including *The Routledge Companion to the Frankfurt School*, with Espen Hammer and Axel Honneth (2018).

WARREN BRECKMAN is the Sheldon and Lucy Hackney Professor of History at the University of Pennsylvania, where he has taught since 1995. He is the author of *Marx, the Young Hegelians, and the Origins of Radical Social Theory* (1999), *European Romanticism: A Brief History with Documents* (2008), and *Adventures of the Symbolic: Postmarxism and Radical Democracy* (2013). He served as co-editor of the *Journal of the History of Ideas* (2006–2016), and co-edited the volume *The Modernist Imagination: Essays in Intellectual History and Critical Theory* (2008), also with Peter E. Gordon.

THE CAMBRIDGE HISTORY OF
MODERN EUROPEAN THOUGHT

The Cambridge History of Modern European Thought is an authoritative and comprehensive exploration of the themes, thinkers, and movements that shaped our intellectual world from the late eighteenth century to the present. Representing both individual figures and the contexts within which they developed their ideas, this two-volume history is rich with original interpretive insight, and is written in a clear and accessible style by leading scholars in the field.

Renouncing a single "master narrative" of European thought across the period, Warren Breckman and Peter E. Gordon establish a formidable new multi-faceted vision of European intellectual history for the global modern age.

VOLUME I
The Nineteenth Century
EDITED BY WARREN BRECKMAN AND PETER E. GORDON

VOLUME II
The Twentieth Century
EDITED BY PETER E. GORDON AND WARREN BRECKMAN

THE CAMBRIDGE
HISTORY OF
MODERN EUROPEAN THOUGHT

*

VOLUME II
The Twentieth Century

*

Edited by
PETER E. GORDON
Harvard University

WARREN BRECKMAN
University of Pennsylvania

CAMBRIDGE
UNIVERSITY PRESS

CAMBRIDGE
UNIVERSITY PRESS

University Printing House, Cambridge CB2 8BS, United Kingdom

One Liberty Plaza, 20th Floor, New York, NY 10006, USA

477 Williamstown Road, Port Melbourne, VIC 3207, Australia

314–321, 3rd Floor, Plot 3, Splendor Forum, Jasola District Centre,
New Delhi – 110025, India

79 Anson Road, #06–04/06, Singapore 079906

Cambridge University Press is part of the University of Cambridge.

It furthers the University's mission by disseminating knowledge in the pursuit of
education, learning, and research at the highest international levels of excellence.

www.cambridge.org
Information on this title: www.cambridge.org/9781108677462
DOI: 10.1017/9781316160879

© Cambridge University Press 2019

This publication is in copyright. Subject to statutory exception
and to the provisions of relevant collective licensing agreements,
no reproduction of any part may take place without the written
permission of Cambridge University Press.

First published 2019
Paperback edition first published 2021

Printed in the United Kingdom by TJ Books Ltd, Padstow, Cornwall

A catalogue record for this publication is available from the British Library.

Library of Congress Cataloging-in-Publication Data
NAMES: Breckman, Warren, 1963– editor. | Gordon, Peter Eli, editor.
TITLE: The Cambridge history of modern European thought / edited by Warren Breckman,
Peter Gordon.
DESCRIPTION: Cambridge, United Kingdom ; New York, NY : Cambridge University Press, 2019–
| Includes bibliographical references. Contents: volume I. The nineteenth century.
IDENTIFIERS: LCCN 2018046335 | ISBN 9781107097759 (vol. 1) | ISBN 9781107097780 (vol. 2) |
ISBN 9781108677462 (set)
SUBJECTS: LCSH: Europe – Intellectual life – 19th century. | Europe – Intellectual life – 20th
century. | Philosophy, European – History.
CLASSIFICATION: LCC D359 .C226 2019 | DDC 190–dc23
LC record available at https://lccn.loc.gov/2018046335

Two Volume Set ISBN 978-1-108-67746-2 Hardback
Volume I ISBN 978-1-107-09775-9 Hardback
Volume II ISBN 978-1-107-09778-0 Hardback
Two Volume Set ISBN 978-1-108-67744-8 Paperback
Volume I ISBN 978-1-107-48376-7 Paperback
Volume II ISBN 978-1-107-48380-4 Paperback

Cambridge University Press has no responsibility for the persistence or accuracy of
URLs for external or third-party internet websites referred to in this publication
and does not guarantee that any content on such websites is, or will remain,
accurate or appropriate.

Contents

List of Contributors page vii
Preface xi

Introduction 1
PETER E. GORDON AND WARREN BRECKMAN

1 · Sociology and the Heroism of Modern Life 18
MARTIN JAY

2 · Psychoanalysis: Freud and Beyond 44
KATJA GUENTHER

3 · Modern Physics: From Crisis to Crisis 72
JIMENA CANALES

4 · Varieties of Phenomenology 102
DAN ZAHAVI

5 · Existentialism and the Meanings of Transcendence 128
EDWARD BARING

6 · Philosophies of Life 153
GIUSEPPE BIANCO

7 · The Many Faces of Analytic Philosophy 176
JOEL ISAAC

8 · American Ideas in the European Imagination 200
JAMES T. KLOPPENBERG AND SAM KLUG

9 · Revolution from the Right: Against Equality 233
UDI GREENBERG

Contents

10 · Western Marxism: Revolutions in Theory   259
MAX PENSKY

11 · Anti-imperialism and Interregnum   289
KRIS MANJAPRA

12 · Late Modern Feminist Subversions: Sex, Subjectivity, and Embodiment   311
SANDRINE SANOS

13 · Modernist Theologies: The Many Paths between God and World   336
PETER E. GORDON

14 · Modern Economic Thought and the "Good Society"   361
HAGEN SCHULZ-FORBERG

15 · Conservatism and Its Discontents   391
STEVEN B. SMITH

16 · Modernity and the Specter of Totalitarianism   417
SAMUEL MOYN

17 · Decolonization Terminable and Interminable   438
JUDITH SURKIS

18 · Structuralism and the Return of the Symbolic   464
CAMILLE ROBCIS

19 · Post-structuralism: From Deconstruction to the Genealogy of Power   490
JULIAN BOURG AND ETHAN KLEINBERG

20 · Contesting the Public Sphere: Within and against Critical Theory   517
DAVID INGRAM

21 · Restructuring Democracy and the Idea of Europe   545
SEYLA BENHABIB AND STEFAN EICH

Index   569

Contributors

EDWARD BARING is Associate Professor of European History at Drew University. He is the author of *The Young Derrida and French Philosophy, 1945–1968* (Cambridge University Press, 2011) and *Converts to the Real: Catholicism and the Making of Continental Philosophy* (Harvard University Press, 2019).

SEYLA BENHABIB is the Eugene Meyer Professor of Political Science and Philosophy at Yale University. Her recent books include *Exile, Statelessness, and Migration: Playing Chess with History from Hannah Arendt to Isaiah Berlin* (Princeton University Press, 2018) and *Dignity in Adversity: Human Rights in Troubled Times* (Polity Press, 2011).

GIUSEPPE BIANCO is a postdoctoral researcher at the Universidade de São Paulo and at the EHESS. His more recent books include *Après Bergson: Portrait de groupe avec philosophe* (Presses Universitaires de France, 2015), and he edited the volume *Georges Politzer, le concret et sa signification: Psychologie, philosophie et politique* (Hermann, 2016).

JULIAN BOURG is Associate Professor of History at Boston College. His books include, *From Revolution to Ethics: May 1968 and Contemporary French Thought* (McGill-Queen's University Press, 2007; rev. edn., 2017) and the edited collection *After the Deluge: New Perspectives on the Intellectual and Cultural History of Postwar France* (Lexington Books, 2004).

WARREN BRECKMAN is the Sheldon and Lucy Hackney Professor of Modern European Intellectual History at the University of Pennsylvania. He is the author of *Marx, the Young Hegelians, and the Origins of Radical Social Theory: Dethroning the Self* (Cambridge University Press, 1998) and *Adventures of the Symbolic: Postmarxism and Radical Democracy* (Columbia University Press, 2013), and he was the executive editor of *Journal of the History of Ideas* from 2006 to 2016.

JIMENA CANALES is faculty at the Graduate College of University of Illinois at Urbana-Champaign. Recent books include *A Tenth of a Second* (one of the *Guardian*'s Top 10 Books About Time) and *The Physicist and the Philosopher: Einstein, Bergson, and the Debate That Changed Our Understanding of Time* (Best Science Books 2015 Science Friday, NPR, and Brainpickings, Top Reads 2015, the *Independent*, Books of the Year 2016, the *Tablet*).

List of Contributors

STEFAN EICH is Perkins-Cotsen Postdoctoral Fellow in the Society of Fellows in the Liberal Arts at Princeton University.

PETER E. GORDON is Amabel B. James Professor of History and Faculty Affiliate in the Department of Philosophy at Harvard University. His more recent books include *Continental Divide: Heidegger, Cassirer, Davos* (Harvard University Press, 2010) and *Adorno and Existence* (Harvard University Press, 2016).

UDI GREENBERG is an associate professor of European history at Dartmouth College. He is the author of *The Weimar Century: German Émigrés and the Ideological Foundations of the Cold War* (Princeton University Press, 2014).

KATJA GUENTHER is Associate Professor in the History of Science at Princeton University. She published *Localization and Its Discontents: A Genealogy of Psychoanalysis and the Neuro Disciplines* (University of Chicago Press, 2015), and is currently completing a history of mirror self-recognition in the human sciences.

DAVID INGRAM is Professor of Philosophy at Loyola University Chicago. His most recent books are *World Crisis and Underdevelopment: A Critical Theory of Poverty, Agency, and Coercion* (Cambridge University Press, 2018) and *The Ethics of Development: An Introduction* (co-author Thomas Derdak) (Routledge, 2018).

JOEL ISAAC is Associate Professor of Social Thought in the John U. Nef Committee on Social Thought at the University of Chicago. He is the author of *Working Knowledge: Making the Human Sciences from Parsons to Kuhn* (Harvard University Press, 2012) and the co-editor of *The Worlds of American Intellectual History* (Oxford University Press, 2017).

MARTIN JAY is Ehrman Professor of European History Emeritus. Among his many books are *The Dialectical Imagination: A History of the Frankfurt School and the Institute of Social Research, 1923–50* (Little, Brown and Co., 1973) and, more recently, *Reason after its Eclipse: On Late Critical Theory* (University of Wisconsin Press, 2016).

ETHAN KLEINBERG is Professor of History and Letters at Wesleyan University. He is the author of *Haunting History: For a Deconstructive Approach to the Past* (Stanford University Press, 2017) and *Generation Existential: Heidegger's Philosophy in France, 1927–1961* (Cornell University Press, 2005).

JAMES T. KLOPPENBERG is Charles Warren Professor of American History at Harvard University. His recent books include *Reading Obama: Dreams, Hope, and the American Political Tradition*, 2nd edn. (Princeton University Press, 2011); *Toward Democracy: The Struggle for Self-Rule in European and American Thought* (Oxford University Press, 2016); and *The Worlds of American Intellectual History*, co-edited with Joel Isaac, Michael O'Brien, and Jennifer Ratner Rosenhagen (Oxford University Press, 2017).

SAM KLUG is a Ph.D. candidate in History at Harvard University and a Graduate Student Fellow at the Radcliffe Institute for Advanced Study. His dissertation is entitled "Making

List of Contributors

the Internal Colony: Black Internationalism, Development, and the Politics of Colonial Comparison in the United States, 1940–1975."

KRIS MANJAPRA is Associate Professor in the Department of History at Tufts University. His books include *M. N. Roy: Marxism and Colonial Cosmopolitanism* (Routledge, 2010), and *Age of Entanglement: German and Indian Intellectuals across Empire* (Harvard University Press, 2014).

SAMUEL MOYN is Professor of History at Yale University. His most recent book is *Not Enough: Human Rights in an Unequal World* (Harvard University Press, 2018).

MAX PENSKY is Professor of Philosophy at Binghamton University. His books include *Melancholy Dialectics: Walter Benjamin and the Play of Mourning* (University of Massachusetts Press, 1993) and *The Ends of Solidarity: Discourse Theory in Ethics and Politics* (SUNY Press, 2008).

CAMILLE ROBCIS is Associate Professor of French and History at Columbia University. She is the author of *The Law of Kinship: Anthropology, Psychoanalysis, and the Family in France* (Cornell University Press, 2013).

SANDRINE SANOS is Associate Professor of Modern European History at Texas A&M University – Corpus Christi. Her most recent publications include *The Aesthetics of Hate: Far-Right Intellectuals, Antisemitism, and Gender in 1930s France* (Stanford University Press, 2013) and *Simone de Beauvoir: Creating a Feminist Existence in the World* (Oxford University Press, 2016).

HAGEN SCHULZ-FORBERG teaches modern global and European history and thought at Aarhus University. He is the co-author with Bo Stråth of *The Political History of European Integration: The Hypocrisy of Democracy-through-Market* (Routledge, 2010) and is currently preparing *Contemporary Europe since the 1970s: (Re-)birth of the Political* (Wiley, 2020).

STEVEN B. SMITH is the Alfred Cowles Professor of Political Science at Yale University. He is the author of *Reading Leo Strauss: Politics, Philosophy, Judaism* (University of Chicago Press, 2006), and most recently *Modernity and its Discontents: Making and Unmaking the Bourgeois from Machiavelli to Bellow* (Yale University Press, 2016).

JUDITH SURKIS is Associate Professor of History at Rutgers University. She is author of *Sexing the Citizen: Morality and Masculinity in France, 1870–1920* (Cornell University Press, 2006) and *Sex, Law, and Sovereignty in French Algeria, 1830–1930* (Cornell University Press, 2019).

DAN ZAHAVI is Professor of Philosophy at the University of Copenhagen and the University of Oxford, and Director of the Center for Subjectivity Research in Copenhagen. His most recent books include *Self and Other: Exploring Subjectivity, Empathy, and Shame* (Oxford University Press, 2014) and *Husserl's Legacy: Phenomenology, Metaphysics, and Transcendental Philosophy* (Oxford University Press, 2017).

Preface

When one steps back to reflect upon the historical course of modern European thought since the French Revolution, it is difficult to avoid the impression that the old master narratives have lost all credibility. It is one of the characteristics of the modern condition that our stories and conceptual schemes have grown increasingly pluralistic: fragmentation, not unity, is the sign of the modern. In this regard, cultural and intellectual activity followed a general trend of modernity toward greater differentiation of spheres and tasks. Relations between workplace and home, public and private, state and society, secular and sacred all changed as modern Europe redefined or created new boundaries between these domains. Likewise, modernity has witnessed an ever more complex division of labor. Just as much as other members of society, intellectuals and artists have been affected by these changes, which have drawn (or blurred) anew the lines between producers and consumers of ideas and between mental and manual labor, even while they have also spawned new subcultures of expertise and disciplinary practice. These larger societal conditions and the torsions they produced are an important factor in the extraordinary creativity of European intellectual life in all fields during the nineteenth and twentieth centuries. Political ideologies have multiplied, and so too have the various fields of philosophical, theological, and scientific inquiry. Intellectual and cultural movements have waxed and waned; various schools have come into being, declaring themselves as avant-garde before hardening into new orthodoxies. Intellectuals announce a breakthrough only to be overtaken in turn by new currents of restoration or rebellion; and yet even those phenomena that seemed to vanish without a trace have in fact left an enduring mark on future generations. Nothing is ever truly past. Our present intellectual and cultural life remains unintelligible without some awareness of the persistent force of debates, problems, and styles of thought that emerged over the course of the nineteenth and twentieth centuries.

The Cambridge History of Modern European Thought offers a capacious and detailed survey of this rich and varied intellectual terrain. It combines state-of-the-art research with accessible presentations that can serve as both touchstones for the seasoned scholar and points of entry for students both beginning and advanced. Individual chapters trace crucial movements and figures across a broad range of disciplinary fields and domains of thought; they do so with sensitivity to the complexities both of the internal debates and traditions of intellectual life and of the larger contexts within which writers and artists have pursued their work. The focus is on intellectual concerns that fall roughly into the domain of humanistic inquiry and artistic practice – questions of the self, knowledge, and truth, human nature, the political order, ethics, justice, religion, ontology, psychology, and the symbolic modes whereby humans represent their ideas and experiences. More or less absent are the natural sciences and medicine. While these did of course exercise an important influence, they have their own deep and complicated histories. Their inclusion might have toppled the scale of even the most ambitious compendium of European thought in this period. The two notable exceptions, however, are the Darwinian revolution and the twentieth-century revolution in physics, both truly paradigmatic shifts that found strong resonances in the broader culture. The focus is also narrowed to emphasize the major countries of Western and Central Europe, chiefly but not exclusively France, Germany, Austria, and Great Britain. These were the national cultures that, during the modern era, could be said to have exercised the greatest influence on the intellectual life of the European continent and beyond. But the volumes and chapters also recognize the many entanglements across time and space that must defeat any attempt to narrate a merely provincial history of European ideas. Especially in the modern era during the age of imperialism and decolonization, the intellectual history of Europe cannot be confined within the boundaries of a single nation or geography. Ideas travel, and they also travel back, enriched and transformed by their peregrinations around the globe.

Absent from *The Cambridge History of Modern European Thought* is any master narrative that would tightly unify all of the numerous strands that thread through these volumes. If the French Revolution brought to an end the feudal age of absolutist monarchy, we would do well to recognize that in the history of ideas there is likewise no sovereign theme that wields all of the threads of intellectual history in its powerful hands. But differentiation does not entail chaos. Even as we recognize the manifold of themes and ideas we also understand that nothing in intellectual history can remain wholly apart from the world. Amply present in this volume is an awareness of the irreducible complexity – the ambiguity but also the creativity – of European intellectual life during these two centuries, alongside a recognition that intellectual history shares in whatever has been good and bad in modern European history. As we embark on the twenty-first century we trust that the ideas of the past may still provide us in some modest way with guidance for the future no matter how formidable its challenges.

Introduction

PETER E. GORDON AND WARREN BRECKMAN

In November, 1917, the German sociologist Max Weber delivered a now-famous lecture, "Science as a Vocation," before an assembly of students and faculty at the University of Munich. "The fate of our times," he declared, "is characterized by rationalization and intellectualization and, above all, by the 'disenchantment of the world.'"[1] Weber intended this remark as a global characterization of a modern society in which the natural sciences and bureaucratic rationality had conspired to undermine confidence in religious values and traditional sources of meaning. But we may also take his words as a more general verdict on the condition of modern European thought at the dawn of the twentieth century, when intellectuals from across the continent looked upon the wreckage of the First World War as a turning point in civilization, as a violent end to the nineteenth century and a grim foretaste of the world to come. Weber himself remained in a posture of ambivalence: He feared that the higher ideals of the Enlightenment were "irretrievably lost" and that only the imperative of "economic compulsion" would prevail.[2] He clung to the ideal of objectivity in social research even while he acknowledged that questions of ultimate significance demanded a species of personal decision exceeding the bounds of rational debate.[3] When we survey the

---

[1] Max Weber, "Wissenschaft als Beruf," translated as "Science as a Vocation" in *From Max Weber: Essays in Sociology*, ed. and trans. H. H. Gerth and C. Wright Mills (Oxford: Oxford University Press, 1946), 142.

[2] Max Weber, *The Protestant Ethic and the "Spirit" of Capitalism*, ed. and trans. Peter Baehr and Gordon C. Wells (London: Penguin, 2002), 121.

[3] For an excellent general portrait of Max Weber, see Fritz Ringer, *Max Weber: An Intellectual Biography* (Chicago: The University of Chicago Press, 2004); for Weber's intellectual reception, see Joshua Derman, *Max Weber in Politics and Social Thought: From Charisma to Canonization* (Cambridge: Cambridge University Press, 2013); for the classic analysis of Weber and German political history, see Wolfgang J. Mommsen, *Max Weber and German Politics, 1890–1920* (Chicago: The University of Chicago Press, 1990); and for a recent study of Weber's classic work on the "Protestant Ethic," see Peter Ghosh, *Max Weber and the Protestant Ethic: Twin Histories* (Oxford: Oxford University Press, 2014).

intellectual history of twentieth-century Europe a similar ambivalence confronts us at almost every turn.[4]

In the years leading up to the Great War, many intellectuals retained their confidence in the natural sciences and in science as a paradigm for human inquiry. The sociologist Émile Durkheim inherited from Comtean positivism the strong belief that science would eventually supersede religion and that the modern division of labor would lead to a new era of individualism in which social solidarity could be achieved on the basis of purely secular ideals.[5] The 1905 Law of Separation in France seemed to validate this secularist confidence even while it also reinforced the political chasm between modernists and traditionalists that had yawned wide in France in the wake of the Dreyfus Affair. Elsewhere in pre-war Europe intellectuals expressed themselves with similar optimism regarding the future for scientific progress. In philosophy, dominant movements such as neo-Kantianism and phenomenology subscribed to rationalist principles that harmonized well with the high-minded liberalism of the modern research university. In 1911 the founder of phenomenology Edmund Husserl combated what he saw as the relativistic threats of both psychologism and historicism and extolled the ideal of philosophy as a "rigorous science."[6] And in the closing years of the nineteenth century, the Viennese physician Sigmund Freud promoted psychoanalysis as a rational science of the irrational. In the clinical setting even the darkest powers of sexual desire could be drawn into the light; patients suffering from hysteria or other neuroses were promised if not a complete cure then at least the possibility of a livable truce among the warring factions of the psyche.[7]

---

[4] For a general portrait of European intellectual history in the years of transition from the nineteenth century to the interwar years, see the classic survey by H. Stuart Hughes, *Consciousness and Society: The Reorientation of European Social Thought, 1890–1930* (New York: Vintage, 1961).

[5] Steven Lukes, *Emile Durkheim: His Life and Work. A Historical and Critical Study* (Stanford: Stanford University Press, 1973).

[6] For the classic historical introduction to phenomenology, see Herbert Spiegelberg, *The Phenomenological Movement: A Historical Introduction*, 2 vols. (The Hague: Martinus Nijhoff, 1971); and for a biographical survey of Husserl's life and work, see Maurice Natanson, *Edmund Husserl: Philosopher of Infinite Tasks* (Evanston: Northwestern University Press, 1974).

[7] The classic biography is Peter Gay, *Freud: A Life for Our Time* (New York: Norton, 1988). More recent biographies include Joel Whitebook, *Freud: An Intellectual Biography* (Cambridge: Cambridge University Press, 2017); and Élisabeth Roudinesco, *Freud: In His Time and Ours*, trans. Catherine Porter (Cambridge: Harvard University Press, 2016). For a general account of the rise of psychoanalysis, see William J. McGrath, *Freud's Discovery of Psychoanalysis: The Politics of Hysteria* (Ithaca: Cornell University Press, 1986); and for a methodological reflection on Freud's biography and the general history of

Introduction

With the outbreak of the War in 1914 much of this late-bourgeois optimism in science and technology was shattered. Many intellectuals and artists shared the dark vision of the Irish poet William Butler Yeats, whose 1919 poem "The Second Coming" portrayed the postwar landscape as a secular apocalypse:

> Things fall apart; the centre cannot hold;
> Mere anarchy is loosed upon the world,
> The blood-dimmed tide is loosed, and everywhere
> The ceremony of innocence is drowned.

Between 1918 and 1923, the German writer Oswald Spengler published his bestselling work *The Decline of the West*, a dramatic and speculative inquiry into the philosophy of history that warned of a tragic future awaiting the "Faustian" spirit of Western civilization.[8] Freud himself, despite his understanding of psychoanalysis as a modern science, also permitted himself to speculate in a more tragic key: In *Beyond the Pleasure Principle* (1919) he introduced the notion of a "death drive" that stood in seemingly irresolvable conflict with the creative power of the libido or "eros." The new emphasis on the irrational became a prominent theme in social and political theory as well. Even before the war Georges Sorel had published his *Reflections on Violence*, a theory of mass-mobilization that emphasized the role of emotion-laden beliefs or "myths" in collective actions such as the mass-strike. Among Sorel's disciples was Benito Mussolini, who came to power as the leader of the Italian Fascist party in 1922. The rise of European fascism in the 1920s and 1930s had many causes, but it clearly signals the loss of confidence in rational deliberation and the gradual dissolution of liberal-parliamentary forms of government after the catastrophe of the Great War.[9]

The interwar years were a time of intellectual disorientation and experimentation in which many philosophers struggled to resist pessimistic feelings

---

psychoanalysis, see John Toews, "Historicizing Psychoanalysis: Freud in His Time and for Our Time," *The Journal of Modern History*, 63(3) (September 1991), 504–545. An accessible history is Stephen A. Mitchell and Margaret J. Black, *Freud and Beyond: A History of Modern Psychoanalytic Thought* (New York: Basic Books, 2016); Freud's own controversial views of this history are recorded in Sigmund Freud, *The History of the Psychoanalytic Movement and Other Papers* (New York: Collier Books, 1963). Also see Eli Zaretsky, *Political Freud: A History* (New York: Columbia University Press, 2015).

8 For Spengler in comparative perspective, see Jeffrey Herf, *Reactionary Modernism: Technology, Culture and Politics in Weimar and the Third Reich* (Cambridge: Cambridge University Press, 1984).

9 Zeev Sternhell, Mario Sznajder, and Maia Ashéri, *The Birth of Fascist Ideology: From Cultural Rebellion to Political Revolution* (Princeton: Princeton University Press, 1994); and Ernst Nolte, *Three Faces of Fascism: Action Française, Italian Fascism, National Socialism* (New York: New American Library, 1969).

of civilizational decline and yearned for new or long-forgotten modes of "re-enchantment."[10] Even before the war, in his last major work of sociology, *The Elementary Forms of Religious Life* (1912), Durkheim had turned in the direction of comparative ethnography and introduced the startling notion that all societies whether modern or "primitive" adhere to certain categories of the "sacred," a suggestion that would inspire students such as Marcel Mauss to turn a nostalgic eye toward ritual celebrations such as the Native American "potlatch" that seemed to promise an alternative to the rationalized forms of capitalist exchange.[11] A related interest in the "sacred" and irrational character of the social bond would inspire the circle of French intellectuals, including Georges Bataille and Roger Callois, that briefly formed in the later 1930s under the fanciful name of the "Collège de Sociologie."[12] The years leading up to and following World War I also saw an explosion of new movements in both philosophy and theology. In his 1907 *Creative Evolution*, the French philosopher Henri Bergson introduced the notion of an *élan vital*, a mystical or intuitive "vital force" that was to become a major theme in the European movement of *vitalism* or *Lebensphilosophie* that also included thinkers such as the sociologist Georg Simmel and the philosopher Max Scheler.[13] In the school of phenomenology as well, the 1920s was an era of rebellion against the rationalist and scientific ambitions of its founder Edmund Husserl. By 1927, Martin Heidegger, Husserl's most prominent student, had emerged as the exponent of a new style of "existential" phenomenology that called

---

10 For general portraits of European intellectual history in the first portion of the twentieth century, see H. Stuart Hughes, *The Obstructed Path: French Social Thought in the Years of Desperation, 1930–1960* (Middletown: Wesleyan University Press, 1987); on interwar Germany, see Peter Gay, *Weimar Culture: The Outsider as Insider* (New York: W. W. Norton, 2001); and Peter E. Gordon, *Continental Divide: Heidegger, Cassirer, Davos* (Cambridge: Harvard University Press, 2010).

11 The definitive biographical study is Marcel Fournier, *Marcel Mauss: A Biography*, trans. Jane Marie Todd (Princeton: Princeton University Press, 2015); for a superb collection of critical essays, see Wendy James and N. J. Allen (eds.), *Marcel Mauss: A Centenary Tribute* (New York: Berghahn Books, 1998); and for a later assessment by the doyen of French structuralist anthropology, see Claude Lévi-Strauss, *Introduction to the Work of Marcel Mauss* (London: Routledge, 1987 [1950]).

12 See Michele H. Richman, *Sacred Revolutions: Durkheim and the Collège de Sociologie* (Minneapolis: University of Minnesota Press, 2002); also see Frank Pearce, "Introduction: The Collège de Sociologie and French Social Thought," *Economy and Society*, 32(1) (February 2003), 1–6.

13 On Bergson's philosophy, see Frédéric Worms and Camille Riquier (eds.), *Lire Bergson*, 2nd edn. (Paris: Presses Universitaires de France, 2013); also see Giuseppe Bianco, *Après Bergson: Portrait de groupe avec philosophe* (Paris: Presses Universitaires de France, 2015). For German *Lebensphilosophie* and the natural sciences in Germany, see Anne Harrington, *Reenchanted Science: Holism in German Culture from Wilhelm II to Hitler* (Princeton: Princeton University Press, 1999).

philosophers to turn away from the erroneous path of post-Cartesian reason and return to the long-forgotten understanding of "Being." In the coming years, and notwithstanding his shameful record of political enthusiasm for Nazism, Heidegger would emerge as one of the most consequential philosophers of the twentieth century.[14]

Alongside existentialism and vitalism, however, the yearning for new kinds of experience and meaning beyond the constraints of modern rationalism also helps to explain the emergence of new trends in modern theology in the years following the War. In 1918 Karl Barth published the first edition of his *Epistle to the Romans*, an explosive challenge to the forms of liberal Protestantism that had remained dominant throughout the nineteenth century. Barth was only the most prominent among the Protestant thinkers of the twentieth century who found new inspiration in Søren Kierkegaard's rebellion against Kantian-liberal and establishment Protestantism and sought to affirm the absolute reality of God in an otherwise godless age.[15] Jewish philosophers such as Franz Rosenzweig and Martin Buber spoke to a similar yearning; Christian intellectuals such as Gabriel Marcel and Paul Tillich interlaced their theologies with existentialism; and beginning in the 1920s many Catholic intellectuals followed the example of Jacques Maritain in a so-called *"renouveau catholique"* that broke with the anti-modernist tendencies of nineteenth-century Roman Catholicism and led to a revival of Thomism.[16]

In European politics and in the sciences, the first decades of the twentieth century were a time of revolution and dramatic innovation. The Bolshevik revolution in Russia brought to power a regime that claimed to follow the

---

14 For a judicious introduction, see Mark Wrathall, *How to Read Heidegger* (New York: W. W. Norton, 2006); excellent and relatively accessible interpretative essays are collected in Charles Guignon (ed.), *The Cambridge Companion to Heidegger*, 2nd edn. (Cambridge: Cambridge University Press, 2006); for an assessment of Heidegger's political record, see Tom Rockmore, *On Heidegger's Nazism and Philosophy* (Berkeley: University of California Press, 1991); also see Hans Sluga, *Heidegger's Crisis: Philosophy and Politics in Nazi Germany* (Cambridge: Harvard University Press, 1995).
15 Bruce L. McCormack, *Karl Barth's Critically Realistic Dialectical Theology: Its Genesis and Development, 1909–1936* (Oxford: Clarendon Press, 1997); also see Gary Dorrien, *The Barthian Revolt in Modern Theology: Theology without Weapons* (Louisville: Westminster John Knox Press, 2000).
16 Peter E. Gordon, *Rosenzweig and Heidegger: Between Judaism and German Philosophy* (Berkeley: University of California Press, 2003); Paul R. Mendes-Flohr, *From Mysticism to Dialogue: Martin Buber's Transformation of German Social Thought* (Detroit: Wayne State University Press, 1989); Stephen Schloesser, *Jazz Age Catholicism: Mystic Modernism in Postwar Paris, 1919–1933* (Toronto: University of Toronto Press, 2005); on Maritain's inspirational role in modernist aesthetics, see Rajesh Heynickx and Jan de Maeyer (eds.), *The Maritain Factor: Taking Religion into Interwar Modernism* (Leuven: Leuven University Press, 2010).

explicit doctrines of Marxism as modified by V. I. Lenin, whose theory of the party vanguard furnished a justification for one-party rule and had already set the Soviet Union on a path toward dictatorship by the end of the 1920s. Meanwhile in Western Europe, aborted attempts at revolution (such as in Munich in 1918–1919) briefly awakened the utopian hopes of left-wing intellectuals who thereafter would spend the interwar era locked in theoretical and practical disputes over the respective merits of revolution versus political reform. Revolution was also on the horizon in the physical sciences. Just as Charles Darwin's theories had dramatically transformed our understanding of evolution and natural selection in the nineteenth century, so too Albert Einstein would transform our understanding of the nature of space and time in the twentieth century. In 1905 Einstein published his paper "On the Electrodynamics of Moving Bodies," in which he introduced the theory of special relativity that dramatically revised longstanding principles of Newtonian physics. This was complemented some years later by the theory of general relativity that transformed our understanding of gravity and presaged astronomical discoveries of the later twentieth century such as black holes and the cosmic microwave background radiation that confirmed the "Big Bang" theory of the origin of the universe.[17]

British intellectual life in the 1920s and 1930s remained more or less immune from the disorientation and political radicalism that dominated public discussion on the European Continent. But in London, a small group of intellectuals known as the "Bloomsbury Circle" nourished progressive thinking about diverse topics including feminism, literature, and economics.[18] In 1929 the novelist Virginia Woolf published "A Room of One's Own," a central text in early-twentieth-century feminism; and in 1936 John Maynard Keynes published his magnum opus, *A General Theory of Employment, Interest, and Money*, a major challenge to neoclassical economics and a foundational text in the development of the modern welfare state. Meanwhile, in academic circles England also served as the site for the emergence of a revolutionary new style of "analytic philosophy." Building on the achievements of Rudolf Carnap and the "Vienna Circle" of logical

---

[17] For a general account of Einstein's achievements, see Abraham Pais, *"Subtle is the Lord ...": The Science and the Life of Albert Einstein* (Oxford: Clarendon Press, 1982); for a broader perspective, see Helge Kragh, *Quantum Generations: A History of Physics in the Twentieth Century* (Princeton: Princeton University Press, 2002).

[18] For a general portrait of the Bloomsbury group, see Leon Edel, *Bloomsbury: A House of Lions* (Philadelphia: J. B. Lippincott, 1979); for a collection of memoirs and criticism, see S. P. Rosenbaum, *The Bloomsbury Group: A Collection of Memoirs and Commentary* (Toronto: University of Toronto Press, 1995).

positivism, Ludwig Wittgenstein wrote a pathbreaking work, the *Tractatus Logico-Philosophicus* (1921) that captured the attention of both Bertrand Russell and Alfred North Whitehead at the University of Cambridge.[19] It was through the combined efforts of Wittgenstein and philosophers at Cambridge that the new species of "analytic philosophy" was born and spread to Anglophone countries and eventually to Europe in the decades following World War II.[20] Over the course of the decades, as it came to dominate the Anglophone philosophical profession, analytic philosophy took on an increasingly academic character and assumed a posture of political neutrality.[21]

From the 1920s until the end of World War II, political theorists and cultural critics on the European Continent were drawn increasingly away from the "consensus" politics of liberal democracy and toward the political extremes.[22] On the right, many thinkers such as the Italian philosopher Giovanni Gentile and the German legal theorist Carl Schmitt turned against democratic pieties and affirmed the unity of the people and the primacy of the absolutist state.[23] For Gentile the terms "state" and "individual" belonged in a "necessary synthesis," while for Schmitt the state must always defend its unity: the essence of "the political" was the distinction between friend and enemy in which there always lurked the possibility of war. On the left, advocates of communist revolution in the West struggled with the question as to why the proletariat had not come to power as Marx had predicted. In reflecting on this problem, more sophisticated intellectuals were drawn into theoretical debates concerning the nature of working-class consciousness and

---

19 The classic portrait of Wittgenstein is Ray Monk, *Ludwig Wittgenstein: The Duty of Genius* (London: Penguin, 1991); for a brilliant if historically inventive novel that portrays Wittgenstein and his circle in Cambridge see Bruce Duffy, *The World as I Found It* (New York: New York Review Books, 2010). For an engaging if impressionistic cultural portrait of intellectual movements before World War I, see Allan Janik and Stephen Toulmin, *Wittgenstein's Vienna* (New York: Simon and Schuster, 1973).
20 For a philosophical history that emphasizes its Austrian roots see Michael Dummett, *Origins of Analytic Philosophy* (Cambridge: Harvard University Press, 1996).
21 Thomas L. Akehurst, "British Analytic Philosophy: The Politics of an Apolitical Culture," *History of Political Thought*, 30(4) (2009), 678–692. For a general overview of post-1945 intellectual life in Great Britain, see Stefan Collini, *Absent Minds: Intellectuals in Britain* (London: Oxford University Press, 2006).
22 Sandrine Sanos, *The Aesthetics of Hate: Far-Right Intellectuals, Antisemitism, and Gender in 1930s France* (Stanford: Stanford University Press, 2012). For a synthesis of fascism in Europe, see Robert Paxton, *The Anatomy of Fascism* (New York: Vintage, 2005); for a classic critique of the intellectual romance with communism during the 1940s and 1950s, see Raymond Aron, *The Opium of the Intellectuals* (New York: Routledge, 2001 [1955]).
23 John P. McCormick, *Carl Schmitt's Critique of Liberalism: Against Politics as Technology* (New York: Cambridge University Press, 1999).

the possibility that it had become denatured in bourgeois society. Founding theorists in the tradition of "Western Marxism" such as Antonio Gramsci in Italy and the Hungarian-born Georg (or György) Lukács developed subtle and even rarefied philosophical answers to this problem that often drew them away from the frequently dogmatic slogans that were favored among Marxist ideologues in the Soviet sphere.[24] The philosophers and cultural theorists associated with the Institute for Social Research, or "Frankfurt School," including Theodor W. Adorno, Max Horkheimer, Herbert Marcuse, and Walter Benjamin, developed an especially sophisticated social-theoretical critique of modern capitalist society that married Marxism with psychoanalysis to explain both the social-structural and the psychological aspects of social domination.[25]

During World War II many intellectuals and artists were compelled to flee the Continent, some because they were known to oppose or suspected of opposing the rising forces of fascism and others because they feared capture by regimes that now identified them as "racial" enemies. These intellectuals comprised what has been called the great intellectual migration that brought new talent from Europe to America. Others fled to Great Britain or Palestine, and to Central and South America. Many swore never to return to Europe or, after the war, would make only occasional visits back to the countries in which they had suffered persecution and where friends or even members of their immediate family had been murdered. Among those who left the Continent were novelists such as Thomas and Heinrich Mann, political theorists and philosophers such as Hannah Arendt and Hans Jonas, and composers and writers such as Arnold Schoenberg, Kurt Weill, and Berthold Brecht.[26] The core members of the Frankfurt School emigrated to

[24] See Andrew Arato and Paul Breines, *The Young Lukács and the Origins of Western Marxism* (New York: Seabury Press, 1979); and James Joll, *Antonio Gramsci* (New York: Viking Press, 1977). For a general overview, see Perry Anderson, *Considerations on Western Marxism* (London: Verso, 1976); also see Martin Jay, *Marxism and Totality: The Adventures of a Concept from Lukács to Habermas* (Berkeley: University of California Press, 1984).

[25] Martin Jay, *The Dialectical Imagination: A History of the Frankfurt School and the Institute of Social Research, 1923–1950* (Berkeley: University of California Press, 1996).

[26] On the intellectual migration to Los Angeles, see Ehrhard Bahr, *Weimar on the Pacific: German Exile Culture in Los Angeles and the Crisis of Modernism* (Berkeley: University of California Press, 2007); for the classic edited collection, see Bernard Bailyn and Donald Fleming (eds.), *The Intellectual Migration: Europe and America 1930–1960* (Cambridge: Harvard University Press, 1969); also see H. Stuart Hughes, *The Sea Change: The Migration of Social Thought 1930–1965* (New York: Harper and Row, 1975). On Hannah Arendt, see Elisabeth Young-Bruehl, *Hannah Arendt: For Love of the World*, 2nd edn. (New Haven: Yale University Press, 2004); and for a comprehensive philosophical analysis, see Seyla Benhabib, *The Reluctant Modernism of Hannah Arendt* (Lanham: Rowman & Littlefield, 2003).

New York and Los Angeles; Walter Benjamin, who had remained in France during the 1930s, sought escape but died in 1940 at the Spanish border. The political philosopher Leo Strauss found refuge at the University of Cambridge before eventually emigrating to the United States. The great literary historian and philologist Erich Auerbach fled Germany to Istanbul.

The painful memory of discrimination and persecution in Europe left many intellectuals with a strong need to comprehend the nature of fascist rule. Some who inclined to Marxist historical categories clung to the explanation that fascism represented the final phase of capitalism in crisis; others such as Hannah Arendt identified traits shared in common by both Nazism and Stalinism and analyzed the general phenomenon of "totalitarianism."[27] Conservative political philosophers tended to see Nazism as an upsurge of mass-society or an expression of a modern and merely "technical" approach to politics that ignored the wisdom of tradition. The British political philosopher Isaiah Berlin spoke of a contrast between "negative" and "positive" liberty, and warned of the overzealous attempt by political philosophers since the Enlightenment to impose a single standard of value upon the diversity of human nature.[28] After the war, European intellectuals and academics who had been either reluctant or enthusiastic supporters of the fascist regimes or who had remained silent were now seen as collaborators.[29] Martin Heidegger underwent a short period of scrutiny during the postwar Allied occupation but, despite his record of zealous support of Nazism, managed to revive his philosophical career and enjoyed a new prestige, especially in France.[30] The pro-fascist and anti-Semitic novelist Louis-Ferdinand Céline fled France to Denmark after the war and was convicted in absentia for collaboration, but later returned to France and continued to write fiction. The German novelist Ernst Jünger went through a similar process of rehabilitation and in the postwar years was celebrated for his fiction despite continued controversies regarding his affinities with the ideologies of the "conservative revolution."[31]

27 Hannah Arendt, *The Origins of Totalitarianism* (New York: Schocken Books, 1951).
28 Joshua Cherniss, *A Mind and Its Time: The Development of Isaiah Berlin's Political Thought* (Oxford: Oxford University Press, 2013); and Michael Ignatieff, *Isaiah Berlin: A Life* (New York: Metropolitan, 1998).
29 For a fascinating reconstruction of the controversy surrounding the French author Robert Brasillach, see Alice Kaplan, *The Collaborator: The Trial and Execution of Robert Brasillach* (Chicago: University of Chicago Press, 2000).
30 Ethan Kleinberg, *Generation Existential: Heidegger's Philosophy in France, 1927–1961* (Ithaca: Cornell University Press, 2007); for the reception of Carl Schmitt's work see Jan Werner-Müller, *A Dangerous Mind: Carl Schmitt in Post-War European Thought* (New Haven: Yale University Press, 2003).
31 Elliott Y. Neaman, *A Dubious Past: Ernst Jünger and the Politics of Literature after Nazism* (Berkeley: University of California Press, 1999).

Such instances of intellectual complicity with fascism were widespread; but it is no less instructive to recall cases of heroism and resistance, by authors such as Albert Camus and Samuel Beckett, both of whom were active members of the French Resistance. Beckett's play, "Waiting for Godot," originally composed in French and premiered on the French stage in 1953, is widely esteemed as one of the finest specimens of European modernism – in 1969 Beckett would receive the Nobel Prize for Literature. But its great abstraction often leaves readers with the impression that the play has little political content, whereas in fact Beckett was a deeply *engagée* author who remained throughout his life thoroughly committed to the causes of political freedom and human rights.[32]

The rebirth of European democracy after World War II brought renewed legitimacy and prestige to the "public intellectual," a species of institutionally unaffiliated writer or critic who claimed to speak for ostensibly universal ideas.[33] The nineteenth-century prototype of the public intellectual was Émile Zola, the novelist who came to political prominence during the Dreyfus Affair. After the Great War, the French novelist Julien Benda assumed a similar role in *La Trahison des Clercs* (*The Treason of the Intellectuals*, published in 1927) in which he asserted that public intellectuals should not betray their true commitment to universal and eternal norms by embracing the temporary idols of nationalism. Intellectual life in *fin-de-siècle* Europe was often found in *La Bohème* or "bohemia," the counter-cultural sphere made famous by Giacomo Puccini in his 1896 opera. As the historian Jerrold Seigel observed, bohemia and bourgeois society emerged simultaneously but in opposition to one another.[34] Intellectuals unattached to the research university often felt themselves drawn to the romantic ideal of the outsider's society, and typically convened in small groups of like-minded writers and critics such as the "Bloomsbury" group in London, the George Circle in Germany, or the Collège de Sociologie in Paris.

After 1945, however, public intellectuals gained new importance. In part because so many career academics in the universities had compromised themselves during the era of fascism, those individuals who could plausibly claim to have participated in the resistance, such as Albert Camus and Jean-

---

32 Emilie Morin, *Beckett's Political Imagination* (Cambridge: Cambridge University Press, 2017).
33 Benjamin Aldes Wurgaft, *Thinking in Public: Strauss, Levinas, Arendt* (Philadelphia: Penn Press, 2015).
34 Jerrold Seigel, *Bohemian Paris: Culture, Politics, and the Boundaries of Bourgeois Life, 1830–1930* (Baltimore: Johns Hopkins, 1999).

Paul Sartre, appeared to many as heroes with the moral authority to speak for higher ideals.[35] In Paris special prominence came to *Les Temps Modernes*, the journal of philosophy and political criticism founded in 1945 by Sartre along with his associates Simone de Beauvoir, Maurice Merleau-Ponty, and Raymond Aron. The English journalist and essayist George Orwell enjoyed a comparable authority in the immediate postwar years for his criticism of totalitarianism in political allegories such as *Animal Farm* (1945) and *Nineteen Eighty-Four* (1949); while the philosopher Bertrand Russell become a public firebrand in Cold War debates over imperialism and nuclear disarmament. In Germany, philosophers such as Karl Jaspers helped to promote the refounding of democracy, while members of the Frankfurt School who had spent the war years in exile returned in the 1950s as critics of what they considered the persistent strains of authoritarianism in German culture.[36]

The new ethos of public criticism in postwar Europe should not be exaggerated. The surrounding culture remained deeply conformist and fearful of any tendencies that threatened the uncertain ideological consensus that had formed under the aegis of anti-communism and Christian Democracy. Theologians such as Jacques Maritain helped to forge a new language of human rights that was installed in the founding charter of the United Nations, even while it was not always clear that Europeans were willing to extend these rights to colonial peoples beyond the European sphere.[37] The dissonance between universal ideals and colonial reality became a major theme in the writing of anti-colonial intellectuals and political dissidents such as Mohandas K. Gandhi and Frantz Fanon, who bore witness to the humiliation of non-European subjects in colonized territories. Fanon, a psychiatrist born in Trinidad, would emerge as an especially trenchant critic of colonial conditions in French Algeria in classic works such as *Les damnés de la terre* (*The Wretched of the Earth*, 1961) for which Sartre wrote an admiring preface.[38]

---

35 See, for example, Mark Poster, *Existential Marxism in Postwar France: From Sartre to Althusser* (Princeton: Princeton University Press, 1976).
36 On the intellectual debate over the Nazi legacy in Germany, see A. Dirk Moses, *German Intellectuals and the Nazi Past* (Cambridge: Cambridge University Press, 2009).
37 Samuel Moyn, *Christian Human Rights* (Philadelphia: Penn Press, 2015).
38 On Sartre and French intellectuals' responses to decolonization, see James D. Le Sueur, *Uncivil War: Intellectuals and Identity Politics during the Decolonization of Algeria* (Lincoln: University of Nebraska Press, 2005), 32–61. On the history of anti-colonial thought, see Gary Wilder, *Freedom Time: Negritude, Decolonization, and the Future of the World* (Durham: Duke University Press, 2015); and David Macey, *Frantz Fanon: A Biography* (London: Verso, 2012). For a critical reading of European literature in the matrix of the imperialist imagination, see the classic work by Edward Said, *Culture and Imperialism* (New York: Knopf, 1993).

Challenges to the conservative ethos of postwar Europe also came from feminist intellectuals such as Simone de Beauvoir, whose pathbreaking work *The Second Sex* (1949) sought both to diagnose the condition of women's subordination and to advance the cause of feminist freedom.[39] For Beauvoir there was nothing natural or foreordained about women's subjection – in her famous phrase, "One is not born, but rather becomes, a woman." Alongside Beauvoir were early contributors to feminist psychoanalytic theory such as Karen Horney and Joan Riviere.[40] Although the culture of sexism and male dominance remained largely undisturbed throughout the 1950s, the cultural rebellion of the late 1960s helped to destabilize conservative and patriarchal norms, and in the last third of the twentieth century a new wave of feminist intellectuals and critics had emerged especially (though not exclusively) in France, including philosophers such as Luce Irigaray and literary critics such as Hélène Cixous, Catherine Clément, and Julia Kristeva.[41]

The Cold War era in Western Europe may have been a period of political consensus, but in intellectual circles it was an era of fierce contestation concerning the merits of communism and the meaning of political commitment. Sartre enjoyed ongoing prestige as the embodiment of the public intellectual, and he attempted to promote a new model of intellectual engagement in an uncertain alliance with Marxism; his colleague Albert Camus, however, expressed far greater skepticism about communism, a disagreement that eventually led to a permanent break in their relations.[42] Meanwhile, however, another theoretical formation was emerging in the 1950s that was to present a challenge to Sartre and the fashion for existentialism.[43] Drawing upon the

---

39 For an excellent assessment, see Sandrine Sanos, *Simone de Beauvoir: Creating a Feminist Existence in the World* (Oxford: Oxford University Press, 2016); also see Emily R. Grosholz (ed.), *The Legacy of Simone de Beauvoir* (New York: Oxford University Press, 2004); and Nancy Bauer, *Simone de Beauvoir, Philosophy, and Feminism* (New York: Columbia University Press, 2000).
40 For a detailed history of the productive encounter between feminism and psychoanalysis, see Mary Jo Buhle, *Feminism and Its Discontents: A Century of Struggle with Psychoanalysis* (Cambridge: Harvard University Press, 2000). An important collection of critical and historical essays is Nancy Chodorow, *Feminism and Psychoanalytic Theory* (New Haven: Yale University Press, 1991).
41 The classic anthology is Elaine Marks (ed.), *New French Feminisms* (New York: Pantheon, 1987); also see Kelly Oliver (ed.), *French Feminism Reader* (Lanham: Rowman & Littlefield, 2000).
42 See Ronald Aronson, *Camus and Sartre: The Story of a Friendship and the Quarrel That Ended It* (Chicago: University of Chicago Press, 2004); for a critical appraisal of French intellectuals and Marxism that expresses greater sympathies for Camus, see Tony Judt, *Past Imperfect: French Intellectuals, 1944–1956* (New York: NYU Press, 2011).
43 François Dosse, *History of Structuralism, Volume 1: The Rising Sign, 1945–1966*, trans. Deborah Glassman (Minneapolis: University of Minnesota Press, 1997); François

insights of structuralist linguistics, the anthropologist Claude Lévi-Strauss introduced the notion that all human culture might be understood as a vast system of differences or contrasting terms.[44] This insight became the foundation for the structuralist movement not only in anthropology but across the human sciences, in psychoanalysis, and in literary criticism.[45] Louis Althusser applied structuralist principles to Marxist theory in *For Marx* (1965); Jacques Lacan argued that the unconscious itself is structured like a language; and Roland Barthes drew inspiration from structuralism in *The Fashion System* (1967). For the structuralists, Sartre's existential ideal of unconditional freedom and humanist self-invention rested on a mistake: The human being was less the cause of culture than its precipitate. The tensions between structuralism and existential phenomenology came to the fore in the concluding chapter to Lévi-Strauss's *The Savage Mind* (1962), where Sartre was accused of subscribing to history as a "myth."[46]

The politics of structuralism were by no means self-evident. In an era of capitalist modernization in Europe the new campaign for a "science" of cultural systems struck some critics as a retreat from the burdens of political responsibility, while the structuralists defended their project and faulted existentialists for making humanism into a philosophical shibboleth. Meanwhile, structuralism itself began to show signs of internal fracture; by the later 1960s a new and more anarchistic sensibility had seized the tools of structuralist analysis and turned them against the ideal of a science. Michel Foucault's *Les mots et les choses* (1966; published in English as *The Order of Things*) seemed to ally itself with the structuralist principles only to enlist the anarchistic memory of Friedrich Nietzsche as a prophet for a coming age beyond both humanism *and* science.[47] The belated return of Nietzsche was only one sign for the emergence of a diverse movement in philosophy and the human sciences

---

Dosse, *History of Structuralism, Volume 2: The Sign Sets, 1967–Present*, trans. Deborah Glassman (Minneapolis: University of Minnesota Press, 1997); Edith Kurzweil, *The Age of Structuralism: From Lévi-Strauss to Foucault* (New York: Columbia University Press, 1980); and John Sturrock, *Structuralism and Since: From Lévi-Strauss to Derrida* (New York: Oxford University Press, 1989).

44 Marcel Hénaff, *Claude Lévi-Strauss and the Making of Structural Anthropology*, trans. Mary Baker (Minneapolis: University of Minnesota, 1998).

45 John Sturrock, *Structuralism and Since: from Levi-Strauss to Derrida* (Oxford, 1979).

46 Claude Lévi-Strauss, *The Savage Mind* (Chicago: University of Chicago Press, 1966), esp. Chapter 9, "History and Dialectic." For the debate with Sartre, see Robert Doran, "Sartre's 'Critique of Dialectical Reason' and the Debate with Lévi-Strauss," *Yale French Studies*, No. 123, *Rethinking Claude Lévi-Strauss (1908–2009)* (2013), 41–62.

47 Hubert L. Dreyfus and Paul Rabinow, *Michel Foucault: Beyond Structuralism and Hermeneutics* (London: Routledge, 2014). Also see the superb volume of classic essays Arnold Davidson (ed.), *Foucault and His Interlocutors* (Chicago: University of Chicago Press, 1996).

that eventually came to be known as "post-structuralism." Both for its proponents and for its critics post-structuralism seemed to express the spirit of student rebellion that had swept through the cities and universities of Western Europe in May, 1968.[48] It promised not the stability of structure but its instability, not a science of meaning but what Jacques Derrida called its "deconstruction."[49] By the later 1970s and the 1980s, the avatars of post-structuralism (who were still not always accepted at home) had gained considerably greater renown in the United States, where they were often marketed under the ambiguous name of "French theory."[50] But post-structuralism was never a unified doctrine or movement. By the 1970s Foucault had developed a new strategy of historical criticism that drew inspiration from Nietzsche's "genealogy" of morality. In works such as *Discipline and Punish* (1975) and *The History of Sexuality* (1976) Foucault sought to identify the ways in which modern society amplified the effects of power through various techniques of knowledge, discipline, and surveillance that extended through all domains of life, from the prison to the hospital to the privacy of the psychoanalytic session.[51] Derrida, by contrast, adopted a more philosophical approach that radicalized Heidegger's "destruction" of metaphysics to explore the ways in which all textuality, both literary and philosophical, remained captive to a dream of uncontaminated meaning that language could not fulfill.

Meanwhile, in Germany the new generation of students turned a critical eye on the conduct of their parents during the Nazi era. The founding members of the Frankfurt School encouraged the difficult task of "working through the past," but by the end of the decade felt themselves increasingly besieged by a new spirit of radicalism and militancy that they poorly understood.[52] By the time of his death in 1969 Theodor W. Adorno had

[48] Luc Ferry and Alain Renault, *French Philosophy of the Sixties: An Essay on Antihumanism* (Amherst: University of Massachusetts Press, 1990). For an important criticism of the way in which the memory of the events of May 1968 has been sanitized of its more political meanings, see Kristin Ross, *May '68 and Its Afterlives* (Chicago: University of Chicago Press, 2008).

[49] For an intellectual history of the emergence of Derrida's thought, see Edward Baring, *The Young Derrida and French Philosophy, 1945–1968* (Cambridge: Cambridge University Press, 2011).

[50] François Cusset, *French Theory: How Foucault, Derrida, Deleuze, & Co. Transformed the Intellectual Life of the United States*, trans. Jeff Fort (Minneapolis: University of Minnesota Press, 2008).

[51] The two best biographies are Didier Eribon, *Michel Foucault*, trans. Betsy Wing (Cambridge: Harvard University Press, 1991); and David Macey, *The Lives of Michel Foucault* (New York: Pantheon, 1994).

[52] Theodor W. Adorno, "The Meaning of Working Through the Past," in *Critical Models: Interventions and Catchwords*, trans. Henry W. Pickford (New York: Columbia University Press, 2005), 89–103.

Introduction

become a controversial figure whom some students criticized as an embodiment of the establishment. In the coming years the mantle of the Frankfurt School was passed from the first to the second generation of critical theorists, foremost among them the gifted philosopher Jürgen Habermas.[53] Beginning with his early contribution to critical sociology *The Structural Transformation of the Public Sphere* (1962), Habermas set about revising the foundations of critical theory by securing its normative status as a practice of rational communication, a philosophical project that reached its culmination in 1981 with the publication of the two-volume work *The Theory of Communicative Action*.[54]

For most intellectuals the 1970s were an age of diminishing political ambitions that saw a shift of concern from utopian and revolutionary thinking toward themes of ethics and human rights.[55] The 1973 recession and the oil crisis brought to an end the three decades of economic growth ("les trentes glorieuses") that had followed World War II. Dissident movements among scientists, poets, and playwrights in the Soviet Union and its communist satellite states made it abundantly clear that the utopia of communism was in full eclipse. In 1973 *The Gulag Archipelago*, a novel by Aleksandr Solzhenitsyn that documented the vast and terrifying system of Soviet labor camps, was published in the West, first in a Russian edition in France and then in an English translation.[56] The radical group in Germany known as the "Red Army Faction" committed acts of terrorism, while popular intellectuals such as Bernard-Henri Lévy in France now spoke of Marxism as "barbarism with a human face."[57] In 1979 the conservative Margaret Thatcher was elected Prime Minister in the UK as a confirmation of the rightward shift in European consciousness. During the 1980s German historians and philosophers (including Habermas) engaged in the "Historians' Controversy"

---

53 Rolf Wiggershaus, *The Frankfurt School: Its History, Theories, and Political Significance*, trans. Michael Robertson (Cambridge: MIT Press, 1994).
54 Stefan Müller-Doohm, *Habermas: A Biography* (Cambridge: Polity Press, 2016).
55 On the shift to ethics, see Julian Bourg, *From Revolution to Ethics, May 1968 and Contemporary French Thought*, 2nd edn. (Montreal: McGill-Queen's University Press, 2017); on the rise of human rights discourse during the Cold War, see Samuel Moyn, *The Last Utopia: Human Rights in History* (Cambridge: Harvard University Press, 2012).
56 The authoritative portrait is Michael Scammell, *Solzhenitsyn: A Biography* (New York: W. W. Norton, 1984); but see also the historically comprehensive account by D. M. Thomas, *Alexander Solzhenitsyn: A Century in His Life* (Boston: Little, Brown and Company, 1998).
57 Hans Kundnani, *Utopia or Auschwitz: Germany's 1968 Generation and the Holocaust* (New York: Columbia University Press, 2009); and Michael Scott Christofferson, *French Intellectuals against the Left: The Antitotalitarian Moment of the 1970s* (New York: Berghahn Books, 2004).

(*Historikerstreit*), a fierce debate over the legacy of National Socialism that was only exacerbated by the decision in 1985 by the US President Ronald Reagan to visit a cemetery in Bitburg, Germany that included gravesites for members of the Waffen SS.[58]

The collapse of the Soviet Union and Soviet-bloc regimes throughout Eastern Europe in 1989–1990 inaugurated a new era of reckoning with the legacy of communism and also raised questions concerning the future of European democracy. For intellectuals the 1990s seemed to open fresh horizons that were unclouded by old dogmas and definitions: Habermas spoke of the challenge of "post-metaphysical thinking," while French philosophers such as Derrida, Emmanuel Lévinas, and Jean-Luc Marion often spoke in a theological register, placing great emphasis on questions of ethical responsibility.[59] The expansion of the European Union seemed to herald a new age of pan-European cooperation, even while the formerly communist regimes in the East struggled with economic recovery and a new spirit of bellicose nationalism that grew especially violent in the new states that emerged after the breakup of Yugoslavia and in the Caucasus. Ethno-racial and religious minorities in Europe, especially Muslims from Africa and the Middle East, were often singled out as the targets of discrimination and violence, and some conservative intellectuals lent their voices to the growing chorus of complaints regarding a supposed threat to Europe's traditionally Christian heritage. Neo-nationalist and neo-fascist sentiments long seen as discredited gained in strength even in the core states of the European Union, partly as a reaction against the intensifying interdependence of global markets. Major terrorist strikes included the bombing of a train in Madrid and of the London subway in 2005. The growing fear of terrorism at the dawn of the new millennium contributed to the new feeling of a shared European identity. In response to the United States' invasion of Iraq in 2003, intellectuals such as Habermas and Derrida overcame their theoretical differences as co-signatories of a statement that affirmed the common values of Europe.[60]

---

58 Charles S. Maier, *The Unmasterable Past: History, Holocaust, and German National identity* (Cambridge: Harvard University Press, 1998).
59 Dominique Janicaud, *Phenomenology and the "Theological Turn": The French Debate* (Fordham, 2000); for an excellent historical treatment of Lévinas, see Samuel Moyn, *Origins of the Other: Emmanuel Levinas between Revelation and Ethics* (Ithaca: Cornell University Press, 2005); on the Catholic dimension of phenomenology, see Edward Baring, *Converts to the Real: Catholicism and the Making of Continental Philosophy* (Cambridge: Harvard University Press, 2019).
60 Jürgen Habermas and Jacques Derrida, "February 15, or What Binds Europeans Together: A Plea for a Common Foreign Policy, Beginning in the Core of Europe," reprinted in *Constellations*, 10(3) (September 2003), 291–297.

Introduction

Today, when one looks back upon the intellectual history of Europe in the twentieth century it is difficult to suppress the thought that the noblest ideals of democracy and creativity have been too often shattered in the name of security and national integrity. But as Adorno once observed, "open thinking points beyond itself."[61] It is in the nature of intellectual ideals that they endure for the future no matter how deeply their authority may be compromised in the present. It therefore seems relevant to conclude this introduction by quoting the final lines from Samuel Beckett's 1953 modernist masterpiece *The Unnameable*: "You must go on. I can't go on. I'll go on."[62]

---

61 Theodor W. Adorno, "Resignation," in *Critical Models: Interventions and Catchwords*, trans. Henry W. Pickford (New York: Columbia University Press, 2005), 289–293, p. 293.
62 Samuel Beckett, *Three Novels: Molloy, Malone Dies, The Unnamable* (New York: Grove Press, 2009), 407.

I
Sociology and the Heroism of Modern Life

MARTIN JAY

> Andrea: Unhappy is the land that breeds no hero.
> Galileo: No, Andrea: Unhappy is the land that needs a hero.
> Bertolt Brecht, *Life of Galileo* (1938), Scene 12, p. 115

Among the plethora of efforts to define modernity, Michel Foucault's attempt in an essay answering the question "What is Enlightenment?," which was famously posed by the eighteenth-century-Germany *Aufklärer*, is particularly suggestive.[1] Modernity, he argued, is neither a temporal period nor adherence to a set of progressive beliefs and practices; it is instead an attitude, "the attitude that makes it possible to grasp the 'heroic' aspect of the present moment. Modernity is not a phenomenon of sensitivity to the fleeting present; it is the will to 'heroize' the present."[2] Here Charles Baudelaire's seminal essays "The Salon of 1846: On the Heroism of Modern Life" and "The Painter of Modern Life" (1863), which celebrated the illustrator Constantin Guys's depiction of the unsettled, turbulent world of the modern city, served Foucault as a recipe for a more general response to "modernity" in all of its motley variety.[3]

What makes that response a heroization is the unflinching affirmation of our world as inherently superior to what preceded it. No nostalgia for a lamented past, no pining for a world of lost traditions or shattered communities, no fantasies of a golden age from which we have fallen. It takes, however, a measure of courage to live in the modern world, a world without the

---

1 For the original debate, its context and aftermath, see James Schmidt (ed.), *What Is Enlightenment? Eighteenth-Century Answers and Twentieth-Century Questions* (Berkeley: University of California Press, 1996).
2 Michel Foucault, "What Is Enlightenment?," in *The Foucault Reader*, ed. Paul Rabinow (New York: Pantheon, 1984), 40.
3 Charles Baudelaire, "The Salon of 1846: The Heroism of Modern Life," in *Selected Writings on Art and Literature*, trans. P. E. Charvet (London: Penguin, 1972); and *The Painter of Modern Life and Other Essays*, ed. and trans. Jonathan Mayne (London: Phaidon, 1970). For a discussion of Foucault on Baudelaire and modernity, see Alan Swingewood, *Cultural Theory and the Problem of Modernity* (New York: St. Martin's Press, 1998), 142–144.

comforting illusion of settled norms, prescribed practices, and unquestioned authorities. Impelled by no inherent telos, modernity is a constant flux of transformations, a maelstrom of destruction and creation, in which we can rely on no one but ourselves to provide any purpose, order, or stability. It is a world of opportunity and self-fashioning, as well as risk and danger, a world in which the horizon of past experience, as Reinhart Koselleck noted, is no longer capable of orienting our expectations about the future.[4] It thus demands a constant exercise of heroism, as Baudelaire already noted in the middle of the nineteenth century, to cope with the shocks and assaults of life in a fast lane going to an unknown destination, whose speed limit always seems to be increasing at an accelerating rate.

And yet, if Foucault is right, the heroization of the present, and by extension our self-image as heroes courageously responding to its demands, must be understood ironically.[5] Or rather, the modern attitude is always already itself ironical about what it heroically celebrates.[6] As Foucault notes, "for the attitude of modernity, the high value of the present is indissociable from a desperate eagerness to imagine it, to imagine it otherwise than it is, and to transform it not by destroying it but by grasping it in what it is."[7] That is, the present for the modern attitude is always understood as a transition to something other than it is, potentially – although not necessarily – better, a way-station to a different future. Thus the rhetoric of "modernization" as a conscious project that understands itself as an endless task of emancipating our species from what Kant, answering the question about the meaning of the Enlightenment, called our "self-incurred immaturity," a condition which we are always in the uncompletable process of leaving behind.[8]

Rather, in other words, than complacently heroizing the present as an accomplished end-state, the modern attitude acknowledges both its necessity

---

4 Reinhart Koselleck, "'Space of Experience' and 'Horizon of Expectation': Two Historical Categories," in *Futures Past: On the Semantics of Historical Time*, trans. Keith Tribe (Cambridge: MIT Press, 1985).
5 For an argument that Baudelaire's essay on the Salon of 1846 might best be understood itself in terms of a destabilizing irony, see David Carrier, "The Style of Argument in Baudelaire's 'Salon de 1846,'" *Romance Quarterly*, 41(1) (1994), 3–14, p. 3.
6 A comparable point might be made about the modern villain, who is often far more complex and nuanced than his predecessors. The rise of the anti-hero as the protagonist of much modern fiction was accompanied by what we might call the "anti-villain," ironically understood as more interesting than his heroic counterpart. Only in melodrama and the comics, where superheroes abound, are the older black and white alternatives still maintained.
7 Foucault, "What Is Enlightenment?," 41.
8 Immanuel Kant, "An Answer to the Question: What Is Enlightenment?," in Schmidt, ed., *What Is Enlightenment?*, 58. This definition, of course, has generated a considerable amount of criticism for its elitist premise, but the point that is relevant here is Kant's assumption that it is a telos that is still to be realized, and is unlikely ever to be.

and its insufficiency. We are living, it tacitly concedes, not in a fully realized modern age, but only in an age of unending modernization. Not only, as Bruno Latour provocatively put it, have we never been modern, but on some level we know we never will be.[9] We realize that the uncompleted "project of modernity," to borrow Jürgen Habermas's formulation, will remain indefinitely open-ended, and so "modernity" is precisely not a condition or state of being, but an ongoing process without closure. To cite Foucault again, "the attitude of modernity does not treat the passing moment as sacred in order to try to maintain or perpetuate it. It certainly does not involve harvesting it as a fleeting and interesting curiosity."[10] Rather than passively spectatorial, the modern attitude is active, "an exercise in which extreme attention to what is real is confronted with the practice of a liberty that simultaneously respects this reality and violates it."[11]

In addition to the ironic heroization of a transient present that knows we are perpetually en route, but never quite there, modernity has also adopted an increasingly ironic attitude toward many of its substantive self-understandings. Thus, to cite obvious examples, belief in the scientific method, the virtues of technological innovation, and the superiority of reason to its various "others" have all been subjected to serious doubt. What following Horkheimer and Adorno has come to be recognized as the ambiguous "dialectic of enlightenment" has spread to virtually all variants of the project of modernity.[12] The origins of that project in a Western culture whose motives in "civilizing" the rest of the world have seemed, to put it mildly, less than pure have been invoked to undermine virtually all of its claims to emancipation. Or, to be more precise, those claims have been subjected to rigorous reflection about their often contradictory implications, allowing a more nuanced judgment about their costs and benefits. Indeed, it is sometimes argued that a main characteristic of modernity, or at least "late" modernity, is precisely its ambivalent reflexivity, its willingness to step back from its earlier unproblematized commitments and aspirations and take on board the lessons learned from its unexpected negative consequences. What for a while was called "postmodernity," prematurely suggesting that modernism had in fact somehow ended, is now widely

---

9 Bruno Latour, *We Have Never Been Modern*, trans. Catherine Porter (Cambridge: Harvard University Press, 1993).
10 Foucault, "What Is Enlightenment?," 40.   11 Foucault, "What Is Enlightenment?," 41.
12 Max Horkheimer and Theodor W. Adorno, *Dialectic of Enlightenment*, ed. Gunzelin Schmid Noerr, trans. Edmund Jephcott (Stanford: Stanford University Press, 2002).

acknowledged as little more than a moment of heightened reflexivity that was a fold within modernity itself.

In fact, if Walter Benjamin is right in an earlier invocation of Baudelaire's consideration of the heroism of modern life, self-critical doubt about the project of modernity was already evident in the nineteenth-century poet's inconclusive search for a type to play the role of the modern hero, who could somehow exhibit the noble traits of a classical character in contemporary garb. After noting that, both for Honoré de Balzac and for Baudelaire, "the hero is the true subject of modernism" because "it takes a heroic constitution to live modernism," Benjamin observes that while for the novelist it was the *commis voyageur* (traveling salesman) who is the modern version of the ancient gladiator, for the poet instead it is the proletariat that is the modern incarnation of the ancient fencing slave.[13] But then Benjamin quickly admits that there were many other candidates for the role of the modern hero in Baudelaire's eyes: the artist, the rag-picker, the *flâneur*, the apache, the dandy, the lesbian, the conspirator, even the suicide, whose self-destruction may well have been "the only heroic act that had remained for the *multitudes maladives* [sickly multitudes] of the cities in reactionary times."[14] In fact, as shown by the threadbare and inauthentic heroism of that imposter emperor Napoleon III, so devastatingly mocked by Marx and Hugo, it is not easy to play the hero convincingly in the modern world. Indeed, according to Benjamin, Baudelaire himself knew this all too well: "Because he did not have any convictions, he assumed ever new forms himself. *Flâneur*, apache, dandy and ragpicker were so many roles to him. For the modern hero is no hero; he acts heroes. Heroic modernism turns out to be a tragedy in which the hero's part is available."[15]

Whereas Foucault read Baudelaire in a cautiously optimistic mood – the heroism of modern life is a "practice of a liberty" that actively violates the present, while nonetheless not trying to escape it – the more saturnine Benjamin understood that the poet's quest for a new constellation of the eternal values of antiquity with the flux of modernity would likely be in vain. What both shared, however, is the recognition that the smooth flow of progress assumed by liberal historicists is the antithesis of a genuinely modern heroism, which appreciates that time is out of joint and that the "now" is more than a moment in an inexorable evolutionary drive upward toward enlightenment, however it might be defined. Both Foucault and Benjamin

13 Walter Benjamin, *Charles Baudelaire: A Lyric Poet in the Era of High Capitalism*, trans. Harry Zohn (London: NLB, 1973), 74.
14 Benjamin, *Charles Baudelaire*, 76.   15 Benjamin, *Charles Baudelaire*, 97.

knew, in other words, that heroizing the present, although necessary, can be attempted only in an ironic mode. For even when you try to write it as a tragedy, there is no obvious candidate to play the role of tragic hero.[16]

***

What are we to make of the provocative claim that modernity can best be understood as the heroization of the present, a claim first introduced by Baudelaire and then given an ironic twist by Benjamin and Foucault?[17] "The heroism of modern life," as we know, has become a frequent trope in cultural studies – symptomatically, two books and one film on the great visual artists Daumier, Eakins, and Manet borrow it for their subtitles[18] – and cultural critics, such as Marshall Berman, have been characterized as its contemporary exponents.[19] But can it be reconciled – and this is really the primary question I want to address – with the more ambitious explanations offered by the leading sociologists of modernization, Émile Durkheim, Max Weber, and Georg Simmel? Does it comport with their analytic attempts to differentiate modernity from what preceded it, attempts that went beyond the brilliant, but underdeveloped insights of a Baudelaire?[20]

***

Before tackling that question head on, we must acknowledge the importance of two very modern different attitudes toward heroism, which were anything but ironic and, as will become apparent, had little resonance

---

16 Any serious account of Benjamin's thoughts on the trope of tragedy without a tragic hero would have to address his discussion of the early-modern German *Trauerspiel*, which was not equivalent to classical tragedy, but to do so is beyond the scope of this chapter.

17 It also, of course, might be asked whether it helps to distinguish modernity from its alleged postmodern successor, but that is a can of worms best left tightly closed in a modest exercise such as this one.

18 John Berger, *Daumier: The Heroism of Modern Life* (London: Royal Academy, 2013); Elisabeth Johns, *Thomas Eakins: The Heroism of Modern Life* (Princeton: Princeton University Press, 2013); and Lizzie Barker and Juliet Wilson-Bareau, *Manet: The Heroism of Modern Life*, video for the National Gallery (London, 1992).

19 James Meehan, "Marshall Berman, November 24, 1940–September 11, 2013: Chronicler of the Heroism of Modern Life," *Humanity and Society*, 41(1) (2015), 3–12, http://has.sagepub.com/content/early/2015/12/18/0160597615622232.full.pdf.

20 The question of heroism has, in fact, rarely been addressed by sociologists. A quick perusal of the indexes of ambitious general overviews of sociological thought, such as Raymond Aron, *Main Currents of Sociological Thought*, trans. Richard Howard and Helen Weaver, 2 vols. (New York: Basic Books, 1965 and 1967); Robert A. Nisbet, *The Sociological Tradition* (New York: Basic Books, 1966); Lewis A. Coser, *Masters of Sociological Thought: Ideas in Historical and Social Context* (New York: Harcourt Brace Jovanovich, 1977); Tom Bottomore and Robert Nisbet (eds.), *A History of Sociological Analysis* (New York: Basic Books, 1978); and Richard Münch, *Sociological Theory from the 1850s to the Present* (Chicago: Nelson-Hall, 1994), will not find a single entry devoted to it.

among sociologists. They were narrated instead in what might be called romantic and comic modes. In the former, the historical field is understood to be a chaos of contingency in which only the will of the great man, who is engaged in an endless romantic quest, might fashion meaning, however fleeting, from the flux. As Hayden White puts it in his analysis of metahistorical romance, "the appearance of a hero represents a 'victory' of 'human Free-will over Necessity' ... The 'Chaos of Being' [is] the situation the heroic individual faces as a field to be dominated, if only temporarily and in the full knowledge of the ultimate victory this 'Chaos' will enjoy over the man who seeks to dominate it."[21] Eric Bentley, writing in the middle of World War II, discerned a tradition of what he called irrationalist "heroic vitalism," exemplified by Thomas Carlyle, Friedrich Nietzsche, Richard Wagner, Oswald Spengler, Stefan George, and D. H. Lawrence. All were repelled by the mechanization of modern life, the mediocrity of political democracy, and the banality of mass culture.[22] Here the founding premise was expressed in Carlyle's 1840 lectures *On Heroes, Hero-Worship, and the Heroic in History*: "Universal History, the history of what man has accomplished in the world, is at bottom the History of the Great Men who have worked there."[23] Focusing on six categories of heroes – divinities, prophets, poets, priests, men of letters, and kings – Carlyle advocated the return of an unapologetically worshipful, that is, religious, attitude toward them in an age that he lamented "denies the existence of great men; denies the desirableness of great men."[24] As Nietzsche likewise proclaimed in his *Untimely Meditations*, "the goal of humanity cannot lie in its end but in its highest exemplars."[25] They enjoyed a "pathos of distance" from the common man, whose ignoble status could not be remedied through resentful efforts to

---

[21] Hayden White, *Metahistory: The Historical Imagination in Nineteenth-Century Europe* (Baltimore: Johns Hopkins University Press, 1973), 148.

[22] Eric Bentley, *A Century of Hero-Worship*, 2nd edn. (Boston: Beacon Press, 1957). The first edition appeared in 1944. It is worth noting that not all attitudes toward the role of heroes in history were as critical. See, for example, the more ambivalent assessment in Sidney Hook, *The Hero in History: Study in Limitation and Possibility* (Boston: Beacon Press, 1955).

[23] Thomas Carlyle, *On Heroes, Hero-Worship and the Heroic in History*, ed. Carl Niemeyer (Lincoln: University of Nebraska Press, 1966), 1. For a discussion of the nuances of Carlyle's argument and the differences in his attitudes toward figures in his pantheon, see Robert A. Donovan, "Carlyle and the Climate of Hero-Worship," *The University of Toronto Quarterly*, 42(2) (1973), 122–141.

[24] Carlyle, *On Heroes, Hero-Worship and the Heroic in History*, 12. Carlyle's general distaste for irony in comparison with Kierkegaard is discussed in Eric J. Ziolkowski, *The Literary Kierkegaard* (Evanston: Northwestern University Press, 2011), Chapter 5.

[25] Friedrich Nietzsche, *Untimely Meditations*, ed. Daniel Breazeale, trans. R. J. Hollingdale (Cambridge: Cambridge University Press, 1997), 111.

revenge themselves on their betters.[26] An ideology of "heroic realism" was kept alive in the writings of such twentieth-century glorifiers of the technological sublime as Ernst Jünger, whose armored warriors were impervious to pain, both suffered and inflicted.[27] Belief in the exceptional role of the hero in history was still potent as late as Freud's last work *Moses and Monotheism*, in which he criticized history based entirely on impersonal forces, and concluded "we will keep, therefore, a place for the 'great man' in the chain, or rather in the network of determining causes."[28]

The defense of those highest exemplars could, however, also be based on very different premises from the ones motivating the elitist irrationalists identified by Bentley, who wrote in an essentially romantic mode. They could instead be read as playing a role in an essentially comic narrative, in the sense of an ultimately happy ending, in which all contradictions come to be harmoniously reconciled. Here Hegel is the main exemplar. He not only pondered the role of the hero in such Greek tragedies as *Antigone*, but also celebrated the important role of "world-historical" figures like Napoleon in his own day. From the subjective point of view, such heroes were best understood as tragic figures, who achieved little satisfaction or happiness in their own lives. But from the objective point of view of History as a whole, the one with which Hegel himself identified, they performed necessary functions in an ultimately triumphal story.

When it came to the contemporary distrust of heroes, Hegel famously noted that no hero is a hero to his valet, "but that is not because heroes are not heroes, it is because valets are valets."[29] The deeper meaning of this celebrated observation has recently been glossed by the Brazilian philosopher Vladimir Safatle, who writes

> What this witticism gestures at is a certain problem of perspective: a viewpoint (such as the valet's) that erases the notion of historical subject

26 Friedrich Nietzsche, *Beyond Good and Evil*, trans. Marianne Cowan (Chicago: Henry Regnery, 1955), 200.
27 For an excellent introduction to Jünger and his continuing influence in the postwar era, see Elliot Y. Neaman, *A Dubious Past: Ernst Jünger and the Politics of Literature after Nazism* (Berkeley: University of California Press, 1999).
28 Sigmund Freud, *Moses and Monotheism*, trans. Katharine Jones (New York: Alfred A. Knopf, 1939), 138. There may, to be sure, be a difference between Moses as the transmitter of laws and the heroic vitalists who often favored their transgression. But it should be remembered that Freud also suggested to Otto Rank that he write a book on the hero, which became *The Myth of the Birth of the Hero: A Psychological Interpretation of Mythology*, trans. F. Robbins and Smith Ely Jelliffe (New York: The Journal of Nervous and Mental Disease Publishing Company, 1914). The book argued that mythic heroes define themselves by rebelling against the rule-giving father in a family romance.
29 Georg Wilhelm Friedrich Hegel, *The Philosophy of History*, trans. J. Sibree (New York: Dover, 1956), 32.

reduces sequences of events to the lesser condition of collections of random occurrences, which is to say, to occurrences bereft of history ... What the sneering chamber valet fails to grasp is how one's interests lose their particularistic traits once they become integral to the unfolding of historical processes.[30]

That is, for Hegel, the hero is not merely a powerful and inspirational figure; he is also the vehicle through which Reason enters the seeming contingency of history, the means by which manifest disorder reveals itself as latent order. The valet is too short-sighted to grasp what is happening beyond his ken.

It was, however, against both the romantic, irrationalist, worship of savior figures in the heroic vitalist tradition and the comic Hegelian celebration of great men as the vehicles of Reason in history that we have to understand the ironic heroism of modern life defended by Baudelaire, Benjamin, and Foucault. They distrusted both the elevated rhetoric of salvation via sacrifice and the faith in history as a story of redemption, rational or otherwise. Instead, they acknowledged that the world had been irrevocably disenchanted and that the course of history could not be accounted a narrative of reason's increasing emergence amidst the flux of contingency. And yet, although they focused new attention on the little rather than the great man, they did not adopt wholesale the cynicism of the valet, who denied all claims to heroism as fraudulent in the modern world. Ironic distance, if we follow Foucault's formulation, was not directed at heroization *per se*, but rather at modernity's aspiration to realize its romantic hopes or achieve a state of harmonious, "comic" reconciliation. For despite everything, it was still possible for some individuals to confront the challenges of unredeemed modern life without resignation or despair.

* * *

Was there, to turn finally to the main subject of this exercise, a comparable attitude expressed in the work of the founding fathers of modern sociology? Emerging as a distinct discipline in the early nineteenth century in the wake of the French and Industrial Revolutions, when the name was coined by the Positivist August Comte, sociology came of age only in the decades before

---

30 Vladimir Safatle, *Grand Hotel Abyss: Desire, Recognition and the Restoration of the Subject*, trans. Lucas Carpinelli (Leuven: Leuven University Press, 2016), 116–117. In *Negative Dialectics*, however, Adorno wrote of "the master class joke of the hero and the valet" that it demonstrated Hegel's over-rating of the exceptional individual and neglect of his real counterpart. The larger-than-life publicity of geniuses, especially military and political ones, he argued, compensates for the weakness of the latter: "projections of the impotent longings of all, they function as an *imago* of unleashed freedom and unbounded productivity, as if those might be realized always and everywhere." Theodor W. Adorno, *Negative Dialectics*, trans. E. B. Ashton (New York: Seabury Press, 1973), 342.

World War I. Despite the occasional exception, such as the German nationalist Werner Sombart who thought he belonged to a nation of heroes,[31] its proponents have often been assumed to share the debunking perspective of the valet, who looks behind the façade of his master's pretensions to reveal the latent forces and embedded structures that really affect society. Although Comte had included a roster of secular heroes of progress to replace the discredited Christian saints in his Religion of Humanity, sociologists with less exalted goals tended to stress impersonal processes instead. Herbert Spencer, for example, railed against Carlyle's great-man theory of history in his 1860 *Study of Sociology*: "you must admit that the genesis of a great man depends on the long series of complex influences which has produced the race in which he appears, and the social state into which that race has slowly grown ... Before he can remake his society, his society must make him."[32] Although Spencer still believed in the idea of progress of the species, he did not think humanity's "highest exemplars" were necessary to bring it about.

By the time of Durkheim (1857–1917), Weber (1864–1920), and Simmel (1858–1918), sociologists were also growing far more skeptical of progress, at least as an evolutionary necessity, and the collective subjects who allegedly brought it about.[33] Instead, they had grown far more sensitive to the challenges of a modernity whose costs seemed as great as its benefits. Even when they worked within a broad framework of narrative change, allowing them to understand modernity as a meaningful rupture with what preceded it, they resisted a triumphalist account, which glossed over the multiple discontents

---

31 Werner Sombart, *Händler und Helden: Patriotische Besinnungen* (Munich: Duncker & Humblot, 1915). For a discussion, see Arthur Mitzman, *Sociology and Estrangement: Three Sociologists of Imperial Germany* (New York: Knopf, 1973), Chapter 22. His critique of the British as a nation of mere merchants presaged his later demonization of the Jews and embrace of the Nazi "heroic popular community."

32 Herbert Spencer, *The Study of Sociology* (London: Appleton, 1896), 15. For a discussion of Spencer's personal antipathy towards Carlyle, see William Baker, "Herbert Spencer's Unpublished Reminiscences of Thomas Carlyle: The 'Perfect Owl of Minerva for Knowledge' on a 'Poet without Music,'" *Neophilologus*, 60(1) (December 1975), 145–152.

33 As Peter Weingart notes in a discussion of the differentiation of sociological from biological claims about human development, "the modernist turn that characterized the work of this 'second generation' of sociologists – Weber, Simmel, Durkheim – centered on their renunciation of the idea of social progress which had dominated sociology through the nineteenth century. One crucial move in this respect was for sociology to abdicate the role of prophet of a future society and to limit itself to those social phenomena that could be experienced." Peter Weingart, "Biology as Social Theory: The Bifurcation of Social Biology and Sociology in Germany, *circa* 1900," in *Modernist Impulses in the Human Sciences, 1870–1930*, ed. Dorothy Ross (Baltimore: Johns Hopkins University Press, 1994), 270.

Sociology and the Heroism of Modern Life

fostered by the change.[34] The rhetoric of crisis or even decline often accompanied their account of the transition away from the comparatively settled, inert, and integrated world modernity had irrevocably left behind.

But when they attempted to identify the source of that crisis and explain modernity's discontents, they infrequently, if at all, pondered the issue of heroism and its apparent irrelevance. The reason for this indifference is most explicit in the case of Durkheim, whose seminal works on the division of labor, suicide, and elementary forms of religious life were all motivated by a desire to discover and foster the sources of social integration after the decline of traditional institutions and practices. His life-long animus was directed against the corrosive power of excessive individualism, which had become a disturbing "cult" in the modern world, in favor of the maintenance of social solidarity. On a methodological level, this meant resisting the reduction of "social facts" to the level of the psychological or the whole of society to its component parts.[35] For Durkheim, society was ontologically *sui generis*, prior to and distinct from the individuals within it, who were wrongly thought to have constituted it by an act of contractual consent.[36] The structural forces that enabled social action were, he argued, more fundamental than the agency of the actors themselves.[37] Nor could a heroic meta-subject be construed as the genetic origin of the social totality. Durkheim's image of the human condition was that of *homo duplex*, in

---

[34] For a short, but comprehensive, survey of the attempts made by sociologists to analyze modernity, see Donald N. Levine, "Modernity and its Endless Discontents," in *After Parsons: A Theory of Social Action for the Twenty-first Century*, ed. Renée C. Fox, Victor M. Lidz, and Harold J. Bershady (New York: Russell Sage, 2005). He identifies several candidates for the primary characteristic posited by different sociologists: functional specialization, individuation, political unification, jural equalization, extension of new forms of discipline, normative universalization, and cultural rationalization, as well as the discontents associated with each.

[35] Émile Durkheim, *The Rules of Sociological Method*, ed. George E. G. Catlin, trans. Sarah A. Solovay and John H. Mueller (New York: Free Press, 1938).

[36] For Durkheim's polemic against contractualism, which was directed largely at Herbert Spencer, see *The Division of Labor*, trans. George Simpson (New York: Free Press, 1933), Chapter 7. His understanding of the priority of the community over the individual has sometimes been interpreted as anticipating the evolutionary biological belief that individual members of a species are merely vehicles for the transmission of genetic material, as well as structuralist linguistics. See Talcott Parsons, "Durkheim Revisited: Another Look at *The Elementary Forms of the Religious Life*," in *Beyond the Classics?: Essays in the Scientific Study of Religon*, ed. Charles Y. Glock and Phillip E. Hammond (New York: Harper and Row, 1973).

[37] The simple opposition between structuralist and social-action approaches to society has, to be sure, often been called into question, with many attempts to see them as reciprocally intertwined, but it is fair to say that Durkheim leaned heavily toward the priority of structure and system over action and agency, especially when the latter was understood in individualist terms.

which the desires and interests of embodied egos are in tension with the cognitive and moral imperatives they internalize from their society as a whole. Thus even extraordinary individuals were subjected to the "external constraint" exercised by social facts, which were collective representations that can be examined as if they were objective "things" in the world. As such, they could be subjected to a rigorous scientific analysis, fulfilling the hopes of Comtean positivism.

Against the Nietzschean ideal of heroic supermen who posited and followed their own individual morality, Durkheim was concerned with the recovery of a robust moral community, which he feared was undermined by the rampant individualism of modernity. Indeed, he thought that the science of sociology would provide a means to that end. What he famously bemoaned as anomie, a pathological erosion of the norms that bind a society together, sometimes leading to suicide,[38] could be countered only by the restoration of institutions, such as the family or corporation, that might foster the meaningful cohesion and unalienated sense of belonging that no individual hero – even one inspiring a rejuvenated nation-state – could provide.

Similar premises underlay his thoughts on politics. Appalled by *soi-disant* political heroes like General Georges Boulanger, whose coup to overthrow the Third Republic ended in a fiasco in 1889, Durkheim remained a staunch supporter of solidaristic republican values throughout his career.[39] Although there was, in fact, a hyper-masculinist, anti-republican cult of heroism in pre-World War I France, which sought to counter the alleged decadence of the times through a revitalization of the military ideal and the cultivation of competitive sports, Durkheim was not tempted by its regressive solutions to the ills of the modern world.[40] Nor did he succumb to the cult of vitalist *élan* spawned by the writings of Henri Bergson.

---

38 Anomic normlessness was, of course, only one of the explanations Durkheim provided for the etiology of suicide. The others were egoistic, altruistic, and, rarely, fatalistic (which resulted from too many norms, the opposite of the normlessness of anomie). See Émile Durkheim, *Suicide: A Study in Sociology*, ed. George Simpson, trans. John A. Spaulding and George Simpson (New York: Free Press, 1951).
39 Solidarism was a specific political movement during the Third Republic, led by Léon Bourgeois. For a discussion of Durkheim's loose affiliation with its goals, see Steven Lukes, *Emile Durkheim: His Life and Work* (London: Allen Lane, 1973), 50–54.
40 See Paul Gerbod, "L'éthique héroïque en France (1870–1914)," *La Revue historique*, 268(2) (1983), 409–429; and Robert A. Nye, *Masculinity and Male Codes of Honor in Modern France* (New York: Oxford, 1993), 218–222. Restoring ideals of military valor and courage meant reversing a trend that has been traced as far back as the reign of Louis XIV. According to Paul Rabinow, "during his reign there emerged a discourse of discipline and machine-like regulation of the body; the representation of the soldier as a controlled parallelogram of forces replaced that of the heroic warrior." Paul Rabinow, *French Modern: Norms and Forms of the Social Environment* (Chicago: University of Chicago Press, 1995), 117.

Even when it came to religion, whose "elementary" or primitive forms Durkheim explored late in his career, heroic founding figures played a very minor role. Although there were, he conceded in his discussion of the religious lives of Australian aboriginals, what he called "civilizing heroes," their function was entirely symbolic: "the fabulous beings whom we call by this name are really simple ancestors to whom mythology has attributed an eminent place in the history of the tribe, and whom it has, for this reason, set above the others."[41] They are often simulacra of a great god, who is an ancestral spirit given a special place in a totemic system and who is cast in turn in the image of individual souls. But these "are only the form taken by the impersonal forces which we found at the basis of totemism, as they individualize themselves in the human body."[42] Whatever the source of Durkheim's understanding of the sacred as a category rooted in the collective consciousness of society – sometimes it is attributed to his nostalgia for the concretely embodied, organic Jewish community out of which he had come[43] – it was prior to the utilitarian pursuit of individual self-interests or the hedonistic satisfaction of appetitive desires. Its role, moreover, was still central in even the allegedly secularized society of the present.[44] For Durkheim, who has rightly been called a "symbolic realist," the internalization of moral norms created an internal moral environment, which was the source of even the apparently spontaneous actions of a genius.[45] Insofar as rituals and shared behavioral patterns are prior to conscious beliefs, heroes are the effects of collective effervescence and not its causes.

Thus, although it might be possible to see some residues of Baudelaire's symptomology of modernity in Durkheim's description of anomie or interest in the issue of suicide,[46] it would be difficult to attribute to him

---

41 Émile Durkheim, *The Elementary Forms of the Religious Life*, trans. Joseph Ward Swain (New York: Free Press, 1968), 328.
42 Durkheim, *The Elementary Forms of the Religious Life*, 333.
43 For a discussion of Durkheim's complex relation to his Jewish identity, see Ivan Strenski, *Durkheim and the Jews of France* (Chicago: University of Chicago Press, 1997).
44 The general recognition among sociologists of the abiding power of religion or its functional equivalents in modernity has long been acknowledged; see, for example, Nisbet, *The Sociological Tradition*, Chapter 6.
45 Durkheim's disdain for the inner spontaneity of the individual genius was directed against the defense of it made by Gabriel Tarde. See the discussion in Dominick LaCapra, *Emile Durkheim: Sociologist and Philosopher* (Aurora: The Davies Group, 2001), 216–217. He points out that Durkheim sought to go beyond the dichotomy between external, conventional persona and internal, authentic self.
46 For an attempt to do so, see Stjepan G. Meštrović, *The Coming Fin de Siècle: An Application of Durkheim's Sociology to Modernity and Postmodernism* (London: Routledge, 1991), Chapter 5. He claims that Benjamin's "observation that for Baudelaire, modernism exists under the sign of suicide, resonates with Durkheim's claim that suicide is the 'ransom

any notion of individual heroism as an antidote to it. The sociological tradition inspired by Durkheim and institutionalized in the university system of France after his death retained a strong disdain for the priority of the individual over society, and was accordingly uninterested in whatever residues of heroism might be active in the modern world.[47] Despite the occasional desperate appeal to self-sacrificial heroism by the outlier "sacred sociologists" who gathered around the Collège de Sociologie in the 1930s, French sociology resisted even an ironic valorization of the "heroism of modern life."[48]

**

What can be said of his two great German counterparts, Weber and Simmel?[49] The former did pioneering work on the rationalization, secularization, and bureaucratization of the "disenchanted" world that emerged from the rise of capitalism, which he explained through the sociology of religion combined with economic analysis. The latter investigated modern art and culture, the experience of metropolitan life in all its motley variety, the forms of social interaction, the philosophy of money, and a welter of seemingly marginal topics such as fashion, flirtation, and the stranger. In contrast to Durkheim, both came to sociology filtered through German historicism's validation of the unique individual, and thus resisted the

> money' of civilization" (75–76), and that "Durkheim was indirectly mirroring Baudelaire's indictment of the modern dandy in his own comments on French Romanticism." (78). David Frisby also notes Benjamin's observation that for Baudelaire suicide was the quintessence of modernity, and adds "several decades after Baudelaire's death, the sociologist Emile Durkheim felt compelled to assess the role of 'the different currents of collective sadness' and 'collective melancholy' in causing the 'morbid effervescence' of suicide." David Frisby, *Fragments of Modernity: Theories of Modernity in the Work of Simmel, Kracauer and Benjamin* (Cambridge: MIT Press, 1986), 263. These are odd arguments insofar as Baudelaire didn't indict dandyism, but defended it, and Durkheim never turned suicide into an act of heroic rebellion.

47 For an account of the institutional success of the Durkheimians, see Terry Nichols Clark, *Prophets and Patrons: The French University and the Emergence of the Social Sciences* (Cambridge: Harvard University Press, 1973).

48 In his report of a meeting to discuss the crisis of democracy at the Collège in December, 1938, Bertrand d'Astorg records without attribution the sentiment that "a country unable to rouse a hero to defend it, or better to cultivate it, is dead. But any system breaking the human will to heroism is criminal." Denis Hollier (ed.), *The College of Sociology 1937–39*, trans. Betsy Wing (Minneapolis: University of Minnesota Press, 1988), 195.

49 Comparisons between Weber and Durkheim are more plentiful in the secondary literature than comparisons between Simmel and Durkheim. For a good short instance of the former, see Reinhard Bendix, "Two Sociological Traditions," in Reinhard Bendix and Guenther Roth, *Scholarship and Partisanship: Essays on Max Weber* (Berkeley: University of California Press, 1971). For examples of the latter, see Kurt H. Wolff, "The Challenge of Durkheim and Simmel," *American Journal of Sociology*, 63(6) (May 1958), 590–596; and Meštrović, *The Coming Fin de Siècle*, Chapter 4.

Sociology and the Heroism of Modern Life

Frenchman's insistence on the *sui generis* quality of constraining "social facts" understood objectively from the outside. However much they sought to understand the regularities of social life in the spirit of scientific disinterest, they still pitted what the neo-Kantian Heinrich Rickert famously called the "idiographic" against the "nomothetic" impulse in historical and social analysis. Weber's celebrated reliance on "ideal types" as heuristic devices drew on an ontology that was more nominalist than realist when it came to the general patterns of social life. Although resisting what he saw as Simmel's problematic effacing of the boundary between psychology and sociology, Weber stressed social action and its motivations rather than focusing, as had Durkheim, on the level of constraining structures. Moreover, unlike Durkheim, neither Simmel nor Weber entertained much hope for the restoration of collectively binding meaning via the expedient of restored corporative institutions (or what another founding father of sociology, Ferdinand Tönnies, had famously called "community" [*Gemeinschaft*] as opposed to "society" [*Gesellschaft*]). Despite their enthusiasm for the German cause in World War I, they were reluctant to follow Sombart in applying the category of "hero" to their own nation and contrasting it to so-called "merchant" nations on the enemy side.[50]

When it came to heroic individuals, Weber and Simmel were more ambivalent than their French counterpart, and traces of the heroic vitalism of *Lebensphilosophie* can be found at points in their work. Admiring Nietzsche's diagnosis of the crisis of meaning in modernity, both Weber and Simmel were deeply impressed by his validation of the nobility of character and distrust of egalitarian leveling.[51] Weber's celebrated concept of "personality" (*Persönlichkeit*) resonated with Nietzsche's disdain for the impersonality and functionality of modern existence, in which a yawning gap

---

50 Weber, to be sure, was also fervently nationalist and defended German imperialism. For a discussion of his theory of leadership in the context of German elitist political thought, see Walter Struve, *Elites against Democracy: Leadership Ideals in Bourgeois Political Thought in Germany, 1890–1933* (Princeton: Princeton University Press, 1973), Chapter 4. And for a short period during World War I, Simmel too joined the chorus of German jingoists.

51 For a comparison of their reactions to Nietzsche, see Lawrence A. Scaff, *Fleeing the Iron Cage: Culture, Politics, and Modernity in the Thought of Max Weber* (Berkeley: University of California Press, 1989), 127–133. For discussions of Weber and Nietzsche, see Robert Eden, *Political Leadership and Nihilism: A Study of Weber and Nietzsche* (Tampa: University Presses of Florida, 1983); Tracy B. Strong, "Love, Passion, and Maturity: Nietzsche and Weber on Science, Morality and Politics," in *Confronting Mass Democracy and Industrial Technology: Political and Social Theory from Nietzsche to Habermas*, ed. John P. McCormick (Durham: Duke University Press, 2002); and Ralph Schroeder, "Nietzsche and Weber: Two 'Prophets' of the Modern World," in *Max Weber, Rationality and Modernity*, ed. Sam Whimster and Scott Lash (London: Allen and Unwin, 1987).

had opened between inner life and external role, subjective feelings and objective norms.[52] Responding to the imperative of what Weber understood as a secularized version of the Calvinist "calling" (*Beruf*), which evoked an ascetic constraint disdained by Nietzsche in his Dionysian moods, meant more than internalizing conventional social norms.[53] At a time of value relativism, it required choosing one's own ethical code, even worldview, and having the fortitude to live by it. It involved maintaining a dignified inner life rather than succumbing to base interests, needs, or desires, the driving motivations ascribed to men by the utilitarian tradition. It demanded a "pathos of distance," to cite once again Nietzsche's *Genealogy of Morals*, that was especially valuable in a political leader.[54]

In his wide-ranging ruminations on comparative religion, Weber in fact fully acknowledged the seminal role of heroes in founding many traditions.[55] It is indirectly evident, for example, in the lessons of an "ethical prophet," who provides a code of moral conduct that demands to be rigorously followed. In a letter of 1907 expressing his cautiously respectful view of Freudian psychoanalysis, Weber specifically referred to a "heroic" ethic, "which imposes on men demands of principle to which they are generally *not* able to do justice, except at the high points of their lives, but which serve as signposts pointing the way for man's endless *striving*."[56] Even more directly, he argued, religious

---

52 See Wilhelm Hennis, "Personality and Life Orders: Max Weber's Theme," in *Max Weber, Rationality and Modernity*, ed. Sam Whimster and Scott Lash (London: Allen and Unwin, 1987); and David Owen, *Maturity and Modernity: Nietzsche, Weber, Foucault and the Ambivalence of Reason* (London: Routledge, 1994), Chapter 7. Owen points out that whereas Nietzsche endorsed turning one's life into a work of art, Weber's personality realized himself through works in the world.

53 Weber's own wrestling with the concept of *Beruf* is traced in Arthur Mitzman, *The Iron Cage: An Historical Interpretation of Max Weber* (New York: Grosset and Dunlop, 1969). He cites a letter from the young Weber to his fiancée in which he confesses "I never had any kind of respect for the concept of 'calling,' since I thought I knew I fitted into a large number of positions, to a certain extent." (65). But then he notes that at the end of Weber's life, when he adopted a more realistic notion of politics, "the key concept which binds together aristocracy, charisma and political leadership is *Beruf* (calling) – i.e. precisely that concept from which, in *Wirtschaft und Gesellschaft*, Weber had clearly separated charisma." (247).

54 Max Weber, "Politics as Vocation," in *From Max Weber: Essays in Sociology*, ed. Hans Gerth and C. Wright Mills (New York: Oxford University Press, 1958), where he asserts that "'Lack of distance' *per se* is one of the deadly sins of every politician." (115).

55 See the discussion in Joseph W. H. Lough, *Weber and the Persistence of Religon: Social Theory, Capitalism and the Sublime* (New York: Routledge, 2006), Chapter 6.

56 Weber, letter to Edgar Jaffé, September 13, 1907, in *Weber: Selections in Translation*, ed. W. G. Runciman, trans. Eric Matthews (Cambridge: Cambridge University Press, 1978), 385. He cites older Christianity, "before it had lost its integrity," and Kantianism as examples, and contrasts their idealism with a more modest "ethic of the mean," which accepts man's nature as it is and puts no pressure on him to behave with ethical heroism. Freud, it should be noted, is included in the latter category.

Sociology and the Heroism of Modern Life

heroism is manifested in an "exemplary prophet," one who enjoins his followers to imitate his virtuous example. In such cases, discrete instances of heroic behavior can congeal into a characterological essence, as "formal sanctification by the good works shown in external actions is supplanted by the value of the total personality pattern, which in the Spartan example would be an habitual temper of heroism."[57] Such heroism can manifest itself in the inspirational courage of a warrior, who enacts righteous justice on the foes of God, but also in the loving mercy of a follower of a God whose measure of justice is ineffable to mere humans: "Unconditional forgiveness, unconditional charity, unconditional love even of enemies, unconditional suffering of injustice without requiting evil by force – these products of a mystically conditioned acosmism of love indeed constituted demands for religious heroism."[58] Religious heroism appeared, however, most explicitly in Weber's celebrated concept of charisma, which, although often compared to Durkheim's idea of the sacred, stressed with Nietzsche the importance of unique individuals rather than cultural symbols or ritual practices.[59]

An enormous amount of interpretive energy has been exercised in explicating the origins, meaning, and implications of this seminal idea, whose applicability Weber extended well beyond the religious sphere, but only a few points can be made here.[60] Weber, who prided himself on being a value-neutral social scientist, introduced charisma as an ideal type to characterize one of three major forms of "imperative coordination," or legitimate authority, that generated voluntary submission to a social order.[61] The other two were "traditional" and "rational–legal" authority. He was careful to note that

> it will be applied to a certain quality of an individual personality by virtue of which he is set apart from ordinary men and treated as endowed with

---

57 Max Weber, *The Sociology of Religion*, trans. Ephraim Fischoff (Boston: Beacon, 1964), 156.
58 Weber, *The Sociology of Religion*, 273.
59 For the comparison with Durkheim, see, for example, Nisbet, *The Sociological Tradition*, 252; and Edward Tiryakian, "Emile Durkheim," in *A History of Sociological Analysis*, ed. Tom Bottomore and Robert Nisbet (New York: Basic Books, 1978), 220. For the comparison with Nietzsche, see Wolfgang J. Mommsen, *The Age of Bureaucracy: Perspectives on the Political Sociology of Max Weber* (New York: Harper, 1977), 79.
60 The concept is most elaborately presented in Max Weber, *The Theory of Social and Economic Organization*, ed. Talcott Parsons (New York: Free Press, 1964), 358–392. For an insightful discussion, see Luciano Cavalli, "Charisma and Twentieth-Century Politics," in *Max Weber, Rationality and Modernity*, ed. Sam Whimster and Scott Lash (London: Allen and Unwin, 1987).
61 Parsons's awkward translation of *"Herrschaft"* as "imperative coordination" has generated considerable comment, as it could just as easily be translated as "domination" or "rulership." See the discussion in Richard Swedberg, *The Max Weber Dictionary: Key Words and Central Concepts* (Stanford: Stanford University Press, 2005), 64–66.

supernatural, superhuman, or at least specifically exceptional powers or qualities. These are such as are not accessible to the ordinary person, but are regarded as of divine origin or as exemplary, and on the basis of them the individual concerned is treated as a leader.[62]

By carefully noting that a charismatic leader functions as such only so far as those who follow him believe that he – and the pronoun is apt, as women are never among his examples – has certain gifts, Weber was distancing himself from the assumption that such a leader possesses intrinsically heroic qualities. He notes that the "gift of grace" attributed to the charismatic leader works only so long as he delivers what his followers expect of him; if not, the magic fades and the leader's feet of clay crumble. Charisma, in other words, is a relational concept based on intersubjective recognition, not inherent worth; and nor is it an ascribed role in a traditional hierarchy or a bureaucratic office.

Weber wore his disinterested "scientific" hat in identifying charisma's possible instantiations – in addition to religious prophets and magicians, he included political leaders, military heroes, gang leaders, and all who demonstrate the "rule of genius" as opposed to socially defined status – as well as its ability to be "routinized" in institutions that outlive its original moment, such as the Catholic Church.[63] He took pains to stress that false prophets, demagogic politicians, shamans, and "berserkers" must also be included in the category, for "sociological analysis, which must abstain from value judgments, will treat all of these on the same level as the men, who according to conventional judgments, are the 'greatest' heroes, prophets, and saviors."[64]

Weber saw charismatic leadership as increasingly rare in a spiritually disenchanted world that honored only rational–legal authority. Instrumental reason, privileging efficiency and formal regularity, had undermined the rule-bending power of a leader who could proclaim, as often had Jesus, "it is written, but I say unto you." Because it comes unprepared and its tenure is uncertain, charismatic appeal, in fact, has never existed in its pure form for very long, even if its after-effects can linger in the new routinized order that solidifies after its brief disruptive moment. It does, to be sure, always have the potential – and here Weber was acknowledging that his ideal types were normally mixed in

---

62 Weber, *The Theory of Social and Economic Organization*, 358–359.
63 For an insightful discussion of routinization, which distinguishes between depersonalized and impersonalized variations, see Wolfgang Schluchter, *The Rise of Western Rationalism: Max Weber's Developmental Theory*, trans. Guenther Roth (Berkeley: University of California Press, 1979), 124–125.
64 Swedberg, *The Max Weber Dictionary*, 359. Berserkers were old Norse warriors who went into battle in a trance-like state.

practice – to enhance the authority of those whose legitimacy was primarily derived from traditional or rational–legal sources.

More purely charismatic authority, Weber did, however, concede in one of his heroic vitalist moods, was still possible as an enlivening intervention in the prevailing order, an unexpected disruption of the everyday life that somehow can start something new in the world. But whether or not Weber, despite his efforts to mask his own emotional, political, and moral investments behind a façade of scientific value neutrality, covertly yearned for its emergence as a deliverance from what he famously described as the "iron cage" of bureaucratic rationalization has been much disputed.[65] In the last years before his death in 1920, so a number of commentators have argued, Weber did indeed flirt with the idea of such a solution to the impoverished life he lamented in modernity. "The extreme rationalization of the modern world," writes Harry Liebersohn, "set the stage for extreme heroism. Those who really wished to prove their personal charisma had to test it in an impersonal world: the scholar in the modern factory of learning, the politician amid the bureaucratic machine."[66] According to Wolfgang Mommsen, Weber, disillusioned by the failures of liberalism but not willing to scorn the masses, yearned for a Caesarist "plebiscitarian leader-democracy" to break the stalemate of modern politics.[67] This sympathy may well have found its logical conclusion in the anti-normative "decisionism" of Carl Schmitt and practical realization, in a sinister form Weber would never have embraced, thirteen years after his death in 1920.[68]

---

65 The original term *"stahlhartes Gehäuse"* was rendered as "iron cage" by Talcott Parsons in his influential translation of *The Protestant Ethic and the Spirit of Capitalism*, but has also been translated as "a shell as hard as steel" or "a steel-hard casing." For a discussion of the controversy over and afterlife of this metaphor, see Swedberg, *The Max Weber Dictionary*, 132–133.
66 Harry Liebersohn, *Fate and Utopia in German Sociology, 1870–1923* (Cambridge: MIT Press, 1988), 124.
67 Mommsen, *The Age of Bureaucracy*, Chapter 4.
68 The connection with Schmitt seems to have been first suggested by Jürgen Habermas, who originally called him "a legitimate pupil" of Weber and then modified the metaphor to "a natural son," that is, one born out of wedlock. See Jürgen Habermas, "The Discussion on Value-Freedom and Objectivity," in *Max Weber and Sociology Today*, ed. Otto Stammer (New York: Harper and Row, 1971), 66. The same volume contains a spirited discussion of Mommsen's argument and the role of nationalism, imperialism, and great-power politics in Weber's worldview: Raymond Aron, "Max Weber and Power-Politics," with comments by Carl J. Friedrich, Hans Paul Bahrdt, Wolfgang J. Mommsen, Karl W. Deutsch, Eduard Baumgarten, and Adolf Arndt, in *Max Weber and Sociology Today*, ed. Otto Stammer (New York: Harper and Row, 1971), 83–132. For one discussion of the connection, see Stephen Turner and Regis Factor, "Decisionism and Politics: Weber as a Constitutional Theorist," in *Max Weber, Rationality and Modernity*, ed. Sam Whimster and Scott Lash (London: Allen and Unwin, 1987).

On a more specifically cultural level, Weber's ambivalent attitude toward the lure of heroism has often been inferred from his complicated relationship with the poet Stefan George, the leader of an anti-modern, aristocratic cult in the years before World War I.[69] Weber was introduced to the George Kreis by Friedrich Gundolf in 1910 and deeply admired the charismatic poet's verse, which he saw as harnessing the formalist rigor of asceticism in the service of ecstatic transformation. But he soon became disillusioned with the snobbish elitism and political posturing of George's circle, differing, for example, over the justification of women's emancipation – George's homoeroticism was infused with explicit misogyny – as well as over "the meaning of heroism, which George considered insufficiently physical in the modern age and Weber, insufficiently intellectual."[70] Because its members foolishly mistook their cult for a genuinely revolutionary movement, the circle around George seems to have disabused Weber of his heroic vitalist belief, always tenuous, that charismatic leadership was an antidote to the ills of the modern world. By the time he delivered his celebrated lectures on "Politics as Vocation" and "Science as Vocation" a few years before his death in 1920, Weber seems to have increasingly embraced a non-charismatic politics, based more on an "ethics of responsibility" than an "ethics of ultimate ends," even if the former might reach a limit with what he called a *"mature* man" who felt the imperative to stand by his convictions.[71]

The revolutionary events at the end of the war further dampened any belief Weber might have had in charismatic heroes, and he grew increasingly estranged from friends like the Hungarian Marxist Georg Lukács, who embraced the revolutionary heroism of Lenin.[72] And yet, even in the famous final paragraph of his great lecture on the political vocation, in which he introduced the poignant metaphor of politics as "the strong and slow boring of hard boards," Weber could still acknowledge that attaining the possibility for someone with a political "calling" sometimes meant reaching for the impossible:

> But to do that a man must be a leader, and not only a leader but a hero as well, in a very sober sense of the word. And even those who are neither leaders nor heroes must arm themselves with that steadfastness of heart

---

[69] See, for example, Mitzman, *The Iron Cage*, 216–270; Scaff, *Fleeing the Iron Cage*, 106–108; and Liebersohn, *Fate and Utopia in German Sociology*, 150–151.

[70] Mitzman, *The Iron Cage*, 267.   [71] Weber, "Politics as Vocation," 127.

[72] For a comparison, see Árpád Kadarkay, "The Demonic Self: Max Weber and Georg Lukács," *Hungarian Studies*, 9(1/2) (1994), 77–102; and Liebersohn, *Fate and Utopia in German Sociology*, Chapter 6.

which can brave even the crumbling of all hopes. This is necessary right now, or else men will not be able to attain even that which is possible today."[73]

However, for a man such as Weber himself, whose vocation was that of a scientist, even a sober heroism was less important than acknowledging that "the fate of our times is characterized by rationalization and intellectualization, and, above all, by the 'disenchantment of the world.'"[74] For those too weak to bear this disillusionment, there was always the option of making an "intellectual sacrifice" and retreating into the bosom of the Church, which was more laudable than the academic prophecy that sought to use the lecture hall as a platform for demagoguery. But for those with the integrity to face the end of the age of heroes, there was only one course: "We shall set to work and meet the 'demands of the day,' in human relations as well as in our vocation. This, however, is plain and simple, if each finds and obeys the demon who holds the fibers of his very life."[75] It was sober sentiments like these that allowed many in the Weimar Republic to see Weber as an anti-utopian realist, a "heroic skeptic" who was right for "an age of iron."[76]

***

How did the other German founding father of modern sociology, Georg Simmel, comprehend the role of heroes in the modern world? He was, it seems, often more seriously tempted by Nietzsche's heroic vitalism than Weber, and was far less suspicious of the cultic pretensions or anti-feminism of Stefan George.[77] He specifically embraced the virtue of distinction (*Vornehmheit*), which he had praised in his study of *Schopenhauer and Nietzsche*, as an antidote to the homogenizing pressures of modern life.[78] Identified with an inner quality of character that transcended deeds in the world, it suggested an aristocratic state of being, an autonomous bearing, that was very different from the bourgeois stress on mundane actions. Against what he saw as the "Roman" or Enlightenment version of egalitarian, quantitative individualism, Simmel

---

73 Weber, "Politics as Vocation," 128.
74 Weber, "Science as Vocation," in *From Max Weber: Essays in Sociology*, ed. Hans Gerth and C. Wright Mills (New York: Oxford University Press, 1958), 155.
75 Weber, "Science as Vocation," 156. The phrase "demands of the day" was Goethe's, as was the idea of a personal "daemon," understood not in the sense of a Satanic minion, but as a source of spiritual inspiration. See Angus Nicholls, *Goethe's Concept of the Daemonic: After the Ancients* (Rochester: Camden House, 2006).
76 For a selection of these characterizations by intellectuals such as Ernst Troeltsch, Siegfried Kracauer, Karl Mannheim, and Christoph Steding, see Joshua Derman, "Skepticism and Faith: Max Weber's Anti-Utopianism in the Eyes of his Contemporaries," *Journal of the History of Ideas*, 71(3) (July 2010), 481–503.
77 Liebersohn, *Fate and Utopia in German Sociology*, 151; Scaff, *Fleeing the Iron Cage*, 144–149.
78 For a discussion, see Liebersohn, *Fate and Utopia in German Sociology*, 141–144.

favored a "German" or Romantic alternative that stressed qualitative difference instead.[79] "For Nietzsche," he approvingly wrote, "it is the qualitative *being* of the personality which marks the stage that the development of mankind has reached; it is the highest exemplars of a given time that carry humanity beyond its past. Thus Nietzsche overcame the limitations of merely social existence, as well as the valuation of man in terms of his sheer effects."[80] But, unlike Weber, Simmel never seems to have been tempted by the role such "highest exemplars" might play as political leaders. Nor did he theorize charisma as a relationally grounded mode of legitimate authority, even if for a while he too was caught up in the enthusiasm for the German war effort in 1914.

When it came to the mass society of modernity, Simmel contended that it was a new phenomenon "made up, not of the total individualities of its members, but only of those fragments of each of them in which he coincides with all others. These fragments, therefore, can be nothing but the lowest and most primitive."[81] Pondering Hegel's interpretation of the relationship between heroes and valets, Simmel blamed the latter for not tendering the respect owed to the former, thus failing to display the "inner compulsion which tells one to keep at a distance and which does not disappear even in intimate relations with him. The only type for whom such distance does not exist is the individual who has no organ for perceiving significance. For this reason, the 'valet' knows no such sphere of distance; for him there is no 'hero'; but this is due not to the *hero*, but to the valet."[82]

But without Hegel's "comic" faith in the ultimate rationality of history, Simmel resisted casting the hero in the role of world-historical agent of that rationalization and disdaining the ignoble valet for failing to appreciate his larger function. "However true it may be that the valet does not understand the hero because he cannot rise to his height," he wrote, "it is equally true that the hero does not understand the valet because he cannot lower himself

---

79 For a discussion, see Efraim Podoksik, "Georg Simmel: Three Forms of Individualism and Historical Understanding," *New German Critique*, No. 109 (Winter 2010), 119–145, which argues that there was an often ignored third meaning in his *lebensphilosophische* later work, which understood the individual as a reflection of the totality of life.
80 Georg Simmel, "Individual and Society in Eighteenth- and Nineteenth-Century Views of Life: An Example of Philosophical Sociology," in *The Sociology of Georg Simmel*, ed. and trans. Kurt H. Wolff (New York: Free Press, 1964), 63.
81 Georg Simmel, "The Social and the Individual Level: An Example of General Sociology," in *The Sociology of Georg Simmel*, ed. and trans. Kurt H. Wolff (New York: Free Press, 1964), 33.
82 Georg Simmel, "Types of Relationships by Degrees of Reciprocal Knowledge of their Participants," in *The Sociology of Georg Simmel*, ed. and trans. Kurt H. Wolff (New York: Free Press, 1964), 321.

to his subordinate level."[83] Because of Simmel's relativist perspectivism, which abjured Durkheim's objectivist stance and belief in observable "social facts," and his scorn for the disinterested scientific rigor sought by Weber, it is difficult, in fact, to define a conclusive position on the question of heroism or much else in modern life.[84] Although he was initially attracted to Spencer's scientific theory of evolutionary social differentiation, Simmel went through a neo-Kantian phase and ultimately embraced the *lebensphilosophische* stress on the ineffable qualities of a "life" that defied subsumption into conceptual categories or long-term historical patterns. As much a philosopher and aesthetician as a sociologist, Simmel was a self-defined formalist, interested in the abiding interactions of social life, the web or labyrinth of inter-related connections in which fragmented personal experience took place, rather than their historical development over time or their coalescence into a coherent community above the shifting social relations between and among individual selves. Even the meta-category of "society," which was so crucial for such sociologists as Durkheim, Simmel found wanting.[85]

Simmel's increasing attraction to vitalism did not, however, lead him to embrace the heroic variety emplotted in a romantic mode described by Eric Bentley. As a shrewd phenomenologist of the modern experience, a micro-logical analyst of the endless differentiations of everyday life, he in fact earned the plaudits of those who saw him as developing the ironic insights of Baudelaire so valued by such later thinkers as Benjamin and Foucault.[86] Steeped in the aestheticism that Weber knew only from the outside and a gifted interpreter of the fleeting, surface manifestations of modern culture, Simmel wrote extensively about the arts and adopted a method that often invited comparison with the impressionist painters of his era. When he wrote

83 Simmel, "The Social and the Individual Level," 39.
84 Simmel's approach is often called impressionistic and anti-systematic, with a typical description of the characteristics of his style reading as follows: "different problems more or less simultaneously and without any clear indication of how they are linked, the inclination to eschew careful analysis and detailed argument in favor of pregnant examples and glittering insights, and the playful and inconclusive quality of the inquiry itself, in which aesthetic considerations frequently seem to outweigh the requirements of science." Guy Oakes, "Introduction," to *Georg Simmel: On Women, Sexuality and Love*, trans. Guy Oakes (New Haven: Yale University Press, 1984), 58. Useful introductions to his thought include David Frisby, *Georg Simmel* (Chichester: Horwood, 1984); and Rudolf H. Weingartner, *Experience and Culture: The Philosophy of Georg Simmel* (Middletown: Wesleyan University Press, 1962).
85 For a general analysis of the idea of "society," see David Frisby and Derek Sayer, *Society* (Chichester: Horwood, 1986), which compares Durkheim and Simmel.
86 Frisby, *Fragments of Modernity*; Swingewood, *Cultural Theory and the Problem of Modernity*; and Elizabeth S. Goodstein, *Experience without Qualities: Boredom and Modernity* (Stanford: Stanford University Press, 2005).

about economic themes – as he did in his magisterial *Philosophy of Money* in 1900 – it was more in terms of their effects on personal experience than in those of historically discrete modes of production or the rise of capitalist industrialization; value, he insisted, was a subjective not an objective category, and the exchange value of a commodity was more important than the labor congealed in it.[87] Simmel was an acute diagnostician of the interaction of technological innovations, epitomized by the emergence of electricity as a radical new source of energy in the lives of urban dwellers, and the emotional stresses of those subjected to them, producing the epidemic of "neurasthenia" suffered by many in the modern world.[88] Even for those who escaped its pathological consequences, Simmel argued in his most influential essay "The Metropolis and Mental Life," "the psychological basis of the metropolitan type of individuality consists in the *intensification of nervous stimulation* which results from the swift and uninterrupted change of outer and inner stimuli."[89] As a reaction to over-stimulation, the typical attitude of the modern urban dweller was one of blasé indifference and cautious, self-protective reserve, providing the beleaguered individual space to enable some exercise of personal freedom. His dispassionate "cool conduct" may have preserved a certain interpersonal distance, but it did not provide that "pathos" of elevation of mankind's "highest exemplars" over the herd extolled by Nietzsche.[90]

Where, if anywhere, we might ask, was the ironic heroism in Simmel's analysis of modern life? One obvious place to look for an answer would be his invocation of the model of tragedy to characterize enduring aspects of modern life, which appeared in at least two places in his work. In his essay on "The Individual's Superiority over the Mass," Simmel introduced the term "the sociological tragedy." He defined it as the tension between people understood as unique individuals, where they might become figures of distinction

87 Georg Simmel, *The Philosophy of Money*, trans. Tom Bottomore and David Frisby (Boston: Routledge & Kegan Paul, 1978). The concept of personal experience underlying Simmel's analysis was more that of transitory *Erlebnis* than cumulative *Erfahrung*, a distinction more explicitly thematized by Benjamin. See Frisby, *Fragments of Modernity*, 63. For my own attempt to sort out different modes of experience, see Martin Jay, *Songs of Experience: Modern European and American Variations on a Universal Theme* (Berkeley: University of California Press, 2005).
88 For an analysis of this interaction, which discusses Simmel and the city he knew so well, see Andreas Killen, *Berlin Electropolis: Shock, Nerves, and German Modernity* (Berkeley: University of California Press, 2006).
89 Georg Simmel, "The Metropolis and Mental Life," in *The Sociology of Georg Simmel*, ed. and trans. Kurt H. Wolff (New York: Free Press, 1964), 409–410.
90 For a discussion of the widespread culture of self-armoring in Weimar Germany, especially during the mid-1920s period of the "Neue Sachlichkeit," see Helmut Lethen, *Cool Conduct: The Culture of Distance in Weimar Germany*, trans. Don Reneau (Berkeley: University of California Press, 2002).

and refinement, and people in their role as members of the "folk" or "mass," where they are reduced to their "lower and primitively more sensuous levels."[91] Exposure to collective pressures, Simmel lamented, "corrupts the character. It pulls the individual away from his individuality and down to a level with all and sundry."[92] That is, heroes are turned into valets when they make common cause with the masses. This was a sociological tragedy because it prevented men of distinction from assuming leading public roles.

Simmel's even more influential notion of the "tragedy of culture," which he developed in a series of essays that culminated in "The Conflict of Modern Culture," written shortly before his death in 1920, pointed to the unbridgeable gap between the act of subjective creation and the objective world of enduring prior creations. This type of tragedy resulted from the ineluctable conflict between dynamic, creative life and the reified "spiritual" forms that it left behind, forms that could only confront the creative subject as external constraints.[93] Although it is a cultural constant, the gap seems to have widened in the modern world. According to Simmel, "the real cultural malaise of modern man is the result of this discrepancy between the objective substance of culture, both concrete and abstract, on the one hand, and, on the other, the subjective culture of individuals who feel this objective culture to be something alien, which does violence to them and with which they cannot keep pace."[94] Attempts to reassert the dominance of life, whether in philosophy with pragmatism, in art with expressionism, or in religion with mysticism, were doomed to fail, for no one was able to reconcile life and forms, subjective and objective culture.

The tragedies of society and culture are ongoing, indeed accelerating, dramas in the modern world, and Simmel had no faith in a future comic resolution to their tensions. Nor was the romantic quest to do so, extolled by the heroic vitalists, really worth pursuing. What is even more important, for our purposes, is that these tragedies lack what might be called a tragic hero, whose courageous, if vain, quest for redemption is thwarted by fate. Even the outsider figures extolled by Baudelaire – prostitutes, artists, rag-pickers, *flâneurs*, dandies, lesbians, apaches, conspirators, suicides – are unable for Simmel to play this heroic role, which, it will be recalled, Benjamin had said was still "available" to be filled in the poet's lifetime. As one commentator has

91 Georg Simmel, "The Individual's Superiority over the Mass," in *The Sociology of Georg Simmel*, ed. and trans. Kurt H. Wolff (New York: Free Press, 1964), 32.
92 Simmel, "The Individual's Superiority over the Mass," 32.
93 Georg Simmel, "The Conflict of Modern Culture," in *Georg Simmel: Sociologist and European*, ed. Peter Lawrence (Sunbury-on-Thames: Nelson, 1976).
94 Georg Simmel, "The Future of our Culture" (1909), in *Georg Simmel: Sociologist and European*, ed. Peter Lawrence (Sunbury-on-Thames: Nelson, 1976), 251.

noted, "while sharing Baudelaire's emphasis on the fragment and the micrological, Simmel's modernity departs radically from Baudelaire through grounding modernity in the metanarrative of irreconcilable tragedy of culture, its failure to generate unity in the face of commodity fetishism and reification."[95]

Whereas Simmel's student and friend Georg Lukács came to believe the conflict between form and life was only a feature of bourgeois society and not of culture in general, and was thus able to identify a class hero – the proletariat – as the means to overcome it, Simmel himself never did.[96] The noble personalities he valued for their Nietzschean *Vornehmheit* and pathos of distance were inner émigrés from the modern world without the will or means to transform it. The distinction between healthy objectification and pathological reification, which allowed Marxists like Lukács to believe the latter could be overcome through the overthrow of capitalism, was not for him a meaningful alternative. As Jürgen Habermas was to put it,

> [Simmel] detached the pathologies unveiled in the modern lifestyle from their historical connections and attributed them to the tendency, embedded with the process of life, towards the estrangement between the soul and its forms. A strangeness that is so deeply rooted in metaphysics robs the diagnosis of the times of the power and courage of political–practical conclusions.[97]

But despite all of his ahistorical fatalism, there was still in Simmel a glimmer of the ironic heroism that Foucault had discerned in Baudelaire's response to modern life, and one which ties him to the attitude we have already noted in Durkheim's cool observation of "social facts" from the outside and Weber's ruminations on science as a vocation. In "The Salon of 1846," Baudelaire had identified the black frock-coat of the dandies of his day as the "outer skin of the modern hero" and called it "the inevitable uniform of our suffering age, carrying on its very shoulders, black and narrow, the mark of perpetual mourning." And then added, "a uniform livery of grief is a proof of equality."[98] Foucault understood the implications of this

---

95 Swingewood, *Cultural Theory and the Problem of Modernity*, 146.
96 In his essay collection of 1909, *Soul and Form*, trans. Anna Bostock (Cambridge: MIT Press, 1974), Lukács adopted the same argument we have traced in Simmel, but after his conversion to Marxism in 1918, he explicitly repudiated it, as well as any romanticization of the *Lumpenproletariat* praised by Baudelaire. For an analysis of their relationship, see Liebersohn, *Fate and Utopia in German Sociology*. It should be noted that the German word "*Seele*," which is sometimes translated as "soul" and sometimes as "psyche" could be counterposed not only to "form," but also to *Geist*, "intellect" or "spirit."
97 Jürgen Habermas, "Georg Simmel on Philosophy and Culture: Postscript to a Collection of Essays," *Critical Inquiry*, 22(3) (Spring 1996), 403–414, p. 413.
98 Baudelaire, "The Salon of 1846," 105.

insight, which he said was as much a mode of relationship with the self as with the present moment: "the deliberate attitude of modernity is tied to an indispensable asceticism."[99]

Although Foucault went on to say that Baudelaire understood this asceticism to be the special preserve of artists alone, with no place in society or politics, it may well be that it found a place as well in modern sociology, at least in the varieties inspired by the founding fathers we have examined. Simmel's project in particular drew, as David Frisby has pointed out, on the qualities Baudelaire attributed to the painter of modern life. Both valued a certain mode of experiencing the present, a mode involving ascetic self-distancing: "its presentation carries with it a necessary confrontation with the reflexivity of his analysis since the mode of accounting for *modernité* also belongs to the modernist tradition itself."[100] That is, Simmel tells us that the heroic ironization of the present extends as well to the sociologist's own attitude toward modern society. And as such, it also extends to the modern self, including that of the sociologist. For all of Weber's ambivalent attraction to charismatic authority, he too, as we have seen, interpreted the calling of the scientist, a calling that echoed the Calvinist tradition of ascetic constraint, as one of ironic restraint.[101] In fact, the "heroic renunciation" of the Puritans who espoused the "Protestant ethic" and delayed material gratification may well have been the ideal model for Weber's man of science.[102]

This insight leaves us with an unexpected conclusion. The hero of modern life, it turns out, may not be that romantic man of action on an infinite quest for whom the heroic vitalists so passionately yearned, nor the comic world-historical leader who is an agent of historical reason, as Hegel had hoped. He – or she – may be instead the ascetic, distant observer of a rapidly unfolding tragedy, who has only ironic reflexivity to ward off the lure of false solutions to intractable problems that remain, alas, far easier to acknowledge than to solve. *Pace* the latter-day devotees of Marx's eleventh *Thesis on Feuerbach*, the hero of modern life may well be the one who soberly interprets the world rather than tries rashly and, alas, vainly to change it.

---

99 Foucault, "What Is Enlightenment?," 41.   100 Frisby, *Fragments of Modernity*, 41.
101 As David Kettler and Colin Load note in their discussion of the legacy of Weber and Simmel, "Weimar sociology took its brief from their newly ironic orientation." David Kettler and Colin Load, "Weimar Sociology," in *Weimar Thought: A Contested Legacy*, ed. Peter E. Gordon and John P. McCormick (Princeton: Princeton University Press, 2013), 18.
102 Frédéric Vandenberghe, "Simmel and Weber as Ideal-Typical Founders of Sociology," *Philosophy and Social Criticism*, 25(4) (1999), 57–80, p. 59.

2

Psychoanalysis: Freud and Beyond

KATJA GUENTHER

Freud's Psychoanalysis

Perhaps more than any other discipline, psychoanalysis is intimately associated with its founder, Sigmund Freud (1856–1939). That is, of course, no coincidence. From the beginning, Freud bound his new science to his life and psychic world: *The Interpretation of Dreams* (1899/1900) – to many the Ur-text of psychoanalysis – is informed predominantly by Freud's self-analysis. Despite the enormous variety of psychoanalytic practice, Freud's centrality to the field's self-understanding only increased over the course of the twentieth century, when his legacy was bolstered by a series of hagiographic biographies, the best known of which was published in three volumes by Ernest Jones in the 1950s.[1] Moreover, it has been common to apply psychoanalytic insights to Freud's life in order to explain the development of his science.[2]

And yet there is an irony to this attempt to privilege Freud in psychoanalysis, which is a form of thought and medical practice that considers individuals to be constituted by their social relationships and experience of the world. Consequently, in what John C. Burnham has called "The New Freud Studies," a group of revisionist scholars has sought to place Freud in context.[3] Today, we are seeing the benefits of this approach for examining

---

[*] I would like to thank Edward Baring, Giuseppe Bianco, Michael Gordin, Peter E. Gordon, and Eli Mandel for their insightful comments and suggestions.

[1] Ernest Jones, *The Life and Work of Sigmund Freud*, 3 vols. (New York: Basic Books, 1953–1957). The work was commissioned by Freud's daughter Anna after several sensationalist biographies had been published. Elisabeth Young-Bruehl, "A History of Freud Biographies," in *Discovering the History of Psychiatry*, ed. Mark Micale (New York: Oxford University Press, 1994), 157–173.

[2] For example Peter Gay, *Freud: A Life for Our Time* (New York: Norton, 1988).

[3] John C. Burnham, "The 'New Freud Studies': A Historiographical Shift," *The Journal of the Historical Society*, 6(2) (2006), 213–233. See John Forrester, *Language and the Origins of Psychoanalysis* (London: MacMillan, 1980); Lydia Marinelli and Andreas Mayer, *Dreaming*

both Freud's life and the history of psychoanalysis more generally.[4] Scholars are becoming increasingly aware that one can understand the movement only by displacing its most famous proponent from center-stage.

Freud's Early Scientific Work

Despite this historiographical development, and perhaps due to the Freud Wars of the 1980s and 1990s, where the scientificity of Freud's claims was placed in doubt, there have been few attempts to examine the scientific context of Freud's work, which nevertheless shaped much of his early career.[5] Before settling down as a physician in private practice in 1886, Freud had spent over a decade working in laboratories – dissecting eels and staining cells and examining them under a microscope. Freud worked at Vienna's Institute for Comparative Anatomy under the zoologist and Haeckel-opponent Carl Claus (and for a while at his marine research station in Trieste), and in the laboratory of physiologist Ernst Brücke.[6] On the basis of this laboratory work, he was able to submit his Habilitation (a second doctorate, which in the German-speaking world made one eligible for academic positions) and become a Privatdozent in 1885.[7]

Arguably the most important scientific influence on Freud's early career was that of the neuropsychiatrist Theodor Meynert. Freud worked with Meynert at the Second Psychiatric Clinic in the Vienna General Hospital in 1883 and, for two years afterwards, conducted research at Meynert's neuropathological laboratory. There, Freud had ample opportunity to learn about the major tenets of Meynert's work. Following the doyen of psychiatry Wilhelm Griesinger's dictum that mental disease was brain disease, Meynert sought to explain psychiatric conditions through brain pathology, which for him meant correlating mental dysfunction with damage to the

---

by the Book: Freud's Interpretation of Dreams and the History of the Psychoanalytic Movement, trans. Susan Fairfield (New York: Other Press, 2003); Andreas Mayer, Sites of the Unconscious: Hypnosis and the Emergence of the Psychoanalytic Setting, trans. Christopher Barber (Chicago: University of Chicago Press, 2013); and George Makari, Revolution in Mind: The Creation of Psychoanalysis (New York: HarperCollins, 2008).

4 Burnham, "The 'New Freud Studies.'" See also the more recent Dagmar Herzog, Cold War Freud: Psychoanalysis in an Age of Catastrophes (Cambridge: Cambridge University Press, 2017); and Élisabeth Roudinesco, Freud, in His Time and Ours, trans. Catherine Porter (Cambridge: Harvard University Press, 2016).

5 There is early scholarship that contextualizes Freud's work within science, for example Maria Dorer, Historische Grundlagen der Psychoanalyse (Leipzig: Felix Meiner, 1932).

6 Todd Dufresne, Against Freud: Critics Talk Back (Stanford: Stanford University Press, 2007), 1.

7 Although, as is well known, an academic career did not work out for Freud, for reasons of anti-Semitism amongst others, the title of Privatdozent allowed Freud to have a socially elevated practice.

brain, as revealed in autopsy. Through this work he hoped to localize the parts of the brain responsible for different psychological functions.[8]

Freud was not fully convinced by Meynert's model.[9] In particular, he found it difficult to relate its explanation of mental pathology to a disease that he confronted with increasing regularity in his private practice: hysteria. Freud had first become acquainted with hysteria during his 1885–1886 stay with the prominent French neurologist Jean-Martin Charcot at the Salpêtrière hospital in Paris. And while Meynert explained mental disease by physical damage, Charcot had argued that hysteria was caused by psychological experience. In the 1890s, Freud's uneasiness with Meynert's theory only became more pronounced, when he started a collaboration with the more senior physician Josef Breuer. Because Breuer had a successful private practice, and was the source of many patient referrals, his support was crucial for Freud in those early, financially insecure years of his career. Their shared interest in hysteria, a disease frequently diagnosed in their patients, led to the *Studies on Hysteria* (1895). In the jointly written "Preliminary Communication," used as an introduction to the book, Freud and Breuer formulated the insight that would sharpen their dissatisfaction with neuropsychiatric localization and later serve as the basis of Freud's psychoanalysis: "[h]ysterics suffer mainly from reminiscences."[10]

While this claim was at odds with Meynert's lesion-based theory, Freud thought that the latter could be revised to make sense of it. When he had applied the localization model to higher functions, Meynert had drawn on the work of association psychologists, for whom mental activity could be explained by the association of different *Vorstellungen* (sensations, or images). The simultaneous consciousness of the image of a lamb and bleating, for instance, allowed the mind to associate the two, such that a future experience of bleating would recall the image of a lamb. Meynert translated this psychological model into neurological language. Each *Vorstellung* resided in a separate cortical nerve cell, connected to the sense organs via a system of projection fibers. If two of these *Vorstellungen* appeared in consciousness

---

8 Theodor Meynert, *Psychiatrie: Klinik der Erkrankungen des Vorderhirns, begründet auf dessen Bau, Leistungen und Ernährung* (Vienna: Wilhelm Braumüller, 1884).
9 For a history of the Meynert–Wernicke model and Freud's engagement with it, see Katja Guenther, *Localization and Its Discontents: A Genealogy of Psychoanalysis and the Neuro Disciplines* (Chicago: University of Chicago Press, 2015).
10 Josef Breuer and Sigmund Freud, "On the Psychical Mechanism of Hysterical Phenomena: Preliminary Communication," in *Studies on Hysteria* (1893–1895), in *The Standard Edition of the Complete Psychological Works of Sigmund Freud*, ed. and trans. James Strachey, 24 vols. (London: Hogarth Press, 1953–1974) (henceforth *SE*), vol. II, 1–17, p. 7.

together, this would lead the two to be connected through another "association" fiber.[11]

In order to account for hysteria, Freud took the association model a step further. Since, as Meynert had argued, associations were forged by experience, perhaps certain experiences could produce pathological associations, which would not show up as brain damage, and yet could still cause mental illness. Meynert's associative model, that is, could be reworked to explain how hysteria might be caused by memories. This is the argument Freud set out to make in his 1895 *Project for a Scientific Psychology*. As Freud put it, diseases such as hysteria corresponded to what he called a "pathological symbol-formation," which, though repressed (*verdrängt*) and pushed out of consciousness, could still cause disturbances there.[12]

The Birth of Psychoanalysis

The idea that certain associations had been effectively forgotten and yet could still impinge on the psychic life of the present informed Freud's ideas about the unconscious. In what came to be known as Freud's first topography, Freud distinguished three domains of the human psyche.[13] First, there was consciousness, the realm of the psyche of which the individual was aware. Of course, not all aspects of our psychic life were conscious at all times, so second, Freud posited the existence of the pre-conscious, which included those elements that could be brought into consciousness but were not present in consciousness at any particular time. Some memories, however, that were too threatening to the psyche to be allowed free access to our waking life, could not be instantly recalled. These rather inhabited the third realm: the unconscious.

Freud's associative model also opened up a path toward treatment. Already in the 1895 *Studies on Hysteria* Freud had discussed the cases of five patients – one, the famous Anna O. (in reality, Bertha Pappenheim), had been treated by Breuer; the other four were treated by Freud. As Freud presented them, these cases showed that, while the offending memories had been

---

11 Theodor Meynert, "Anatomie der Hirnrinde als Träger des Vorstellungslebens und ihrer Verbindungsbahnen mit den empfindenden Oberflächen und den bewegenden Massen," in *Lehrbuch der psychischen Krankheiten*, ed. Maximilian Leidesdorf (Erlangen: Enke, 1865), 45–73, pp. 52–53.
12 Sigmund Freud, *Project for a Scientific Psychology*, in SE, vol. I, 281–391, p. 350.
13 Sigmund Freud, *The Interpretation of Dreams*, in SE, vol. V (1901), Chapter 7. It has been proposed, however, that Freud had developed his conceptualization earlier, in the *Project*, and since then in his correspondence with Wilhelm Fließ; see Jean Laplanche and Jean-Bertrand Pontalis, *The Language of Psychoanalysis* (New York: Norton, 1974), 450.

repressed, they could be accessed in the process of analysis. Once the repressed memories were brought to light, the patient got better. Breuer had called this approach the "cathartic method," but Anna O.'s name for the treatment has lodged itself more securely in the popular imagination: She called it the "talking cure."[14]

The critical therapeutic question thus concerned the best way to bypass repression and access the relevant memories. At the time of Freud's *Studies on Hysteria*, he placed his faith in hypnosis. Freud thought that shutting off the conscious brain, which repressed memories, would allow them to return to the surface. Hypnosis, however, had been criticized by Hippolyte Bernheim at the Nancy school of psychotherapy because it seemed to produce the symptoms of hysteria artificially through a process of "suggestion," and Freud became increasingly convinced of this criticism himself. Thus, at the turn of the century, Freud came to favor instead the method of "free association," following the "fundamental rule of psychoanalysis" whereby the patient was asked to say whatever comes to his or her mind.[15] As we have seen, though repressed memories had been expunged from conscious life, they could still distort it through their association with other, non-repressed elements. A careful survey of the conscious surface could thus lead the analyst to discern the hidden masses lying beneath. That is, psychoanalytic symptoms pointed to underlying traumas, but only obliquely; they first had to be interpreted.

A likely suspect for such interpretation was our dream life, which Freud, in his *Interpretation of Dreams*, famously presented as the "royal road [...] to the unconscious."[16] Dreams seemed to be absurd, but this was by design: Their true meaning had been masked. Their manifest content (what happened in them, the images from which they were constructed), pointed to a latent content (the memories or desires with which the dream imagery was associated but which had been repressed). Though the dreamer was necessarily unaware of the latent content, it could become clear to the analyst through a process of interpretation. In particular Freud sought to read the dream to reveal the deep and shameful wish of which he thought it was the imaginary fulfillment.[17]

---

14 Josef Breuer (1893), "Fräulein Anna O.," Case Histories from *Studies on Hysteria*, in SE, vol. II (1893–1895), 19–47, p. 30.
15 Sigmund Freud, "Two Encyclopaedia Articles" (1923a [1922]), in SE, vol. XVIII, 233–260, p. 238.
16 Sigmund Freud, *The Interpretation of Dreams*, in SE, vol. V, 608. See also part II ("Dreams") of Freud's *Introductory Lectures* (1915–1916), in SE, vol. XV.
17 Sigmund Freud, *The Interpretation of Dreams* (1900), in SE, vols. IV–V, Section VI: The Dream-Work, 277–508.

In the book, Freud used many of his own dreams as examples. "Irma's injection" concerned a patient who had not accepted Freud's proposed treatment. In the dream, Freud ran into the patient at a party where she complained about a choking pain. Looking into her throat, Freud saw a white patch, gray scabs, and a curly structure. After consulting a Dr. M., who was present at the party and who also examined her, Freud decided that she had an infection gained after his "friend Otto," a junior colleague, had injected her using a dirty syringe. Freud argued that the dream sought to absolve him of the guilt he felt over the woman's treatment. The dream expressed his wish that the mistakes he had made could be attributed to others.[18]

By extending psychoanalysis to dreams, Freud moved it beyond the realm of what was traditionally understood as pathology. He implied that we all had repressed desires, and all struggled to come to terms with these dark forces in our daily lives. A similar argument runs through Freud's texts *The Psychopathology of Everyday Life* (1901) and *Jokes and Their Relation to the Unconscious* (1905). Here Freud deciphered the workings of the unconscious and how it manifested itself in everyday situations in the "normal" mind. The *Psychopathology* is concerned with the parapraxes, that is, errors in language or memory, such as the famous slip of the tongue, which Freud explained by the way in which our repressed desires bypassed the normal censorship of the mind.[19] In *Jokes*, Freud worked out the parallels between the functioning of jokes and the workings of the unconscious and dreams: Both involved a "process of condensation," whereby certain associations were lost and others became more pronounced. In contrast to the interpretation of dreams, in "joke-work" the retrieving of latent content produced a sentiment of pleasure.[20]

The necessity of interpretation in psychoanalysis suggests that it is best understood as a form of practice, and indeed Freud long sought to write a book on psychoanalytic technique.[21] In the end he only managed to write six papers on the topic, composed between 1911 and 1915, which were later collected in *Papers on Technique*.[22] The most comprehensive methodological account of psychoanalysis was rather written by Freud's close associate, Sándor Ferenczi, in the 1909 essay "Introjection and Transference."[23] In the

---

18 Sigmund Freud, *The Interpretation of Dreams* (1900), in *SE*, vol. IV, 106ff.
19 Sigmund Freud, *The Psychopathology of Everyday Life* (1901), in *SE*, vol. VI, vii–296, pp. 6–7.
20 Sigmund Freud, *Jokes and Their Relation to the Unconscious* (1905), in *SE*, vol. VIII, 1–247, pp. 20 and 54.
21 A book project with the title *A General Exposition of the Psychoanalytic Method*, see Makari, *Revolution in Mind*, 241.
22 Sigmund Freud, *Papers on Technique* (1911–1915), in *SE*, vol. XII.
23 See Makari, *Revolution in Mind*, 241.

absence of a definitive volume on technique, the best introductions to psychoanalysis are still the long case studies, which Freud published in the first two decades of the twentieth century. Freud had worried earlier that the genre "lack[ed] the serious stamp of science";[24] but cases were well suited to explaining key psychoanalytic concepts *in situ*, such as transference (*Übertragung*; the redirection of emotions onto the analyst), resistance (*Widerstand*; the force in treatment that prevents the analyst from getting through to the unconscious), conversion (*Konversion*; the translation of a psychological complaint into a physical symptom), and displacement (*Verschiebung*; the substitution of a goal by another one, sometimes because it was considered less dangerous). By using and interpreting these processes in a psychoanalytic session, Freud thought he could both reveal the underlying trauma and bring the patient, despite his or her resistance, to recognize it too (and thus achieve a cure).

Take for instance the 1905 *Fragments of an Analysis of a Case of Hysteria*. The eighteen-year-old Dora had been brought to Freud by her father in 1900 after threatening to commit suicide. She presented a number of hysterical symptoms including a nervous cough and an occasional tightening of her chest. Dora also reported the following "periodically recurrent"[25] dream:

> A house was on fire. My father was standing beside my bed and woke me up. I dressed myself quickly. Mother wanted to stop and save her jewel-case; but Father said: "I refuse to let myself and my two children be burnt for the sake of your jewel-case." We hurried downstairs, and as soon as I was outside I woke up.[26]

Dora first had the dream four times in quick succession, during a vacation with her parents' friends, Herr and Frau K. On a walk to the lake with Dora, Herr K. had declared his love for her, which Dora rejected. Through further analytic sessions with Dora, Freud settled on the following interpretation of the dream. Dora had felt sexually threatened by Herr K., which was expressed in her fears for the jewel case, a symbol of the female genitals.[27] The dream thus was the result of Dora's "intention" to flee the vacation home. Because "[a]n intention remains in existence until it has been carried out," the dream kept recurring during the remainder of her stay.[28]

---

24 Freud (1893), *Studies on Hysteria*, in SE, vol. II, 160.
25 Freud (1893), *Studies on Hysteria*, in SE, vol. II, 64.
26 Freud (1893), *Studies on Hysteria*, in SE, vol. II, 64.
27 Freud (1893), *Studies on Hysteria*, in SE, vol. II, 69.
28 Freud (1893), *Studies on Hysteria*, in SE, vol. II, 67.

The overall implications seemed clear, but Freud was confused by the role played by Dora's father. Freud thought that it could only be explained by a deeper attraction to Herr K., an attraction Dora had disavowed. Freud argued that Dora really was "more afraid of [her]self, and of the temptation [she] feel[s] to yield to him."[29] She needed her father to save her from herself. This reading was corroborated by another moment from the dream: her father rousing her from sleep. The scene recalled a time when Dora was about six years old and had begun to wet her bed; her father had sought to bring it to an end, by waking her up. For Freud the bed wetting suggested masturbation as a child and thus sexual feelings about which Dora was ashamed, like her desire for Herr K.[30]

As the treatment continued other reasons emerged for this "supervalent train of thought" that her father was responsible for not protecting her.[31] Dora had explained her father's actions by his own affair with another woman, Frau K. Dora thought that she had been offered as a reward for Herr K.'s acceptance of the affair. But in addition, Freud argued that Dora had homoerotic feelings for Frau K., eliciting feelings of jealousy. In Freud's language, Dora's inability to forgive her father was *overdetermined*, the coalescing of multiple psychic forces. Dora's disavowed love for Herr K. also explained her other symptoms including the cough. The feeling of stricture in Dora's chest could be explained by a previous encounter with Herr K., when he had pressed himself against her body and she had felt his erection. Dora had repressed the memory of this sensation around her genital region, but it had returned in a less sensitive area: her chest. This was, as Freud argued, a *displacement* "from the lower part of the body to the upper."[32] The cough was an example of *conversion*, the "translation of a purely psychical excitation into physical terms," for it was maintained by Dora's repressed sexual fantasy of oral sex.[33] Most famously Dora's case is a fine example of mishandled *transference*. Transference here referred to the reanimation of previous psychic experiences in the relationship of patient to doctor. Transference could be of great use in treatment because it gave the psychoanalyst powerful affective tools for intervening in the patient's psychic life, but it could also lead to disaster. In Freud's own post-mortem of the case after Dora had ended the treatment abruptly, he interpreted her behavior as

---

29 Freud (1893), *Studies on Hysteria*, in SE, vol. II, 70.
30 Freud (1893), *Studies on Hysteria*, in SE, vol. II, 74.
31 Freud (1893), *Studies on Hysteria*, in SE, vol. II, 88.
32 Freud (1893), *Studies on Hysteria*, in SE, vol. II, 30.
33 Freud (1893), *Studies on Hysteria*, in SE, vol. II, 53.

transferential revenge: Dora "took her revenge on me as she wanted to take her revenge on [her father], and deserted me as she believed herself to have been deceived and deserted by him."[34]

A Sexual Revolution?

Freud's increasing emphasis on the role of sexuality in the etiology of hysteria had already led to his estrangement from Breuer by 1894. After the break, Freud only became more convinced of its importance, as demonstrated by his *Three Essays on the Theory of Sexuality* (1905), the second most canonical work by Freud after *The Interpretation of Dreams*. The *Three Essays* went a long way in establishing Freud's reputation, no longer as neuroscientist and private doctor, but as a theoretician of the human mind, and, in some circles, as a sexual libertine. Of the three parts of the book (The Sexual Aberrations; Infantile Sexuality; and The Transformations of Puberty), the second is the best known and most controversial. In Viennese society at the time, it was widely believed that sexual life started in puberty. Freud claimed otherwise: Sexuality began at birth. Although he was not the only scientist maintaining the existence of infantile sexuality,[35] Freud invested it with the greatest explanatory power by claiming that its repression was the cause for later neuroses and perversions.

Freud distinguished five stages of psychosexual development, the oral, the anal, the phallic, the latent, and the genital, in each of which the libido fixates on a different part of the body.[36] Freud thought that his famous "Oedipus complex" developed during the phallic stage (between three and five years of age).[37] Drawing from the Greek tragedy, Freud argued that the child experienced an unconscious desire for the parent of the opposite sex, and a feeling of rivalry for the parent of the same sex, to the point of desiring his or her death. But at the same time, the child developed feelings of guilt about these desires, which for boys resulted in castration anxiety. Freud claimed the Oedipus complex was universal, visible across most of human history and across most differences of geography and culture, and could explain, for example, Hamlet's inability to act against the uncle in Shakespeare's play of

---

34 Freud (1893), *Studies on Hysteria*, in *SE*, vol. II, 119.
35 Henri Ellenberger, *The Discovery of the Unconscious* (New York: Basic Books, 1970), 504.
36 Though note that these stages are the result of a series of modifications over the course of the different editions of the *Three Essays*, building on and developing Freud's original distinction between adult and infantile sexuality; see Laplanche and Pontalis, *The Language of Psychoanalysis*, 237.
37 On Freud's sometimes contradictory accounts of the complex, see Laplanche and Pontalis, *The Language of Psychoanalysis*, 282–287.

the same name. Freud argued that Hamlet had been unable to kill his uncle because the latter had fulfilled the deepest wishes of his own Oedipus complex, killing Hamlet's father and marrying his mother.[38]

Freud's Oedipus complex led him to revise the claims of the first topography, of the conscious, pre-conscious, and unconscious, to create the "second topography" which he laid out in its fullest form in *The Ego and the Id* (1923). The id (*Es*) referred to the realm of the (mostly sexual) instincts, and sought only their satisfaction (this is what Freud called the pleasure principle). The id was kept in check by the ego (*Ich*), which was governed by the reality principle, and the super-ego (*Über-Ich*), which imposed moral imperatives.[39] According to Freud, the super-ego could be traced to the dissolution of the Oedipus complex. As Freud pointed out, the super-ego internalized parental discipline so that it "retains the character of the father."[40] Freud illustrated the new topography in a famous diagram for the *New Introductory Lectures* (1933), shown as Figure 2.1.

As the diagram shows, the new topography did not simply replace the old. Rather the two coexisted, if uneasily: "the three qualities of the characteristic of consciousness and the three provinces of the mental apparatus do not fall together into three peaceable couples ... we had no right to expect any such smooth arrangement."[41]

Soon, Freud extended his theory in a more sinister direction. In *Beyond the Pleasure Principle* (1920), Freud argued that humans were not simply controlled by the sexual instinct (libido), or pleasure principle, but rather by the two opposing forces of libido and death drive (*Todestrieb*), which were "locked in eternal battle."[42] Freud had been led to posit the death drive by what he termed repetition compulsion.[43] Revisiting themes from his 1914 essay "Remembering, Repeating, Working-Through," Freud noted that neurotics were prone to act out unpleasant events repeatedly. For example, dreams following traumatic neuroses such as war neuroses "repeatedly br[ought] the patient back into the situation of his accident." Similarly, in the game of "Fort–Da," the child enacted repeatedly the trauma of separation from the mother by moving back and forth

---

38 Freud, *The Interpretation of Dreams*, in *SE*, vol. V, 260–266.
39 Sigmund Freud, *The Ego and the Id* (1923), in *SE*, vol. XIX, 1–66. See also Sigmund Freud, *Inhibitions, Symptoms and Anxiety* (1926), in *SE*, vol. XX, 75–176.
40 Freud, *The Ego and the Id* (1923), in *SE*, vol. XIX, 34.
41 Sigmund Freud, *New Introductory Lectures on Psychoanalysis*, in *SE*, vol. XXII, 1–182, p. 72.
42 Quoted in Gay, *Freud*, 401.
43 An important source for the death drive was a paper by Sabina Spielrein, "Die Destruktion als Ursache des Werdens," in *Jahrbuch für psychoanalytische und psychopathologische Forschungen*, ed. E. Bleuler and S. Freud (Leipzig and Vienna: Franz Deuticke, 1912), vol. IV, part 1, 465–503.

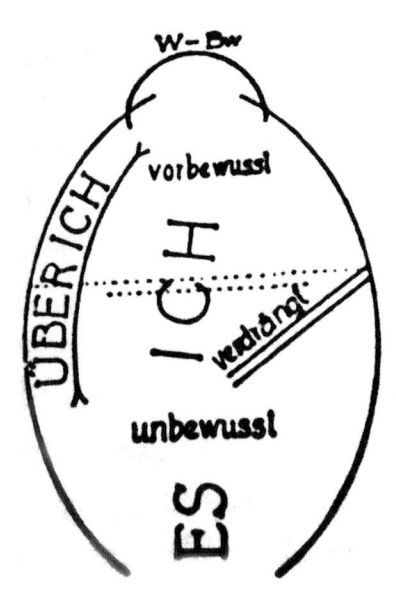

Figure 2.1 Freud, "Neue Folge der Vorlesungen zur Einführung in die Psychoanalyse," Chapter 31.

a reel.[44] This compulsive repetition could not be explained by the pleasure principle, as it brought discomfort. Instead, Freud posited "an urge inherent in organic life to restore an earlier state of things," the "expression of the *conservative* nature of living substance."[45] And this restoration of an earlier state was a reduction to nothingness, the drive toward death.

Freud's positing of the death drive in *Beyond the Pleasure Principle* has often been explained by the context of Freud's experience of war, more specifically his anxieties over his three sons. But if the war produced Freud's most pointed formulations of the idea, the basic insight of a reduction to nothingness can be found much earlier. Indeed, in *Beyond the Pleasure Principle*, Freud famously returned to the biological language he had used in his work before 1900. Just as in the 1895 *Project* Freud had argued that the nervous system aimed at the total discharge of excitation,[46] so too now he argued that organic entities had an urge to return to their earlier state of inorganic being: "the aim of all life is death."[47]

---

44 Sigmund Freud, *Beyond the Pleasure Principle*, in *SE*, vol. XVIII, 1–64, pp. 13 and 15.
45 Freud, *Beyond the Pleasure Principle*, in *SE*, vol. XVIII, 36.
46 Freud, *Project for a Scientific Psychology*, in *SE*, vol. I, 295–297.
47 Freud, *Beyond the Pleasure Principle*, in *SE*, vol. XVIII, 38.

With the second topography, psychoanalysis had become a science of the mind more broadly. It also came to concern itself with cultural issues. In *Civilization and Its Discontents* (1930), for example, Freud's argument is grounded in his model of the id, ego, and super-ego. Because, in this model, the mind is already plural, and formed by its relationship with other individuals, Freud was able to extend it to society as a whole, following his belief that ontogenesis recapitulates phylogenesis. For instance, Freud related his individual model of the mind, where the super-ego turns the subject's aggression back onto itself, producing guilt, to his social model, in which a collective aggression against the "Father" by a primal band of brothers was turned inward as a form of social control.[48]

These arguments allowed Freud to elaborate on our ambivalent relationship with society and culture; they were both necessary to modern life and they made us unhappy. Culture, according to Freud, "serve[d] two purposes – namely to protect men against nature and to adjust their mutual relations."[49] These goals, however, could only be achieved at a cost: "civilization [wa]s built up upon a renunciation of instinct."[50] The pleasure principle and the drive to avoid un-pleasure were not compatible with our social lives: We had to constrain our instincts and repress our most fundamental desires in order to live harmoniously with others. The pressures of these social constraints explained the allure of intoxication, psychosis, or neurosis, and they also, as Freud had argued in *The Future of an Illusion*, revealed the social function of religion.[51] Freud developed these two main if related themes – religion and social control – in his other cultural writings, which, with the exception of *Totem and Taboo* (1913), were all composed after World War I: *Group Psychology and the Analysis of the Ego* (1921), *The Future of an Illusion* (1927), *Civilization and Its Discontents* (1930), and *Moses and Monotheism* (1939).

Global Psychoanalysis

While Freud turned to the psychoanalysis of society only in his later work, the society of psychoanalysis had preoccupied him early on. When Freud wrote his *On the History of the Psychoanalytic Movement* in 1914, he was eager to protect the legacy of his new science. Though the title suggests that the text

---

48 Freud, *Civilization and Its Discontents*, in *SE*, vol. XXI. Freud only sketches this argument here, referring to his fuller analysis in *Totem and Taboo*.
49 Freud, *Civilization and Its Discontents*, in *SE*, vol. XXI, 57–146, p. 89.
50 Freud, *Civilization and Its Discontents*, in *SE*, vol. XXI, 97.
51 Sigmund Freud, *The Future of an Illusion*, in *SE*, vol. XXI, 1–56.

would concern psychoanalysts in general, Freud placed himself at the center of the story. The book had three parts, and only the central section was dedicated to the history of psychoanalysis narrowly defined. That history was sandwiched between two sections which had as their main goal the elaboration of a psychoanalytic orthodoxy. In part one, Freud offered a pre-history of psychoanalysis, in order to argue that his work with Breuer should be seen as pre-analytic, and thus that he alone was responsible for the new science. Breuer remained stuck at the level of the cathartic method, rather than free association, and he had not been receptive to Freud's theory of sexuality. Indeed, the *History of the Psychoanalytic Movement* is a rare occasion where Freud gave a definition of sorts of psychoanalysis, which, to him, consisted of three elements: repression and resistance; infantile sexuality; and the interpretation of dreams.[52]

Part three is an extended account of Freud's differences from Alfred Adler and Carl Jung. Adler had split from Freud over the former's theory of masculine protest.[53] According to Adler, neuroses resulted from the attempts to compensate for a real or perceived bodily defect; for instance Adler explained "masculine protest" as an attempt to affirm virility, where that virility was in doubt for anatomical reasons. While Freud acknowledged Adler's attempt to work out "the biological foundations of instinctual processes,"[54] he disliked Adler's de-emphasis of the psychosexual etiology of the neuroses, as well as what Freud thought was an overly facile psychology of the ego, directly contradicting the basic insights of psychoanalysis. Conflict erupted at the society meetings, and on March 1, 1911, Adler resigned his post as chairman of the Vienna Psychoanalytic Society.

The conflict with Jung was more threatening. Jung held enormous institutional power within the psychoanalytic movement. Seeing in Jung a future heir, not least because Freud thought that a non-Jewish figurehead would aid the acceptance of psychoanalysis, Freud had named the young Swiss the first president of the International Psychoanalytic Association (IPA) in 1910, and he was editor of the *Jahrbuch für psychoanalytische und psychopathologische Forschungen*. Jung accompanied Freud on his first trip to the United States in 1909, where he delivered his famous lectures at Clark University, at the invitation of the American psychologist G. Stanley Hall. As has recently been suggested, even though Hall was clearly interested in Freud, Jung was the

---

52 Sigmund Freud, *The History of the Psychoanalytic Movement*, in SE, vol. XIV, 1–66, p. 15.
53 Rubén Gallo, *Freud's Mexico: Into the Wilds of Psychoanalysis* (Cambridge: MIT Press, 2010), 63–66.
54 Freud, *The History of the Psychoanalytic Movement*, in SE, vol. XIV, 50.

better known of the two, due to his prominent institutional position at the Burghölzli hospital near Zurich.[55]

Nevertheless, in the years before World War I, the two men began to diverge over a number of theoretical questions. First, Jung found Freud's view of the unconscious limiting, arguing for a second, "collective," unconscious, which comprised ubiquitous "archetypes." In extending the reach of the unconscious to the level of a collective, Jung opened it up to the realm of religion and ethics. Second, Jung, much like Adler, de-emphasized sexuality, which for Freud was sufficient to exclude him from the psychoanalytic fold.[56]

The history of the psychoanalytic association, especially as it started to reach beyond Vienna, is then also a story about asserted orthodoxy and resistance to it. The IPA can trace its roots back to 1902, when Freud had established the "Wednesday Psychological Society," a meeting group with five original members (in addition to Freud, Wilhelm Stekel, Alfred Adler, Max Kahane, and Rudolf Reitler), which met once a week at Freud's home on Berggasse 19 in Vienna. The Society began to grow, until, in 1906, there were seventeen members, and the group changed its name in 1908 to the Vienna Psychoanalytic Society.[57] The growth in interest also began to transcend national borders, and further societies were established abroad: By 1911, two American societies had been founded, the New York Psychoanalytic Society and the American Psychoanalytic Association. The London Society for Psychoanalysis was formed in 1913, the Berlin Psychoanalytic Institute in 1920, and the Paris Psychoanalytic Society in 1926. As the IPA grew, regulations were devised to forge greater unity. Of special importance was the so-called training analysis (*Lehranalyse*), which was instituted to bring training under the auspices of psychoanalytic societies rather than individuals. The IPA then was not simply content to organize the movement, but also aimed to police its boundaries. As George Makari has noted, the IPA was founded on the contradictory principles of moving beyond Freud and controlling his followers.[58]

Freud was not able to eliminate dissent. One early and persistent controversy revolved around the question whether or not a medical degree (M.D.) should be required before training as a psychoanalyst. It is here that

---

55 Richard Skues, "Clark Revisited: Reappraising Freud in America," in *After Freud Left: A Century of Psychoanalysis in America*, ed. John C. Burnham (Chicago: University of Chicago Press, 2012), 49–84, e.g. p. 53. Jung was well known for his association test; his writings were published in English earlier than Freud's.
56 Freud, *The History of the Psychoanalytic Movement*, in SE, vol. XIV, 61.
57 Gay, *Freud*, 175.
58 Makari, *Revolution in Mind*, 249.

a major rift opened between the European "orthodoxy" (mostly represented by Freud and Ferenczi) and the Americans; the latter required a medical degree. The question of orthodoxy was rendered even more important by public concern over Freud's emphasis on sexuality. As Eduard Hitschmann pointed out in his *Freud's Theory of the Neuroses* (1913), an early attempt to provide a systematic presentation of Freud's psychoanalysis, "[b]y far the greatest and most universal opposition raised against the Freudian doctrines has been because of the disclosure of an unfailing sexual agency in the causation of neurotic manifestations. Here the resistance, a normal one, lies in the nature of the thing itself, since healthy and slightly neurotic individuals are inclined for intelligible reasons to deny the paramount importance of sexuality: the healthy, because it constituted no problem for them; the others because of their unconscious need to spread a veil over their own weaknesses."[59] More controversial still were Freud's theories about infantile sexuality. As Freud put it in his *Autobiographical Study*, these theories were a "contradiction of one of the strongest of human prejudices," children's sexual innocence.[60]

The public prejudice against psychoanalytic claims regarding sexuality was only deepened by a handful of psychoanalysts who radicalized Freud's theories on this point. Georg Groddeck, from whom Freud adopted the idea of the id,[61] and who called himself a "wild analyst," was infamous for the vigorous massage treatments he offered in his sanatorium in Baden-Baden.[62] The Austrian Wilhelm Reich was perhaps most noted for connecting psychoanalysis with free sexuality in the public imagination. In his 1936 book *The Sexual Revolution*, he argued that sexual conflicts imposed on us by modern norms (monogamous relationships, etc.) gave rise to the neuroses and, potentially, violence. In response, he promoted general sexual liberation. Reichian ideas fed into the tumult of the 1960s and the formulation of that era's tagline: "Make love not war."

The question of "orthodoxy" became even more complicated upon Freud's death, especially given the role he had assumed in the movement. One distinct strand of self-proclaimed orthodoxy developed out of the work of Freud's daughter, Anna, who contributed to what came to be called ego

---

59 Eduard Hitschmann, *Freud's Theory of the Neuroses* (New York: The Journal of Nervous and Mental Disease Publishing Company, 1913), 2.
60 Sigmund Freud, *An Autobiographical Study*, in SE, vol. XX, 1–74, p. 33.
61 Georg Groddeck, *The Book of the It* (New York: New American Library, 1961).
62 Veronika Fuechtner, *Berlin Psychoanalytic: Psychoanalysis and Culture in Weimar Republic Germany and Beyond* (Berkeley: University of California Press, 2011), 66 and 89.

psychology. This orthodoxy found its base in the English-speaking world, especially after the rise of Nazism had led to the emigration of major psychoanalysts from Vienna and Berlin, including Freud himself. Through Anna Freud, London became a center of gravity for psychoanalysis; Ernest Jones was the long-term president of the IPA (between 1920 and 1924, and again during the years 1932–1949). But the United States did not lag far behind in importance, and the other ego psychologists, almost without exception, were Viennese émigrés from Freud's inner circle who had fled to New York City. The ego-psychological "triumvirate" in America consisted of Heinz Hartmann, Ernst Kris, and Rudolph Loewenstein. They considered themselves orthodox Freudians, but they also wanted to broaden the base of psychoanalysis, making it part of mainstream medicine and science, which they sought to achieve through a pronounced medicalization, strictly regulating the access to training to those with medical degrees.

The Anglo-American orthodoxy homed in on the autonomous functions of the ego. Drawing on Freud's "structural model" that presented the ego as a mediator between the id and the super-ego, the ego psychologists moved away from a psychology of drives, which attributed primacy to the libido and aggression.[63] While, in *The Ego and the Id*, Freud had compared the ego to the rider of a horse, who sought to guide the animal, but was subject to its whims,[64] the ego psychologists suggested that the ego was more like the driver of a car that (under normal circumstances at least) could be fully controlled. The experience of war and exile – paired with American technological optimism – made this idea highly attractive; the ego psychologists constructed the ego as a bulwark against the upheavals of the age.

In Anna Freud's seminal book *The Ego and the Mechanisms of Defense* (published in German in 1936, in English in 1937), she listed and extended Sigmund Freud's mechanisms of defense, the unconscious functions of the ego that sought to control the forces of the id, and linked them to the psychosexual stages of development. In analysis, these defense mechanisms could be brought out through an analysis of the patient's associations.[65] In Freud's second topography, resistance too counted as a mechanism of defense, and, as has been shown, he thought that the doctor had to use the

---

63 See especially Freud, *The Ego and the Id* (1923), in *SE*, vol. XIX and *Inhibitions, Symptoms and Anxiety* (1926), in *SE*, vol. XX.
64 Freud, *The Ego and the Id* (1923), in *SE*, vol. XIX, 25. Note the influence of evolutionary theory and hierarchical conceptions of mind and brain in Freud's thinking.
65 Anna Freud, *The Ego and the Mechanisms of Defense* (London: Hogarth Press, 1937). See also Elisabeth Young-Bruehl, *Anna Freud: A Biography* (New Haven: Yale University Press, 2008), 208ff.

patient's resistances to uncover past trauma and then deploy the arsenal of psychoanalysis to overcome them.[66] For Anna Freud, in contrast, the defenses of the ego needed to be strengthened, because only thus could it gain the control over its desires that healthy living required.

Anna Freud also departed from her father in terms of institutional setting. Unlike her father's private practice, where he treated the daughters of the haute bourgeoisie, Anna Freud redeployed psychoanalysis as a socially engaged practice.[67] Together with Dorothy Burlingham in Vienna, Anna had founded and directed a nursery for children under two, mostly from destitute families. The nursery was funded by and named after the American Edith Jackson, who had been analyzed by Sigmund Freud and trained by Anna Freud as a child analyst at the Vienna Institute. Through her work at the Jackson Nursery, Anna Freud sought to gain "knowledge about a child's first steps out of the biological unity between infant and mother."[68] When she fled Vienna in 1938, Anna Freud sought to recreate the experiment, drawing on the help of Princess Marie Bonaparte to ship the Jackson Nursery equipment – small tables and chairs, feeding equipment, and toys – to London, where it became part of the Hampstead War Nurseries. There, Anna Freud and Burlingham continued to support children from poor backgrounds – many of the children came from London's East End – though now the situation was shaped by the war as well. Many of the admitted children had fled from the bombing of London, or were casualties of family break-ups caused by the pressures of the conflict.[69] As Anna Freud observed, the children were most troubled not by the bombing itself, but by the process of evacuation, which meant separation from their mothers. Consequently, she encouraged parental visits at any time of day, a departure from the norm at similar institutions at the time.[70]

Whereas Anna Freud centered her work on the ego's defenses, the Viennese émigré psychoanalyst to the United States Heinz Hartmann emphasized the ego's adaptive functions.[71] He believed that the ego

---

66 As Laplanche and Pontalis point out, this is a departure from Freud's pre-second-topographical view that allowed for a different reading: that the forces driving the resistance lie within the repressed, that is, the unconscious. See Laplanche and Pontalis, *The Language of Psychoanalysis*, 395.
67 See Elisabeth Danto, *Freud's Free Clinics: Psychoanalysis and Social Justice, 1918–1938* (New York: Columbia University Press, 2005), who shows that Sigmund Freud advocated free psychoanalytic clinics.
68 Anna Freud, cited in Young-Bruehl, *Anna Freud*, 219.
69 Michal Shapira, *The War Inside: Psychoanalysis, Total War, and the Making of the Democratic Self in Postwar Britain* (Cambridge: Cambridge University Press, 2013), 70.
70 Shapira, *The War Inside*, 75–76.
71 Heinz Hartmann, *Ego Psychology and the Problem of Adaptation*, trans. David Rapaport (New York: International Universities Press, 1958 [1939]).

possessed several autonomous functions (perception, attention, memory, concentration, motor coordination, and language), which could flourish in an "average expectable environment."[72] In development, these autonomous ego functions would grow out of the "conflict-free ego sphere." Of course, there could be conflict as well, which led to disease. Therefore, the ego psychologist had to promote and extend the conflict-free ego sphere of the ego to ease the patient's adaptation to the environment.[73]

Ego psychology dominated the medical landscape in the United States from the 1950s to the 1970s. There were alternative visions, such as that of the Chicago group, but they never presented a real threat to ego psychology, whose hegemonic position began to crumble only when Heinz Kohut (an émigré from Vienna based in Chicago) formulated another, uniquely American, version of psychoanalysis in his self psychology and most importantly his concept of narcissism.[74] A "healthy narcissism,"[75] Kohut thought, differed from the Freudian conception, which was a pathological fixation at the childhood stage of development, but was rather necessary for the development of a robust self.[76] Like Hartmann before him, Kohut, in the words of Elizabeth Lunbeck, "managed simultaneously to kill off Freud and to insure [sic] his survival in America."[77]

As this account shows, even though they saw themselves as faithful followers of Freud, the ego psychologists did not simply reiterate Freud's theories. In fact, by emphasizing the ego and endowing it with normative value, the ego psychologists challenged some of the central tenets of psychoanalysis: psychosexuality and the predominance of the unconscious. And by privileging certain aspects of Freud's work over others, the ego psychologists opened their ideas to attacks from rivals who could equally invoke the legacy of psychoanalysis's Viennese founder: above all Melanie Klein and Jacques Lacan.

Melanie Klein

In the early 1930s, Klein had held a relatively secure position within the British Psychoanalytical Society (BPAS).[78] But Ernest Jones's heroic endeavor to aid

---

72 Hartmann, *Ego Psychology and the Problem of Adaptation*, 51.
73 Hartmann, *Ego Psychology and the Problem of Adaptation*.
74 Elizabeth Lunbeck, *The Americanization of Narcissism* (Cambridge: Harvard University Press, 2014).
75 Cited in Elizabeth Lunbeck, "Heinz Kohut's Americanization of Freud," in *After Freud Left: A Century of Psychoanalysis in America*, ed. John C. Burnham (Chicago: University of Chicago Press, 2012), 209–231, p. 220.
76 Lunbeck, "Heinz Kohut's Americanization of Freud," 220.
77 Lunbeck, "Heinz Kohut's Americanization of Freud," 211.
78 Klein had come to London in 1926 at the invitation of her supporter Ernest Jones; Anna Freud came with her family in 1938 fleeing the Nazis.

psychoanalysts fleeing the Nazis shifted the balance of psychoanalytic power in Britain: By 1938, around a third of analysts came from Continental Europe, and most often they opposed Klein's work. In particular Melanie Klein clashed with Anna Freud over their common interest in child analysis. The differences first came to light when Anna Freud criticized Klein in her 1927 book *Introduction to the Technique of Child Analysis*. Consequently Ernest Jones organized the Symposium on Child-Analysis in London the same year Klein responded to Freud's critique, in turn sharply criticizing her.[79] In the early 1940s, the debates between the two child analysts intensified, to such an extent that the BPAS attempted to mediate between the two in a number of "Controversial Discussions." The discussions did little to resolve theoretical and practical difference between the two schools, but they did end in an institutional compromise. In 1944, after Ernest Jones and Edward Glover had both withdrawn, Sylvia Payne, an analyst committed neither to Anna Freudian nor to Kleinian approaches, became president of the society. Under her leadership, three separate training tracks were established, one Freudian, one Kleinian, and one independent. Moreover, to mitigate the rupture, each candidate required a second supervisor from the independent/middle group.[80]

The institutional clash between Anna Freud and Klein can be traced to their differing views of the development of transference neurosis during treatment.[81] For Klein, transference was established immediately by the child, and consequently the analysis would follow the same principles as that of an adult. In contrast, for Anna Freud, there was no transference neurosis that stood in for the child's relationship with his or her parents: "a child is not ready to produce a new edition of his love relationships because, as one might say, the old edition is not yet exhausted."[82] This led Freud to include the child's parents in the analysis. These differences had also implications for their understanding of children's play. While Freud introduced play into her psychoanalytic session, only Klein gave that play symbolic meaning, comparable to adult free association. For her, a child crashing a horse and

---

79 Anna Freud, *Einführung in die Technik der Kinderanalyse* (Vienna: Internationaler Psychoanalytischer Verlag, 1927); and Melanie Klein, "Symposium on Child Analysis," *The International Journal of Psychoanalysis*, 8 (1927), 339–370.
80 Makari, *Revolution in Mind*, 472.
81 Additional points of contestation included the existence of a pre-Oedipal period, the uses of pedagogy in therapy, and the role of internal psychic or environmental factors for psychopathology, Makari, *Revolution in Mind*, 427ff.
82 Cited in Young-Bruehl, *Anna Freud*, 168.

a carriage together in play represented parental sexual intercourse, reliving the child's previous observance of the primal scene.[83]

One can readily grasp why Klein has often been seen as heretical, and Anna Freud as orthodox. Anna Freud was Sigmund Freud's favorite child, a close companion and scientific co-worker who had been analyzed by the master himself. But it is important to recognize that Klein could also appeal to the founder's work in presenting her theories. She argued that her child analysis followed directly from Sigmund Freud's treatment of Little Hans in 1909, one of Freud's long case histories that dealt with the five-year-old boy and his fear of horses.[84] Klein argued that it was Anna Freud who had departed from the Freudian orthodoxy when she claimed children to be special.[85]

So too Klein, like Sigmund Freud, worked mostly in private practice. Klein did not follow Anna Freud in presenting psychoanalysis as a tool for social reform. In contrast to Anna Freud, who considered the interplay between inner life and outer factors, Klein de-emphasized external contextual factors in the development of the child. The emphasis on the inner is evident in Klein's object relations theory, which is concerned with the relations between the self and its inner objects.[86] For example, an infant had two representations of the mother's breast, one good (nurturing), one bad (not satisfying his or her hunger). The child lived in a state of paranoia of the bad breast, and attempted to attenuate this threat by identifying with the good breast. This state of being was, however, not tenable, and the child at some point began to see the mother as a whole; this realization led the child from the paranoid state to the depressive state, a shift that occurred around the fifth month of life.[87]

Despite her clashes with Anna Freud, the systematic nature of Klein's ideas allowed them to spread quickly. In Argentina, the country with probably the most active psychoanalytic culture today, child psychoanalysis became an important way of making psychoanalysis acceptable to the middle classes. Klein's ideas had been introduced by the wives of the founders of the Argentine Psychoanalytic Association (APA). Arminda Aberastury (wife of the psychiatrist and psychoanalyst Enrique Pichon Rivière) translated Melanie Klein's works into Spanish. Though at first there had been an equally

---

83 Melanie Klein, *The Psychoanalysis of Children*, trans. Alix Strachey (New York: Grove Press, 1960 [1932]), 41.
84 Klein, *The Psychoanalysis of Children*, 17. Sigmund Freud, *Little Hans*, in *SE*, vol. X (1910), 1–150.
85 Young-Bruehl, *Anna Freud*, 169.   86 Makari, *Revolution in Mind*, 436.
87 Makari, *Revolution in Mind*, 435f. Melanie Klein, "Notes on Some Schizoid Mechanisms," *The International Journal of Psychoanalysis*, 27 (1946), 99–110, p. 100.

strong interest in the work of Anna Freud, Argentinians thought that Klein offered certain practical advantages, primarily a set of guidelines for how to conduct child analysis, a possibility that they did not see in Anna Freud's work. Further, the esoteric nature of Klein's writings was considered a professional advantage. Finally, the embrace of Kleinianism served to demarcate Argentinian psychoanalysis from the US school, which had embraced Anna Freud's ego psychology.[88] From Argentina, Kleinianism spread, between the 1950s and 1970s, to Mexico, Uruguay, and Brazil, and indeed, back to Continental Europe, most importantly to France.[89]

Jacques Lacan

The second major heterodoxy in psychoanalysis was that presented by Jacques Lacan, who advocated his own "return to Freud." Freud, according to Lacan, had challenged the dominant position of an autonomous ego in Western philosophy through his concept of the unconscious.[90] While the IPA and the ego psychologists – one of whom, Rudolf Loewenstein, had been responsible for Lacan's training – sought to strengthen the ego through therapy, Lacan argued that the ego was itself the cause of mental pathology and had to be dissolved.

For Lacan, the ego ("moi") was formed during the mirror stage – between six and eighteen months – when the infant first identified with her or his image in the mirror. At this time, Lacan argued, the infant was "still trapped in his motor impotence,"[91] not able to walk or even stand. Owing to this lack of coordination, the child experienced his or her body as fragmented, and thus desired the apparent unity that the mirror presented. The infant identified with the image, in a moment of "jubilant activity."[92] But because of the persistent mismatch between the child's own body and the image, this identification involved misrecognition, and thus instituted feelings of

---

88 Mariano Ben Plotkin, *Freud in the Pampas: The Emergence and Development of a Psychoanalytic Culture in Argentina* (Stanford: Stanford University Press, 2001), 65ff.
89 Alejandro Dagfal, "Paris–London–Buenos Aires: The Adventures of Kleinian Psychoanalysis between Europe and South America," in *The Transnational Unconscious: Essays in the History of Psychoanalysis and Transnationalism*, ed. Joy Damousi and Mariano Ben Plotkin (London: Palgrave Macmillan, 2009), 179–198, esp. 194. However, it is likely that French analysts like Jacques Lacan and Didier Anzieu knew Klein's work independently of a South American route.
90 Nevertheless, in the 1930s and early 1940s, Lacan had been highly critical of the notion of the unconscious.
91 Jacques Lacan, "The Mirror Stage as Formative of the *I* Function," in *Écrits*, trans. Bruce Fink (New York: W. W. Norton, 2006), 75–81, p. 76.
92 Lacan, "The Mirror Stage as Formative of the *I* Function," 76.

alienation. That is why Lacan thought that therapy was necessary to deconstruct the ego.

Lacan's "Mirror Stage as Formative of the *I* Function" (1949) is perhaps his best-known text from this period. But his argument gained a fuller meaning due to developments in his thought over the 1950s. At that time, the mirror stage became the foundation of the imaginary order where the subject is caught under the thrall of his or her own image. But the imaginary order was only one of three. In his "The Function and Field of Speech and Language in Psychoanalysis" of 1953 (often referred to as the Rome Discourse), Lacan presented his broader structure: Along with the imaginary, Lacan posited a real and a symbolic order. Of the three, the symbolic was of crucial importance, and it shaped the other two: The core of psychoanalysis was language, which Lacan thought Freud had acknowledged in his discussion of dreams, symbolism, and jokes. The way different mental elements could stand in for others, the processes of association that Lacan labeled metaphor and metonymy, showed that "the unconscious is structured like a language."[93] As a form of language, the unconscious was cut off from the real, gaining its meaning rather from the relationship among mental elements.

But how did this fit with the imaginary? The imaginary created distortions within the symbolic, which caused the unconscious to be untrue to itself. The desires of the ego as imaginary clashed with the desires of the unconscious. It therefore resulted in what Lacan called "empty speech."[94] That is why the analyst sought to break the grip of the ego, move from empty speech to full speech, of which the unconscious itself was the subject. To achieve this the analyst had to wait for the unconscious to break through in the analysis,[95] in slips of the tongue, or in unexpected revelations. The incongruence of these moments suggested that the unconscious was expressing itself, while the "ego" was silent. That is why, in his practice, Lacan advocated variable-length sessions. Since therapy required waiting for moments of truth that the ego hoped to avoid, a variable-length session prevented the patient from simply running down the clock, holding out until the hour had passed and the ego was safe again. Lacan's variable-length sessions exacerbated pre-existing tensions between Lacan and the psychoanalytic establishment. Lacan had left the Société Psychanalytique

---

[93] Jacques Lacan, "Science and Truth," in *Écrits*, trans. Bruce Fink (New York: W. W. Norton, 2006), 726–745, p. 737.

[94] Jacques Lacan, "The Function and Field of Speech and Language in Psychoanalysis," in *Écrits*, trans. Bruce Fink (New York: W. W. Norton, 2006), 197–258, pp. 206ff.

[95] Lacan, "The Function and Field of Speech and Language in Psychoanalysis," 212–213.

de Paris (SPP) in 1953 because of this issue.[96] Ten years later, in 1963, the IPA gave Lacan's new home at the Société Française de Psychanalyse an ultimatum: The IPA would recognize it, but only under the condition that Lacan's name was taken off the list of training analysts. Excluded again, Lacan found another receptive community teaching at the Parisian École Normale Supérieure (ENS), where he encountered many students of Louis Althusser, and later at his own École Freudienne de Paris.[97]

Even though Lacan had gained fame in the 1930s within certain intellectual circles in France, it was only after 1966 and especially after 1968 that his form of psychoanalysis achieved more popular success. Lacanian psychoanalysis helped keep together the peculiar constellation of French Marxism, feminism, (post-)structuralism, and anti-psychiatry.[98] It was at this time that Lacan's unique brand of psychoanalysis began to travel internationally. The most important country to adopt Lacanian ideas and practices was Argentina, as it had been for Kleinianism. Lacanian psychoanalysis is still central there today (comparable in numbers of Lacanian analysts only to France), finding success across wide swathes of society.[99] Lacanianism entered Argentina in the 1960s through two channels. One route involved the Argentine psychoanalyst Oscar Masotta, who formed the Grupo Lacaniano de Buenos Aires in 1969 (which, in turn, founded its own journal, the *Cuadernos Sigmund Freud*) and later founded the Escuela Freudiana de Buenos Aires, the "first formal Lacanian analytic institution in the Spanish-speaking world," according to Mariano Ben Plotkin.[100] The second channel was that Lacan gained traction due to the international success of his ENS colleague Althusser, who became an iconic figure among the Argentine left.[101]

Within the APA, the Lacanians remained faithful to Lacan's anti-institutional principles. They contested training analysis (Lacan's "analyst authorizes himself") and the fixed duration of the analytic session – the

---

96 Lacan had joined Daniel Lagache in the newly founded Société Française de Psychanalyse in 1953.
97 Élisabeth Roudinesco, *Jacques Lacan and Co.: A History of Psychoanalysis in France* (Chicago: University of Chicago Press, 1990).
98 For an account of Lacan's relationship to other political and philosophical movements at the time, see Chapter 18 by Camille Robcis.
99 Plotkin, *Freud in the Pampas*, 208.
100 Oscar Masotta, "Jacques Lacan, o El inconsciente en los fundamentos de la filosofía," *Pasado y Presente*, 3(9) (April–September 1965), 1–15. Plotkin, *Freud in the Pampas*, 208.
101 See Louis Althusser "Freud et Lacan," *La Nouvelle Critique*, nos. 161–162 (1964–1965), 88–108. The article "legitimized psychoanalysis for the left as a legitimate science," Plotkin, *Freud in the Pampas*, 209

very aspects that had led to Lacan's exclusion from the SPP. This is not to say that Argentine Lacanians rejected all rules. In fact, Argentinian and South American Lacanianism more broadly developed into a distinctly clinical discipline, which is quite different from its status in the United States, where the use of Lacanian insights is almost entirely limited to academia.

As had occurred with Kleinianism, Lacan's success in South America later helped it expand its reach in Europe. Soon after founding the Escuela, Masotta moved to Europe and founded other Lacanian schools in Spain.[102] The diffusion of Lacanianism is not limited to the Latinate world. It also played a role in the Soviet Union.[103] And Lacan found receptive ground in the colonial context. Many colonial elites had presented the ego as a quintessentially western force, which they often juxtaposed to the dominance of instincts and the id amongst "primitive" populations. In his rich correspondence with Sigmund Freud and other writings, the Hungarian psychoanalyst and anthropologist Géza Róheim, for instance, used Freud's account of the Oedipus complex to present so-called "primitives" as more childlike than their European counterparts.[104] In this context, Lacan seemed to provide arguments against European domination, and found significant support in Africa and beyond. The French colonial psychiatrists, such as Marie-Cécile and Edmond Ortigues, used Lacanian psychoanalysis in their influential work *Œdipe africain*.[105] More prominently still, the Martiniquan psychiatrist Frantz Fanon, who was a major voice during the Algerian revolution, discussed Lacan in his work.[106] Later psychoanalysis more broadly has come to play an important role in postcolonial theory, in the work of Homi K. Bhabha and others.[107]

---

102 Sergio Eduardo Visacovsky, "Origin Stories, Invention of Genealogies and the Early Diffusion of Lacanian Psychoanalysis in Argentina and Spain (1960–1980)," in *The Transnational Unconscious: Essays in the History of Psychoanalysis and Transnationalism*, ed. Joy Damousi and Mariano Ben Plotkin (London: Palgrave Macmillan, 2009), 227–256, pp. 240ff.
103 For example N. S. Avtonomova, "The Psychoanalytic Conceptions of Jacques Lacan," cited in Martin Miller, *Freud and the Bolsheviks: Psychoanalysis in Imperial Russia and the Soviet Union* (New Haven: Yale University Press, 1998), 146.
104 Géza Róheim, *Australian Totemism: A Psychoanalytic Study in Anthropology* (London: G. Allen and Unwin, 1925).
105 Marie-Cécile Ortigues and Edmond Ortigues, *Œdipe africain* (Paris: Librairie Plon, 1966).
106 Warwick Anderson, Deborah Jenson, and Richard Keller, *Unconscious Dominions: Psychoanalysis, Colonial Trauma, and Global Sovereignties* (Durham: Duke University Press, 2011), 12; see p. 24 for parallels between Fanon and Lacan's work.
107 Homi K. Bhabha, *The Location of Culture* (London: Routledge, 1994); and Anderson, Jenson, and Keller, *Unconscious Dominions*.

Beyond the Analytic Session

While psychoanalysis gained traction around the world as a medical practice, it also attracted the interest of other intellectuals. On the one hand, Freud's theory of art in his cultural writings gained the interest of art historians, philosophers, and literary critics. For example Freud's psychopathographic approach finds its Ur-form in the 1910 essay *Leonardo da Vinci and a Memory of His Childhood*, where unconscious motives – usually caused by early childhood trauma or conflict – are used to explain artistic work.[108] In a different vein, in his *Moses of Michelangelo* (1914), Freud analyzes his response to a specific work of art that had produced in him a strong affective reaction.[109] Even more prominent are the works by the Surrealists – André Breton, Louis Aragon, Salvador Dalí, Max Ernst, Joan Miró – who found inspiration in psychoanalysis. They sought to express the unconscious in their work, and to explore the complex connections between reality and dream. Thus moving beyond the ego to the unconscious, they prefigured elements of Lacan, who would later draw on their work.

Social theorists, too, have been profoundly influenced by psychoanalysis. Psychoanalysis found one path into the realm of academic social theory and philosophy through the work of the Frankfurt School, members of which (such as Herbert Marcuse and Max Horkheimer) had been attracted to psychoanalysis since the late 1920s. Through this contact, members of the Frankfurt Psychoanalytic Institute (the second psychoanalytic institute in Germany after Berlin, founded in 1929), such as Karl Landauer, Heinrich Meng, Frieda Fromm-Reichmann, and Erich Fromm, were offered working space in the Frankfurt Institute for Social Research.[110] Psychoanalysis was attractive to members of the Frankfurt School because it provided a means to understand the unpredictable and irrational aspects of human behavior that often ran counter to the individual's interest, and thus troubled the overarching theories of classical Marxism. Freud's theory of the unconscious informed Adorno's analyses of the authoritarian character and fascist propaganda, and Fromm's understanding of authority and the family. Along with Wilhelm Reich, the Frankfurt School has been a major influence on what later was known as "Freudomarxism."

---

108 Sigmund Freud, *Leonardo da Vinci and a Memory of His Childhood* (1910), in *SE*, vol. XI, 57–138.
109 Sigmund Freud, *Moses of Michelangelo* (1914), *SE*, vol. XIII, 209–238.
110 Fuechtner, *Berlin Psychoanalytic*, 76 and 135.

The marriage between the Frankfurt School and psychoanalysis was not stable over time. In one of the key works of the Frankfurt School, Horkheimer and Adorno's *Dialectic of Enlightenment*, written in 1944 while in exile in Southern California, the authors critically engaged with and moved away from Freud, who, according to them, aimed for a rationalism that was both impoverished and harmful. This changing perspective can be attributed in part to their experience of psychoanalysis in America, which was both medicalized and dominated by ego psychology. According to Adorno, this psychoanalysis was nothing but "a part of hygiene," a science of the normal. In his characteristically elliptical style, Adorno declared "[i]n psychoanalysis nothing is true except the exaggerations."[111] The engagement of the Frankfurt School sociologist Marcuse was, on the other hand, more optimistic and more sustained. While criticizing some of the more conservative themes in Freud, in *Eros and Civilization* (1955), Marcuse used psychoanalysis to help him imagine a civilization that was free from repression.[112]

Finally, psychoanalysis has offered inspiration to feminism and gender studies, even if the response has often been highly critical. As early as the 1930s, psychoanalyst Karen Horney had attacked the perceived biological determinism in Freud, developing her "feminist psychology" in response.[113] These claims were picked up in the 1960s and 1970s, when writers like Kate Millett and Betty Friedan criticized Freud for assuming that "anatomy is destiny" and measuring women against a male norm, for instance in his theory of "penis envy." And yet at the same time, both Lacanianism and Kleinianism became areas of productive mutual engagement, for instance in the work of American sociologists Nancy Chodorow and Dorothy Dinnerstein, who used object relation theory to understand individual development, and in the reformulation of Freudian psychoanalysis through French philosophers such as Luce Irigaray, Hélène Cixous, and Julia Kristeva.

Conclusion

Over the last twenty-five years, psychoanalysis has lost much of the appeal and excitement that drove its expansion in the second half of the twentieth century. It no longer has the broad cultural reach of the postwar period, from

---

111 Theodor Adorno, *Minima Moralia: Reflections from Damaged Life* (London: Verso, 1999 [1951]), 58–59 and 49.
112 Herbert Marcuse, *Eros and Civilization: A Philosophical Inquiry into Freud* (Boston: Beacon Press, 1955).
113 Karen Horney, *Feminine Psychology* (New York: W. W. Norton, 1967).

Benjamin Spock to Hollywood.[114] Undergraduates in universities today are rarely more than vaguely familiar with the person of Freud, or even with basic psychoanalytic concepts.[115] As Samuel Moyn has recently observed, Freud's popularity has been the victim of a broader move away from synthetic theories of social reality.[116] Nevertheless, there are still moments of engagement. For example, some have turned to Freud in their attempt to overcome the fragmentation of contemporary neuroscience. In the words of Nobel laureate Eric Kandel, psychoanalysis "still represents the most coherent and intellectually satisfying view of the mind."[117] Kandel and other neuro-psychoanalysts such as the South American Mark Solms like to present Freud as a neuroscientist manqué, who chose another path because he lacked the technologies of today's state of the art. Neuro-psychoanalysis also matches psychoanalysis's global reach, with researchers in South Africa, the United States, Germany, and elsewhere; it is part of a new *biological* global. And yet, as Nima Bassiri has pointed out, the relationship between psychoanalysis and neuroscience is asymmetrical: "while psychoanalysis might *inform* neuroscience conceptually, it is neuroscience that can *ultimately* ground psychoanalysis scientifically."[118]

Psychoanalysis is legion, covering a vast array of different ideas and practices, taking place in countries across the world. The philosopher Jacques Derrida once posed the problem of psychoanalysis thus: "How can an autobiographical writing, in the abyss of an unterminated self-analysis, give birth to a world-wide institution?"[119] But it would be wrong to see the personal and the global aspects of psychoanalysis as opposed. First, the vast and multi-faceted nature of psychoanalysis has made the appeal to its founding figure all the more important. Freud's work has become a privileged means, both for scholars of the movement and for participants in it, for sorting through and organizing its otherwise unmanageable variety. But second, that variety can be traced back to Freud's work. The conflicts

---

114 This is true for Europe and the United States. Although, of course, as we have seen, in South America, psychoanalysis is still *en vogue*.
115 Except in humanities departments in the United States, where psychoanalysis still has a significant following.
116 Samuel Moyn, "Freud's Discontents," *The Nation*, November 2, 2016, 25–28.
117 Eric R. Kandel, "Biology and the Future of Psychoanalysis: A New Intellectual Framework for Psychiatry Revisited," *American Journal of Psychiatry*, 156(4) (1999), 505–524, p. 505.
118 Nima Bassiri, "Freud and the Matter of the Brain: On the Rearrangements of Neuropsychoanalysis," *Critical Inquiry*, 40(1) (Autumn 2013), 83–108, p. 88.
119 Quoted in John Forrester, "Dream Readers," in *Dispatches from the Freud Wars: Psychoanalysis and Its Passions* (Cambridge: Harvard University Press, 1997), 138–183, p. 140.

between psychoanalysts, which fueled the diffusion of Freud's ideas around the world, the battles between ego psychologists and Lacanians, between Anna Freud and Melanie Klein, are not simply the result of a disorder caused by the death of the father. Rather they are the product of deeper conflicts, that Freud, better than anyone else, understood to lie at the depths of every individual mind, including his own.

3

Modern Physics: From Crisis to Crisis

JIMENA CANALES

The first decades of the twentieth century were marked by two revolutionary scientific accomplishments, the theory of relativity and quantum mechanics, with repercussions still felt today. Relativity theory and quantum mechanics became the two most important branches of "Modern Physics" that emerged as an alternative to "Classical Physics" (a term often used interchangeably with that of "Newtonian" or "Galilean" physics). No field of science (from astronomy to the life sciences), no field of knowledge (from philosophy to sociology), and no artistic practice (from architecture to the fine arts) was left untouched by these investigations into the nature of our physical universe.

For many observers far and near, modern physics became a catalyst for much that was new about the modern world. For the most part, cultural ramifications were celebrated and promoted, sometimes considered as emerging from a kind of "genetic connection," while at other times they were seen as unwarranted extensions of science into unrelated territories.[1] Particularly controversial was the relation of relativity theory to other forms of relativism (cultural, moral, and popular). When Einstein was asked to comment about the similarities between his work and the "new artistic 'language'" associated with Picasso, cubism, and modern art, he answered decisively: It had "nothing in common" with it.[2]

---

[1] Gerald Holton, "Introduction: Einstein and the Shaping of Our Imagination," in *Albert Einstein: Historical and Cultural Perspectives*, ed. Gerald Holton and Yehuda Elkana (Mineola: Dover, 1997).

[2] Einstein to Paul M. Laporte, May 4, 1946, reprinted in Paul M. Laporte, "Cubism and Relativity with a Letter of Albert Einstein," *Leonardo*, 21(3) (1988), 313–315. For other accounts about the relation of relativity and the arts see Arthur I. Miller, *Einstein, Picasso: Space, Time and the Beauty That Causes Havoc* (New York: Basic Books, 2001); and Linda Dalrymple Henderson, "Einstein and 20th-Century Art: A Romance of Many Dimensions," in *Einstein for the 21st Century: His Legacy in Science, Art, and Modern Culture*, ed. Peter L. Galison, Gerald Holton, and Silvan S. Schweber (Princeton: Princeton University Press, 2008).

How did the new physics affect European intellectual thought? Not only did new insights into the nature of the physical universe affect how intellectuals across fields thought about basic concepts (such as time, space, and the nature of matter and light), but they also had to contend with the growing status of physics as a field of knowledge in the public sphere. The question of how non-scientists (philosophers, intellectuals, or humanists) should react and adapt to these changes became a concern for decades to come. Increasingly after World War I, a tightknit community of expert elite physicists played prominent roles in public spheres, far surpassing the influence that nineteenth-century scientists, such as Louis Pasteur, Charles Darwin, and Alexander von Humboldt, had once had on the culture of their time. The new role of physicists as spokespersons for the universe disrupted traditional hierarchies between physics and philosophy, as well as that between the sciences and the humanities and arts.

The main scientific insights of these scientific revolutions remain, for the most part, valid today. Both fields opened up fertile research programs leading generations of scientists to many future discoveries. Modern physics paved the way for the development of entire new fields of research, from nanoscience to, most recently, gravitational waves. A host of new technologies central to the modern world were widely understood as "spin-off" effects emerging from theoretical research, further securing the status of theoretical physics in public and academic circles. The world of radio, of electrical, telephone, and telegraph communications, of nuclear energy, satellites, space exploration, and global positioning systems (GPS) became associated with the lessons of the theory of relativity (and mostly with Einstein), while the world of microelectronics (transistors and semiconductors), lasers, atomic clocks, electron microscopy, magnetic resonance imaging (MRI), and light-emitting diodes (LEDs) was associated with quantum mechanics. New laws sought to explain the universe at two extremes, microscopic and macroscopic, as the world became more extreme in other ways too.

The relation of theoretical science to pure knowledge and of technology to applied knowledge became a topic of wide concern. In addition, a growing number of thinkers attributed to technology an outsized role in modernity, some celebrating its benefits while others stressed its perils (the latter often citing military innovations). Widespread fears of the potential of science and technology running amok led to new discussions about the role of human agency within larger technological systems and networks.

The Modern in Modern Physics

What exactly is *modern* about modern physics? A common way of understanding the main scientific purport of these fields has been in terms of their radical redefinition of traditional concepts of time and space. As is well known, the theory of relativity took time to be a fourth dimension next to the three dimensions of space. Although this insight can be found in different forms before the twentieth century (and can even be traced to ancient philosophy), Einstein's theory of relativity introduced it alongside the more radical claim that no privileged "frame of reference" existed, that is, that for every point in space-time the laws of physics are the same, or invariant. These two insights were related to the discovery of time and length dilation: Measurements of time and length were proven to vary in relation to the velocity of translation of a system in motion relative to another one. In 1908 the mathematician Hermann Minkowski explained the importance of the theory of relativity in these terms: "Henceforth, space by itself, and time by itself, are doomed to fade away into mere shadows, and only a kind of union of the two will preserve an independent reality."[3]

Quantum mechanics changed our common perception of space and time in yet other ways. First, the "uncertainty relation" (associated with the work of Werner Heisenberg) posed an absolute limit on the knowledge that could be obtained (non-commuting observables such as position and momentum could not be determined beyond a certain limit, $\Delta x \, \Delta p \geq \hbar/2$). Second, the possibility of "non-locality" and "entanglement," showing how one particle could affect simultaneously another one separated at arbitrarily large distances, violated the theory of relativity. Third, quantum mechanics introduced essentially discrete changes in the state of nature, called "quantum jumps," to explain certain characteristics of atoms. In addition to these revolutionary claims, scientists noted that light seemed to behave as both wave and particle, leading some scientists to advocate for a more general "theory of complementarity" where every object in the universe was considered as having both particulate and wavelike qualities. Finally, by showing how performing a measurement could change the phenomenon under investigation (as in the "double-slit experiment"), quantum mechanics introduced new questions about the relation of the universe to consciousness. To explain the philosophical and physical meaning of these effects, the Danish physicist Niels Bohr developed an explanatory

---

3 Address to the 80th Assembly of German Natural Scientists and Physicians (September 21, 1908). Hermann Minkowski, "Raum und Zeit," *Jahresbericht der Deutschen Mathematiker-Vereinigung*, 18 (1909), 75–88.

framework known as the "Copenhagen interpretation," stressing indeterminism in the laws of the universe.

Modern physics emerged from the research of many investigators across Europe. Einstein emerged as an outsized public figure, towering above other scientists in terms of public recognition. Max Planck, Erwin Schrödinger, Werner Heisenberg, Max Born, Pascual Jordan, Wolfgang Pauli, John von Neumann, and Paul Dirac, among others, were other key contributors to quantum mechanics.

The history of modern physics is one of the most scrutinized yet also most distorted topics in the history of science. What follows is an attempt to bring precision to some of the most controversial aspects of these revolutions in relation to intellectual thought. These topics – ideal cases for understanding the relation between theory and experiment and the relation of science to other areas of knowledge – show how the public was mobilized by a community of experts. Scientists divided their time between private research and public dissemination, promoting science as associated with moral values (objectivity, civil discourse, democracy, and anti-totalitarianism).

The Turn of the Century (1898–1902)

Before there can be a solution to a problem, there must be a problem. Two scientists and close collaborators, Henri Poincaré in France and Hendrik Lorentz in the Netherlands, were most responsible for articulating the challenges faced by science at the turn of the century. Both ended up by having complicated relationships to Einstein's proposed solution to the "crisis" of science they described, and both in many ways anticipated – but did not follow through – the research programs associated with Einstein's work.[4]

At the turn of the century a number of prominent scientists and intellectuals perceived that science was "bankrupt" and in "crisis." The legacy of anti-clerical writers of the previous century, such as Hippolyte Taine and Ernest Renan, faced a backlash as intellectuals noted that these authors had placed too much hope in science. In France, "the crisis of science" movement encapsulated one aspect of widely noted societal ills connected to a generalized crisis of authority and widespread discontent with various aspects of life at the *fin de siècle*.

---

4 Stanley Goldberg, "Poincaré's Silence and Einstein's Relativity: The Role of Theory and Experiment in Poincaré's Physics," *British Journal for the History of Science*, 5(1) (1970), 73–84; Peter Galison, *Einstein's Clocks, Poincaré's Maps: Empires of Time* (New York: W. W. Norton, 2003); and Olivier Darrigol, "The Mystery of the Einstein–Poincaré Connection," *Isis*, 95(4) (2004), 614–626.

Signs that a crisis in science was brewing came to a tipping point when Poincaré, a highly respected mathematician and scientist (cousin of Raymond Poincaré, President of France during the years 1913–1920), noted how, in the realm of electricity and magnetism, the laws of physics seemed radically different. In work published in 1898 Poincaré explained how these laws showed a completely new aspect of time where it was no longer a single or unified concept and where no master clock connected to the universe could ever be found. In the *Revue de Métaphysique et de Morale* he stated that, "Of two watches, we have no right to say that the one goes true, the other wrong; we can only say that it is advantageous to conform to the indications of the first."[5] In light of this research, Poincaré argued that another of the most cherished principles associated with Newton, the principle of reaction, should no longer be considered universally valid. Poincaré concluded by leaving physicists with two options: either abandon cherished principles based on the old concepts of time and space, action and reaction (basically, all of Newtonian mechanics) or change the current understanding of physics: "Ainsi se trouveraient condamnées en bloc toutes les théories qui respectent ce principe, *à moins que nous ne consentions à modifier profondément toutes nos idées sur l'électrodynamique.*"[6]

By the end of the nineteenth century, Poincaré had already seen many of the revolutionary consequences of the "new dynamics." But instead of pushing for radical changes in the discipline of physics, he opted for a conservative approach that safeguarded long-held beliefs by applying minor corrections to particular scientific theories.

Poincaré studied the work of Lorentz closely. "The Dutch Poincaré" had made a reputation for himself by focusing on electricity rather than on traditional mechanics.[7] Lorentz revealed how different the laws of the former were, and investigated instances when the two could be reconciled and when they could not. He published prolifically on these topics, establishing a new relation between energy and mass that depended on acceleration.[8] Thereafter the

---

5 Henri Poincaré, "La mesure du temps," *Revue de Métaphysique et de Morale*, 6(1) (1898), 1–13, p. 6.
6 Henri Poincaré, "La théorie de Lorentz et le principe de réaction," *Archives Néerlandaises des Sciences Exactes et Naturelles*, 5 (1900), 252–278, p. 278.
7 Charles Nordmann, "Einstein à Paris," *Revue des Deux Mondes*, 8 (April 1922), 925–937, p. 926.
8 Hendrik A. Lorentz, "Vereenvoudigde theorie der electrische en optische verschijnselen in lichamen die zich bewegen," *Verslag der Koninklijke Akademie van Wetenschappen*, 7 (1899), 507–522; and Hendrik A. Lorentz, "Electromagnetic phenomena in a system moving with any velocity smaller than that of light," *Proceedings of the Koninklijke Akademie van Wetenschappen*, 6 (1904), 809–831.

relation between the concepts of mass and energy, in addition to new space-time relations, became an active area of research that would characterize modern physics, culminating with Einstein's General Theory of Relativity.

The St. Louis World's Fair

Poincaré's widely anticipated conference at the Congress for Arts and Sciences at the St. Louis World's Fair (September 24, 1904) laid out "The Present State and Future of Mathematical Physics."[9] His presentation portrayed physics at the cusp of a "transformation profonde."[10] On account of its non-technical language, the lecture was quickly reprinted in the *Revue des Idées*.[11] Poincaré noted that "nous sommes assurés que la malade n'en mourra pas et même nous pouvons espérer que cette crise sera salutaire," recounting how – despite the revolutionary implications of the new physics – it remained identical to the old physics at a first-order approximation.[12]

Poincaré followed this presentation with the publication the following year of "Sur la dynamique de l'électron," which he presented on June 5, 1905 to the Académie des Sciences.[13] Therein he explained how the "Lorentz transformations" (the new formulae of time and space describing electrodynamic phenomena central to Einstein's theory) could be expressed in terms of the quadratic expression "$x^2 + y^2 + z^2 - t^2$" with "invariant" properties in a "space of four dimensions."[14] In both papers, Poincaré discussed the possible existence of gravitational waves and expressed how further astronomical tests would be possible. Poincaré considered these insights as an important "modification" of the laws of Newton (in the shorter *Comptes Rendus* version) and as "analogous" to the Copernican revolution (in the longer text). He warned readers that, if one changed how physicists traditionally conceived of time to match the new insights, a cataclysm would follow, comparable to that which "befell the system of Ptolemy due to the intervention of Copernicus."[15] His research reached an

---

9 Henri Poincaré, "L'état actuel et l'avenir de la physique mathématique," *Bulletin des Sciences Mathématiques*, 28 (1904), 302–324.
10 Poincaré, "L'état actuel et l'avenir de la physique mathématique," 302.
11 Henri Poincaré, "L'état actuel et l'avenir de la physique mathématique," *Revue des Idées*, 1 (1904), 801–814.
12 Poincaré, "L'état actuel et l'avenir de la physique mathématique," 303.
13 A summary appeared in Henri Poincaré, "Sur la dynamique de l'électron," *Comptes Rendus des Séances de l'Académie des Sciences*, 140 (1905), 1504–1508. The full text published in the *Rendiconti* was submitted on July 23, 1905. Henri Poincaré, "Sur la dynamique de l'électron," *Rendiconti del Circolo Matematico di Palermo*, 21 (1906), 129–175.
14 Poincaré, "Sur la dynamique de l'électron," 168.
15 Poincaré, "Sur la dynamique de l'électron," 131–132.

even wider public with the appearance of the widely read *The Value of Science* (1905) describing the "new mechanics."

Einstein followed the work of both men closely. His areas of interest focused on the same topics, mainly the nature of light and electricity, Brownian motion, the relativity principle, and the relation between mass and energy and acceleration and gravitation. In the *annus mirabilis* of 1905, Einstein published four ground-breaking papers that positioned him as one of the most promising young physicists of his generation. For the next decade he would continue to labor on these topics, respond to criticisms, and eventually integrate most of these insights into a single theory known as the General Theory of Relativity – the fulfillment of his "boldest dreams."[16]

In 1916 Einstein developed a set of "field equations," simultaneously with the mathematician David Hilbert, showing how these new concepts of time and space, matter and energy, inertia and gravitation matched against actual astronomical measurements of our solar system. The new theory was a great scientific achievement, but for many physicists the price to pay seemed too high, since not only did it require changing the definitions of the most basic concepts in physics, but it was also based on a complex non-Euclidean mathematical structure which then had virtually no applicability beyond explaining previously known results.

The Eclipse Expedition

Attention to General Relativity came not from physics but from astronomy. A group of astronomers led by Frank Watson Dyson, the Astronomer Royal of the Greenwich Observatory, and his chief assistant Arthur Eddington organized an eclipse expedition to test one of the central claims of the General Theory: the bending of light by the gravitational pull of the sun. Einstein argued that light should be considered as an ideal measurement standard for both time (frequency) and space (wavelength), so gravitational effects on light could be used as evidence for the warping of the very fabric of time and space itself.

The expedition results "confirmed" Einstein's theory and were announced with great fanfare at the Royal Astronomical Society in Burlington House in London.[17] Although Einstein's theory was neither the first nor the only one to

---

16 Einstein to Michel Besso, December 10, 1915, Berlin, in *The Collected Papers of Albert Einstein*, ed. Diana Kormos Buchwald, 15 vols. (Princeton: Princeton University Press, 1987–), vol. VIII, Doc. 162, 159–160, p. 160.

17 Frank Watson Dyson, Arthur Stanley Eddington, and C. Davidson, "A Determination of the Deflection of Light by the Sun's Gravitational Field, from Observations Made at the Total Eclipse of May 29, 1919," *Philosophical Transactions of the Royal Society of London, Series A*, 220 (1920), 291–333.

propose that gravity would affect light, the published article on the expedition results laid out in its first paragraphs only three possible explanations for the behavior of the light measured during the eclipse. The first option proposed that there was no gravitational effect, the second one concerned an effect equivalent to that of gravity on "ordinary matter" (as in the traditional Newtonian law of gravitation and theory of matter), and the third one would explain a result twice that amount "in accordance with Einstein's generalized relativity theory."[18] The measurements of the photographic plates from the expedition matched with confidence the value for deflection given in the third case.[19]

The public presentation of the eclipse results was covered widely by the popular press, inaugurating a means of dissemination of science via press release that would later become common practice for large-scale projects. In 1919 Einstein's name appeared on the cover of newspapers around the world announcing a revolution not only for physics, but for our general understanding of time and space. The headline of *The Times* read "Revolution in Science/ New Theory of the Universe/ Newtonian Ideas Overthrown," and the *New York Times* announced "The Lights of the Heavens Askew."[20] Shortly after the widespread news coverage, Einstein explained that in Berlin "every child knows me from photographs" and described himself as a media King Midas, who turned everything he touched into news: "Like the man in the fairy tale, whose touch turned everything into gold, thus it is with me, with everything turning into banner line news."[21]

Most accounts of the importance of Einstein's work after the eclipse expedition were based on a standard model where the value of science was understood in terms of hypothesis creation, theoretical prediction, and experimental confirmation. The model for this kind of scientific production became popular after the French astronomer Urbain Le Verrier's discovery of Neptune was widely publicized in 1846. At that time, Le Verrier's discovery became a symbol for how mathematics and theoretical physics could be used

---

18 The third option was twice the amount of the first one because in Einstein's theory the displacement "becomes magnified as the speed increases, until for the limiting velocity of light it doubles the curvature of the path." Dyson, Eddington, and Davidson, "A Determination of the Deflection of Light by the Sun's Gravitational Field," 291–292.
19 The first should show no displacement on the measured photographs, the second 0″.87, and the third option 1″.75.
20 *The Times* (November 7, 1919); and *New York Times* (November 10, 1919).
21 Einstein to Ehrenfest, before September 9, 1920, Berlin, in *The Collected Papers of Albert Einstein*, vol. X, Doc. 139, 264–265, p. 265; Einstein to Max and Hedwig Born, September 9, 1920, Berlin, in *The Collected Papers of Albert Einstein*, vol. X, Doc. 140, 265.

to predict new phenomena. The astronomer was widely applauded for discovering a planet not with a telescope, but *"avec la pointe de sa plume."*[22]

Le Verrier's success in leading observers to find a new planet (which was eventually named Neptune) fueled a race to explain another anomaly in Newtonian celestial mechanics: the perihelion of Mercury. Observations of its actual movement differed greatly from the value obtained through mathematical calculations.

The problem of the perihelion of Mercury captivated some of the most ambitious scientists of the nineteenth and twentieth centuries. In *Science and Method* (1908), Poincaré asked whether the motion of the perihelion of Mercury was "an argument in favor of the new Dynamics" or "an argument against it" concluding that it was *"the only appreciable effect upon astronomical observations"* of the new theories. The most recent calculations using the new theories showed that the perihelion occurred *"in the same direction as that which has been observed without being explained, but [was] considerably smaller"* than the one obtained with a traditional (Newtonian) definition of mass.[23] In the years that followed, Einstein decided to explore other ways to explain the observed value of the perihelion by proposing changes in mass due to velocity. In 1915 he proposed a theory that "has as a consequence a curvature of light rays due to gravitational fields twice as strong" as previously thought. With these adjustments, he matched the value of the most trustworthy observations (Einstein's calculations resulted in 43″ per century while observations amounted to 45″ ± 5″).[24] The new calculated number (nearly double the Newtonian one) would also produce a doubling in the amount of light deflection by gravitational forces that would be tested during the eclipse expedition.

Einstein's magisterial publication "The Foundation of the General Theory of Relativity" appeared the following spring in March 1916. It conformed to the model of scientific discovery that had buttressed the prestige of science in the nineteenth century after Le Verrier's discovery. The text mentioned the effects of the bending of light by gravity, the perihelion of Mercury, and the red-shift of the spectrum of light as possible tests for this theory. These effects

---

22 Observations of the planet Uranus had shown that its orbit did not move exactly as predicted by the laws of Newton. Le Verrier hypothesized that the gravitational pull of another planet could be used to explain this discrepancy and accurately calculated where the planet could be found. François Arago, *Astronomie populaire*, ed. L. Guérin, 4 vols. (Paris: T. Morgand, 1867), vol. IV, 515.
23 Henri Poincaré, "The New Mechanics and Astronomy," in *Science and Method* (New York: Dover Publications, 1952 [1908]), 242.
24 Albert Einstein, "Erklärung der Perihelbewegung des Merkur aus der allgemeinen Relativitätstheorie," *Sitzungsberichte der Königlich Preußische Akademie der Wissenschaften* (1915), 831–839.

came to be known as the "three classic tests" of relativity. While the value of the perihelion of Mercury had been known for decades, at the time of publication experimental work on the other two related phenomena was still incipient and inconclusive.

While the three classic tests were used to prove General Relativity, after 1907 Einstein increasingly invoked the Michelson–Morley experiment as evidence in favor of the Special Theory of Relativity. Historians and philosophers of science, however, have noted that in both cases the actual reliance of Einstein's work on experiment is more complicated than how it was presented in his scientific papers and by the press.[25]

Einstein Simplified

Newspapers of the time reported local news alongside science with cosmological and universal implications to recruit even larger audiences.[26] During the Victorian era science popularization had occurred mainly through large public lectures and specialized journals, such as Norman Lockyer's *Nature* and Camille Flammarion's *Cosmos*, but in the twentieth century newspapers and the daily press increasingly took on the role of publicizing science to an expanding public.

The *New York Times* coverage of Eddington's packed Trinity College lecture to students was announced with the headline "Professor Eddington, 6 Feet to the Eye, Explains How It May Be Really Only 3 Feet."[27] The astronomer asked readers to imagine an aviator traveling at 161,000 miles per second, about nine-tenths the speed of light. The aviator's watch would seem, to a stationary observer, to tick twice as slowly. He invited students to "suppose that you are in love with a lady on Neptune and that she returns the sentiment" to illustrate the complexities behind the scientific understanding of the "now" concept.[28] The mathematician Bertrand Russell continued these popularization efforts, warning readers that circular dinner plates in the dining car on a speedy train would look oval to stationary outsiders. He used the example of flies landing on stagnant pools as models

25 The classic text re-evaluating the role of experiment in Einstein's work is Gerald Holton, "Einstein, Michelson, and the 'Crucial' Experiment," *Isis*, 60(2) (1969), 132–197.
26 Katy Price, *Loving Faster Than Light: Romance and Readers in Einstein's Universe* (Chicago: University of Chicago Press, 2012).
27 "How Tall Are You, Einstein Measure? Prof. Eddington, 6 Feet to the Eye, Explains How It May Be Really Only 3 Feet," *New York Times*, December 4, 1919.
28 Arthur Stanley Eddington, *The Nature of the Physical World* (London: J. M. Dent & Sons, 1935 [1928]), 49.

for stars bending space-time, and recounted other similarly astounding examples, such as cigars and dental appointments lasting twice as long: "What a situation for envy! Each man thinks that the other's cigar lasts twice as long as his own. It may, however, be some consolation to reflect that the other man's visit to the dentist also lasts twice as long."[29]

The most successful of these evocative stories became known as the twin paradox. It was originally due to the physicist Paul Langevin, who did not mention twins, but referred to a voyager on the rocket ship of Jules Verne. Einstein considered it "the thing at its funniest." Later even more colorful examples featured twins, with one of them leaving Earth to travel at close to the speed of light and eventually returning to see that he had aged less rapidly than the sibling who remained at home.[30]

Popularization accounts often stressed that the layman's understanding of such complex theories was necessarily limited. The *New York Times* special cable from Berlin reported Einstein as claiming that, despite the revolutionary importance of his theory, "no more than twelve persons in all the world could understand it."[31] This message was reinforced through other means, including film. An American short film produced by Fleischer Studios of Superman and Betty Boop cartoons spread the message "that only twelve men in the world could understand" Einstein's theory.[32]

The narrative of prediction of observables from abstract mathematics drew from another trope prevalent in accounts of science from the time of Newton, where genius men were portrayed as working in isolation and at a distance from mundane concerns. Einstein was described in the daily press as working "close to the stars he studies, not with a telescope, but rather with the mental eye, and so far only as they come within the range of his mathematical formulae."[33] A title card from the film *The Einstein Theory of Relativity* read "there sits in a quiet little study in Europe a genius."[34] These depictions glossed over Einstein's close attention to experimental work and astronomical measurements, his experience as a patent clerk, and his work as a consultant for the military and industry.[35]

---

29 Bertrand Russell, *The ABC of Relativity* (London: George Allen & Unwin, 1958), 53.
30 Albert Einstein, "Relativitätstheorie," *Vierteljahrsschrift der Naturforschenden Gesellschaft Zürich*, 56 (1911), 1–14.
31 "Einstein Expounds His New Theory," *New York Times*, December 3, 1919.
32 David Fleischer, *The Einstein Theory of Relativity*, film (1923).
33 "Einstein Expounds His New Theory." 34 Fleischer, *The Einstein Theory of Relativity*.
35 József Illy, *The Practical Einstein: Experiments, Patents, Inventions* (Baltimore: Johns Hopkins University Press, 2012); and Jimena Canales, "The Media of Relativity: Einstein and Communications Technologies," *Technology and Culture*, 56(3) (2015), 610–645.

Conventionalism and Differences with Poincaré

The portrayal of Einstein and theoretical physics in public forums stood in sharp contrast with the view of science held and promoted by some of Einstein's most prominent interlocutors. In France, Poincaré's philosophical stance with regard to science was known as "conventionalism" or "commodisme." The value of scientific theories resided in how they helped scientists describe physical phenomena in a useful and pragmatic manner. Conventionalism stressed the tight relation between theory and experiment, highlighted the reliance of theoretical science on practical mathematics, underlined the role of technological context, and stressed the benefits of practical considerations in the production of knowledge. It was a far cry from more sensationalist accounts of science where unexpected discoveries arose from theoretical predictions emerging from the mind of isolated scientists, and which did not capture dramatic headlines.

Conventionalism was amply criticized by its detractors for proposing a view of science as somewhat provisory, tentative, and opportunistic. Yet Poincaré considered scientific theories not as conventions that could be created or changed willy-nilly, but as being so strong that they reflected the true nature of the phenomenon under investigation. However, because Poincaré placed an emphasis on the practice and ease of use of theories and mathematical tools, his accounts contrasted starkly with naïve realist or platonic explanations, on one extreme. On the other hand, he differed from thinkers who believed that science's grasp of absolute truth was even weaker. Poincaré thus differed from some Catholic scientists and philosophers, such as Pierre Duhem, who described scientific theories as matching very imperfectly against nature (the "underdetermination" thesis), and the philosopher Édouard Le Roy, a student of Henri Bergson, whom Poincaré considered a nominalist for proposing a view of science that considered its power as essentially descriptive.[36]

Poincaré's philosophical understanding of the nature of scientific labor affected his estimation of Einstein's scientific work. In a letter of recommendation written to support Einstein's application for a professorship in theoretical physics at Zurich, Poincaré described the work of the theoretical physicist as a kind of guided guesswork. This labor could sometimes result in the prediction of new effects that could be corroborated by experimentalists. Einstein's future success, wrote Poincaré, stemmed from his perseverance and originality

---

36 Henri Poincaré, *Science and Hypothesis* (New York: Dover, 1952 [1902]); and Henri Poincaré, *The Value of Science* (New York: Dover, 1958).

rather than from anything else: "Since he seeks in all directions one must, on the contrary, expect most of the trails which he pursues to be blind alleys. But one must hope at the same time that one of the directions he has indicated may be the right one, and that is enough."[37]

Poincaré's conventionalist approach to science also informed his understanding of relativity theory. In 1902 he wrote to the Nobel Prize committee arguing that Lorentz should receive the prize for discovering some of the central aspects associated with relativity theory. These included the discovery of time dilation, a correct explanation of the Michelson–Morley experiment, and invariance. Poincaré's letter was signed by some of the most renowned physicists of the time, including Wilhelm Röntgen, Henri Becquerel, and Planck, clearly showing that most of these physicists also attributed some of the central ideas of relativity theory to Lorentz.[38] Poincaré's report on Lorentz's work in 1910 stressed that, in the case of traveling clocks, Lorentz had shown why it was "impossible to detect anything other than relative velocities of bodies with regard to one another, and we should also renounce the knowledge of their relative velocities with regard to the ether as much as their absolute velocities."[39] On May 4, 1912, two months before his death, Poincaré delivered a lecture in London that would be his last significant statement on the theory of relativity, and that did not even mention Einstein.

Differences with Lorentz

While Poincaré gave a central importance to utility and convention in science, Lorentz's understanding attributed a strong role to epistemology, especially in determining the merits of competing scientific theories.[40] For him, our understanding of time and space as connected to everyday experiences should be accorded strong epistemological value. This benefit should

---

37 Poincaré to Pierre Weiss (November 1911), Henri Poincaré Papers, ed. Scott A. Walter et al., Doc. 2-59-3, http://henripoincarepapers.univ-nantes.fr/chp/text/weiss-1911-11-00.html.

38 Poincaré to Physics Nobel Committee, received January 31, 1902, Nobel Archives of the Royal Swedish Academy of Sciences, Henri Poincaré Papers, ed. Scott A. Walter et al., Doc. 2-62-7, http://henripoincarepapers.univ-nantes.fr/chp/text/nobel1902.html.

39 "This principle must be regarded as rigorous and not only as approximate." Henri Poincaré, "Rapport sur les travaux de H. A. Lorentz, *ca.* 31 January 1910," in *La Correspondance entre Henri Poincaré et les physiciens, chimistes et ingénieurs*, ed. Scott Walter, Étienne Bolmont, and André Coret (Basel: Birkhäuser, 2007), 438.

40 On the place of epistemology in Lorentz's attempts to distinguish his work from Einstein's, see Richard Staley, *Einstein's Generation: The Origins of the Relativity Revolution* (Chicago: University of Chicago Press, 2008), 329.

be taken into consideration when debating about the merits of scientific theories. Einstein disagreed. He at first attached Lorentz's name to the theory of relativity, referring to it as "the theory of Lorentz and Einstein," but started to separate himself from Lorentz's position in 1907, referring separately to "the H. A. Lorentz theory and the principle of relativity."[41] Einstein claimed that his particular contribution resided in considering Lorentz's "local time" to be time in general.[42] Lorentz, in contrast, would continue to refer to the change in magnitude of time measurements as local time, contrasting it with time in general. In the case of length, he referred to the change in magnitude as apparent length in contrast to length in general. Einstein eventually became convinced that there was nothing "local" or "apparent" about these time measurements and that one was as general as the other.

Lorentz, conceding that Einstein could "take credit" for relativity, explained how "Einstein simply postulates what we have deduced, with some difficulty and not altogether satisfactorily."[43] Lorentz accepted that Einstein was right but claimed that he was right too: "Which of the two ways of thinking you would like to join, is a decision that depends entirely on each individual."[44] The issues at stake, Lorentz insisted, were epistemological: "The evaluation of these concepts belongs largely to epistemology, and the verdict can also be left to this field." Scientists were free to chose between them depending on "the mindset to which one is accustomed, and whether you feel most attracted to one or the other view."[45]

Lorentz's popular book *The Einstein Theory of Relativity* called the theory "a monument of science" and extolled the "indefatigable exertions and

---

41 Albert Einstein, "Über eine Methode zur Bestimmung des Verhältnisses der transversalen und longitudinalen Masse des Elektrons," *Annalen der Physik*, 21 (1906), 583–586, p. 586; and Albert Einstein, "Über das Relativitätsprinzip und die aus demselben gezogenen Folgerungen," *Jahrbuch der Radioaktivität und Elektronik*, 4 (1907), 411–462.
42 Staley, *Einstein's Generation*, 311.
43 Hendrik A. Lorentz, *The Theory of Electrons and Its Applications to the Phenomena of Light and Radiant Heat: A Course of Lectures delivered in Columbia University, New York, in March and April 1906* (Leipzig: B. G. Teubner, 1909), 230.
44 "Welcher der beiden Denkweisen man sich anschließen mag, bleibt wohl dem einzelnen überlassen." Hendrik A. Lorentz, "Alte und neue Fragen der Physik," *Physikalische Zeitschrift*, 11 (1910), 1234–1257, p. 1234.
45 "Die Bewertung dieser Begriffe gehört größtenteils zur Erkenntnislehre, und man kann denn auch das Urteil ihr überlassen, im Vertrauen, daß sie die besprochenen Fragen mit der benötigten Gründlichkeit betrachten wird. Sicher ist es aber, daß es für einen großen Teil von der Denkweise abhängen wird, an die man gewöhnt ist, ob man sich am meisten zur einen oder zur andern Auffassung angezogen fühlt." Hendrik A. Lorentz, *Das Relativitätsprinzip: Drei Vorlesungen gehalten in Teylers Stiftung zu Haarlem*, ed. W. H. Keesom, Beihefte zur Zeitschrift für mathematischen und naturwissenschaftlichen Unterricht aller Schulgattungen nr. 1 (Leipzig: B. G. Teubner, 1914 [1913]), 23.

perseverance" of its author.[46] Nonetheless, Lorentz cautioned that "in my opinion it is not impossible that in the future this road [research on the ether], indeed abandoned at present, will once more be followed with good results."[47] He continued to search for a stable background that could serve as an anchor for an absolute concept of time, be it the ether, a concept of space that could serve as reference point, or some fixed stars in the universe.[48] He still insisted that "one may, in all modesty, call true time the time measured by clocks which are fixed in this medium [space], and consider simultaneity as a primary concept."[49] Special and general relativity were undoubtedly correct, but they were not the only way to see things: "They will just not impose themselves on us so much as the only possible ones."[50] The differences between a "physicist of the old school" and the "relativist" resided in the fact that, while both agreed that nobody could "make out which of the two times is the right one," the old-school physicist was ready to acknowledge that he "preferred" one of them, whereas, for the relativist, "there cannot be the least question of one time being better than the other." Lorentz's personal preference was to maintain "notions of space and time that have always been familiar to us, and which I, for my part, consider as perfectly clear and, moreover, as distinct from one another."[51] While he had introduced the concept of local time, he "never thought that this had anything to do with the real time. The real time for me was still represented by the old classical notion of an absolute time, which is independent of any reference to special frames of co-ordinates. There existed for me only this one true time."[52] Lorentz continued to believe in his hypothesis: "Asked if

46 Hendrik A. Lorentz, "The Einstein Theory of Relativity," in *The Einstein Theory of Relativity: A Concise Statement by Prof. H. A. Lorentz of the University of Leiden* (New York: Brentano, 1920 [1919]), 25–64, p. 62.
47 Lorentz, "The Einstein Theory of Relativity," 61–62.
48 The existence of the ether was questioned years before Einstein. Some of the most severe attacks on it came from Poincaré, who is ironically remembered as one of its defenders. "Whether the ether exists or not matters little." Poincaré, *Science and Hypothesis*, 211. For the argument that Einstein's contribution resided in dropping the ether, see John J. Stachel, "1905 and All That, How Einstein Claimed His Place in the Changing Landscape of Physics during His Annus Mirabilis," *Nature*, 433(7023) (2005), 215–217, p. 217.
49 Hendrik A. Lorentz, "The Principle of Relativity for Uniform Translation," in *Lectures on Theoretical Physics at the University of Leiden*, vol. III, ed. A. D. Fokker, trans. L. Silberstein and A. P. H. Trivelli (London: Macmillan, 1931 [1922]), 179–326, p. 211.
50 Lorentz to Einstein, June 6, 1916, Haarlem, in *The Collected Papers of Albert Einstein*, vol. VIII, Doc. 225, 218–221, p. 220.
51 Hendrik A. Lorentz, *Problems of Modern Physics: A Course of Lectures Delivered in the California Institute of Technology*, ed. H. Bateman (Boston: Ginn and Company, 1927), 221.
52 Hendrik A. Lorentz, "Report," *The Astrophysical Journal*, 68(5) (1928), 345–351, p. 350.

I consider [my hypothesis] a real one, I should answer 'yes.' It is as real as anything we observe."[53]

The presenter of Einstein's Nobel Prize (given in 1922 for the previous year) explained why the prize was not awarded for relativity, restating (almost verbatim) the view that the validity of Einstein's theory of relativity *"pertains to epistemology* and has therefore been the subject of lively debate in philosophical circles," citing additionally the recent criticism leveled by Bergson during Einstein's visit to Paris.[54]

Ernst Mach, The Vienna Circle, and Logical Positivism

During the 1910s and 1920s, Einstein worked hard to combat philosophical or scientific accounts that considered the validity of competing theories in terms of epistemological, practical, or aesthetic considerations. In an article published for general audiences in *Die Kultur der Gegenwart* (1915), he argued against the view that considered a decision on the merits of his theory versus competing interpretations as a matter of choice.[55]

Einstein's opinion about Lorentz's contributions reveals the influence of Ernst Mach's philosophy on his work. Mach had earlier argued that the most parsimonious theories described the world most accurately, and Einstein explained the benefit of his work over Lorentz's in these terms. Because there were no "physical grounds (accessible in principle to observation)" for selecting a privileged frame of reference, that concept should not be used. "A worldview that can do without such arbitrariness is preferable, in my opinion," he concluded, citing Mach.[56]

Einstein's strongest critique against the conventionalism of Poincaré appeared nearly a decade after the mathematician had died. "Geometry and Experience" successfully argued that the mathematics used in the theory of relativity should not be considered just a set of convenient tools for describing the universe, but rather as a reflection of the structure of the universe itself. Einstein employed non-Euclidian (more precisely,

---

53 Lorentz, "Report," 351.
54 Svante Arrhenius, "Presentation Speech," December 10, 1922, in *Nobel Lectures in Physics (1901–1921)* (Singapore: World Scientific, 1998), 479.
55 "Lorentz's theory arouses our mistrust." Albert Einstein, "Die Relativitätstheorie," in *Die Kultur der Gegenwart: Die Physik*, ed. Emil Warburg (Leipzig: Teubner, 1915), 703–713, p. 706.
56 Einstein to Lorentz, January 23, 1915, Berlin, in *The Collected Papers of Albert Einstein*, vol. VIII, Doc. 47, 59–63, p. 60.

Riemannian) mathematics that broke with long-cherished principles (that parallel lines can never cross, that the shortest path between two points is a straight line, and so on) not because these calculating techniques were useful, but rather because the universe itself should be considered as non-Euclidean.

Mach's philosophical understanding of science was expanded by members of the Vienna Circle, initially known as the Verein Ernst Mach. The group consisted of committed philosophers and scientists who met regularly at the University of Vienna from the mid 1920s to the mid 1930s. For the most part, they promoted a "logical empiricist" view of science that, with few exceptions, considered Einstein's relativity as a paragon for intellectual achievement. The circle served as a launching pad for logical positivism in the United States after many of its members were forced into exile with the rise of Nazism. Despite the diverse views of many of its members, one unifying goal across various strands of the movement consisted in trying to ground modern scientific knowledge as a structure built up from sense impressions using analytical mathematics. In influential works, and as founders of the journal *Erkenntnis*, its members defended the value of Einstein's work, the exceptionalism of science, and why science rightfully stood apart from common sense or non-expert knowledge practices.

Einstein's own view about science and its relation to philosophy and metaphysics changed significantly throughout his life. During the years when his theory was amply contested and before he received the accolades that would follow, he insisted on a Machian, anti-metaphysical, and objective view of science. But in later years he denounced Mach's approach as sterile, defended the value of metaphysics, and explained that the differences between physics and metaphysics were of degree and not of kind.

Hans Reichenbach, who had studied with Einstein in Berlin, became one of his most prominent defenders after World War I. Together with other members of the Vienna Circle, Reichenbach developed an epistemological framework for science that would dominate analytical Anglo-American philosophy well into the 1960s. *Experience and Prediction*, one of the most influential books in the field of philosophy of science (first published in 1938), was notable for its articulation of the logical structure of science and for its account of scientific rationality. Reichenbach separated science into two main parts in order to highlight those process which could be explained logically and separate them from those that could not, arguing that philosophical studies of science should be concerned solely with the former: "I shall introduce the term context of discovery and context of justification to mark this distinction ... epistemology is only occupied in constructing the context of justification." The logical structure of scientific thinking appeared to him "a better way of thinking than actual thinking." The price to pay for this logical structure was to completely divorce it from actual scientific practices: "What epistemology intends is to construct thinking processes in a way in which they *ought* to occur ... *replacing the real* intermediary links. Epistemology thus considers a logical *substitute* rather than *real* processes."[57] By portraying science as necessarily logical and rational, Reichenbach downplayed those aspects of it that could be seen as merely conventional or dependent on epistemological assumptions.

With Rudolf Carnap, also of the Vienna Circle, logical positivism expanded its criticism to the German philosophers Fichte, Schelling, Hegel, and Heidegger and in France, Bergson. Carnap found no use for "alleged knowledge ... which transcends the realm of empirically founded, inductive science."[58] For many members of the Vienna Circle, metaphysics appeared as a defect to be eliminated from empirically based rational thought instead of being a label for aspects of science that could not be tested empirically but that necessarily accompanied it.[59] Carnap's *Der logische Aufbau der Welt* (1928) attempted to show how a complete scientific system could be built by combining clear observations with logical mathematics.

Karl Popper's *The Logic of Scientific Discovery* (1934) appeared a few years after Carnap's *Der logische Aufbau der Welt*. Like Carnap, Popper was concerned with the problem of "demarcation," establishing clear criteria for distinguishing between scientific knowledge and unscientific or pseudo-scientific beliefs. He proposed a new model for scientific practices based on a process of hypothesis creation whose strength resided not in how the hypotheses would be verified by experiments but in their potential for falsification. The theory of relativity was a central example for Popper, serving as an aspirational standard for proper scientific work for years to come.

The aims, methods, and professionalization standards of Analytic (mainly Anglo-American after World War II) versus Continental philosophy started

---

57 Hans Reichenbach, *Experience and Prediction: An Analysis of the Foundations and Structure of Knowledge*, 4th impression, 1952 edn. (Chicago: University of Chicago Press, 1938), 5–7.
58 Remarks by Carnap written in 1957 appended to Rudolf Carnap, "Überwindung der Metaphysik durch logische Analyse der Sprache," *Erkenntnis*, 2 (1932), 219–241, translated by Arthur Pap and reprinted in A. J. Ayer, *Logical Positivism* (New York: The Free Press, 1959), 80.
59 Peter Galison, "Aufbau/Bauhaus: Logical Positivism and Architectural Modernism," *Critical Inquiry*, 16(4) (1990), 709–752.

differing radically during these years. For the most part, the Analytical school saw philosophy as a discipline that could function as a jury by providing standards of reasonability (a task that can be traced back to Kant's epistemology, and was rejected later by some postmodern philosophers). It often set science apart from technology, stressed its empirical and rational foundations, and was completely unconcerned with actual scientific practices or historical reality. It was largely this legacy that the anti-logical positivists of the 1970s and the "laboratory studies," "turn to practice," and "science in action" movements of the 1980s and 1990s aimed to correct.

Anti-Semitism and Modern Physics

Einstein's and his allies' response to criticisms needs to be placed in the context of direct anti-Semitic attacks, such as those that took place in Berlin (August 1920) and in Bad Nauheim (September 1920). During these years, Einstein considered assessments of his theory as completely politicized: "Belief in this matter [whether relativity theory is correct] depends on political party affiliation," he wrote to a friend.[60] The relation of modern physics and anti-Semitism became even more charged as Einstein and other physicists took on increasingly public positions on the pressing political questions of their time, such as the League of Nations and Zionism. In certain cases, the links between certain scientific views, philosophical stances, and political affiliations were clear and sometimes extreme.[61]

The relation between Einstein, anti-Semitism, and politics informed how many thinkers conceived of a general relation between science and politics more generally for the rest of the century.[62] Some of the first sociological studies of science, such as Robert K. Merton's "Science and the Social Order" (1938), described an inevitable "conflict between the totalitarian state and the scientist" by reference to attacks against Einstein's theory of relativity by Johannes Stark and Philipp Lenard.[63]

---

60 Einstein to Marcel Grossmann, September 12, 1920, in *The Collected Papers of Albert Einstein*, vol. X, Doc. 148, 271–272, p. 272.
61 The Russian revolutionary Vladimir Lenin attacked Ernst Mach in his defense of Marxist materialism; the physicist Philipp Lenard was nearly killed by students protesting against his views about the murder of Walther Rathenau; Friedrich Adler, a candidate at the ETH for the physics professorship later held by Einstein, shot and killed the Austrian president; Moritz Schlick of the Vienna Circle was murdered by a student with radical national socialist views.
62 For a book-length account see Mark Walker, *Nazi Science: Myth, Truth, and the German Atomic Bomb* (New York: Plenum Press, 1995).
63 Robert K. Merton, "Science and the Social Order," *Philosophy of Science*, 5(3) (1938), 321–337, p. 326.

Anti-Semites, such as Stark and Lenard, frequently co-opted non-anti-Semitic critiques, making it difficult to separate politically or racially motivated attacks from other kinds of critiques. Those scientists and philosophers who questioned the merits of Einstein's work, but did not want to be associated with anti-Semitism, often stressed their support for Einstein as an individual. Lorentz, for example, actively supported Einstein personally and professionally, despite their differences. Similarly, Bergson expressed his admiration for Einstein as a person and physicist, limiting his critique to certain key points around his theory.[64]

In Germany, Stark and Lenard, two of the most vocal opponents of Einstein, expanded their target to theoretical physics in general. They protested against a particular way of doing and presenting science that they considered dangerous, foreign, and associated with the Jewish race. In *Nature*, Stark complained that "a flood of propaganda for them is started by articles in journals and newspapers, by text-books and by lecture tours, if possible around the world." Arguing that "whether the culprit is a Jew or not" was irrelevant, but lamenting that they were securing power by acquiring "numerous chairs in physics, and above all in theoretical physics," his targets were nonetheless clear.[65]

National Socialist and anti-Semitic critiques were part of a larger *Deutsche Physik* movement, a nationalistic initiative that argued for science by and for the state limited to practical and social usefulness. In their role as public servants, professors of physics and heads of national institutes and laboratories represented the state and were often judged in terms of their contribution to it.[66]

The idea that science was and should be international emerged only during this period and in direct response to these historical events. Einstein's "Internationalism and Science" (*circa* 1922) cited with approval the words delivered by the chemist Emil Fischer at the Royal Prussian Academy of Sciences: "Whether you like it or not, gentlemen, science is and always will

---

[64] Jimena Canales, *The Physicist and the Philosopher: Einstein, Bergson and the Debate That Changed Our Understanding of Time* (Princeton: Princeton University Press, 2015).

[65] Johannes Stark, "The Pragmatic and the Dogmatic Spirit in Physics," *Nature*, 141(1938), 770–772, pp. 771–772.

[66] Anti-Semitism flared up in earlier debates about Einstein's priority, as his enemies volunteered lesser-known researchers as deserving of credit. In some cases, alternative theories of credit attribution and accounts of what amounts to a "discovery" in science in general were proposed, but, for the most part, these alternative proposals were quickly delegitimized. Milena Wazeck, *Einsteins Gegner: Die öffentliche Kontroverse um die Relativitätstheorie in den 1920er Jahren* (Frankfurt: Campus Verlag, 2009); and Milena Wazeck, "Marginalization Processes in Science: The Controversy about the Theory of Relativity in the 1920s," *Social Studies of Science*, 43(2) (2013), 163–190.

be international."[67] This characterization of science replaced the older view that considered it as defined by "national" styles of thinking, such as Duhem's characterization of British science as emerging from the "ample and shallow" minds of the British compared with the "narrow and deep" ones of his compatriots.[68]

Bergson and Continental Philosophy

A key moment in the relation of physics to European thought revolved around Einstein's assertion, during a meeting at the Société française de philosophie (April 6, 1922) with Bergson present, that "il n'y a donc pas un temps des philosophes."[69] Bergson objected to the shutting out of philosophy from discussions about the nature of time during the meeting and in *Durée et simultanéité*. When Einstein was finally awarded the Nobel Prize the presenter noted that "it will be no secret that the famous philosopher Bergson in Paris has challenged this theory."[70]

The debate between Bergson and Einstein became a reference point in discussions about how philosophers and other intellectuals should engage with science for the rest of the century. Bergson argued that a hidden philosophy underlay Einstein's science, concluding that "Einstein is the continuator of Descartes."[71] Although Bergson was frequently considered to have misunderstood the facts of science, he considered his critique philosophical: "The theory was studied with the aim of responding to a question posed by a philosopher, and not by a physicist."[72] Bergson argued that some of Einstein's most outlandish claims (such as time dilation and the twin paradox) seemed to rest on unacknowledged assumptions (such as differences in travel trajectories). For him, the "really real" aspects of the theory hardly called for such a revolutionary interpretation. Bergson considered

---

67 Albert Einstein, "Internationalism and Science," reprinted in Chapter 4, "Internationalism and European Security, 1922–1932," in *Einstein on Politics: His Private Thoughts and Public Stands on Nationalism, Zionism, War, Peace and the Bomb*, ed. David E. Rowe and Robert Schulmann (Princeton: Princeton University Press, 2007), 192–194, p. 193.
68 Pierre Duhem, *La théorie physique: Son objet et sa structure* (Paris: Chevalier & Rivière, 1906).
69 "La Théorie de la Relativité," *Bulletin de la Société française de philosophie*, no. 22, part III (April 6, 1922), 349–370.
70 Arrhenius, "Presentation Speech," 479.
71 Henri Bergson, *Durée et simultanéité: À propos de la théorie d'Einstein*, ed. Élie During, 4th edn. (Paris: Quadrige/Presses Universitaires de France, 2009), 180.
72 Henri Bergson, "Les temps fictifs et le temps réel," *Revue de Philosophie*, 31 (1924), 241–260, p. 248.

Lorentz's stance on relativity as "irreproachable" and was also an admirer of Poincaré's philosophy of science.

Bergson lauded Poincaré as the main representative of a French tradition in which "mathematicians wrote the philosophy of their science, and even of science in general," and showed the "symbolic and provisional character" of scientific knowledge.[73] He sided with Poincaré in having "a strong repugnance toward a philosophy that wants to explain all reality mechanically."[74] Bergson included in this camp prominent psychologists (Théodule Ribot, Pierre Janet, Alfred Binet, Georges Dumas) and sociologists (Émile Durkheim and Lucien Lévy-Bruhl) who held implicitly mechanistic, reductionist, and materialistic stances. Bergson's critique influenced generations of thinkers seeking to investigate the role played by convention, choice, convenience, and epistemology in the selection and construction of theories and even, crucially, the role of science-fiction literature and popularization.

From Husserl to Heidegger

German philosophers often focused on some of the same themes raised by Bergson (characteristic of vitalism and *Lebensphilosophie*) in their assessments of relativity. While Bergson tackled the particular interpretation of observed results and formulae, Husserl's critique of relativity was incorporated into the general framework of phenomenology. In 1935, during a Vienna lecture, he enumerated problems facing science, blaming Einstein for some of them. Einstein's revolution had resulted in the distancing of science from those aspects that had "meaning" for us, mainly our everyday sense of time flowing:

> Einstein's revolutionary innovations concern the formulae through which the idealized and naïvely objectified *physis* is dealt with. But how formulae in general, how mathematical objectification in general, receive meaning ... – of this we learn nothing; and thus Einstein does not reform the space and time in which our vital life runs its course.[75]

A year later, in *The Crisis of European Sciences and Transcendental Phenomenology: An Introduction to Phenomenological Philosophy*, one of his most influential texts

---

73 Bergson to V. Norström, April 12, 1910, in Henri Bergson, *Correspondances* (Paris: Presses Universitaires de France, 2002), 348.
74 Bergson to V. Norström, April 12, 1910, 350.
75 Edmund Husserl, "The Vienna Lecture," in *The Crisis of European Sciences and Transcendental Phenomenology: An Introduction to Phenomenological Philosophy*, ed. John Wild (Evanston: Northwestern University Press, 1970), 295.

about science that was foundational for philosophers to come, he provided a particular interpretation of Einstein's theory of relativity in relation to Michelson's experiment. While "Einstein [used] Michelson experiments" to reach his conclusions, he used them in a particularly delimited way.[76] One could envision researchers taking more aspects of science into consideration: "There is no doubt that everything that enters here – the persons, the apparatus, the room of the institute, etc. – can itself become a subject of investigation in the usual sense of objective inquiry, that of the positive science."[77] But there were good reasons why these additional topics should and did not matter to scientists. "Einstein," he explained, "could make no use whatever of the theoretical psychological–psychophysical construction of the objective being of Mr. Michelson." These boundaries, necessary for scientific work, arose from "pre-scientific" "presuppositions" that were "common to all" and arose from "the world of experience." Offering to investigate the "premises" of scientific knowledge, he left its results and conclusions untouched.[78]

Similarly, in his early work, Heidegger did not argue for or against the merits of Einstein's theory, stressing instead the need to think about "the problem of the *measurement* of time as treated in the theory of relativity."[79] Measurement could not simply *give* answers about time, since it itself occurred *in time*. The "temporal meaning of measurement" itself had to be considered, and it had to be considered *first*, before anything else, since it was more basic and more essential than any derivative scientific results. Heidegger's lecture "The Concept of Time" diagnosed a damaging divide in the two dominant ways of thinking about time: the scientific notion of time and the lived notion. In this short lecture, Heidegger explained how a renewed interest in the concept of time was largely due to Einstein.

The physicist, argued Heidegger, used clock time. And clock time, he repeated, was a grossly inadequate concept for understanding time: "Once time has been defined as clock time then there is no hope of ever arriving at its original meaning again," he warned.[80] Heidegger's "The History of the

---

76 Edmund Husserl, *The Crisis of European Sciences and Transcendental Phenomenology: An Introduction to Phenomenological Philosophy*, ed. John Wild (Evanston: Northwestern University Press, 1970), 125.
77 Husserl, *The Crisis of European Sciences and Transcendental Phenomenology*, 125.
78 Husserl, *The Crisis of European Sciences and Transcendental Phenomenology*, 126.
79 Martin Heidegger, *Being and Time* (New York: Harper-Collins, 1962 [1927]), 499 n. iv.
80 Martin Heidegger, *The Concept of Time*, trans. William McNeill (Oxford: Blackwell, 1992). Originally the lecture "Der Begriff der Zeit" given at Marburg Theological Society (July 1924).

Concept of Time" was motivated by "the present crisis of the sciences," which, like Husserl, he blamed largely on Einstein.[81]

Although Heidegger was a Nazi sympathizer and at times enthusiast, his philosophy of science differed greatly from the standard fare of *Deutsche Physik* or Nazi racial science.[82] Initially, Heidegger's critique of Einstein was similar to that of Bergson and Husserl, but he soon distanced himself from their approaches by rejecting purely subjective notions of lived time as much as objective ones.

Being and Time (1927) sketched a new relation of philosophy to science, and of both to rational discourse and logical structure. "As regards the title 'Being and Time,' 'time' means neither the calculated time of the 'clock,' nor 'lived time' in the sense of Bergson and others," he wrote. Heidegger contested an Aristotelian notion of temporality from which (in his view) derived Einstein's notion of time. It represented the culmination of a denial of differences between past and future, left and right, or up and down, and so on. In "everydayness," he argued, these differences mattered substantially. His focus on eyeglasses, radio, telephone, trains, and streets introduced a host of objects that had traditionally been left out from accounts of technology based largely on the machines of the Industrial Revolution. His later analysis of dictation, typewriters, the printing press, and paper represented the beginning of a media history *avant la lettre* by focusing on the sources of support and materiality of ratiocination itself.

Heidegger's philosophy of technology and science rejected the common understanding of technology as a tool or as a machine. His perspective left no room for the politicization of science in terms of its supposed usefulness to the state that was part of the reductive biology of Nazi "scientific" racism and eugenics, nor did he fall into line with the denigration of theoretical physics and an exaltation of the experimental and technological that was typical amongst critics of Einstein. He also differed from most right-wing or left-wing scientists, artists, and intellectuals whose focus on technology was either of effusive celebration or reactionary rejection: "The much discussed question of whether technology makes man its slave or whether man will be able to be the master of technology is already a superficial question." In arguing against common views that considered that "'technology' and 'man' were two 'masses,'" he not only unsettled the understanding of both,

---

[81] "In physics the revolution came by way of relativity theory," in Martin Heidegger, *History of the Concept of Time: Prolegomena* (Bloomington: Indiana University Press, 1979), 2–3.

[82] Trish Glazebrook (ed.), *Heidegger on Science* (Albany: SUNY Press, 2013).

but called into question the typical "anthropological" conceptualization of the human as *homo faber* and *homo sapiens*.[83]

Quantum Mechanics

The conflict between relativity and quantum mechanics intensified with the political tensions of the time. Although historians have attempted to draw strict parallels between these fields and particular political stances (identifying the indeterminism of quantum mechanics with the irrationalism of German *Kultur*), these associations break down upon close analysis.[84]

The conflict between a quantum-mechanical description of the world and a relativistic one was articulated clearly during a discussion between Bohr and Einstein at the Fifth Solvay International Conference (1927). The discussion revived with renewed force questions about the role of philosophy and epistemology in science. "This epistemology-soaked orgy out to burn itself out," Einstein insisted to Schrödinger. Relativity theory, during these years, ran the risk of appearing conservative and retrograde. "No doubt, however, you smile at me and think that, after all, many a young whore turns into an old praying sister, and many a young revolutionary becomes an old reactionary," wrote Einstein to Schrödinger.[85] Rather than be forced to rethink our common understanding of physical reality, Einstein would insist that quantum mechanics was incomplete. Others, led by David Bohm, would argue for the existence of "hidden variables" that could revert the theory's ostensible indeterminism back to traditional determinism.

The discussions between Einstein and quantum physicists brought to light the question of how general beliefs and even religious ones affected science. Bohr denounced Einstein's now famous remark – "God does not play dice with the universe" – worrying that "utterances of this kind would naturally in many minds evoke the impression of an underlying mysticism foreign to the spirit of science."[86]

---

83 Martin Heidegger, *Parmenides*, trans. André Schuwer and Richard Rojcewicz (Bloomington: Indiana University Press, 1992), 86–87.
84 Paul Forman, "Scientific Internationalism and the Weimar Physicists: The Ideology and Its Manipulation after World War I," *Isis*, 64(2) (1973), 150–180; and Helge Kragh, *Quantum Generations: A History of Physics in the Twentieth Century* (Princeton: Princeton University Press, 2002), Chapter 10.
85 Einstein to Schrödinger, June 17, 1935, cited in Arthur Fine, *The Shaky Game: Einstein, Realism and the Quantum Theory*, 2nd edn. (Chicago: University of Chicago Press, 1996), 68.
86 Niels Bohr, "Discussion with Einstein on Epistemological Problems in Atomic Physics," in *Albert Einstein: Philosopher-Scientist*, ed. Paul Arthur Schilpp (La Salle: Open Court, 1949), 236.

The lack of public understanding and the "mystical" tenor of scientific discourse concerned the highest echelons of the intellectual elites of the 1930s. In 1938 the International Commission for Intellectual Cooperation under the auspices of the League of Nations tried to moderate the conflict during a meeting in Warsaw, but these efforts broke down as tensions across Europe intensified.

Postwar Continental Thought

Public accounts of the development of the atomic bomb affected the way in which many intellectuals thought of the relation of physics to general culture. Most accounts of its development stressed the role of Einstein, Robert Oppenheimer, and theoretical physicists rather than chemistry and industrial engineering, placing it within a narrative of scientific rather than military innovation. Censorship about the science of radioactivity and the industrial chemistry work necessary for uranium-isotope isolation contributed to the attribution of an exaggerated importance to physics and even to relativity theory.[87] While relativity theory was credited with "saving lives," the atomic bomb's destructive power could not be ignored.[88]

In the post-World War II years the negative consequences of science were explored by Max Horkheimer and the Frankfurt School, who saw them as arising mainly from an over-specialized "instrumental rationality" that led scientists, especially those working on the applied sciences, to ignore the broader meaning of their work and neglect their social responsibility.[89]

Heidegger attempted a different approach, setting himself apart from the critiques of instrumental reason of the Frankfurt School, by inquiring into the "essence" of technology and questioning the concept of instrumentality itself. Following the work of Heisenberg on quantum mechanics closely, he introduced a critique of theories of causality into his philosophy of technology, leading him to a different understanding of the concept of instrumentality itself. By reference to Heisenberg, he considered a common conception of instrumentality as tied to particular causal forms of reasoning and urged his listeners to question these links in order to gain a better understanding of the

---

[87] Jimena Canales, "The Secret PR Push That Shaped the Atomic Bomb's Origin Story," *The Atlantic*, April 18, 2017.

[88] "Thousands of young Americans thus may owe their lives to the theory of relativity." William Laurence, *Dawn over Zero: The Story of the Atomic Bomb* (New York: Alfred A. Knopf, 1946).

[89] Max Horkheimer, *Eclipse of Reason* (New York: Oxford University Press, 1947). Later published in German as *Zur Kritik der instrumentellen Vernunft*.

failure to control our destiny in relation to things in general. "So long as we do not allow ourselves to go into these questions, causality and with it instrumentality, and with the latter the accepted definition of technology, remain obscure and groundless."[90] In the context of these investigations, he was heard drawing offensive parallels between concentration camps and modernized agriculture (in an unpublished lecture given in Bremen on December 1, 1949).[91] In the published version of these lectures, Heidegger described connections between different technologies in terms of an "essence" that was neither causal nor moral, placing mundane technologies next to "demonic" ones.

"Das Ding" placed the atomic bomb and the hydrogen bomb next to radio and film, arguing for the need to think of them by reference to a simple ceramic jug (and the table and bench on which it may be placed) as part of his continuing effort to understand the mundane next to the "terrifying," and the new next to the ancient, in his attempts to change our common understanding of technology and "instrumental" reason. Rejecting accounts based on the use of technology (and the morality thereof), he strove to get at a deeper ethical structure of the thinking processes themselves that gave rise to an understanding of our environment as "instrumental" in the first place. "The Question Concerning Technology" concerned itself with atomic energy, radar, hydroelectric power, the mechanized food industry, airliners, paper, magazines, and cyclotrons (among other things) to define an "essence" cutting across all these systems. In *What Is Called Thinking?*, the first post-World War II university lectures Heidegger gave to students and the last ones before his retirement, one can see Heidegger attempting to ground logic and thinking in post-Kantian terms by considering thinking in relation to memory and thankfulness.[92]

In France, discussions about modern physics by prominent intellectuals often discussed the perils of unbridled "rationality" and continued to draw on themes about Einstein's role as a public intellectual. Maurice Merleau-Ponty's "Einstein and the Crisis of Reason" centered on how an all-pervading scientism had overtaken experience: "The experience of the perceived world with its obvious facts is no more than a stutter which precedes the clear speech of science." Merleau-Ponty questioned the common deference of most

90 Martin Heidegger, "The Question Concerning Technology," in *The Question Concerning Technology and Other Essays* (New York: Harper and Row, 1977 [1954]).
91 Quoted in Philippe Lacoue-Labarthe, *Heidegger, Art, and Politics*, trans. Chris Turner (Oxford: Blackwell, 1990), 34.
92 Martin Heidegger, *What Is Called Thinking?*, trans. J. Glenn Gray (New York: Harper & Row, 1968).

intellectuals toward physics and physicists and how they were consulted as authorities about everything from the arts to government: "And since it was precisely Einstein who showed that at a great distance a present is contemporaneous with the future, why not ask him the questions which were asked of the Pythian oracle?"[93]

Roland Barthes in "The Brain of Einstein" (originally 1956) covered some similar themes:

> Einstein fulfills all the conditions of myth ... at once magician and machine, eternal researcher and unfulfilled discoverer, unleashing the best and the worst, brain and conscience, Einstein embodies the most contradictory dreams, and mythically reconciles the infinite power of man over nature with the "fatality" of the sacrosanct, which man cannot yet do without.[94]

Gilles Deleuze also rethought the relation of science to philosophy in relation to Einstein and Bergson, outlining two possible ways for philosophy to interact with science. In one instance "philosophy can renounce its rivalry with science, can leave things to science and present itself solely in a critical manner, as a reflection." In the alternative case, philosophy competed against science as an alternative form of knowledge, seeking "to establish, or rather restore, another relationship to things, and therefore another knowledge, a knowledge and a relationship that precisely science hides from us, of which it deprives us."[95] With some notable exceptions, the work of most post–World War II intellectuals fell into these either–or camps, as they were no longer able to imagine a form of knowledge that affected philosophy, science, and general culture simultaneously.

Like other intellectuals at the time, and in stark contrast to logical positivists and analytical philosophers, continental thinkers such as Deleuze and Barthes argued against the benefits (and even possibility) of separating science from other areas of general culture and against setting it aside as a privileged form of knowledge. Gaston Bachelard, for the anniversary of Einstein's seventieth birthday, revived questions about the relation of relativity theory to the stories through which it was popularized, asking the following question: "All the tales of passing trains which signal an observer standing in a station, of aviators who smoke cigars in lengthened or

---

[93] Maurice Merleau-Ponty, "Einstein and the Crisis of Reason," in *Signs*, ed. John Wild (Evanston: Northwestern University Press, 1964), 194.
[94] Roland Barthes, "The Brain of Einstein," in *Mythologies* (New York: Hill and Wang, 1972).
[95] Gilles Deleuze, "Bergson, 1859–1941," in *Les philosophes célèbres*, ed. Maurice Merleau-Ponty (Paris: Lucien Mazenod, 1956).

contracted periods of time – to what purpose are they?" He argued against the usual science-popularization explanation, where they were considered to be made for "those who have not understood" and considered them instead as an essential part of a broader reconfiguration of a "space-time notion" that could not be limited to specialized science. In addition, he asked readers to accept paradoxical aspects of science (such as the presence of the concrete in the abstract and the abstract in the concrete) as essential, even when these did not fit within traditional divisions between science and the humanities, or between scientific and poetic truth.

From Quine to Kuhn

Particular insights of late-nineteenth- and early-twentieth-century Francophone philosophy were revived by post-World War II Anglophone philosophers. The "Duhem–Quine thesis," which combined some of the insights of W. V. O. Quine with those of Duhem, became a powerful anti-logical positivist argument for the need to consider how theoretical presuppositions could not be completely eliminated from scientific descriptions of the world.[96]

Kuhn's *Structure of Scientific Revolutions* (first published in 1962 as part of the Foundations of the Unity of Science series) can be considered as marking the end of an era characterized by a particular understanding of science. While part of Kuhn's analysis was based on insights from applied experimental psychology (the inverted goggle experiments of the Hanover Institute), much of the discussion around it centered on its repercussions for a more general conception of knowledge bounded by "paradigms," a term closely related to the terms "worldview" (*Weltanschauung*) and "conceptual structure" (*Begriffssystem*) that had been widely used by relativity and quantum physicists to describe their new theories. By considering key episodes in the history of science as involving paradigm shifts, Kuhn's account closely followed a model associated with the work of Alexandre Koyré and the "history of ideas" movement. Yet his historical recounting of theory choice during periods of revolution was most similar to Poincaré's. When exploring the Copernican case, he claimed that "available observational tests ... provided no basis for a choice between them [Ptolemy and Copernicus]."[97] Much earlier, at the Congrès International de Philosophie of 1900, Poincaré

---

96 Sandra G. Harding (ed.), *Can Theories Be Refuted? Essays on the Duhem–Quine Thesis* (Dordrecht: D. Reidel, 1976).
97 Thomas S. Kuhn, *The Structure of Scientific Revolutions*, 2nd edn. (Chicago: University of Chicago Press, 1970), 76.

had framed Copernicus's revolution as nothing more than a more convenient formulation than the preceding ones.[98]

The Social Studies of Knowledge (SSK) movement of the late 1970s and 1980s responded to the "sociology of knowledge" movement of Merton and his school by incorporating a more subtle understanding (partly inspired by Michel Foucault) of the category of "the political" in science as embodied in subtle intersubjective power relations. For the most part, SSK practitioners stressed the primacy of theory and even language in comparison with the value of observations, borrowing as well from the "linguistic turn" affecting philosophy more generally. Some of these insights, which were often introduced as a corrective to the "naïve realism" of the logical positivists, were associated with "postmodernity" and "French theory."

Even as intellectuals, historians, and philosophers continued to develop novel accounts about science and technology, the trauma from Nazi critiques of relativity theory in modern physics continued to mark modern European thought. For Jürgen Habermas, overt interference with the processes of consensual scientific deliberation was clearly and simply identified as the process that had led to the "freak of a [German] natural physics."[99] The importance of detailed and careful historical and philosophical accounts of actual scientific practices, instruments, experiments, and debates paled in comparison with these world historical events.

---

98 Henri Poincaré, "Sur les principes de la mécanique," in *Bibliothèque du Congrès international de philosophie* (Paris: Armand Colin, 1901).
99 Jürgen Habermas, *Knowledge and Human Interests* (Cambridge: Polity Press, 1987), 315.

4
Varieties of Phenomenology

DAN ZAHAVI

Introduction

Phenomenology counts as one of the most influential philosophical movements in twentieth-century philosophy. Edmund Husserl (1859–1938) was its founder, but other influential proponents were Max Scheler (1874–1928), Martin Heidegger (1889–1976), Jean-Paul Sartre (1905–1980), Maurice Merleau-Ponty (1908–1961), and Emmanuel Lévinas (1906–1995). Over the years, phenomenology has made major contributions to many areas of philosophy, including transcendental philosophy, philosophy of mind, social philosophy, philosophical anthropology, aesthetics, ethics, philosophy of science, epistemology, theory of meaning, and formal ontology. It has offered important analyses of topics such as intentionality, embodiment, self-consciousness, intersubjectivity, temporality, historicity, truth, evidence, perception, and value theory. It has delivered a targeted criticism of reductionism, objectivism, and scientism, and argued at length for a rehabilitation of the lifeworld. By presenting a detailed account of human existence, where the subject is understood as an embodied and socially and culturally embedded being-in-the-world, phenomenology has provided crucial inputs to a whole range of empirical disciplines, including psychiatry, sociology, psychology, literary studies, and architecture.

One reason for its influence is that almost all subsequent theory formations in continental philosophy can be understood as either extensions of or reactions to phenomenology. A proper grasp of phenomenology is consequently important not only for its own sake, but also because it remains a *sine qua non* for an understanding of what later happened in French and German philosophy.

When providing a historical overview of phenomenology, however, one is faced with some initial challenges. What topics should one cover and which figures should be included? Both choices depend upon one's definition of phenomenology. But the question of how to define phenomenology remains contested even today, almost 120 years after the publication of Husserl's *Logical Investigations* (1900–1901), the work that he himself considered his "breakthrough" in phenomenology,[1] and which stands out not only as one of his most important works, but also as a key text in twentieth-century philosophy.

Husserl, whose inclusion in any overview of phenomenology is undisputed, came to philosophy at a relatively late age. Born in Proßnitz, Moravia (then part of the Austrian Empire), Husserl was primarily trained as a mathematician. It was only after obtaining his doctorate in mathematics in Vienna in 1883 that Husserl became seriously interested in philosophy. Prolonged reflections on foundational problems in epistemology and theory of science eventually culminated in the publication of his monumental *Logical Investigations*.

A central ambition in *Logical Investigations* was to explore the intentionality of consciousness, the fact that our perception, thinking, judging, etc. is of or about something. Some of Husserl's central claims were that (1) every intentional experience is an experience of a specific type, i.e., an experience of perceiving, judging, hoping, desiring, regretting, remembering, affirming, doubting, wondering, fearing, etc., (2) that each of these experiences is characterized by being directed at an object in a particular way, and (3) that none of these experiences can be analyzed properly without considering their objective correlate, i.e., the perceived, doubted, expected object. The very attempt to offer a careful description of our psychological life, the very idea that intentionality is a distinctive feature of mental states can, however, already be found in the work of the prominent psychologist and philosopher Franz Brentano, whose lectures in Vienna Husserl had attended in the early 1880s. It is consequently natural to ask whether Husserl was not simply continuing the project commenced by Brentano. If so, one might eventually end up opting for a definition of phenomenology akin to the one provided by Siewert, who writes that one is doing plain phenomenology, if one (1) makes and explains mental or psychological distinctions, (2) shows why those distinctions are theoretically important, (3) relies on a source of first-person warrant, and (4) does not assume that first-person warrant derives from some source of third-person warrant.[2]

---

1 Edmund Husserl, *Logical Investigations I–II*, trans. J. N. Findlay (London: Routledge, 2001 [1900–1901]), vol. I, 3.
2 Charles Siewert, "In Favor of (Plain) Phenomenology," *Phenomenology and the Cognitive Sciences*, 6(1–2) (2007), 201–220, p. 202.

On such a definition, many philosophers not normally considered part of the phenomenological movement, like Searle, for instance, would count as phenomenologists.

There are good reasons to resist this conclusion, however. One reason to insist on the difference between Brentano and Husserl can be found in the first part of *Logical Investigations* entitled *Prolegomena to Pure Logic*. Whereas Brentano had defended the claim that psychology is the theoretical science on which other disciplines including logic ought to be based,[3] Husserl was keen to protect the purity and irreducibility of logic. As Husserl pointed out in his famous attack on *psychologism*, which can be found in the *Prolegomena*, the domain of logic is a domain of ideal structures and laws, and the proposal that such universally valid laws can be reduced to and explained by psychic processes is ultimately incoherent and countersensical.

Husserl's *Logical Investigations* was a resounding success. It secured him a permanent position in Göttingen, where he would remain until 1916. It also inspired a number of former students of the psychologist Theodor Lipps (including Johannes Daubert, Alexander Pfänder, and Adolf Reinach) to move from Munich to Göttingen in order to study with Husserl. This move is sometimes referred to as the Munich invasion of Göttingen, and is generally considered to be the starting point of the phenomenological movement proper.[4]

How should one explain this early enthusiasm? Phenomenology was seen by many as offering a refreshingly new way to conduct research, one that connected with everyday experience in a way not normally seen in philosophy.[5] As Husserl declared in *Logical Investigations*,

> We can absolutely not rest content with "mere words" . . . Meanings inspired only by remote, confused, inauthentic intuitions – if by any intuitions at all – are not enough: we must go back to the "things themselves."
>
> (Husserl, *Logical Investigations I–II*, vol. I, 168)

---

3 Franz Brentano, *Psychology from an Empirical Standpoint*, trans. A. C. Rancurello, D. B. Terrell, and L. L. McAlister (London: Routledge, 1973 [1874]), 15–16.
4 Alessandro Salice, "The Phenomenology of the Munich and Göttingen Circles," *The Stanford Encyclopedia of Philosophy*, ed. Edward N. Zalta (Winter 2015 Edition), http://plato.stanford.edu/archives/win2015/entries/phenomenology-mg/.
5 A similar reaction occurred in France some decades later. In her autobiography, Simone de Beauvoir recounts how Sartre's interest in phenomenology was originally aroused. She and Sartre were both visiting a cocktail bar with their friend Raymond Aron, who had just returned from Germany. At one point, Aron pointed to the apricot cocktail he had ordered and said to Sartre, "You see, my dear fellow, if you are a phenomenologist, you can talk about this cocktail and make philosophy out of it!" (Simone de Beauvoir, *The Prime of Life*, trans. Peter Green (Harmondsworth: Penguin, 1962 [1960]), 135). When Sartre heard this, he turned pale with excitement.

Husserl's initial criticism of psychologism, his sustained defense of the irreducibility of ideality, and his focus on things as they are encountered in experience were interpreted by many of his early followers as a turn away from subjectivity and toward the objects, and as a legitimization of essentialism. Consider, for example, an introductory lecture on phenomenology given by Adolf Reinach (1883–1917) in Marburg in 1914. Reinach starts out by insisting that phenomenology, rather than being a comprehensive system of philosophical propositions, is a specific method of philosophizing, a particular philosophical attitude. What characterizes this attitude? Its aim is to grasp the essence or what-ness of the object under investigation, whereas its singularity or actuality is of no concern. Reinach concedes that eidetic intuition (*Wesensschau*) is also required in other disciplines. The specific task of phenomenology, however, is to lay bare the lawful connections that hold between these essences. Moreover, it has to clarify the very scope and nature of the *a priori*, and in particular reject any (Kantian) subjectification of the latter. Reinach concludes his lecture by arguing that the phenomenological return to "the things themselves" is a turning away from theories and constructions, in order to obtain a "pure and unobscured intuition of essences."[6]

Such an attempt to identify phenomenology with a particular kind of eidetic intuition is not unique to Reinach. Max Scheler also understood Husserl's phenomenological method as involving a form of eidetic reduction, where one disregards the *hic et nunc* of objects in order to focus on their essential features. As Scheler writes, the aim of phenomenology is to provide a rigorous intuitive method that will allow a disclosure of *a priori* structures.[7] For the same reason, Scheler also distanced himself from Husserl's subsequent turn towards transcendental philosophy, which Scheler characterized as a turn towards epistemological idealism and as a curbing of phenomenology to a mere eidetics of consciousness.[8]

The early realist phenomenologists were indeed unhappy about Husserl's philosophical development after *Logical Investigations*. His next major work from 1913, *Ideas Pertaining to a Pure Phenomenology and to a Phenomenological Philosophy, First Book* (commonly referred to as *Ideas I*), which involved an endorsement of a form of transcendental idealism, was seen by many of these

---

6 Adolph Reinach, "What Is Phenomenology?," trans. D. Kelly, *The Philosophical Forum*, 1(2) (1968 [1914]), 234–256.
7 Max Scheler, *Die deutsche Philosophie der Gegenwart*, in *Gesammelte Werke*, ed. Manfred S. Frings, 15 vols. (Bern and Munich: Francke-Verlag, 1973 [1922]), vol. VII, 259–326, p. 309.
8 Scheler, *Die deutsche Philosophie der Gegenwart*, 311.

early followers as a betrayal of the core ideas of phenomenology. Husserl on his side complained that their reluctance to follow his transcendental turn simply meant that they had failed to really understand his philosophical project, had failed to fully grasp what phenomenology is all about. I am inclined to think that Husserl was right. In the following sections, I will outline some core ideas and then explore how these ideas also continued to be operative in Heidegger's and Merleau-Ponty's thinking.[9]

Husserl's Correlationism

One idea common to both *Logical Investigations* and *Ideas I* is that we need to recognize the decisive difference between the act and the object of experience. But although Husserl insists that the most fundamental ontological distinction is the one between the being of consciousness and the being of that which reveals itself for consciousness,[10] such a radical difference does not prevent the two types of being from being essentially related. Indeed, as Husserl puts it in *Ideas I*, an "objectively" oriented phenomenology has as its main theme intentionality, and any proper investigation of intentionality must include an investigation of the intentional correlate.[11] In *Logical Investigations*, this is expressed slightly differently. After having first established the irreducible difference between the subjective act of knowing and the object of knowledge, Husserl insists that one is still confronted with the apparent paradox that objective truths are known in subjective experiences. And as he then continues, this relation between the objective and the

---

9 I have discussed these issues on a number of previous occasions. For some partially overlapping and partially complementary texts, see Dan Zahavi, "Merleau-Ponty on Husserl: A Reappraisal," in *Merleau-Ponty's Reading of Husserl*, ed. T. Toadvine and L. Embree (Dordrecht: Kluwer Academic Publishers, 2002), 3–29; Dan Zahavi, "How to Investigate Subjectivity: Heidegger and Natorp on Reflection," *Continental Philosophy Review*, 36(2) (2003), 155–176; Dan Zahavi, "Phenomenology," in *The Routledge Companion to Twentieth-Century Philosophy*, ed. Dermot Moran (London: Routledge, 2008), 661–692; Dan Zahavi, "Husserl and the Transcendental," in *The Transcendental Turn*, ed. S. Gardner and M. Grist (Oxford: Oxford University Press, 2015), 228–243; and Søren Overgaard and Dan Zahavi, "Phenomenological Sociology: The Subjectivity of Everyday Life," in *Encountering the Everyday: An Introduction to the Sociologies of the Unnoticed*, ed. Michael Hviid Jacobsen (Basingstoke: Palgrave Macmillan, 2009), 93–115. For an extensive interpretation of Husserl's phenomenology, see Dan Zahavi, *Husserl's Legacy: Phenomenology, Metaphysics, and Transcendental Philosophy* (Oxford: Oxford University Press, 2017).
10 Edmund Husserl, *Ideas Pertaining to a Pure Phenomenology and to a Phenomenological Philosophy, First Book: General Introduction to a Pure Phenomenology*, trans. F. Kersten (The Hague: Martinus Nijhoff, 1982 [1913]), 171.
11 Husserl, *Ideas Pertaining to a Pure Phenomenology and to a Phenomenological Philosophy, First Book*, 199–201.

subjective has to be investigated and clarified, if we wish to attain a more substantial understanding of the possibility of knowledge.[12] What Husserl is ultimately aiming at is something he many years later in *Crisis* (1936) would refer to as his discovery of the *correlational a priori*:

> The first breakthrough of this universal a priori of correlation between experienced object and manners of givenness (which occurred during work on my *Logical Investigations* around 1898) affected me so deeply that my whole subsequent life-work has been dominated by the task of systematically elaborating on this a priori of correlation.
> (Husserl, *The Crisis of European Sciences and Transcendental Phenomenology*, 166)

One important difference between *Logical Investigations* and *Ideas I* is that Husserl in the intervening years came to the realization that certain methodological steps – the famous epoché and transcendental reduction – were required if phenomenology were to accomplish its designated task. Whereas both notions were absent in *Logical Investigations*, they came to play a decisive role after Husserl's transcendental turn. Indeed, as Husserl would repeatedly insist, if one considers the epoché and the phenomenological reduction irrelevant peculiarities, one will have no chance of comprehending what phenomenology is all about.[13] But what is the epoché and what is the reduction? One way to answer this question is by inquiring into their motivation. Why were they introduced in the first place?

Husserl often contrasts philosophy proper with the work done by the positive sciences. The latter are so absorbed in their investigation of the natural (or social/cultural) world that they do not pause to reflect upon their own presuppositions and conditions of possibility. According to Husserl, they all operate on the basis of a tacit belief in the existence of a mind-, experience-, and theory-independent reality. This realist assumption is so fundamental and deeply rooted that it is not only operative in the positive sciences, but also permeates our daily pre-theoretical life, for which reason Husserl calls it the *natural attitude*. Regardless of how natural this attitude might be, if philosophy is supposed to amount to a radical form of critical elucidation, it cannot simply take our natural realism for granted, but must instead engage in a reflective move that allows it to explore the epistemic and metaphysical presuppositions of the latter. To argue that the natural attitude must be

---

12 Husserl, *Logical Investigations I–II*, vol. I, 166–170.
13 Husserl, *Ideas Pertaining to a Pure Phenomenology and to a Phenomenological Philosophy, First Book*, 211.

philosophically investigated is not to endorse skepticism, however. That the world exists is, as Husserl writes, beyond any doubt. However, it is our duty as philosophers to truly understand this indubitability (which sustains life and positive science) and to clarify (rather than justify) its legitimacy.[14]

Philosophy has its own aims and methodological requirements, and is engaged in a type of inquiry that *"is prior to all natural knowledge and science and is on an entirely different plane than natural science."*[15] Ordinary science takes it for granted that there are worldly objects that can be investigated, but it does not reflect upon what it means for something to be given as an object of investigation, nor how this givenness is possible in the first place. Rather than simply taking reality as the unquestioned point of departure, rather than focusing on *what* the world contains, we need to attend to the question of what it means for something to be given as real in the first place, we need to focus on the *how* of its givenness. To do so calls for a number of methodological preparations. In order to avoid simply presupposing realism, it is necessary to suspend our acceptance of the natural attitude. We keep the attitude (in order to investigate it), but we bracket its validity. This procedure of suspension is what Husserl calls the *epoché*. Strictly speaking, the epoché can be seen as the first step toward what Husserl terms the *transcendental reduction*, which is his name for the systematic analysis of the correlation between subjectivity and world. This is a more prolonged analysis that *leads* from the natural sphere *back to* (*re-ducere*) its transcendental foundation.[16] Both the epoché and the reduction can consequently be seen as elements of a transcendental reflection, the purpose of which is to liberate us from our natural(istic) dogmatism and make us aware of our own constitutive contribution.

The purpose of the epoché and the reduction is not to doubt, ignore, neglect, abandon, or exclude reality from our research; rather their aim is to suspend or neutralize a certain dogmatic *attitude* toward reality, thereby allowing a decisive discovery. They permit us to investigate reality in a new way, namely in its significance and manifestation for consciousness. In short, they entail a change

---

14 Edmund Husserl, *Ideas Pertaining to a Pure Phenomenology and to a Phenomenological Philosophy, Second Book: Studies in the Phenomenology of Constitution*, trans. R. Rojcewicz and A. Schuwer (Dordrecht: Kluwer, 1989 [c. 1912–1928]), 420; and Edmund Husserl, *The Crisis of European Sciences and Transcendental Phenomenology: An Introduction to Phenomenological Philosophy*, trans. D. Carr (Evanston: Northwestern University Press, 1970 [1936]), 187.
15 Edmund Husserl, *Introduction to Logic and Theory of Knowledge: Lectures 1906/07*, trans. Claire Ortiz Hill (Dordrecht: Springer, 2008), 173–174.
16 Edmund Husserl, *Cartesian Meditations: An Introduction to Phenomenology*, trans. Dorion Cairns (The Hague: Martinus Nijhoff, 1960 [1931]), 21.

of attitude toward reality, and not an exclusion of reality.[17] As Husserl explains in *Crisis*, "one of the most common misunderstandings of the transcendental epoché" is that it involves a "turning-away" from "all natural human life-interests."[18] This is a misunderstanding, for

> if it were meant in this way, there would be no transcendental inquiry. How could we take perception and the perceived, memory and the remembered, the objective and every sort of verification of the objective, including art, science, and philosophy, as a transcendental theme without living through these sorts of things as examples and indeed with [their] full self-evidence?
> (Husserl, *The Crisis of European Sciences and Transcendental Phenomenology*, 176)

To perform the epoché and the reduction is to effectuate a thematic reorientation. It is not as if we cannot continue to observe, thematize, and make judgments concerning the world, but we must do so in a reflective manner that considers the world as intentional correlate.[19] To put it differently, by adopting the phenomenological attitude, we do not turn the gaze inwards in order to examine the happenings in a private interior sphere. Rather we look at how the world shows up for the subject. We pay attention to how and as what worldly objects are given to us. But in doing so, in analyzing how and as what any object presents itself to us, we also come to discover the intentional acts and experiential structures in relation to which any appearing object must necessarily be understood. We realize our own subjective accomplishments and the intentionality that is at play in order for worldly objects to appear in the way they do and with the validity and meaning that they have. The topic of Husserl's phenomenological analyses is consequently not a worldless subject, and he does not ignore the world in favor of consciousness. On the contrary, he is interested in consciousness precisely because it is world-disclosing, because it, rather than merely being an *object in the world*, is also *subject for the world*, i.e., a necessary condition of possibility for any entity to appear as an object in the way it does and with the meaning it has. To put it differently, for Husserl, the *transcendental* dimension of consciousness is something that realists and naturalists alike have failed to recognize. This is why phenomenology has to be appreciated as a form of transcendental philosophy and not as a kind of (Brentanian) descriptive psychology.

---

17 Husserl, *The Crisis of European Sciences and Transcendental Phenomenology*, 151.
18 Husserl, *The Crisis of European Sciences and Transcendental Phenomenology*, 176.
19 Edmund Husserl, *Zur phänomenologischen Reduktion: Texte aus dem Nachlass (1926–1935)*. Husserliana XXXIV (Dordrecht: Kluwer, 2002), 58.

In *Crisis*, Husserl describes phenomenology as the final gestalt (*Endform*) of transcendental philosophy.[20] When accounting for the history of transcendental philosophy, however, Husserl insists that he is operating with a broader conception of transcendental philosophy than Kant did, namely as referring to a fundamental reflective inquiry into the first-personal basis of all knowledge formations.[21] A couple of pages later, he adds that transcendental philosophy is characterized by its criticism of objectivism and by its elucidation of subjectivity as the locus of all objective formations of sense and validity.[22]

Rather than merely amounting to a limited exploration of the psychological domain, for Husserl an in-depth investigation of intentionality paves the way for a proper understanding of reality and objectivity. This is why transcendental phenomenology should not be conceived merely as a theory about the structure of subjectivity, nor is it merely a theory about how *we* understand and perceive the world, rather its proper theme is the mind–world dyad. To construe Husserlian phenomenology in such a way that being and reality are topics left for other disciplines would neither respect nor reflect Husserl's own assertions on the matter. As he declares in § 23 of *Cartesian Meditations* (1931), the topics of existence and non-existence, of being and non-being, are all-embracing themes for phenomenology, themes addressed under the broadly understood titles of reason and unreason.[23] Husserl's investigations of intentionality, his exploration of the correlation between experiential acts and objects of experience, ultimately led him to embrace a form of transcendental idealism that insisted on the essential interconnection between reason, truth, and being, and on the for-us-ness of any coherent notion of reality. By rejecting the Kantian notion of an unknowable thing in itself as nonsensical, Husserl also removed any reason to demote the status of the reality we experience to being "merely" for us.

Expanding the Framework

One way to think of Husserl's philosophical development is to view it as a continuous expansion and elaboration of the basic correlationist framework. For Husserl, the dative of manifestation, the subject of intentionality, is not merely a formal principle of constitution; it is not, as he puts it, "a dead

---

20 Husserl, *The Crisis of European Sciences and Transcendental Phenomenology*, 70.
21 Husserl, *The Crisis of European Sciences and Transcendental Phenomenology*, 97.
22 Husserl, *The Crisis of European Sciences and Transcendental Phenomenology*, 99.
23 Husserl, *Cartesian Meditations*, 56.

pole of identity."[24] This is why he stresses the importance of an in-depth investigation of consciousness and why he argues that this will necessitate an extension of Kant's concept of the transcendental. In the end, it will even prove necessary to include the humanities and the manifold of human sociality and culture in the transcendental analysis.[25]

Let me focus on three distinct domains where this expansion can be observed, namely *embodiment*, *temporality*, and *intersubjectivity*. Whereas each of these three domains was initially treated and analyzed in separation, in his late thinking, Husserl increasingly came to see them as deeply intertwined.

Already early on, in lectures on *Thing and Space* from 1907, Husserl stressed the importance of embodiment for perceptual intentionality. Spatial objects appear perspectivally. When we perceive an object, it never appears in its totality, but always from a certain limited perspective. When we realize that that which appears spatially always appears at a certain distance and from a certain angle, the implication is straightforward: Every perspectival appearance presupposes that the experiencing subject is itself located in space, and since the subject possesses a spatial location only due to its embodiment,[26] spatial objects can only appear for and be constituted by embodied subjects. There is no pure point of view and there is no view from nowhere, there is only an embodied point of view. More generally, Husserl argues that the body is essentially involved in the perception of and interaction with spatial objects,[27] and that every worldly experience is mediated by and made possible by our embodiment.[28] In fact, we cannot first study the body, and next investigate it in its relation to the world. The world is given to us as bodily explored, and the body is revealed to us in its exploration of the world.[29]

Husserl's first significant writings on temporality are also to be found early on, namely in his *Lectures on the Phenomenology of the Consciousness of Internal Time* (1905). As Husserl realized, any investigation of intentionality will remain

---

24 Edmund Husserl, *Phenomenological Psychology: Lectures, Summer Semester, 1925*, trans. J. Scanlon (The Hague: Martinus Nijhoff, 1977), 159.
25 Edmund Husserl, *Erste Philosophie (1923/24). Erster Teil: Kritische Ideengeschichte.* Husserliana VII (The Hague: Martinus Nijhoff, 1956), 282.
26 Husserl, *Ideas Pertaining to a Pure Phenomenology and to a Phenomenological Philosophy, First Book*, 125; and Husserl, *Ideas Pertaining to a Pure Phenomenology and to a Phenomenological Philosophy, Second Book*, 36.
27 Edmund Husserl, *Zur Phänomenologie der Intersubjektivität III. Texte aus dem Nachlass. Dritter Teil: 1929–1935*. Husserliana XV (The Hague: Martinus Nijhoff, 1973), 540.
28 Husserl, *Ideas Pertaining to a Pure Phenomenology and to a Phenomenological Philosophy, Second Book*, 61.
29 Husserl, *Zur Phänomenologie der Intersubjektivität III*, 287.

incomplete as long as one ignores the temporal dimension of the intentional acts and intentional objects. We can explore the different sides of a table; we can hear an enduring tone; we can see the flight of a bird. In each of these cases, the object under investigation is temporally extended. But how is it that the different sides of the table are perceived as synthetically integrated moments, rather than as disjointed fragments? How is it that we can actually see the smooth continuous movement of the bird? Husserl's answer is that consciousness must itself be experientially unified if we are to perceive an object as enduring over time. More specifically, Husserl argues that the basic unit of temporality is not a 'knife-edge' present, but a 'duration-block,' i.e., a temporal field that comprises all three temporal modes of present, past, and future. Husserl employs three technical terms to describe the temporal structure of consciousness. There is (i) a 'primal impression' narrowly directed toward the strictly circumscribed now-slice of the object. The primal impression never appears in isolation and is an abstract component that by itself cannot provide us with a perception of a temporal object. The primal impression is accompanied by (ii) a 'retention,' or retentional aspect, which provides us with a consciousness of the just-elapsed slice of the object, thereby furnishing the primal impression with a past-directed temporal context; and by (iii) a 'protention,' or protentional aspect, which in a more-or-less indefinite way intends the slice of the object about to occur, thereby providing a future-oriented temporal context for the primal impression.[30] According to Husserl, the concrete and full structure of all lived experience is consequently *protention–primal impression–retention*. Although the specific experiential contents of this structure change progressively from moment to moment, at any given moment this threefold structure of inner time-consciousness is present as a unified field of experiencing.

An idea of Husserl's that gained increasing prominence in his later thinking is that a transcendental clarification of objectivity in the sense of 'being valid for everybody' requires a further analysis of intersubjectivity.[31] This is so, not only because my apprehension of objects as real and objective is mediated by and depends upon my encounter with other world-directed subjects, but also because Husserl considers objectivity the correlate of an ideal intersubjective concordance.[32] There is no other meaningful true reality than the one we agree

---

30 Husserl, *Phenomenological Psychology*, 154.
31 Edmund Husserl, *Formal and Transcendental Logic*, trans. Dorion Cairns (The Hague: Martinus Nijhoff, 1969 [1929]), 236.
32 Edmund Husserl, *Erste Philosophie (1923/24). Zweiter Teil: Theorie der phänomenologischen Reduktion*. Husserliana VIII (The Hague: Martinus Nijhoff, 1959), 47–48.

upon at the end of the road of inquiry. It is considerations like these which led Husserl to argue that "as long as one interprets transcendental subjectivity as an isolated ego and – like the Kantian tradition – ignores the whole task of establishing the legitimacy of the transcendental community of subjects, any prospect of a transcendental knowledge of self and world is lost."[33] In lectures given in London in 1922, Husserl even declared that the development of phenomenology necessarily implied the step from an "'egological' ... phenomenology into a transcendental sociological phenomenology having reference to a manifest multiplicity of conscious subjects communicating with one another."[34]

During the thirties, Husserl came to suffer from the conditions imposed by the German National Socialist Regime. Barred from any kind of official academic activity due to his Jewish ancestry, Husserl in turn lost his right to teach, his right to publish, and eventually also his German citizenship. Deeply affected by this development, Husserl nevertheless continued his work, insisting even more passionately on the relevance of philosophy at a time when Europe was descending into irrationalism.

In Husserl's last writings, the topics of embodiment, intersubjectivity, and temporality are brought and thought together. There is also a diachronic dimension to intersubjectivity. Ultimately, Husserl would consider the subject's birth into a living tradition to have constitutive implications. It is not merely the case that I live in a world, which is permeated by references to others, and which others have already furnished with meaning, or that I understand the world (and myself) through a traditional, handed-down, linguistic conventionality. The very meaning that the world has for me is such that it has its origin outside of me, in a historical past. As Husserl writes in *Crisis*, being embedded in "the unitary flow of a historical development" – in a generative nexus of birth and death – belongs as indissolubly to the I as does its temporal form.[35] For the very same reason, creatures who are unaware that they are born and will die, i.e., unaware of their own participation in a transgenerational chain, will be unable to fully share the constitutive accomplishment of generative intersubjectivity[36] and therefore also lack the capacity to constitute a truly objective world.

---

[33] Edmund Husserl, *Die Krisis der europäischen Wissenschaften und die transzendentale Phänomenologie. Ergänzungsband. Texte aus dem Nachlass 1934–1937*. Husserliana XXIX (Dordrecht: Kluwer, 1993), 120.
[34] Edmund Husserl, *Shorter Works*, ed. P. McCormick and F. A. Elliston (Notre Dame: University of Notre Dame Press, 1981), 68.
[35] Husserl, *The Crisis of European Sciences and Transcendental Phenomenology*, 253.
[36] See Sara Heinämaa, "The Animal and the Infant: From Embodiment and Empathy to Generativity," in *Phenomenology and the Transcendental*, ed. Sara Heinämaa, Mirja Hartimo, and Timo Miettinen (London: Routledge, 2014), 129–146, p. 139.

In his early works, Husserl practised a form of phenomenological analysis that he would later call *static phenomenology*. It studied intentional correlations with no regard for genesis and temporality. The type of object and the type of intentional act were both considered readily available. Subsequently, however, Husserl came to realize that both sides of the correlation had an origin and a history. He described how patterns of understanding and expectations are gradually established and how they come to influence and enable subsequent experiences. Certain types of intentionality (pre-linguistic experiences, for example) condition later and more complex types of intentionality (scientific analyses, for instance), and he took the task of what he called *genetic phenomenology* to involve the examination of the temporal becoming of these different forms of intentionality, one that also traced higher-order forms of objectivity back to lower-order forms.[37] The scope of genetic phenomenology remained restricted to the experiential life of an individual ego, however. In the last phase of his thinking, Husserl ventured into what has been called *generative phenomenology*.[38] The focus was broadened to investigate the constitutive role of tradition and history. In what way are the accomplishments of previous generations operative in our individual experiences? As Husserl writes in a manuscript from the twenties,

> That which I have constituted originally (primally instituted) is mine. But I am a 'child of the times'; I am a member of a we-community in the broadest sense – a community that has its tradition and that, for its part, is connected in a novel manner with the generative subjects, the closest and the most distant ancestors. And these have 'influenced' me: I am what I am as an heir. What is really and originally my own? To what extent am I really primally instituting [*urstiftend*]? I am it on the basis of the 'tradition'; everything of my own is founded, in part through the tradition of my ancestors, in part through the tradition of my contemporaries.
> (Husserl, *Zur Phänomenologie der Intersubjektivität III*, 223)

The fact that Husserl eventually included topics such as embodiment and intersubjectivity in his transcendental analysis is the reason why Merleau-Ponty in the preface to *Phenomenology of Perception* could write "Husserl's transcendental is not Kant's."[39] The fact that Husserl significantly broadened

---

37 Edmund Husserl, *Analyses Concerning Passive and Active Synthesis: Lectures on Transcendental Logic*, trans. Anthony Steinbock (Dordrecht: Kluwer, 2001 [1918–1926]), 634.
38 Anthony J. Steinbock, *Home and Beyond: Generative Phenomenology after Husserl* (Evanston: Northwestern University Press, 1995).
39 Maurice Merleau-Ponty, *Phenomenology of Perception*, trans. D. Landes (London: Routledge, 2012 [1945]), lxxvii.

and transformed the scope of transcendental philosophy gave rise to new challenges. If a transcendental investigation cannot ignore the historicity of human life, if transcendental structures develop over the course of time and can be modified under the influence of experience, it is, for instance, faced with the task of countering the threat of historical relativism. By endorsing the view that the only justification obtainable and the only justification required is one that is internal to the world of experience and to its intersubjective practices, it should be clear, however, that Husserl offers a view on the transcendental that points forward in time rather than backwards to Kant. In that sense, and to that extent, Husserl's conception of the transcendental is distinctly modern.

Post-Husserlian Phenomenology

The relation between Husserl and the post-Husserlian phenomenologists remains controversial. Opinions diverge widely regarding the extent to which figures such as Heidegger and Merleau-Ponty remained indebted to Husserl. Whereas Carman has argued that "Heidegger's fundamental ontology cannot be understood as a mere supplement or continuation, let alone 'translation,' of Husserl's philosophy,"[40] Merleau-Ponty declared that the whole of *Being and Time* was nothing but an explication of Husserl's notion of the lifeworld.[41] And whereas Merleau-Ponty himself repeatedly emphasized his indebtedness to Husserl and occasionally presented his own work as an attempt to unearth the implications of Husserl's late philosophy and to think his "unthought thought,"[42] numerous Merleau-Ponty scholars have insisted that the Husserl Merleau-Ponty found reason to praise was primarily an extrapolation of Merleau-Ponty's own philosophy.[43]

There are certainly significant differences between Husserl, Heidegger, and Merleau-Ponty. Whatever influence Husserl exerted on Heidegger and Merleau-Ponty, the latter two were also indebted to other seminal figures in the philosophical tradition, including Aristotle, Descartes, Kierkegaard, Nietzsche, Bergson, and Sartre. But much of Heidegger's and Merleau-Ponty's

---

40 Taylor Carman, *Heidegger's Analytic: Interpretation, Discourse and Authenticity in Being and Time* (Cambridge: Cambridge University Press, 2003), 62.
41 Merleau-Ponty, *Phenomenology of Perception*, lxx.
42 Maurice Merleau-Ponty, *Signs*, trans. R. C. McClearly (Evanston: Northwestern University Press, 1964 [1960]), 160.
43 Gary Brent Madison, *The Phenomenology of Merleau-Ponty* (Athens: Ohio University Press, 1981), 70; and M. C. Dillon, *Merleau-Ponty's Ontology* (Evanston: Northwestern University Press, 1997), 27.

disagreement with Husserl takes place within a horizon of shared assumptions. It is an immanent criticism, a criticism internal to phenomenology, and not a break with or general rejection of it. To put it differently, in order to understand and appreciate the *phenomenological* aspect of Heidegger's and Merleau-Ponty's thinking, a familiarity with Husserl remains indispensable.

In the following, my modest aim will be to point to certain Husserlian themes that continue to be operative in the writings of Heidegger and Merleau-Ponty. By focusing on the similarities rather than on the differences, I hope to make it clear why it makes sense to speak of phenomenology as a tradition rather than as the work of a single author.

A first point of contact concerns the transcendental character of Heidegger's and Merleau-Ponty's thinking. Just like Husserl, both Heidegger and Merleau-Ponty remained interested in the intentionality of our experiential life. As Heidegger writes, if we really are to understand the fundamental structures of life, a radically new methodology is called for, a new phenomenological methodology.[44] This is also why Heidegger repeatedly speaks of phenomenology as an "originary science of life."[45] What such an investigation will reveal is that traditional categories such as inner and outer or transcendence and immanence are all misplaced when it comes to the study of pure life-experience.[46] Experiential life is, as Heidegger says, as such world-related, it is always already living in the world; it does not have to seek it out.[47] Life-experience is literally speaking "worldly tuned," it always lives in a world, it is properly speaking a worldlife, and it always finds itself in a lifeworld.[48] These ideas are forcefully articulated in the following quote from *Being and Time* (1927):

> When Dasein directs itself towards something and grasps it, it does not somehow first get out of an inner sphere in which it has been proximally encapsulated, but its primary kind of Being is such that it is always 'outside' alongside entities which it encounters and which belong to a world already discovered. Nor is any inner sphere abandoned when Dasein dwells alongside the entity to be known, and determines its character; but even in this 'Being-outside' alongside the object, Dasein is still 'inside,' if we understand this in the correct sense; that is to say, it is itself 'inside' as a Being-in-the-world which knows. (Heidegger, *Being and Time*, 89)

---

44 Martin Heidegger, *Grundprobleme der Phänomenologie (1919/1920)*, in *Gesamtausgabe*, ed. Vittorio Klostermann, 102 vols. (Frankfurt am Main: Verlag Vittorio Klostermann, 1993), vol. LVIII, 237.
45 Heidegger, *Grundprobleme der Phänomenologie*, 233.
46 Heidegger, *Grundprobleme der Phänomenologie*, 253.
47 Heidegger, *Grundprobleme der Phänomenologie*, 34.
48 Heidegger, *Grundprobleme der Phänomenologie*, 250.

Heidegger has occasionally been interpreted as a radical critic of the notion of subjectivity. It is certainly true that Heidegger rejects the idea of subjectivity as some kind of isolated, self-contained, worldless soul substance and instead employs the notion of *Dasein* (which is composed of '*Da*,' meaning 'there,' and '*sein*,' meaning 'being,' i.e., there-being or being-there) to designate the kind of beings we ourselves are. But as he also makes clear, his own exploration of the structure of Dasein is really a phenomenological analysis of the subjectivity of the finite subject.[49] More importantly, Heidegger explicitly denies that his analysis of Dasein is in any way a psychological analysis,[50] just as he writes that any attempt to interpret Husserl's investigations as a kind of descriptive psychology completely fails to do justice to their transcendental character. In fact, as Heidegger adds, phenomenology will remain a book sealed with seven or more seals to any such psychological approach.[51] A similar sentiment is expressed in *Phenomenology of Perception* (1945), where Merleau-Ponty declares that phenomenology is distinguished in all its characteristics from introspective psychology and that the difference in question is a difference in principle. Whereas the introspective psychologist considers consciousness as a mere sector of being, and tries to investigate this sector in the same way the physicist tries to investigate his, the phenomenologist realizes that an investigation of consciousness cannot take place as long as the absolute existence of the world is left unquestioned. Consciousness cannot be analyzed properly without leading us beyond common-sense assumptions and toward a transcendental clarification of the constitution of the world.[52] Rather than taking the world as described by science for granted, phenomenology asks how the world can be given as objective in the first place. How is objectivity constituted and to what extent is our theoretical exploration of the world enabled by our pre-theoretical embodied embedding in the world?

Heidegger and Merleau-Ponty both deny the self-contained nature of the mind and argue that it is intrinsically world-involved. They also defend the reverse claim, however, and argue that the world is tied to the mind. To put it differently, both of them would argue that the relation between mind and world is an internal relation, a relation constitutive of its relata, and not an

---

49 Martin Heidegger, *Being and Time*, trans. J. Macquarrie and E. Robinson (New York: Harper & Row, 1962 [1927]), 45, 418, and 434; and Martin Heidegger, *The Basic Problems of Phenomenology*, trans. A. Hofstadter (Bloomington: Indiana University Press, 1982 [1927]), 146 and 155.
50 Heidegger, *Being and Time*, 71–76.
51 Heidegger, *Grundprobleme der Phänomenologie*, 15–16.
52 Merleau-Ponty, *Phenomenology of Perception*, 59–60.

external one of causality. As Heidegger writes in the lecture course *The Basic Problems of Phenomenology* from 1927,

> World exists – that is, it is – only if Dasein exists, only if there is Dasein. Only if world is there, if Dasein exists as being-in-the-world, is there understanding of being, and only if this understanding exists are intraworldly beings unveiled as extant and handy. World-understanding as Dasein-understanding is self-understanding. Self and world belong together in the single entity, the Dasein. Self and world are not two beings, like subject and object, or like I and thou, but self and world are the basic determination of the Dasein itself in the unity of the structure of being-in-the-world.
> (Heidegger, *The Basic Problems of Phenomenology*, 297)

A similar commitment to correlationism is found in Merleau-Ponty, who toward the end of *Phenomenology of Perception* declares that

> The world is inseparable from the subject, but from a subject who is nothing but a project of the world; and the subject is inseparable from the world, but from a world that it itself projects. The subject is being-in-the-world and the world remains 'subjective,' since its texture and its articulations are sketched out by the subject's movement of transcendence.
> (Merleau-Ponty, *Phenomenology of Perception*, 454)

Our relation to the world is so fundamental, so obvious and natural, that we normally take it for granted. It is this domain of obviousness that phenomenology seeks to investigate. Its task is not to uncover new empirical knowledge about different areas in the world, but rather to comprehend the basic relation to the world that is presupposed in any such empirical investigation. In our ordinary pre-philosophical life, we are so absorbed in daily activities, so focused on worldly matters, that our own self-understanding tends to be characterized by a certain self-forgetfulness and self-objectification. Phenomenology can also be described as a struggle against this leveling self-understanding, this objectifying self-alienation. This is why Heidegger in *Being and Time* writes that the phenomenological analysis is characterized by a certain violence, since its disclosure of the being of Dasein is only to be won in direct confrontation with Dasein's own tendency to cover things up. In fact, it must be wrested and captured from Dasein.[53] In *Phenomenology of Perception*, Merleau-Ponty likewise argues that we have to break with our familiar acceptance of the world if we are to understand the latter properly. The world is, as Merleau-Ponty writes, wonderful. It is a gift

---

53 Heidegger, *Being and Time*, 359.

and a riddle. But in order to fully appreciate this, we must undertake a methodological suspension of our ordinary blind and thoughtless taking the world for granted. Normally, we live in a natural and engaged world-relation. But as philosophers, we cannot make do with such a naïve world-immersion. We have to distance ourselves from it, if ever so slightly, in order to be able to account for it. It is only by slackening them slightly that we can make the intentional threads that connect us to the world visible. This is also why Merleau-Ponty argues that a proper analysis of our being-in-the-world presupposes the phenomenological reduction.[54]

Husserl's dictum "to the things themselves" was interpreted by Merleau-Ponty as a criticism of scientism, and as a call for a return to the perceptual world that is prior to and a precondition for any scientific conceptualization and articulation. Scientism seeks to reduce us to objects in the world. It argues that the methods of natural science provide the sole means of epistemic access to the world, and that entities that cannot be captured in terms accepted by natural science are non-existent. As Merleau-Ponty insists, however, we should never forget that our knowledge of the world, including our scientific knowledge, arises from a bodily anchored first-person perspective, and that science would be meaningless without this experiential dimension. The scientific discourse is rooted in the world of experience, in the experiential world, and if we wish to comprehend the performance and limits of science, we have to investigate the original experience of the world of which science is a higher-order articulation. The one-sided focus of science on what is available from a third-person perspective is for Merleau-Ponty both naïve and dishonest, since the scientific practice constantly presupposes the scientist's first-personal and pre-scientific experience of the world.[55] For both Merleau-Ponty and Heidegger, positive science takes certain ideas about the mind-independent nature of reality for granted and seems to consider such ideas exempt from critical scrutiny. But the aim of phenomenology is to question such objectivism, and to investigate all objects, scientific findings, cultural accomplishments, social institutions, etc., with an eye to how they present or manifest themselves to us.

Such a focus on givenness is no restriction and limitation, is not about banning questions of being and of ontology, since, as Heidegger declares, there "is no ontology *alongside* a phenomenology. Rather, *scientific ontology is nothing but phenomenology.*"[56] When speaking of the phenomenon, it is

---

54 Merleau-Ponty, *Phenomenology of Perception*, lxxviii.
55 Merleau-Ponty, *Phenomenology of Perception*, lxii.
56 Martin Heidegger, *History of the Concept of Time: Prolegomena*, trans. Th. Kisiel (Bloomington: Indiana University Press, 1985 [1925]), 72.

consequently decisive not to understand it as something that conceals something more fundamental, which it merely represents, but instead as that which shows itself. As Heidegger writes in the lecture course *History of the Concept of Time* from 1925,

> It is phenomenologically absurd to speak of the phenomenon as if it were something behind which there would be something else of which it would be a phenomenon in the sense of the appearance which represents and expresses [this something else]. A phenomenon is nothing behind which there would be something else. More accurately stated, one cannot ask for something behind the phenomenon at all, since what the phenomenon gives is precisely that something in itself.
> (Heidegger, *History of the Concept of Time: Prolegomena*, 86)

If we, as phenomenologists, are to engage with fundamental ontological questions, we must, according to Heidegger, proceed via an investigation of Dasein's understanding of being, that is, we have to investigate being "in so far as Being enters into the intelligibility of Dasein."[57] It is consequently no coincidence that Heidegger calls the science of being a transcendental science.[58]

Husserl's late ideas regarding the intertwinement between self, others, and world is from early on also pursued by Heidegger and Merleau-Ponty, who likewise insist that self, world, and others belong together; that they reciprocally illuminate one another, and can only be understood in their interconnection. In an early lecture, Heidegger describes the lifeworld as an interpenetration of the three domains: surrounding world (*Umwelt*), with-world (*Mitwelt*), and self-world (*Selbstwelt*),[59] and argues that Dasein as world-experiencing is always already being-with (*Mitsein*). As he would put it in later lectures from 1927,

> ... just as the Dasein is originally being with others, so it is originally being with the handy and the extant. Similarly, the Dasein is just as little at first merely a dwelling among things so as then occasionally to discover among these things beings with its own kind of being; instead, as the being which is occupied with itself, the Dasein is with equal originality being-with others *and* being-among intraworldly beings.
> (Heidegger, *The Basic Problems of Phenomenology*, 297)

As for Merleau-Ponty, he argues that subjectivity is essentially oriented and open toward that which it is not, and that it is in this openness that it

---

57 Heidegger, *Being and Time*, 193.
58 Heidegger, *The Basic Problems of Phenomenology*, 17.
59 Heidegger, *Grundprobleme der Phänomenologie*, 33, 39, and 62.

reveals itself to itself. What is disclosed by the cogito is consequently not an enclosed immanence, a pure interior self-presence, but an openness toward alterity, a movement of exteriorization and perpetual self-transcendence. It is by being present to the world that we are present to ourselves, and it is by being given to ourselves that we can be conscious of the world.[60] The subject has no priority over the world, and truth is not to be found in the interiority of man. There is no interiority, since man is in the world, and only knows him- or herself by means of inhabiting a world. To put it differently, the subjectivity disclosed by the phenomenological reflection is not a concealed interiority, but an open world-relation.[61] As a careful phenomenological analysis will also reveal, however, I do not simply exist for myself, but also for others, just as others do not simply exist for themselves, but also for me. There are aspects of myself and aspects of the world that become available and accessible only through others. Merleau-Ponty consequently insists that a phenomenological description, rather than disclosing subjectivities that are inaccessible and self-sufficient, reveals continuities between intersubjective life and the world. The subject realizes itself in its presence to the world and to others – not in spite of, but precisely *by way of* its corporeality and historicity.[62] In short, my existence is not simply a question of how I apprehend myself, it is also a question of how others apprehend me. Subjectivity is necessarily embedded and embodied in a social, historical, and natural context. The world is inseparable from subjectivity and intersubjectivity, and the task of phenomenology is to think world, subjectivity, and intersubjectivity in their proper connection.[63] As Merleau-Ponty fully realizes, such a conception of the intertwinement of self, others, and world will not leave the traditional conception of transcendental philosophy untouched:

> ... how can the borders of the transcendental and the empirical help becoming indistinct? For along with the other person, all the other person sees of me – all my facticity – is reintegrated into subjectivity, or at least posited as an indispensable element of its definition. Thus the transcendental descends into history. Or as we might put it, the historical is no longer an external relation between two or more absolutely autonomous subjects but has an interior and is an inherent aspect of their very definition. They no

---

60 Merleau-Ponty, *Phenomenology of Perception*, 311, 396, and 448.
61 Merleau-Ponty, *Phenomenology of Perception*, lxxiv.
62 Merleau-Ponty, *Phenomenology of Perception*, 478.
63 Merleau-Ponty, *Phenomenology of Perception*, lxxvi and lxxxv.

longer know themselves to be subjects simply in relation to their individual selves, but in relation to one another as well. (Merleau-Ponty, *Signs*, 107)

How does the phenomenological work of Merleau-Ponty and Heidegger diverge from that of Husserl? One way to conceive of the divergence is by seeing both of them as pursuing ideas already found in Husserl in a more radical manner than Husserl himself.

Merleau-Ponty attributes more significance to the role of embodiment and facticity than Husserl, and is also going further in his attempt to rethink the traditional divide between the transcendental and the empirical and between mind and world. This is already evident in Merleau-Ponty's first major work, *The Structure of Behavior* (1942), where Merleau-Ponty engages extensively with empirical science and on the final page calls for a redefinition of transcendental philosophy.[64] Rather than making us choose between a scientific explanation and a phenomenological reflection, Merleau-Ponty asks us to respect the living relation between consciousness and nature and to search for a dimension that is beyond both objectivism and subjectivism. What is of particular importance is that Merleau-Ponty clearly believes that transcendental phenomenology itself can be changed and modified through its dialogue with the empirical disciplines. In fact, it needs this confrontation if it is to develop in the right way.

Heidegger is a far more attentive reader of the history of philosophy than Husserl and is also to a larger extent than Husserl emphasizing the extent to which our current thinking is influenced by the tradition. For Heidegger, one important task of phenomenology is to disclose and deconstruct some of the metaphysical conceptions that for centuries have tacitly enframed and constrained philosophical thinking. In the course of his own phenomenological analysis, Heidegger comes to question the traditional privileging of theoria, of object-givenness, and of temporal presence. He argues that one of Husserl's limitations was that he operated with too narrow a concept of being and givenness. Rather than letting his investigation be guided by the things themselves, Husserl was – according to Heidegger – instead led by traditional, or, to be more specific, Cartesian, presuppositions and decisions. By privileging the active ego, and by reducing givenness to object-givenness, Husserl not only failed to disclose the unique mode of being peculiar to intentional subjectivity, but also failed to engage

---

[64] Maurice Merleau-Ponty, *The Structure of Behavior*, trans. A. L. Fisher (Boston: Beacon Press, 1963 [1942]), 224.

adequately with the truly transcendental question concerning the nature of phenomenality as such.[65] In works succeeding *Being and Time*, Heidegger's own wrestling with these issues led him to question his own privileging of Dasein. Whereas he in *Being and Time* still argued that a fundamental ontology must be rooted in human existence and that we have to approach the ontological questions via an investigation of Dasein's understanding of being, he subsequently came to hold the view that Dasein's own understanding is enabled by a more fundamental clearing (*Lichtung*) that belongs to being itself. As Heidegger writes in his *Letter on "Humanism"* (1946),

> The human being is rather 'thrown' by being itself into the truth of being, so that ek-sisting in this fashion he might guard the truth of being, in order that beings might appear in the light of being as the beings they are. Human beings do not decide whether and how beings appear, whether and how God and the gods or history and nature come forward into the clearing of being, come to presence and depart. The advent of beings lies in the destiny of being. But for humans it is ever a question of finding what is fitting in their essence that corresponds to such destiny; for in accord with this destiny the human being as ek-sisting has to guard the truth of being. The human being is the shepherd of being. (Heidegger, *Pathmarks*, 252)[66]

Phenomenological Sociology

Obviously, phenomenology did not come to an end with the passing of Merleau-Ponty and Heidegger, nor was its influence restricted to philosophy. Sociology was among the disciplines that already early on incorporated ideas from phenomenology.

Alfred Schutz (1899–1959) is often considered the founder of phenomenological sociology. Initially, Schutz was inspired by Max Weber's interpretive sociology. However, although Weber regarded meaningful action as the central topic of the social sciences, and although he emphasized the importance of explicating the meaning that the individual agent attributes to her own action, Weber did not concern himself with the constitution of social meaning as such. It was this omission that Schutz attempted to

---

65 Heidegger, *History of the Concept of Time: Prolegomena*, §§ 10–13; cf. Jean-Luc Marion, *Reduction and Givenness: Investigations of Husserl, Heidegger, and Phenomenology*, trans. T. A. Carlson (Evanston: Northwestern University Press, 1998 [1989]), 204.
66 Martin Heidegger, *Pathmarks*, ed. W. McNeill (Cambridge: Cambridge University Press, 1998 [1976]).

address by combining Weber's sociology with Husserl's phenomenological methodology.[67]

According to Schutz, sociology should take its point of departure in the lifeworld – since it is this world that constitutes the frame and stage of social relations and actions – and engage in a systematic examination of everyday life. Drawing on Husserl's analyses, Schutz claimed that the social world reveals and manifests itself in various intentional experiences. Its meaningfulness is constituted by subjects, and in order to understand and scientifically address the social world it is therefore necessary to examine the social agents for whom it exists; agents that possess consciousness, understanding, motives, etc. As a result, Schutz emphatically rejected reductionist programs, such as behaviorism and positivism, which attempted to reduce human action to observable behavior and stimulus–response mechanisms.

Schutz's phenomenological perspective emphasizes that the primary object of sociology is not institutions, market conjunctures, social classes, or structures of power, but *human beings*, that is, acting and experiencing individuals, considered in their myriad relations to others, but also with an eye to their own, meaning-constituting subjective lives. As Schutz writes, every science of social meaning must refer to our meaning-constituting life in the social world: to our everyday experience of other persons, to our understanding of pre-given meanings, and to our initiation of new meaningful behavior.[68] Schutz's point, of course, is not that sociology should have no interest whatsoever in institutions, power structures, and the like. Rather, he merely insists that a concept such as 'power structure' must be regarded as a sort of 'intellectual shorthand,' which can be useful for certain purposes, but must never lead us to forget that, in the end, power structures presuppose experiencing, interpreting, and acting individuals.[69]

In the course of his investigation, Schutz emphasizes the heterogeneity of the social world. It is structured in multiple ways. The same holds true for interpersonal understanding, which differs in character depending on whether the one to be understood is bodily present, or, rather, removed in space or time. It depends in short on whether the other belongs to the world

---

67 Alfred Schutz, *The Phenomenology of the Social World*, trans. G. Walsh and F. Lehnert (Evanston: Northwestern University Press, 1967 [1932]), 13.
68 Schutz, *The Phenomenology of the Social World*, 9.
69 Alfred Schutz, *The Problem of Social Reality: Collected Papers I* (The Hague: Martinus Nijhoff, 1962), 34–35; and Alfred Schutz, *Studies in Social Theory: Collected Papers II* (The Hague: Martinus Nijhoff, 1964), 6–7.

of our associates, contemporaries, predecessors, or successors, or, to use Schutz's original terms, whether the other belongs to our *Umwelt*, *Mitwelt*, *Vorwelt*, or *Folgewelt*.[70]

It might seem natural to focus on social encounters that take place within our *Umwelt*, i.e., those that involve direct bodily interaction, but ultimately such a focus is far too narrow and limited; it covers only a small, though admittedly central and fundamental, part of the social world. I am also able to understand those whom I have previously encountered face to face but who now live abroad, or those of whose existence I know, not as concrete individuals, but as points in social space defined by certain roles and functions, say, tax officials or railway guards. Thus, Schutz repeatedly stresses the multi-layered character of the social world, and argues that one of the important tasks of a phenomenological sociology is to conduct a careful analysis of these different strata.

In ordinary life, we move between *Umwelt* and *Mitwelt* constantly and effortlessly. This is so because we increasingly interpret our own behavior and that of the other within contexts of meaning that transcend the here and now. To that extent, our stock of knowledge influences our face-to-face interactions and comes to serve as interpretative scheme even in the world of direct social experience.[71]

Some of Schutz's central ideas were subsequently taken up by two of his former students, Peter Berger and Thomas Luckmann. In their influential book *The Social Construction of Reality: A Treatise in the Sociology of Knowledge*, Berger and Luckmann sought to understand how knowledge is produced, distributed, and internalized, and how the validity of any form of knowledge (be it that of the Tibetan monk or the American businesswoman) becomes socially established.[72]

For Berger and Luckmann, social reality is a product of human activity; it is neither biologically determined, nor in any other way determined by facts of nature.[73] The task of social theory is to provide an account of how human beings, through manifold forms of interaction, create and shape social structures and institutions, which may at first simply have the character of a shared intersubjective reality, but which eventually become

---

70 Schutz, *The Phenomenology of the Social World*, 30.
71 Schutz, *The Phenomenology of the Social World*, 185.
72 Peter L. Berger and Thomas Luckmann, *The Social Construction of Reality: A Treatise in the Sociology of Knowledge* (Harmondsworth: Penguin, 1991 [1966]), 15.
73 Berger and Luckmann, *The Social Construction of Reality*, 70.

'externalized' and with time appear inevitable and natural. But, as Berger and Luckmann insist,

> It is important to keep in mind that the objectivity of the institutional world, however massive it may appear to the individual, is a humanly produced, constructed objectivity ... The paradox that man is capable of producing a world that he then experiences as something other than a human product will concern us later on. At the moment, it is important to emphasize that the relationship between man, the producer, and the social world, his product, is and remains a dialectical one. That is, man (not, of course, in isolation but in his collectivities) and his social world interact with each other. The product acts back upon the producer. (Berger and Luckmann, *The Social Construction of Reality*, 78)

Social reality is thus not only an externalized and objectified human product. It is also something that individual human beings 'internalize.' We are not raised outside society, but grow up in it. And, as part of our socialization, we take over roles, attitudes, and norms from others. Human society, Berger and Luckmann emphasize, must therefore be "understood in terms of an ongoing dialectic of the three moments of externalization, objectivation and internalization."[74]

Conclusion

After World War II, France replaced Germany as the phenomenological powerhouse. Thinkers like Emmanuel Lévinas, Michel Henry, Jacques Derrida, and Paul Ricœur all questioned the adequacy of the classical phenomenological investigations of intentionality, time-consciousness, intersubjectivity, and language. In their attempt to radicalize phenomenology, they disclosed new types and structures of manifestation, and thereby made decisive contributions to the development of phenomenology. Insofar as phenomenology in the twenty-first century is concerned, recent studies and collections[75] show that a lot of work is currently being done in two directions: inward (and backward) and outward (and forward). On the one hand, we find a continuing engagement and conversation with the founding fathers (and mothers). The philosophical resources and insights to be found in Husserl's, Heidegger's, and Merleau-Ponty's work have evidently not yet been exhausted. On the other hand, an increasing amount of

---

74 Berger and Luckmann, *The Social Construction of Reality*, 149.
75 For example Dan Zahavi (ed.), *The Oxford Handbook of Contemporary Phenomenology* (Oxford: Oxford University Press, 2012).

dialogue is taking place between phenomenology and other philosophical traditions and empirical disciplines. Ideas from phenomenology have, for instance, started to impact discussions of self-consciousness and social cognition in analytic philosophy of mind,[76] just as the currently prominent 4E (i.e., embodied, embedded, extended, and enactive) approaches to cognition have drawn inspiration from the phenomenological tradition.[77]

---

[76] Shaun Gallagher and Dan Zahavi, *The Phenomenological Mind*, 2nd edn. (London and New York: Routledge, 2012); and Dan Zahavi, *Self and Other: Exploring Subjectivity, Empathy, and Shame* (Oxford: Oxford University Press, 2014).

[77] See Francisco J. Varela, Evan Thompson, and Eleanor Rosch, *The Embodied Mind: Cognitive Science and Human Experience* (Cambridge: MIT Press, 1991); and Giovanna Colombetti, *The Feeling Body: Affective Science Meets the Enactive Mind* (Cambridge: MIT Press, 2014).

5

Existentialism and the Meanings of Transcendence

EDWARD BARING

In one of the most famous set pieces of Jean-Paul Sartre's *Being and Nothingness* (1943), he describes running into a café. He looks through the smoky atmosphere to the patrons. He hears "sounds of voices, rattling saucers, and the footsteps that fill it." But despite this "fullness of being," the scene is structured by an absence. For Sartre has come looking for a friend, who, he argues, is palpably not there.[1] Sartre's description draws attention to the two elements of his philosophy announced in the book's title. An embodied and situated "being," the human individual nonetheless participates in "nothingness" such that it is never fully controlled by physical or moral laws. How we act determines who we are, not vice versa. Or, in the laconic style of his 1945 slogan: "Existence precedes essence."

Sartre's watchword does not hold for all existentialists,[2] but it is a response to a common question: how to reconcile our concrete particularity with freedom, understood as a movement of transcendence. In his 1932 book, *Towards the Concrete*, the French philosopher Jean Wahl articulated one of the driving concerns of existentialism: the desire to move beyond the sterility and abstraction of much earlier philosophy.[3] Existentialists wanted to replace the theoretical and universal subject of idealism by the singular individual understood in broader and richer terms: We grasp the world not simply intellectually, but as bodily (affective, volitional, and acting) beings. Considering the

---

[1] Jean-Paul Sartre, *Being and Nothingness*, trans. H. Barnes (New York: Washington Square Press, 1993), 40–42.
[2] Heidegger famously rejected it in his "Letter on Humanism," as did most other so-called "existentialists." In this article I will use the term "existentialism" to describe the work of all the relevant actors. Nevertheless, within the existentialist community there was a considerable debate over the name, and at times other alternatives such as "the philosophy of existence" and "existential philosophy" held sway. I discuss this debate and its effects on the constitution of an international existentialist community in "Anxiety in Translation: Naming Existentialism before Sartre," *History of European Ideas*, 41(4) (2015), 470–488.
[3] Jean Wahl, *Vers le concret* (Paris: Librairie Philosophique J. Vrin, 1932).

human individual in this way showed that it was impossible to imagine the subject as a disengaged spectator. We are necessarily in a "situation," members of a particular nation, family, and class, with particular concerns and responsibilities. These concrete aspects of existentialism helped it forge strong connections with literature. It is not a surprise that many of the most important existentialists, Sartre, Albert Camus, and Simone de Beauvoir, but also Gabriel Marcel and Richard Wright, were novelists and playwrights too.

Nonetheless, existentialists argued that this thick particularity did not exhaust the individual; they were wedded to a conception of human freedom. The situation, they argued, was contingent, more a set of conditions to which we have to respond, rather than being absolutely determinative. As de Beauvoir wrote, the individual exists "only by transcending himself ... He justifies his existence by a movement which, like freedom, springs from his heart but which leads outside of him."[4] And while the emphasis on the concrete encouraged existentialists to pay attention to human singularity, because they took this movement of transcendence to be common to all, it gave existentialism the shading of universalism.

The tension between particularity and transcendence at the level of existentialist thought is mirrored at the level of its intellectual community. On the one hand, existentialism is so closely associated with an area of Paris that one is tempted to put a name to the café in Sartre's vignette: the *Café de Flore* or perhaps *Les Deux Magots*, which were situated only a few meters from each other in Saint-Germain-des-Prés on the left bank of the Seine.[5] The major figures of French existentialism – Sartre, de Beauvoir, Camus, and Maurice Merleau-Ponty – all knew each other and, at least before they became so famous as to make it impossible, often frequented those establishments. On the other hand, existentialism stands out amongst twentieth-century philosophies for its geographic reach. In the 1940s, 1950s, and 1960s, there were self-identified existentialists in Germany, Italy, Belgium, Spain, and the United States. In Paris too, the existentialists were a cosmopolitan community, welcoming émigrés from Russia, America, and elsewhere.

The theoretical and sociological tensions are related. For the various ways existentialists figured the movement of transcendence allowed them to tap

---

4 Simone de Beauvoir, *The Ethics of Ambiguity*, trans. Bernard Frechtman (New York: Philosophical Library, 1949), 156.
5 For an evocative account of the social scene in these cafés in the 1930s and 1940s see Herbert Lottman, *The Left Bank: Writers, Artists, and Politics from the Popular Front to the Cold War* (San Francisco: Halo Books, 1991); and Sarah Bakewell, *The Existentialist Café: Freedom, Being and Apricot Cocktails* (New York: Other Press, 2016).

into transnational networks that shuttled their ideas across the world. Some existentialists invested transcendence with religious meaning, which spoke to Christian philosophers across Europe and beyond. Others gave it political significance, producing the close but fraught relationship between existentialism and international communism. Finally, the ethical demand to acknowledge human transcendence drove existentialists to participate in large-scale, transnational projects of social change: anti-colonialism, anti-racism, and feminism amongst others.

The Kierkegaard Renaissance in Germany

The existentialist movement in postwar France drew inspiration from the Kierkegaard Renaissance in Germany in the period following World War I, which Peter E. Gordon discusses in Chapter 13 on modern theology. Kierkegaard had been read in literary and philosophical circles in Germany at the turn of the century, but the experience of war and defeat catapulted him to the center of the intellectual world.[6] Responding to the political and economic blows that shook the fledgling Weimar Republic, from the early attempted putsches to the hyperinflation of 1923, thinkers of various stripes criticized the alienating forces of modernity and the philosophies that acquiesced to its illusory sense of progress and rationality. Though many disagreed with the details of Oswald Spengler's catastrophic vision in *The Decline of the West* (1918) they saw it as a symptom of a pervasive crisis, extending even to the principles of scholarly work.[7]

It was thus with a sense of philosophical and historical kinship that thinkers like Karl Barth, Martin Buber, Theodor Haecker, and Paul Tillich picked up Kierkegaard's protest against the system-building Hegelians in mid-nineteenth-century Denmark. It was not just his rejection of philosophical systems that made Kierkegaard so relevant at the time, but the way in which he emphasized the priority of the concrete singular individual or "existence." Confronting this individual and the higher religious demands he or she faces, Kierkegaard thought, could lead us to "suspend the ethical," our

---

[6] For the early reception of Kierkegaard up until the end of World War I, see Habib C. Malik, *Receiving Søren Kierkegaard: The Early Impact and Transmission of His Thought* (Washington: Catholic University Press, 1997), Chapter 8.

[7] See Peter E. Gordon, *Continental Divide: Heidegger, Cassirer, Davos* (Cambridge: Harvard University Press, 2010), 43–51.

commitment to universal moral principles, and take a "leap of faith" to an absolutely transcendent God.[8]

Most important for the emergence of European existentialism were the Kierkegaard readings of Karl Jaspers and Martin Heidegger. Heidegger (1889–1976) had begun his career as a student of Catholic philosophy in Freiburg, but already in his 1916 doctorate he was moving away from his childhood faith, and in the early 1920s he turned to predominantly Protestant thinkers: Kierkegaard, but also Martin Luther, Rudolf Otto, and others.[9] The result of these readings was less a conversion to Protestantism than a self-conscious distancing from the philosophy of religion, culminating in Heidegger's 1927 masterwork, *Being and Time*.[10] *Being and Time* is concerned with what Heidegger calls "the analytic of Dasein," the slow and careful investigation of that entity "which each of us is himself."[11] Heidegger called this entity "Dasein," rather than "man" or "the subject," because he had wanted to distance his work from the forms of thought with which those words had been associated. Instead, Heidegger followed Kierkegaard in presenting Dasein in terms of existence (*Existenz*).[12] Though, as Theodore Kisiel has shown, this language was added only in the final draft of *Being and Time*, Heidegger's choice would have far-reaching consequences for the intellectual history of modern Europe.[13]

Heidegger opposed Dasein to the Cartesian subject, which was distinct from the world it sought to know. Descartes's account is plausible if we foreground representation, a theoretical account, where the subject peruses a world composed of distinct objects in space. But for Heidegger, representation was secondary to a more fundamental form of understanding. Most of the time, in our "everyday" existence, we do not examine objects as detached spectators. Rather we are engaged with them, using pens, sitting on chairs. In

---

8 Søren Kierkegaard, *Fear and Trembling*, trans. A. Hannay (London: Penguin, 1986), 65.
9 For these readings see Judith Wolfe, *Heidegger's Eschatology: Theological Horizons in Martin Heidegger's Early Work* (Oxford: Oxford University Press, 2013).
10 For Heidegger's work in this period see Steven Galt Crowell, *Husserl, Heidegger, and the Space of Meaning: Paths toward Transcendental Philosophy* (Evanston: Northwestern University Press, 2001).
11 Martin Heidegger, *Being and Time*, trans. J. Macquarrie and E. Robinson (London: SCM Press, 1962), 27.
12 Heidegger, *Being and Time*, 67. In 1920 Heidegger started to name "concrete actual Dasein" "life." Theodore Kisiel, *The Genesis of Heidegger's Being and Time* (Berkeley: University of California Press, 1993), 117. As Heidegger made clear, the term existence "formally indicates" Dasein's being. Heidegger, *Being and Time*, 274. For Heidegger's reading of Kierkegaard see Vincent McCarthy "Martin Heidegger: Kierkegaard's Influence Hidden and in Full View," in *Kierkegaard and Existentialism*, ed. Jon Stewart (Farnham: Routledge, 2011), 95–125.
13 See Kisiel, *The Genesis of Heidegger's Being and Time*, 397 and 421–451.

Heidegger's terminology, this "equipment" (*Zeug*) was "ready-to-hand" (its mode of being was *Zuhandenheit*). Further, while Descartes's objects were separate and discrete, the equipment of our everyday experience participated in a system of references; the pen is used to write on paper, to record a thought for future use, the chair stands at a table so that we can eat.[14] Following these references, it became clear that Dasein was situated in a meaningful totality, in Heidegger's language it was "being-in-the-world" (*In-der-Welt-sein*).[15] This is what Heidegger meant when he said that we were "thrown" (*geworfen*); we find ourselves involved in and open to a world of meanings that precedes us. Second, while Cartesian metaphysics began with an individual detached subject and thus posed the existence of other selves as a problem, Dasein was social from the start. The "world" for Heidegger was already invested with social meanings: the chair that is designed for people to sit on, the lectern from which I speak to a class.[16] By working through its "being in the world," it would become clear that Dasein was also "being-with." For everyday Dasein, being-with didn't refer to any particular individual, but rather to the neutral and faceless "One" (*das Man*) of common opinion, of received practices, the public sphere (*Öffentlichkeit*).[17]

In addition to this concrete particularity, Heidegger placed great emphasis on Dasein's transcendence. As *Existenz* (or later "ek-sistence" from the Latin to "stand out") Dasein was always "ahead-of-itself," constituted by possibilities it was called upon to choose.[18] We could flee this choice, mindlessly following the customs of the "One." Or, in what Heidegger called "authenticity" (*Eigentlichkeit*), we could embrace the possibilities as our own (*eigen*). Authenticity did not mean that Dasein could free itself from the "One," which, as we saw, was constitutive of its being. Rather it entailed a different way of relating to it, in Heidegger's language, an "existentiell [*existenzielle*] modification."[19]

For Heidegger, our choices could be authentic only if they included our "ownmost possibility," namely death, which, because it could never be experienced by anyone else, foregrounded our individuality. Moreover, in one of his most famous analyses, where the influence of Kierkegaard is particularly clear, Heidegger argued that our authentic being was revealed

---

14 Heidegger, *Being and Time*, 95–107.
15 Heidegger, *Being and Time*, 78. For a very clear exposition of this idea and a criticism of the priority Heidegger gave to the ready-to-hand, see Gordon, *Continental Divide*, 217–234.
16 Heidegger, *Being and Time*, 153.   17 Heidegger, *Being and Time*, 163–164.
18 Heidegger, *Being and Time*, 33.   19 Heidegger, *Being and Time*, 168.

in "anxiety." Anxiety was not directed toward a specific object like fear (fear of heights, spiders, etc.). Rather it was an indeterminate mood in which the world and the shared meanings of the "One" appeared detached and strange, losing their grip over us. Anxiety confronted Dasein with its freedom.[20]

Heidegger's emphasis on transcendence and authenticity should be understood in relation to his broader project. The analytic of Dasein within the published portion of *Being and Time* was only a first step toward an ontology, that is an answer to the "question of being": What does it mean to say that something *is*? Ontology was important because the work of the sciences, understood broadly to include history and anthropology, as well as physics and mathematics etc., depended upon understanding the being of their object, what history, humanity, matter, number etc. *was*.[21] Despite the centrality of the question, Heidegger thought that philosophy had failed to provide satisfactory answers. Historically, most accounts treated being (*Sein*) as an entity (a *Seiendes*), an error equivalent to mistaking a material object for matter itself.[22] This had led philosophers to consider being either as the source of everything, like a creator God, or as a mysterious ground, in which all things participated. The pervasiveness of this error in the history of philosophy meant that Heidegger's project of reviving the question of being required first a "destruction" of the ontological tradition.[23]

Heidegger's analytic of Dasein provided a new way of approaching the question of being. The fact that we (as Dasein) could even pose the question suggested that we must already have an inkling about what being meant. As Heidegger wrote *"understanding of being is itself a definite characteristic of Dasein's being."*[24] For Heidegger, this understanding was a direct consequence of Dasein's transcendence: "if Dasein's being is completely grounded in temporality, then temporality must make possible being-in-the-world and therewith Dasein's transcendence; this transcendence in turn provides the support for concernful being alongside entities within-the-world."[25] To come to know the meaning of being in general thus required as a preliminary step

---

20 Heidegger, *Being and Time*, 228–235.   21 Heidegger, *Being and Time*, 29.
22 Heidegger, *Being and Time*, 26.
23 The dual aspect of these ontologies, their rooting in primordial experience, but betrayal of it through a process of "hardening," meant that destruction would never be entirely negative. Heidegger, *Being and Time*, 43–44.
24 Heidegger, *Being and Time*, 32. Heidegger distinguished here between "understanding being" and "knowing the meaning of being."
25 Heidegger, *Being and Time*, 415. See also Heidegger *Being and Time*, 183–188, where he links understanding and projection; and Martin Heidegger, "What Is Metaphysics," in Martin Heidegger, *Basic Writings*, ed. David Farrell Krell (San Francisco: Harper, 1993), 106.

the clarification of the meaning of our own type of being, which in turn required the authentic grasp of Dasein's possibilities.[26] That is why Heidegger could argue in *Being and Time* that *"fundamental ontology, from which alone all other ontologies can take their rise,"* must be sought in the *"analytic of Dasein."*[27] The promised second volume, which would move from this analytic to raise the question of the "meaning of being in general," never came.[28] As Herbert Spiegelberg has written, Heidegger's book is an "astonishing torso."[29]

The question of transcendence and authenticity informed Heidegger's understanding of historicity. We are embedded in a context and tradition, which could become authentic only if we "resolutely" make it our own.[30] As Heidegger explained to his student Karl Löwith in 1936, this reasoning had led him to embrace Nazism. In 1933, just after Hitler's seizure of power, Heidegger placed his ideas at the service of the new regime. In return he was appointed Rector of the University of Freiburg, and he participated in the Aryanization of the university, a process that led to the exclusion of Heidegger's teacher and mentor, Edmund Husserl. Though Heidegger's tenure was short and his enthusiasm for the Nazis may have waned, Heidegger never publicly renounced his allegiance, either before or after World War II. Moreover, his recently published "Black Notebooks" reveal how pervasive anti-Semitism was in his thinking; he grafted his arguments about the fallen nature of philosophy and the forgetting of being onto racist tropes about Jewish rootlessness. How Heidegger, probably the most influential European philosopher of the twentieth century, could have been such an enthusiastic and apparently unrepentant supporter of the Nazis has become one of the most pressing questions of modern intellectual history.[31]

---

26 See Heidegger, *Being and Time*, 276; and Thomas Sheehan's reconstruction of the argument in his *Making Sense of Heidegger: A Paradigm Shift* (Lanham: Rowman & Littlefield, 2014), 170–177.
27 Heidegger, *Being and Time*, 34.   28 Heidegger, *Being and Time*, 486.
29 Herbert Spiegelberg, *The Phenomenological Movement*, 3rd edn. (The Hague: Martinus Nijhoff, 1982), 360.
30 See Heidegger, *Being and Time*, 343–348.
31 The literature on Heidegger and Nazism is vast. Classic studies include Tom Rockmore, *On Heidegger's Nazism and Philosophy* (Berkeley: University of California Press, 1991); Hugo Ott, *Martin Heidegger: A Political Life* (New York: Basic Books, 1993); Hans Sluga, *Heidegger's Crisis* (Cambridge: Harvard University Press, 1993); and Julian Young, *Heidegger, Philosophy, Nazism* (Cambridge: Cambridge University Press, 1997). On the "Black Notebooks" in particular, see Andrew J. Mitchell and Peter Trawny (eds.), *Heidegger's Black Notebooks: Responses to Anti-Semitism* (New York: Columbia University Press, 2017). For further evidence that Heidegger's Nazism and his philosophy cannot easily be separated, see, for example, Martin Heidegger, *Nature, History, State: 1933–1934*, ed. Gregory Fried and Richard Polt (London: Bloomsbury, 2013).

It was a question that troubled Karl Jaspers (1883–1969), the man who had introduced Kierkegaard to Heidegger in the first place. Jaspers had been close to Heidegger in the 1920s, and the two of them shared a sense of historical and social crisis, which the former diagnosed in his 1931 bestseller *Die geistige Situation der Zeit*. There Jaspers lamented contemporary nihilism, and the threat posed to the individual by the "masses," a product of modern industry and standardization. But Jaspers broke with Heidegger over the latter's embrace of Nazism. Given his hostility to the regime, Jaspers was removed from his university post in 1937, and he and his Jewish wife were saved from deportation to the camps only by the allied victory over Germany in April 1945.[32]

Jaspers's most important contribution to existentialism was the three-volume *Philosophie* from 1932, his first major publication in over ten years. The first volume dealt with the objective sciences, which sought to study humanity like any other object. But, as Jaspers argued, such studies necessarily missed concrete human subjectivity, what Jaspers, following Kierkegaard, called *Existenz*.[33] First, *Existenz* was a condition for the objective sciences, and so could not be their object.[34] Second, these sciences ignored human freedom. *Existenz* was *possible* existence, and, because they could not foreclose a future choice, all descriptions were provisional. For Jaspers as for Kierkegaard, the individual was higher than the universal, and couldn't be exhaustively determined. Instead Jaspers declared that *Existenz* could only be "clarified"; this was the subject of the second volume of his *Philosophie*.

Up to this point, Jaspers was not too far from Heidegger. Indeed, he too posed *Existenz* in terms of transcendence, the "transcending" of any particular situation, which was crucial to human freedom. In "limit situations," such as struggle, death, guilt, and suffering, our comfortable self-understandings broke down.[35] We were in Jaspers's terms "shipwrecked," confronted with our finitude, our inability to grasp being as such. Nevertheless, in these moments we became aware of what surpassed our finite horizons, a transcendence, which we could either choose to follow or deny.[36] As Jaspers

---

32 Charles Frederic Wallraff, *Karl Jaspers: An Introduction to his Philosophy* (Princeton: Princeton University Press, 1970), 8–9.
33 See Karl Jaspers, *Existenzphilosophie* (Berlin: Walter de Gruyter, 1938), 1. For Jaspers's reading of Kierkegaard, see the survey by István Czakó, "Karl Jaspers: A Great Awakener's Way to Philosophy of Existence," in *Kierkegaard and Existentialism*, ed. Jon Stewart (Farnham: Routledge, 2011), 155–198.
34 See Karl Jaspers, *Philosophie*, 4th edn., 3 vols. (Berlin: Springer, 1973), vol. I. *Existenz*, along with the World and Transcendence, was what Jaspers later called the "encompassing" (*das Umgreifende*). See Jaspers, *Existenzphilosophie*, 15.
35 See Jaspers, *Philosophie*, vol. II, 201–254; and vol. III, 68.
36 Jaspers, *Philosophie*, vol. III, 4–5.

wrote, in these situations transcendence "reaches out its hand, if only I take it."[37]

Heidegger and Jaspers understood this transcendence in different ways.[38] For Jaspers transcendence didn't allow Dasein to move from entities to their being, and thus open up the possibility of a general ontology. Rather it showed that such an ontology was impossible, and it pointed to a beyond that on occasion Jaspers identified with God.[39] Jaspers's account sought to ward off two errors, which in different ways failed to recognize how transcendence troubled human cognitive mastery. First, he attacked secular philosophy for shutting out and ignoring transcendence. Second, influenced by Nietzsche's "Death of God," he criticized the way in which religious traditions had substantialized it, in particular by their appeal to revelation.[40] Jaspers tried to carve a path between the two: a purely philosophical account of transcendence, which nonetheless did not shoehorn it into conceptual form, an ontology. Though we couldn't give a fully fleshed-out account of transcendence, Jaspers thought, we were able to contemplate its "ciphers," in art, religion, philosophy, or nature, where transcendence was disclosed, even if never fully.[41]

Christian Existentialism

German existentialism thus was divided on its understanding of transcendence. Did the movement of transcendence reawaken the question of being through a clear-sighted recognition of human finitude, or did it rather show how the finite human being was touched by a higher power? In the first flowering of existentialism outside of Germany, the second option had precedence, for it rendered existentialism susceptible to religious appropriation. Crucial to this appropriation was the work of Gabriel Marcel (1889–1973) in France. Marcel had read Jaspers's *Philosophie* in early 1932, and published the first article on it outside of Germany two years later.[42] Moreover, in the

37 Jaspers, *Philosophie*, vol. III, 68.
38 For an analysis of these differences, especially with respect to the "limit situation," see Peter E. Gordon, "German Existentialism and the Persistence of Metaphysics," in *Situating Existentialism*, ed. Robert Bernasconi and Jonathan Judaken (New York: Columbia University Press, 2012), 65–88.
39 See for instance Jaspers, *Existenzphilosophie*, 17–18.
40 See Jaspers, *Existenzphilosophie*, 72–78. For Jaspers's reading of Nietzsche, see C. Bambach, "Rethinking the 'Existential' Nietzsche in Germany," in *Situating Existentialism*, ed. Robert Bernasconi and Jonathan Judaken (New York: Columbia University Press, 2012), 305–335.
41 Jaspers, *Philosophie*, vol. III, 160.
42 Gabriel Marcel, "Situation fondamentale et situations limites chez Karl Jaspers," in *Recherches Philosophiques*, 2 (1932/1933), 317–348, p. 348.

famous soirées at his Latin Quarter home, Marcel presented Jaspers and existentialism more generally to a number of the most important philosophers in France, including Paul Ricœur, Emmanuel Lévinas, Maurice Merleau-Ponty, de Beauvoir, and Sartre.[43]

Like Jaspers, Marcel constructed his philosophy around the concrete and embodied subject. For Marcel objects could be said to exist only to the extent that they were, or could be, placed in relationship to the body. But this imposed limits upon the objective sciences. We could only examine existence objectively, presenting it as something "before me," by denying our embodiment, our own participation in existence. Questions in which we were ourselves implicated – questions about being, God, or evil for instance – were "mysteries." They escaped objective analysis and could be approached only through non-objectifying means: fidelity, hope, and love. Moreover, such mysteries, Marcel argued, suggested that we participated in a transcendent reality, which we could experience but never fully grasp, while fidelity, hope, and love could be fully explained only if they were secured by a transcendent God.[44] For Marcel, then, the way the existential subject challenged the objective sciences made room for faith. The strongly religious tones of Marcel's philosophy informed his critique of Jaspers's purely "philosophical" account of transcendence. For Marcel, if transcendence were deprived of its religious meaning, it would lose its "vital drive."[45]

While transcendence pointed toward God, Marcel nonetheless thought that it posed a challenge to Catholic orthodoxy, with which he had struggled in part due to his friendship with the Thomist Jacques Maritain. Thomists sought a conceptual understanding of being as a first step toward proving the existence of God; the order we could discern in the created universe was evidence that it was God's handiwork. For Marcel, however, Thomists had failed to see the "obscurity" at the heart of being, the way transcendence necessarily escaped our intellectual grasp. For Marcel, God was accessed through faith and prayer, and it was a mistake to think that his existence could ever simply be known.[46]

We see similar understandings of the relationship between the concrete and transcendence in other members of Marcel's study circle: An analysis of

---

43 See François Dosse, *Paul Ricœur: Un philosophe dans son siècle* (Paris: Armand Colin, 2012), 28–30.
44 See especially Gabriel Marcel, *Être et avoir*, new edn. (Paris: Presses Universitaires de France, 1995), 82–87.
45 Marcel, "Situation fondamentale et situations limites chez Karl Jaspers," 346–348.
46 Marcel, *Être et avoir*, 73.

the existential subject implied the inadequacy of objective knowledge, and pointed to a form of transcendence. Take, for instance, René Le Senne (1882–1954) in his *Obstacle et valeur* (1934). Le Senne argued that an examination of human experience in its existential fullness showed that we constantly confronted "obstacles" that challenged our attempts to grasp the world. Nevertheless, the fact that we experienced obstacles as something in our way suggested that they did not limit us in any simple sense. We must be able to "transcend" them and enlarge our conceptual categories, even if a new obstacle would inevitably challenge this new "determination" in turn.[47] For Le Senne the ability to transcend the obstacle was evidence of our participation in the divine.[48]

The attempt to articulate a heterodox religious philosophy out of existentialism, to see in the limits of human rational knowledge the intimations of a higher power, allowed these thinkers to break out of the parochialism to which philosophy is often consigned. This was the case in Paris, where a common religious sensibility and resistance to Thomism brought Marcel close to the Russian Orthodox Nikolai Berdyaev (1874–1948). Expelled from Russia after the revolution, Berdyaev had arrived in Paris in the 1920s. He participated in Marcel's soirées and first aligned himself with existentialism in the 1933 French translation of his book *Esprit et liberté*. Just as for Marcel, existentialism affirmed Berdyaev's attempt to place the concrete human subject at the center of the philosophical project, what he termed "personalism."[49] If we understood humans as emotional and willing beings, in addition to thinking ones, Berdyaev argued, we would recognize the inadequacy of all, but especially Thomist, accounts of being, and the priority of our personal relationship to God. Formed in the image of God, humans were creative and free.[50] The close association Berdyaev constructed between freedom and faith allowed him to relate existentialism to his own Russian literary tradition, especially Dostoyevsky.[51] Similar arguments resonated in the émigré Russian community in Paris, and informed the work of

---

47 René Le Senne, *Obstacle et valeur* (Paris: F. Aubier, 1934), 149–152.
48 Le Senne, *Obstacle et valeur*, 10.
49 Nikolai Berdyaev, *Cinq Méditations sur l'existence* (Paris: F. Aubier, 1936), 21. See also pp. 37, 49, and 74.
50 This stance also strongly influenced Berdyaev's understanding of God as a person, see Antoine Arjakovsky, *The Way: Religious Thinkers of the Russian Emigration in Paris and Their Journal, 1925–1940*, ed. John A. Jillions and Michael Plekon, trans. Jerry Ryan (Notre Dame: University of Notre Dame Press, 2013), 297.
51 See Val Vinokur, "Russian Existentialism, or Existential Russianism," in *Situating Existentialism*, ed. Robert Bernasconi and Jonathan Judaken (New York: Columbia University Press, 2012), 37–64.

Existentialism and the Meanings of Transcendence

Lev Shestov (1866–1938). Shestov used existentialist ideas to break out from the imprisoning rationalism of "Athens" (associated in Shestov's eyes with Thomism), toward the liberating faith of "Jerusalem."[52]

The value of existentialism for comprehending religious transcendence while distancing it from Catholic orthodoxy also helped gain it adherents outside of Paris. It allowed the writings of heterodox Catholic Miguel de Unamuno in Spain to be incorporated into the existentialist canon,[53] and marked much of the early reading of Heidegger in both Europe and America.[54] So too existentialism spread along an axis of non-Thomist Catholic thinkers reaching from Le Senne in Paris, through his student Gaston Berger in Marseille, to Augusto Guzzo in Turin.[55] The precedence of religious networks meant that many Italians first came to the German existentialists through the French. As Guzzo wrote, Marcel's work "led many Italians to take an interest in Jaspers, in existentialism in general, and also in Heidegger."[56] On this basis Guzzo sent his student Luigi Pareyson to Germany and France to study the movement at its source.[57] When Pareyson returned, he became an important writer on existentialism, and his essays collected in the 1943 *Studi sull'esistenzialismo* brought him to the heart of the conversation. Like his teacher, Pareyson leaned toward the more "optimistic" and religious account of the French existentialists, arguing that "the true master of true existentialism is without doubt Augustine."[58]

Christian existentialists claimed that transcendence could not be identified with any determined account of God. Others, like Marcel's friend Jean Wahl (1888–1974), wondered whether it needed to be understood as divine at all.

52 For the relationships between the two see Arjakovsky, *The Way*, 282–285 and 296–303.
53 See Eduardo Mendieta, "Existentialisms in the Hispanic and Latin American Worlds: El Quixote and Its Existential Children," in *Situating Existentialism*, ed. Robert Bernasconi and Jonathan Judaken (New York: Columbia University Press, 2012), 180–207; and George Pattison, *Anxious Angels: A Retrospective View of Religious Existentialism* (New York: St. Martin's Press, 1999), 194–201.
54 For the impact of religious philosophy on the reception of Heidegger, see for instance, Roberto Tommasi, *"Essere e tempo" di Martin Heidegger in Italia (1928–1948)* (Rome: Glossa, 1993); Martin Woessner, *Heidegger in America* (Cambridge: Cambridge University Press, 2011); and Samuel Moyn, *Origins of the Other: Emmanuel Levinas between Revelation and Ethics* (Ithaca: Cornell University Press, 2005).
55 Augusto Guzzo, "Gaston Berger et l'Italie," *Les Études Philosophiques*, 16(4) (1961), 401–405, pp. 401–402.
56 See Augusto Guzzo, "Bilancio dell'esistenzialismo in Italia," *Logos: Rivista Internazionale di Filosofia*, 1 (1942), 103–107, p. 104.
57 The lectures were collected in his 1940 book, Augusto Guzzo, *Sguardi su la filosofia contemporanea* (Rome: Parella, 1940). For Le Senne see pp. 35–38.
58 Luigi Pareyson, "Genesi e significato dell'esistenzialismo," in *Giornale Critico della Filosofia Italiana*, 5 (1940), 326–337, pp. 334–335; and Luigi Pareyson, *La filosofia dell'esistenza e Carlo Jaspers* (Naples: Loffredo, 1940), x.

Taking Jaspers's account of transcendence, Wahl provided the opposite criticism to Marcel. Jaspers did not err in failing to take religious orthodoxy seriously; he went wrong in thinking that transcendence necessarily pointed to a religious "beyond."[59] Wahl wondered whether this was not simply "the product of one of those objectifications, of those fixations Jaspers denounces."[60] In the language he would adopt later in the decade, it remained unclear to Wahl whether the movement Jaspers described was a trans-ascendance or a trans-descendance, toward Gods or demons, or perhaps simply toward nature: Did it really touch the divine?[61]

Communism and Existentialism

The close relationship between Jaspers's thought and the rise of Christian existentialism suggested that a truly secular form of existentialism might find surer ground in the work of Martin Heidegger. Such an idea informed the writings of Jean-Paul Sartre (1905–1980). Sartre grew up in a bourgeois family in Paris, and was a star student at the elite Parisian École Normale Supérieure at the end of the 1920s. Disillusioned with academic philosophy in France, he had been attracted to Husserlian phenomenology in the 1930s, and in the midst of the Nazi seizure of power had traveled to Berlin in 1933 to read more.[62] After his return, Husserl became the major influence on Sartre's essays. Nevertheless, an important turning point in Sartre's philosophy was his reading of Heidegger, which he began to do seriously only after he had been captured following the disastrous French defeat in 1940. In a German prison camp Sartre managed to get his hands on a copy of Heidegger's *Being and Time*, which helped inspire his own major philosophical contribution from 1943, *Being and Nothingness*.

Sartre argued that, in our experience of the world, we were confronted not simply with appearances, but with "being-in-itself." Consciousness is intentional, which means that it is always consciousness *of* something (see Chapter

---

59 Jean Wahl, "Le problème du choix, l'existence et la transcendance dans la philosophie de Jaspers," *Revue de Métaphysique et de Morale*, 41(3) (1934), 405–444, p. 429.
60 Wahl, "Le problème du choix," 441–442. See also Jean Wahl, "Subjectivité et transcendance," *Bulletin de la Société Française de Philosophie*, 37(5) (1937), 161–211, which deals with the attempt to secularize Jaspers's thought. For Jean Wahl, see Stefanos Geroulanos, *An Atheism That Is Not Humanist Emerges in French Thought* (Stanford: Stanford University Press, 2010).
61 See Wahl, "Subjectivité et transcendance," 161–162.
62 For Sartre's life see Annie Cohen-Solal, *Sartre: A Life*, trans. Anna Cancogni (New York: Pantheon, 1987); and Thomas R. Flynn, *Sartre: A Philosophical Biography* (Cambridge: Cambridge University Press, 2014).

4 by Dan Zahavi). In his early essay on intentionality, Sartre described consciousness as a strong wind constantly casting us out into the world.[63] That is why Sartre rejected both the Kantian idea that the real thing lay in some way behind appearances, and the Berkeleyan idea that it could be identified with them.[64] In an experience that corresponds to Heidegger's "anxiety," we are confronted with brute existence, being that simply is, without rhyme or reason. In his earlier novels, such as *Nausea* (1938), Sartre had described the massiveness of this "being-in-itself" in the language of excess; surpassing all our attempts to define it, it was vast and inexplicable.[65]

The way we encountered being-in-itself, Sartre thought, shed light on the being of human consciousness, or "being-for-itself." Though we grasped the in-itself in perception, we could not grasp a whole entity in one go; we perceived only one aspect at a time. To move beyond finite manifestations, Sartre argued, the subject had to be able to "transcend the appearance towards the total series of which it is a member," toward the "transphenomenal" being which was the condition of appearance.[66] This movement of transcendence showed that, unlike the in-itself, the for-itself could not be characterized by absolute presence or self-identity. Its condition was "nonbeing," which was, in Sartre's language, like a "worm" constantly disrupting being-in-itself.[67] That is, while the in-itself is stable and self-identical, the for-itself is "what it is not and ... not what it is."[68] These analyses led Sartre to a dualist ontology of for-itself and in-itself, which informed all of his work.

By rooting transcendence in "nothingness" Sartre cast Kierkegaard's subject in profane terms.[69] He no longer coupled human freedom to religious faith. Thus, when Sartre famously presented humans as those beings for whom "existence precedes essence," he did so by rejecting the idea of a creator God, who could create the human essence in advance.[70] Instead we are left alone in the world with the terrible responsibility to choose our own

---

63 Jean-Paul Sartre, "Intentionality: A Fundamental Idea of Husserl's Phenomenology," *Journal for the British Society for Phenomenology*, 1(2) (1970), 4–5, p. 5.
64 Sartre, *Being and Nothingness*, 3.
65 Jean-Paul Sartre, *Nausea*, trans. Lloyd Alexander (New York: New Directions, 1975), 131.
66 Sartre, *Being and Nothingness*, 7–9. He related this to Heidegger's transcendence to being. See also Sartre, *Being and Nothingness*, 24.
67 Sartre, *Being and Nothingness*, 49–56. 68 Sartre, *Being and Nothingness*, 785.
69 For an incisive analysis of Sartre's debt to Kierkegaard, especially concerning the concept of "authenticity," see Noreen Khawaja, *The Religion of Existence: Asceticism in Philosophy from Kierkegaard to Sartre* (Chicago: Chicago University Press, 2017).
70 Jean-Paul Sartre, *Existentialism Is a Humanism*, trans. Carol Macomber (New Haven: Yale University Press, 2007), 22.

ends. We were, Sartre argued, "condemned to be free." The denial of this freedom was itself an act of freedom, and thus self-contradictory, what Sartre called "bad faith."

In the immediate postwar period, Sartre's thought caused a sensation. For an older generation, existentialism represented all that was immoral and crude. For many young people, however, it heralded new forms of liberation. Existentialism's influence in the period can be attributed to the way Sartre was able to insert his thought into the post-liberation moment. He engaged with the central debates of the French national election at the time and discussed writerly responsibility and choice, which had become major issues for a nation trying to grapple with a legacy of collaboration during the Nazi occupation.[71] But, most importantly, Sartre was able to find relevance for his thought by aligning it with one of the dominant political forces of the moment: Communism. In a period when Communists had gained great prestige through their service to the French resistance and the Soviet role in World War II, the French Communist Party (PCF) grew quickly to become the largest party in the nation and Sartre began his thirty-year struggle with "the unsurpassable philosophy of our time."[72]

Sartre engineered this alignment through his analysis of transcendence. In *Existentialism Is a Humanism*, Sartre took transcendence as his starting point: "man is always outside of himself ... it is in pursuing transcendent goals that he is able to exist."[73] But while the choice of goals was an individual one, Sartre was also adamant that it was not a "gratuitous act" subject to our fleeting whim. For human anxiety arose from the fact that, when we chose, we necessarily chose "for all men."[74] To proclaim that others "do as I say and not as I do" was for Sartre a form of bad faith, simultaneously affirming an action as wrong (what I say) and as right (what I do). Further, since good faith, or authenticity, depended upon an acceptance of our own freedom, it demanded that we fight for that freedom for all.[75] In laying out a common human "condition," Sartre posed transcendence, the struggling against the limitations of a situation, as a form of human universality, an "absolute" free commitment above the "relativity of the cultural ensemble."[76] As Sartre implied, it required that we fight against slavery, fight against colonialism,

---

[71] See Patrick Baert, *The Existentialist Moment: The Rise of Sartre as a Public Intellectual* (Cambridge: Polity Press, 2015).

[72] Jean-Paul Sartre, *The Search for a Method*, trans. Hazel E. Barnes (New York: Alfred A. Knopf, 1963).

[73] Sartre, *Existentialism Is a Humanism*, 52.   [74] Sartre, *Existentialism Is a Humanism*, 24.

[75] Sartre, *Existentialism Is a Humanism*, 48–49.   [76] Sartre, *Existentialism Is a Humanism*, 43.

and fight against capitalist exploitation.[77] Sartre's desire to link his philosophy to revolutionary socialism is also visible in his new journal *Les Temps Modernes,* which he founded with Raymond Aron, Simone de Beauvoir, and Maurice Merleau-Ponty in 1945. Though he denied that the journal had a political program, Sartre did assert that it was concerned with social transformation, and he spoke approvingly of revolutionary action by the proletariat.[78]

Using his account of transcendence to graft his philosophy onto revolutionary socialism raised the question of relating the individualist project of existentialism to the communal political action demanded by the Communists. Over the next fifteen years, this would be Sartre's greatest theoretical and practical challenge. As de Beauvoir wrote, "in 1944 [Sartre] thought that any situation could be transcended by a subjective movement ... by 1951, he knew that circumstances sometimes rob us of our transcendence; against them no individual salvation is possible, only a collective struggle."[79] Sartre began to develop his arguments in a set of articles from 1952, *The Communists and the Peace,* which, against the more pessimistic conclusions of *Being and Nothingness,* argued that class solidarity could produce a real and meaningful "we-subject," one that found its champion in the Communist party acting in the interests of "all men." The importance of communism for this political goal led Sartre to become during the years 1952–1956 a "fellow traveler" of the PCF, putting his pen at the service of a party he nonetheless never joined.

Sartre published his developed ideas on this subject in the 1960 *Critique of Dialectical Reason,* where he shifted the movement of transcendence from consciousness to *praxis,* a human and social engagement with the so-called "practico-inert," calcified and oppressive social structures.[80] Sartre's friend and collaborator Maurice Merleau-Ponty (1908–1961) also came to embrace communism in the immediate postwar period, most famously in the 1947 *Humanism and Terror.*[81] History did not have a meaning, which was why it

---

77 See for instance Sartre, *Existentialism Is a Humanism,* 36, 42, 47, and 48. See Edward Baring, "Humanist Pretensions: Catholics, Communists, and Sartre's Struggle for Existentialism in Postwar France," *Modern Intellectual History,* 7(3) (2010), 581–609.
78 Jean-Paul Sartre, "Présentation," *Les Temps Modernes,* no. 1 (1945), 1–21, pp. 14–19.
79 Quoted in Jonathan Judaken, "Introduction" to *Race after Sartre: Antiracism, Africana Existentialism, Postcolonialism,* ed. Jonathan Judaken (Albany: SUNY Press, 2008), 2. See also the argument in Thomas R. Flynn, *Sartre and Marxist Existentialism* (Chicago: University of Chicago Press, 1984).
80 For an account of Sartre's critique, see Mark Poster, *Sartre's Marxism* (Cambridge: Cambridge University Press, 1982).
81 For the relationship between Merleau-Ponty's views on religion and on Marxism, see Albert Rabil, *Merleau-Ponty: Existentialist of the Social World* (New York: Columbia University Press, 1967), 215–235.

was necessary to give it one, and Merleau-Ponty found the meaning offered by communism – a story of progressive liberation – the most compelling.[82]

In the period following the fall of the Berlin Wall, Sartre and others have been widely criticized for their embrace of communism. Most famously in his *Past Imperfect*, Tony Judt painted Sartre and Merleau-Ponty as apologists for the Soviet Union.[83] But it is important to recognize that doubts about communism gnawed at Sartre. Indeed, right from his earliest engagement with the Communist Party he did not hide his criticism. Because he was attracted to communism by the way in which it promised a universal liberation of human transcendence, Sartre also attacked what he sometimes called "scholastic Marxism" for denying the agency of the proletariat and claiming that the revolution would occur as a result of the operation of impersonal economic laws. Merleau-Ponty too explained his embrace of communism by citing the lack of better options, and by the early 1950s had come to reject even this stance. In the *Adventures of the Dialectic* he criticized communism for assuming that it could divine the meaning of history, thus shutting out all forms of resistance or criticism.

Most importantly, even at their most enthusiastic, Sartre and other existentialists tended to distance themselves from the institutional heart of Marxism, Stalin's USSR. In *What Is Literature?* (1947) Sartre explicitly repudiated the idea of an alliance with Stalinist communism, which was "incompatible in France with the honest practice of the literary craft";[84] in the 1957 essay "The Phantom of Stalin" Sartre rejected the guiding role of the Communist Party and the Soviet Union; and in the 1960 *Critique* Sartre explained how the pressures of industrialization in the USSR and geopolitical isolation had led to the deformation of Marxism into a form of economic reductionism. True Marxism lay beyond the Soviet Union's institutional reach, and Sartre showed greater sympathy for Trotskyists, anarchists, syndicalists, and later the 68ers, with their demands for "autogestion," than for what he sometimes referred to as the "imperial" ambitions of the Communist East. Democratic revolution, not bureaucratic communism, was always his goal.[85] This idea of an autonomous left, aligned with, but independent of, institutional Communism found concrete form when Sartre partnered with David Rousset in 1947 to found the Rassemblement Démocratique

---

82 See Martin Jay, *Marxism and Totality: The Adventures of a Concept from Lukács to Habermas* (Berkeley: University of California Press, 1984), 370.
83 Tony Judt, *Past Imperfect* (Berkeley: University of California Press, 1992).
84 See Baert, *The Existentialist Moment*, 119.
85 See Ian H. Birchall, *Sartre against Stalinism* (New York: Berghahn Books, 2004), 211–224.

Révolutionnaire, an organization which attempted to find a "third way" between capitalism and communism.[86] Only when this enterprise failed did Sartre declare himself a fellow traveler, and then only until 1956, when the Soviet invasion of Hungary made that position untenable, for Sartre as for many intellectuals on the left.[87]

Sartre dramatized the conflict between doctrinaire Communism and a more pragmatic Communism in his play *Dirty Hands* (1948), where the sympathetic Hoederer is assassinated by the bourgeois intellectual Hugo at the behest of party leaders. The Communist Party responded aggressively. *Dirty Hands* was picketed by angry PCF activists,[88] and from the mid 1940s they sent wave upon wave of party intellectuals to challenge existentialism, even drafting at one point the Hungarian Marxist Georg Lukács.[89] For the Communists, Sartre's emphasis on human transcendence showed him to be the archetypal petit-bourgeois philosopher, and his philosophy, in Henri Lefebvre's memorable words, "the metaphysics of shit."[90]

The existentialists' negotiation with Communism, affirming human transcendence and autonomy against Stalinism even while holding on to the goal of a socialist revolution, raised their profile in the non-French community in Paris. Merleau-Ponty's critical engagement with communism made him an unavoidable interlocutor for the Greek émigrés Cornelius Castoriadis and Kostas Axelos, at the journals *Socialisme ou Barbarie* and *Arguments*, respectively, the latter of which itself had international affiliations to the Italian heterodox Marxist journal *Argomenti*.[91] Similarly, as with the Christians, existentialism's heterodox stance gave it traction further afield. In the United States, Sartre, de Beauvoir, and Merleau-Ponty found a receptive audience in the first years after World War II amongst the anti-Stalinist but Marxisant writers for the *Partisan Review*, and later with the Trotskyist-turned-anti-communist crusader Dwight Macdonald, editor of the leftist

---

86 Birchall, *Sartre against Stalinism*, 94.
87 During this period *Les Temps Modernes* under Sartre's leadership continued to publish criticisms of the Soviet Union and Stalinist Marxism.
88 See Raymond Aronson, *Camus and Sartre: The Story of a Friendship and the Quarrel That Ended It* (Chicago: University of Chicago Press, 2004), 106–107; and Birchall, *Sartre against Stalinism*, 84–89.
89 Georges [Georg] Lukács, *Existentialisme ou marxisme*, trans. E. Kelemen (Paris: Nagel, 1948). For their attacks see Mark Poster, *Existential Marxism in Postwar France: From Sartre to Althusser* (Princeton: Princeton University Press, 1975), Chapter 4.
90 Henri Lefebvre, *Existentialisme* (Paris: Sagittaire, 1946), 82.
91 This did not mean that they were uncritical. For the sharp differences between them, see Poster, *Existential Marxism in Postwar France*, 222–227; and Warren Breckman, *Adventures of the Symbolic: Post-Marxism and Radical Democracy* (New York: Columbia University Press, 2013), 100–112.

review *Politics*, which published translations of their essays.[92] Sartre's essay "Existentialism and Marxism" first appeared in the Polish journal *Twórczość*, and Sartre forged a strong bond with the Italian Communist Party, many of whose members wrote for *Les Temps Modernes*.[93]

Nevertheless, Sartre's misgivings about institutionalized communism provided a possibility for others to attack communism *tout court*, in a way that recalls Wahl's rejection of Christian existentialism. The debate cut right to the heart of the existentialist movement: the friendship between Sartre and Camus. Albert Camus (1913–1960) was one of the early stars of the movement. Camus, who grew up in a working-class district of Oran in Algeria, was a *pied-noir*, a descendant of the European settlers whose families had been embraced as French by the colonial government in the late nineteenth century. Camus's early work was a meditation on the "absurd," which arose from the clash between the human search for meaning and the refusal of the world to furnish it. In *The Myth of Sisyphus*, Camus rejected Kierkegaard's leap of faith and Jaspers's transcendence as vain attempts to flee this absurdity. As Camus argued, we must reject all such transcendent justification and "find out if it is possible to live *without appeal*."[94]

For Camus, appealing to transcendence to impose order on an absurd world produced human suffering and required the brutal silencing of critics. Camus had recognized this in his native Algeria, where poverty was less a result of natural processes than the product of French colonial policy; he railed against these colonial policies in his pre-war journalism. But it became abundantly clear in the Nazis' new order, with its cruel, eliminatory racism. As Camus argued in his 1944 "Letters to a German Friend," the German actions provided a rare justification for violent resistance, and, in the closing years of the war, Camus became an important figure in the French fight against the Nazis, editing the resistance journal *Combat*.

In the postwar period, Camus turned his sights on communism. In his 1951 *The Rebel* (*L'Homme révolté*), Camus argued that, like the Christian heaven, the future communist society was at best a hopeful dream, and yet, it was used to sacrifice the concrete present, justifying violent revolution and the taking of

---

92 See Birchall, *Sartre against Stalinism*, 59; and Mark Greif, *The Age of the Crisis of Man: Thought and Fiction in America, 1933–1973* (Princeton: Princeton University Press, 2015), 66–70.

93 See Michel-Antoine Burnier, *Choice of Action: The French Existentialists on the Political Front Line*, trans. Bernard Murchland (New York: Random House, 1968), 87, 115–116, and 140–141.

94 Albert Camus, *The Myth of Sisyphus*, trans. Justin O'Brien (New York: Vintage, 1991), 53.

lives.[95] From this, Camus famously concluded that Marxism led inevitably to "murder." Instead, Camus put forward Kaliayev, the 1905 Russian Revolutionary who was the central character in Camus's 1949 play *The Just Assassins*, as a model. Kaliayev did not deny the necessity of violent struggle, after all he was a political assassin. But he refused to justify murder to himself or to others by an appeal to a greater, but future and so only potential, good. That is why the play reached its climax with Kaliayev on the scaffold. As Camus wrote, "he kills and dies so that it shall be clear that murder is impossible. He demonstrates that in reality, he prefers the 'We are' to the 'We shall be.'"[96]

Camus's attack on Communism set off a series of events that would lead to his rupture with Sartre.[97] When Sartre, as editor of *Les Temps Modernes*, was sent *The Rebel* for review, he passed it on to his young protégé, Francis Jeanson. Sartre's decision was mostly an attempt to avoid confronting the book himself, and thus antagonizing a friend, but the decision only made the situation worse; Camus read it as a slight. The review itself did not help things. Jeanson was unsparing, piling *ad hominem* attacks on top of an unrelenting and often unfair criticism of Camus's work. He argued that Camus had dispensed with any real analysis of material conditions, seeing oppression merely as a result of ideas. The book was thus the product of a detached intellectual, blithely unaware of the real struggle of the proletariat. Camus complained in a long and embittered letter to Sartre. In Sartre's response, he broke all ties: "Our friendship was not easy, but I will miss it."[98]

In the debate both sides tried to assume the role of the good existentialist, rejecting the ideal and abstract. Camus argued that the communism in which Sartre had placed his faith was an idealist illusion, a new God, who (like the old) demanded bloody sacrifice. Sartre, however, turned this argument against Camus. Camus's rejection of God was so absolute that it blinded him to the true cause of oppression. Sartre claimed that "when a child died, [Camus] blamed the absurdity of the world and this deaf and blind God that [he] created in order to be able to spit in his face. But the child's father ... blamed men." By figuring rebellion as a fight against Gods – by being an "anti-theist" rather than simply an "atheist" – Camus had chosen to ignore the fact that the fundamental

---

95 Albert Camus, *The Rebel: An Essay on Man in Revolt*, trans. Anthony Bower, new edn. (New York: Vintage, 1992), 69.
96 Camus, *The Rebel*, 282.
97 For a narrative account see Aronson, *Camus and Sartre*, 131–154.
98 Jean-Paul Sartre, "Reply to Albert Camus," in *Sartre and Camus*, ed. David Sprintzen (New York: Humanity Press, 2004), 131.

struggle in history was between humans, and consequently that we had to choose a side.[99] For Camus, to be attentive to the concrete was to foreswear violence in the present; for Sartre, it was to recognize that the battle had already been engaged and there was no haven for "beautiful souls."[100]

The Other

Behind the fraught existentialist engagement with communism, one can see the outlines of other social and political projects, the key to which was the existentialist analysis of transcendence and its intersubjective corollary: "othering." In *Being and Time*, Heidegger had paid relatively little attention to this question, and Emmanuel Lévinas (1908–1995) would later deploy our ethical relationship to the Other in order to disrupt what he saw as the deleterious political consequences of Heidegger's ontology.[101] In our face-to-face encounter with other people, Lévinas argued, we encountered an "infinity" that exceeded our conceptual categories, and called us to ethical responsibility. For this reason, ethics, not ontology, counted as "first philosophy."[102]

Others took a different tack. In his famous course on Hegel's *Phenomenology* in the 1930s, the Russian émigré Alexandre Kojève (1902–1968) presented the meeting between two consciousnesses in confrontational terms. A common desire for recognition inaugurated a tragic dialectic of domination and submission between individuals. Though a "slave" chose submission over death, his subordinate position to the "master" undercut the value of his recognition.[103] Sartre rehearsed a similar scenario in *Being and Nothingness*. In what he called the "gaze" (*le regard*), the other reduced us to being-in-itself, "transcended our transcendence."[104] In more prosaic terms, Sartre suggested that other people pigeonholed us, gave us an essence, and thus denied our freedom. This is why, in his play *No Exit*, Sartre could famously claim that "hell is other people."

Sartre first worked out the concrete social consequences of this argument in the 1946 *Anti-Semite and Jew*.[105] Though Sartre argued here that only a social

---

99 Sartre, "Reply to Albert Camus," 153–154.   100 Sartre, "Reply to Albert Camus," 137.
101 See Moyn, *Origins of the Other*.
102 Emmanuel Levinas, *Totality and Infinity: An Essay on Exteriority*, trans. Alphonso Lingis (Pittsburgh: Duquesne University Press, 1969).
103 Alexandre Kojève, *Introduction to the Reading of Hegel*, trans. J. Nichols (New York: Basic Books, 1969).
104 Sartre, *Being and Nothingness*, 352.
105 For an analysis, see Jonathan Judaken, *Jean-Paul Sartre and the Jewish Question: Anti-antisemitism and the Politics of the French Intellectual* (Lincoln: University of Nebraska Press, 2006), 134; and Sarah Hammerschlag, *The Figural Jew: Politics and Identity in Postwar French Thought* (Chicago: Chicago University Press, 2010), Chapter 2.

revolution (implicitly a Communist one) would lead to the end of anti-Semitism, he presented the main problem of racism not as economic exploitation, but rather as "bad faith," the denial of transcendence. Drawing on analyses of the "gaze," Sartre argued that anti-Semites had decided to see the "Jew" as "other," in order to flee their own freedom. They secured their sense of superiority in a racial essence rather than in their own actions.[106] The situation produced by anti-Semites both creates and traps the Jew, according to Sartre, who "cannot choose not to be a Jew."[107] In his argument, Sartre rejected the assimilationist policies of the "democrat," who wishes to "destroy him as a Jew and leave nothing in him but the man." His argument nonetheless fed into a universalizing project of liberation.[108] Sartre claimed that the common recognition of the human condition, both concrete situation and transcendence, was necessary for the freedom of all. As he concluded, "not one Frenchman will be free so long as the Jews do not enjoy the fullness of their rights."[109]

Sartre's argument against othering found its most potent application in the struggle against colonialism, which during France's brutal and costly war of decolonization in Algeria (1954–1962) became a lightning rod for political engagement. Sartre gave a speech at the Salle Wagram in 1956 openly supporting Algerian independence, and was pivotal for the organization of the 1960 "Manifesto of the 121," which affirmed the right of French citizens to "refuse to take arms against the Algerian people." Jeanson, Sartre's protégé in Paris, became a famous "porteur de valises" during the Algerian War, transporting money and medical supplies for the FLN.[110]

The existentialist understanding of colonial othering found resonance around the world. The Barbadan Georges Lamming used Sartre's language when he identified the "Negro" as a "man whom the Other regards as a Negro," while the Franco-Tunisian Albert Memmi drew on Sartre in his *Portrait of the Colonized*.[111] The most famous thinker who reworked existentialist ideas for the colonial situation, however, was Frantz Fanon (1925–1961). Fanon was born and grew up in the French possession of Martinique, fought for the Free French Forces during World War II, and arrived in France for medical training in 1946, first in Paris and then in Lyon. Fanon practised as a psychiatrist

---

106 See Jean-Paul Sartre, *Anti-Semite and Jew*, trans. George J. Becker (New York: Schocken, 1992), 27 and 53–54.
107 Sartre, *Anti-Semite and Jew*, 89.   108 Sartre, *Anti-Semite and Jew*, 57.
109 Sartre, *Anti-Semite and Jew*, 153.
110 See Paige Arthur, *Unfinished Projects: Decolonization and the Philosophy of Jean-Paul Sartre* (London: Verso, 2010).
111 Quoted in David Macey, *Frantz Fanon: A Biography* (New York: Verso, 2012), 165.

in Algeria in the 1950s, where he treated both the victims and the perpetrators of torture, and from early on he made contacts with the anti-colonial forces of the FLN, becoming by the later stages of the war a mouthpiece of the organization.

Though he would not meet Sartre until 1961 in conversations over the latter's preface to Fanon's *The Wretched of the Earth*, Fanon had read Sartre's *Anti-Semite and Jew* and later the *Critique of Dialectical Reason* with great interest. Drawing on the existentialist arguments about how the "Other" creates the self, especially in the unequal situation of colonialism, Fanon nonetheless affirmed human transcendence: "I am not a prisoner of history. I should not seek there for the meaning of my destiny. I should constantly remind myself that the real *leap* consists in introducing invention into existence."[112] As Macey has argued, for Fanon, Sartre's philosophy had to be reformulated to accord with the experience of a black Martiniquan.[113] Fanon too would struggle between the specificity of his own situation and the broader application of an anti-colonial message, a question that has come to the fore in the secondary literature concerning the violence, or more properly counter-violence, that Fanon supported as part of the anti-colonial struggle in Algeria.[114]

The analysis of othering helped raise the profile of existentialism amongst Americans, especially at the beginnings of the Civil Rights movement. After World War II, Sartre's reputation helped shift the center of what Tyler Stovall has called "Paris Noir," the African-American émigré community in the French capital, from Montmartre to Saint-German-des-Prés.[115] Existentialism proved a valuable resource and point of engagement for Richard Wright (1908–1960), who had first met Sartre in New York, and who moved to the Left Bank in 1946. He became friends with de Beauvoir, for whom his wife later became a literary agent, and worked with Camus and Merleau-Ponty, amongst others. In

[112] Frantz Fanon, *Black Skin, White Masks*, trans. C. Markmann (London: Pluto Press, 1986), 179, see also pp. 105–106.
[113] Macey, *Frantz Fanon*, 163–164. See also Peter Hudis, *Frantz Fanon: Philosophy of the Barricades* (London: Pluto Press, 2015), 30–32. Hudis emphasizes how Fanon's optimism about intersubjective relations distances him from Sartre, for whom "Hell is other people."
[114] Camus famously opposed the FLN because of the use of violence, a position which brought great controversy, but has been compellingly defended by David Carroll, *Albert Camus, the Algerian: Colonialism, Terrorism, Justice* (New York: Columbia University Press, 2007). For a contrasting analysis see James D. Le Sueur, *Uncivil War: Intellectuals and Identity Politics during the Decolonization of Algeria* (Philadelphia: University of Pennsylvania Press, 2001).
[115] See Tyler Stovall, *Paris Noir: African Americans in the City of LIght*, 2nd edn. (Boston: Houghton Mifflin, 2012), 169.

Existentialism and the Meanings of Transcendence

1947 Wright was one of the sponsors, alongside Sartre and Camus, of the journal *Présence Africaine*. The engagement between Wright and the existentialists was two-way. Sartre famously quoted Wright in *Anti-Semite and Jew*, arguing that there wasn't a "Negro problem in the United States ... only a White problem,"[116] and Wright drew on existentialist themes in his 1953 novel *The Outsider*.[117] Through Wright existentialist ideas came to be embraced in the African American community in New York, by such writers as Ralph Ellison. As Ellison affirmed, there was "an existential tradition within American Negro life."[118]

The analysis of othering also occupied a central place in the work of Simone de Beauvoir (1908–1986). De Beauvoir's close relationship with Sartre since the late 1920s has raised a significant debate about her own contribution to the development of the latter's ideas. But regardless of the result of that discussion, her 1949 *The Second Sex* shows her to be a powerful thinker in her own right. In that book, de Beauvoir argued in existentialist language that man was the Absolute, woman was the "other," and that this relationship, bolstered by social and economic inequality, defined women's situation. As she put it, because of her situation, a woman's transcendence is "forever transcended by another essential and sovereign consciousness."[119] De Beauvoir's feminism attracted great interest in her work abroad, especially America. Her *Second Sex* was a bestseller there when it was translated in 1953, and both Betty Friedan and Hazel Barnes drew on her example to develop broadly existentialist approaches to feminism.[120]

Conclusion

Existentialism is Janus-faced. Turned toward the concrete, it cautions us against abstract dreams or delusions of universality, and urges us to pay attention to existing reality. But existentialists also claim that we are free, that we can transcend the situation into which we are thrown. Indeed, the way existentialists understood the individual as ek-sistence, both concretely situated and standing out, was crucial to their success. It recommended existentialism to Christians, Communists, anti-colonial revolutionaries, civil rights

---

116 Sartre, *Anti-Semite and Jew*, 152.   117 Stovall, *Paris Noir*, 182–199.
118 George Cotkin, *Existential America* (Baltimore: Johns Hopkins University Press, 2005), 162–167 and 175–184.
119 Simone de Beauvoir, *The Second Sex*, trans. Constance Borde and Sheila Malovany-Chevallier (New York: Vintage, 2011), 16–17.
120 See Cotkin, *Existential America*, 151–158.

protesters, and feminists the world over. By the early 1950s existentialism was a "French" philosophy that could be found everywhere. But it proved difficult to define precisely what existentialist transcendence meant. Moreover, the appeal to transcendence disrupted the institutions to which various intellectuals attempted to graft their thought. Some tried to square this circle by adopting oppositional stances; they were Christians, but not orthodox; they were communists, but critical of the Soviet Union. But even these positions proved difficult to maintain, and opened multiple fissures between leading proponents of the movement. Ironically, the very aspects of existentialism that gave it international reach also pulled it apart.

6
Philosophies of Life

GIUSEPPE BIANCO

"Philosophy of life" is currently employed as a synonym or as a hyponym of "vitalism," "philosophy of nature," and "biological philosophy," labeling texts produced in completely different historical, geographic, and disciplinary contexts and bearing only certain family resemblances.[1] The expressions *"Philosophie des Lebens"* and *"Lebensphilosophie"* first appeared during the 1770s in the writings of mutually independent, non-academic German authors linked to the Romantic movement, such as Karl Philipp Moritz (1756–1793). Starting from the 1910s, they re-emerged in two essays written respectively by the Neo-Kantian philosopher Heinrich Rickert (1863–1936) and by the phenomenologist Max Scheler (1874–1928). With these key expressions, the two philosophers designated the doctrines of three other, older producers of philosophy, Friedrich Nietzsche (1844–1900), Henri Bergson (1859–1941), and Wilhelm Dilthey (1833–1911), who, nonetheless, never quoted one another, never met, and did not explicitly define their own work as a "philosophy of life"; after World War I, Rickert added to this small group of authors select other philosophers such as his colleague Georg Simmel (1858–1918), the phenomenologist Edmund Husserl (1859–1938), and the pragmatist William James (1842–1910), despite the fact that they were not connected in any way. They also did not employ these expressions. Starting from the 1920s, the expressions *Philosophie des Lebens*

---

[1] Recent studies on the topic include Karl Albert, *Lebensphilosophie: Von den Anfängen bei Nietzsche bis zu ihrer Kritik bei Lukács* (Freiburg im Breisgau: Alber, 1995); Ferdinand Fellmann, *Lebensphilosophie: Elemente einer Theorie der Selbsterfahrung* (Reinbek bei Hamburg: Rowohlt, 1993); Ferdinand Fellmann, "Lebensphilosophie," in *Enzyklopädie Philosophie*, vol. 2, ed. Hans Jörg Sandkühler (Hamburg: Felix Meiner, 2010); Jürgen Große, *Lebensphilosophie* (Stuttgart: Reclam, 2010); Robert Josef Kozljanič (ed.), *Lebensphilosophie: Eine Einführung* (Stuttgart: Kohlhammer, 2004); Volker Schürmann, *Die Unergründlichkeit des Lebens: Lebens-Politik zwischen Biomacht und Kulturkritik* (Bielefeld: Transcript, 2011); and Gerald Hartung, Lebensphilosophie, in *Das Leben II: Historisch-Systematische Studien zur Geschichte eines Begriffs*, ed. Stephan Schaede, Gerald Hartung, and Tom Kleffmann (Tübingen: Mohr Siebeck, 2012), 309–326.

and *Lebensphilosophie* spread in Germany, being used both by non-academic producers of philosophy – such as Oswald Spengler (1880–1936) and Ludwig Klages (1872–1956) – and by such academics as Dilthey's former student Georg Misch (1878–1965). During the Third Reich, while *völkisch* ideology took over Germany, many other minor cultural producers, promoting the regime's bio-political agenda, presented themselves, or were treated, as *Lebensphilosophen*; however, starting from the 1940s, their work was quickly forgotten. Between the end of the 1920s and the 1940s, with the translation of some of the aforementioned authors' works into other languages, and the production in various languages of secondary literature dedicated to their work, the expression "philosophy of life" entered more common usage, being applied to the doctrines of other authors whose work was supposedly characterized by a metaphysical conception of life conceived as an original transformative force, and by their reliance on a method or a faculty irreducible to the ones used by science. Finally, from the 1970s on, the expression "philosophy of life" – *"philosophie de la vie," "filosofia della vita," "Lebensphilosophie"* – began to designate non-empirical doctrines stating the priority of "life" conceived as a principle irreducible to physico-chemical causality or theories concerning "life" addressed to a broad lectureship. The work of philosophers as different as Georges Canguilhem (1904–1995), Maurice Merleau-Ponty (1908–1961), Gilles Deleuze (1925–1995), and Michel Foucault (1924–1984), or even that of early modern philosophers such as Baruch Spinoza, started being classed under the banner "philosophy of life," again despite the fact that none of these authors ever employed the expression.

To understand this process of growing polysemy of the expression, it is necessary to consider it as the effect of a transformation that affected the terms "philosophy" and "life"; this transformation was the result of the increasing division and specialization of intellectual labor which triggered polemics and negotiations among protagonists of four types: (a) academic philosophers, (b) non-academic producers of philosophy, (c) academic producers of empirically based knowledge about biological and human phenomena – mainly naturalists, embryologists, physiologists,[2] and, later on, psychologists and sociologists – and, finally, starting from the 1930s, (d) ideologists tied to state apparatuses.

---

2 Robert J. Richards, *Darwin and the Emergence of Evolutionary Theories of Mind and Behaviour* (Chicago: University of Chicago Press, 1987).

The Birth of "Life" and the Birth of "Philosophy"

Since the time of early modernity the word "life" (*vita, vie, Leben*) had been used to designate both human existence and what characterizes a particular class of phenomena, living beings. To differentiate the first meaning from the second, one used theological expressions, such as *"vie spirituelle," "geistiges Leben,"* or *"vie intérieure,"* and, starting from the 1870s, *"Erlebnis."* According to Giorgio Agamben's controversial thesis, this ambiguity was already present in ancient philosophy, in the distinction between *bios* (βίος) – or "qualified life," life proper to man, a political animal (*zōon politikon*) – and *zoê* (ζωή) – "bare life," biological life, the life proper to individuals deprived of rights inside the Greek *polis*.[3]

According to Michel Foucault's *The Order of Things*, it is only at the end of the eighteenth century that a consistent notion of biological life appears. Before, as Foucault famously wrote, "life did not exist."[4] Two key phenomena had been essential for the emergence of the modern notion of life: The first is the appearance of "vitalism," a type of endeavor proper to medical theories and practices, which isolated a distinct class of phenomena; the second is the work of naturalists, who contributed by unifying and specifying this class. In 1802, the term "biology" had been used by Treviranus, in his *Biology, or Philosophy of Living Nature*, and by Jean-Baptiste de Lamarck (1744–1829), in his *Research on the Organization of Living Bodies*. Both affirmed the existence of a science having a peculiar object: life. The "birth" of life, located at the convergence of the practice of medicine and natural sciences, implied a mutation of the image of nature, which was conceived as an historical and unitary process. Biology changed also the image of "man": By inscribing the history of humanity inside the history of life and by reducing man to one living being among others, the newborn science represented an impressive blow both against anthropocentrism and against the religious beliefs supporting it.

At the same moment, the word "philosophy" became involved in a transformation related to the one involving the term "life." During the seventeenth and eighteenth centuries, the term had been semantically unstable, designating texts produced both inside and outside academic spaces, a part of which would today be labeled as "science." By contrast, at the beginning of the nineteenth century, the word was used to indicate

---

3 Giorgio Agamben, *Homo Sacer: Sovereign Power and Bare Life*, trans. Daniel Heller-Roazen (Stanford: Stanford University Press, 1998).
4 Michel Foucault, *The Order of Things*, trans. Alan Sheridan (London: Routledge, 1970), 139.

a particular cognitive practice, taking place mainly inside the university, aimed at providing a logical and synthetic ground for the totality of human knowledge and values. Immanuel Kant (1724–1804) was among the protagonists of this change, which led to institutional consequences throughout Europe because of the Humboldtian reform of the medieval university:[5] He granted the "scientists" – a word that progressively came to substitute for the term "natural philosopher" – the task of explaining phenomena, and to the "philosophers" he gave the responsibility of studying their conditions of possibility. On the one hand, the natural world would be studied experimentally following the *a priori* categories of causality, space and time, etc., thus it would perforce be deprived of all purposiveness. On the other hand, the idea of will and agency would henceforth be limited to human subjectivity.

Even if Kant had placed life in continuity with inanimate matter, in his *Critique of Judgment* (1790), he left a breach open for a possible dynamic and teleological description of it. By admitting that the hypothesis of the existence of purposiveness in nature had a heuristic utility, he suggested to naturalists notions such as *Bildungstrieb* (formative force) and *Lebenskraft* (vital force).[6] After Kant, thinkers such as Johann Wolfgang Goethe (1749–1852) and Friedrich Schelling (1775–1854) opposed the limitations imposed by the author of the three *Critiques*. Their doctrines, known as *Naturphilosophie*, attempted to provide a metaphysical framework capable of giving a meaning to the new science of life and to discoveries such as electromagnetism. These authors, who were describing a non-deterministic universe animated by spiritual forces, were influenced by Romanticism's reaction against a narrow Enlightenment rationalism and the Industrial Revolution, namely by its emphasis on feeling and immediacy, by its insistence on affective and intuited experience as opposed to the narrowness of rationality, and, finally, by its search for a unifying principle prior to the "abstractions" of scientific reason. In France, Schelling influenced the work of the philosopher Félix Ravaisson (1813–1900), who, in his *On Habit* (1837), reintroduced agency and freedom into the mechanistic natural world of Cartesianism, describing a universe organized according to a hierarchy of growing degrees of perfection and freedom. Ravaisson also inherited from Schelling the idea that, because of

---

5 See Randall Collins, *The Sociology of Philosophies: A Global Theory of Intellectual Change* (Boston: Belknap, 1998).
6 See Timothy Lenoir, *The Strategy of Life* (Chicago: Chicago University Press, 1982); and Robert J. Richards, *The Romantic Conception of Life: Science and Philosophy in the Age of Goethe* (Chicago: Chicago University Press, 2002).

nature's purposiveness and creativity, the only way to understand it was by supplementing intellect with an aesthetic intuition.

Meanwhile, in Germany, by 1828, the synthesis of urea – which was aimed at proving the continuity between animate and inanimate matter – and the discovery of the conservation of energy and the formulation of the laws of thermodynamics had caused the decline of *Naturphilosophie* and tipped the scales in favor of the mechanistic theory of life. In 1842, the physiologist and philosopher Hermann Lotze (1817–1881) published an article, "Leben, Lebenskraft," and a book, *Allgemeine Pathologie*, which together constituted an attack against the notion of a "vital force" and, more generally, against all speculative theories of life such as the ones proposed by the *Naturphilosophen*. As a result, starting from the beginning of the 1850s, the majority of German physiologists found themselves in agreement on rejecting vitalism and teleology and supporting a mechanistic view. In France, Auguste Comte (1798–1857) played the same role: He opposed metaphysical notions such as "vital force" and "soul," and refused to draw any analogy between living beings and the human mind.[7]

From the 1860s until the end of the century, the relation between philosophy, dominated by the Kantian approach, and the life sciences, progressively unified by the theory of evolution, had been regulated by a compromise: To the biologists were allocated the facts as interpreted according to a mechanistic causality; to the philosophers, their conditions of possibility.

However, in France, the referential works of Jules Lachelier (1832–1918) – *The Foundation of Induction* (1872) – and Émile Boutroux (1845–1921) – *The Contingency of the Natural Laws* (1874) – which were guided by an original interpretation of the third *Critique*, and influenced by Félix Ravaisson, left the door open for a different approach to nature, once conceived as a universe organized hierarchically according to growing degrees of contingency, freedom, and spirituality. The orientation proper to these philosophers had often been called *"spiritual realism"*,[8] following the expression coined by Ravaisson.

---

7 John A. McCarthy, Stephanie M. Hilger, Heather I. Sullivan, and Nicholas Saul (eds.), *The Early History of Embodied Cognition from 1740–1920: The Lebenskraft-Debate and Radical Reality in German Science, Music, and Literature* (Leiden: Brill, 2016).

8 For "spiritualist realism" and its heritage, see Dominique Janicaud, *Ravaisson et la métaphysique: Une généalogie du spiritualisme français* (Paris: J. Vrin, 1997); François Azouvi, *La Gloire de Bergson: Essai sur le magistère philosophique* (Paris: Presses Universitaires de France, 2007); Giuseppe Bianco, *Après Bergson: Portrait de groupe avec philosophe* (Paris: Presses Universitaires de France, 2015); and Larry S. McGrath, "Alfred Fouillée between Science and Spiritualism," *Journal of the History of Ideas*, 12(2) (2015), 295–323.

On the one hand, these thinkers inscribed man inside the process of evolution and, on the other hand, they insisted that this process was not mechanical, but was teleological or, at least, indeterminate. Nonetheless, just like Eduard von Hartmann (1842–1906) and Nietzsche, these "spiritual realists" occupied peripheral positions in the academic space: Alfred Fouillé (1838–1918) – author of *The Evolutionism of the Ideas-Forces* (1890), his stepson Jean-Marie Guyau (1854–1888) – author of *A Sketch of Morality Independent of Obligation or Sanction* (1885), which deeply influenced Nietzsche – and, finally, Henri Bergson. In his bestseller *The Creative Evolution* (1907), Bergson discussed in detail the theory of evolution, proposing an idea of life as a unitary process of creation irreducible both to mechanical and to teleological explanations. This process was likely to be grasped through the collaboration between biology and philosophy. The latter, using a particular faculty, intuition, was able to guide science and redirect its intellectual efforts. Bergson characterized life by analogy with the *duration* of the human subject he studied in his first two monographs, *Time and Free Will* (1889) and *Matter and Memory* (1898): He conceived both phenomena as temporal processes of enrichment and continuous production of novelty.

"Philosophy of Life" Outside and Inside Academia

During the long nineteenth century, because of the polysemy of the words "life" and "philosophy" and because of the process of disciplinarization, the expression "philosophy of life" was used with two meanings. While in English, French, Spanish, and Italian, the expression was used, though very seldom, as a synonym of biology, in France, in 1838, Auguste Comte introduced the expression "biological philosophy" in his *Cours de philosophie positive* to designate the life sciences. "Biological philosophy" retained this meaning at least until the mid 1920s.

Contrasting with France, in Germany from the 1770s onwards, the terms *Philosophie des Lebens* and *Lebensphilosophie* designated a peculiar literary genre consisting in edifying tales, aphorisms, and "psychological" analysis indicating a wise way of conducting one's existence.[9] The emergence of this popular philosophy had been made possible by the expansion of the book market, by

---

9 See Georg Pflug, "Lebensphilosophie," in *Historisches Wörterbuch der Philosophie*, ed. Joachim Ritter, Karlfried Gründer, and Gottfried Gabriel, 12 vols. (Basel: Schwabe Verlag, 1980), vol. V, 135–140; and Gertrude Kühne-Bertram, *Aus dem Leben, zum Leben: Entstehung, Wesen und Bedeutung populärer Lebensphilosophien in der Geistesgeschichte des 19. Jahrhunderts* (Bern: Peter Lang, 1989).

the existence, since Christian Wolff (1679–1754), of a *"Philosophia practica,"* and, finally, by the existence of a field called "anthropology."[10] This field was popularized by books such as *Anthropologie für Aerzte und Weltweis (Anthropology for Physicians and the Worldwise,* 1772) by the physician Ernst Platner (1744–1818), whose work played a formative role for the most important of these *"Lebensphilosophen,"* namely Karl Philipp Moritz (1756–1793). Moritz had been the author of *Beiträge zur Philosophie des Lebens aus dem Tagebuch eines Freimäurers (Contributions to the Philosophy of Life from the Diary of a Freemason,* 1780), but had also been the editor of one of the first journals of psychology, the *Magazin zur Erfahrungsseelenkunde* (1783–1793). As a result, from the 1780s onward, in connection with a new interest in the French moralists, terms such as *Lebenskunst* (art of living), *Lebenslehre* and *Lebensweisheit* (wisdom in life) began to appear.

This kind of *Lebensphilosophie* shared many features with the Romantic Movement – namely its eclecticism, anti-scholasticism, and anti-academicism. In the years following 1800, the philosopher Wilhelm Traugott Krug (1770–1842) – who would later become Kant's successor in the chair of logic and metaphysics at the University of Königsberg – gave a first formal definition of *"Lebensphilosophie."* He defined it as a *"Philosophie für die Welt"* – a philosophy for everyone, constructed fragmentarily – opposing it to the *"Schulphilosophie"* – the systematic philosophy practised in the academic spaces. This definition appears again in a dictionary published by Krug in 1828[11] and, the same year, in a book by Friedrich von Schlegel (1772–1829), *Philosophie des Lebens*, a collected volume of lectures he gave in Vienna. By defining the object of philosophy as the "inner spiritual life" (*geistige Leben*), Schlegel counterposed the "philosophy of life" to "scholastic philosophy," implicitly designating with this expression the idealism dominating German institutions. In fact, at the same moment, in his *Lectures on the History of Philosophy*, published posthumously (1836), Hegel discredited the genre, considering it a mere continuation of Wolff's *"Philosophia practica."*

After the decline of German idealism, the heritage of this popular and extra-academic "philosophy of life" – combined with that of Romanticism – influenced cultural producers peripheral to the academic institutions, such as

---

10 See Odo Marquard, "Anthropologie," in *Historisches Wörterbuch der Philosophie*, ed. Joachim Ritter, Karlfried Gründer, and Gottfried Gabriel, 12 vols. (Basel: Schwabe Verlag, 1971), vol. I, 362–374; John H. Zammito, *Kant, Herder, and the Birth of Anthropology* (Chicago: University of Chicago Press, 2002).

11 Wilhelm Traugott Krug, *Allgemeines Handwörterbuch der philosophischen Wissenschaften nebst ihrer Literatur und Geschichte* (Leipzig: Brockhaus, 1828).

Schopenhauer and Nietzsche. Both harshly criticized Kantianism and Idealism, the German academic system, and the supposed dogmatism of the empirical sciences; both were influenced by the French moralists and authored books whose titles evoked the approach and the aims of *Lebensphilosophie*. These include, for instance, Schopenhauer's *Aphorisms on the Wisdom of Life* (1841) and Nietzsche's *Gay Science* (1882). Nonetheless, neither Schopenhauer nor Nietzsche used the expressions *"Lebensphilosophie"* or *"Philosophie des Lebens,"* which circulated widely outside of the university.

These expressions appeared again under the pen of an academic in 1913, in an essay entitled "Versuche einer Philosophie des Lebens,"[12] authored by Max Scheler, a disciple of Rudolf Eucken (1846–1926). With this manifesto Scheler tried to intervene strategically in a context marked by a *"Streit,"* a quarrel that appeared between 1895 and 1910 in a conflictual space created by the interaction of protagonists of three types who were fighting to monopolize control of the term "life": (a) academic philosophers, (b) non-academic philosophers, and (c) biologists. This quarrel around life could be renamed the *"Biologismus-Streit"* by analogy with the more renowned *Psychologismus-Streit* to which it was related,[13] and can be considered the origin of the "philosophy of life" of the 1920s, 1930s, and 1940s.

At the center of the *Biologismus-Streit* there was one problem, which can be summarized by the title of the most famous of Scheler's books, namely *The Position of Man in the Cosmos* (1928). This problem was not exclusively theoretical, but practical, as well: Once the place of man had been established, one could also establish what type of knowledge had the last word on man's "human" essence.

Kant and Darwin

Ever since Darwin's *The Descent of Man* (1871), the theory of evolution had tried to give an account of the human phenomenon by locating humans within the framework of a history of life: Hominization was nothing but the result of the combined effect of the process of adaptation and genetic variations. This apparently simple explanation was the result of the convergence of different areas of science that had emerged during the nineteenth

---

12 Max Scheler, "Versuche einer Philosophie des Lebens" (1913–1915), in *Vom Umsturz der Werte: Abhandlungen und Aufsätze* in *Gesammelte Werke*, ed. M. S. Frings and Max Scheler, 16 vols. (Bern: Franke Verlag, 1954–1998), vol. III, 313–339.
13 See Martin Kusch, *Psychologism: A Case Study in the Sociology of Philosophical Knowledge* (London: Routledge, 1998).

century, such as comparative anatomy, paleontology, embryology, and genetics. Since 1860, "philosophy" – intended as a specialized form of knowledge practised in the academic spaces – had been providing, along with religion, a moral and epistemological "spiritual supplement" aimed at organizing empirical knowledge and reflecting on its grounds and consequences; nonetheless philosophy started coming under attack from the empirical psychology proposed by authors such as Gustav Theodor Fechner (1801–1887), Wilhelm Wundt (1832–1920), and their students, whose ambition was to naturalize man's behavior and cognition. To survive as a discipline, philosophy had to be able to counter the attacks of both biology and psychology and to locate an object that it could claim as its own. During the 1910s and 1920s, a part of philosophy had to turn itself into a "philosophy of life" able to resist biology's "mechanical reductionism" and, then, it had to turn into a "philosophical anthropology" able to counter psychology's and sociology's supposed "reductionisms."

From the 1870s onwards, after the decline of German idealism and of *Naturphilosophie*, two intellectual forces were dominant; the Neo-Kantians, divided between the Baden School and the Marburg School, and the Darwinians, whose most famous spokesman was Ernst Haeckel (1834–1919).[14] Haeckel was both the main introducer of Darwinism and a scholar whose authority and originality had been internationally recognized. The alliance that the Neo-Kantians signed with the Darwinians was similar to the one they made with the German "positivists." Both alliances were strategic: They were aimed at opposing the old idealistic philosophy and the religious and reactionary forces of *Thron und Altar*.[15] Furthermore, they were meant to counter the doctrine of the unconscious – which was anti-Kantian, anti-scientific, and anti-academic – which was being promoted by von Hartmann and by other authors inspired by Schopenhauer, who were gaining much success during the 1870s. The Neo-Kantians were satisfied with evolution theory's methodological mechanism, and with its opposition to the metaphysical idea of vital teleology; but they demanded as well that the disciplinary frontiers established by Kant, according to which German academia was structured, be respected.

Nonetheless, both the biologists and the philosophers expressed a growing dissatisfaction with the limits that this pact imposed on their activity. These

---

14 See Fredrick Beiser, *The Genesis of Neo-Kantianism, 1796–1880* (Oxford: Oxford University Press, 2014); and Robert J. Richards, *The Tragic Sense of Life: Ernst Haeckel and the Struggle over Evolutionary Thought* (Chicago: University of Chicago Press, 2011).
15 See Beiser, *The Genesis of Neo-Kantianism*.

limits were traced over onto the totality of the object they were supposed to be studying from two completely different points of view: *life*. It is not by chance that the term *Erleben* (and *Erlebnis*) acquired a technical meaning during the 1870s, namely after the success of Darwinism and the emergence of scientific psychology.

Wilhelm Dilthey was among those most influential in this direction. He had systematically used the two terms in his *The Life of Schleiermacher* (1870), and conceptually defined them in his *Introduction to the Human Sciences* (1883). In the concept of *Erleben* there converged three different conceptual aspects that were already present in the Romantic movement: (a) the immediacy (*Unmittelbarkeit*) of the relation between man and world, preceding any rational construction; (b) the meaningfulness (*Bedeutsamkeit*) of life, which was tied to its interconnected historical totality; and (c) the incommensurability of life's content itself, which gave the concept an aesthetic dimension.[16] Starting from this concept, Dilthey created a series of categories derived from the root "*Leben.*" Even though he "manifested no special interest in biology and did not use the term 'life' in a biological sense,"[17] Dilthey was witnessing both the success of Darwinism and that of empirical psychology. One of his objectives in the *Introduction to the Human Sciences* was explicit: to subtract a part of human psychology, which he called "descriptive," from the grasp of the sciences of nature (*Naturwissenschaften*) so as to annex it to the sciences of the spirit (*Geisteswissenschaften*). According to Dilthey, descriptive psychology's object was historical, and therefore this science had to use a particular hermeneutical method, that of "understanding" (*Verständnis*), which was irreducible to the one used by the natural sciences.

The case of Rudolf Eucken, Scheler's mentor, a Catholic philosopher and Haeckel's colleague at the university of Jena, is similar to that of Dilthey. Eucken criticized materialism for being the cause of the loss of real values in modern society, proposing instead an idealistic philosophy based on the concept of *Geistesleben*, or "spiritual life." According to Eucken, only idealism would be able to save civilization, by promoting the "spiritual" dimension proper to human life. Ever since his first works from the late 1870s, until *Der*

---

16 Konrad Cramer, "Erleben, Erlebnis," in *Historisches Wörterbuch der Philosophie*, ed. Joachim Ritter, Karlfried Gründer, and Gottfried Gabriel, 12 vols. (Basel: Schwabe Verlag, 1972), vol. II, 702–711; and Georg Gadamer, *Truth and Method*, trans. Joel Weinsheimer and Donald G. Marshall (London: Bloomsbury, 2007).

17 Theodore Plantinga, *Historical Understanding in the Thought of Wilhelm Dilthey* (Toronto: Toronto University Press, 1980), 74. See also Rudolf A. Makkreel, *Dilthey: Philosopher of the Human Studies* (Princeton: Princeton University Press, 1992).

Sinn und Wert des Lebens (*The Sense and Value of Life*, 1908), a book for which he was awarded a Nobel prize, Eucken's production had been characterized by a progressive multiplication of concepts and terms derived from the root *Leben*. Much like Dilthey, Eucken did not conceive of "*Leben*" in a biological way; on the contrary, both of them made biological life subordinate to a "spiritual" life, which could be grasped only by philosophy, the queen of the *Geisteswissenschaften*. Even though both Dilthey and Eucken were completely uninterested in the advancements of the *Naturwissenschaften*, their usage of concepts derived from the root *Leben* is the clear sign of a growing concern that was being felt by the academic philosophers.

At the end of the nineteenth century Ernst Haeckel broke the non-aggression pact between the biologists and the philosophers. With the publication of his bestseller *The Riddle of the Universe* (1899), Haeckel became the herald of Monism, a totalizing and supposedly scientific vision of the world, which claimed to liberate man from both religion and philosophy. The philosopher he most wanted to vanquish was Immanuel Kant, whose legacy still dominated the German university system. *Die Welträthsel*, which was also a plea for empirical psychology against all the philosophical and theological descriptions of man, raised a general outcry from the entire philosophical community. From that moment on, all Neo-Kantians became hostile toward most of the Darwinians.[18]

A few years later, a new outrage emerged from the field of the life sciences, in the person of Hans Driesch (1867–1941), one of Haeckel's pupils. During the 1890s Driesch abandoned his master's rigid mechanical reductionism, separated himself from Darwinism, and formulated a new teleological approach to living organisms that he named "neo-vitalism." In an essay of 1893, *Die Biologie als selbständige Grundwissenschaft*, Driesch defended biology as an "independent basic science," and in the following years, imitating Haeckel, he progressively abandoned the laboratory to produce writings targeting a broader readership. This evolution led him to a *Habilitationsschrift* – under the supervision of the Neo-Kantian philosopher Wilhelm Windelband (1841–1915) and the experimental psychologist Oswald Kulpe (1862–1915) – and, in 1911, to an appointment to the chair of "natural philosophy" at the University of Heidelberg, one of the strongholds of Neo-Kantianism. Because of its content, Driesch's work had attracted the attention of some philosophers: Heinrich Rickert mentioned *Die Biologie als selbständige Grundwissenschaft* in his *The Limits of Concept Formation in the Natural*

---

18 Beiser, *The Genesis of Neo-Kantianism*.

Sciences (1897), where he established the difference between the sciences of man or of culture (*Kulturwissenschaften*) and the natural sciences (*Naturwissenschaften*), and Eduard von Hartmann discussed Driesch's *The History and Theory of Vitalism* (1905) in his *The Problem of Life* (1906).[19] Driesch's research initially could have looked like a possible step in the direction of a less imperialistic conception of biology, a conception more friendly to philosophy. But in 1907, two years after the publication of his book on vitalism, in *The Science and Philosophy of the Organism* (1908), Driesch decided to aggressively face some problems that, until then, had been considered exclusively philosophical. That was evident from the book's title, which announced itself as both scientific *and* philosophical. By doing that, Driesch followed the path taken by Haeckel in his two bestsellers, *The Riddle of the Universe* and the following *Wonders of life: A Popular Study of Biological Philosophy* (1904). Here, he dared to treat his work as "biological philosophy."

In the last chapter of *The Science and Philosophy of the Organism*, "The History of Humanity," Driesch directly criticized Rickert: Against the division he had established between *Kulturwissenschaften* and *Naturwissenschaften*, Driesch was advocating the possibility of understanding the history of human culture on the basis of the positive knowledge proper to the sciences of life. He was also advocating a reform of German universities going against the distinction between the two types of knowledge. Finally, in 1908, Driesch published "Bergson, der biologische Philosoph," a positive review of Bergson's *L'Évolution créatrice*, a book which had already caused outrage among the French Neo-Kantians. In the review he praised Bergson for his philosophical understanding of life and on account of the possible alliance between a neo-vitalist biology and an anti-Kantian metaphysics.

Rickert's reaction came some years later, and it was indirect. In 1912, Windelband's protégé published in *Logos* – the journal of the Neo-Kantian Baden School, to which he belonged – an article entitled "Life-Values and Cultural Values." As the title clearly stated, Rickert's point of view was that of *Wertphilosophie* ("philosophy of value"), a specialty proper to the school of his master Windelband. The essay was directed against what he called *"Lebensphilosophie"* or *"biologistische Modephilosophie"* ("fashionable biological philosophy"), and its arguments were very similar to the ones presented nine years later in the book *The Philosophy of Life* (1920). Under the category of *Lebensphilosophie* Rickert placed all the discourses pretending to explain

---

19 Maurizio Esposito, *Romantic Biology, 1890–1945* (London: Routledge, 2003).

human values, norms, and culture from a purely biological standpoint. This explanation consisted in what Rickert called a reduction of everything to *"bloßen Leben,"* namely to "mere life," "bare life," or "naked life," an expression that was to be used, no more than one year later, by Walter Benjamin (1892–1940) in an essay on violence[20] from which Agamben drew inspiration when he wrote *Homo Sacer*. *Lebensphilosophie*, inspired by modern biology, and especially by evolutionism, gave priority to a notion of life which was, nonetheless, metaphysical and potentially irrational. Life was conceived as a force, accessible through a particular method or faculty, which was irreducible to the scientific ones.

Epistemological Borders

The Science and Philosophy of the Organism represented only the last of a series of writings that the German Neo-Kantian mandarins perceived as attacks on the legitimacy of academic philosophy.[21] Rickert's first polemical target was neither Driesch nor Haeckel, but Friedrich Nietzsche, who was receiving belated success both inside and outside the academic space.

Until the mid 1890s, the author of the *Genealogy of Morals* was almost unknown: He was just one of the several writers who had tried to respond to the problem of the collapse of transcendent certainties and values caused by the growing success of the life sciences, by the failure of the revolution of 1848, and, finally, by the economic crash of 1873. The "death of God," far from being Nietzsche's trademark, was a recurrent theme before him. The crisis into which German culture plunged starting from the 1860s provoked the belated success of Schopenhauer, who had been ignored until then. In his *The World as Will and Representation* (1818, expanded in 1844), influenced by readings in the life sciences, Schopenhauer described the phenomenal world as the product of an unconscious, blind, and insatiable will to live, academic philosophy as useless, and renunciation of the world as the only solution to the suffering caused by life. The belated success of Schopenhauer's philosophy starting from the mid 1860s, increased by that of von Hartmann's *Philosophy of the Unconscious* (1869), caused an intellectual dispute around the value of "life," understood as

---

20 Walter Benjamin, "Critique of Violence," in *Reflections: Essays, Aphorisms, Autobiographical Writings*, ed. Peter Demetz, trans. Edmund Jephcott (New York: Schocken Books, 1986), 277–300.
21 See the essential book by Fritz K. Ringer, *The Decline of the German Mandarins: The German Academic Community, 1890–1933* (Cambridge: Harvard University Press, 1969).

human existence: the *Pessimismus-Streit*.[22] This dispute mobilized several academic and non-academic actors: the first to respond was the positivist philosopher and economist Karl Eugen Dühring (1833–1921), in a book paradigmatically entitled The Value of Life (1865), but the following years were especially marked by the reaction of the Neo-Kantian community. Both the Neo-Kantians and the positivists could not accept anything of Schopenhauer's philosophy. His misanthropy, his pessimistic ascetic ethics, his jointly anti-Kantian and anti-scientific endeavor, and, finally, his contempt for academia, were all going against everything that both academic philosophers and scientists were defending. Nietzsche's books started having success both in the academic world and in popular culture toward the end of the century;[23] a few years before the publication of Rickert's essay, literary journals such as *Die Tat*[24] were contributing to the constitution of new ideologies promoting life, energy, and youth, and were mixing Nietzsche's vitalism, Haeckel's monism, and Bergson's spiritualism.

In 1907, the sociologist Georg Simmel (1858–1918), one of Rickert's colleagues and friends, published a monograph, *Schopenhauer und Nietzsche*, which was the result of a series of lectures he had been giving at the University of Berlin. At the turn of the century, because of the development of German universities, lecturers like Simmel abandoned academia, or struggled to prove their talent to the institutions by attracting to their courses as many students as possible. One way to attract more students was by introducing new questions and new authors: This is what Simmel did with Nietzsche, whom he started reading while he was finishing his book on money, at the precise moment in which the author of *Also sprach Zarathustra* was having success. Simmel's *Philosophie des Geldes* treated, through the question of money, a topic which was a trademark of the Southwestern School, or Baden School: that of values. In the book on Schopenhauer and Nietzsche, Simmel treated the two authors as serious philosophers able to respond to philosophical questions such as those of values and historicity, and he used them to discuss the "vital" origin of values, reconnecting to a discussion which had originally started during the 1870s, during the *Pessimismus-Streit*.

---

22 Fredrick C. Beiser, *Weltschmerz: Pessimism in German Philosophy, 1860–1900* (Oxford, Oxford University Press, 2016).
23 Steven E. Aschheim, *The Nietzsche Legacy in Germany* (Berkeley: University of California Press, 1992).
24 Marino Pulliero, *Une modernité explosive: La revue* Die Tat *dans les renouveaux religieux, culturels et politiques de l'Allemagne d'avant 1914–1918* (Geneva: Labor et Fides, 2008).

With this book, Simmel started locating his former "sociological philosophy" in a metaphysical framework inspired by Nietzsche, Schopenhauer, and Bergson.[25] This development, which led to the publication of his last book, *The View of Life* (1918), progressively irritated his former friend and colleague Rickert.

The second of Rickert's targets was Henri Bergson (1859–1941). After the publication of the *Évolution créatrice*, Bergson's texts began to enjoy some success in Germany,[26] especially in cultural milieus that the Neo-Kantians disliked: idealistic and religious, such as Eucken's circle; and artistic and sometimes reactionary, such as the groups gathering around Stefan George (1867–1933), that Simmel participated in, or the one gathering around the publisher Eugen Diederichs (1867–1930). The naturalization of man that Bergson seemed to be proposing in the *Évolution créatrice*, his pragmatist conception of scientific knowledge, his anti-intellectualistic idea of an intuition able to grasp the flux of life without mediations, and, last but not least, his manifest detestation of Kant made him, both in France and in Germany, a true *bête noire* of the Kantians.

Rickert also criticized the American pragmatists and, without naming them, Haeckel and Driesch. Hence, Rickert's essay constituted an attempt to put in their place all those who, from different perspectives, were trying to contest the disciplinary divisions existing in German academia. The targets were non-academic and anti-academic philosophers such as Nietzsche and Schopenhauer, academic philosophers advocating a non-academic practice of philosophy such as Bergson, and biologists with hegemonic ambitions, such as Driesch and Haeckel.

The "Plenitude of Life": Phenomenology and *Lebensphilosophie*

Scheler's manifesto for the philosophy of life should be interpreted as a strategic intervention in a debate polarized along two axes: on the one hand, by the tensions between mechanist biologists, such as Haeckel, and vitalists or holists, such as Hans Driesch and Jakob Johann von Uexküll (1864–1944); and, on the other hand, between philosophers and biologists. Scheler smartly picked up the expression used by Rickert, "philosophy of life." Because of the particular academic conjuncture of 1895–1910, the

---

25 Gregor Fitzi, *Soziale Erfahrung und Lebensphilosophie: Georg Simmels Beziehung zu Henri Bergson* (Konstanz: Universitätsverlag Konstanz, 2002).
26 Caterina Zanfi, *Bergson et la philosophie allemande, 1907–1932* (Paris: Armand Colin, 2013).

younger producers of philosophy, who were not likely to be published in scientific journals, were hosted in non-academic ones, and, therefore, they had to conform to the expectations of a different readership. Scheler published his essay in a literary journal, *Die weißen Blätter*, promoted an expression, "Philosophie des Lebens," which had been used at the end of the eighteenth century by non-academic authors, and used a literary and prophetic style. Finally, Scheler was presenting the philosophy of life not as a stable set of theories, but as a program inspired by three philosophers, Nietzsche, Bergson, and Dilthey, whose works had to be appropriated by the new generation. These three authors, who had never been in contact with each other, nonetheless had something in common: their reaction to positivism and to the mechanistic interpretation of the life sciences, and their hostility, or at least indifference, to Kantianism. They also shared a non-reductionist view of life as a phenomenon likely to be accessed through an inner experience. According to Scheler the "philosophy of life" was a philosophy springing "out of the plenitude of the experience of Life." The genitive "of" implied precisely that "life" had to be both the object and the subject of philosophy. But this "life" was not the one studied by biologists, but the pre-objective felt or "lived life" (*Erlebnis des Lebens*). By contrast, Scheler considered that the biologists were studying merely an objectified life or, in the case of Haeckel, a mechanized one. Therefore science needed a philosophy rooted in life "itself," namely in "lived life."

Now, the problem of life was not solvable without an anthropological framework likely to provide a stable ground to justify philosophy's epistemological claims. That's the reason why, simultaneously with the "Versuche," Scheler published an essay, "Zur Idee des Menschen" ("On the Idea of Man," 1913), which provided the basis for his last and most famous book, *Die Stellung des Menschen im Kosmos*. In his formulation of this theoretical framework Scheler was strongly influenced by Husserl's phenomenology, conceived as part of *Lebensphilosophie* too. This unusual usage of phenomenology was made possible by the Austrian philosopher's own philosophical development. Husserl, whose intellectual formation had taken place within the Austro-Hungarian academic system, which was strongly anti-Kantian, started using the concepts of *Erleben* and *Erlebnis* after his appointment at the University of Göttingen, in an environment very different from the Austrian one, marked by a fight between philosophers and physiological psychologists over some university chairs. It is during this period that Husserl began reading his German colleagues and started responding to their critiques: He engaged with the Neo-

Kantians, who accommodated his manifesto "Phenomenology as a Rigorous Science" in their journal *Logos*, but also with Eucken and Dilthey, from whom he picked up the language of "vitalism" and the concept of the *Lebenswelt*.[27] This concept appears only from 1917 onwards, when Husserl inherited the philosophy chair in Freiburg from Rickert after the latter's departure for Heidelberg.

It was phenomenology conceived as a "philosophy of life" that, according to Scheler, constituted the best candidate for giving an explanation of human cognition and behavior and, thereby, for giving a new meaning to the concept of "value," the trademark of the Baden School. Phenomenology was the best candidate for replacing Neo-Kantianism. The philosophers of the Baden and Marburg Schools had been able, until then, to maintain the exceptionality of man amidst the natural world, and the exceptionality of philosophy amidst the disciplines.

To conclude, despite the sympathies that some philosophers had toward some biologists, and beyond the quarrels between different biologists – especially between the neo-vitalists, represented by Driesch, and the mechanists, represented by Haeckel – there was a clear conflict between the biologists, who were often close to the psychologists because of their medical training, and the "pure" philosophers. The dispute around psychologism which began around 1870, the *Psychologismus-Streit*, was therefore accompanied by a *Biologismus-Streit*, which gave birth to the "philosophies of life." These two disputes were largely resolved after World War I, when neo-Kantianism was slowly eclipsed and the "philosophy of life" assumed a renewed prominence.

Lebensphilosophie and Bio-politics

At the end of World War I, in the new Republic of Weimar, one of the dominant debates concerned the causes of the past four years of killings and destruction. The disastrous situation of postwar Germany provided the perfect sounding board for the spiritualist and even religious claims of certain philosophers, such as Eucken and Scheler, who, since the end of the nineteenth century, had been criticizing the supposed abstraction and inhumanity of the scientific rationality promoted by positivism and Neo-Kantianism, incarnated by industrialization and technical development, which they

---

27 For the philosophical appropriation of the concept of *Lebenswelt*, which appeared initially in the work of Haeckel, see Carl Bermes, *"Welt" als Thema der Philosophie: Vom metaphysischen zum natürlichen Weltbegriff* (Hamburg: Meiner, 2004).

considered incapable of fostering moral progress.[28] The philosophers who had shown their fidelity to the nationalist cause during the war – when they opposed, in propagandist publications, the German "spiritual" *Kultur* to the French "materialistic" *Zivilisation* – were often able to gain a central spot on the intellectual scene. This applied to the case of Scheler, who – after having actively been engaged in the production of propaganda like his mentor Eucken[29] – had finally been hired by the University of Cologne.

At that moment, another "philosopher of life" was having an impressive success: Oswald Spengler. Even though Spengler did not present himself as a *Lebensphilosoph*, he clearly appeared as such to his readership. In his two-volume bestseller *The Decline of the West* (1919–1923) he classified societies as the naturalists were doing with organisms and, in the follow-up, *Man and Technics* (1931), explicitly subtitled *A Contribution to a Philosophy of Life*, he described technology as humanity's external organs. On the one hand, much like Nietzsche, his main inspiration along with Goethe, Spengler naturalized technique, science, morality and, in general, humanity. On the other hand, he used a non-scientific and "spiritual" notion of life, appealing to an extra-rational solution to the supposed crisis of civilization. *Der Untergang des Abendlandes* had a massive success, selling more than 100,000 copies within six years, but Spengler's position as an "independent scholar," and his despisal of academia blocked the breakthrough of his *Lebensphilosophie* inside the university. Both the phenomenologists and the Neo-Kantians wasted no opportunity to crucify *Lebensphilosophie* as irrational and politically dangerous: In 1920 there appeared both Rickert's *Das Philosophie des Lebens* and a whole issue of the journal *Logos* dedicated to a criticism of the now-fashionable "movement."

To be academically "presentable" *Lebensphilosophie* had to be turned into something else, namely a *philosophische Anthropologie*, and the best instrument to make this transformation possible was phenomenology. In the climate of general revolt against "abstraction" characteristic of the Weimar Republic, Scheler had been smart enough to present phenomenology as an intuitive and concrete philosophy (or *"Sachlichkeit,"* following the Husserlian motto *"Zu den Sachen selbst"*), quite the opposite of Neo-Kantianism.[30] Thanks to phenomenology, "philosophy of life" survived as philosophical anthropology

---

28 See Paul Forman, "Weimar Culture, Causality, and Quantum Theory, 1918–1927: Adaptation by German Physicists and Mathematicians to a Hostile Intellectual Environment," *Historical Studies in the Physical Sciences*, 3 (1971), 1–115.
29 See Kusch, *Psychologism*; and Ringer, *The Decline of the German Mandarins*.
30 See Kusch, *Psychologism*.

in different forms, very biological (in the case of Arnold Gehlen), tied to psychopathology (in the case of Karl Jaspers and Ludwig Binswanger), or more historical and interested in the social sciences (in the case of Helmuth Plessner and Georg Misch).

In the 1930s, after the deaths of Dilthey (1913), Simmel (1918), and, finally, Scheler (1928), the jargon of life – which started circulating in the 1870s and had progressively invaded literature, philosophy, and political discourses – became an essential piece of the *völkisch* ideology promoted by the Nazi regime in publications such as *Gestalt und Leben* (1938) by Alfred Rosenberg (1893–1946). Nonetheless, it would be to say the least imprecise to speak of National Socialism's ideology as a "philosophy of life," and not only because "philosophy of life" wasn't a coherent set of discourses. Modern *Lebensphilosophie* emerged as a tool to save the practice of philosophy from its possible disappearance under the pressure of the life and human sciences. On the one hand, the critiques that some *Lebensphilosophen* addressed against the abstraction of "intellectualism" served as an appeal to "spiritual" forces that was easily appropriated by Nazi propaganda. On the other hand, the National Socialist discourses on "life" were connected with something apparently incompatible with this philosophy, namely the racial bio-politics inspired by a particular eugenic interpretation of social Darwinism.[31]

In many cases, similar theoretical positions – both philosophical and scientific – were followed by very different political choices, or the other way around. The cases of Ernst Haeckel, Helmuth Plessner, Arnold Gehlen, Hans Driesch, and Martin Heidegger are interesting. Despite his rationalism and mechanical reductionism, Haeckel supported German nationalism and imperialism; he was a social Darwinist and a eugenist, therefore his work was held in the highest respect by the Nazi ideologists. Both Plessner and Gehlen had been pupils of Scheler, and both of them were *philosophische Anthropologen*, but in 1933 their paths separated: While the first, of Jewish ancestry, had to flee Germany, the second had no compunction about taking Paul Tillich's chair in Frankfurt, once the latter had been forced from his post by the authorities of the Third Reich. Despite the fact that some aspects of neo-vitalism[32] had been used by Nazi ideology, Hans Driesch was a strong

---

31 George L. Mosse, *Masses and Man: Nationalist and Fascist Perceptions of Reality* (New York: Howard Fertig, 1980); George L. Mosse, *Nazi Culture: Intellectual, Cultural and Social Life in the Third Reich*, trans. Salvator Attanasio and others (New York: Grosset and Dunlap, 1966); and George L. Mosse, *The Crisis of German Ideology: Intellectual Origins of the Third Reich* (New York: Howard Fertig, 1998).

32 Anne Harrington, *Reenchanted Science: Holism in German Culture from Wilhelm II to Hitler* (Princeton: Princeton University Press, 1999).

supporter of pacifism and universalism, which cost him his position.[33] Finally, Martin Heidegger, an active member of the Nazi Party since 1933, in a series of lectures of 1929 – later published under the title *The Fundamental Concepts of Metaphysics* – opposed both Driesch's and Uexküll's doctrines, and criticized his master Scheler's *Lebensphilosophie* for being a disguised form of "biologism."

During the late 1920s and the early 1930s, before the complete imposition of the Nazi ideology, many intellectuals in Germany expressed harsh critiques of *Lebensphilosophie*, from different points of view. They were often inspired by Rickert, who mentored, or at least influenced, German intellectuals as different as Martin Heidegger, Rudolf Carnap (1891–1970), and Max Weber (1864–1920). They criticized not only *Lebensphilosophie*, but also vitalism and holism in biology. This had been the case for Ernst Cassirer (1874–1945), the last adherent of the Marburg School, in *Philosophie der symbolischen Formen: Phänomenologie der Erkenntnis* (*The Philosophy of Symbolic Forms: Phenomenology of Knowledge*, 1929). This was also the case for the members of the neo-positivist circle of Vienna around Rudolf Carnap – Austrian philosophers such as Moritz Schlick (1882–1936), Philipp Franck (1884–1966), and Edgar Zilsel (1891–1944) – who followed the path taken by Bertrand Russell (1872–1970), who criticized "The Philosophy of Henri Bergson" and its "irrationalism" in the eponymous article he published in the 1912 issue of the journal *The Monist*. In the field of social philosophy, especially in the Marxist Frankfurt school, *Lebensphilosophie* was almost immediately treated as ideological, irrational, and, therefore, potentially dangerous.[34]

Post-structuralism: A "Philosophy of Life"?

In France the expression *"philosophie de la vie"* appeared for the first time during the 1920s, from the pen of the German-speaking philosopher Vladimir Jankélévitch (1903–1985) to designate Bergson's, Simmel's, and Scheler's writings. In 1947 Georges Canguilhem remarked that the strong Cartesian heritage in France did not provide the conditions for the emergence of a "philosophy of life" and of a "biological philosophy" there during the

---

33 Harrington, *Reenchanted Science*.
34 Max Horkheimer's (1895–1973) review of Bergson's *The Sources of Morals and Religion*, "Zu Bergsons Metaphysik der Zeit," published in 1934 in the *Zeitschrift für Sozialforschung*, György Lukács's (1885–1971) *The Destruction of Reason* (1955), Herbert Marcuse's (1898–1979) *One-Dimensional Man: Studies in the Ideology of Advanced Industrial Society* (1964), and Jürgen Habermas's *The Philosophical Discourse of Modernity* (1985) all belong to this half-century-long Marxist tradition.

nineteenth century.[35] During the interwar period, and even more so between 1945 and the mid 1960s, the heritage of the Neo-Kantian critiques of Bergson's philosophy (such as was addressed by René Berthelot in his famous book from 1911–1920, *Un romantisme utilitaire*), the association of *Lebensphilosophie* with Nazi ideology, the critiques that communist philosophers such as Georges Politzer (1903–1942) advanced against Bergson and many German philosophers, and the neat academic division between the humanities and the natural sciences blocked the breakthrough of *Lebensphilosophie*, which would later enter filtered through the prism of existential phenomenology. In most cases – such as that of Jean-Paul Sartre (1905–1980) – French phenomenologists did not engage in a reflection on biological life and its relation with the human, conforming instead to the classic French Cartesianism. Only a few philosophers – such as Merleau-Ponty, in his *La structure du comportement* (*The Structure of Behavior*, 1942), and, later on, in his posthumously published lectures on *Nature* (1959–1961); Raymond Ruyer (1902–1987), in his book *Éléments de psychobiologie* (*Elements of psychobiology*, 1946); and Georges Canguilhem, in *Le Normal et le Pathological* (1943) and in *The Knowledge of Life* (1952) – drew inspiration from Nietzsche and Scheler, and from German biologists and physicians such as Driesch, Uexküll, and Kurt Goldstein (1878–1965), with the aim of promoting a holistic and anti-mechanist view of life able to give meaning to the peculiarity of human behavior and cognition. Nonetheless, with the exception of Georges Canguilhem, these thinkers never used the expression *"philosophie de la vie"* or *"philosophie biologique."*

The works of these authors had a great importance for a new generation of thinkers who, during the 1960s, promoted a new interpretation of Nietzsche, used as a tool to read the socio-cultural context of the French Sixth Republic. The most important of them was, beyond any doubt, Gilles Deleuze (1905–1995), who published his seminal *Nietzsche et la philosophie* (*Nietzsche and Philosophy*) in 1961. Nietzsche's philosophy, conceived as an anti-subjectivist and anti-dialectical post-Kantian "philosophy of life," combined with the influence of Bergson and Spinoza, influenced the interpretation that Deleuze would later give of Marxism and psychoanalysis in the highly influential book he published with Félix Guattari (1930–1992), *L'anti-Œdipe: Capitalisme et Schizophrénie* (*Anti-Oedipus: Capitalism and Schizophrenia*, 1972). This work was the result of the new importance that the works of Freudo-

---

35 Georges Canguilhem, "Note sur la situation faite en France à la philosophie biologique," in *Résistance, philosophie biologique et histoire des sciences 1940–1965*, in *Œuvres complètes*, 5 vols. (Paris: Vrin, 2015), vol. IV, 307–320.

Marxists – especially Wilhelm Reich (1897–1957) and Herbert Marcuse (1898–1979) – had in French culture during the 1960s and especially in the aftermath of May 1968. *L'anti-Œdipe* not only tried to provide a critique both of Marxism and of psychoanalysis, but also combined the two in a synthesis centered around the concept of "productive desire." This notion was a means by which to criticize both consumerist society and the classic notion of desire as lack, which grounded psychoanalysis. In *L'anti-Œdipe* and in its 1980 companion text *Mille plateaux* (*A Thousand Plateaus*), Deleuze and Guattari constructed a philosophical system that looked like the ones produced by the *Naturphilosophen*, insofar as it considered "spirit" and "matter," culture and nature, as the static result of a productive desire prior to the all-too-human distinctions and dualisms. The effects of this work both inside and outside of France were impressive – Jean-François Lyotard's (1924–1998) *Libidinal Economy* (1974) was deeply influenced by it, and it stimulated a renewal of interest in authors such as Nietzsche, Bergson, and even Schelling.

During the 1960s, the French Nietzschean legacy not only had to make sense of the new social situation of postwar European society, but also had to deal with the recent developments in genetic biology. In 1970, in *The Logic of Life*, the French biologist and historian of the life sciences François Jacob (1920–2013) declared that life was "no longer interrogated in the laboratories." The following year, and more boldly still, his colleague Jacques Monod (1910–1976) affirmed, in *Chance and Necessity*, that, while the secret of life had once seemed inaccessible, it was, by then, mostly solved. With such claims, the two scientists who, together with André Lwoff (1902–1994), had been awarded the 1965 Nobel Prize for their work on molecular biology, wished to emphasize the trend toward the reduction of biological phenomena to the laws governing the inanimate world. They interpreted life as a "code" or a "message" inscribed in every living being and reproduced through the self-copying of the DNA strand. Because the "question of life" was progressively fading away, it was no longer possible to consider the various versions of "vitalism" as viable orientations in biology or "philosophy of life" as an acceptable orientation in philosophy. During the 1960s a "philosophy of biology" adopting a strictly analytical and anti-metaphysical approach emerged as an independent sub-discipline of philosophy of science.[36]

---

36 See for instance David L. Hull, *Philosophy of Biological Science* (Englewood Cliffs: Prentice Hall, 1974); and David L. Hull, "Biology and Philosophy," in *Contemporary Philosophy: A New Survey, Volume 2: Philosophy of Science*, ed. Guttorm Fløistad (The Hague: Martinus Nijhoff, 1982), 281–316.

From the late 1960s onwards, it was the very concept of life itself that could sound useless, or at least could be seen as the inscription of a false problem. In 1966 Michel Foucault published *The Order of Things*, a book that sketched an "archeology of the human sciences." While Jacob and Monod claimed that life was a useless concept in biology, Foucault suggested that the historical transcendental, or *episteme*, which had dominated Western culture for 150 years was about to change. Together with "man," also "life" was destined to disappear.

In Foucault's visionary evocation of a future disappearance of man at the very end of *The Order of Things*, one can clearly hear the echo of Nietzsche's prophecy about the overcoming of man. But, just as in Nietzsche, the prophecy concerning the overcoming of man was essentially ambiguous. The notion of life was not about to disappear entirely: It was destined to go through mutations, in the life sciences as well as in the humanities.

7
The Many Faces of Analytic Philosophy

JOEL ISAAC

Analytic philosophy emerged from a stew of ideas in philosophy and mathematics, which, especially in Britain and German-speaking Europe, was brought slowly to a simmer in the closing decades of the nineteenth century. Many of these ideas were, naturally enough, highly technical, and thus intelligible only within the philosophical and scientific discourses on which they drew. It is worth stressing, then, that these conceptual developments were infused with the ambient cultural and political values of their time, especially those of the diffuse cultural moment known as modernism. The radicalism of analytic philosophy was of a piece with the broader sense of rupture and renewal that defined *fin-de-siècle* Europe.[1]

Three ingredients stand out as being of special importance to the formation of the tradition. The first is the legacy of German Idealism. It has often been said that analytic philosophy was born in revolt against Kant and Idealism – a claim based, in large part, on Bertrand Russell's and G. E. Moore's explicit repudiation of specific doctrines of Kant and Hegel, as well their broader scorn for the metaphysics of British Idealism.[2] Similarly, Gottlob Frege's treatment of the laws of arithmetic as deducible from the purely analytic truths of logic was

---

1 See, for example, Moore and Russell's connections with the Bloomsbury Group, or the Vienna Circle's famous affiliation with modernist movements in design and architecture. Paul Levy, *Moore: G. E. Moore and the Cambridge Apostles* (London: Weidenfeld & Nicolson, 1979); and Alan Richardson, "Philosophy as Science: The Modernist Agenda of Philosophy of Science, 1900–1950," in *In the Scope of Logic, Methodology and Philosophy of Science*, ed. Peter Gärdenfors, Jan Woleński, and Katarzyna Kijania-Placek, 2 vols. (Dordrecht: Kluwer, 2002), vol. II, 621–639.

2 This is a claim that can be traced back to the testimony of Russell and Moore themselves. It is a view that scholars still proffer today, even though it is now widely recognized that matters are more complex than the "rebellion" narrative suggests. See Juliet Floyd and Sanford Shieh, "Introduction," to *Future Pasts: The Analytic Tradition in Twentieth-Century Philosophy*, ed. Juliet Floyd and Sanford Shieh (Oxford: Oxford University Press, 2001), 5; Hans-Johann Glock, *What Is Analytic Philosophy?* (Cambridge: Cambridge University Press, 2008); and Stephen P. Schwartz, *A Brief History of Analytic Philosophy: From Russell to Rawls* (Chichester: Wiley-Blackwell, 2012), 27–29.

also seen as a rejection of Kant's account of arithmetic as an instance of synthetic *a priori* judgments.[3] However, analytic philosophy's relations with idealism are not so clear-cut, or antagonistic, as these claims suggest. Recent scholarship has shown that analytic philosophers like Frege and Russell by no means rejected outright the teachings of Kant and Hegel; their developments of analytic methods were forged in dialogue with German and British variants of Idealism, not in flight from them.[4]

Another crucial intellectual context for the emergence of analytic philosophy was the rapid development of the natural and historical sciences during the second half of the nineteenth century. It has often been said that analytic philosophy was born in revolt, not only against Idealism, but also against the claims of those great Victorian doctrines: psychologism and historicism.[5] The central thesis of psychologism, on this account, was that the objectivity of judgment and truth was to be explained in terms of the processes by which warranted judgments were formed: In its various modes, psychologism might assert that these processes involved the interaction of mental faculties, or the causal processes of perception and action in the human nervous system. In a similar fashion, historicism asserted the historically derived nature of human beliefs and values – the situatedness of those beliefs and values within evolving social practices. Early analytic philosophers railed against what was in their view a conflation of the processes (social or psychological) by which judgments were formed, on the one hand, and what made them true, on the other. Nevertheless, early analytic philosophy did not involve the blanket rejection of the empirical findings of the psychological and historical sciences. A better way of conceiving of analytic philosophy's relationship with the empirical and transcendental theories of mind is to say that the early analytic philosophers wanted to renegotiate philosophy's relationship with the physical and mathematical sciences – and to do so precisely in the light of nineteenth-century upheavals in the study of physics, psychology, and the foundations of mathematics. It was an open question exactly what this new bearing should be: Frege emphasized that philosophical logic had revealed a "third realm" beyond physical objects and mental processes; on the other hand, as we shall see, Ludwig Wittgenstein (1889–

---

3 Michael Potter, "Introduction" to *The Cambridge Companion to Frege*, ed. Michael Potter and Tom Ricketts (Cambridge: Cambridge University Press, 2010), 8–9.
4 On Russell's debts to Hegel, see Nicholas Griffin, *Russell's Idealist Apprenticeship* (Oxford: Clarendon Press, 1991).
5 See, for example, Michael Dummett, *Origins of Analytic Philosophy* (Cambridge: Harvard University Press, 1994); Floyd and Shieh, "Introduction," 5; and Glock, *What Is Analytic Philosophy?*, 124–127.

1951) thought modern logic and mathematics empty and thus radically distinct from natural science, while Rudolf Carnap (1891–1970) and Willard Van Orman Quine (1908–2000) insisted that philosophy was in some sense continuous with the process of scientific inquiry.

The problem of defining philosophy's role among the special sciences in the *fin-de-siècle* points toward a third and final feature of the intellectual context from which analytic philosophy emerged. This is its commitment to "analysis" as an ideal of philosophical inquiry. Obviously enough, the goal of performing an analysis on some object of philosophical puzzlement goes back to the very origins of Western philosophy. Contemporary philosophers often distinguish – as a step toward a full description of modern philosophical analysis – between three different forms of analysis, each of which has found advocates, and each of which has been combined with the others.[6] Decompositional analysis is perhaps the most common form: the breaking down of an object of analysis into its elemental forms, with the aim of accounting for this object in terms of its parts. Regressive analysis, in contrast, seeks to account for an object of analysis in terms of first principles or axioms from which the object in question can be deduced: In this case, decompositional analysis, or something akin to it, is the prolegomenon to a *synthetic* understanding of the object in question. Finally, the philosopher Michael Beaney has identified what he calls interpretive analysis as a method distinct to early analytic philosophy.[7] Before an object of analysis can be disarticulated into its constituent parts, or treated as the synthetic product of more basic principles, it may first be necessary to *interpret* or *transform* it – to look below its surface structure to find the elements of which it is composed. The logical notations of Giuseppe Peano and, especially, Frege, encouraged these interpretive reconstructions of judgments, and made interpretive analysis central to the revival of interest in the possibilities of "analysis" at the dawn of the analytic project. The new logic was used to display a logical structure of propositions that was otherwise invisible in the statements of natural languages. Armed with the new logic, philosophy (it was argued) could thus take up the unique role of laying bare the ontological commitments and conceptual structure of modern science.

---

6 These distinctions are drawn from Michael Beaney, "Analysis," in *Stanford Encyclopedia of Philosophy*, ed. E. N. Zalta (Summer 2016), https://plato.stanford.edu/archives/sum2016/entries/analysis.

7 Beaney, "Analysis." See also Michael Beaney, "The Analytic Revolution," *Royal Institute of Philosophy Supplements*, 78 (2016), 227–249.

Bertrand Russell: From Idealism to Logic

These three elements – the legacy of Idealism, the place of philosophy among the special sciences, and the possibilities of analysis – were developed in different ways by the founding thinkers of the tradition. Bertrand Russell (1872–1970), above all, played the central role in generating momentum for the new philosophy. Born into the British nobility, he was the son of Lord and Lady Amberly, and the grandson of former Prime Minister Lord John Russell. Russell's parents were among the radical followers of John Stuart Mill, who was Russell's godfather. (For more on Mill and his contributions to political thought, see Chapter 8 by Jerrold Seigel in Volume I.) Russell's parents died when he was very young, and he was raised in the house of his grandparents. Russell was brought up by a string of "German nurses, German and Swiss governesses, and finally by English tutors"; he saw little of other children and found refuge in his grandfather's resplendent library, "which became my schoolroom."[8] Russell steeped himself in great literature, from the major Florentine and Enlightenment historians – Guicciardini, Machiavelli, Gibbon – to the Romantic poets. He also immersed himself in the writings of Mill, in whom he found a kindred spirit and guide. The crucial event in his education was his discovery of Euclid, and his subsequent revelation of his aptitude for mathematics. When the time came for Russell to go up to Cambridge, it was to prepare for examination in the Mathematical "Tripos" (as undergraduate examinations in a given subject are called in Cambridge). Only in his fourth year did he switch to the study of philosophy, under the auspices of what was then called the Moral Sciences Tripos.

At Cambridge, Russell was quickly recognized as a brilliant student. He was also a young man of deep yet shifting passions. The presiding spirit of the Moral Sciences during Russell's time in Cambridge was Henry Sidgwick (1838–1900), the latter-day incarnation of the utilitarian and empiricist traditions in British philosophy. Yet Russell, as later with Moore, found Sidgwick old-fashioned and uninspiring as a teacher. He gravitated instead toward Idealism, although in a peculiarly Cantabridgian form. British Idealism was principally an Oxonian phenomenon: By the 1890s, its pre-eminent representative was F. H. Bradley (1846–1924), whose *Appearance and Reality* (1893) was the most important philosophical work of its time in Britain. Russell's encounter with Kant, Hegel, and Bradley came through two sources: the teaching of G. F Stout (1860–1944), a follower of Idealism at Cambridge; and

---

8 Bertrand Russell, "My Mental Development," in *The Philosophy of Bertrand Russell*, ed. Paul Arthur Schilpp, 2nd edn. (Evanston: Library of Living Philosophers, 1946), 6–7.

Russell's interactions with a young fellow at Trinity, J. M. E. McTaggart (1866–1925), who would go on to become a leading figure within British philosophy. Between them, Stout and McTaggart "caused [Russell] to become a Hegelian."[9] After he graduated in 1894, Russell produced a fellowship dissertation on the foundations of geometry that attempted to apply Hegel's categories to the mathematical sciences.[10] For a time, he envisaged a series of works on the philosophy of the natural and moral sciences – a Hegelian synthesis of theory and practice in a single, encyclopedic work.

Two developments led Russell toward his eventual break with Idealism. The first was his discussions with his friend G. E. Moore (1873–1958) in and around the year 1898, when Moore was preparing a Prize Fellowship dissertation for Trinity College. Moore was two years Russell's junior, and had taken Part II in the Moral Sciences Tripos at Russell's suggestion, after reading Classics in Part I. Like Russell, Moore had been much impressed by the teachings of Stout and McTaggart, but his Idealist period was briefer than Russell's. Already in his first, unsuccessful fellowship dissertation of 1897, Moore had been critical of the metaphysical underpinnings of Kant's theory of freedom, as well as the German philosopher's related view of practical reason. By 1898, Moore had generalized this argument into a critique of Kant's account of the *a priori*, which was, in Moore's eyes, guilty of psychologism: Kant, Moore contended, elided the crucial distinction between the psychological processes of judgment and inference, on the one hand, and the truth or objectivity of the propositions that were involved in such processes of cognition, on the other. For Moore, Kant made a profound mistake in claiming that the content and truth of judgments were the product of human mental faculties. In fact, he argued, propositions were neither reducible to the operation of the cognitive faculties nor representations of facts or states of affairs; rather, they were themselves facts.[11] This position implied its own kind of idealism: The objects of thought are here treated as the only world we can know. However, such arguments were characterized by Moore, and then by Russell, as a kind of direct realism, in which all the truths of common sense were held to be straightforwardly real and objective.[12] In contrast, the Absolute of Idealism, supposedly existent beneath the realm of mere appearance, was dismissed as so much metaphysical hogwash. These ideas took time

---

9 Russell, "My Mental Development," 10.
10 On Russell's Hegelian period, see Griffin, *Russell's Idealist Apprenticeship*, 62–99.
11 George Edward Moore, "An Autobiography," in *The Philosophy of G. E. Moore*, ed. Paul Arthur Schilpp (Evanston: Northwestern University Press, 1942), 21–22.
12 Moore's evolving view of propositions is traced in Thomas Baldwin, *G. E. Moore* (London: Routledge, 1990).

to form in Moore's philosophy, but Russell was immediately moved by Moore's rejection of the fundamental tenets of Idealism. "With a sense of escaping from prison," Russell wrote, "we allowed ourselves to think that grass is green, that the sun and stars would exist if no one was aware of them, and also that there is a pluralistic and timeless world of Platonic ideas."[13]

The second event that altered the course of Russell's philosophical development was his encounter in 1900 with the mathematician Giuseppe Peano (1858–1952) at the International Congress of Philosophy in Paris. Here Russell opened another breach with the philosophy of Kant and Hegel. Even during the height of his Hegelian enthusiasm, Russell had found Hegel's statements on the foundations of mathematics to be misguided. More generally, Russell was unconvinced by Kant's treatment of the laws of arithmetic as synthetic *a priori* truths. Yet he was no more impressed by Mill's treatment of arithmetical laws as empirical generalizations. In contradistinction to these speculative attempts to account for the laws of arithmetic, Peano's work provided something more practical and conceptually powerful: a basic notation in which could be derived all the theorems and formulae of mathematics.[14] Integrating Peano's logic into his own mathematical inquiries, Russell set to work providing logically rigorous definitions of such basic mathematical concepts as series, cardinals, ordinals, and so on. Russell and his collaborator Alfred North Whitehead (1861–1947) saw how the whole of mathematics could be reduced to basic logical concepts, thus simplifying, yet also making more rigorous, the discourse of the mathematical sciences. In the short term, this enterprise produced Russell's important early treatise *The Principles of Mathematics* (1903).[15] In the longer term, and after some twists and turns that we shall presently consider, it resulted in Russell and Whitehead's epochal, if flawed, treatise on the logical foundations of mathematics, *Principia Mathematica* (1910–1913).

Gottlob Frege: Mathematical Logic and the Foundations of Mathematics

As Russell was at work on the logical foundations of mathematics, he came across the writings of an obscure German mathematician based at the

---

13 Russell, "My Mental Development," 12.
14 Russell, "My Mental Development," 12. It should be stressed that Russell adapted Peano's logic to his own work, rather than slavishly following the Italian's example. See Peter Hylton, *Russell, Idealism, and the Emergence of Analytic Philosophy* (Oxford: Clarendon Press, 1992), 168.
15 Bertrand Russell, *The Principles of Mathematics* (Cambridge: Cambridge University Press, 1903).

University of Jena. In the work of Gottlob Frege (1848–1925), Russell found a project much like his own, in which the fundamental concepts of number theory and arithmetic were extracted from a basic set of logical terms and operations. Frege's major text at this time was the first volume of the *Grundgesetze der Arithmetik* (1893), which was itself a technical working out of a theory of the foundations of arithmetic stated in more accessible form in Frege's earlier book, *Die Grundlagen der Arithmetik*.[16] The analytical machinery underpinning these two important studies was Frege's "conceptual notation" – a calculus for logical reasoning that he had outlined in his first book, the *Begriffsschrift* of 1879.[17] It is with the *Begriffsschrift* that one must begin an account of Frege's thought.

Frege's aim was to show how, with just a few basic logical notions, one could give a logical definition of the concept of number, and thereby adduce from the principles of logic the laws of arithmetic. Simply put, Frege was after a calculus that could lay bare the basic structure of human thought. This was, Frege insisted, something quite different from an empirical account of the psychological processes underpinning cognition. As he made clear in his very earliest notes on logic, the so-called "Kernsätze zur Logik," it made no sense to ask of a psychological process whether it was true or false: "associations of ideas are neither true nor untrue."[18] Thoughts, on the other hand, were defined precisely by their normative standing, their susceptibility to assessment in terms of their truth or falsity. Logic, for Frege, dealt with truth: the laws of inference that determined the relations between thoughts – the contents of judgments.

What such an account required was a full analysis of the structure of "thoughts," and the laws that guided their relations with one another in the making of judgments. Yet the principles of logic that confronted Frege when he began his work in this field were manifestly inadequate for that task. The conventional method of logical analysis, which traced its roots all the way

---

16 Gottlob Frege, *Grundgesetze der Arithmetik*, 2 vols. (Jena: Verlag Hermann Pohle, 1893/1903), ed. and trans. Philip A. Ebert and Marcus Rossberg (with Crispin Wright) as *Basic Laws of Arithmetic: Derived Using Concept-Script*, 2 vols. (Oxford: Oxford University Press, 2013); and Gottlob Frege, *Die Grundlagen der Arithmetik: Eine logisch-mathematische Untersuchung über den Begriff der Zahl* (Breslau: Verlag Wilhelm Koebner, 1884), trans. J. L. Austin as *The Foundations of Arithmetic: A Logico-Mathematical Enquiry into the Concept of Number*, 2nd edn. (Oxford: Blackwell, 1974).
17 Gottlob Frege, *Begriffsschrift, eine der arithmetischen nachgebildete Formelsprache des reinen Denkens* (Halle: Louis Nebert, 1879), trans. Stefan Bauer-Mengelberg as *Concept Script, a Formal Language of Pure Thought Modelled upon that of Arithmetic*, in *From Frege to Gödel: A Source Book in Mathematical Logic, 1879–1931*, ed. Jean van Heijenoort (Cambridge: Harvard University Press, 1967).
18 Quoted in Potter, "Introduction," 2.

back to Aristotle's treatment of the syllogism, was to break down statements into subject–predicate form. According to this analysis, in the statement "All logicians are human," the subject was "All logicians" and the predicate was "human." The subject and predicate were united by the copula "are." We should note two problems with this method of analysis. First, it is not well equipped to handle relational statements such as "Smith is taller than Jones." Second, and more importantly, the standard approach to logic treated indifferently two kinds of subject: subjects that clearly denoted a particular individual, and subjects that were qualified by markers of quantity. The analysis for "Gottlob is a human" was the same as the analysis for "All logicians are human" and "Some logicians are human." In what amounted to a reinvention of modern logic, Frege was able to show that these statements had very different underlying logical forms. It followed that any coherent account of correct inference from one "thought" to another had to depend on a clear analysis of what was being said of what – the semantic machinery that underpinned the expression of propositional contents.

Frege's first move was to bring function–argument analysis into logic.[19] This involved treating predicates as functions and subjects as arguments. Thus "Gottlob is a logician" became "La," where L is the function "is a logician," defined over the argument a, which in this case is the individual Gottlob. (The more general form of this statement is to replace the argument with the variable x, giving Lx.) The function–argument method made it much easier to handle relational sentences: "Smith is taller than Jones" can be written as "Rxy," where R is defined as the relation "is taller than," and Smith and Jones can be taken as the arguments of x and y, respectively. Crucially, Frege's use of function theory allowed him to handle statements involving multiple generality. Frege thus developed a quantificational logic that could mark the difference between subjects involving single names or descriptions ("Gottlob," "The King of France"), circumscribed groups ("Some logicians"), and universal groups ("Every," "All").

Frege's apparatus of quantifiers and function–argument analysis appeared to resolve a number of philosophical puzzles. For example, the conventional subject–predicate logic raised lots of troubling questions about assertions of existence: If every true statement had to correspond to something in the world, what was one to make of true statements like "Unicorns do not exist"? How can one say something true about an entity that does not exist?

---

19 My exposition of Frege's innovations in logic draws on Michael Beaney's excellent account in Beaney, "The Analytic Revolution."

Notoriously, the Austrian philosopher Alexius von Meinong (1853–1920) argued that one had to attribute to such fantastical entities a putative form of objecthood, because they were the objects of denoting terms like "unicorn" or "the present King of France." The members of this range of impossible entities were characterized by Meinong as "existent" but not "subsistent"; only real entities were subsistent. The problem with this solution, as Russell would point out in his famous article "On Denoting" (1905), was that these kinds of non-existent objects "were apt to infringe the law of contradiction. It is contended, for example, that the King of France exists, and also does not exist; that the round square is round, and also not round."[20] Frege's logic, in contrast, did not render the subject "unicorns" as a subject at all. Rather, it could "analyze away" this *apparently* denoting subject term by interpreting the statement "Unicorns do not exist" as "It is not the case that there is some x that is a U."[21] We must take care to record the crucial analytical feature of Frege's quantificational logic: Frege's analysis converts what looks like a statement about a peculiar kind of entity – a unicorn – into a statement about whether there is an argument for x that falls under a concept U, "is a unicorn." And, of course, the statement says that there is *not* some x that is a U. More technically, the logical interpretation of "Unicorns do not exist," as given by Frege's quantificational logic, asserts only that the concept U is not instantiated: It says that there are no entities that instantiate the concept. Using Frege's techniques, Meinong's problem of having to posit a non-existent object was dissolved.

When Frege turned to revise the logical foundations of arithmetic in the *Grundgesetze der Arithmetik*, he generalized this point. In Frege's logic, quantified statements were *always* statements about *concepts*: They asserted of a concept to what degree, if any, a concept was instantiated. This made concepts involving quantification second-order concepts – concepts about concepts. The contrast here was with concepts that could be identified with classes of objects that existed in the world (e.g., "Gottlob," "is a human"): These were, for Frege, first-order concepts. The point that Frege sought to drive home was that quantified statements were but one way of saying something about numbers. After all, what they said about a concept was that it was instantiated by a certain number of entities. In seeking to build on this thesis, Frege asserted that *all* statements about numbers involved assertions, not about actual objects in the world of common-sense experience, but

---

20 Bertrand Russell, "On Denoting," in *Essays in Analysis*, ed. Douglas Lackey (London: George Allen & Unwin, 1973), 107. First published in the journal *Mind* in 1905.
21 In formal notation: $\neg\,(\exists x)\,Ux$.

about concepts.[22] Accordingly, the only means of grasping the concept of number and the laws of arithmetic was to analyze the concept of number as it was used in statements involving numbers. This was the basis for what has become known as Frege's "context principle": the treatment of the concept of number in terms of the kinds of statements in which claims about numbers, or quantities, were made. In this way, the basic concepts of arithmetic could (so Frege hoped) be derived from quantificational logic.

Frege perceived a major challenge here. If he was right that numbers had to be treated as logical concepts – and thus not as either empirical generalizations of experience (Mill's view) or features of the pure forms of intuition (as in Kant) – they would need to be identified with logical objects. That is to say, an explanation was needed of the objects to which statements about numbers (which are, let us remember, statements about concepts) corresponded. This way of posing the problem rested upon a prior thesis in Frege's theory: namely, that the objects of all concepts were their *extensions*, the class of things of which they were true. For example, the object of the concept "is red" is the class of all things that are red. This class of red things is what the concept "red" denotes. As we have seen, numbers, as Frege had defined them, were statements about concepts: Specifically, they were statements about the *classes* of things about which concepts were true. Talk of numbers in arithmetical statements could therefore be reduced to an exclusively *logical* vocabulary that concerned classes (the extensions of concepts). Arithmetic, in other words, could be derived from logic, and from there the whole apparatus of mathematics could be constructed out of a logical notation.

This was the edifice into which Russell tore when, in a letter of June 1902, he outlined his famous paradox, nowadays known as Russell's Paradox. As he pondered the arguments of the *Grundgesetze*, Russell realized that there was a problem with treating classes as logical objects. Such an approach was prone to vicious contradictions, which threatened the foundations of mathematical knowledge. Frege's reliance on constructing classes of other classes – this as a means of making his logical concept of numbers correspond to their own logical objects – opened up possibilities for paradox. Specifically, it occurred to Russell that talk of "classes of classes" could not rule out questions such as the following: Was the class of all classes that were not members of themselves a

---

22 Frege spelled out the philosophical foundations of his view of concepts and meaning in three papers published shortly before the appearance of the *Grundgesetze*: "Function and Concept" (1891), "On Concept and Object," and "On Sense and Meaning" (both 1892), all published in *Translations from the Philosophical Writings of Gottlob Frege*, ed. and trans. Peter Geach and Max Black, 3rd edn. (Oxford: Basil Blackwell, 1980), 21–78.

member of itself? If it was not a member of itself, then it was a member of itself, whereas if it was a member of itself then it was not. When one allowed such objects as classes of classes into one's logical system, one could not, it appeared, disallow such insoluble paradoxes. This, Russell concluded, was where the treatment of classes as self-subsistent logical objects led. Frege's project of reducing arithmetic to logic never recovered from Russell's revelation.[23]

Russell himself labored to rescue the logicist enterprise with the Theory of Types, which he elaborated with Whitehead in *Principia Mathematica*.[24] In his more explicitly philosophical work from this time, Russell filled out his view of talk of classes. Unlike Frege, for whom classes were logical objects with their own Platonic realm of existence, Russell viewed classes merely as "useful fictions": By carving the world up into classes, we are enabled to use concepts and thus make judgments. But classes themselves do not have an independent existence; only the things that instantiate them do.[25] On Russell's view, humans are discursive creatures who use concepts to make assertions, both about the world and about other concepts. Logical analysis can reveal the semantic elements that make such talk possible. But the concepts such analysis reveals are themselves, in the final analysis, merely posits, or logical constructs, which, if need be, can be eliminated or revised. Russell thus revealed himself as an "eliminativist" in his view of concepts, while Frege remained a "reductivist," who believed that mathematical laws reduced to logical truths that were themselves ontologically independent, in the sense that they were at once objective, yet neither physical nor mental entities.[26] As Frege famously put it, logical truths existed in a timeless "third realm" of sense, between the physical and psychological realms.

Analytic Philosophy in the Interwar Years: From Vienna to Cambridge

With Russell's and Frege's differing visions of the logicist project, we have reached an inflection point in the history of the analytic tradition. For soon

---

23 Which is not to say that there have not been later attempts to salvage Frege's logicism (and, for that matter, his Platonism about logical and mathematical concepts). See Bob Hale and Crispin Wright, *The Reason's Proper Study: Essays toward a Neo-Fregean Philosophy of Mathematics* (Oxford: Oxford University Press, 2001).

24 Russell, "The Theory of Logical Types" (1910), *Essays in Analysis*, ed. Douglas Lackey (London: George Allen & Unwin, 1973), 215–252.

25 For Russell's defense of the "no classes" theory – the theory that "all significant propositions concerning classes can be regarded as propositions about all or some of their members" – see Bertrand Russell, "On 'Insolubilia' and Their Solution by Symbolic Logic" (1906), in *Essays in Analysis*, ed. Douglas Lackey (London: George Allen & Unwin, 1973), 190–214.

26 Beaney, "The Analytic Revolution," 245–246.

after they had laid out their positions, there was a shift away from logicism toward a new view of logic that would propel the emergence of a much wider philosophical program. The bulk of Frege's and Russell's most important work was completed in the years before World War I. After 1914, and into the interwar years, the next generation of analytic philosophers radicalized the findings of their forebears. To understand how they did so, we should begin by noting that both Frege and Russell had at least some faith in the idea that the principles of logic and mathematics revealed something foundational about the nature of human knowledge. Frege posited an entirely separate ontological realm for the laws of logic; and Russell, despite his treatment of classes as logical fictions, also believed that logical notation tracked in some significant way the pathways of human reasoning. These convictions were overturned by Russell's protégé, Ludwig Wittgenstein. In his epoch-making *Tractatus Logico-Philosophicus* (1921), Wittgenstein argued that Frege and Russell, far from uncovering deep truths about the nature of logic or the mental faculties, had revealed the essential emptiness of logical and mathematical concepts.[27] The only statements that had content were those that pictured "facts," or "states of affairs." Logical analysis could show how these contentful statements were articulated with one another according to logical rules to form coherent scientific theories of the world; but once this structure was displayed there was no more, philosophically, to say.

In the light of Wittgenstein's analysis, it seems clear that the kind of logical analysis both Frege and Russell favored encouraged the treatment of logic and mathematics as purely formal or "analytic" – even if Frege, in particular, never intended to render logic and mathematics an epistemically and ontologically empty realm. Wittgenstein's originality in grasping that, nevertheless, this was the lesson to be drawn from his mentors must be attributed, in part, to his unusual path to the study of philosophy.[28] His background was not in philosophy but in mechanical engineering. The son of one of Austria's wealthiest industrialists, Wittgenstein had taken a degree from the Technische Hochschule in Charlottenburg, Berlin, before going to the Victoria University of Manchester to study for a Ph.D. in aeronautics. Around this time, he came across Russell's *Principles* and Frege's *Grundgesetze*; he soon

---

27 Ludwig Wittgenstein, *Tractatus Logico-Philosophicus*, trans. D. Pears and B. McGuiness (London: Routledge & Kegan Paul, 1961). First published in German in 1921, and in English translation in 1922.
28 On Wittgenstein's early life, see Ray Monk, *Ludwig Wittgenstein: The Duty of Genius* (London: Cape, 1990); and Alexander Waugh, *The House of Wittgenstein: A Family at War* (London: Bloomsbury, 2008).

became smitten with mathematics, and abandoned his Ph.D. so that he could devote himself full-time to inquiries in logic and the foundations of mathematics. Wittgenstein sought out Frege at the University of Jena over the summer of 1911. On the basis of their discussions, Frege recommended that Wittgenstein go to Cambridge to work with Russell, which he duly did beginning in the autumn of that year. Wittgenstein's manner was infamously odd, and his remarks on philosophical matters initially struck Russell as by turns peculiar and naïve. Yet Wittgenstein's eagerness to abandon his vocation as an engineer and plunge into the esoteric world of the philosophy of mathematics also expressed a striking cultural self-confidence, which went hand in hand with periods of often-chronic self-doubt. In Vienna, the Wittgensteins, representatives of the most assimilated milieu of Central European Jewry, were a brilliant and troubled family – patrons of the arts, and often gifted musicians and thinkers in their own right. (Paul Wittgenstein, Ludwig's brother, was a highly esteemed pianist.) The modernism of turn-of-the-century Vienna coursed through the life of the Wittgenstein family, and underpinned Ludwig's own eccentric but profound meditations on philosophy.[29] Russell himself was quickly won over, and saw in his student someone who would "solve the problems I am too old to solve."[30]

In fact, Wittgenstein did not solve any of Russell's technical problems, such as his famous paradox of classes; instead, the purpose of his *Tractatus* was to draw a radical lesson from recent work on the foundations of mathematics. According to Wittgenstein, Russell's and Frege's logical form of analysis had shown that, beneath ordinary language, one could discern a system of logically interconnected propositions, with each proposition holding, in principle, a determinable truth-value. In the case of the propositions of logic – which had been the focus of Peano's, Russell's, and Frege's studies in the foundations of mathematics – these truth values could be computed automatically using truth tables. This was because logical propositions were either tautological or self-contradictory: They *asserted* nothing about the world, but *displayed* its logical structure (including where it had departed the bounds of sense). Equally, mathematical propositions were "equations, and therefore pseudo-propositions." Hence there were determinable truth values in logic and mathematics, but they depended on formal relations alone, not on anything in the world. They gave the world its form, but not its content: "The logic of the world, which is shown by tautologies in the

---

29 See, most famously, Allan Janik and Stephen Toulmin, *Wittgenstein's Vienna* (New York: Simon and Schuster, 1973).
30 Quoted in Monk, *Ludwig Wittgenstein*, 41.

propositions of logic, is shown by equations in mathematics."[31] The only other propositions that had determinable truth-values were those of natural science. For Wittgenstein, all meaningful statements were composed of elementary propositions that described or "pictured" simple states of affairs in the world; the more complicated concepts of the natural sciences were composed of elementary propositions drawn from direct experience that were combined according to the (purely formal or analytic) rules of logic and mathematics. There were of course many other things one could say in language, but if they were neither the pseudo-propositions of mathematics nor the verifiable propositions of natural science, they were simply nonsense – they had no meaning at all. Wittgenstein did not intend to say that "meaningless" statements had no *value*, ethically or spiritually. It was simply that the propositions of ethics, aesthetics, and religious experience were not candidates for assessment in terms of their truth or falsity.

In Wittgenstein's view, his work had left nothing else to be said in philosophy. While the natural sciences would add to the stock of knowledge, and logical propositions would continue to knit elementary propositions together, the *Tractatus* had set the proper bounds of philosophy; any attempts to go beyond it would take philosophers into the realm of nonsense – or, at any rate, toward what was mystical, not philosophical *sensu stricto*. After completing the *Tractatus* in 1918, Wittgenstein abandoned philosophy; he failed to get his text published in either English or German, and handed the manuscript over to Russell to deal with it as he saw fit. In the end, the *Tractatus* was published in a German-language journal in 1921, and then in English in 1922, translated by C. K. Ogden and with an introduction by Russell. As Wittgenstein embarked on an ill-fated career as a school teacher in rural Austria, however, his philosophy took on a new life. In Cambridge, the *Tractatus* continued to be read and discussed, above all by Moore, who became in the 1920s the leading figure of the so-called "Cambridge school of analysis."[32] Wittgenstein's book also found an admirer in Frank Ramsey, a mathematician at King's College who made, in his short life, a series of seminal contributions to mathematics, economics, and philosophy.[33] It was in Wittgenstein's native Vienna, however, that the *Tractatus* had its most forceful impact.

---

31 Wittgenstein, *Tractatus Logico-Philosophicus*, 6.2 and 6.22.
32 Thomas Baldwin, "G. E. Moore and the Cambridge School of Analysis," in *The Oxford Handbook of the History of Analytic Philosophy*, ed. Michael Beaney (Oxford: Oxford University Press, 2013), 431–451.
33 On the Ramsey–Wittgenstein relationship, see Monk, *Ludwig Wittgenstein*, 215–224.

Scientific Philosophy in Interwar Europe

The universities and café culture of Vienna had been a hotbed of radical thought since the turn of the century. The break-up of the Austro-Hungarian Empire, and the coming to power of a socialist government in Austria after the war, had intensified the fertile, febrile intellectual climate.[34] In this context, the *Tractatus* was read by some as an anti-metaphysical tract, which offered a vision of all substantive human knowledge as reducible either to the purely analytic truths of logic, or to the substantive, empirical truths of the elementary propositions of natural science.[35] This interpretation of the *Tractatus* fit neatly some ideas already in play, notably those of the physicist and philosopher Ernst Mach (1838–1916), who was seen as the standard bearer of a new, strict positivism.[36] The key figure in this reception of Wittgenstein's thought was Moritz Schlick (1882–1936), who held the Chair in the Philosophy of the Inductive Sciences at the University of Vienna – a position he held from 1922 until his death in 1936. Schlick was trained in physics, but he gathered around him a remarkable group of mathematicians, philosophers, physicists, and social scientists. In addition to hosting a salon at his home and presiding over the mathematics seminar at the university, Schlick was also chairman of the Verein Ernst Mach, which became the main focal point of the Wiener Kreis, the Vienna Circle. Among its members were Rudolf Carnap, Otto Neurath, Friedrich Waismann, Hans Hahn, Gustav Bergman, Philipp Frank, and Kurt Gödel.

Schlick and some of his colleagues – notably Carnap, Hahn, and Waismann – spotted in the *Tractatus* a way of repurposing the logic of Frege and Russell to their own ends. For them it was a vehicle for the reconstruction of all knowledge on the basis of verifiable propositions and logical principles alone. This was in some respects a forcible act of appropriation. They did not just make Wittgenstein's arguments more resolutely anti-metaphysical and empiricist than Wittgenstein himself had intended; toward the end of the

---

34 For a general account of bourgeois intellectual life in Vienna during this period, see Deborah R. Coen, *Vienna in the Age of Uncertainty: Science, Liberalism, and Private Life* (Chicago: University of Chicago Press, 2007); and Janik and Toulmin, *Wittgenstein's Vienna*.

35 Brian McGuinness, "Wittgenstein and the Vienna Circle," *Synthese*, 64(3) (1985), 351–358; and David G. Stern, "Wittgenstein, the Vienna Circle, and Physicalism: A Reassessment," in *The Cambridge Companion to Logical Empiricism*, ed. Alan Richardson and Thomas Uebel (Cambridge: Cambridge University Press, 2008), 305–331.

36 The best general guide to the history of the circle is Friedrich Stadler, *The Vienna Circle: Studies in the Origins, Development, and Influence of Logical Empiricism*, 2nd edn. (Dordrecht: Springer, 2015).

1920s and into the early 1930s, they also adapted Wittgenstein's account of the principles of logic and mathematics. New currents in the foundations of mathematics in the 1920s revealed that there were more bases for arithmetic than Frege and Russell's "logicism": logic was not a finished system, as Wittgenstein had supposed. In due course, members of the Vienna Circle such as Rudolf Carnap seized on this plurality of logical systems to argue that the language of science (and so of knowledge *tout court*) could be reconstructed in different ways depending on which logical system (or "logical syntax") one employed.[37] Although members of the Vienna Circle, and Schlick especially, were much taken with Wittgenstein, they often adopted an instrumental approach to his findings in the *Tractatus*. Unsurprisingly, perhaps, on the occasions when Schlick, Carnap, and others succeeded in coaxing Wittgenstein into engaging them in discussion, they did not often see eye-to-eye.

These tensions notwithstanding, Wittgenstein's thought was crucial in sustaining new currents in the analytic tradition in the 1920s. The logical empiricism of the Vienna Circle was one of several interdisciplinary groups binding together philosophy, the mathematical sciences, and (in many cases), a secular, left politics during this era. To be sure, logical empiricism was much more diverse, and riven by much more disagreement, than conventional accounts of "logical positivism" suggest.[38] Everything from the status of "protocol sentences" (the elementary propositions on which the edifice of scientific knowledge was built) to the nature of "analytic" truths was up for discussion, as were the social and political implications of the new "scientific philosophy." When it was published in 1931, the manifesto of the circle around Schlick (*Wissenschaftliche Weltauffassung: Der Wiener Kreis* – The Scientific World Conception: The Vienna Circle) was markedly eclectic, and purposefully vague in its pronouncements.[39] Still, this diversity was a sign of a vibrant intellectual movement, which was united by its sense that breakthroughs in logic, mathematics, physics, and psychology were pointing toward a new unified and universal science, which would serve as a bulwark

---

37 See Steve Awodey and A. W. Carus, "The Turning Point and the Revolution: Philosophy of Mathematics in Logical Empiricism from *Tractatus* to Logical Syntax," in *The Cambridge Companion to Logical Empiricism*, ed. Alan Richardson and Thomas Uebel (Cambridge: Cambridge University Press, 2008), 165–192; and Michael Friedman, *Reconsidering Logical Positivism* (Cambridge: Cambridge University Press, 1999).

38 Alan Richardson, "The Scientific World Conception: Logical Positivism," in *The Cambridge History of Philosophy, 1870–1945*, ed. Thomas Baldwin (Cambridge: Cambridge University Press, 2003), 391–400.

39 Otto Neurath, Hans Hahn, and Rudolf Carnap, *Wissenschaftliche Weltauffassung: Der Wiener Kreis* (Vienna: Artur Wolf Verlag, 1929).

against the political and theological dogma suffusing European culture and society.[40] Sister groups sprang up in Berlin, for example, while important clusters of logicians and positivists were found in such places as Warsaw and Lwów in Poland, where Alfred Tarski (1901–1983) was one among a number of leading lights, and in Uppsala University under the jurist and philosopher Axel Hägerström (1868–1939).[41] This network would be rent asunder as Europe succumbed to fascism and war in the 1930s, but before it sank it drew in figures from Britain and the United States who would make "logical positivism" a word with which to conjure in philosophical circles after World War II.

The Turn from Empiricism

From the intellectual world of logical empiricism there emerged a second inflection point in the analytic tradition. The followers of Russell and the Wittgenstein of the *Tractatus* were, broadly speaking, empiricists, in the sense that, for them, any genuinely meaningful statement had to have correlates, however far removed by logical steps of inference, in experience. Perhaps the simplest way of stating the form that this commitment to empiricism took is to say, in the language of the *Tractatus*, that the "truth-values" of all meaningful propositions were fixed by *facts*, and that these facts were known only through experience.

This statement captures the essence of the new, 'logical' empiricism of the interwar analytic philosophers. The tools of logical analysis provided by Frege and Russell allowed one to make a seemingly crystal-clear distinction between those items of knowledge known *a priori* (which were described by the new logic) and those objects of knowledge derived from experience. But this apparently robust distinction, precisely because it isolated the domain of empirical knowledge so sharply, left the way open for a resurgence of what had traditionally been the Achilles Heel of empiricism, namely, skepticism, if not outright solipsism. It is not hard to see why a whole set of skeptical doubts soon returned within the heartlands of analytic philosophy. Truths

---

40 On the political and cultural program of the Circle, see, for example, Peter Galison, "Aufbau/Bauhaus: Logical Positivism and Architectural Modernism," *Critical Inquiry*, 16(4) (1990), 709–752; and George A. Reisch, *How the Cold War Transformed Philosophy of Science: To the Icy Slopes of Logic* (Cambridge: Cambridge University Press, 2005).

41 Richardson, "Scientific World Conception," 393; and Dieter Hoffmann, "The Society for Empirical/Scientific Philosophy," *The Cambridge Companion to Logical Empiricism*, ed. Alan Richardson and Thomas Uebel (Cambridge: Cambridge University Press, 2008), 41–57.

known by experience were by definition subjective. Yet, if all experience was given to individual consciousness and accessible only to the person undergoing the experience, then in what sense was the basis of knowledge truly objective?

After Wittgenstein's *Tractatus*, analytic philosophers' turn toward an epistemology of propositions and facts reopened this very old philosophical can of worms by making empirical verification the hinge between propositions and their truth-values. At issue for the logical empiricists was how verification-by-experience could be made safe for the logical construction of knowledge.[42] The nub of the issue was how to embrace empiricism while evading the problems of skepticism and solipsism. What emerged from the deliberations of figures like Wittgenstein, Carnap, and Schlick was what Peter Strawson would later call the "no-ownership theory" of sensations.[43]

The claim that sensations have no owners – no persons to whom they are given – is perhaps less absurd that it sounds. It was couched as a rebuttal of the view that the appeal to elementary experiences as the basis of human knowledge led ineluctably to solipsism. Logical empiricists rejected the idea that the basis of their logical constructions of knowledge had to be "subjective" experiences. Already in the *Tractatus*, Wittgenstein presented the no-ownership theory of sensations to analytical philosophers. He admitted the truth of solipsism: the problem that using experience as a bedrock of objective knowledge left one making an appeal to sensations given to a particular person. But he argued further that this dilemma entailed not Cartesian skepticism but rather the elimination of the "metaphysical subject" from the theory of knowledge altogether.

These arguments resonated with members of the Vienna Circle and their followers. For example, in his first major book, *Der logische Aufbau der Welt* (1928), Rudolf Carnap took as the basis of his constructional system what he called "the stream of experience" or "the given," but he was quick to point out that this choice of "methodological solipsism" contained no subjectivist or idealist assumptions. Basing one's system on the given did not "presuppose somebody or something to whom the given is given." Carnap breezily affirmed that the given "does not have a subject" (§65). Emboldened both by recent work in empirical psychology and by the metaphysical critique of Nietzsche, Carnap cited the lists of philosophers who agreed with him that

---

42 Thomas Uebel, *Overcoming Logical Positivism from Within: The Emergence of Neurath's Naturalism in the Vienna Circle's Protocol Sentence Debate* (Amsterdam: Rodopi, 1992).
43 Peter F. Strawson, *Individuals: An Essay in Descriptive Metaphysics* (London: Routledge, 1990 [1959]), 95.

"the self is not implicit in the data of cognition." This, as we have seen, was precisely Wittgenstein's claim in the *Tractatus*. In fact, the holistic understanding of "experience" emerging from the discipline of psychology showed that the very notion of a subject–object split, which Frege had simply assumed in his account of "ideas," was itself a construction out of more elementary "total impressions." Hence Carnap saw no absurdity in speaking of a "subjectless given." Moreover, he sidestepped the worry that solipsism would make the objectivity of science impossible by insisting that what made for objectivity was in any case *not* the basis of a constructional system – i.e., statements about sense data or states of affairs in the world – but only that "certain *structural properties* [of that system] are analogous for all streams of experience."[44] Those structural properties were precisely what Carnap's constructional system would delineate; objectivity was the *intersubjectivity* of a shared logical structure of knowledge.

The most trenchant version of the no-ownership theory of sense-experiences was presented by the leader of the Vienna Circle, Moritz Schlick. In 1936, he gave a defense of Viennese positivism to an American audience. He insisted that the thoroughgoing empiricism of the logical positivists provided no grounds for the skeptical or solipsistic worries generated by the egocentric predicament. Indeed, "one of the greatest advantages and attractions of true positivism," Schlick maintained, was "the antisolipsistic attitude that characterizes it from the very beginning." The mistaken notion that immediate experience was in the "first person" was itself a product of ungrounded *a priori* assumptions that the "genuine positivist" could never accept. Thus, for the positivist, "this predicament does not exist."[45]

In advocating this theory, the logical empiricists and their allies pushed the new empiricism as far as it could go. Whether they succeeded in evading the dilemmas of skepticism is less clear. As we shall see in the next section, the epistemic status of sensations and mental states was an issue that Wittgenstein and his later students would address in their "grammatical" approach to conceptual analysis. From the hard-edged empiricism of the interwar scientific philosophers there developed concern with questions of personhood, intentionality, and morality. This brought about a transformation that helped to renew the analytic tradition in the decades after 1945.

---

44 Rudolf Carnap, *The Logical Construction of the World, and Pseudoproblems in Philosophy*, trans. Rolf A. George (Peru: Carus Publishing, 2003), 101–109. First published in German in 1928.
45 Moritz Schlick, "Meaning and Verification," *Philosophical Review*, 45(4) (1936), 339–369, pp. 358–359.

Toward Ordinary Language Philosophy

In retrospect, it is clear that Schlick published his remarks at a crucial juncture in the history of the analytic tradition. In the same year of 1936, Schlick was killed by a deranged and likely politically motivated student while leaving class. Schlick's murder precipitated the break-up of the Vienna Circle. In the following years, exponents of scientific philosophy in Europe began to go into exile, often in the United States. Even before Schlick's untimely death, logical empiricism was beginning to make its presence felt in English-speaking philosophy – a process that was accelerated by the intellectual migration before and during the war. Indeed, Schlick's 1936 paper was a rejoinder to a critique of "logical positivism" advanced by the Harvard logician and latter-day pragmatist Clarence Irving Lewis. Lewis's skepticism about the doctrines of the Vienna Circle, which he felt merely reinforced the "egocentric predicament," was itself a sign that the work of figures like Wittgenstein and Carnap was being taken increasingly seriously outside of German-speaking Europe.[46] In the early 1930s, figures such as the American logician Willard Van Orman Quine (1908–2000) and the Oxford-trained British philosopher Alfred Jules Ayer (1910–1989) had made the pilgrimage to Vienna to absorb the new scientific philosophy.[47] Soon after – again, in 1936 – Ayer published what would become the single most important English-language textbook on "logical positivism," *Language, Truth, and Logic*.[48] Quine, from his perch at Harvard, began to position himself as Carnap's foremost expositor and critic in the United States.[49]

In Britain, too, it was a time of transition. Already in the later 1920s, Gilbert Ryle (1900–1976) was at the forefront of a group of philosophers at Oxford who were increasingly resistant to its ambient Idealism. Ryle read Russell and befriended Wittgenstein when the latter returned to Cambridge in 1929. Ryle was especially taken with the positivist insistence on distinguishing between sense and nonsense. Emboldened, he began to inject a hard-edged style of

---

46 Clarence Irving Lewis, "Experience and Meaning," *Philosophical Review*, 43(2) (1934), 125–146.
47 See Willard V. O. Quine, *The Time of My Life: An Autobiography* (Cambridge: MIT Press, 1985), 92–95; and Ben Rogers, *A. J. Ayer: A Life* (New York: Grove Press, 1999), 97–106.
48 Alfred Jules Ayer, *Language, Truth, and Logic* (London: Gollancz, 1936).
49 Peter Hylton, "'The Defensible Province of Philosophy': Quine's 1934 Lectures on Carnap," in *Future Pasts: The Analytic Tradition in Twentieth-Century Philosophy*, ed. Juliet Floyd and Sanford Shieh (Oxford: Oxford University Press, 2001), 257–275; and Alan Richardson, "Logical Empiricism, American Pragmatism, and the Fate of Scientific Philosophy in North America," in *Logical Empiricism in North America*, ed. Gary L. Hardcastle and Alan W. Richardson (Minneapolis: University of Minnesota Press, 2003), 1–24.

German-influenced analysis into the complacent philosophical scene at Oxford.[50] By the mid 1930s, Ayer's polemical interventions on behalf of the new positivism generated yet more discussion, and encouraged younger figures, such as J. L. Austin (1911–1960) and Isaiah Berlin (1909–1997), to join the fray.[51] In Cambridge, too, analysis was making inroads, thanks in large part to Wittgenstein's return to philosophy, but also owing to the growing prominence of students mentored by Moore, such as John Wisdom (1904–1993) and Susan Stebbing (1885–1943).[52] The upheavals caused by the war cleared the path for this new generation to take up the mantle of philosophical analysis, and to do so often through direct engagement with legatees of central European scientific philosophy, who were attempting to find a home within British and American universities.

Schlick's 1936 lecture on sensory knowledge also marked the limit of logical empiricism's attempt to conjure away the problem of solipsism that Lewis thought beset their approach. The dispersal of scientific philosophers might have made analytic philosophy no more than a rump movement, were it not for the fact that Wittgenstein began to change his mind about the salience of the problem of solipsism within his philosophical system. As he came to appreciate the difficulties of the "no-ownership" theory during the 1930s, Wittgenstein developed a notion of conceptual analysis less absolute than the one he had offered in the *Tractatus*. If, as he started to insist, our grasp of concepts that pertained to sensations relied on an intuitive grasp of their "grammar," of the way they were properly used in ordinary speech, then it was less clear that questions of subjectivity could be excluded from the discussion. The deeper one delved into the grammatical differences in the use of terms, and into the human ability to understand the norms underpinning the use of concepts, the more it seemed that the phenomena of meaning and understanding were grounded in more basic features of human life that were not reducible to philosophical first principles. By the time he came to write what has become his second major work, the posthumously published *Philosophical Investigations* (1953), Wittgenstein was speaking of his aim as that of uncovering what he called "the natural history of the human."[53]

---

50 Gilbert Ryle, "Autobiographical," in *Ryle*, ed. Oscar P. Wood and George Pitcher (London: Macmillan, 1971), 1–12.
51 Isaiah Berlin, "Austin and the Early Beginnings of Oxford Philosophy," in Isaiah Berlin, L. W. Forguson, D. F. Pears, G. Pitcher, J. R. Searle, P. F. Strawson, and G. J. Warnock, *Essays on J. L. Austin* (Oxford: Clarendon Press, 1973), 6–7.
52 See Baldwin, "G. E. Moore and the Cambridge School of Analysis."
53 Ludwig Wittgenstein, *Philosophical Investigations*, trans. G. E. M. Anscombe, 3rd edn. (Oxford: Blackwell, 2001 [1953]).

Inspired by Wittgenstein's example, a generation of analytic philosophers began to explore the languages of human intention and motivation, a field known as "philosophical psychology."

One thesis in particular underpinned Wittgenstein's approach: The ability to grasp mental states, or to follow rules of thought and action, presupposed a concept of ourselves and others as *persons*. The grammar of a given concept usually hinged on this underlying sense of personhood. For example, it was part of one's understanding of the concept of pain that the person in pain would *have* it: They would not have to check, or test, whether they were in pain; if someone did, say, insist on examining their behavior to determine whether or not they were in pain, we would think them odd. On the other hand, to say one knew that another person was in pain was not to say that *their* behavior met with certain outward behavioral criteria; it was to know that they suffered. To say that one knew that another was in pain was to express – barring special circumstances – one's sympathy with their plight. It was this kind of implicit understanding of these bounds of personhood that allowed us to intuit the grammar of psychological or mental concepts, whether those of sensations like pain, or those of moral emotions and attitudes.[54]

The reception of Wittgenstein's later philosophy turned to a considerable degree on the fleshing out of this kind of analysis, and its extension into the realms of social theory and moral philosophy. It was used to buttress a trenchant critique of positivism in psychology and social science – a line of attack most easily seen in the Wittgensteinian "red books" of the 1950s and 1960s, the most famous of which was Peter Winch's *The Idea of a Social Science* (1958).[55] Wittgenstein's approach was also used by philosophers such as Elizabeth Anscombe and Philippa Foot in Great Britain, and John Rawls in the United States, in their search for a grammar of moral emotions and natural attitudes – pride, guilt, shame, anger.[56] The aim was to outline a new

---

54 For a fuller discussion, see Joel Isaac, "Pain, Analytical Philosophy, and American Intellectual History," in *The Worlds of American Intellectual History*, ed. Joel Isaac, James T. Kloppenberg, Michael O'Brien, and Jennifer Ratner-Rosenhagen (New York: Oxford University Press, 2016), 202–217.

55 Peter Winch, *The Idea of a Social Science and Its Relation to Philosophy* (London: Routledge & Kegan Paul, 1958).

56 Elizabeth Anscombe, "Intention," *Proceedings of the Aristotelian Society*, 57 (1956), 321–332; Elizabeth Anscombe, "Modern Moral Philosophy," *Philosophy*, 33(124) (1958), 1–19; Elizabeth Anscombe, "On the Grammar of 'Enjoy.'" *Journal of Philosophy*, 64(19) (1967), 607–614; Philippa Foot, "Moral Beliefs," *Proceedings of the Aristotelian Society* 59 (1958), 83–104; and John Rawls, *A Theory of Justice* (Oxford: Oxford University Press, 1971).

kind of moral psychology, on the basis of which philosophical analysis could be extended to questions of ethics and politics.[57]

A notable feature of this Wittgensteinian philosophy was that its appeal to "ordinary" or everyday uses of words by no means entailed a commitment to the study of empirical usage. On the contrary, the aim was to uncover the transcendental conditions of meaning and understanding, even if these turned out to be grounded in little more than the "whirl of organism" that underwrote the human ability to acknowledge and intelligibly respond to one another.[58] Nevertheless, the methods of Wittgenstein and his followers held something in common with the more empirical approach to ordinary language being developed in postwar Britain by two leading lights at Oxford, Gilbert Ryle and J. L. Austin. Ryle's own "logical behaviorism" – which defended the notion that psychological concepts were irreducible to physical ones – was not directly influenced by Wittgenstein. Austin, meanwhile, cited Moore, not Wittgenstein, as his principal inspiration in his analysis of the performative aspects of human speech and their role in the production of meaning. Still, both recognized that they shared with Wittgenstein an emphasis on the importance of the use of words in everyday, established contexts in determining their meaning. Alongside Wittgenstein's *Philosophical Investigations*, their key works – notably Ryle's *The Concept of Mind* (1949) and Austin's *How to Do Things with Words* (1955) – helped to define a new kind of linguistic analysis within the analytic tradition.[59]

In the United States, the analytic tradition took a somewhat different course. Because so many of the leading logical empiricists emigrated to the United States, their positivism was imbibed more directly. At the same time, many of the philosophers who introduced the work of the Vienna Circle to American audiences were interested in questions that the later Wittgenstein had bypassed. W. V. Quine, who had been trained by Whitehead and taken under Carnap's wing, presented the analytic tradition as a retooled form of empiricism, which was nonetheless beholden to two older dogmas: namely, that there was a sharp distinction between analytic and synthetic truths, and that meaningful statements within a language must be reducible to immediate

---

57 For a full discussion of this mid-century program in Wittgensteinian moral psychology, see P. MacKenzie Bok, "The Early Rawls and His Path to *A Theory of Justice*," Ph.D. Thesis, University of Cambridge, 2015.
58 Stanley Cavell, *Must We Mean What We Say?* (Cambridge: Cambridge University Press, 1969), 52.
59 Gilbert Ryle, *The Concept of Mind* (London: Hutchinson's University Library, 1949); and John L. Austin, *How to Do Things with Words: The William James Lectures Delivered at Harvard University in 1955* (Oxford: Clarendon Press, 1962).

experience.[60] This way of framing the logical empiricist project obscured its animating philosophical (and for that matter political) concerns.[61] But it did bring onto the agenda questions about epistemology and ontology that would be central to North American variants of analytic philosophy. By the late 1950s, currents of Quinean naturalism were beginning to mix with the philosophy of language associated with Wittgenstein and Oxford, to create an increasingly rich and pluralistic intellectual scene.[62]

In the 1970s, with Quine's Harvard and Oxford at the apex of their power, analytic philosophy had become a globe-straddling tradition. Its Central European and Cantabridgian roots had been augmented by an Anglo-American alliance that propelled various forms of logical and linguistic analysis to the forefront of philosophical inquiry. Americans – senior and junior – came through Oxford on visiting fellowships; British philosophers took up visiting or full-time positions in North America. The powerful Harvard philosophy department began to clone itself elsewhere in the United States. Even insurgent movements – the turn to analytic metaphysics at Princeton, for example, under David Lewis and Saul Kripke – bore the stamp of Quine's Harvard.

Putting all of this together into a single, coherent intellectual tradition is, of course, a different matter. Like an impressionist painting, the analytic tradition is easy to see at a distance, but apt to dissolve into a thousand brushstrokes when examined up close. Still, although the pointillist treatment has its virtues, this chapter has tried to show how the main contours are visible even when we are careful to acknowledge the diversity of the tradition.

---

60 Willard V. O. Quine, "Two Dogmas of Empiricism," *Philosophical Review*, 60(1) (1951), 20–43.
61 For a critique of Quine in this regard, see Richardson, "Logical Empiricism, American Pragmatism, and the Fate of Scientific Philosophy in North America."
62 See, for example, G. Pitcher, "Austin: A Personal Memoir," in Isaiah Berlin, L. W. Forguson, D. F. Pears, G. Pitcher, J. R. Searle, P. F. Strawson, and G. J. Warnock, *Essays on J. L. Austin* (Oxford: Clarendon Press, 1973), 17–30; and Stanley Cavell, *Little Did I Know: Excerpts from Memory* (Stanford: Stanford University Press, 2010), 322–326.

8

American Ideas in the European Imagination

JAMES T. KLOPPENBERG AND SAM KLUG

By the time Jean-Paul Sartre first visited the United States in the winter of 1945, he was already fascinated by American culture. A bookish child, he had grown up reading not only French classics but also American detective novels; he romanticized the Wild West along with medieval France. While teaching in a lycée in Le Havre in 1931–1932, he discovered the fiction of William Faulkner and John Dos Passos, whom he described in an essay six years later as "the greatest writer of our time." Like many Europeans experiencing the United States for the first time, Sartre saw much to like and much to loathe. New York City, he wrote in 1945, "is for far-sighted people, people who can focus on infinity." Sartre and his fellow French visitors were put up at the Plaza and welcomed in New York by members of the École Libre des Hautes Études, which had already greeted many French and German émigrés fleeing the Third Reich. During their eight-week stay, the French guests of the US government traveled to Pittsburgh, Chicago, Hollywood, Washington, D.C., and rural Georgia, and – from a plane swooping too close for comfort – marveled at the Grand Canyon. Sartre noted that the American bourgeoisie, unlike their French counterparts, seemed to him indistinguishable, in appearance and behavior, from the white working class. The "misery of the farmer" in the South reminded him of that of colonized peoples in North Africa. "Negroes" everywhere in the United States were rigidly segregated "untouchables," "pariahs" with "absolutely no political rights." Sartre lamented the loss of glamor in the new movies being released but hailed the rise of film noir and singled out *Casablanca* for special praise. The French journalists met with European refugees and prominent Americans ranging from the writer Walter Lippmann to Franklin D. Roosevelt. They did not know that the FBI was monitoring every step they took.

In a gushing letter to the editor of the *New York Times*, Sartre proclaimed his "deep affection" for the United States, not merely for its role in the (nearly complete) liberation of Europe, but also "because men of our generation have been influenced by your literature, and because during the Occupation we turned our spirits toward you, the greatest of all free countries." When Sartre returned to the new world a year later, primarily to visit one of the many women in his life, he gave lectures at Yale, Harvard, Princeton, Columbia, and Carnegie Hall. He promised that the rising writers of postwar France would return to America "the techniques you have lent us," primarily Faulkner's stream of consciousness and Dos Passos's celebration of ordinary people bucking the system. In two brief trips to the United States, Sartre managed to articulate all four dimensions of European intellectuals' persistent fascination with – and contempt for – the culture across the Atlantic.[1]

America has enchanted Europeans for more than five centuries. From the moment Columbus landed, through the bloody conquest of the continent by European settlers, and up until the present, Europeans have viewed the new world as a magic screen, onto which they have projected their wildest hopes and deepest fears, often simultaneously. Before and since France enabled the United States to establish its independence and the new nation developed a culture of its own, Americans have produced ideas that Europeans have found sublime and ideas that Europeans have found odious.

Of the four dimensions of the intellectual relations between Europe and the United States, the first is the puzzle of émigrés. When do thinkers born elsewhere become American? Right away? Never? What if they never return "home" but spend their remaining years in America, as did Francis Lieber, Ayn Rand, Friedrich Hayek, Hannah Arendt, Leo Strauss, Herbert Marcuse, and countless others who fled Europe?[2] What about those who traveled east and stayed, such as Henry James, Gertrude Stein, T. S. Eliot, Richard Wright, and William Forsythe? Did they remain American or become something else? Second is the impact of European ideas on American thinkers, a topic that has received a great deal of scholarly attention and continues to illuminate American intellectual history. No one who wants to study

---

[1] Annie Cohen-Solal, *Sartre: A Life*, ed. Norman MacAfee, trans. Anna Cancogni (New York: Pantheon, 1987), provides a vivid account of Sartre's American visits.

[2] Studies of this phenomenon include, among many others, Laura Fermi, *Illustrious Immigrants: The Intellectual Migration from Europe, 1930–1941* (Chicago: University of Chicago Press, 1971); Martin Jay, *The Dialectical Imagination: A History of the Frankfurt School and the Institute for Social Research, 1923–1950* (Boston: Little, Brown & Co., 1973); and Anthony Heilbut, *Exiled in Paradise: German Refugee Artists and Intellectuals in America, from the 1930s to the Present* (Boston: Beacon Press, 1983).

American thought can afford to stop at the shore of the Atlantic.[3] Third is the enormous impact of American popular culture in Europe: movies and cartoons, music and television, advertising and consumer goods (such as the once notorious and now ubiquitous Coca-Cola).[4] Fourth is the significance of American thinkers for European intellectual history, a dimension of the topic that has not received equal attention. In this "needs-and-opportunities-for-study" essay, we will concentrate on this fourth dimension, particularly in relation to social theory, because it seems to us that students of European intellectual history often pay less attention to American thinkers than did the people whose ideas they study.

The possibility that the new world – and it is worth pondering the significance of that phrase – might be the source of new ideas, and might enable Europeans to experiment with new forms of life, beckoned from the beginning. Hints of dramatic differences shimmered in early travelers' accounts. Amerigo Vespucci, writing to Lorenzo de' Medici in 1503, set the tone that would endure for most of the sixteenth century. He reported that "the inhabitants of the New World do not have goods of their own, but all things are held in common. They live together without king, without government, and each is his own master." Not only did they organize their own economic and political affairs, they "live according to nature," and the "great abundance of gold" meant it could be taken for granted rather than "esteemed or valued." It was, in short, a "terrestrial paradise." In Thomas More's *Utopia*, his imaginary friend Raphael Hythloday has just returned from a voyage with Vespucci, and his account of utopian social life closely resembles that outlined in Vespucci's letter.[5] More and other humanists also knew the writings of Peter Martyr, who described the inhabitants of the New World in similar terms: "amongst them the land belongs to everybody, just as does the sun or the water. They know no difference between mine and yours, that source of all evils." Martyr too wistfully invoked paradise: "It is indeed

---

[3] Joel Isaac, James T. Kloppenberg, Michael O'Brien, and Jennifer Ratner-Rosenhagen (eds.), *The Worlds of American Intellectual History* (New York: Oxford University Press, 2017).

[4] Richard Pells, *Not Like Us: How Europeans Have Loved, Hated, and Transformed American Culture since World War II* (New York: Basic Books, 1997); Richard Pells, *Modernist America: Art, Music, Movies, and the Globalization of American Culture* (New Haven: Yale University Press, 2011); Michael Ermarth (ed.), *America and the Shaping of German Society, 1945–1955* (Oxford: Berg, 1993); and Victoria de Grazia, *Irresistible Empire: America's Advance through Twentieth-Century Europe* (Cambridge: Harvard University Press, 2005).

[5] Amerigo Vespucci, "Mundus Novus: Letter on his Third Voyage to Lorenzo Pietro Francesco de Medici," March or April 1503, reprinted in *The Letters of Amerigo Vespucci*, ed. Clements R. Markham (London: Hakluyt Society, 1894), 46–48.

a golden age, neither ditches nor hedges, nor walls enclose their domains; they live in gardens open to all, without walls, without judges."[6]

Where some saw Eden, others saw opportunity.[7] Columbus reckoned from the start that the friendly Indians who met his ships would make "good servants," and the merciless *conquistadores* who followed in his wake aimed to exploit the qualities the humanists admired. The French Calvinist minister Jean de Léry recounted that the Indians he encountered in the new world had "neither kings nor princes, and consequently each is more or less as much a great lord as the other."[8] The Spanish historian José de Acosta, who spent seventeen years in Spanish America, published a *History* in the 1580s that perpetuated such visions: "Surely the Greeks and Romans, if they had known the Republics of the Mexicans and the Incas, would have greatly esteemed their laws and governments. We today only enter there by the sword, giving them no heed, no hearing, no more consideration than a venison taken in the forest." Acosta shared the idea that Europeans had much to learn from the new world. Many of the "peoples and nations of the Indies have never suffered kings or Lords of an absolute and sovereign sort," precisely the sort judged indispensable in early modern Europe. Instead "they live in common and create and ordain certain Captains and Princes for certain occasions only, during which time they obey their rule. Afterward, these leaders return to their ordinary status."[9] The prospect that such peaceful, benevolent, and self-governing cultures might exist at all – and Acosta insisted that "the greatest part of the New World governs itself in this fashion" – electrified European readers. No one used the differences between the old and new worlds more effectively than Michel de Montaigne, who

---

6 Peter Martyr, *De Orbe Novo: The Eight Decades of Peter Martyr d'Anghera*, trans. Francis Augustus MacNutt, 2 vols. (New York: G. P. Putnam's Sons, 1912), vol. I, 103–104.
7 On the impact of early images of American Indian cultures, see Karen Ordahl Kupperman (ed.), *America in European Consciousness* (Chapel Hill: University of North Carolina Press, 1995); J. H. Eliot, *The Old World and the New, 1492–1650* (Cambridge: Cambridge University Press, 1972); J. Martin Evans, *America: The View from Europe* (New York: Norton, 1976); Mary B. Campbell, *The Witness and the Other World: Exotic European Travel Writing, 400–1600* (Ithaca: Cornell University Press, 1988); C. Vann Woodward, *The Old World's New World* (New York: Oxford University Press, 1991); Anthony Pagden, *European Encounters with the New World* (New Haven: Yale University Press, 1993); Jack P. Greene, *The Intellectual Construction of America: Exceptionalism and Identity from 1492 to 1800* (Chapel Hill: University of North Carolina Press, 1993); and Stephen Greenblatt, *Marvelous Possessions: The Wonder of the New World* (Chicago: University of Chicago Press, 1991).
8 Jean de Léry, *History of a Voyage to the Land of Brazil*, trans. Janet Whatley (Berkeley: University of California Press, 1992), 113.
9 José de Acosta, *Natural and Moral History of the Indies*, ed. Jane Mangan, trans. Frances Lopes-Morillas (Durham: Duke University Press, 2002), 330.

leveraged travelers' accounts and perceptions of indigenous people visiting France to unsettle assumptions about the universality of European values.[10]

From the earliest days of contact until today, awareness of the contrasts between American and European cultures has inspired self-criticism among some observers and reinforced others' arrogance. The English Levellers took the experience of their co-religionists in New England as evidence that self-governing communities of saints could redeem the promise of Christianity. John Locke built his version of contract theory on the idea that once "all the world was America" – in his estimation, propertyless and ungoverned. Jean-Jacques Rousseau and other *philosophes* deployed the customs of American Indians, as Montesquieu used his Persian travelers, to show the artificiality of the *salonier* in contrast to the "natural man" freely roaming American forests. Only with the appearance in 1770 of one the most widely read works of the Enlightenment, the Abbé Raynal's *Histoire philosophique et politique des établissements et du commerce des européens dans les Deux Indes*, did Europeans begin thinking of Europeans rather than Indians as "Americans." Raynal was among the first to predict that one day those outposts on the periphery of European culture might outshine – and overpower – the metropole, a perception that spread rapidly once the United States had been established. St. Jean de Crèvecœur explained in his *Letters from an American Farmer* (1782) that the new nation was filled with equal, independent, self-governing landowners liberated from outdated old-world impediments, an intoxicating prospect for subjects of the King of France.[11]

Radicals all over continental Europe devoured the writings of young American firebrands such as John Adams, Thomas Paine, and Thomas Jefferson. Adams later earned a reputation as a conservative because of his emphasis on the separation of powers, his opposition to Jacobinism (and Jeffersonian Democratic-Republicans), and his cantankerousness, but before the outbreak of the French Revolution he was a passionate critic of aristocracy and partisan of popular government. Adams's *Thoughts on Government* (1776) provided the template for the state and national constitutions; he described his Constitution for the Commonwealth of Massachusetts (1780),

---

10 Michel de Montaigne, "Of Cannibals" and "Of Coaches," in Michel de Montaigne, *The Complete Works*, trans. Donald Frame (New York: Knopf, 2003), 182–193 and 831–849.
11 On the effects of America on European theorists, see James T. Kloppenberg, *Toward Democracy: The Struggle for Self-Rule in European and American Thought* (New York: Oxford University Press, 2016); and Denis Lacorne, Jacques Rupnik, and Marie-France Toinet (eds.), *L'Amérique dans les têtes: Un siècle de fascinations et d'aversions* (Paris: Hachette, 1986). Since its founding in 1979, the bilingual journal *La Revue Tocqueville/The Tocqueville Review* has focused on transatlantic cultural and political connections.

still in force today, as "Locke, Sidney, Rousseau, and de Mably reduced to practice." The American Revolution was widely thought to mark the beginning of a new age, which explains why Paine, active in the French Revolution before his Girondin leanings put him in prison, was entrusted to deliver the key to the Bastille to George Washington. Many of the new nation's defining documents, including Jefferson's Declaration of Independence, were quickly translated into European languages and devoured by radicals eager to import self-rule to Europe. Before Jefferson left Paris in 1789, he worked with the Marquis de Lafayette to draft a Charter of Rights designed to graft institutions of representative democracy onto the French monarchy. Like some of Jefferson's agricultural experiments with grapes and rice, the hybrid failed to reproduce.[12]

Louis Alexandre Frédéric, duc de la Rochefoucauld d'Enville helped explain the new nation to European readers. He produced one of the first translations of the state constitutions in 1783. In a two-volume account of his extensive travels through the United States in 1795–1796, his cousin François Alexandre Frédéric, duc de la Rochefoucauld-Liancourt, introduced themes that have endured. He was favorably impressed by the "simplicity" of American manners and the industriousness of the people. It is not clear whether he had read Adam Smith, but he reported that although Americans' "love of money" might be thought to "harden the heart," there was in America a "universal interest, which unites and supports society," that "no member can enrich himself, without promoting at the same time the prosperity of others." The progeny of commerce and democracy, which Alexis de Tocqueville would later dub "self-interest properly understood" ("*l'intérêt bien entendu*"), Rochefoucauld-Liancourt found already thriving less than a decade after the ratification of the Constitution. The American aspiration to do well while doing good, or vice versa, has fascinated European observers ever since.[13]

When nineteenth-century European travelers to the United States, including Harriet Martineau and Charles Dickens as well as Tocqueville, recounted their adventures, they shared Rochefoucauld-Liancourt's assessment of Americans' "simple" manners but found them appalling rather than

---

12 John Adams, *Works*, ed. Charles Francis Adams, 10 vols. (Boston, 1850–1856), vol. IV, 216. On the lines of influence running across the Atlantic in both directions during the late eighteenth century, see Kloppenberg, *Toward Democracy*, Chapters 5–12.
13 Louis Alexandre Frédéric, duc de la Rochefoucauld, *Constitutions des treize États-Unis de l'Amérique* (Paris: Ph.-D. Pierres, 1783); and François Alexandre Frédéric, duc de la Rochefoucauld-Liancourt, *Travels through the United States of North America, the Country of the Iroquois, and Upper Canada in the Years 1795, 1796, and 1797*, 2 vols. (London: R. Phillips, 1799), vol. I, 64–66.

charming. Thus was inscribed on the European imagination the notion of the United States as a nation of country bumpkins, people incapable of what Walt Whitman later mocked as "politesse" and whose behavior many European intellectuals either lampooned as crude or celebrated, as Sartre did, as a sign of unvarnished authenticity. Tocqueville's *Democracy in America* (vol. I, 1835; vol. II, 1840), then as now the most widely read portrait of the early United States, was hailed right away as an ambitious work of social theory rather than a mere travelogue. Tocqueville's vivid accounts of the New England town as the seedbed of democracy, his description of the magic metamorphosis of the ancient vice of egoism into the spirit driving vibrant political participation, and his warnings about the explosive contradiction between the fact of slavery and the ideal of freedom fixed in the minds of Europeans a complex image of the United States. A nation simultaneously benevolent and cold-hearted, boisterous and oppressive, it was the land of the future conceived as potentially more egalitarian and potentially more stultifying than the present or the past.

Most Europeans, however, did not understand (then or now) that the heart of Tocqueville's analysis derived as much from his reading of Adams, Jefferson, and James Madison as from his own experiences. Nor did they realize how much of his writing reflected the understanding of American democracy that he took from his lengthy conversations and correspondence with former President John Quincy Adams and a future president of Harvard College, Jared Sparks. These anti-slavery New Englanders not only formed Tocqueville's – and his European readers' – views of the United States, both North and South, but also powerfully shaped the broader assessments of the possibilities of democratic culture that Tocqueville's allies, notably John Stuart Mill, bequeathed to later European thinkers.[14]

If the influence of American thinkers was masked in Tocqueville's work, the influence of nineteenth-century Americans on other Europeans was less obscure. Thomas Carlyle and John Ruskin corresponded with Ralph Waldo Emerson, and Friedrich Nietzsche later claimed that Emerson had been a powerful influence on his own developing ideas. Emerson's friend Henry David Thoreau was known primarily through his books on Walden Pond and the Merrimack River, and his sense of the proper relation between humans and the non-human world would inspire later environmentalists on both sides of the Atlantic. Thoreau's other most influential writings, including his

---

14 On the American sources of Tocqueville's ideas, see Kloppenberg, *Toward Democracy*, Chapters 12 and 13.

essay on civil disobedience and his defense of John Brown, were prompted by his hatred of slavery, a sentiment widely shared among European abolitionists. Among the other Americans most influential among European thinkers in the middle decades of the nineteenth century were anti-slavery activists, notably Frederick Douglass, whose powerful autobiography was only the best-known of the many American slave narratives that circulated among Europeans appalled by the discrepancy between American tributes to liberty and their acquiescence in its antithesis. Both the literary form and the content of Douglass's autobiography were recognizable to Europeans familiar with the writings of black abolitionists in eighteenth-century England, such as Olaudah Equiano and Ottobah Cugoano. Abraham Lincoln, at least when he was finally transformed by anti-slavery activists such as Douglass (and by military expediency) from a moderate opposing slavery's expansion into the Great Emancipator, became, in the eyes of Europeans ranging from Mill to Marx, the American most admired on the other side of the Atlantic.[15]

Another set of American reformers who likewise identified a longstanding form of hierarchy as intolerable oppression attracted Europeans' attention. Women's rights advocates in the United States had kept alive the ideas of Mary Wollstonecraft and Olympe de Gouges, even though many people on both sides of the Atlantic thought Wollstonecraft's scandalous life discredited her writings. The women who gathered in Seneca Falls, New York, in 1848 had cut their teeth in anti-slavery activism during the 1830s, and they stayed in contact with like-minded European women. When the Americans gathered in Worcester, Massachusetts, in 1851, they highlighted an essay received from the British radical Harriet Taylor Mill. They also read a translated letter from the French writers Jeanne Deroin and Pauline Roland, who sent a message of solidarity from the prison where they had been incarcerated for their role in the revolution of 1848. Lucretia Mott and Elizabeth Cady Stanton, two of the women who drafted the Declaration of Sentiments and Resolutions in Seneca Falls, patterned their arguments after Jefferson's in the Declaration of Independence. They reasoned, as did Taylor Mill, Deroin, and Roland, that it was past time to extend, in the domestic, civic, and economic spheres, these "natural rights" from one half of the human race to the other. As all involved

---

15 Olaudah Equiano, *The Interesting Narrative of the Life of Olaudah Equiano; or, Gustavus Vassa, the African; Written by Himself*, ed. Robert J. Allison (New York: Palgrave MacMillan, 2007 [1789]); Caleb McDaniel, *The Problem of Democracy in the Age of Slavery: Garrisonian Abolitionists and Transatlantic Reform* (Baton Rouge: Louisiana State University Press, 2013); and Leslie Butler, *Critical Americans: Victorian Intellectuals and Transatlantic Reform* (Chapel Hill: University of North Carolina Press, 2007).

agreed, in the mid-to-late-nineteenth-century and early-twentieth-century transatlantic women's rights movement, the lines of influence ran in both directions.[16]

With the rise of research universities in the United States in the closing decades of the nineteenth century, the nation's previously parochial colleges began to play a larger role in scholarly discourse. In some disciplines, American thinkers remained consumers rather than producers of knowledge until the middle of the twentieth century. In other domains it took decades for American-born ideas to register in Europe. The remainder of this chapter sketches some of the principal contributions of American thinkers to conversations that have become, as many of the chapters in these two volumes make clear, *transatlantic* rather than strictly European.

Charles Sanders Peirce (1839–1914) labored in obscurity for most of his life. Despite his widely acknowledged brilliance and the efforts of his friend William James, the irascible Peirce had trouble observing the Victorian proprieties considered necessary for holding down an academic job. Partly as a result, and partly because many of his ideas remained buried in fragmentary manuscripts unpublished during his lifetime, Peirce received widespread attention only long after his death. Peirce worked for years on the US Coast and Geodesic Survey, and he produced valuable scholarship on mathematics, chemistry, and geodesy even though his real passion was not the accuracy of scientific measurements but philosophy of science. A pioneer in logic and what he called "semiotic," Peirce has become most widely known for having sparked William James's interest in the ideas that came to be known as pragmatism. The influence of Peirce's own ideas, though, has proved equally enduring. Against the standard approach to logic, Peirce added abduction, or hypothesis, to deduction and induction, an insight that has been pursued by scholars in fields ranging from analytic philosophy to computer science. Against Cartesian mind–body dualism, Peirce argued that experience should be understood with reference to two different kinds of relations. An object in the world (a "first") is represented by a sign (a "second") to a mind (a "third"). In contrast to the understanding of semiotics associated with Ferdinand Saussure and Roland Barthes, Peirce argued that the adequacy or accuracy of a sign must be tested against objects and events external to the human using the signs.[17]

---

16 Bonnie Anderson, *Joyous Greetings: The First International Women's Movement, 1830–1860* (Oxford: Oxford University Press, 2000).
17 Vincent Colapietro and Thomas Olshewsky (eds.), *Peirce's Doctrine of Signs: Theory, Applications, and Connections* (Berlin: Mouton de Gruyter, 1995), is an essay collection that manifests Peirce's wide and continuing influence on both sides of the Atlantic.

It was Peirce's insistence on assessing the truth of our representations through experimentation that James took to be the heart of Peirce's philosophy. Peirce disagreed. When he became exasperated by the popularity of James's more free-flowing conception of truth-testing, Peirce renamed his philosophy "pragmaticism," a term sufficiently ugly, he hoped, to safeguard it from kidnappers. Things, from Peirce's perspective, exist independently of humans, but as humans apprehend objects ("firsts") and their representations ("seconds") in thought, they take on meanings for us. It is that meaning-laden quality that Peirce intended to convey with the concept of "thirds," and it is the centrality of communication for his philosophy that inspired the German philosopher Karl-Otto Apel to credit Peirce with having inaugurated a new stage in the history of philosophy: "transcendental semiotic, or transcendental pragmatics, with its insight that the thinking (and by this I mean 'arguing') subject must necessarily conceive itself as a member of the communication community." Lived experience thus conceived, Apel argued, provides a sturdy basis for ethics. Because of the fragmentary nature of Peirce's writings and the intricacy of his arguments, interpretive disputes over his ideas, especially in mathematics and logic, are bound to continue. It is possible, though, that his conception of a relational self, a self existing only in community and through communication with other selves, provides as solid a foundation for social philosophy as do the better known ideas of his three pragmatist successors, Peirce's friend William James, Peirce's student John Dewey, and one of the most important early American sociologists, James's student and Dewey's colleague George Herbert Mead.[18]

William James (1842–1910) lived a transatlantic life. His independently wealthy father, the Swedenborgian philosopher Henry James, Sr., believed that his children should be spared the tedium of schooling, so they were educated by tutors in several European nations. Having grown up fluent in German, French, and Italian, James met and corresponded with prominent European thinkers in a variety of disciplines. He earned only one degree, in medicine, which he never practised. At Harvard, where he spent his entire working life and taught anatomy, psychology, and philosophy, he remained a self-proclaimed outsider anxious that the emerging "Ph.D. Octopus" would strangle originality by shunting independent minds into the grooves of conventional thinking. James himself escaped that fate, but the price of his quirky intellectual ramblings was the condescension of specialists in his day

18 Karl-Otto Apel, *Charles S. Peirce: From Pragmatism to Pragmaticism*, trans. J. M. Krois (Amherst: University of Massachusetts Press, 1981); and Richard J. Bernstein, *The Pragmatic Turn* (Cambridge: Polity Press, 2010).

and ever since. He gloried in his eclecticism, defiantly writing and lecturing for popular rather than scholarly audiences. His books ranged from the first work of existential phenomenology, *The Principles of Psychology* (1890), where he introduced the fertile ideas of consciousness as a stream and experience as necessarily social and irreducibly meaning-laden; through a pioneering work in the field that became religious studies, *The Varieties of Religious Experience* (1902); to several unclassifiable works of philosophy, including *Pragmatism* (1907), where he specified, fruitlessly, that "our ideas must agree with realities," *The Meaning of Truth* (1909), *A Pluralistic Universe* (1909), and two volumes published posthumously. James taught, and by their reckoning shaped the sensibilities of, students ranging from Theodore Roosevelt (whom James detested for his bluster and his militarism) to Gertrude Stein, W. E. B. Du Bois, Walter Lippmann, Horace Kallen, and Alain Locke, all of whom influenced European thinkers and all of whom admired James for his wide-ranging inquisitiveness, the same reason he delighted in them. James also intervened politically. He celebrated the Union cause in a brilliant address at the unveiling of Augustus St. Gaudens's tribute to the African American soldiers of the Massachusetts 54th and their commanding officer, Robert Gould Shaw (whose adjutant happened to be James's brother Wilky). James condemned his nation's slide toward empire in the Philippines at the end of the Spanish–American War, and he proudly adopted the designation "intellectuel" from the Dreyfusards whose commitments to exposing bigotry and injustice he shared.[19]

James's British friends and colleagues included the moral philosopher Henry Sidgwick, whom James invited to spend a year teaching politics at Harvard, and his fellow pragmatist F. C. S. Schiller. His admirers among English philosophers included Alfred North Whitehead and Ludwig Wittgenstein, his critics Bertrand Russell and A. J. Ayer. James's French allies included the neo-Kantian Charles Renouvier, whose ideas James credited with pulling him back from a near-suicidal depression, Henri Bergson, and Théodore Flournoy. Like many of James's readers, Émile Durkheim misunderstood and rejected what he took to be James's pragmatism. Italians who championed James included Giovanni Papini and Giuseppe Prezzolini, whose versions of "magic pragmatism" substituted willfulness for truth-testing. They also paved the way for Giovanni Gentile and Benito Mussolini, who found in muscle-flexing just the sort of truth-testing that

---

19 Trygve Throntveit, *William James and the Quest for an Ethical Republic* (New York: Palgrave Macmillan, 2014).

James had discerned and condemned in the future Rough Rider Roosevelt. Although James studied with the psychologist Wilhelm Wundt and was acquainted with the philosopher Wilhelm Dilthey, most of his German contemporaries were less responsive to James's ideas than were later thinkers such as Max Wertheimer, Kurt Koffka, Wolfgang Köhler, and Alfred Schutz. Among the most tantalizing aspects of James's influence is the role played by his analysis of the perception of time and of space, specifically the line drawings of a reversible cube and a bent greeting card that he examined in *The Principles of Psychology*, in Picasso's development of cubism. When Picasso claimed that modernism, although "born in France," was "the product of Spaniards and Americans," he might have been referring to one of James's former students or to James himself, a visitor to Stein's Paris apartment at the time of Picasso's experiments with faceting. Picasso's cubist painting "The Architect's Table" (1912) includes a bent greeting card, like the one in James's *Principles*, bearing the name of Gertrude Stein.[20]

The writings of John Dewey (1859–1952), as voluminous as Peirce's although less complex, have been perhaps more widely influential than those of any other American philosopher. Dewey wrote about psychology, logic, metaphysics, aesthetics, religion, education, and politics. A relentless critic of laissez-faire capitalism and oligarchic government, Dewey started out among liberal Protestant social gospelers and progressive reformers in Ann Arbor and Chicago, where he collaborated with Jane Addams at Hull House and established, at the University of Chicago, the still-thriving Laboratory School to test his educational theories in practice. In 1904 he moved to Columbia in New York City, where he lived and wrote until his death in 1952. Dewey produced books on a staggering array of topics, the most lastingly influential of which are *Democracy and Education* (1916), *The Public and Its Problems* (1927), *Art*

---

20 On the continuing vitality of James's ideas in contemporary philosophical debates on both sides of the Atlantic, see Martin Halliwell and Joel D. S. Rasmussen (eds.), *William James and the Transatlantic Conversation: Pragmatism, Pluralism, and Philosophy of Religion* (Oxford: Oxford University Press, 2014); and Robert B. Brandom, *Perspectives on Pragmatism: Classical, Recent, and Contemporary* (Cambridge: Harvard University Press, 2011). For different perspectives on the responses of James's European contemporaries, see Hans Joas, *Pragmatism and Social Theory* (Chicago: University of Chicago Press, 1993); John R. Shook, "F. C. S. Schiller and European Pragmatism," in *A Companion to Pragmatism*, ed. John R. Shook and Joseph Margolis (Oxford: Blackwell, 2009), 44–53; Susanne Rohr and Miriam Strube (eds.), *Revisiting Pragmatism: William James in the New Millennium* (Heidelberg: Universitätsverlag Winter, 2012); Francesca Bordogna, "Unstiffening Theory: The Italian Magic Pragmatists and William James," in *The Worlds of American Intellectual History*, ed. Joel Isaac, James T. Kloppenberg, Michael O'Brien, and Jennifer Ratner-Rosenhagen (New York: Oxford University Press, 2017), 155–181; and Eliza Jane Reilly, "Concrete Possibilities: William James and the European Avant-Garde," *Streams of William James*, 2(3) (Fall 2000), 22–29.

as Experience (1934), and *Liberalism and Social Action* (1935). Dewey campaigned tirelessly for democracy as he understood it, as a way of life rather than merely a set of institutions. Through his students, his influence extended from the pre-World War I progressive era through the New Deal (even though Dewey believed Franklin Roosevelt was too timid in moving the United States in the direction of social democracy), and beyond the nation's borders. The most prominent of the founders of China's reformist May Fourth movement, Hu Shih, the father of India's Constitution, B. R. Ambedkar, and several of the most important reformers in modern Mexico studied with Dewey at Columbia and traced their devotion to constitutional democracy to his teaching. Dewey's ideas have been influential, but they have also been mangled, especially in the field of education, and as much by his self-proclaimed followers as by his critics. Dewey followed James in insisting that knowledge comes from active engagement. Particularly in a democracy, passivity is the enemy of learning, and the teacher's goal should be to inculcate habits of inquiry rather than merely transmit information. As Dewey's revolutionary ideas progressed from scandalous to conventional, however, their radical thrust was blunted, and "progressive" education devolved from his rigorous insistence on developmentally appropriate problem-solving to the routinized, banal "child-centered" classroom in which disciplined investigations give way to entertainment and "adjustment."[21]

Dewey's ideas have continued to attract attention outside as well as within the United States. Although many Anglo-American analytic philosophers have dismissed Dewey as a well-meaning but muddled thinker, he remains alive in continental philosophy. Gérard Deledalle has translated many of Dewey's books into French, and he and his students have been instrumental in disseminating the ideas of more recent American pragmatist philosophers such as Hilary Putnam, who established himself in the philosophy of mathematics before turning to the tradition of James and Dewey, Richard J. Bernstein, who taught with Jürgen Habermas for years and has been a conduit linking American and continental thought, and Richard Rorty, the most widely read and most idiosyncratic of these thinkers.[22]

---

21 On Dewey's impact, see James T. Kloppenberg, *Uncertain Victory: Social Democracy and Progressivism in European and American Thought, 1870–1920* (New York: Oxford University Press, 1986); Robert B. Westbrook, *John Dewey and American Democracy* (Ithaca: Cornell University Press, 1991); Alan Ryan, *John Dewey and the High Tide of American Liberalism* (New York: Norton, 1995); and Ruben Flores, *Backroads Pragmatists: Mexico's Melting Pot and Civil Rights in the United States* (Philadelphia: University of Pennsylvania Press, 2014).
22 On Putnam, Bernstein, and Rorty, see James T. Kloppenberg, "Pragmatism: An Old Name for Some New Ways of Thinking?," *The Journal of American History*, 83(1) (June

Habermas has long referred to himself as a "good Deweyan pragmatist," and the German critical theorist Axel Honneth has drawn directly on Dewey to develop his own radical democratic theory grounded on social cooperation. "Dewey was able to derive from the interconnection of values with technical knowledge," Habermas wrote as early as *Theory and Practice* (1971), "the expectation that the deployment of continually multiplied and improved techniques" would not stay tied to existing values, "but also would subject the values themselves indirectly to a pragmatic test of their viability."[23] In Honneth's recent work *Freedom's Right: The Social Foundations of Democratic Life* (2015), he offers an extended commentary on Dewey's political ideas to advance his concept of "social freedom." Honneth points out that Dewey, like Habermas, argued "that cooperative interaction in public will-formation is both the means and the end of individual self-realization."[24]

Of equal significance for these German thinkers, and for their contemporary Hans Joas, is George Herbert Mead (1863–1931), whose ideas helped shape the disciplines of social psychology and sociology. Having studied at Harvard and tutored one of James's children, Mead continued his studies in Germany with Wundt, Dilthey, and Hermann Ebbinghaus before taking positions teaching with Dewey at Michigan and, from 1894 until Mead's death in 1931, at the University Chicago. Mead drew ideas from Peirce, James, and Dewey to construct his theory of the "social self." He argued that the capacity to communicate through symbols and the capacity to see situations from the perspective of the "generalized other" enable humans to develop both a particular kind of self-consciousness and forms of social organization of which other animals are incapable. Like Peirce, James, and Dewey, Mead contended that the meanings of our experience come from the role played by the external world in presenting us with situations in which we must actively select what to do.

In Mead's version of organic functionalism, consciousness serves, as it did for Dewey, as a mid-point between the stimuli we receive and the response – never purely mechanical or limited to external behavior – that we choose. Consciousness is constantly engaged in assessing the adequacy of our conduct to solve the problems or resolve the ambiguities we encounter. Human self-consciousness is a social achievement, made possible by our capacity to

---

1996), 100–138; Alan Malachowski (ed.), *The Cambridge Companion to Pragmatism* (Cambridge: Cambridge University Press, 2013); and Bernstein, *The Pragmatic Turn*.
23 Jürgen Habermas, *Theory and Practice*, trans. John Viertel (Boston: Beacon, 1973), 272.
24 Axel Honneth, *Freedom's Right: The Social Foundations of Democratic Life*, trans. Joseph Ganahl (New York: Columbia University Press, 2015), 271–274.

use language, a set of socially meaningful symbols, to make sense of our experience and make decisions. Mead envisioned ethical reasoning as a thoroughly naturalistic form of scientific inquiry: Instead of falling back on dogmatism when we confront conflicts of values, we should think creatively and openly test hypotheses in experience so that "all the ends, all the valuable objects, institutions, and practices which are involved, must be taken into account."[25]

Habermas has drawn extensively on Mead in developing his arguments concerning the communicative community of the lifeworld, but the most important contemporary interpreter of Mead is Hans Joas (1948–). From his early work on Mead and on the impact (and misperception) of pragmatism in Europe, Joas has developed an ambitious social theory centered on the inescapable value orientation of human experience. By emphasizing the precognitive social ties that bind humans to each other, in *The Theory of Creative Action* (1996) Joas insisted, as did Mead, that philosophical and social-scientific assumptions of purely instrumental reasoning must be rejected because they lack any empirical foundation. The intersubjectivity that Peirce linked with "thirds" and that Mead examined in greater detail than did James or Dewey (although it seems clear that they took for granted some version of it) has served as the principal focus of Joas's scholarship. Not content with descriptions of behavior or abstractions concerning supposedly "rational" self-interest, Joas has urged scholars in the human sciences to concentrate on investigating the sources of values and the possibilities of self-transcendence, whether in religious experience or in the experiences of interpersonal love or communion with nature. From Joas's perspective, the American pragmatists' focus on the contingency of situations and the agency and perspective of actors makes them a richer source of insight than the abstract discourse ethics of either Apel or Habermas.[26]

As that brief survey suggests, the founders of American pragmatism have had a broad, deep, and continuing impact on European thought. Later pragmatists, such as C. I. Lewis, W. V. Quine, Nicholas Rescher, Rorty, Bernstein, Putnam, Nancy Fraser, Richard Shusterman, and Robert Brandom, among others, have also contributed to debates in the fields of language and logic, ethics and aesthetics, law and politics, in ways discussed

---

25 George Herbert Mead, *Selected Writings*, ed. Andrew J. Reck (Chicago: University of Chicago Press, 1964), 256.
26 Hans Joas, *G. H. Mead: A Contemporary Re-examination of His Thought* (Cambridge: MIT Press, 1985); and Hans Joas, *The Creativity of Action* (Chicago: University of Chicago Press, 1996).

elsewhere in these volumes. Joel Isaac's Chapter 7 shows how mid-century American pragmatists engaged with Anglo-American analytic philosophers, and Edward Baring's Chapter 5 on existentialism makes clear the parallels between some of the thinkers in that tradition and the emphases on both freedom and social embeddedness characteristic of Peirce, James, Dewey, and Mead.

Indeed, since 1945 it has become increasingly difficult to separate European from American scholarly discourses, particularly in the natural sciences but also in the human sciences. In the remainder of this chapter, we will briefly highlight a few American thinkers who have figured especially prominently in the shaping of different disciplines, beginning with psychology and continuing through sociology, anthropology and linguistics, economics, and political science, then concluding with brief comments on the broader themes of race, religion, gender, and cultural criticism.

Psychology has splintered since James's *Principles of Psychology* was published to wide acclaim, on both sides of the Atlantic, in 1890. His Harvard colleague Hugo Münsterberg left his native Germany to add Teutonic *gravitas* to James's efforts to bring laboratory methods to American psychology. During their careers the discipline of philosophy and the fledgling field of psychology inhabited the same physical space in Cambridge, but psychology soon split off from that older home and divided into the fields of social, behavioral, developmental, cognitive, clinical, Freudian, and, most recently, evolutionary psychology and the psychology of perception, separate discourses that at times seem to have as little to do with each other as they do with scholarship in philosophy. In the early twentieth century, Harvard sponsored a lecture series in psychology and philosophy in honor of William James. After the Gestalt psychologist Wolfgang Köhler delivered those lectures in 1934, however, the series came to an end. The two disciplines had fractured, with philosophy heading toward logic and language and psychology toward various forms of experimentation and behaviorism. In neither of those emerging disciplines did the pragmatists' orientation toward studying the formation of value judgments remain an urgent concern.

American psychology, under the leadership of G. Stanley Hall, who invited Sigmund Freud to lecture at Clark University in 1910, was already beginning its long march back toward the biological sciences and technocratic applications, which is where it began with Francis Galton in England, Alfred Binet in France, and Hermann Helmholtz, Gustav Fechner, Wundt, and Ebbinghaus in Germany. Americans quickly took up the challenge of building laboratories where "brass instrument psychology" replaced the now-discredited "introspection." The battle between students of consciousness and volition such as James and Mead, on the one hand, and the positivism of the many American psychologists following Edward Titchener, on the other, was resolved with the triumph of behaviorism. First in John B. Watson's 1913 article proscribing explorations of the conscious mind in favor of predicting and controlling behavior, and gathering momentum with the fame accorded B. F. Skinner's flamboyant reductionism, American-style studies using quantitative measures and classification schemes rapidly established themselves as the dominant methodologies on both side of the Atlantic. When the purpose of psychology was to address the crisis of intelligence that alarmed the US army in World War I and those dealing with returning GIs after World War II, concerns about worker performance in Britain and France, and the German fascination with "psychotechnics" as a means of improving battlefield decision-making and officer selection, the original tools and orientation of Alfred Binet and Théodore Simon's intelligence scale proved irresistible. In light of imperatives to improve performance on tests of all kinds, and to "adjust" individuals to the imperatives of organizations from the military to industry, the concerns of symbolic interactionists and Gestalt psychologists with consciousness and communication seemed downright quaint.[27]

Nevertheless, dissenting voices continued to be heard on both sides of the Atlantic. The Swiss-born developmental psychologist Jean Piaget advanced a theory of cognitive stages that proved widely influential, especially in early-childhood education. Clinical psychology, not always behaviorist in orientation, exploded in popularity in the United States and Britain. Psychiatry too split into biological/pharmacological and culture and personality schools. The latter, founded in the United States by Harry Stack Sullivan and later dominated by émigrés such as Erich Fromm and Erik Erikson, grew into a prominent presence. Many of its leading figures, including Margaret Mead, Ruth Benedict, and Karen Horney, were widely read on both sides of the Atlantic. The disordered band of "humanistic psychologists" following Abraham Maslow and Carl Rogers continued to insist on the importance of

---

27 A fine overview that spans the Atlantic is Mitchell G. Ash, "Psychology," in *The Cambridge History of Science, Volume 7: The Social Sciences*, ed. Theodore M. Porter and Dorothy Ross (Cambridge: Cambridge University Press, 2003); see also James T. Kloppenberg, "The Place of Values in a Culture of Facts," in *The Humanities and the Dynamic of Inclusion since World War II*, ed. David A. Hollinger (Baltimore: Johns Hopkins University Press, 2006), 126–158; and Ellen Herman, *The Romance of American Psychology: Political Culture in the Age of Experts* (Berkeley: University of California Press, 1995).

qualitative rather than quantitative measures of human flourishing. Gestalt psychologists, at least until they were banished from German universities by the Nazis, held positions of visibility and influence and sustained interest in ideas of the sort later revivified by Apel, Habermas, Honneth, and Joas.[28]

Variants on Freudian psychoanalysis, curiously, blossomed more luxuriantly in Britain and the United States than in Freud's central European homeland. Despite the best efforts of many Americans in the Freudian diaspora to return psychoanalysis to its roots, the versions of Freudian theory that developed in continental Europe bore less direct relation to practices of psychotherapy in the United States, or to the soft Freudianism of Benjamin Spock's best-selling *Baby and Child Care* (1946), which sold tens of millions of copies and was translated into dozens of languages, than to the French or German philosophical traditions from which they descended. On this dimension of the story, see Katja Guenther's Chapter 2 in this volume.

Sociology followed a similar pattern of early westward movement, fragmentation, and re-export, after World War II, in a "scientifically" processed form. Originating in the positivism of Auguste Comte and Herbert Spencer, sociology was enlisted on both sides of the late-nineteenth-century battle over "social Darwinism" in Europe and the United States. Quantitative analysis emerged as part of the effort to make sociology "scientific." Adolphe Quetelet and Frédéric Le Play thought that tabulating statistics would enable government officials to manage their nations' populations more effectively. In the United States, as in Britain, sociology grew from the efforts of social reformers to show the urgency of the problems they wanted to see addressed. These pioneers, Charles Booth, B. Seebohm Rowntree, and Patrick Geddes in Britain; Robert Park, Jane Addams, and W. E. B. Du Bois in the United States; and Ferdinand Tönnies and Max Weber in Germany, emphasized the importance of impersonal forces that shaped and limited individuals' options, but they kept the focus on lived experience, even though that dimension of Weber's thought was muted when his writings were translated into English by American sociologists with a different agenda. In his quest to establish "social facts," Émile Durkheim experimented with quantitative measures to explain suicide rates before turning his attention to questions of social structure and ritual.

---

28 Elizabeth Lunbeck, *The Psychiatric Persuasion: Knowledge, Gender, and Power in Postwar America* (Princeton: Princeton University Press, 1994); and Peter Mandler, *Return from the Natives: How Margaret Mead Won the Second World War and Lost the Cold War* (New Haven: Yale University Press, 2013).

For more on these founding theorists of modernity, see Chapter 1 by Martin Jay.[29]

The reformist purposes of these founders and their immediate followers, L. T. Hobhouse and Beatrice and Sidney Webb in Britain, and Albion Small, Franklin Giddings, E. A. Ross, and Charles Cooley in the United States, persisted in the work of stubborn progressives such as Erving Goffman and Robert and Helen Lynd, but they found themselves challenged by the self-consciously value-free inquiries of interwar scholars more intent on scientific rigor than on reform. William Ogburn had engraved on the Social Science Research Building at Chicago the words of Lord Kelvin: "When you cannot measure, your knowledge is meager and unsatisfactory." Talcott Parsons (1902–1979) organized at Harvard an interdisciplinary Department of Social Relations and produced an ambitious "systems theory" purporting to explain norms and institutions in relation to the social functions they serve. He attempted to place his project in a direct line of descent from Weber and Durkheim, which required some creative reinterpretations of their work. As Parsons continued to refine his ideas, he tried to integrate subsystems into a grand synthesis that showed why cultures resist radical change. Although Parsons himself was a New Deal liberal, his insistence on social stasis made him a target of younger scholars who considered their "stable" society the opposite of "functional" for everyone but a small managerial elite. The methods and techniques of quantitative and statistical analysis developed in American universities such as Chicago and Harvard made their way back across the Atlantic to European social scientists, who likewise began to deploy multivariate analyses to make sense of vast quantities of data.[30]

But the ideas of American dissenters traveled too. Columbia sociologist Robert K. Merton (1910–2003) not only challenged Parsons's ideas about successful social integration, but also pioneered the field of the sociology of science. Merton conceived of scientific communities as the embodiments of democratic values and procedures. What he called the "ethos of science" included disinterestedness, skepticism, universalism, and collective rather than individual ownership of whatever science produced. That view of

---

29 Craig Calhoun (ed.), *Sociology in America: A History* (Chicago: University of Chicago Press, 2007); and Aldon Morris, *The Scholar Denied: W. E. B. Du Bois and the Birth of Modern Sociology* (Berkeley: University of California Press, 2015).
30 Dorothy Ross, *The Origins of American Social Science* (Cambridge: Cambridge University Press, 1991); and Joel Isaac, *Working Knowledge: Making the Human Sciences from Parsons to Kuhn* (Cambridge: Harvard University Press, 2012).

science was later challenged by Thomas Kuhn in *The Structure of Scientific Revolutions* (1962). Kuhn's analysis of the ways in which "normal science" proceeds until anomalies pile up, and its assumptions are undone by "paradigm shifts," transformed understandings of science. It also gave rise to the critical, and now burgeoning, Science and Technology Studies movement. Also at Columbia, Merton's renegade colleague C. Wright Mills exposed the declining status and blinkered lives of America's vaunted middle class in *White Collar* (1951). Mills urged his fellow scholars and his students to cultivate what he called a radical sociological imagination to unseat the privileged triumvirate of business, government, and the military that he dissected in *The Power Elite* (1956). As Merton and Mills illustrate in different ways, the earlier Peircean and Deweyan emphasis on the compatibility between scientific inquiry and radical democracy persisted in many precincts of American sociology. The rise of quantification did not necessarily mean the end of ethical inquiry. To those post-progressive social scientists who had hoped to escape partisanship for the neutrality or objectivity of scholarship as they understood it, however, the persistence of these stinging critiques was merely an atavistic annoyance.[31]

In the aftermath of World War II, and under the pressure of the Cold War, many mainstream social scientists in Western Europe as well as the United States thought the time had come to close ranks and, in the words of the radical writer Dwight Macdonald, "choose the West" over the Soviet Union. The American historian Arthur Schlesinger, Jr., urged his countrymen to discard the contentious politics of the depression era and embrace what he called *The Vital Center* (1949). One of the most prominent American sociologists, Daniel Bell, proclaimed "the end of ideology" in an essay collection of 1962. Bell's friend and associate Raymond Aron, named to a chair in sociology at the Sorbonne in 1955 – still one of the few chairs in the field in French universities – shared Bell's perspective on the exhaustion of ideas. Aron and Bell, like Parsons, occupied prestigious positions: Bell moved from Columbia to Harvard, Aron from the Sorbonne to the Collège de France. Because they thought of themselves as also occupying positions slightly left of the political center in France and the United States, they were unprepared for the volcanos that were about to erupt only a few years after they thought

---

[31] Andrew Jewett, *Science, Democracy, and the American University: From the Civil War to the Cold War* (Cambridge: Cambridge University Press, 2012); and Daniel Geary, *Radical Ambition: C. Wright Mills, the Left, and American Social Thought* (Berkeley: University of California Press, 2009).

a consensus had formed around the rationality and desirability of the postwar liberal capitalist welfare state.[32]

If sociologists were puzzling over the nature of modern social organization, anthropologists since the founding of the discipline in the 1850s and 1860s were exploring the origins and development of those societies. Inspired by work in Biblical criticism, geology, and archaeology, and by Darwin's theory of natural selection, scholars from the humanities and the natural sciences converged on a common set of questions. They offered a wide variety of answers, which have been grouped conventionally into three categories and periods: evolutionary (1850s–1920s); social psychological or structural (1920s–1970s), and cultural (1970s–present). Seeking the foundations of kinship networks, language groups, races, and social and political institutions, scholars differed on whether all cultures passed through a single set of stages or developed in fundamentally different ways. European anthropologists, following the lead of E. B. Tylor, generally adopted versions of Enlightenment stadial theories, but Germans followed Rudolf Virchow in emphasizing the contingent factors of environment and haphazard cultural borrowings to account for variations. A pioneering figure in American anthropology, Lewis Henry Morgan (1818–1881), derived from his studies of Iroquois kinship networks a set of cross-cultural typologies for kinship and social organization. He aligned himself with Tylor's evolutionary account of cultural development rather than Virchow's diffusionism.

By the turn of the twentieth century, Morgan's followers found themselves challenged by one of Virchow's students, Franz Boas (1858–1942), who secured a position at Columbia and established the first graduate program in anthropology in an American university. Among his students was the anthropological linguist Edward Sapir (1884–1939), who in turn mentored Benjamin Whorf (1897–1941), whose work on the Hopi sought to show how the maps of a particular language enable and constrain thought. What came to be known as the Sapir–Whorf hypothesis concerning the effects of language on perception became one of the most influential and controversial touchstones in modern linguistics. Boas, who was in contact with both Du Bois and Addams as early as the first years of the twentieth century, and his students disputed the claim that all cultures pass through the same series of steps and advanced

---

32 Howard Brick, *Daniel Bell and the Decline of Intellectual Radicalism* (Madison: University of Wisconsin Press, 1986); Iain Stewart, "The Origins of the 'End of Ideology'? Raymond Aron and Industrial Civilization," in *The Companion to Raymond Aron: Recovering Political Philosophy*, ed. José Colen and Elisabeth Dutartre-Michaut (New York: Palgrave Macmillan, 2015), 177–190.

a theory of cultural pluralism. They contended that all human cultures, despite the wide range of patterns of belief and behavior that emerge and persist over time, are unique and equally valuable, despite their differences. Boasians shared with Morgan only the sense of urgency sparked by their perception that America's indigenous cultures were fast disappearing under the pressure of contact with a culture radically unlike their own.

That conflict gradually eased as a result of the shift in emphasis from diachronic to synchronic analysis in the work of the British anthropologist A. R. Radcliffe-Brown (1881–1955) and the Polish-born Bronisław Malinowski (1884–1942) and their students. These scholars redirected the attention of anthropologists from questions of origin and development to intensive field research focused on generating studies that revealed the function served by myths and rituals and the gaps separating stated beliefs from behaviors. Many German anthropologists, inheriting a Romantic interest in the vitality of folk cultures, slid toward the ideas on eugenics and race theory that briefly sustained the Third Reich and largely collapsed with it. Anthropology in France remained focused on the questions posed by Durkheim and Mauss: What are the categories of thought, or the forms of reason, that undergird a culture's myths and rituals? Although American followers of Boas gradually, and grudgingly, adopted the syncretic approach of the British and French, they remained committed to the uniqueness of each culture and the necessity of using psychology and sociology – the "culture and personality" approach associated with Margaret Mead and Ruth Benedict – to make sense of what they observed.[33]

In *The Social System* (1952), Parsons announced his ambitious plan to colonize anthropology within a model patterned on Harvard's all-encompassing Department of Social Relations: He allocated the study of individuals to psychology, that of societies to sociology, and that of culture, by which he meant values, norms, and beliefs, to anthropology. Not surprisingly, many American anthropologists demurred. Although major figures such as Alfred Kroeber (1876–1960) and Clyde Kluckhohn (1905–1960)

---

[33] George W. Stocking, Jr., *After Tylor: British Social Anthropology, 1888–1951* (Madison: University of Wisconsin Press, 1995); George W. Stocking (ed.), *Volksgeist as Method and Ethic: Essays on Boasian Ethnography and the German Anthropological Tradition* (Madison: University of Wisconsin Press, 1996); and George W. Stocking (ed.), *Malinowski, Rivers, Benedict, and Others: Essays on Culture and Personality* (Madison: University of Wisconsin Press, 1986). See also Regna Darnell, *And Along Came Boas: Continuity and Revolution in Americanist Anthropology* (Philadephia: John Benjamins, 1998); and Regna Darnell, *Edward Sapir: Linguist, Anthropologist, Humanist* (Berkeley: University of California Press, 1990).

continued to direct their studies toward aspects of cultures that Parsons assigned to other disciplines, versions of structural functionalism nevertheless spread quietly through much of American anthropology. It was adopted at the University of Chicago by Parsons's student Clifford Geertz (1926–2006) and at Yale by George Murdock (1897–1995), and it was widely disseminated by their students, who dismissed the Boasians as insufficiently committed to the project of a unified social science oriented toward generating laws instead of collecting exotica.

Things began to change on both sides of the Atlantic as "primitive" cultures studied by anthropologists freed themselves from the grip of empire. The Cold War generated widespread interest in the "modernization" of "primitive" peoples thought susceptible to communism, and western governments sought to enlist anthropologists in that cause. Many of these scholars came to be housed in area studies programs, which were often created and funded – either openly or covertly – by government agencies seeking to enlist anthropologists' specialized knowledge in Cold War projects ranging from international development work to counterinsurgency. Tensions over anthropologists' ties to the state and rising uneasiness about overly ambitious aspirations to scientific status, expressed as early as 1950 by Oxford's E. E. Evans-Pritchard, who urged anthropologists to renounce the search for laws and return to the interpretation of meanings, left the discipline poised for another shift. Geertz, who in the early 1960s was a firm believer in the precepts of modernization theory, made it official in 1973, when his widely read essay collection *The Interpretation of Cultures* ratified the transition from explanatory science to hermeneutics. The European as well as American anthropologists who had adopted versions of the structural functionalist model now had to defend themselves on two fronts, from the political charge of complicity with imperialism and the philosophical charge of scientistic reductionism. Chapter 11 by Kris Manjapra and Chapter 17 by Judith Surkis provide further analysis of these developments.[34]

Some anthropologists, of course, adopted other positions, including Claude Lévi-Strauss's or Noam Chomsky's strikingly different but influential versions of structuralism. Lévi-Strauss derived his theory, which promised a universal science based on signs rather than structures and functions, from the structural linguistics he learned from Roman Jakobson while taking refuge in New York and teaching at the École Libre des Hautes Études during

---

34 David H. Price, *Cold War Anthropology: The CIA, the Pentagon, and the Growth of Dual Use Anthropology* (Durham: Duke University Press, 2016).

World War II. Chomsky's voluminous and controversial writings about linguistics challenged behaviorists as well as cultural pluralists. Chomsky posited an innate human capacity for language use and insisted that, at the deepest level, all languages share certain universal characteristics. On the topics of structuralism and post-structuralism more generally, see Chapter 18 by Camille Robcis and Chapter 19 by Julian Bourg and Ethan Kleinberg.

Some anthropologists rejected both pluralism and structuralism. Some followed Marx, himself influenced by Lewis Henry Morgan's work, and rejected the notion that any culture's "superstructure," its myths, rituals, or language, could be divorced from its economic base. Others followed E. O. Wilson into sociobiology, searching for a new scientific ground in the lessons to be learned about humans from the behavior of ants and apes. Still others in anthropology, taking their cues from thinkers such as Frantz Fanon, Edward Said, and Talal Asad, extended the critique of scholarship's imbrication with imperialism from direct, material connections between academics and state power to broader cultural and literary tropes that undergird the exoticization and oppression of the global South. When younger American anthropologists followed the lead of James Clifford, George Marcus, Renato Rosaldo, Michelle Zimbalist Rosaldo, Sherry Ortner, and others who not only denied the possibility of neutrality or objectivity but also explicitly undertook to give voice to the oppressed, on their own terms rather than those of the imperialist West, some not only encountered people watching American sit-coms and eating hamburgers but also found themselves unsettled by their awareness of the privileges they enjoyed. Geertz and others – on both sides of the Atlantic – have observed in recent decades that the illumination accompanying self-consciousness can be paralyzing.[35]

As that self-consciousness has spread from anthropology across the academy, propelled by the studies of disciplinary regimes, biopower, and governmentality produced under the sign of the French philosopher Michel Foucault (1926–1984), and of the careerist maneuverings within academic cultures produced under the sign of the French sociologist Pierre Bourdieu (1930–2002), it has produced a turn inward among many intellectuals, who have become concerned with deconstructing the internal codes and power structures of their own disciplines. This shift has included a welcome and overdue attempt at what Bourdieu called "reflexivity," but it has also led some intellectuals to fully fledged denunciations of social-scientific practices.

---

35 See for example James Clifford and George Marcus, *Writing Culture: The Poetics and Politics of Ethnography* (Berkeley: University of California Press, 1986); and Ellen Lewin (ed.), *Feminist Anthropology: A Reader* (Oxford: Blackwell, 2006).

Striking the perfect balance between disciplinary self-criticism and active use of the tools these disciplines have bequeathed is a difficult – perhaps, ultimately, impossible – task for contemporary scholars, but it is a worthy aspiration.

The influence of American thinkers in economics and politics has received a lot of attention; as a result, it requires less discussion here. In both domains that influence has divided into paths leading left and right, both of which, oddly enough, can be traced to the career of Walter Lippmann (1889–1974). Lippmann, who was one of James's favorite students at Harvard, made such a strong impression on visiting professor Graham Wallas that the British Fabian dedicated his book *The Great Society* (1914) to his former student. After a short stint in politics, Lippmann set to work writing *A Preface to Politics* (1913), the first American book to reflect the influence of Freud and Nietzsche, and *Drift and Mastery* (1914), which reflected Lippmann's deeper debts to James's pragmatism and to the radical critiques of early feminists and renegade economists such as Thorstein Veblen (1857–1929). Like Veblen, Lippmann lampooned the shallow and showy displays that drove the rich and those who aped their ways. He urged his readers to adopt a "scientific" approach toward social and economic problems rather than resting content with the "panacea habit of mind" favored by thinkers on the left as well as on the right. No single solution would suffice, Lippmann insisted. Only continuous inquiry of the sort recommended by James and Dewey, spearheaded by highly trained investigators freed of fixed ideas and committed to problem-solving, would enable the United States to cope with the unprecedented challenges of democratic governance in an urban industrial world.

Lippmann joined with another of James's students, Herbert Croly (1869–1930), and the economist Walter Weyl (1873–1919) to edit the new progressive periodical *The New Republic*, which was deliberately patterned after the Webbs's *New Statesman*. There Lippmann found himself in contact with Dewey, a frequent contributor, and his commitment to pragmatism solidified. Lippmann's brilliance brought him to the attention of Woodrow Wilson, who named him to the Inquiry, a top-secret group convened not only to drum up support for the war and draft the Fourteen Points that Wilson took with him to Versailles but also to draw national lines for a post-World War I Europe consistent with the principle of the "self-determination of peoples." This was heady stuff for a young man in his twenties, even one with Lippmann's talent and self-confidence.[36]

---

36 On Lippmann's early career, see Kloppenberg, *Uncertain Victory*, Chapters 8–10.

In the aftermath of the war and the Paris peace conference, Lippmann's already stirring skepticism about popular decision-making deepened. In his controversial *Public Opinion* (1922), he expressed doubts about the public's ability to penetrate the subtleties of social problems. The distorting role of "stereotypes," which humans use to filter, simplify, and make comprehensible information too complex for the "common man," would stymie reasoned debate. Although this book set off a flurry of critical responses, including Dewey's *The Public and Its Problems* (1927), Lippmann was unrepentant. He continued to sharpen his critique of the positions that James, Dewey, and their fellow progressive democrats had taken, so that by the time his book *The Good Society* appeared in 1937, he had become the darling of cultural conservatives on both sides of the Atlantic. A glowing review of *The Good Society* by the University of Chicago economist Frank Knight highlighted the same themes that prompted twenty-six intellectuals to convene in Paris in August 1938, as the "Colloque Lippmann."

This group of European intellectuals wanted to discuss with Lippmann not only his recent book but also their broader concerns about the dual threats of relativism and social democracy. Whereas many pre-World War I progressives called themselves "new liberals," those gathering in the Colloque Lippmann wanted a return to the stable principles of nineteenth-century classical liberalism, suitably refashioned for new circumstances. Convinced that an alternative had to be found between the poles of socialism and fascism, some members of the group that first gathered around Lippmann's ideas, including Friedrich Hayek, Ludwig von Mises, Michael Polanyi, Wilhelm Röpke, and Raymond Aron, later formed the Mont Pèlerin Society (MPS) that gave birth to renewed forms of conservative activism in Europe as well as in the United States. Did any individual have a more lasting impact on Europe than the man who was charged first with trying to redraw the boundaries of the former Austro-Hungarian empire and then, two decades later, with laying the foundations for the rise of the New Right?[37]

The principal contributions of American economists in the early twentieth century had been on the left side of the political spectrum. Veblen's critiques of "conspicuous consumption" and "conspicuous waste" as the twin engines driving modern capitalist culture resonated with many Europeans critical of inequity but unpersuaded by the rigid orthodoxy of European communist parties. Henry George's idea of a single tax on rent,

---

37 Angus Burgin, *The Great Persuasion: Reinventing Free Markets since the Depression* (Cambridge: Harvard University Press, 2012).

which attracted considerable attention during his electrifying lecture tour of Great Britain, converted many listeners – not least George Bernard Shaw and others soon to be attracted to Fabianism – to the socialist cause. American economists trained in Germany, such as Richard T. Ely, helped challenge the hegemony of laissez-faire. They insisted, as did their German teachers and their own students, such as John Commons, that economic theory develops historically rather than existing timelessly in the rarified air of pure theory.

American economists played minor roles in the Marginal and Keynesian Revolutions, but Paul Samuelson and Kenneth Arrow were crucial figures in refining Keynes's *General Theory*. Samuelson's *Foundations of Economic Analysis* (1947) and his *Economics: An Introduction* (1948) added comparative statics analysis and the concept of a social welfare function, which raised the question of equity as well as efficiency and showed that market mechanisms are inadequate to provide public goods. Not only did Arrow's work refine general equilibrium theory by probing economic decision-making under conditions of risk, uncertainty, and incomplete information, but his impossibility theorem also cast doubt on the adequacy of Samuelson's social welfare function.[38]

With the rise of the University of Chicago School, microeconomics emerged as the central concern of economics as a discipline, and the reorientation of politics later accomplished by Ronald Reagan and Margaret Thatcher found its rationale. Knight, Hayek, and the young Milton Friedman targeted central aspects of Keynesian theory and the mildly redistributionist public policies it underwrote. Their ideas, presented in easily digestible form in Friedman's *Capitalism and Freedom* (1962), in the popular book *Free to Choose* (1970) that he wrote with his wife Rose Friedman, and in a widely viewed ten-part television series with the same title, persuaded many American and British readers and viewers that only free market capitalism is compatible with individual freedom. Although the Russian émigré Ayn Rand reached an even wider audience with the libertarian nostrums of her popular novels *The Fountainhead* (1943) and *Atlas Shrugged* (1957), the Chicago School of economists helped give anti-government politicians such as Barry Goldwater, Reagan, and Thatcher a patina of legitimacy they had lacked. The philosopher Robert Nozick aimed to provide a cogent argument for radical libertarianism in *Anarchy,*

---

[38] Agnar Sandmo, *Economics Evolving: A History of Economic Thought* (Princeton: Princeton University Press, 2011); and Eric MacGilvray, *The Invention of Market Freedom* (Cambridge: Cambridge University Press, 2011).

State, and Utopia (1974). Nozick's book gave Anglo-American conservatives an academic philosopher of their own, which added ballast to the tireless but previously unsuccessful efforts of conservative writers such as William Buckley, Russell Kirk, Frank Meyer, and the European refugees Eric Voegelin and Leo Strauss. For more about these thinkers, see Chapter 15 by Steven B. Smith.

On the other side of the political spectrum, where most American practitioners of political science have resided in recent decades, surely the most widely read American political philosopher was John Rawls (1921–2002), whose books provided a philosophical rationale for just those policies targeted by conservatives. First in the articles from the 1950s that he elaborated in *A Theory of Justice* (1971) and later in *Political Liberalism* (1993), Rawls argued that rational individuals, deliberating behind a "veil of ignorance" that keeps them from knowing their own talents or particular predispositions, would seek to maximize their access to "primary goods" including rights, opportunities, wealth, and self-respect. To accomplish that goal, they would establish a society based on two principles of justice. The first, the principle of liberty, would secure for each person an equal right to the most extensive liberty compatible with similar liberty for others. The second, known as the difference principle or the "maximin," would stipulate that social and economic inequalities should be (a) for the greatest benefit of the least advantaged and (b) attached to positions and offices open to all under conditions of fair and equal opportunity. The individuals entering this compact, Rawls argued, would give priority to the liberty principle over the difference principle.

Although none of his critics has approached the fame or influence achieved by Rawls, whose books have been translated into every major European language and have been the subject of unparalleled scrutiny by philosophers and political theorists, other American thinkers such as Michael Walzer, Michael Sandel, Seyla Benhabib, Richard Rorty, and the Canadian philosopher Charles Taylor invigorated scholarly debates by challenging the individualism at the core of Rawls's theory. They insisted, as Hegel, Marx, and the American pragmatists Peirce, James, Dewey, and Mead had done, that humans never exist outside communities. Moreover, these critics contended, it is precisely the self-awareness, inherited traditions, and commitments that Rawls tried to bracket in "the original position" that constitute us as individuals. For that reason Rawls's version of liberalism, although compelling within the framework of "rational choice" that governed so much post-

World War II social science, was false to the lived experience of real as opposed to theoretical persons.[39]

The influence of African American intellectuals on European social thought in the twentieth century extended from literature and the arts to philosophy and critical theory. For much of the twentieth century, the most fertile route for intellectual exchange between African American thinkers and the European continent went through France. In the 1920s, the Harlem Renaissance attracted attention from writers, artists, and philosophers in Paris. While for many white Parisians this intellectual milieu fit into a broader and often paternalistic cultural fascination with Caribbean, African, and African American cultural production – the famed *"vogue nègre"* – many black students, workers, and writers developed deeper links to both the literature and the politics of the Harlem Renaissance. The Martiniquan-born sisters Paulette and Jane Nardal translated Alain Locke's collection *The New Negro* into French. They also held salons in Paris in the 1920s and early 1930s that planted the seeds for the publication of *La revue du monde noir*, a bilingual journal that brought together anti-colonial political tracts and modernist poetry from African American, Caribbean, and African sources. It also set the stage for Aimé Césaire, Léopold Senghor, and Léon-Gontran Damas to articulate the ideas of racial consciousness and anti-colonialism that came to be known by the term *"Négritude."* The intellectual interchange between African American and Francophone black writers in the interwar period was multidirectional and multivalent, as writers discussed the relation of Africa to black people in the West, differential systems of racial oppression in Europe and the United States, and the possibilities of international solidarity in a multilingual, transatlantic conversation.[40]

African American influences on European thought continued after World War II. Paris remained the main site for this transmission, particularly

---

39 P. Mackenzie Bok, "To the Mountaintop Again: The Early Rawls and Post-Protestant Ethics in Postwar America," *Modern Intellectual History*, 14(1) (2017), 153–185; and see Bok's forthcoming book on Rawls's ideas; Robert Adcock, Mark Bevir, and Shannon C. Stimson (eds.), *Modern Political Science: Anglo-American Exchanges since 1880* (Princeton: Princeton University Press, 2007); S. M. Amadae, *Rationalizing Capitalist Democracy: The Cold War Origins of Rational Choice Liberalism* (Chicago: University of Chicago Press, 2003); and Catherine Audard (ed.), *Individu et justice sociale: Autour de John Rawls* (Paris: Éditions du Seuil, 1988).

40 Brent Hayes Edwards, *The Practice of Diaspora: Literature, Translation, and the Rise of Black Internationalism* (Cambridge: Harvard University Press, 2003); Jennifer Anne Boittin, "In Black and White: Gender, Race Relations, and the Nardal Sisters in Interwar Paris," *French Colonial History*, 6 (2005), 119–135; and Gary Wilder, *Freedom Time: Negritude, Decolonization, and the Future of the World* (Durham: Duke University Press, 2015).

through the expatriate writers Richard Wright, Chester Himes, and James Baldwin. Simone de Beauvoir cited the influence of her friend Wright at several points in *The Second Sex*, drawing on his phenomenological depictions of racism to evoke the issues of alterity and sexism. Although women and black people share the experience of being seen as other, according to Beauvoir they are socially conditioned to respond in different ways to their distinct oppressions: "The Negroes submit with a feeling of revolt, no privileges compensating for their hard lot, whereas the woman is offered inducements to complicity."[41]

African American ideas also spread through Britain. When Malcolm X spoke at the Oxford Union in 1964, at the height of the civil rights movement in the United States, he attracted the attention of the black British community, which had played host in the interwar years to an important network of anti-colonial intellectuals and political leaders that included C. L. R. James, Kwame Nkrumah, and George Padmore, among others. Malcolm X's Oxford address sought to place the American civil rights movement in a global context, and it influenced the spread of Black Power-inflected ideologies among the increasing number of black immigrants to Britain from its former colonies.[42]

Another important avenue of African American influence on European intellectual life came through post-1968 French thinkers' engagements with African American writings on the prison, an influence reflected in Michel Foucault's *Discipline and Punish: The Birth of the Prison* (1975). Foucault was the principal spokesperson of the Groupe d'Information sur les Prisons (GIP), an activist group founded in 1971 that documented and reported on French prisons. The GIP emphasized the voices of prisoners themselves and tried to forge alliances between professionals and intellectuals and the incarcerated, a move that reflected the transatlantic shift in left thinking away from an identification of the industrial working class as the necessary agent of social transformation.[43]

---

41 Simone de Beauvoir, *The Second Sex*, ed. and trans. H. M. Parshley (New York: Vintage, 1989 [1949]), 297–298.
42 Minkah Makalani, *In the Cause of Freedom: Radical Black Internationalism from Harlem to London, 1917–1939* (Chapel Hill: The University of North Carolina Press, 2011); Marc Matera, *Black London: The Imperial Metropolis and Decolonization in the Twentieth Century* (Berkeley: University of California Press, 2015); Stephen Tuck, *The Night Malcolm X Spoke at the Oxford Union: A Transatlantic Story of Antiracist Protest* (Berkeley: University of California Press, 2014); and Saladin Ambar, *Malcolm X at Oxford Union: Racial Politics in a Global Era* (New York: Oxford University Press, 2014). See also the essays in Robin D. G. Kelley and Stephen Tuck (eds.), *The Other Special Relationship: Race, Rights, and Riots in Britain and the United States* (New York: Palgrave Macmillan, 2015).
43 Julian Bourg, *From Revolution to Ethics: May 1968 and Contemporary French Thought* (Montreal: McGill-Queen's University Press, 2007).

Through Jean Genet (1910–1986), a prominent supporter of the Black Panther Party in the United States, Foucault and other members of the GIP became acquainted with the work of incarcerated Black Panthers Angela Y. Davis (1944–) and George Jackson (1941–1971). Genet, who had been in and out of prison as a young man, wrote the preface to the first edition of George Jackson's collection of prison letters, *Soledad Brother*, published in English in 1970 and in French in 1971. *Soledad Brother* quickly became a canonical text of radical black anti-prison activism in the United States and gained attention on the French left. The GIP published a pamphlet, written by Foucault with Catharine von Bülow and Daniel Defert, publicizing Jackson's writings and analyzing the media coverage of his killing by prison guards after his attempted takeover of a section of the San Quentin Correctional Facility in 1971. In *The Assassination of George Jackson*, Foucault and his co-authors dissected the official story of Jackson's death and reframed his killing as an "act of war" committed against a potential threat to the state.[44]

Foucault's engagement with black radical thought in the United States, although largely unacknowledged in his published work, was an important influence on several elements of his analysis of penal institutions. George Jackson's portrayals of the prison as an institution that functioned through a combination of daily procedures of surveillance and ritual humiliation prefigured central components of Foucault's depiction of disciplinary power. Jackson's descriptions of the spiritual as well as material degradations of prison life reverberated in Foucault's portrait of the prison as an institution that penetrated prisoners' souls. More generally, the writings and activism of many African Americans, including Du Bois, Ida B. Wells, Ralph Ellison, James Baldwin, Martin Luther King, Jr., Malcolm X, Stokely Carmichael, Toni Morrison, bell hooks, and Barack Obama have undermined smug but stubborn assumptions of white supremacy in Europe as they have done in the United States.[45]

---

[44] Dan Berger, *Captive Nation: Black Prison Organizing in the Civil Rights Era* (Chapel Hill: University of North Carolina Press, 2014); Brady Heiner, "Foucault and the Black Panthers," *City: Analysis of Urban Trends, Culture, Theory, Policy, Action*, 9(3) (December 2005), 313–356; and Michel Foucault, Catharine von Bülow, and Daniel Defert, "The Masked Assassination," trans. Sirène Harb, in *Warfare in the American Homeland: Policing and Prison in a Penal Democracy*, ed. Joy James (Durham: Duke University Press, 2007).

[45] Alexander Weheliye, *Habeas Viscus: Racializing Assemblages, Biopolitics, and Black Feminist Theories of the Human* (Durham: Duke University Press, 2014); Heiner, "Foucault and the Black Panthers"; and Berger, *Captive Nation*.

A more comprehensive analysis of the impact of American intellectuals in Europe would have to attend to additional topics that cannot be addressed here. The lively debates about religious faith and secularism that have roiled European and American cultures since the eighteenth century have been the subject of widely read texts by Americans ranging from Emerson to James, from Walter Rauschenbusch to Reinhold Niebuhr, and from John Courtney Murray to Robert Bellah. Likewise, the ideas of feminists from Charlotte Perkins Gilman and Jane Addams through Betty Friedan, Gloria Steinem, and Adrienne Rich to Gerda Lerner, Linda Gordon, Gloria Azaldúa, Andrea Dworkin, Nancy Chodorow, and Judith Butler have contributed to transatlantic conversations concerning gender and sexuality. Some of the American contributions to discourses on religion and gender are discussed elsewhere in this volume, particularly in Chapters 12 and 13 by Sandrine Sanos and Peter E. Gordon, respectively.

Finally, there are American cultural critics who do not fit neatly into the categories of academic disciplines but who nevertheless contributed significantly to intellectual life across the Atlantic. That list would include figures such as Norbert Wiener, Rachel Carson, Michael Harrington, Gore Vidal, Susan Sontag, Ralph Nader, Jane Jacobs, Stewart Brand, and the countless painters, architects, choreographers, composers, graphic artists, poets, novelists, playwrights, and film makers who have helped transform the life of the mind in the modern North Atlantic world. Of course there remain Europeans who sniff disdainfully at the very idea of an American intellectual tradition, let alone the claim that American ideas have had any impact on European thought. Plenty of American intellectuals have internalized such assessments of America's cultural inferiority. Americans impatient with European condescension, however, and intent on making the case for acknowledging the impact of American ideas in Europe, should remember this wise observation from the Russian-born choreographer George Balanchine. "Publicity overrates everything. Picasso's overrated. I'm overrated. Even Jack Benny's overrated."

In the twenty-first century, communication has been unshackled from the printed page. Words, music, images, and videos move instantly not just across the Atlantic but around the globe. Given the breadth of the communities of discourse in which we now move, the very notion of a distinctive "American" or "European" intellectual history might be in the process of becoming an artifact from an earlier era. While the supply of ideas at our fingertips has become almost infinite, and the volume of transatlantic exchanges of information and ideas has reached unprecedented levels, the depth of these exchanges, as we hope our essay has shown, depends on shared and contested philosophical traditions, methodological commitments, and understandings of the social world, none of which can be produced simply through technological advance. It is an open question whether European and American thinking will become richer – and less parochial – or merely more frantically self-absorbed.

9

Revolution from the Right: Against Equality

UDI GREENBERG

The early decades of the twentieth century initially seemed devastating for the European Right, especially for its adherence to traditional hierarchies. The spread of democracy and rise of mass politics undermined the rule of the nobility and the monarchy; feminism questioned established gender roles; industrialization and urbanization swallowed up the cherished countryside; increasingly militant workers challenged the economic order. The slaughterhouse of World War I and the political upheavals that followed seemed to only accelerate this crisis. Across Central Europe, monarchical empires collapsed in democratic revolutions, women gained legal equality, and socialist mass parties entered the realm of power. On the most profound level, some of the traditional Right's most basic ideological pillars, especially the belief that society had to relish "natural" and traditional inequalities, seemed deeply shaken. While Europeans continued to live in a tight web of hierarchies – whether colonial, religious, gendered, or economic – many contemporaries believed that with the new society of the masses, equality was sweeping the continent.

From the crucible of this perceived emergency a novel and ambitious intellectual movement was born. Composed of prominent scholars, artists, and philosophers, it sought to revitalize the Right and overcome the logic of equality, ultimately becoming known under the paradoxical monikers "revolution from the Right" or "conservative revolution" (terms popularized in 1927 by the novelist Hugo von Hofmannsthal).[1] Like conservatives of earlier generations, members of this group shared a profound suspicion toward reason and progress, which they dismissed as "artificial" inventions of an overly rational Enlightenment. They reserved particular ire for liberal democracy, in their minds the ultimate expression of atomized individualism, and socialism, which they derided as a "materialist" ideology that diminished human spirituality.

---

1 Martin Travers, *Critics of Modernity: The Literature of the Conservative Revolution in Germany, 1890–1933* (New York: Peter Lang, 2001), 2.

Unlike other thinkers of the older or conventional Right, however, members of the conservative revolution were not infatuated with tradition, and were typically uninterested in the monarchical or agrarian past. The future, most of them believed, belonged to an "organic" national body, which would bind its members in spiritual solidarity, transcend historical class divisions, and facilitate an urban, industrialized, and technologically advanced existence. Most importantly, their writings sought to "rescue" Europeans from what they believed was their misguided focus on socio-economic security and material convenience. They called for the formation of a new consciousness, one that embraced the irrational, tragic, and dangerous elements of existence.

This intellectual project animated writers and thinkers across Europe, who offered diverse visions for an anti-Enlightenment, anti-liberal, and anti-Marxist existence. The French political thinker Georges Sorel (1847–1922) called on Europeans to break with their alleged belief in reason, stability, and order, qualities he associated with a "decadent" bourgeoisie. In his *Reflections on Violence* (1908), he celebrated the motivating power of collective "myths" and acts of collective violence, such as riots and mass strikes, which he hoped would replace the liberal focus on individual rights with a communal and irrational solidarity.[2] The Italian philosopher Giovanni Gentile (1875–1944) similarly celebrated mass politics, and proclaimed radical nationalism the antidote to modernity's atomization. Only by conceiving of themselves as cells in a national body and accepting the state's authority over their lives, he wrote, could people enjoy moral and fulfilling lives, a conviction that led him to support the Italian Fascist regime and serve as its chief theoretician and minister of education.[3] The French essayist Charles Maurras (1868–1952) envisioned an "integral nationalism," which would unify the nation around authoritarian monarchism, abolish the separation between church and state, and combat the rights of minorities, such as Jews and freemasons. The influential journal he edited, *Action française*, became the central mouthpiece of the French radical right, while his books and pamphlets circulated among nationalists in Spain and Belgium.[4] Novelists such as Louis-Ferdinand Céline (1894–1961), in his *Journey to the End of the Night* (1932), and Robert Brasillach (1909–1945), in his *The Seven Colors* (1939), also railed

---

2 Georges Sorel, *Reflections on Violence* (Cambridge: Cambridge University Press, 1999).
3 See for example Giovanni Gentile, *The Theory of Mind as Pure Act*, trans. H. Wildon Carr (London: Macmillan, 1922); and Giovanni Gentile, *Origins and Doctrine of Fascism*, ed. and trans. A. James Gregor (London: Routledge, 2004).
4 See for example Charles Maurras, *L'action française et la religion catholique* (Paris: Nouvelle librairie nationale, 1913); and Charles Maurras, *L'Allée des philosophes* (Paris: Société littéraire de France, 1923).

against the nihilism and anxiety of "materialist" society, which they depicted with innovative artistic techniques such as non-linear narratives, a mixture of literary genres, and the heavy usage of colloquial language. This belief in modernity's "emptiness" ultimately led them to embrace fascism, writing texts that celebrated the nation's transcendental quality, glorified war, and engaged in vile anti-Semitic conspiracy theories.[5]

While the revolution from the Right had intellectual representatives across Europe, it reached its peak of influence in Germany. Even before World War I, the country's shockingly quick industrialization and urbanization (which exceeded any other European country) and the meteoric rise of its socialist party (which was by 1912 the largest in the world) led some thinkers on the Right to proclaim the need for an updated and modern conservatism. Germany's humiliating defeat in 1918 and the democratic revolution that followed lent special urgency to these efforts, which exploded in a new intellectual galaxy of journals (such as *Gewissen* and *Tat*), seminars, and clubs. In particular, the German conservative revolution was centered around four fields of knowledge, each dominated by an especially influential figure. Oswald Spengler introduced a new approach to the writing of history; Carl Schmitt revolutionized political theory; Ernst Jünger produced innovative literary forms; and Martin Heidegger developed a new philosophy of authenticity. While these thinkers (and the others who considered themselves their allies) often disagreed with each other, they nevertheless were part of a broad and distinct intellectual undertaking. Their writings became a significant presence in the landscape of modern European thought.

This intellectual project was contentious from its very inception, but the question of its relationship to fascism, and especially German Nazism, has been especially controversial. Many scholars in fact have treated the works of the new Right mainly as forerunners and enablers of the Third Reich.[6] Indeed, though both the conservative revolution and Nazism entailed diverse and even contradictory strands of thought, the overlaps between them were glaring. Both were animated by fierce hostility to "decadent" liberalism, socialism, and feminism; both were possessed by radical nationalism and

---

5 Louis-Ferdinand Céline, *Journey to the End of the Night*, trans. Ralph Manheim (New York: New Directions, 2004); and Robert Brasillach, *Les sept couleurs* (Paris: Plon, 1939). More broadly, see David Carroll, *French Literary Fascism: Nationalism, Anti-Semitism, and the Ideology of Culture* (Princeton: Princeton University Press, 1994).
6 Jeffrey Herf, *Reactionary Modernism: Technology, Culture, and Politics in Weimar and the Third Reich* (New York: Cambridge University Press, 1984); Roger Woods, *The Conservative Revolution in the Weimar Republic* (New York: St. Martin's Press, 1996); and Ernst Nolte, *Three Faces of Fascism* (New York: Holt, Rinehart and Winston, 1965).

authoritarianism; and both placed "authentic" communal belonging above rational discourse. The biographies of the conservative revolution's prominent figures similarly point to the two movements' affinities. Schmitt and Heidegger, for example, joined the Nazi party, took part in the regime's brutal policies – including its harsh anti-Semitic discrimination – and endorsed its imperialistic war designs. The conservative revolution, then, was deeply entangled with extreme oppression and violence. Its works provided an intellectual arsenal for unspeakable atrocities.

Yet other scholars have insisted that the movement was not identical to the political goals it ended up serving, and that many of its assumptions actually distinguished it from Nazi ideology.[7] Perhaps most importantly, these historians have emphasized that the thinkers of the new Right did not share the Third Reich's biological fixation, and were not animated by extreme racism; they conceived the nation as a spiritual and ideological community, rather than a biological one. Indeed, the difference between the two camps was just as apparent as their similarities. Even those who initially supported Hitler had a falling out with his new regime, whether out of disappointment at the Reich's actions or because they were dismissed by Nazi authorities for being insufficiently racist. These distinctions meant that the conservative revolution's most important works were not discredited by Nazism's demise. Unlike Nazi historical scholarship, political theory, literature, and philosophy, which have largely been forgotten, the writings of the new Right continued to attract a wide array of readers for the rest of the twentieth century. For many readers, the Revolution from the Right provided crucial tools for understanding modern and liberal society, especially its persistent shortcomings, failures, and inner contradictions. Far beyond mere apologia for fascism, they claimed, the movement left a distinct and enduring intellectual legacy, which should far outlive the moment of its creation.

Oswald Spengler and Cultural Pessimism

More than anyone, it was the historian Oswald Spengler (1880–1936) who articulated the new right's dismay at the rise of mass politics and demands for

---

7 The most important work to do so remains Armin Mohler, *Die Konservative Revolution in Deutschland, 1918–1932: Ein Handbuch*, 2nd edn. (Darmstadt: Wissenschaftliche Buchgesellschaft, 1972). See also Rolf Peter Sieferle, *Die Konservative Revolution: Fünf biographische Skizzen* (Frankfurt: Fischer, 1995); and Volker Weiß, *Moderne Antimoderne: Arthur Moeller van der Bruck und der Wandel des Konservatismus* (Paderborn: Schöningh, 2012).

equality. Even prior to World War I, working as a high-school teacher and then independent scholar in Munich, Spengler became convinced that Europe was in the process of slow but decisive decay. Despite its technological development and global political dominance, the norms and traditions that had sustained European growth were disintegrating into chaos. In 1911, Spengler embarked on an ambitious effort to identify the source of this tragic development, a task which gained a heightened urgency with the violence of war. By looking at the history of past civilizations, he believed, it would be possible to distil universal and recurring rules, that would explain the ills plaguing modern Europe. The 1,200-page tome that emerged from this work, *The Decline of the West* (first published in 1918, reissued in an expanded and revised version in 1922), became one of the period's greatest intellectual sensations. It sold more than 100,000 copies – a rare feat for such a lengthy and scholarly text – and received more than 400 reviews. Europe's leading sociologists, philosophers, and novelists, such as Max Weber and Robert Musil, hotly debated its claims. The prominent novelist Thomas Mann went so far to call it the era's "most important book."[8]

At its core, *The Decline of the West* was an assault on the Enlightenment's understanding of history. According to Spengler's pessimistic view, thinkers such as Immanuel Kant and his successors were wrong to claim that human history was the unfolding of universal progress, whereby reason would bring about gradual liberation, prosperity, and peace. Humanity was instead subjected to recurrent cycles, in which civilizations (which were made of several tribes of nations) emerged, flourished, and then declined into entropy. In Spengler's mind, there were eight civilizations that best reflected this ironclad rule: Babylonian, Egyptian, Indian, Chinese, Mesoamerican (Mayan/Aztec), Greco-Roman, Arabian, and Western (Euro-American). Those, he claimed, were humanity's most "advanced" civilizations, which consciously developed a sense of "mission" (in contrast to the rest of humanity, which Spengler dismissed as lacking "historical awareness" and thus unworthy of attention). What is more, Spengler claimed that in contrast to the Enlightenment belief in humanity's ability to converge around universal norms, these civilizations were profoundly distinct, each of them guided by its own idea or "world feeling" that manifested itself in all areas of life, from political institutions to economic relations, artistic and philosophical

---

8 Oswald Spengler, *The Decline of the West*, trans. Charles Francis Atkinson, 2 vols. (New York: Alfred A. Knopf, 1926–1928). On the book's reception, see John Farrenkopf, *Prophet of Decline: Spengler on World History and Politics* (Baton Rouge: Louisiana State University Press, 2001), 100–112.

production, and religious tradition. For example, the Egyptians were preoccupied with the sequential passage of the soul, while the Greco-Romans were consumed by a fascination with the present.[9]

Though *The Decline of The West* claimed to offer an overarching theory of civilization across thousands of years, its most significant and lengthy portions were dedicated to modern Europe. Both Spengler and his reviewers, after all, were most interested in the ability of these allegedly universal laws of civilization to explain their own era of violence and instability. According to Spengler, the West, like the civilizations that preceded it, had enjoyed a long period of spiritual vibrancy, which began in the Middle Ages and reached its zenith in the early modern era. Animated by its own unique "world feeling" to reach new horizons, what Spengler called the "search for the infinite," it gave birth to astounding technological innovation, cultural production, and imperial world domination. Yet ironically, it was these very achievements that led to decadence. Beginning in the late eighteenth century, the people of the West had been corrupted by their wealth. Like the Romans or Mayans before them, they grew accustomed to a life of convenience, and became concerned solely with selfish material pleasure. In fact, *The Decline of the West* maintained that the greatest evil of European modernity's was the rise of "money values," which celebrated profit-making as life's chief goal. This ideology, propagated by plutocrats and financiers, sought to displace notions of tradition, commitment to the community, and loyalty to the family, while destroying the nobility's centuries of control over politics and the economy.[10]

In Spengler's eyes, such abject "materialist" values received their darkest confirmation with the spread of liberal democracy after the French Revolution. Capitalist entrepreneurs, who controlled the media, promoted the notion of political and legal equality because they recognized it would serve their mission of forging a "duty-less" society that they could rule. In this narrative, socialism, too, was a mere variation of this ideology, one that also fetishized wealth but sought to transfer it to a different group. As Spengler put it, "the interest-politics of the workers' movements also belong to it [capitalism], in that their object is not to overcome the money-vales, but to possess them."[11] For Spengler, both democrats and socialists were "parasitic" elements, groups that did not recognize any value beyond material gain.

---

9 Spengler, *The Decline of the West*, vol. I, 3–41.
10 Spengler, *The Decline of the West*, vol. II, 453–465.
11 Spengler, *The Decline of the West*, vol. II, 506.

Their triumph across Europe, especially in Germany (where democractic and socialist representatives came to power just as Spengler finished the book), signaled the West's terminal state. Indeed, Europeans had become so self-absorbed and so averse to sacrifice that they ceased to care about their culture's survival, including procreation. Succumbing to "appalling depopulation," which would soon leave their cities empty, this apathy would lead "the whole pyramid of cultural man" into "final self-destruction."[12] For Spengler, then, the horrors of World War I and the chaos that followed it were not merely the product of individuals' or even nations' choices. They were symptoms of the West's epochal demise, the product of inevitable and impersonal forces that mandated civilizational waning.

Many scholars have described Spengler's sweeping generalizations as pessimism, but his thought entailed more than melancholic resignation.[13] While he claimed that civilizational disintegration was inevitable, it could also be postponed through new spiritual–political arrangements. In *Prussianism and Socialism* (1919), for example, Spengler asserted that Germany still possessed a unique tradition that might enable it to resist the corrosive diffusion of "money values" (which, like many German writers, Spengler associated with Britain and France). It survived among the Prussian conservative elite, which had dominated Germany's pre-democratic legal, military, and political leadership, and still respected values of tradition, patriarchy, and obedience. To regain its authority, however, Spengler claimed that this elite would have to embrace a new alliance with the mass politics embodied by socialism, which was an irreversible product of the modern world. Shedding its "agrarian-feudal narrowness" would allow the Prussian elite to accept the masses as active participants in politics and as equal members in the national community, which Spengler considered the most "natural" and spiritual social association.[14] In Spengler's eyes, such unity would resist materialism by overcoming apathy and thus resurrect the West's earlier commitment to "the infinite," the search for never-ending improvement and sacrifice. A national rebirth entailed nobility and socialists working shoulder to shoulder to build a "German socialism," "both determined to establish a strictly socialist state … both welded together through a shared sense of duty, through the realization that

---

12 Spengler, *The Decline of the West*, vol. II, 103–104.
13 On this point, see for example Matthew W. Slaboch, *A Road to Nowhere: The Idea of Progress and Its Critics* (Philadelphia: University of Pennsylvania Press, 2018), 89–109.
14 Oswald Spengler, *Preußentum und Sozialismus* (Munich: Beck, 1919), 11.

a great task lies ahead, through the will to obey in order to rule, to die in order to be victorious."[15]

There were, of course, considerable tensions and evasions in this vision, most glaringly its relationship to Spengler's broader narrative of decline. If the West – Germany included – had already begun its inevitable fall, what would be the benefits of postponing it to establish "German socialism"?[16] What is more, Spengler's claim to offer a novel plan that integrated socialism into a modern and spiritual society, which would be free of "materialist" decadence, was largely rhetorical. Focused as he was on abstract notions of "duty" and "value," his writings offered few specific economic or political recommendations, and he largely expected workers to unilaterally accept "Prussian" values. Indeed, Spengler's "German socialism" had little to do with the left's historical demands, such as economic redistribution or international solidarity between workers. Rather, his vision of a united spiritual community could materialize only once workers abandoned their political and economic agenda; as he put it in *Prussianism and Socialism*, his goal was to "liberate German Socialism from Marx."[17] Spengler's writings thus captured powerful sentiments on the Right after World War I, especially its simultaneous horror at the demise of traditional hierarchies and hope that they could be reborn, but his political program remained vague and underdeveloped. The task of crafting a new political theory would be left to others.

Carl Schmitt and the "Total State"

By far the most influential political theorist of the new Right was Carl Schmitt (1888–1985), a prolific professor of law in Bonn, who launched a blistering attack on what he saw as liberalism's internal contradictions. Parliamentary democracy, he warned in a series of widely read publications, was ideologically incoherent, and far too weak to address the challenges of the modern era. Schmitt updated conservative ideas about legitimacy and authority and crafted a powerful alternative to the liberal-democratic political system that emerged from World War I. In contrast to pre-war conservatives, Schmitt did not envision a right-wing order rooted in traditional and divinely ordained monarchical regimes. The future, he asserted, lay instead in modern,

---

15 Spengler, *The Decline of the West*, vol. II, 105.
16 Ben Lewis, "Spengler's Prussian Socialism," *European Review*, 25(3) (2017), 479–493.
17 Spengler, *Preußentum und Sozialismus*, 4.

nationalist, and authoritarian dictatorship. Like Spengler, Schmitt grounded his theory in claims of universal, tragic, and timeless facts. Anti-liberalism and authoritarianism, he argued, were a necessary and unavoidable response to the harsh and unchanging realities of human nature.

According to Schmitt, humans had always organized themselves into hostile collectives, seeing some as "friends" and others as "enemies." There was nothing rational or noble about these divisions; they were a hard fact of life, inherent to humanity. In the modern era, the most important divide was along national lines. People's strongest solidarities and hatreds were now national, and the state's most important task was to prepare the people for inevitable national wars.[18] Schmitt, however, claimed that this responsibility was severely undermined by liberalism, and especially its focus on individual freedom and open parliamentary debate. The logic of liberal ideology, he claimed in *The Crisis of Parliamentary Democracy* (1923), came from the apolitical sphere of commerce: In the same manner that merchants believed free competition would lead to universal prosperity, liberal politicians thought that electoral politics and open discussions would eliminate conflict. In Schmitt's eyes, the consequence of this ideology was a catastrophic domestic chaos. The pluralist division of power and the practice of open debate ultimately pitted one group against the other and fomented competition over resources and power: labor unions against businesses, conservatives against feminists, churches against atheist associations. Liberalism, then, divided the nation and undermined leaders' ability to respond to external threats. Both its ideology and its practice were inimical to the nation's political survival.[19]

What is more, Schmitt was convinced that the state must embody a metaphysical quality. The goal of state institutions, he maintained, was to "represent," by which he meant to realize spiritual values. Schmitt, who was fond of theological images, claimed that the mission of political leaders was analogous to that of a Catholic clergy. Just as the Eucharist transformed bread and wine into Christ's body, so were decisions made by state rulers the realization of the political community's essence.[20] Like Spengler, however,

---

18 These ideas were most clearly articulated in Carl Schmitt, *The Concept of the Political*, trans. George Schwab (Chicago: University of Chicago Press, 2006).
19 Carl Schmitt, *The Crisis of Parliamentary Democracy*, trans. Ellen Kennedy (Cambridge: MIT Press, 1985).
20 Carl Schmitt, *Roman Catholicism and Political Form*, trans. G. L. Ulmen (Chicago: University of Chicago Press, 2008). Scholars have debated the relationship between Schmitt's theological analogies and his political theory. For a good study that charts their deep links, see Duncan Kelly, "Carl Schmitt's Political Theory of Representation," *Journal of the History of Ideas*, 65(1) (2004), 113–134.

Schmitt lamented that liberalism and socialism (which he considered liberalism's offshoot) were devoid of such spiritual and metaphysical qualities. They were money-obsessed systems that observed all objects in materialist terms, and thus soulless. "Something dead," he scoffed in his *Constitutional Theory* (1928), "something inferior or valueless, something lowly, cannot be represented."[21] Liberal democracy, then, was not only too weak to defend the national "friends" from their many "enemies," but also too spiritually feeble to sustain the state's true mission. For the nation to regain its "life," liberalism had to be defeated.[22]

As an alternative, Schmitt envisioned an authoritarian and nationalist model, which he hoped would soon emerge. In *Dictatorship* (1921) and subsequent publications, Schmitt claimed that an authoritarian regime was best equipped to prepare the nation against its enemies. Instead of the constant infighting and compromises of a pluralist regime, a strong leader could subject all people, classes, and groups to the nation's cause, coordinate the state's resources for its defense, and remind its citizens of their fate as members of the same community. Even more importantly, a powerful leader could embody the undivided nation, the only modern group that possessed a spiritual quality. By taking decisions that benefited the nation as a whole (and not just a few sectors), the leader would "represent" the nation's essence. Breaking with traditional conservative political theory, Schmitt did not envision this dictatorship as dynastic or monarchical rule, but one that would rely on the active support of the masses. This autocrat, he claimed, would be chosen by direct national referendum; the dictator would also invite the people to confirm or reject proposed policies in national referendums. Indeed, for Schmitt, this plebiscite dictatorship was far more democratic then elected parties and parliaments. Even though it manufactured consent from above (by deciding what choices to present the people), it drew its legitimacy from the whole and unified nation.[23]

Alongside its reliance on popular legitimacy, Schmitt claimed that such a dictatorship would depart from previous political models in its radically expansive authority. And the term that best encapsulated this vision was the

---

21 Carl Schmitt, *Constitutional Theory*, ed. and trans. Jeffrey Seitzer (Durham: Duke University Press, 2008), 243.
22 For an analysis of Schmitt's relationship with theology and theological rhetoric, see for example Heinrich Meier, *The Lesson of Carl Schmitt: Four Chapters on the Distinction between Political Theology and Political Philosophy* (Chicago: University of Chicago Press, 1998).
23 Carl Schmitt, *Dictatorship: From the Origin of the Modern Concept of Sovereignty to Proletarian Class Struggle*, trans. Michael Hoelzl and Graham Ward (Cambridge: Polity Press, 2017); and Schmitt, *The Concept of the Political*.

"total state," a term which Schmitt borrowed from Italian fascists and used with growing frequency from 1930 onward.[24] According to Schmitt, the expansion of suffrage and the politicization of the masses across the industrialized world led to the blurring of the traditional separation between state and society, especially in economic matters. As governments' efforts to respond to the Great Depression showed, citizens now expected states to secure economic stability, even if that meant a proliferation of regulations, taxes, and bureaucratic management. For Schmitt, similar developments characterized the state's approach to religion, education, and the media, which governments increasingly regulated and controlled. The masses' participation in politics meant that the state became "indistinguishable from society," and thus controlled "anything that concerns the collective existence of human beings." Schmitt claimed that this new order, which emerged in the twentieth century, was best described as a "total state." While it took different forms in different countries, its broad contours were similar everywhere, which showed that it was a permanent feature of modern life.[25]

While liberal and parliamentary regimes could try and establish such a "total state," Schmitt warned that they were far too disorganized to effectively fulfill this expansive constellation of state responsibilities. At best, he sneered, they could establish a "weak total state," where authority was compromised by infighting between constituencies and decisions were routinely reversed by elections. A modern authoritarian regime, in contrast, could become what Schmitt called a "strong total state." The nationalist dictator would not only be in charge of political matters and diplomatic affairs (as monarchs traditionally were), but run the entire life of the nation, managing economic policy, deciding on religious issues, and controlling and censoring the media. What is more, a dictator could be freed from liberal democracy's need to rely on the Rule of Law, that is, the need to articulate general and universal principles that would apply to all. In a "strong total state," the sovereign could swiftly decide on all matters, without having to comply with "abstract" rules (for example, exempting one firm from regulations but not another). The future and strong total state, then, would be the ultimate political constellation. It would both fulfill the state's eternal mission – to prepare its people against their enemy – and adapt it to the modern era.[26]

---

24 On the evolution of the term, see John P. McCormick, *Carl Schmitt's Critique of Liberalism* (Cambridge: Cambridge University Press, 1990).
25 Carl Schmitt, *Der Hüter der Verfassung* (Tübingen: Mohr, 1931), 79.
26 Carl Schmitt, *Legality and Legitimacy*, trans. Jeffrey Seitzer (Durham: Duke University Press, 2004).

Like Spengler's theory of decline, Schmitt's vision of "the total state" electrified the German Right. It presented hierarchical and anti-liberal ideas as the natural product of the human condition, and nationalist authoritarianism as the most efficient system in the world of modern economy and mass politics. The term "total state" therefore spread like wildfire in the early 1930s. The historian Otto Hinze, for example, one of Germany's leading thinkers, celebrated it as an astute description of modern political trends; jurist (and former student of Schmitt) Ernst Forsthoff embraced it in a widely read book entitled *The Total State* (1933); and a slew of nationalist journalists and thinkers embraced it to articulate their hopes for an authoritarian future. To be sure, the term was also criticized by more traditional conservatives, who worried that an elected leader who ruled through plebiscites lacked the "natural" authority of dynastic monarchies. The sociologist Heinz Ziegler, for example, lambasted Schmitt and claimed that his "total state" was not substantially different from the elected parliamentary democracy, and thus should be rejected by conservatives. By the 1930s, however, such voices were a minority in the universe of right-wing thought. In the era of mass politics, it was ideas like Schmitt's that seemed to offer more realistic yet enticing possibilities.[27]

While Schmitt claimed to base his ideas on a sober and systematic recognition of life's harsh realities, his writings left much unexplained: If parliamentary and liberal regimes were truly as weak as he supposed, why did Britain and France win World War I and erect massive empires? On a more profound level, Schmitt did not clarify why democratic regimes were *inherently* dysfunctional, or why national differences were fated to erupt into war. The realities of post-World War I Germany, with its unstable republic and boiling resentment over its recent defeat, provided his template for the universal laws of politics. Others on the German new Right, however, were more explicit in acknowledging World War I's formative role in their thought. The war, they claimed, was a watershed experience, which received its best articulation through literature.

Ernst Jünger, War, and Masculinity

Few articulated the radical Right's fascination with violence in artistic form more creatively than Ernst Jünger (1895–1998). Born to a well-off middle-class family from Heidelberg, Jünger served in World War I and became one of Germany's most highly decorated soldiers (he was one of only eleven

---

27 On the reception of Schmitt's work on the "total state," see William E. Scheuerman, *Carl Schmitt: The End of Law* (Lanham: Rowman & Littlefield, 1999), 100 onward.

infantry leaders to receive the *Pour le mérite*, the country's highest honor). Drawing from the well of this experience, he published a series of stylistically innovative war memoirs and novels, which enjoyed both commercial success and critical acclaim. While war had long been an important theme in European literature, Jünger's writings depicted it in a profoundly new way. In contrast to classic literary works like Leo Tolstoy's *War and Peace* (1867), which examined war as the manifestation of broader historical and social trends, Jünger explored the war as an atavistic and psychological event, one that overwhelmed the soldier's senses and forever transformed his psyche. Most importantly, Jünger depicted the war's chaos and destruction as paradoxically liberating both for the individual and for society. Its extreme nature could shock "decadent" industrial society from its slumbers, inject exhilarating vitality into its veins, and inaugurate a new era of collective determination. Expressed with unmatched literary flair, these ideas propelled Jünger to the center of the right-wing intellectual universe in the postwar era. They allowed traumatized nationalists to find meaning and hope in the war's senseless slaughter.[28]

According to Jünger, modern society, with its focus on a stifling routine, work, and material security, had emptied human life of meaning. The world possessed magical and exciting forces, but they had become hidden as people sank into apathy, preoccupied by their petty economic worries. War, however, allowed soldiers to reconnect with those primordial energies. Thrown into unpredictable danger and the constant threat of death, young men experienced emotional extremes and new possibilities for life. In *The Storm of Steel* (1920), which was based on his own experiences on the Western Front, Jünger portrayed the battlefield as a theater for the realization of natural forces in which human action and nature merged. An artillery barrage was a "storm of iron," an exploding shell "a hurricane of fire," troops launching an attack were a "swarm of bees," and houses under shelling collapsed "as if by the power of magic."[29] Indeed, to capture this sensory experience, *Storm of Steel* (like many of Jünger's later novels) did not revolve around a structured narrative, but was instead composed of disparate scenes. War could not be captured by a traditional story of personal and gradual growth (*Bildungsroman*) or by rational interpretation; only a disparate collage could reflect its shattering impact. For Jünger, witnessing such carnage did not spark alarm at the war's horrendous destruction, but on the contrary,

---

28 Thomas R. Nevin, *Ernst Jünger and Germany* (Durham: Duke University Press, 1996).
29 Ernst Jünger, *The Storm of Steel* (New York: Penguin, 2004).

aroused a profound thrill. Battle provided a psychological and spiritual adventure, unshackling the soul from the chains of the familiar. Indeed, even though *The Storm of Steel* was rife with description of gruesome injuries and deaths, it transformed them into a somehow revivifying experience. As Jünger put it, "in among the great, bloody scenes there was a wild, unsuspected hilarity."[30]

If war was such an exhilarating experience, it was to a large extent because violence forged a kind of spiritual camaraderie between male soldiers. According to Jünger, the psychological shock of battle allowed soldiers to transcend their individuality. It was "an intoxication beyond all intoxication," he wrote in *Battle as an Inner Experience* (1922), in which "the individual is like a ranging storm, the tossing sea and roaring thunder. He is melted into everything ... It is as if a wave slipped back into the flowing sea."[31] This breaking of the boundaries in turn furnished the creation of a new and "special community," enforced by atavistic bonds. The soldiers share "a great destiny, ride the same wave, are for once together as an organism in the face of the hostile outside world, encompass a higher mission."[32] In Jünger's deeply gendered vision, this new community was decisively masculine, a quality he associated with creativity, strength, and courage. His writings celebrated war and its glories as the ultimate manifestations of manhood. "Oh," he rhapsodized with evident nostalgia when describing one battle, "the baptism of fire! The air was so laden with an overflowing manliness that every breath was intoxicating! ... Oh hearts of men that could feel this!"[33] In Jünger's eyes, war and the enhancement of masculinity were inseparable. "The battle," he observed, "is not only a process of destruction, but also a masculine form of creation."[34]

In Jünger's eyes, what emerged from this "masculine form of creation" was a new kind of human being, defined by unprecedented firmness and determination. It was man with "a granite face, a voice that rattles order," a body that was "smooth, lined, lean ... with chiseled features, eyes hardened under a thousand horrors."[35] These qualities, Jünger maintained, transformed soldiers into the future leaders of their societies. They were the new aristocracy, anointed for leadership not by birth or tradition but by fire, regardless of their pre-war background. As historian Jeffrey Herf noted, Jünger envisioned war as scorching not only the "feminine" or "bourgeois" traditions of refinement,

---

30 Jünger, *The Storm of Steel*, 24.
31 Ernst Jünger, *Der Kampf als inneres Erlebnis* (Berlin: E. S. Mittler, 1922), 57.
32 Jünger, *Der Kampf als inneres Erlebnis*, 89.   33 Jünger, *Der Kampf als inneres Erlebnis*, 22.
34 Jünger, *Der Kampf als inneres Erlebnis*, 53.   35 Jünger, *Der Kampf als inneres Erlebnis*, 57.

but also the conservative enchantment with custom and tradition-based hierarchies. As *Battle as an Inner Experience* explained, the war created a "new man, the storm pioneer, the elite of Central Europe. A wholly new race, intelligent, strong, and full of will. What emerges here in battle ... tomorrow will be the axis around which life will revolve faster and faster."[36]

In addition to unlocking masculine virility and courage, Jünger's war also forged a new relationship between humans and machines. In works like *Fire and Blood* (1925), Jünger criticized the thinking of traditional conservatives who had decried machines and feared the routinization of labor as detrimental to "natural" life. The war, he claimed, and its reliance on modern technology such as machine guns and poison gas, has shown that machines possessed beauty and energy; the time had come to recognize the splendor of their harsh movement. Indeed, Jünger's writings described with fascination the proliferation of telephone lines, urban transportation, and electric lights, and implored readers to embrace their decimating impact on traditional (and slower) modes of life, especially decaying agrarian communities. Like machine guns, these new technologies were irreversible, and the destruction they inflicted on the world was making way for a new and modern community, one that accepted chaos and danger as the basis for courage. The generation of the front, in Jünger's eyes, would lead the way in building this new approach, and had begun "to reconcile itself with the machine and to see in it not only the useful but the beautiful as well. This reconciliation," he explained, "is an important first step out of a gray, frightful world of utilitarianism."[37]

As this fascination with technology indicates, Jünger's understanding of war was hardly nostalgic. In his eyes, the task of culture and politics was to make the experience of the front *permanent*, to bring soldiers' sense of excitement, masculine community, and wonder about technology back into the home-front of civilian existence. As he put it in a famous 1930 essay, thinkers and politicians had to generate a "total mobilization," "an act through which ... the great current of the energy of war will be transmitted throughout the far-flung and multi-circuited network of modern life."[38] Jünger called on readers to grasp the demonic beauty and danger of everyday experience, and open themselves to the virility that his novels sought to capture. "It suffices simply to consider our daily life," he wrote,

---

36 Jünger, *Der Kampf als inneres Erlebnis*, 76. See Herf, *Reactionary Modernism*, 75 onward.
37 Ernst Jünger, *Feuer und Blut* (Magdeburg: Stahlhem Verlag, 1925), 81.
38 Ernst Jünger, "Total Mobilization," in *The Heidegger Controversy*, ed. Richard Wolin (Cambridge: MIT Press, 1993), 122–139, p. 127. The translation has been slightly modified.

with its inexorability and merciless discipline, its smoking, glowing districts, the physics and metaphysics of its commerce, its motors, airplanes, the burgeoning cities. With pleasure-tinged horror, we sense that here, not a single atom is not in motion – that we are profoundly inscribed in this raging process. Total mobilization is ... in war and peace, the expression of the secret and inexorable claim to which our life in the age of masses and machines subjects us.[39]

To help foster this psychological approach, Jünger complemented his war novels with a photograph collection entitled *The Dangerous Moment*, which reproduced images of sinking ships, colliding cars, and violent demonstrations. The encounter with those acts of sudden and man-made violence was to be the jolt that propelled the reader into a higher form of existence.[40]

More than anywhere, Jünger believed that this morphing of war into perpetual experience would take place among the working masses. In his popular tract, *The Worker* (1932), Jünger broke with traditional conservative disdain for the poor and uneducated classes by claiming that workers could be the vanguard of a psychological revolution. Their physical labor, he maintained, their life of scarcity, their collectivist ethos, and their indifference for refinement replicated the values and experiences of soldiers. Indeed, Jünger depicted factory workers as the reincarnations of his wartime comrades. Like soldiers, they were strong, firm, and healthy; their individuality "melted" into the community of their peers; and they integrated technology into their everyday routine.[41] Jünger went so far as to compare laboring men to the mythical figures of the titans, who defied the Greek gods to realize their monumental power. "The worker," he wrote in one essay, "is a son of the earth, much closer to the great titans, like Antaeus, Prometheus, Atlas, than Heracles."[42] For Jünger, workers had to abandon socialism's "impoverished" focus on economic conditions and class struggle, and instead reconceive themselves as a spiritual community of masculine values. By doing so, they would realize "the German essence," and thus destroy the stale and despised "bourgeois" order of security, femininity, and democracy. Jünger mused that "the worker" was the "nascent power on which the fate of the

---

39 Jünger, "Total Mobilization," 128. The translation has been slightly modified.
40 Ernst Jünger, *Der gefährliche Augenblick* (Berlin: Junker und Dünnhaupt, 1931).
41 Ernst Jünger, *The Worker: Dominion and Form*, ed. Laurence Paul Hemming, trans. Bogdan Costea and Laurence Paul Hemming (Chicago: Northwestern University Press, 2017), 108.
42 Ernst Jünger, "Maxima Minima," in *Sämtliche Werke*, 22 vols. (Stuttgart: Klett-Cotta, 2000), vol. X, 319–387, p. 341.

country rests." The "rise of the worker" was thus "synonymous with a new rise for Germany."[43]

Jünger, of course, was not a political theorist, and he did not pause from his rhapsodies to explain which institutions or politics could sustain such a "total mobilization." For all his fascination for collective community, his vision remained highly individualist: war, labor, and politics all acquired meaning not from their prosaic realities, but from individuals' ability to conceive of them as phenomena charged with transcendent meaning. Indeed, much of the appeal of his work stemmed from its insistence that gigantic and impersonal forces – whether death in war or the rise of industrial society – could open the door for a "real" and "authentic" recognition of the self. However, literature alone could not show how this could occur; instead, this search for authenticity became the task of philosophy.

Heidegger and The Search for "Authenticity"

The most influential philosopher of interwar Germany – and the person whose relationship to the conservative revolution has fostered the most heated debates – was Martin Heidegger (1989–1976). As a young professor in Marburg and then Freiburg, Heidegger offered a radically new approach to our understanding of the human condition. In his eyes, traditional philosophy had asked the wrong questions, especially by emphasizing knowledge, disengaged reasoning, and ethics. Instead, philosophers should seek to recall "the question of Being" by analyzing the nature of lived experience. To begin doing so, Heidegger developed an unusual style of writing. His works, most importantly *Being and Time* (1927), were filled with neologisms, unfamiliar phrasings, and a language that seemed at once starkly concrete and astonishingly abstract. Despite the challenges that this style posed to readers, Heidegger's reputation as a brilliant and revolutionary thinker grew quickly. In the eyes of many, his philosophy represented the most profound challenge to the Enlightenment's modes of thinking.

According to Heidegger, European philosophers had erroneously conceived of humans as potentially rational beings who could analyze the world around them from a position of detachment. Especially since René Descartes proclaimed *cogito ergo sum* (usually translated as "I think, therefore I am"), they had viewed humans as capable of freeing themselves from irrational thinking, and thus capable of approaching all objects in a scientific manner. Heidegger

---

43 Jünger, *The Worker*, 14.

argued that this framework failed to capture the realities of human existence, which were rooted in non-rational being. As he put it, "with the *'cogito sum'* Descartes had claimed that he was putting philosophy on a new and firm footing. But what he left undetermined . . . was the kind of being which belongs to the *res cogitans*, or – more precisely – the meaning of the being of the *sum*." Rather than soberly analyzing the world, humans were always "thrown" into it, shaped by and operating in a world of meaning that existed before them. Indeed, in their "everyday" existence, humans engaged with objects as part of a total system of references. They did not analyze a chair, for example, as a purely independent object. Rather, they approached it through its relation to something else, i.e., as something that stands near a table so they could sit on it in order to eat.[44] Heidegger therefore argued that instead of talking about "individuals" or "subjects," philosophy should explore what he called "Dasein," a term that in German combined "there" (*Da*) and "to be" (*Sein*). Philosophers had to understand that Dasein was situated in an environment of meaning; it was, in Heidegger's phrasing, "being in the world."[45]

Most of the time, Heidegger maintained, Dasein was immersed in its everyday actions, without putting much thought into its engagement with objects. Occasionally, however, this seamless process was disrupted, such as when a useful tool stops working. A chair, for example, could fall to pieces, or a clock might stop showing the time because its inner apparatus had frozen. These moments, in Heidegger's eyes, were instructive insofar as they could awaken philosophical reflection on Dasein's relationship to the world. They reminded Dasein that its actions could be made out of deliberate reflections, rather than automatic gestures. Most famously, Heidegger maintained that the most radical interruption of everyday life came when Dasein was confronted with its own death. In the rare moments when Dasein truly anticipated its end, it was possessed by radical "anxiety," an overwhelming mood that threw all of its quotidian commitments and habits into question. Borrowing from Christian thought and most especially Søren Kierkegaard's *Fear and Trembling* (1843), Heidegger described this existential anxiety as fundamentally different than regular fear (such as fear of insects).[46] It was a shattering of conventional understanding that otherwise held sway in Dasein's worldly experience.

---

44 Martin Heidegger, *Being and Time*, trans. J. Macquarrie and E. Robinson (New York: Harper and Row, 1962), 95–107.
45 Heidegger, *Being and Time*, 78.
46 On the role of Christian theology in Heidegger's thought, see for example Hubert L. Dreyfus, *Being-in-the-World: A Commentary on Heidegger's* Being and Time, *Division I* (Cambridge: MIT Press, 1991).

Anxiety was such a crucial phenomenon or mood for Heidegger because it helped clarify Dasein's relationship to other humans. Because Dasein was always thrown into a world, it was a deeply social entity. Its entire mode of thinking was rooted in the language, community, and order that existed before it. This meant that, most of the time, Dasein followed the norms set by others. It accepted the judgment of what Heidegger called the "one" (*das Man*), a set of shared values, social practices, and common opinion that constituted its own manner of being.[47] The anxiety of death, however, allowed Dasein to break free from this mindless conformity. It allowed it to recognize the artificiality of its social setting, to examine the commitments that inform its automatic and unreflective behavior. For Heidegger, embracing anxiety rather than taking refuge in the comforts of the familiar (like numbing entertainment or senseless political debates) therefore was the key to Dasein's freedom. The dread of human finitude confronted Dasein with its "ownmost possibility."[48]

Such freedom, however, was not the freedom to ignore one's surroundings, which in Heidegger's eyes was in any case impossible. Rather, this confrontation with finitude liberated Dasein to embrace an "authentic" existence, by which Heidegger meant a conscious choice of one's collective fate. According to *Being and Time*, because people are so deeply immersed in their communal surroundings, they cannot help but accept this as their heritage. It was incumbent on people to embrace their community's past, holidays, and works of art, and to understand how integral these were to human thought. But such recognition did not mean an uncritical or mindless celebration of the past and present, which would be a mere submission to the authority of the "one." By actively and consciously accepting the choices set by heritage, Dasein recognized its own "thrownness" and made it its own; it could "understand this thrownness as the null basis which it has to take up into [its] existence."[49] Authenticity, for Heidegger, meant accepting and taking genuine ownership over the possibilities set by Dasein's surroundings. "The resoluteness in which Dasein comes back to itself," he concluded, "discloses current factual possibilities of authentic existing, and discloses them in terms of the heritage which that resoluteness, as thrown, takes over."[50]

Heidegger never clarified in *Being and Time* which element of one's given social being lent itself to the most authentic existence. Was there any hierarchy between the Dasein's adherence to its nationality and its devotion to its sex, generation, class, or religious denomination? And what was the

---

47 Heidegger, *Being and Time*, 163–164.   48 Heidegger, *Being and Time*, 228–235.
49 Heidegger, *Being and Time*, 333.   50 Heidegger, *Being and Time*, 435.

Dasein to do if one part of its heritage conflicted with another? Indeed, Heidegger's writings from the 1920s remained evasive about his philosophy's ethical or political implications. While his longing for authenticity was clear, he did not explain whether it could be more easily achieved through certain ethical commitments or through political action. At least in part, this was a product of the tension between Heidegger's belief that authenticity simultaneously required the recognition of one's membership in a collective (like the nation) *and* the embrace of one's individual finitude. "Once one has grasped the finitude of one's existence," he wrote, "it snatches one back from the endless multiplicity of possibilities which offer themselves as closest to one – those of comfortableness, shirking, and taking things lightly – and brings Dasein into the simplicity of its fate."[51] Ultimately, what animated Heidegger's early writings more than anything was the rejection of complacency. Authenticity, with its harsh recognition of one's mortality and conscious embrace of one's surroundings, was potentially attainable in multiple forms; what furnished one Dasein's life with an authentic existence could be radically different than what did so for another's.[52]

At least in part, the appeal of Heidegger's writings was their comprehensive and radical challenge to the Enlightenment's tradition of reasoning. For a generation of young thinkers, who understood World War I as the refutation of humanity's ability to achieve progress through reason, *Being and Time*'s embrace of anxiety and challenge to spiritual complacency captured the need for a new way of thinking. Yet Heidegger's earlier openness would soon be eclipsed by very concrete allegiances. With the onslaught of the Great Depression and the rise of Nazism, Heidegger threw his support behind the most extreme nationalist convictions, and joined the Nazi party. A similar path, with varying degrees of enthusiasm, was taken also by the rest of the conservative revolutionaries. The consequence for their thought's legacy would be far reaching.

The Revolution from the Right, Nazism, and Beyond

In its ambitious bid to redefine scholarship, politics, gender roles, artistic expression, and social norms, the Revolution from the Right was bound to be

---

51 Heidegger, *Being and Time*, 435.
52 For a brief and clear discussion of *Being and Time*'s complex implications for politics and ethics, see Peter E. Gordon, *Continental Divide: Heidegger, Cassirer, Davos* (Cambridge: Harvard University Press, 2010), 24–37.

one of the twentieth century's most controversial intellectual phenomena. But nothing has fueled as much debate as the movement's relationship to Nazism. It is beyond dispute that the new Right shared profound ideological overlaps with the Nazi movement, especially its blistering attacks on individualism, Marxism, and any notion of human equality. Many of the movement's leading figures recognized these similarities, and once Hitler had come to power in Germany in 1933, they joined the Nazi party and supported the new regime. Yet this embrace was also laced with misgivings and disagreements. These radical conservatives sometimes recoiled at the Third Reich's vulgar racism, and claimed that their broader ideas should not be reduced to mere scaffolding for Nazi politics. These concurrent similarities and differences meant that the Revolution from the Right's legacy in European thought has been contentious but also far-reaching. While some historians have dismissed it as forever "tainted" by the Nazi stain, other scholars and thinkers have continued to mine it for fresh insights, often in the service of surprising and markedly anti-nationalist projects.

The movement's four intellectual luminaries' personal paths clearly demonstrate the new Right's dual relationship to Nazism, and its long-term consequences. Even before the Nazis came to power in 1933, Spengler was interested in their blend of fierce nationalism with a rhetoric of populist economist justice. Hitler's condemnation of "materialist" capitalism, liberalism, and Marxism, and his promise to replace these "empty" concepts with a new order of spiritual solidarity and unity, resonated with Spengler's laments from *The Decline of the West* as well as his hope for rebirth through "German socialism." The Nazis also recognized this overlap between Spengler's vision and their own intellectual agenda, and sought to recruit the renowned historian for their "national revolution." After a lengthy meeting with Hitler in 1933, Spengler joined The German Academy, the country's most prestigious institution of thought and scholarship.[53] Jünger, too, was enthused by much of the Nazi agenda, especially its call to rebuild German life around the "front experience" of World War I. Like *Storm of Steel*, the Nazis constantly idealized soldierly and masculine communities that allegedly transcended social hierarchies and which the Nazis claimed could become permanent. On the basis of this intellectual affinity, the Nazis sought to recruit Jünger to their ranks, offering him a position as a delegate to the Reichstag in 1933. While he declined, stating his preference to focus on his

---

53 Farrenkopf, *Prophet of Decline*, 234–238.

artistic work, he remained loyal to the regime, even volunteering to join the war effort once the hostilities had started.[54]

Even more enthusiastic was Schmitt's and Heidegger's embrace of the Third Reich. While Schmitt disliked the Nazi movement at first, after 1933 he heartily lent his ideas to its service. Celebrating the Third Reich as a "strong total state," he declared in major essays that the Führer embodied the nation and state, and his words were thus law (including the right to murder the regime's enemies).[55] After this support had granted him prestigious positions – he became the head of the "Union of German-Socialist Jurists," the union of Nazi lawyers, and an advisor to the government of Prussia – Schmitt also helped coordinate the regime's anti-Semitic crusade, articulating in public sentiments that he had previously kept private. In books such as *The Leviathan in the State Theory of Thomas Hobbes* (1938), he attacked the "Jewish spirit" as the embodiment of "dead" legalism, and, from his institutional perch within the Nazi legal regime, orchestrated the firing of Jewish jurists from their positions.[56] Heidegger, too, came to view the Nazis as a pathway to realize his quest for authentic existence. As he famously told one of his students in 1936, supporting the regime's celebration of German heritage seemed to fulfill his own philosophy.[57] After his public endorsement of Hitler, Heidegger was appointed rector of the university of Freiburg, a position he used to further promote the ideals of the "national revolution."[58] In one of his more notorious published statements, found in *An Introduction to Metaphysics* (1935), Heidegger disparaged competing philosopher-advocates for Nazism such as Ernst Krieck and Alfred Baeumler, complaining that their work had nothing to do with what he called "the inner truth and greatness" of National Socialism.[59] Like Schmitt, Heidegger's longstanding anti-Semitism also fueled his infatuation with the Nazis. In his mind, it was necessary to eradicate the Jewish "foreign" presence in German

---

54 Nevin, *Ernst Jünger and Germany*, 141–172.
55 An overview of Schmitt's career and writings during the Third Reich's first years can be found in Joseph J. Bendersky, *Carl Schmitt: Theorist for the Reich* (Princeton: Princeton University Press, 1983), 172–273.
56 Carl Schmitt, *The Leviathan and the State Theory of Thomas Hobbes* (Chicago: Chicago University Press, 2008). On Schmitt's long-held anti-Semitism, see Raphael Gross, *Carl Schmitt and the Jews* (Madison: University of Wisconsin Press, 2007).
57 Karl Löwith, "My Last Meeting with Heidegger in Rome, 1936," *The Heidegger Controversy*, 140–143.
58 Heidegger's relationship with the Third Reich is explored in detail in Hugo Ott, *Martin Heidegger: A Political Life* (London: HarperCollins, 1993), 133–260.
59 Martin Heidegger, *An Introduction to Metaphysics*, ed. Gregory Fried and Richard Polt (New Haven: Yale University Press, 2000), 213.

culture, a task he sought to fulfill by supervising the "cleansing" of Jewish academics at the University of Freiburg.[60]

Scholars have long debated the implications of this record. Does the self-proclaimed overlap between their ideas and Nazi ideology reflect the toxic and irredeemable nature of their work? Or does it reflect just *one* interpretation of their ideas, which should not overshadow their many valuable insights?[61] After all, despite the conservative revolution's clear affinities and cooperation with Nazism, this relationship was not always straightforward. The two movements had genuine disagreements, especially about the role of biology in human existence, which meant their relationship also produced tension. For example, while being courted by prominent Nazis, Spengler criticized their movement for its focus on biological racism. His *Hour of Decisions* (1934) dismissed this racial fixation as inimical to the values of honor, which led to a Nazi ban on this text.[62] Jünger similarly held mixed feelings about the Reich, whose rhetoric and politics he sometimes found too vulgar, and openly requested that the regime's newspapers refrain from publishing his work. Many in fact read his novel *On the Marble Cliffs* (1939), which depicted the destruction of a community by an invading force, as a criticism of life under Hitler.[63] A more substantial cleavage opened between the regime and Schmitt, who was accused of brazen opportunism by the Nazi magazine *Das schwarze Korps* in 1936. The magazine derided the theory of "the total state" as deeply un-racial and Schmitt's anti-Semitism as merely rhetorical, accusations on account of which he was stripped of his leadership positions (though he continued to teach).[64] Heidegger, too, quickly grew disappointed with the Reich, which he came to believe was promoting social conformity and "inauthentic" thinking. While he remained hostile to the Enlightenment, democracy, or social pluralism, in 1934, he resigned from his position as rector, and refrained from political activity thereafter.[65]

---

60 Heidegger's anti-Semitism has received heightened attention since the publication of his diaries, known as the "Black Notebooks." For multiple perspectives on this issue, see Andrew J. Mitchell and Peter Trawny (eds.), *Heidegger's Black Notebooks: Responses to Anti-Semitism* (New York: Columbia University Press, 2017).
61 This discussion revolved in particular around Heidegger's philosophy. See for example Hans Sluga, *Heidegger's Crisis* (Cambridge: Harvard University Press, 1993); and Julian Young, *Heidegger, Philosophy, Nazism* (Cambridge: Cambridge University Press, 1997). For a good overview of the debate regarding Schmitt's thought, see Gopal Balakrishnan, *The Enemy: An Intellectual Portrait of Carl Schmitt* (London: Verso, 2000), esp. 176–245.
62 Oswald Spengler, *The Hour of Decision* (New York: Knopf, 1934); Farrenkopf, *Prophet of Decline*, 238–268.
63 Ernst Jünger, *On the Marble Cliffs* (New York: New Directions, 1947); Nevin, *Ernst Jünger and Germany*, 141–172.
64 Bendersky, *Carl Schmitt*, 237–239.   65 Ott, *Martin Heidegger*, 235–261.

To be sure, one should not exaggerate the conservative revolutionaries' aversion to Nazism, as they never openly criticized the regime, critiqued its violent ideology, or condemned its horrific brutalities. Even after the Reich's demise, when the full horrors of its extermination policies became clear, Schmitt, Jünger, and Heidegger (Spengler died before the war) did not express even faint regret for their earlier enthusiasm. Still, the Revolution from the Right was clearly distinguished from the Nazi ideological project, at least from its most biologically obsessed strands of thought. Its thinkers, for example, had little interest in eugenics, a stark contrast to ideologues such as Hans F. K. Günther and Alfred Rosenberg, who sought to root Nazism's legitimacy in Darwinist concepts. Their anti-Semitism similarly departed from the Nazi regime's racial conceptions. Even Schmitt and Heidegger conceived Judaism as "materialist" ideology, and not as genetic destiny that could never be transcended. On the most substantial level, much of the new Right's key terms and frameworks – the belief in historical decline, the need for the total state, the focus on masculine communities, or search for authenticity – could be articulated without reliance on racism. One could find their analysis illuminating even while rejecting the Nazis' bid to reshape society on the basis of eugenics and hereditary "science."

This separation between Nazism and the new Right helped shaped the judgment of later generations, who have found much to admire in the conservative revolution's most prominent texts. Even if they rejected the new Right's politics and at times openly condemned its thinkers' love affair with the Third Reich, readers and thinkers in Germany and beyond continued to rely on its concepts and publications to articulate their own agendas. Spengler's ideas, for example, were resurrected and reformulated by the British historian Arnold Toynbee (1889–1975), whose monumental multi-volume *A Study of History* (1934–1961) was one of the century's most influential scholarly works. Like Spengler, Toynbee conceived humanity as locked in an epic cycle of emerging and declining civilizations. These civilizations, whether Hellenic, Arabic, or Babylonian, operated as autonomous organs, rarely engaging in meaningful interactions. Unlike Spengler, however, Toynbee was optimistic about the West's prospects for self-rejuvenation, and especially the benefits of democracy and capitalism. Recycling British imperial ideology, he claimed that the West could flourish and even unify the entire world under a peaceful world state and globally integrated economy. This conception of world history, which retained Spengler's totalizing assumptions, proved especially popular during the early Cold War, which Toynbee helped explain as a clash of "civilizations."

For this framing, Toynbee's work enjoyed unprecedented success, its abridged version selling 300,000 copies in the United States alone and receiving extensive coverage in mainstream magazines like *Life*.[66]

Even more remarkable was the afterlife of Heidegger's search for an authentic existence, which stood at the center of a boom in philosophical and left-leaning activism in postwar France. The key figure in this process was the French philosopher Jean-Paul Sartre (1905–1980), who first read Heidegger's *Being in Time* in a German prison camp during World War II.[67] Like Heidegger, Sartre described the human condition as a desperate struggle with dread and meaninglessness. This anxiety could be overcome, he claimed, by accepting that humans are responsible for choosing their own ends. People are, as he put it in *Existentialism Is a Humanism* (1946), "condemned to be free."[68] Sartre expanded on Heidegger's early writings, however, to claim that the responsibility for one's own freedom entailed responsibility for *others'* freedom, too. To be authentic required not only that people embrace their own heritage, but also that they struggle to make this possibility relevant to all those who are denied it, whether due to their economic status, gender, or race. Throughout the 1950s, Sartre and his many admirers claimed that Communism best embodied this possibility. Because it was rooted in notions of universal freedom and equality, class solidarity could forge a "we-subject," one that truly drew meaning from embracing its social position. Existentialists therefore often supported other radical political projects. Existentialist philosophers such as Simone de Beauvoir (1908–1986) used existentialist terms to advocate for feminism, while anti-colonialist writer Frantz Fanon (1925–1961) drew on existential language to call for anti-imperialist resistance.

Perhaps the most surprising legacy belonged to Schmitt, whose ideas were embraced by radical New Left groups across Western Europe during the turmoil of the 1960s and 1970s. The German radical Marxist Johannes Agnoli (1925–2003), for example, resurrected Schmitt's attack on parliamentary democracy, which he dismissed as a degenerate "bourgeois state" in the service of capitalism. The entire democratic apparatus, he scoffed, with its parties, elections, and elective assemblies, was a tool of class domination,

---

66 Arnold J. Toynbee, *A Study of History* (London and New York: Oxford University Press, 1934–1961). On the work's reception, see William H. McNeill, *Arnold Toynbee: A Life* (New York: Oxford University Press, 1989).
67 See Chapter 5 on Existentialism by Edward Baring.
68 Jean-Paul Sartre, *Existentialism Is a Humanism* (New Haven: Yale University Press, 2007), 29.

designed to deceive workers into believing their exploitation was legitimate and consensual. As he put it in the book he co-authored with psychologist Peter Brückner, *The Transformation of Democracy* (1968), liberal democracy glorified "the republic of the market" to hide "the despotism of the factory."[69] While Agnoli and his followers scorned Schmitt's nationalist authoritarianism, they nevertheless admired his critique of liberalism as an effort to repress political antagonism. They claimed that the path to liberation and the end of capitalist exploitation required an embrace of political conflict and the eradication of liberal institutions.[70] With different variations, these ideas continued to resonate with left-leaning thinkers for the rest of the twentieth century. The radical thinker Chantal Mouffe (1943), for example, invoked Schmitt in *The Democratic Paradox* (2000) and *On the Political* (2005) to criticize liberal democracy and to insist on the centrality of conflict as the center of political life.[71]

Conclusion

The Revolution from the Right's intellectual diversity meant it was never free of inner tensions and contradictions. Like other movements, such as socialism or existentialism, its most prominent figures were interested in a variety of questions, and often disagreed with each other. Yet their ambitions were united by a unique blend of cultural and ideological dispositions. Alongside a belief in society's decline, the inevitability of conflict, and the limits of rational reasoning, Spengler, Schmitt, Jünger, Heidegger, and their followers also shared a belief in the possibility of regeneration, the formation of a modern and unified nationalist community, based on spiritual solidarity between all its members. It was this simultaneous critique and embrace of modernity that allowed the movement's most important works to transcend their moment of creation. Despite their role in furnishing Europe's most horrific cultural and political experiment, they continued to resonate with new audiences and readers, inspiring new intellectual currents for the rest of the century.

---

69 Johannes Agnoli and Peter Brückner, *Die Transformation der Demokratie* (Frankfurt: Europäische Verlagsanstalt, 1968), 10.
70 On Schmitt and the New Left, see Jan-Werner Müller, *A Dangerous Mind: Carl Schmitt in Post-War European Thought* (New Haven: Yale University Press, 2003), 169–180.
71 Chantal Mouffe, *The Democratic Paradox* (London: Verso, 2000); and Chantal Mouffe, *On the Political* (London: Verso, 2005).

10

Western Marxism: Revolutions in Theory

MAX PENSKY

Western Marxism refers to the broad current of theoretical innovation by a number of Marxist-oriented political theorists and activists, beginning in the period immediately following the end of World War I and the 1918 Russian Revolution, enduring through the rise of European fascism in the early 1930s, and continuing in multiple versions to the present day. With a remarkable range of theoretical creativity, Western Marxists effectively recreated Marxism as an object of philosophical analysis, and rededicated themselves to the idea of Marx's thought as worthy of theoretical reconstruction. In the process, they broke sharply from the rigid and simplified vision of Marxist theory and practice espoused by the official Party hierarchies.

In doing so, Western Marxists both re-appropriated and radically expanded Marx's own early philosophical motivations and positions, insights that had been mostly lost by the 1920s as socialist politics had largely forgotten its origins in the idealist philosophies of the European bourgeoisie, above all that of Hegel. In particular, Marx's relatively underdeveloped concepts of alienation, exploitation, and domination, of the function and effects of bourgeois ideology, and of the role of culture in the dynamic of social change inspired a range of new theorization for Western Marxists. They reread Marx for a reinvigorated theoretical self-understanding of Marxism as a way of better guiding political practices. But they also found in Marx a resource for diagnosing why capitalism, supposedly doomed according to iron-like economic laws, was instead able to survive and thrive by drawing on symbolic, cultural, and ideological resources that scientific socialism could not account for.

In different ways, then, Western Marxists reintroduced the crucial question of the relation between theory and political practice, both in a forensic and in an anticipatory manner. If scientific socialism's dogma of the inevitable collapse of market economies could no longer be defended, then rediscovering the conceptual power and sophistication of Marxism might help to explain capitalism's continued survival. The explanation might be found not in economic laws but rather in the realm of culture. For this reason, Western Marxists developed increasingly sophisticated theories of the efficacy and pervasiveness of bourgeois ideology: of the cultural, rather than the material, reproduction of capitalist society.

Further, insofar as the Third International (1919) had effectively established the Party authority in the Soviet Union as the sole arbiter of doctrinal correctness for the European communist parties, Western Marxists of the first generation (from *circa* 1924 to the mid 1930s) felt obliged to adopt a precarious stance. The Third International left little room for independent Marxist theorizing, since the Party avant-garde claimed a peremptory and exhaustive role as the intellectualizing organ for international communism. Marxist theory outside the Party structure was in principle incompatible with adherence to Party doctrine. On the other side, departure (or expulsion) from the official organs of the Party left it unclear how independent theorizing was meant to connect to organized political action on behalf of the working classes.

While every Western Marxist had to make a personal decision regarding this unattractive trade-off, those of the first or founding generation did so informed by experiences of direct and significant political involvement in European socialism. Those of the later generations, however else they understood their political identities, theorized largely from within the context of an archetypical bourgeois institution, the modern university. As many observers have noted, Western Marxism theorized consistently about the relation between radical or revolutionary theory and practice from epistemic positions that lay at some distance from revolutionary action, increasingly (and, in the years since 1968, nearly exclusively) as university professors.[1] The "academicization" of Western Marxism gave theorists an institutional seat relatively secure from the demands and risks of Party membership. On the other hand, it also realigned the formal and informal incentives that theorists had to negotiate as they tried to connect their theories with political practice.

The result of this increasing autonomy from the demands of Party membership and doctrine has been interpreted variously. On the one hand, commentators such as Perry Anderson have lamented Western

---

[1] See Perry Anderson, *Considerations on Western Marxism* (London: New Left Books, 1976), 49ff. "The most striking single fact about the whole tradition from Lukács to Althusser, Korsch to Colletti, is the overwhelming predominance of professional philosophers within it" (49).

Marxists' growing isolation and remoteness from real politics, as they increasingly turned to cultural and aesthetic problems, drew ever closer to a familiar core of philosophical approaches and methods, and devised an academic specialization out of Marxist thought.[2] On the other hand, other interpreters such as Martin Jay have noted the spectacular creativity and restless curiosity and productivity that resulted once theorists were freed from the strict intellectual discipline of the post-Comintern Party, connecting Marxism creatively with other seemingly remote theoretical approaches (Freudian theory, literary and art criticism, cultural studies, empirical sociology, history, and on).[3] In this sense, the trajectory of Western Marxism offers a paradigmatic case of the dynamics of the modern politically engaged intellectual, even apart from the specific questions and problems of the appropriation of Marxism. Making sense of the Western Marxist tradition requires understanding what motivated these theorists: not just the experience of historical failures and disappointment, but the growing perception that Marxism required a sort of theoretical rescue as the best response.

To do so, Western Marxists frequently appropriated the lost Hegelian, or "dialectical," legacy in the development of Marx's critique of bourgeois ideology. In Hegel's sense, dialectics is the science of the relation between concepts and reality; between forms of subjective consciousness and the actual material, social, and institutional contexts in which subjective consciousness relates to objects. Central for Hegel's vision of dialectical reasoning is the maxim that antinomies such as concept and reality, or subject and object, are not fixed. The opposition between such binaries also contains within itself a moment or aspect of identity as well, and historical duration is structured by the dynamic in which such moments of identity within contradiction are actualized.

The authors associated with Western Marxism were united by no single institution or group, apart from their general (though often quite conflicting) visions of a reformulated Marxism that could respond both to the perceived failures of scientific socialism and to the authoritarian collapse of Soviet communism. Nor did they share a common nationality or language. The lines of demarcation that define who belongs to the broad current of Western Marxism have never been clearly drawn, and interpreters of Marxist theory have often differed sharply concerning just whom, where, and when

---

2 Anderson, *Considerations on Western Marxism*.
3 Martin Jay, *The Dialectical Imagination: A History of the Frankfurt School and the Institute for Social Research, 1923–1950*, 2nd edn. (Berkeley: The University of California Press, 1996).

Western Marxism should encompass.[4] A relatively uncontroversial point of departure is found in the early 1920s with the works of the Hungarian Georg Lukács, the German Karl Korsch, and the Italian Antonio Gramsci, three separate theorists whom we can rightly call the "founders" of the tradition. From the early 1930s, Western Marxism is primarily associated with the Critical Theory of the Frankfurt School, centered at the Institute for Social Research during its relatively brief initial phase at the University of Frankfurt, and its later wartime exile, with brief stays in London and Geneva and its decade-long affiliation with Columbia University in New York before the Institute's return to Frankfurt shortly after the war's end. After this "first generation" of critical theory, a "second generation" arises, represented primarily by the work of Jürgen Habermas. This is followed by a "third generation" composed primarily of Habermas's former students. Others take an even broader temporal and geographical view of the boundaries of the tradition of Western Marxism, and include the creative fusion of Marxism and structuralism in the works of French writers such as Louis Althusser, Lucien Goldmann, and, in an indirect way, Jean-Paul Sartre.

For the purposes of this chapter, it's unnecessary to insist on where and how sharply the lines demarcating the tradition of Western Marxism should be drawn. We will focus first on what is by general consensus the core group generally associated with the term: Lukács, Korsch, and Gramsci before turning to a more brief discussion of the German theorists Walter Benjamin and Ernst Bloch. A second section explores the Critical Theory of the Frankfurt School, with special attention to the classic work by Theodor W. Adorno and Max Horkheimer, *Dialectic of Enlightenment*. A further section surveys the work of Jürgen Habermas and some of the more influential and creative members of a third generation of Critical Theory.

Western Marxism has its origin in the first half of the 1920s, among a scattered group of Marxist theorist-activists, united by a shared recognition that the political failures and frustrations of European Marxist movements in

---

4 See Martin Jay, *Marxism and Totality: The Adventures of a Concept from Lukács to Habermas* (Berkeley: University of California Press, 1984). "There are no easy ways to map the rugged and shifting terrain of the intellectual territory known as Western Marxism. Indeed, its very boundaries and most prominent features have themselves become the source of heated dispute" (1). The dispute referred to was provoked by the publication of Anderson's *Considerations on Western Marxism* in 1976, a highly polemical reconstruction of the Western Marxist tradition that condemned its supposed abandonment of revolutionary commitment, its self-exile into the sterile sanctuary of research universities, its growing esotericism and remoteness from the situation of the international working classes, and its increasingly bleak and hopeless diagnoses of the prospects for radical political change.

implementing a revolutionary program could be traced back to shortcomings in Marxist theory. Demanding that this theory undergo significant revision and renewal, Western Marxists also insisted that political movements could dramatically increase their chances of success if they remained theory-guided, restoring theory – above all a theory explaining the durability of capitalism – as an integral part of their larger political programs.

The works of the first or founding generation of Western Marxists – Karl Korsch, Antonio Gramsci, and Georg Lukács – were thus a re-appropriation of philosophy, and a recovery of Marx's status as a philosophical critic, a project that obviously had to contend with Marx's own famous demand, in the 11th Thesis on Feuerbach, to abandon philosophical interpretation in favor of political transformation.

The effort to reclaim the primacy of theory in Marxism clearly had to contend with a version of Marxism in which theoretical questions had been largely expelled. The scientific socialism (or 'vulgar Marxism') typical of the Second International, supported by influential early German party luminaries such as Karl Kautsky and Isaac Bebel, conceived of Marxism as a set of inflexible and inviolate historical–economic laws, requiring and admitting of no modification or addition, which forecast the impending collapse of capitalism as a form of economic organization as inevitable.[5] Having grasped these objective laws, no further theory was necessary, and further theoretical work was indeed at best a distraction and at worst a form of counter-revolutionary activity. This anti-intellectual bias (after a relative wealth of economic and political Marxist theories in the later decades of the nineteenth century) extended to Leninism as well, according to which the Communist Party, as the intellectual vanguard of the proletariat, assumed sole responsibility for the production and dissemination of intellectual products.

This anti-theoretical attitude of the European socialist parties in the years following the First World War even found support in Marx himself, who after all regarded theory as an independent activity – in its most purified form, the tradition of speculative philosophy from Descartes through Spinoza, Kant, and Hegel – as an ideological product of the dominant economic class, and as therefore bearing a political function (the justification of the existing *status quo*) behind the backs even of theorists themselves. Marx's abandonment of his own early Hegelianism, like his determination to move from philosophy to

---

5 For an analysis of the role of the Second International see Donald Sassoon, *One Hundred Years of Socialism: The Western European Left in the Twentieth Century* (New York: New Press, 1996), Chapter 1. See also the classic discussion in Leszek Kołakowski, *Main Currents of Marxism*, 3 vols. (Oxford: Oxford University Press, 1981), vol. II, Chapter 1, 2–31.

empirically grounded political economy, appeared to justify the prevailing view in the early 1920s that "Marxist theory" had become largely superfluous.

In response, the first-generation Western Marxists sought to re-appropriate the resources and heritage of philosophical thinking as a practical response to the multiple failures of scientific socialism. They were responding, in effect, to the theoretical poverty of the Marxism of the Second International as well as the growing hostility to theoretical innovation of the Third.[6] Particularly in the case of Georg Lukács, as we will see, this project led to a rediscovery of the Hegelian foundation of (and not just the influence on) Marx's thought. This entailed the deeply Hegelian idea that philosophy – theory – could and must set itself the task of grasping the totality of the condition of contemporary society in the medium of theoretical concepts. And this in turn required bringing into full conceptual expression the manifold, often contradictory, ways in which the material and "spiritual" or intellectual–cultural dimensions of contemporary life mutually determine and condition one another.[7]

Georg Lukács (1885–1971) was raised in an affluent assimilated Jewish family in Budapest. Following his university degree, Lukács spent considerable time in Germany, where he read deeply both in aesthetic and literary theory and in the nascent field of sociology. In this connection he was heavily influenced by the early pioneers of German sociology, Max Weber and Georg Simmel.[8]

By the early 1920s, Lukács had established himself as a prominent young literary and cultural critic. He saw capitalist modernity as a profound loss of meaning, an evacuation of modern culture's "soul" and its replacement by increasingly rationalized, formal categories of thought and action.[9] This global critique of the fragmenting, anomic consequences of modern life has

---

6 "Western Marxism, in this reading, was therefore opposed not only to the fatalistic economism of the Second International, but also to the voluntarist vanguardism of the Third. In contrast to both, it insisted that true praxis was a collective expression of self-emancipation involving all of mankind. The reawakening of the potential for such a collective subject was thus a central preoccupation of the Western Marxists who represented what another early exponent, Ernst Bloch, liked to call the 'warm' rather than the 'cold' current of socialism." Jay, *Marxism and Totality*, 2.

7 The classical expression of this view of philosophy as the total conceptual reflection of its own times is in the preface to Hegel's *Elements of the Philosophy of Right*. "To comprehend what is is the task of philosophy, for what is is reason." G. W. F. Hegel, *Elements of the Philosophy of Right* (Cambridge: Cambridge University Press, 1991), 21.

8 For a comprehensive discussion, see Andrew Feenberg, *Lukács, Marx, and the Sources of Critical Theory* (Towanda: Rowman & Littlefield, 1981).

9 Primary among these earlier works is the essay collection *Soul and Form* from 1908 (Georg Lukács, *Soul and Form* (New York: Columbia University Press, 2010)); also significant is *Theory of the Novel*, from 1915 (Georg Lukács, *Theory of the Novel* (Cambridge: MIT Press, 1974)).

been accurately described as "romantic anti-capitalism,"[10] and renders a negative aesthetic and spiritual judgment against modern life, rather than one based on terms of economic or political oppression.[11]

Influenced as much by Nietzsche as by Weber, the political valence of this romantic anti-capitalism could just as easily be conservative as radical-revolutionary. In the case of Lukács, the end of the war saw his abrupt conversion to an orthodox Marxist position, and despite many turns and modifications he would never abandon it. He transformed his earlier cultural critique of the soullessness and fragmentation of modern capitalism into an interrogation of the intellectual foundations of Marx's critical analysis of the relations between productive forces and intellectual and cultural life.

The work in which this reformulation takes place, *History and Class Consciousness* (1923) can be regarded as the founding document of Western Marxism.[12] Perhaps paradoxically, the book was intended as a full-throated defense of Lenin's conception of communist theory and practice, a conception that had little room for, or patience with, abstract theoretical speculation, demanding that "intellectual" dimensions of communist politics be located entirely within the vanguard of the Party and its duly designated officials.[13] Despite this apparent tension, the book is a sophisticated philosophical work that single-handedly recovers and revives the philosophical foundations of Marxism. Among its central claims is that, *contra* Marx, the great philosophical tradition of bourgeois philosophical idealism, from Kant through Fichte and Hegel, remains an essential resource for understanding Marx's message and putting it into practice.

In *History and Class Consciousness* Lukács suggests that dialectical method must be re-appropriated as the quintessential and defining attribute of orthodox communism. For Lukács, despite its bourgeois origins, dialectics is the mode of thought that is definitive for the objective historical position of the global proletariat. He proposes to reintroduce dialectics as a political tool for

---

10 See Michael Löwy, "Naphta or Settembrini? Lukács and Romantic Anticapitalism," *New German Critique*, No. 42 (Autumn 1987), 17–31. In Thomas Mann's *The Magic Mountain*, the doomed intellectual Naphta is a stand-in for Lukács.
11 For a classic study see Andrew Arato and Paul Breines, *The Young Lukács and the Origins of Western Marxism* (New York: Seabury Press, 1979) as well as Andrew Feenberg, *Lukács, Marx, and the Sources of Critical Theory*.
12 Georg Lukács, *History and Class Consciousness: Studies in Marxist Dialectic* (Cambridge: MIT Press, 1971).
13 It was a defense that went unappreciated in the Soviet Union. Party officials swiftly denounced the book at the Fifth World Congress of the Comintern in 1924, and Lukács quickly and publicly retracted most of the book's argument, though he was to offer a qualified defense of it, in various forms, over the following decades.

the proletariat to come to an objectively correct understanding of its historical position – the "subject-object" of history, the class positioned to grasp the truth of its own historical character and significance free of ideological distortion and concealment, and to transform this knowledge into revolutionary action, negating the economic conditions that both define and limit it.

In this sense, as Martin Jay argues, *History and Class Consciousness* reappropriates the central Hegelian category of totality.[14] Hegel saw his own method as the pinnacle of humanity's capacity for self-knowledge. The apogee of philosophical idealism is the capacity to capture a historical totality in the medium of philosophical concepts. Marx sought to "turn Hegel on his head" by demonstrating that dialectical materialism preserves the core of Hegel's insight – that concepts and the material world mutually condition and reproduce one another in a process of contradiction and mediation – but corrects Hegel's error in believing that dialectics was a spiritual reality first, and a material one only derivatively. At the center of *History and Class Consciousness*, the chapter on "Reification and the Consciousness of the Proletariat," Lukács recovers this early Marxian view. Hegelian dialectics remains an indispensable tool for comprehending how a capitalist economy thwarts the capacity of agents to acquire insight into, and resistance to, the socio-economic totality that dominates them.

Hegelian dialectics concerns the relation between subject and object, concepts that share a moment of identity even as they maintain their contradictory relation. Marx drew indirectly from the dialectics of subject and object in his famous analysis of the fetishism of the commodity under capitalism. Deprived of intrinsic value in the exchange process, commodities assume the very aspects of human value that workers in a wage economy lose in the process of producing them.

For Marx, fetishism is an ideological effect of an economic form that demands the dehumanization of wage laborers, who lose sight of their own loss of value by projecting human value onto the intrinsically meaningless objects they produce. It is one of the few moments in Marx's *Capital* that retains a vestige of the young Marx's deep interest the actual dehumanizing effects of capitalism, and recalls the extensive discussion of the concept of alienation in Marx's "1844 manuscripts" – which remained unpublished and unknown in the 1920s.[15] Nevertheless, in *History and Class Consciousness*, Lukács anticipated Marx's

---

14 Jay, *Marxism and Totality*.
15 Marx's *Economic and Philosophical Manuscripts*, originally written in Paris in 1844, were not edited and published until 1932, when a Russian edition edited by David Ryazanov appeared in Moscow.

earlier theory of alienation, recovering and expanding Marx's dialectical analysis of the relation between the subjective consciousness of the alienated worker and the overdetermined status of the economic commodity.

Lukács sees the relation between subject and object in multiple registers. The same process that endows commodities with the illusion of human characteristics is also one in which humans lose their own distinct individuality, their intrinsic value as humans, and take on a thing-like, interchangeable form. They assume a false relationship to the actual value of the things they produce, while losing the capacity to encounter one another as genuine sources of intrinsic value. For Lukács, both sides of this dialectic – the false humanization of things, and the false objectification of humans – are captured in his term "reification" (*Verdinglichung*).

It is important to see this central concept of reification as the outcome of a creative appropriation not just of Marx's conception of "commodity fetishism," but also of the earlier Hegelian dialectics. "Reification" is, by deliberate design, a dialectical concept, in the sense that it makes possible contradictory interpretations. Lukács means *both* to address a theoretical shortfall in contemporary communist politics – a shortfall that lies behind the broad failure of socialist political parties to diagnose properly the intransigence of their opponents – *and* to recover from within the core of Marx's own writings a resource meant to satisfy this shortfall. Reification traces back to the early Marx's more overtly Hegelian, dialectical view on the way subject–object relationships, in their distinctly modern form, generate distinct kinds of alienation and domination. It also offers a deep hypothesis for the shortfall of actually existing class consciousness among the European working classes, compared with what objectively would have been predicted given the actual circumstances of their oppression. Reification thus also offers a far more sophisticated alternative to the older orthodox view of a simple causal relation between "base" and "superstructure," in the process suggesting not just that ideology is to be taken as far more than a false scrim or projection of far more real material processes, but also that the two levels must be accounted for simultaneously.[16]

The proletariat and the bourgeoisie under capitalism both suffer from reified consciousness. An additional goal of *History and Class*

16 As Martin Jay puts it, "This term [reification], one not in fact found in Marx himself, meant the petrification of living processes into dead things, which appeared as an alien 'second nature.' Weber's 'iron cage' of bureaucratic rationalization, Simmel's 'tragedy of culture' and Bergson's spatialization of durée were thus all part of a more general process. Lukács was able to move beyond the stoic pessimism of Weber and Simmel by linking their intellectual dilemmas to the reified nature of bourgeois life, an explanation that grounded them historically." Jay, *Marxism and Totality*, 109–110.

Consciousness, again drawing on Hegel, was to argue that the former, and not the latter, was in an objective position to overcome reification. Through the very dialectical process of history itself, it was up to the proletariat to transform itself into both the subject and the object of true historical consciousness at one and the same time. History, on these terms, is, as Hegel argued, a matter of a dialectical development of consciousness – no longer taking as its ultimate subject the mind of the philosophical idealist, but rather the economic class whose mediation between consciousness and materiality placed it in the unique position of being able to transform, rather than merely grasp, the totality of the social conditions under modern capitalism.[17]

History and Class Consciousness, perhaps paradoxically, also affirmed that the actual agency by which the international proletariat would grasp and transform its concrete historical position – the catalyzing agent for this grand dialectical process – was the Communist Party. In this way, the book both confirmed and challenged the Comintern's doctrinal view that the intellectual content of the international Communist movement was under the authority of the Party as intellectual vanguard. In this sense, as a founding document of Western Marxism *History and Class Consciousness* retains a peculiar position, insofar as Lukács regarded the work as an affirmation of the theoretical authority of Leninism, which of course had to include a doctrinal commitment to vanguardism.

Antonio Gramsci (1891–1937), unlike Lukács, came from very modest circumstances in Sardinia, in southern Italy. After winning a scholarship to study at the University of Turin, Gramsci plunged into the chaotic world of the nascent Italian Communist Party (PCI), in the founding of which in 1921 he was deeply involved. In 1924 he won a parliamentary seat as a representative of the PCI. Gramsci was arrested and imprisoned by the Mussolini government in 1926, and spent the remainder of his short life in prison, under hard conditions and with enormous suffering. Plagued by constant ill health, Gramsci died shortly after his release from prison in 1937.

Apart from a large number of shorter journalistic pieces, Gramsci's work as a theorist of Western Marxism consists primarily of his *Prison Notebooks*,

---

17 As Kołakowski elegantly puts it, "The consciousness of the proletariat may be thought of as the acquisition of self-knowledge by a commodity. In the proletariat's situation the process of reification, the transformation of men and women into things, takes on an acute form. When the proletariat becomes aware of itself as a commodity it will at the same time understand, and rebel against, the reification of all forms of social life." Kołakowski, *Main Currents of Marxism*, vol. III, 276.

written during his eleven years of confinement.[18] While the *Notebooks*, covering a wide range of themes and problems of communist theory and practice, are impossible to summarize, they have been most influential in articulating what Gramsci termed a theory of *hegemony*. With this term, Gramsci offered his own explanation for the range of questions that had also preoccupied Lukács in his conception of reification: What concrete mechanisms did bourgeois, capitalist economies and societies deploy in order to forestall the rise of a collective revolutionary consciousness of the globalized proletariat? How, specifically, does bourgeois capitalism maintain control over an oppressed class not only overtly (through the direct application of force, or through material immiseration), but also indirectly, through the production and dissemination of forms of consciousness that run counter to the interests of those adopting them?

For Gramsci, the answer to these defining questions of Western Marxism lay in the capacity of bourgeois ideology to form a complete or totalizing set of cultural and social institutions and corresponding norms, again encompassing both the macro-level and the micro-level of everyday life: a total spectrum, in short, that includes within itself even the standards by which those norms can be evaluated. Hegemony refers to the exhaustive, all-encompassing nature of capitalist culture's control not only of institutions and practices, but also of the semantic resources to manage their meaning. It follows that, *pace* the theories of scientific socialism, the development of an international working class's awareness of the objective features of its own historical situation will be rendered nearly impossible, since the proletariat will have access only to the hegemonic cultural vocabulary of its oppressor. Ideology, far more than a mere effect or expression of material modes of production, is also creative: It cannot be treated as an epiphenomenon that will simply evaporate once those material conditions are changed.

Bourgeois hegemony is the mechanism by which cultural control gradually replaces brute force as a mode of generating consent; shared by capitalists and workers, it generates modes of normative approval of the status quo in which the proletariat accepts and indeed embraces the terms of its own oppression. On the large-scale level of social and political institutions, hegemony is exerted through the formation of "historic blocs" or alliances between institutions that might otherwise come into material conflict. The modern sovereign state, the market economy, the organized and state-

---

18 The notebooks were composed between 1929 and 1935, though they remained unpublished until the 1950s. Antonio Gramsci, *Prison Notebooks* (New York: Columbia University Press, 2011).

supported churches, and the institutions of a lightly governed civil society such as the press and voluntary organizations all coordinate, disseminating variants of a consistent cultural–ideological content via a multiplicity of organs and languages.

Where such cultural–institutional hegemony does not exist, and blocs have not formed – for Gramsci, in pre-revolutionary Russia – then, as Lenin argued, the revolutionary strategist must think primarily in political and military terms. But in advanced Western capitalist democracies where hegemonic control over aspects of social life has progressed, Gramsci's theory suggests that force alone will not suffice for a successful revolutionary movement. Instead, the *Notebooks* argue for an open-ended cultural struggle of indeterminate length and uncertain outcome. Only by replacing the hegemonic character of bourgeois culture with a proletarian culture, by a transformation of both the mode and the content of cultural reproduction, could European communist parties establish the conditions for a successful material transformation of economic reproduction. The *Notebooks* are filled with observations and speculations on how such a proletarian challenge to bourgeois hegemony might be possible. Gramsci focuses much of his attention on the possibilities of proletarian education and the agency of what he terms "organic" intellectuals – members of the working classes who jettison the vocabulary and values of the bourgeoisie and generate novel, class-specific modes of cultural life from within the experiences and struggles of the working classes.

Like Lukács, German theorist and politician Karl Korsch (1886–1961) was born into comfortably middle-class circumstances; after successful study of law at the University of Jena, Korsch spent two years in the United Kingdom, where he became a member of the Fabian Society. In the summer of 1914 he was called up for military service and returned to Germany; Korsch was radicalized by his wartime experiences, and joined the German Communist Party in 1920. From then until his emigration in 1933, Korsch remained an active and influential political voice in Germany and in broader European debates over the Communist movement, arguing that the vulgar Marxism of the Second International was incapable of either motivating or understanding the working class. Like Lukács, Korsch became convinced that a superior theoretical understanding of the actual historical position of the workers was necessary to explain why they failed to adopt the collective class consciousness necessary as a prerequisite for political transformation. In 1923 (virtually simultaneously with Lukács's *History and Class Consciousness*) Korsch published *Marxism and Philosophy*, a book that argued even more overtly than Lukács that philosophical theory alone could rescue communism from its vulgarization, and that such a theory was already waiting to be recovered in the Hegelian origins of Marx's own writings.

Marxism and Philosophy argues that the truth of a dialectical conception of history – the highest achievement of bourgeois ideology – was also the explanation of why that bourgeoisie itself was incapable of comprehending the theory fully. The historical position of a globalized proletariat nominated it, rather than its oppressors, as the addressee of a fully realized, concrete theory of historical change. That same dialectical theory also provided a key to its own correct interpretation, which had been part of Marx's core insight regarding the transition from philosophy as ideology to theory as the guide of revolutionary politics in his 11th Thesis on Feuerbach.

For Korsch, re-appropriating Marx as a philosopher also demanded a redefinition of "philosophy" once the grand era of (German) philosophical idealism had been historically overcome. As the negation of bourgeois philosophy, materialist *theory* was in Korsch's opinion never meant to abandon dialectical method; rather, dialectical materialism should remain genuinely *dialectical*. Forgetting just this crucial point, Korsch believed, was the central mistake of vulgar Marxism,[19] and it largely explained the generally dismal performance of vulgar Marxism's attempts to predict or respond creatively to the remarkable resilience of the structures of bourgeois ideology.[20]

The Frankfurt School of Critical Theory

The authors affiliated with the Institute for Social Research at the University of Frankfurt are the most prominent and influential thinkers of the tradition of Western Marxism.[21] The Institute was founded originally in 1923, by an initial grant from Felix Weil, the scion of a wealthy grain importer, and between 1924 and 1929 was directed by the Austrian Marxist labor historian

---

19 Karl Korsch, *Marxism and Philosophy*, translated and with an introduction by Fred Halliday (New York: New Left Books, 1970).
20 On Korsch's philosophy see Patrick Goode, *Karl Korsch: A Study in Western Marxism* (London: Macmillan, 1979).
21 The first major study of the Frankfurt School in English, the standard historical reference remains Martin Jay, *The Dialectical Imagination* (Berkeley: University of California Press, 1996). Other worthwhile studies include Rolf Wiggershaus, *The Frankfurt School* (Cambridge: Polity Press, 1995) and David Ingram, *The Frankfurt School and Philosophy* (St. Paul: Paragon House, 1990).

Carl Grünberg. Its affiliation with the University of Frankfurt was a natural fit in many ways. The newly founded University was itself a self-consciously progressive institution, in sharp contrast to the generally conservative tenor and function of the older German universities and faculties. In addition to the standard academic curriculum, the University also devoted considerable attention and resources to the nascent social sciences. The Institute, as an affiliated program of the University, was in this sense part of a broader ambitious and short-lived experiment of the Weimer years of recasting and modernizing traditional German cultural institutions to have an explicitly progressive function. While the original Marxist orientation of the Institute was rarely made explicit, it was not vigorously denied either, and much of its work during the Grünberg years consisted in the compilation of an archive of German labor history.

With the advent of Max Horkheimer (1895–1973) as director in 1930, the Institute took on the more interdisciplinary features that would characterize its work in the decade to come. Under Horkheimer's vision, the Institute was intended as a multidisciplinary group, including political theorists, philosophers, sociologists, economists, legal scholars, and pyschologists, inspired by the idea that only such an innovative cross-disciplinary approach, synthesizing the most up-to-date methodologies of the social sciences, could succeed in generating critical insight into the subtle forms of social domination exemplified both in the rise of advanced industrial capitalism and in the decay of democratic life and the prospect of fascism.

In a foundational essay on "Traditional and Critical Theory" (1937), Horkheimer made a broad distinction between the current predominant practice of the empirical social sciences – "traditional" theoretical efforts to explain social phenomena – and the goal of the Institute, to formulate a truly critical theory of society, inspired by but no longer inflexibly committed to Marxist principles, that would have an explicitly practical, transformative political role even if that role could no longer be understood as a contribution to the goal of a global (or even national) proletarian revolution.[22]

Traditional theory, wrote Horkheimer, remained mired in the ideology of positivism. As a mode of empirical explanation of phenomena from observed facts, traditional social theory could not avoid endowing both the observed facts and the social theorist with the appearance of value neutrality, while in fact both the social theorist and the observations of social phenomena she

---

22 Max Horkheimer, "Traditional and Critical Theory," in *Critical Theory: Selected Essays* (New York: Continuum, 1972), 188–243.

produces are deeply intertwined with the oppressive structure of the social whole. In this sense, traditional theory's very dependence on epistemic neutrality is itself a classic example of the function of bourgeois ideology. Traditional theory, uncritically amassing and rearranging supposedly value-neutral social facts, not only "explains" social structures, but surreptitiously contributes to their maintenance and support via a positivistic epistemology that approaches social facts as quasi-natural facts, and hence resistant to (or not in need of) radical change.

Critical theory, by contrast, would claim a distinctively dialectical epistemology, abandoning both the false objectivity of social facts and the false neutrality of the social theorist. Dialectical criticism openly embraces the status of theory as a part of the social and historical processes it explores. As a method, dialectics therefore must include a constant capacity for self-reflexivity, since the critical capacity to disclose otherwise occluded forms of social domination must also remain conscious that theorizing itself is a social activity, and hence is both the subject and the object of critique at one and the same time. Theoretical success is not a matter of objectivity but of the illumination of otherwise implicit aspects of how those processes replicate themselves behind the backs of, and contrary to the true interests of, social members. Hence critical theory for Horkheimer did not dissolve the distinctions between fact and value, or theory and practice, or scientific truth and political advocacy. Rather, it aimed to show how such binaries were already always dialectically in motion, both generating one another and constantly transgressing their status as mutually exclusive.

"Critique," in the originally Kantian sense, referred to the responsibility of reason to determine by its own application the legitimate extent of its powers. In Marx's largely Hegelian reformulation, critique no longer referred to a merely intellectual exercise, but referred to the capacity of real human agents to think from, and beyond, their material conditions and connect their thinking directly with the practical demand to transform those conditions, in ways that harmonized with their true interests.

For the Frankfurt School, both the Kantian and the Hegelian-Marxist conceptions of critique remain preserved. Critical theory was a predominantly academic exercise that sought to disclose or unmask the ultimately contingent, and hence changeable, features of a world of social practices, cultural formations, and structures of consciousness – in short, a 'superstructure' – both concealing and defending the domination at the core of the capitalist form. Recalling Lukács's exploration of the "antinomies of bourgeois philosophy," critical theory also intended to *make explicit* why these antinomies – between the freedom of the noumenal subject and the subjection to natural necessity of the human considered as part of the natural world – could not be overcome under conditions of capitalism.

Bourgeois philosophy was complicit in the larger social totality in which the very thing that idealist philosophy had always implicitly promised – the unity of subjective freedom and natural existence – would be forever denied or deferred. Hence, inspired by Lukács, critical theory, *contra* Marx, insisted that bourgeois ideology could never have maintained its power over consciousness unless ideology too, precisely as false consciousness, also contains a deep moment of truth. Hence, in Horkheimer's vision, critical theory could oversee cutting-edge, empirically sophisticated social-scientific research on the mechanisms and features of contemporary forms of social domination only by preserving the utopian demand for a redeemed, free, and happy social life that, under conditions of modern social unfreedom, was available only indirectly, as a sense of disappointment or indignation in the face of injustice. No direct grounding of the normative core of critical theory, in the manner of a rational foundationalist argument, was possible. All such direct attempts would necessarily end by recreating the forms of bourgeois idealism. Critical theory, as negative, no longer aspires to connect itself directly with political activism. But it is a form of theorizing that takes itself as a mode of resistance to an otherwise totalizing mode of social domination.

The interdisciplinary team that Horkheimer assembled was impressively broad. A few capsule biographies, together with brief descriptions of principal works and research interests of the core members of the early Institute, should give a sense of how Horkheimer's program of critical theory was put into practice.[23]

Horkeimer himself had trained primarily as a philosopher, and maintained strong philosophical interests throughout a career that focused primarily on the relation between philosophical and sociological forms of socially embedded knowledge. As well as overseeing the Institute's work, Horkheimer participated directly in the Institute's project on "Authority and the Family" in the mid 1930s. Together with Theodor W. Adorno he co-authored the famous work *Dialectic of Enlightenment* in 1944 (about which more below). Horkheimer's collection *The Eclipse of Reason* (1947) served as a kind of *summa* of the major themes of his theoretical trajectory. Together

---

23 In addition to Max Horkheimer, Herbert Marcuse, and Theodor W. Adorno (who would join the Institute only later in the 1930s), core members included Friedrich Pollock (1894–1970), Erich Fromm (1900–1980), and Leo Löwenthal (1900–1993). Additional members included Franz Neumann and Otto Kirschheimer.

with Adorno, Horkheimer returned to Germany and the University of Frankfurt shortly after the end of World War II, assuming a professorship and, ultimately, the office of University Rector.

Theodor Wiesengrund Adorno (1903–1969) is perhaps the most influential and best-known theorist of the "first generation" of critical theory. He trained both in philosophy and in music theory and composition, and joined the Institute only relatively late, after it had already begun its exile in New York in the mid 1930s. Adorno spent the war years in New York and California, deeply involved in a range of empirical research projects on the emergence of new forms of social domination in mass culture, both in the shape of German fascism and in American mass industrial culture, frequently in collaboration with Horkheimer. Returning to Germany with Horkheimer in the early 1950s, Adorno became a professor of sociology (and, later, philosophy) in Frankfurt, where he continued to publish both philosophical works, including his *magnum opus Negative Dialectics* in 1966, and *Aesthetic Theory*, which remained unfinished and was published posthumously.[24] Adorno also authored more popular works as interventions in the nascent democratic political culture of postwar West Germany, and he was a frequent participant in debates over issues of German responsibility and the question of "working through" the darkest chapters of Germany's past.

The work of the Institute in the decades between 1930 and the end of the 1960s is sprawling and resists easy summary. On one side, the empirical work undertaken by members of the Institute focused increasingly on efforts to bring social-scientific methodology to bear on the increasing attractions of fascism and racism for citizens of democratic-capitalist societies. This line included *The Authoritarian Personality*, co-authored by Adorno together with researchers at the University of California at Berkeley, which famously proposed a classification system (the "F-scale") to measure and predict individuals' personality traits associated with support for fascism on the basis of a series of questionnaires.[25]

These studies outlined a global drift toward a form of irrationalism and domination in culture far more pervasive even than the kinds hinted at by theories such as the reification of the consciousness of the proletariat and the hegemonic nature of bourgeois culture. Especially over the course of the late 1930s and throughout the 1940s, critical theorists – above all Horkheimer and

---

24 For a definitive biography see Detlev Claussen, *Theodor W. Adorno: One Last Genius* (Cambridge: Harvard University Press, 2008).
25 Theodor W. Adorno, Else Frenkel-Brunswik, Daniel J. Levinson, and R. Nevitt Sanford, *The Authoritarian Personality* (New York: Harper & Row, 1950).

Adorno in American exile – grew increasingly pessimistic about the prospects for meaningful resistance, not only to the forms of domination characteristic of modern capitalism, but indeed to the rise of a kind of unholy alliance between capitalism and fascism. That fusion would spell the end of the Enlightenment dream, ideologically inflected though it may have been, of a universal basis for the dignity and freedom of individual persons, as well as the Marxist utopia of freedom from conditions of material servitude under wage-based economies. Especially during the war years, Horkheimer and Adorno saw the collapse of European civilization no longer merely as a confluence of recent historical trends, but as the outcome of factors rooted in the nature of the human predicament itself.

This trend culminated in the composition of *Dialectic of Enlightenment*, cowritten by Horkheimer and Adorno in California and first published in 1944 (though it was not widely read until its second publication, in a revised edition, appeared in 1947).[26] The study is a landmark in the development of Western Marxism, and hence a longer excursus is warranted.

The core argument linking the book's diverse chapters is that rational enlightenment, the bedrock claim of the revolutionary eighteenth-century European bourgeoisie, bears a dialectical relation to the forces of mythic nature, the very forces against which it had always defined itself. The claim of enlightenment is that of an internal connection between human rationality and human emancipation. Rationality – the distinctly human capacity for the impartial, logical evaluation of the content, purpose, and value of any human activity, and the systematic and organized exploration, explanation, and control of natural processes – promises to deliver humankind from subjection to the terror and power of external nature. And yet, the rationalization of all aspects of human life results not in emancipation but in a new subjection, now no longer to mythic nature but to modern systems of supposedly value-neutral technologies of manipulation and control.

The book argues that the replacement of one form of domination by another is a repetition of mythic domination in a different form. The relation between myth and enlightenment is not *merely* negation or contradiction, but is deeply dialectical: The moment of logical negation between the two concepts also contains within itself a moment in which the identity between the two concepts is preserved, an identity that compulsively reasserts itself in the course of Western European history. Rational

---

26 Max Horkheimer and Theodor W. Adorno, *Dialectic of Enlightenment: Philosophical Fragments* (Stanford: Stanford University Press, 2007).

enlightenment emancipates from myth, in other words, only to negate itself and revert back to mythic domination, even in newer, more subtle, and more totalizing forms. The fear of loss of self to external nature generates a form of rationality that orients itself against external nature as a hostile, opaque power to be conquered.

And yet the very success of this conquest of nature is bought by the re-domination of *inner* nature – of the human longing for physical well-being, bodily pleasure, and gratification of instinctual drives; of utopian dreams of a peaceful relation between subjectivity and its natural setting.

This startling thesis had both a more and a less concrete context in the chapters of *Dialectic of Enlightenment*. Concretely, Horkheimer and Adorno were attempting to understand the underlying causes of the massive failure of the Enlightenment legacy of high European bourgeois culture to mount any effective psychic resistance to the rise of fascism. Why, they asked, did the revolutionary bourgeois political ideals of individual freedom and equality prove so inadequate as a resource against the reversion to a political ideology with such evidently irrationalist aspects? This question reframes the more familiar Marxist conundrum of how capitalist society and economy proved so resilient to crises, and how the dimension of cultural or symbolic reproduction in advanced industrial societies could produce mechanisms of cultural or even psychic stabilization to offset what Marxist theory had forecast as the impending economic collapse of market economies.

In this more immediate context, *Dialectic of Enlightenment* offers telling analyses of structures of symbolic, cultural, and psychic domination. Its famous chapter on the "culture industry," for instance, argues that the classic distinction between the levels of material and symbolic production – base and superstructure – had badly misdiagnosed capitalism's capacity to combine these two levels, effectively transforming them into mutually supporting moments of a single mechanism. Cultural products could be rationally produced and disseminated with the same considerations of efficiency as any material commodity, and like material commodities had the same sort of double life, as concentrations both of alienated social labor and of suppressed collective wishes and fantasies. Consumption of cultural goods – above all the new media of entertainment such as mass-produced music, cinema, and television – negates the difference between cultural and material consumption, and in the process makes capitalistic social control vastly more efficient.

Other aspects of the argument of *Dialectic of Enlightenment*, however, went well beyond the immediate context of the failure of bourgeois liberal culture and the rise of the irrationalist fascist state. Horkheimer and Adorno understand rationality as what the sociologist Max Weber termed *Zweckrationalität*, or "instrumental rationality," a reasoning process wholly concerned with the formal calculation of efficiency of means, and abandoning the very idea that the evaluation of the substantive good of worthwhile human ends could be a task of reason. From a socially conservative perspective, Weber had famously described this instrumental rationality as the driver behind the "disenchantment" of the world: the evacuation of religious values from public life, the professionalization of matters of ethics and morality into the specialized sphere of modern positive law, and the rise of a notorious "steel-hard casing" of rationality. Once it succeeds in replacing substantive value orientations as the hegemonic index for success, instrumental rationality compels modern subjects to submit their own evaluative normative reasoning to its own standards. One can either be rational, or live a life guided by substantive normative values, but (so Weber argued in *The Protestant Ethic and the Spirit of Capitalism*) one can no longer do both.

In adapting Weber's vision for critical theory, Horkheimer and Adorno make the far more expansive claim that the instrumental rationality at the core of the enlightenment's dialectic extends far beyond the more immediate circumstances of contemporary capitalism and the failure of liberal democracy. It may in fact be the defining feature of the human predicament. In a chapter on "Juliette, or Enlightenment," the authors claim that the Marquis de Sade, rather than Hume, Voltaire, Bentham, or Kant, should be regarded as the quintessential Enlightenment theorist. While the moral theories of these more familiar Enlightenment philosophers settled into a dialogue between utilitarianism and Kantian ethics, de Sade's fiction, Horkheimer and Adorno insist, depicts instrumental rationality at its purest: morally neutral and unconcerned with final ends or highest goods, and dedicated entirely to the maximization of the efficiency of whatever enterprise or pursuit the rational agent directs it toward, be it the fulfillment of duties or the infliction of pain.

Perhaps the book's most famous chapter consists of an "excursus" on Homer's *Odyssey*, and in particular the figure of Odysseus, as the "prototypical bourgeois." The epic presents Odysseus as a cunning hero, mastering and defeating a succession of mythic threats by pitting his own intelligence against intransigent nature. Odysseus wins every time. Yet the rational power by which he defeats and escapes from these threats also subjects him to forms of control and domination far more insidious and severe than the mythic nature from which he has freed himself. The subject is saved from domination by external nature only at the cost of the full domination of inner nature:

Odysseus defeats external temptations only by mastering and defeating his own natural desires. He denies the threat of annihilation by external mythic nature (such as the Cyclops) with cunning (exploiting the ambivalence of the name "no one" to the Cyclops's demand that he reveal his identity), but the cunning is only part of a larger process of denying a genuine identity, a full subjectivity, in the very interest of protecting it from all external threats.

The exegetical excursus reconstructing the *Odyssey* as a prototypical blueprint for modern subjectivity is among the most insightful and thrilling moments of *Dialectic of Enlightenment*, and emblematic of the book and of the larger mood of Critical Theory during the years of and immediately following World War II. And yet the very hermeneutic power of the excursus, like the book itself, raises difficult questions about the course of Critical Theory.

The first is the question of whether a global critique that indicts instrumental rationality as replicating the historical cycle of domination and emancipation is compatible with the central task of Western Marxism, to identify a meaningful connection between theory and political praxis. If it is true that there is no escape from the grip of instrumental reason, and if that form of reason is not merely a product of the constellation of modern conditions of social and economic life but is an anthropological constant, then theory, though it may identify the sources and mechanisms of social domination, may have little to offer regarding how such insights can be translated into effective remedies via political action. The inflation of instrumental rationality into an anthropological universal risks transforming critical theory into a mode of pessimistic quietism.

This conclusion has been reached not infrequently by other Western Marxists themselves. Lukács famously dismissed Horkheimer and Adorno's theory as having been written while in opulent residency at the "Grand Hotel Abyss." From a very different direction, Jürgen Habermas has criticized the conclusions of *Dialectic of Enlightenment* both in the conclusion of the first volume of his *Theory of Communicative Action* and, more pointedly, in *The Philosophical Discourse of Modernity*.

The second question concerns the evidently aporetic aspect of the argument. If it is true that there is no viable alternative to instrumental rationality, and if the role of instrumental rationality has become effectively hegemonic in our major social and economic institutions, then it is not evident why the normal operation of such institutions should even be regarded as oppressive or dominating: After all, what normative standpoint could the critical theorist occupy to generate this critical perspective? In *Dialectic of Enlightenment*,

Horkheimer and Adorno acknowledge this problem without offering any obvious solution. If there is no identifiable alternative to a mode of rationality that is internally linked to domination, then whatever normative, even utopian, content is left in critical theorizing would have to be derived from resources that are other than rational. Indeed, parts of *Dialectic of Enlightenment* hint broadly at modes of thinking and experiencing, such as the mimetic capacity, that survive surreptitiously in modern life and that, under certain conditions, offer an indirect form of normativity to the critique of instrumental reason. Many commentators, however (most notably Jürgen Habermas in his *Philosophical Discourse of Modernity*), have regarded this implied solution to the outstanding problem of the normative foundations of critical theory as deeply unsatisfying.

Some thumbnail biographies of other influential members of the Frankfurt School can conclude this section on Critical Theory. Herbert Marcuse (1898–1979) came to the Institute with strong philosophical interests in Hegel and Heidegger as well as Marx. Unlike Horkheimer and Adorno, Marcuse elected to remain in the United States after World War II, and his postwar works were highly influential for the American Left, in particular the radical democracy of the student movements in the late 1960s and into the 1970s. Among Marcuse's many works, *Eros and Civilization* and *One-Dimensional Man* proved most influential.[27] The former, a philosophical re-appropriation of Freudian theory, argues that human drives, which Freud had regarded as fixed biological inheritances, were in fact historically dynamic and malleable. Beyond the "reality principle," in accord with which infants adapt to the impossibility of unrestricted libidinal gratification through mechanisms of repression and sublimation, capitalist culture installs "surplus repression," thwarting pleasure and libidinal release well beyond what is required to maintain social function. In a parallel with Gramsci's conception of hegemony (albeit now installed at the level of the individual unconscious), this "performance principle" de-eroticizes the body, installs frustration and shame as social dominants, and redirects libidinal energies toward meek acceptance of the repetitive drudgery of endless production and consumption. One telling feature of the success of this unconscious control is the supremacy of technological innovation to generate increased wants, even as technological capacity surpasses the level objectively necessary to meet humanity's most basic material needs.

---

27 Herbert Marcuse, *Eros and Civilization: A Philosophical Inquiry into Freud* (Boston: Beacon Press, 1974); and Herbert Marcuse, *One-Dimensional Man: Studies in the Ideology of Advanced Industrial Society* (Boston: Beacon Press, 1991).

Marcuse's synthesis of Freudian and Marxist ideas argued for a new balance of human libidinal drives beyond the false demands of the performance principle. Such a re-eroticization of repressed and alienated aspects of human existence, not in the sense of a sort of sexualization but rather as the reimagination of bodies and actions as sources of desire and pleasure, was for Marcuse one way of imagining the communist demand for a revolutionary reconstruction of the structure of society.

Ernst Bloch (1885–1971), was not officially a member of the Institute for Social Research and did not share their central commitment to dialectical logic and immanent critique. Nevertheless, Bloch was also an important contributor to the Western Marxist tradition, principally for two large-scale works at roughly either end of his career. In 1918 Bloch published *The Spirit of Utopia*, a reinterpretation of central themes of Marxism through the lens of utopian theology: the longing for the redemption and repair of the world. For Bloch, the power of Marx's revolutionary theory could be preserved only via the disruptive dimension of the utopian impulse.[28] During the years of wartime exile in the United States Bloch produced his chief theoretical work, *The Principle of Hope*, which appeared in three volumes between 1954 and 1959. It radically expands and deepens the earlier work, describing the transgressive power of radical hope as a subterranean intellectual tradition running behind and counter to Western philosophy's tendency toward memory and conservatism. Utopian fantasies are unruly and disruptive; tapping their power from within the heart of Western thought was Marx's distinctive achievement. In a recognizably expressionistic style, covering an astonishing range of cultural, aesthetic, and historical topics, *The Principle of Hope* demanded that anticipation of a fully redeemed future state, rather than a forlorn search for the last traces of socially embedded reason, should drive the project of critical theory. Unlike most other critical theorists, Bloch relocated to East Germany following his return from exile in the United States during the war years, where he remained until 1961, spending the remainder of his life in Tübingen.

Walter Benjamin (1892–1940), like so many other critical theorists, was the product of an affluent, assimilated German Jewish family, and was radicalized over the course of the 1920s by the experiences of war and revolution. A literary and cultural critic as much as a philosopher or political theorist, Benjamin's

---

[28] Ernst Bloch, *The Spirit of Utopia*, trans. Anthony A. Nassar (Stanford: Stanford University Press, 2000 [1918]).

relation to the Frankfurt Institute for Social Research was complex and difficult; his influence on Adorno's thought cannot be underestimated.

Benjamin's writings can be said to move theory from a conceptual–discursive to a visual or pictorial mode and approach. Like other Western Marxists, Benjamin was struck by the capacity of capitalism to generate powerful conscious and unconscious effects extending well beyond the traditional materialist diagnosis of economic exploitation and political domination. He was especially fascinated by the capacity of the commodity-based economy to produce the illusion of newness in the medium of the repetition or return of archaic images and archetypes, and hence the power of capitalism to deploy pre-rational or irrational modes of experience, of myth and mythic time, as mechanisms of control. His never-finished magnum opus, commonly known as the "Arcades Project" (*Das Passagenwerk*), attempted to depict this gradual encroachment of mythic time via the proliferation of a commodity-based culture through an idiosyncratic construction of the material, symbolic–cultural, and literary phenomena of the birth of social-economic modernity in nineteenth-century Paris. The arcades, mid-century covered shopping avenues cut through older, premodern city streets, served as a kind of master metaphor for the collision of the archaic and the contemporary.[29]

As a Marxist theorist, Benjamin was also keenly interested in new modes of art and aesthetic productivity (such as cinema, radio, and Brechtian experimental theater) and their power to produce shock effects that could break through the lulling nature of capitalist modernity. In addition to his unfinished "Arcades Project" Benjamin also produced a series of essays in the 1930s exploring the revolutionary transformation of contemporary art practice, including a famous essay on "The Work of Art in the Age of its Mechanical Reproducibility," "The Author as Producer," which examined the prospects of a proletarianization of literary production in ways that bear interesting parallels to Gramsci, and works on Eduard Fuchs, on storytelling, on Kafka and on Proust, all of which delineate Benjamin's distinctive manner of Marxist literary criticism, one positioned in strong opposition to Lukács's defense of realism.[30]

29 Walter Benjamin, *The Arcades Project*, trans. Howard Eiland and Kevin McLaughlin (Cambridge: Harvard University Press, 2002). Prepared on the basis of the German volume edited by Rolf Tiedemann.
30 Walter Benjamin, "The Work of Art in the Age of Its Technological Reproducibility," in Walter Benjamin, *Selected Writings*, ed. Howard Eiland and Michael W. Jennings, 4 vols. (Cambridge: Harvard University Press, 2002), vol. III, 101–130; and Walter Benjamin, "The Author as Producer," in Walter Benjamin, *Selected Writings*, ed. Michael W. Jennings, Howard Eiland, and Gary Smith, 4 vols. (Cambridge: Harvard University Press, 1999), vol. II, part 2, 768–782. On Benjamin's idiosyncratic reading of Marx, see Susan Buck-Morss, *The Origin of Negative Dialectics* (Hassocks: Harvester Press, 1977).

Given the centrality of the Frankfurt School tradition within Western Marxism, and the role that German philosophical idealism played in shaping the trajectories of so many of the Western Marxists, it is easy to get the impression that Western Marxism is virtually a national intellectual tradition, despite the status of the Hungarian Lukács and the Italian Gramsci among its intellectual progenitors. This impression is not without merit. On the other hand, while Critical Theory essentially focuses on the rediscovery of the resources of (German) philosophy for answers to questions about the practical implications of a political vision that emerged from out of that philosophy, we should be cautious in overemphasizing the national features of Western Marxism.

This caution is justified on two main grounds. First, the diverse concepts and problems that Western Marxism in general and the Frankfurt School specifically confronted were, by their very nature and content, transcendent of national particularities. Problems of modern societies under capitalism, the collapse of liberal democracies and the rise of new forms of authoritarian and totalitarian states, the risk of genocidal violence, and above all the global character of capitalist markets, of instrumental rationality, and of new modes of political oppression all pointed beyond any national context. The rational ideals of personal autonomy and collective well-being, the utopian norms implicit in so much of the Frankfurt School's social critique, are explicitly universalistic in content. Notwithstanding its strong German origin, in other words, both the problems and the proposed solutions of Western Marxists evoke context-transcendent, universal human values. Marxism itself was meant at heart to be a political and theoretical program with an international core. As Perry Anderson has observed, insofar as Western Marxism tended to deliquesce back into nationally inflected variants following the more international tenor and effects of earlier Marxist theories, this can be interpreted as a part of, and measure of, an overall regression.[31]

For these reasons, it is also important to take note of the significant French current within Western Marxism – one that, given the previous point, perhaps not surprisingly tends to draw from French sources as much as or indeed more than from German ones. French Western Marxists, like their German counterparts, developed a critical social science with an emancipatory political intent. Lucien Goldmann (1913–1970), for instance, while deeply influenced by Lukács, also sought to make connections between Marxist

---

[31] See Anderson, *Considerations on Western Marxism*, 69ff.

theory and sources as diverse as Pascal and the developmental theory of Jean Piaget.[32] The philosophers Maurice Merleau-Ponty and Jean-Paul Sartre, although better known for their contributions to existentialism and phenomenology (as discussed by Edward Baring in Chapter 5), also made important theoretical contributions to Marxist debates.[33]

Louis Althusser (1918–1990), the most influential French Marxist theorist in the tradition of Western Marxism, broke sharply from the tradition's more familiar themes and approaches, and rejected both the attempt to reconnect with the humanist heritage of Marxism and the reappropriation of Hegel's dialectics. Instead, Althusser argued (in works such as *Reading Capital*) that there was a sharp discontinuity, rather than a continuity, between Marx's earlier, more humanistic works concerning concepts such as species-being and human alienation in the *Economic and Philosophical Manuscripts*, texts that still dealt with legacies of the tradition of European philosophy, and the later study of political economy that crystallized in *Capital*, a work that for Althusser was unprecedented and could not be interpreted according to anything in Marx's previous thought.[34]

Althusser drew heavily on both Freud and Spinoza to argue that ideology can no longer be taken as a sort of screen through which critical theory can open holes, or a historically contingent suite of illusions in need of critical-theoretical insight. Rather, Althusser insisted that ideology is more comparable to the structure of the unconscious. Ideologies exhibit a global, timeless, and unchanging structure that enables and produces, rather than dominates and constrains, subjects who occupy them. Indeed, Althusser came to regard subjectivity itself as an effect of ideology, one that disabled the prospect for a revolutionary emancipation from forms of social domination.

The influence of Critical Theory did not cease after the end of the 1960s, even though those years saw the ebbing of the "first generation" of critical theory. Even before Adorno's death in 1969, what is frequently referred to as second-generation Critical Theory was already taking shape as Jürgen Habermas, who had served briefly as Adorno's assistant in Frankfurt, rose to prominence as a theorist and philosopher in his own right.

---

32 See Lucien Goldmann, *The Hidden God* (London: Verso, 2016).
33 See Maurice Merleau-Ponty, *Humanism and Terror: An Essay on the Communist Problem* (Boston: Beacon Press, 1969); and Jean-Paul Sartre, *Critique of Dialectical Reason* (London: Verso, 1991).
34 See Louis Althusser, Étienne Balibar, Roger Establet, Pierre Machery, and Jacques Rancière, *Reading Capital*, trans. Ben Brewster and David Fernbach (London: Verso, 2016).

Habermas's contribution to the rebirth of the European public sphere in the post-World War II era will be treated in Chapter 20 by David Ingram. Here we should note how Habermas continued the themes and problems of Western Marxism. Habermas's own relationship with Marxism is indirect and multifaceted; as a lifelong staunch defender of the normative core of European Enlightenment, Habermas has never associated himself with any orthodox Marxist party or movement, even as he has been an advocate of the kinds of social movements and reforms inspired by forms of social domination characteristic of capitalist society. In a programmatic essay from 1975, "Toward a Reconstruction of Historical Materialism," Habermas argued that Marx's dialectical materialism was ultimately unsuited to a reconstruction of specifically modern forms of domination since it lacked a satisfactory account of the social processes whereby modern forms of subjectivity arose in tandem with modern political and economic modes of development.[35] For this, Habermas argued, a critical social theory would have to jettison both the economic primacy and economic determinism of Marx's theory and Marx's distrust of modern modes of individuation. For Habermas, Marxist materialism should give way to a theory of communicative competence – the capacity to structure social practices and institutions via the intersubjective exchange of reasons for actions. This capacity, Habermas argued, made the distinctive achievements of Enlightenment reason possible. At the same time, distortions or failures in a society's capacity to adequately institutionalize intersubjective communication were forms of social domination, and could be criticized in ways more sociologically sophisticated than a materialist method would allow. On this basis Habermas developed a theory of communicative action. The theory reconstructed the promise of rational social life as socially embodied communicative reason. It also diagnosed the dynamic of new forms of social domination as non-communicative modes of rational control, such as economic coordination of individual and society via the medium of profit and price, and political–bureaucratic control via the medium of hierarchically organized power, which gradually crept from their institutional seats in modern economy and modern political institutions to "colonize" the everyday lifeworld of modern subjects, systematically depriving them of their capacity to make full, meaningful use of their communicative competences.

---

35 See Jürgen Habermas, "Toward a Reconstruction of Historical Materialism," in *Communication and the Evolution of Society* (Cambridge: Polity Press, 2015).

This sprawling social theory, Habermas's two-volume work, *The Theory of Communicative Action* (first published in 1981) was followed by a sharp turn to philosophy in the 1990s and beyond. In these later works, Habermas expanded his theory of communicative action to more philosophically familiar areas such as normative ethics and ethical theory. His major work in political and legal philosophy, *Between Facts and Norms* (1992), reconstructed the twin normative foundations of modern positive law and modern rights-based democratic governance as emerging from the basic communicative competence of speakers and hearers who are prepared to coordinate their actions together on the basis of the exchange of reasons.[36]

Critical Theory in the wake of Habermas's work (sometimes referred to as "third-generation" critical theory[37]) is a range of both continuities and discontinuities, not only with Habermas's thought, but indeed with the tradition of Western Marxism to its beginnings in the 1920s. Many of Habermas's former pupils continue his influence by challenging it and attempting to move beyond it. Axel Honneth, for example, has rejected much of Habermas's social-scientific and political–legal theory, embarking instead on yet another strategy for the re-appropriation of Hegel, now focusing less on dialectics than on Hegel's early theory of intersubjective recognition. In this way, Honneth attempts to revitalize and expand the project of a critical theory of society – the critique of forms of social domination – by a recognition-theoretical account of how modern societies suffer from distinct forms of pathology, all of which can be analyzed as modes of lack or failure of the due recognition of persons as rights bearers, as needy of love and caring, and as worthy of respect for their individual accomplishments.[38] In this context, Honneth has even offered a broad reinterpretation of Lukács's concept of reification, translating the subject–object dialectic at the core of the original Lukácsian idea into an intersubjective perspective in which reification registers as "the forgetting of recognition."[39]

---

36 Jürgen Habermas, *The Theory of Communicative Action* (Boston: Beacon Press, 1985); Jürgen Habermas, *Between Facts and Norms* (Cambridge: MIT Press, 1996).
37 See Max Pensky, "Third Generation Critical Theory," in *A Companion to Continental Philosophy*, ed. Simon Critchley and William R. Schroeder (Oxford: Blackwell, 1998), 407–416.
38 See Axel Honneth, *The Struggle for Recognition: The Moral Grammar of Social Conflicts* (London: Polity Press, 1995); Axel Honneth, *Freedom's Right: The Social Foundations of Democratic Life* (New York: Columbia University Press, 2014).
39 Axel Honneth, *Reification: A New Look at an Old Idea* (Oxford: Oxford University Press, 2008).

In the United States, the critical impact of Habermas's work has long combined with other intellectual currents, making possible other kinds of theoretical cross-fertilization. Theorists such as Seyla Benhabib and Nancy Fraser have written broadly at the confluence of critical theory, contemporary feminist theory, and international legal and political theory. Benhabib's work has also been instrumental in moving critical theory into new and timely engagements with international relations and international law, addressing controversies in global justice and migration, and the status of international human rights.[40]

Beyond the transatlantic intellectual relationship between Europe and the United States, Western Marxism also continues to offer resources that inform and challenge political theories in the global south as well. The relation between Critical Theory and postcolonial theory is complex and highly contested,[41] but many theorists continue to draw inspiration from this tangled relationship. The Argentine–Mexican political theorist Enrique Dussel, for instance, has written widely on themes linking critical theory and Latin American political experiences.[42] In a related area, Gayatri Chakravorti Spivak has drawn heavily on Western Marxist themes and approaches in combination with literary theory and criticism to theorize about the status of the postcolonial subject.[43]

Much more could be said concerning the role that Western Marxist approaches, motifs, and concepts continue to play – and should play – for political theorists confronting a global configuration in which even the liberal democracy that Western Marxism had regarded with such deep suspicion has itself come under increasing pressure. The relation between the intellectual

---

40 See Nancy Fraser, *Fortunes of Feminism: From State-Managed Capitalism to Neoliberal Crisis* (London: Verso, 2013); Nancy Fraser, *Scales of Justice: Re-imagining Political Space in a Globalizing World* (Cambridge: Polity Press, 2008); Seyla Benhabib, *Another Cosmopolitanism: Hospitality, Sovereignty and Democratic Iterations*, ed. Robert Post (Oxford: Oxford University Press, 2006); Seyla Benhabib, *Dignity in Adversity: Human Rights in Troubled Times* (Cambridge: Polity Press, 2011); Seyla Benhabib, *Equality and Difference: Human Dignity and Popular Sovereignty in the Mirror of Political Modernity* (Tübingen: Mohr Siebeck, 2013); and Seyla Benhabib, *The Democratic Disconnect: Citizenship and Accountability in the Transatlantic Community* (Washington: Transatlantic Academy, 2013).
41 See most recently Amy Allen, *The End of Progress: Decolonizing the Normative Foundations of Critical Theory* (New York: Columbia University Press, 2016).
42 See Enrique Dussel, *Ethics of Liberation: In the Age of Globalization and Exclusion* (Durham: Duke University Press, 2013).
43 See Gayatri Chakravorti Spivak, "Can the Subaltern Speak?," in *Marxism and the Interpretation of Culture*, ed. Cary Nelson and Lawrence Grossberg (London: Macmillan, 1988); and Gayatri Chakravorti Spivak, *A Critique of Postcolonial Reason* (Cambridge: Harvard University Press, 1999).

tradition of Western Marxism and global democracy has always been fraught. But it has been and remains highly creative as well, and this creative tension is needed more than ever when those core values that motivated Western Marxism's critique of capitalist modernity – freedom from domination, material justice and equality, peaceful living together – are more threatened than ever.

11

Anti-imperialism and Interregnum

KRIS MANJAPRA

The keyword anti-imperialism connotes a set of concepts about the violence of empire and the meaning of freedom. But the history of the usage of this keyword also informs us about the shape of history itself. "Anti-imperialism" came into wide circulation in the late nineteenth century across imperial metropoles and colonial peripheries. Anti-imperialism is not just a term for various concepts that are critical of empire, but also indexes a world-historical shift that occurred between 1898 and 1930, between the end of the Age of Empires (reaching its peak in the 1880s and 1890s with the European scrambles for colonial possessions and US American overseas expansion) and the dawn of the Age of Decolonization and Nation States (resulting in the Non-Aligned Movement of the 1950s and 1960s). We study here the bridge between the age in which discourses of imperialism were hegemonic and the age in which the discourse of postcolonial nation-states became normative. The shift from one historical epoch to another often occurs through a period of transition marked by ongoing crisis, and not through a radical break. Antonio Gramsci called this treacherous transition period between historical times an "interregnum."[1]

"Interregnum" names the transition period when one hegemonic language to speak about the world order breaks down, before a new language is instituted. Keywords that circulate in any particular society serve to record, investigate, and present problems preoccupying that society at a particular historical time.[2] During an interregnum the meanings of keywords, those "strong, difficult and persuasive words" about the world, become volatile and unstable.[3] Terms are redefined at breakneck speed. Once an interregnum is

---

[1] Gramsci, *Selections from the Prison Notebooks*, ed. and trans. Quintin Hoare and Geoffrey Nowell-Smith (London: Lawrence & Wishart, 1971), 276; see Raymond Williams, "Interregnum," in *Culture and Society 1780–1950* (London: The Hogarth Press, 1993 [1958]), 162–198.
[2] Raymond Williams, *Keywords: A Vocabulary of Culture and Society* (New York: Oxford University Press, 1983), 15.
[3] Williams, *Keywords*, 14.

complete, dictionaries need to be rewritten as the "strong words" have undergone dramatic redefinition.[4]

Raymond Williams notes in *Keywords* (1976) that the meaning of "imperialism" drastically changed in the early twentieth century. In the 1870s, imperialism still carried a normal, everyday positive sense of "a political system in which colonies are governed from an imperial center, for economic but also for other reasons held to be important," culminating in the "grant of independence or self-government to these colonies." At the peak of the Victorian era, imperialism was synonymous with patrician ideals of civility and "high culture," but also with populist objectives such as good governance, national vigor, industrial education, and improvement.[5] Richard Koebner noted that "popular imperialism" climaxed around 1898 at the time of the Spanish–American War, as publics across many Western nation-states saw the struggle for colonial possessions as a matter of collective rejuvenation. Imperialist war became a nationalist "rite of spring."[6]

But Williams notes that "imperialism" also took on an unprecedented "negative sense" among a growing group of critics at the very same time. The word was increasingly associated with market penetration, military control, jingoism, barbarism, and warmongering. With the emergence of new anti-imperialist discourse at the turn of the twentieth century, "imperialism" itself came to be redefined. A new way of speaking about empire gained currency on a global scale, from locations across metropole and colony alike. A nineteenth-century mode of speaking of imperialism as a "civilizing mission" was dying out by the early twentieth century, as an emergent anti-imperial language provided a detailed autopsy of capitalist exploitation, militarism, cultural domination, and moral failure. Despite the trenchant critiques, new avatars of imperial force would continue to stalk the earth throughout the twentieth century.

M. K. Gandhi (1869–1948) is a quintessential interregnal thinker. Most of his creative work took place during this period, 1898–1930. In many ways, his

---

4 Raymond Williams comments on the inadequacy of the *Oxford English Dictionary of Historical Concepts*, written in the 1880s, to capture the meaning of words as they had changed by the twentieth century, see Williams, *Keywords*, 13. A different approach to the study of keywords and "conceptual history" is provided in the work of Reinhart Koselleck. Compare Williams's "strong words" with Koselleck's discussion of "fundamental concepts" (*Grundbegriffe*), which act in society to create "effective conditions" for historical events. Reinhart Koselleck, *Begriffsgeschichten* (Frankfurt am Main: Suhrkamp, 2006), 24. On the ways words and concepts mediate historical materiality, also see Raymond Williams, *Culture and Society* (London: The Hogarth Press, 1993 [1958]).
5 Jennifer Pitts, *Turn to Empire* (Princeton: Princeton University Press, 2005).
6 Richard Koebner and Helmut Dan Schmidt, *Imperialism: The Story and Significance of a Political Word, 1840–1960* (Cambridge: Cambridge University Press, 1965), 217–220; and Modris Eksteins, *Rites of Spring* (Toronto: Lester & Orpen Dennys, 1989).

writing and actions manifest the world-historical transition at issue here, and we can study Gandhi's thought to better understand that broad transition. A philosopher, political strategist, moral teacher, Indian nationalist firebrand, and global icon in the struggle against empire, Gandhi gained international status not only because of what he wrote and did, but also because of what he symbolized: the consolidation of a new anti-imperial revolutionary period across the colonized world. He was one among many anti-imperial spokespeople, yet his work soon became a dominant version of thought and action in India, and a touchstone for movements across various colonial territories.

Gandhi was born in Gujarat, studied in London, honed his approaches and commitments in South Africa at the turn of the twentieth century, and orchestrated many phases of anti-colonial resistance in India from the first satyagraha in 1917 to the massive Quit India Movement in 1942. Gandhi was known for his "total" politics – for insisting upon a political program that also demanded the adoption of a different way of life.

His critics, especially anti-colonial Marxists, as well as Dalit and Muslim leaders who perceived the high-caste Hindu bias of his teachings, persistently attacked his metaphysics, and his apparent emphasis on the cultural and religious, instead of the political and economic, determinants of freedom from oppression. In this chapter, I suggest that Gandhi's genius lay in expanding the definition of "freedom" beyond economic and political frameworks alone, to address what I will define as the "sociogeny" of racialization in the lived experience of the colonized. In this respect, Gandhi was emblematic of a larger interregnal shift taking place in response to imperial power on a global scale.

The development of "anti-imperialism" as a keyword from 1898 to 1930 and onwards represented a change of perspective among many in colonized societies: what the Jamaican American philosopher Sylvia Wynter terms a transformation of their "conscious experience." Anti-imperialism was associated increasingly with colony-focused instead of metropole-focused discussion, and less with what imperial lords were doing and more with what colonial subjects were going to do about it. Anti-imperialism came to be actively and creatively articulated by South American, African and African Diasporic, West Asian and Middle Eastern, South Asian, Southeast Asian, and East Asian colonial thinkers from the late nineteenth century onwards and was marked by deliberations over the meaning of freedom and independence from imperial rule.[7]

---

7 Prasenjit Duara, *Decolonization: Perspectives from Then and Now* (London: Routledge, 2004); Nicholas Tarling, *Decolonisations Compared: Central Asia, Southeast Asia, the Caucasus* (London: Palgrave Macmillan, 2017); Odd Arne Westad, *The Global Cold War: Third World Interventions and the Making of Our Times* (Cambridge: Cambridge University

This global age of anti-imperialism has some concrete institutional landmarks. Anti-imperialist societies and clubs, devoted to pacifism and the critique of military and industrial overseas expansion, arose in cities such as San Francisco, Madrid, London, and Paris following the outbreak of the Spanish–American War of 1898, and the British–French Fashoda Crisis of the same year.[8] This was also the era of the 1899–1902 Anglo-Boer war in South Africa, and the international conflagration of the 1899–1901 Boxer Uprising in northern China. By the time of World War I, anti-imperialism was no longer associated with small-scale civic societies in metropolitan capitals and their weedy pacifist fringes, but with an awesome, international constellation of mobilizations worldwide. For example, anti-imperial congresses met in the shadow of the League of Nations, which was inaugurated in Paris starting in 1919. And the League against Imperialism convened in Brussels and Berlin between 1925 and 1929, bringing together more than 200 representatives from around the world, from Black America and South America, from Africa, and from across the Middle East and Asia. Anti-imperialism became what Michael Goebel terms a "revolutionary lingua franca" for colonial activists around the world.[9]

It is worth noting, however, that anti-imperial sentiment was not born for the first time in the late nineteenth century; it had had previous lives. What we might term a first anti-imperial interregnum had already come and gone between the 1770s and the 1830s, inaugurated by the creole independence struggles in North and South America during those decades, by the epochal slave revolution in Haiti 1791–1804, and by groundswells of rebellion across the old multiethnic empires of Asia, including the Mughal, Ottoman, Safavid, and Qing empires.[10] This earlier moment of anti-imperial mobilization differed in historical consciousness from the later one. If keywords such as "revolution," "abolition," and "republicanism" characterized the creole

---

Press, 2007); and Christopher J. Lee, *The Making of a World after Empire: The Bandung Moment and Its Political Afterlives* (Athens: Ohio University Press, 2010).

8 Alyosha Goldstein, *Formations of United States Colonialism* (Durham: Duke University Press, 2014); and Herbert LePore, *Anti-Asian Exclusion in the United States during the Nineteenth and Twentieth Centuries* (Lewiston: Edwin Mellen, 2013).

9 Daniel Brückenhaus, *Policing Transnational Protest: Liberal Imperialism and the Surveillance of Anticolonialists in Europe, 1905–1945* (New York: Oxford University Press, 2017); Jean Jones, *The League against Imperialism* (London: Socialist History Society, 1996); Kris Manjapra, "Communist Internationalism and Transcolonial Recognition," in *Cosmopolitan Thought Zones: South Asia and the Global Circulation of Ideas*, ed. Sugata Bose and Kris Manjapra (Houndmills: Palgrave Macmillan, 2010), 159–177; Michael Goebel, *Anti-Imperial Metropolis: Interwar Paris and the Seeds of Third World Nationalism* (Cambridge: Cambridge University Press, 2015), 176–249; and Minkah Makalani, *In the Cause of Freedom: Radical Black Internationalism from Harlem to London* (Chapel Hill: University of North Carolina, 2011).

10 Benedict Anderson, *Imagined Communities* (London: Verso, 1983).

nationalisms of the earlier period, new keywords were added to the repertoire of anti-imperialist thought by the second phase, especially "sovereignty," "folk," "culture," and "selfhood," suggesting that "imperialism," and resistance to it, had taken on vastly new structures and meanings.[11]

A first imperial system, characterized by unruly and internecine European competition for overseas dominion in the Americas, on the one hand, and by vast, rambling, and restive multiethnic empires across Europe and Asia, on the other, came to an end by the late seventeenth century. This was followed after the 1830s by the consolidation of a more uniform international system, organized around British world order, and by the spirit of liberal imperialism. Liberal imperialism professed the gospel of improvement, productivity, free trade, and industrious free labor. The power of new travel technologies (e.g., the steam ship), new financial arrangements (e.g., the gold standard), and new weaponry (e.g., the machine gun) underpinned the spread of liberal ideology, and helped to accelerate colonial penetration further into the heartlands of the Americas, Africa, and Asia, in order to weld these to the supply curves of international markets.[12]

Different Approaches to Anti-imperial Thought

No wonder, then, that anti-imperial theory at the turn of the century in European and American imperial metropoles was chiefly concerned with the critique of militarism and the socio-economic analysis of imperialist drives. Thinkers writing from New York, London, Paris, Berlin, and Moscow were primarily focused on specifying the relationship between the rise of violent imperial competition and the expansion of industrial capitalism. European anti-imperial thinkers of different political stripes alternatively suggested theories of imperialism as *parasitic* upon, *atavistic* to, or *intrinsic* to capitalism.

John Hobson, a British political scientist disaffected by British foreign policy during the Anglo-Boer war, was perhaps the first and most influential

---

[11] See Reinhart Koselleck on the drastic shift in meaning of the term "revolution" at the end of the eighteenth century from its earlier signification of the "slow return of the same" to its new definition as "singular and unique process" that breaks historical progression. Koselleck, *Begriffsgeschichten*, 64; Uday Singh Mehta, *Liberalism and Empire: A Study in Nineteenth-Century British Liberal Thought* (Chicago: University of Chicago Press, 1999); and David Armitage and Sanjay Subrahmanyam, *The Age of Revolutions in Global Context, c. 1760–1840* (Houdmills: Palgrave Macmillan, 2010).

[12] Thomas McCarthy, *Race, Empire, and the Idea of Human Development* (Cambridge: Cambridge University Press, 2009); and Domenico Losurdo, *Liberalism: A Counterhistory*, trans. Gregory Elliott (London: Verso, 2011).

formulator of a theory of imperialism as parasitic on capitalism. In his 1902 book *Imperialism*, he sought to demolish the claim that imperialism benefited capitalist enterprise by spreading rationality and civilization, by opening up foreign markets for home industry, or by providing a release valve for overpopulation. Rather, the "new imperialism" was driven by "parasites" that would "jeopardize the entire wealth of the nation." There were "sectional interests that usurp control of the national resources and use them for their private gain," he argued. To be specific, these were the interests behind the manufacture or provision of ships, guns, military and naval equipment, foreign investment, consular services, exports, engineering works, and missions – the military–industrial complex.[13] Imperialism allowed a parasitic leeching by business interests on national wealth.

Joseph Schumpeter, the Austrian-born American economist and liberal political philosopher, developed a competing critique of imperialism as an atavistic, feudal form of economic life that persisted into the time of modern capitalism. According to Schumpeter, imperialism was a residue of the pre-capitalist past that flared up in the capitalist present. "*Imperialism is an atavism.* It falls in the great group of those things that live on from earlier epochs, things which play so great a role in every concrete situation and which are to be explained not from the conditions of the present but from the conditions of the past." In his essay "Sociology of Imperialism" (1918), written during the final devastating endgame of World War I, Schumpeter proposed that, like any vestigial limb, imperialism was "object-less." Imperialism is the "objectless disposition of a state to expansion by force without assigned limits." Hence, the "inner logic" of capitalism would ensure that imperialism would disappear over time. Imperialism was no parasite on capitalism, but a residual pre-capitalist form that would be extinguished through the working out of capitalism's evolutionary laws.

Both Hobson's and Schumpeter's critiques of imperialism were strongly in contrast with the Marxist theories that emerged among German- and Russian-speaking thinkers during the same period. For this group, imperialism was neither parasitic on nor atavistic to capitalism, but *intrinsic* to it; its most important vital organ – its beating heart. The German political economist Rudolf Hilferding (1977–1941), in his *Das Finanzkapital* (1909), was one of the first to theorize imperialism as intrinsic to capitalism. Finance capital's key feature was "over-accumulation," or accumulation without productive purpose, and this was a cause of imperialist expansion, Hilferding argued.

---

13 John Hobson, *Imperialism: A Study* (London: Unwin Hyman, 1988 [1902]), 48.

Imperialism was the chief means by which England was able to secure its own industrial development, but now, under the pressure of finance capital, British imperial accumulation continued on without productive end. It was overheated, boundless, and compulsive.[14]

In *The Accumulation of Capital* (1913), the Polish-born Marxist theoretician and revolutionary Rosa Luxemburg (1871–1919) argued that capitalism was itself a colonial endeavor that required a non-capitalist frontier in which to find new consumers and new markets. Luxemburg developed a theory of imperialism as a "stage" of capitalist accumulation. "Just as the substitution of commodity economy for a natural economy and that of capitalist production for a simple commodity production was achieved by wars, social crises and the destruction of entire social systems, so at present the achievement of capitalist autonomy in the hinterland and backward colonies is attained amidst wars and revolutions."[15] For Luxemburg, "primitive accumulation," or accumulation through warfare, was a permanent requirement for the capitalist mode of production.

Finally, V. I. Lenin (1870–1924) drew heavily on Hilferding and Luxemburg in his famous *Imperialism: The Highest Stage of Capitalism* (1917). Following Hilferding, he argued that imperialism was synonymous with "monopoly capitalism." And he developed Luxemburg's argument by laying out the ways in which "high imperialism" served the interests of metropolitan capitalist industry: by providing banks with a new role, by creating spaces for the export of capital, by creating a division of world geography for "capitalist combines," and by permitting the rise of monopolies. Imperialism, Lenin theorized, represented not a parasite on capitalism, but capitalism's "highest stage" before the coming of its own demise.[16]

Metropolitan definitions of anti-imperialism articulated a diverse array of competing visions during the interregnum 1898–1930, even as they all shared a universally derogatory view of empire as a warmongering and jingoistic enterprise. The question was how to record, investigate, and present the problem of imperialism, and how to think beyond its limits. Hobson's critique presented imperialism as parasitic on capitalism, and thus as an infection that could be cured. Schumpeter saw imperialism as atavistic to capitalism, and thus as a vestigial form that would fall away. Meanwhile,

14 Rudolf Hilferding, *Nationalstaat, Imperialistischer Staat und Staatenbund*, (Nuremburg: Fränkische Verlagsanstalt, 1915), 36.
15 Rosa Luxemburg, *The Accumulation of Capital*, trans. Agnes Schwartzchild (New Haven: Yale University Press, 1951), 399.
16 Vladimir Lenin, *Imperialism: The Highest Stage of Capitalism* (London: Junius, 1996), 99.

Hilferding, Luxemburg, and Lenin, and the emerging Communist Third International, saw imperialism as intrinsic, as capitalism's beating heart. As this new keyword, "anti-imperialism," gained currency from 1898 onwards, it was used to signify many things, and to marshal a variety of concepts. And the very volatility in meaning is historically significant in itself.

Gandhi's Moment

M. K. Gandhi's adult life, from the time he left to study in London in 1887 until the time of his assassination in 1948, spanned the shift from old meanings of anti-imperialism to new ones. Theory and practice were imbricated for Gandhi, as they were for so many intellectual-activists from the colonial world at the turn of the twentieth century. His anti-imperial problematic was centered not on deciphering the intentions of the imperial lords, but on defining the path to freedom for colonial subjects. If metropolitan anti-imperialism was mostly a discourse about the nature and sources of exploitation and domination, colonial anti-imperialism was one about the possible cultural, experiential, and political meanings of freedom from imperial exploitation.

From the perspective of the colonized, it was not just militarism and capitalism that experientially defined imperialism, but, importantly, the experience of intensifying and blatant forms of racialization and colonial abjection. The experience of racial violence as a concrete manifestation of imperial power was obvious to people in the colonies, just as warfare and capitalist expansion were obvious to anti-imperial writers watching the world tilt toward a great war. In fact, racialization and dehumanization became *the* concrete, material experience of war and capitalist exploitation, as it filtered down from political economic theory and grand military strategy into the texture of the daily life of colonized peoples. The racial response by the British empire to the Indian Uprising of 1857 and its culmination in the Ilbert Bill of 1883 giving whites in India unprecedented legal privileges; the mass murder of Black Jamaicans after the Morant Bay Uprising of 1865; the Asian Exclusion Laws instituted in the United States and across British settler colonies in the 1880s–1910s; the expansionist racial colonialism of the French Third Republic; the Anglo-American racial supremacy that underpinned US annexations and occupations of Hawaii, the Philippines, Cuba, Puerto Rico, and Haiti after 1898; the extermination campaigns by German and Belgian colonial overlords in southwestern and central Africa; and the Jim Crow backlash in the post-bellum American South made clear to colonial thinkers from different parts of the world that imperialism relied not only on militias and financiers, but also on racist institutions and ideologies of white supremacy.[17] Such a view was floridly articulated in the writings of many imperial racial ideologues from this period, including Frederick Jackson Turner, Lothrop Stoddard, Houston Stewart Chamberlain, and Arthur de Gobineau.[18]

Racial Sociogeny

In response, anti-imperialist thinkers from the colonies were forced to develop ways of conceiving the struggle against imperialism that surpassed the limits of anti-imperialist discourse in European metropolises, in which the *socio-economic* principles were discussed, but the *sociogenic* implication of imperial force remained untheorized. Frantz Fanon proposed that "besides phylogeny and ontogeny there stands sociogeny."[19] The 'sociogenic principle,' as Sylvia Wynter explained, drawing on Franz Fanon, refers to how legacies of racial colonialism overdetermine the "conscious experience" of what it's like to be colonized.

Racial sociogeny is the result of European global expansion from the late fifteenth century onwards, involving the dispossession, forced displacement, imposed cultural conversion, minoritization, and segregationist containment of many kinds of subjected peoples in the spread of European overseas empires. Drawing on Fanon's psychoanalytic writing, Wynter explains that the psyche, or mind, of the colonized is formed not only by biological processes (phylogeny), and interpersonal and family experiences (ontogeny), but also by long-term historical and social logics of race:

> This means that the range of emotional behaviors, experienced by the peoples colonized by the West, rather than being natural, had been "skillfully injected" through processes of cultural socialization as the indispensable condition of the bringing into being of the contemporary order of modernity. These subjective feelings of abjection are therefore ones linked to a non-

---

17 Walter Rodney, *How Europe Underdeveloped Africa* (Washington: Howard University Press, 1974); Gary Wilder, *The French Imperial Nation-State: Negritude and Colonial Humanism between the Two World Wars* (Chicago: University of Chicago Press, 2005); and Moon-Ho Jung, *Coolies and Cane: Race, Labor, and Sugar Production in the Age of Emancipation* (Baltimore: Johns Hopkins University Press, 2006).
18 David Theo Goldberg, *The Racial State* (Malden: Blackwell Publishers, 2002); and George Lipsitz, *The Possessive Investment in Whiteness: How White People Profit from Identity Politics* (Philadelphia: Temple University Press, 1998).
19 Frantz Fanon, *Black Skin, White Masks*, trans. Richard Philcox (New York: Publishers Group West, 2008), 11.

white "native" and, in its extreme form "negro" or "nigger" "sense of self," defined by its enforced position, as the no less invented, Human Other to Man.[20]

The new language of "anti-imperialism" that emerged in Gandhi's moment came to address this racial sociogeny of colonial subjects, of those placed "on the negative or liminally deviant side ... of the *Color line*."[21]

The modern imperialism of European powers drew a line between those who might be deemed fully human, and those savage and backward people who supposedly lacked full human status.[22] The colonized – the blacks, natives, aboriginals, Orientals, islanders, and 'primitives' of the earth – were sociogenically consigned to the racialized domain of the less-than-human, just as they were socio-economically conscripted into globe-spanning capitalist production regimes. As early as 1896, Gandhi had already observed the sociogenesis of the racialized subject:

> The man in the street hates him [the Indian], curses him, spits upon him, and often pushes him off the foot-path ... The tramcars are not for the Indians. The railway officials may treat the Indians as beasts. No matter how clean, his very sigh is such an offence to every White man in the colony that he would object to sit, even for a short time, in the same compartment with the Indian. The hotels shut their doors against them. Even the public baths are not for the Indians no matter who they are ...[23]

Racial sociogenesis disfigured the psyche of the racialized subject. W. E. B. Du Bois used "double consciousness" to describe it as a "peculiar sensation ... of always looking at one's self through the eyes of others, of measuring one's soul by the tape of a world that looks on in amused contempt and pity."[24] This "peculiar sensation" of one's own deformed mental state is captured poetically by Martiniquan philosopher Aimé Césaire, in his famous *Cahier d'un retour au pays natal* (*Return to My Native Land*, 1939):

---

20 Sylvia Wynter, "Towards the Sociogenic Principle: Fanon, Identity, the Puzzle of Conscious Experience, and What It Is Like to be 'Black,'" in *National Identities and Sociopolitical Changes in Latin America*, ed. Mercedes F. Durán-Cogan and Antonio Gómez-Moriana (London: Routledge, 2001), 40.
21 Wynter, "Towards the Sociogenic Principle," 40.
22 Wynter, "Towards the Sociogenic Principle," 23; Fanon, *Black Skin, White Masks*; Dipesh Chakrabarty, *Provincializing Europe: Postcolonial Thought and Historical Difference* (Princeton: Princeton University Press, 2000); Johannes Fabian, *Time and the Other* (New York: Columbia University Press, 1983); and Syed Hussein Alatas, *The Myth of the Lazy Native* (London: Frank Cass, 1977).
23 Mohandas K. Gandhi, *The Collected Works of Mahatma Gandhi*, 100 vols. (New Delhi: Publications Division, Government of India, 1958), vol. I, 360.
24 W. E. B. Du Bois, *The Souls of Black Folk* (Chicago: A. C. McClurg & Co., 1903), 2–3.

> At the end of the dawn ...
> that other dawn of Europe ...
> I would
> Be a jew-man
> A kaffir-man
> A hindu-man-from-Calcutta
> A man-from-Harlem-who-doesn't-vote
> The famine-man, the insult-man, the torture-man one can at any moment seize, beat up or kill – yes really kill him – without having to account to anybody, without having to excuse oneself to anyone.[25]

Frantz Fanon (1925–1961), Afro-Caribbean philosopher, psychiatrist, and Césaire's intellectual protégé, provided the most celebrated description of racial sociogeny in *Black Skin, White Masks*, in the chapter "The Lived Experience of the Black [Person]." Fanon described how everyday encounters with racial colonial societies leave the subordinated feeling "spread-eagled, disjointed, redone," and "fixed" by the white imperial gaze.[26] Given the conditions of the racialized psyche, Fanon prescribed self-assertive acts of individual and collective violence as the source of a "cleansing force. It frees the colonized from his inferiority complex."[27] Gandhi, who was born almost half a century before Fanon, and in a different colonial context, envisioned acts of self-renunciating "non-violence" as the central practice in rehabilitating the psyche and recovering from racial sociogeny.[28]

Gandhi's Anti-imperialism

Gandhi's specific historical significance, I argue here, was to *integrate* the legal and the socio-economic critique of imperialism with a new sociogenic critique. In so doing, he foreshadowed the emergence of a new family relation of vanguard anti-imperialist thought coming out of the colonial world in the early twentieth century.

Gandhi's thought and tactics emerged during the years 1900–1930. During this period he developed new tactics and disciplines, including passive

---

25 Aimé Césaire, *Return to My Native Land* (Paris: Présence Africaine, 1968), 37.
26 Fanon, *Black Skin, White Masks*, 95.
27 Frantz Fanon, *The Wretched of the Earth* (New York: Grove Press, 1963), 74.
28 Ajay Skaria, *Unconditional Equality: Gandhi's Religion of Resistance* (Minneapolis: University of Minnesota Press, 2016).

resistance or "civil disobedience," "satyagraha," and "non-cooperation," and articulated an overall strategy for obtaining "Swaraj" or "rule by self." But, before discussing these constituent elements of Gandhi's anti-imperialism, let us observe the overall arc in his thinking: one that allowed him to multiply the subjects addressed by anti-imperial struggle.

Gandhi's anti-imperialism sought to win freedom for three distinct "selves": the legal person, the cultural spirit, and the laboring body. Gandhi honed a mode of anti-imperial thought and action that addressed each of these subjects, or centers of social action and historical self-consciousness. He thereby developed a way of conceiving anti-imperialism that triangulated the struggle of masses of colonial people in South Africa, and later, India, across different segments of society.

Gandhi's political formation took place in South Africa in the 1890s, when the British were busy implementing racist laws: strengthening the indenture system that conscripted poor Indian migrants for menial and exploitative work, and honing the legal codes of second-class citizenship for the Indian middle classes. In South Africa, Gandhi, like all the Indians in the diaspora, was not granted full legal personhood. Ironically, faith in the possibility of full citizenship for Indians within Empire first inspired Gandhi to travel to Victorian London for law studies as a youth in 1888. But life experience showed him that Empire was not just a practice of economic exploitation and profiteering; it was also an endeavor in racial segregation and white superiority.

In the beginning, Gandhi as a young lawyer, or as a "lawyer-loyalist" as Ramachandra Guha characterized him, envisioned political struggle as a struggle for rights within the state.[29] Gandhi's political aim at this stage was dominion status for India – status as a self-governing polity with a representative national assembly within the British empire. He would quickly set himself up in South Africa as a proponent for middle-class Indians, businessmen and traders. Gandhi sued against segregation laws that affected the Indian middle classes, and against the discriminatory stipulations requiring Indians to obtain internal passports.[30] He also petitioned against laws that assigned "aboriginal races of Asia, including the so-called coolies, Arabs, Malays, and Mahomedan subjects . . ." to "certain streets, wards and locations

---

29 Ramachandra Guha, *Gandhi before India* (New York: Alfred A. Knopf, 2014), 36–54.
30 See Gandhi's "Letter to Colonial Secretary, Natal," July 6, 1899, in *The Collected Works of Mahatma Gandhi*, 100 vols. (New Delhi: Publications Division, Government of India, 1958), vol. III, 96.

for habitation."³¹ Gandhi came to summarize all of these racist laws under the heading of "the Indian Question in South Africa."³² His interest in legal personhood, however, would soon give way to a concern for the colonial subject conceived in different ways.

Yet, even while still a student in London and before traveling to South Africa, Gandhi was taking an interest in the needs of another kind of subject than that of the legal person. He was developing a concern for the freedom of the spirit. This concern was cultivated by his involvement with London counter-cultural circles: the underground world of vegetarians, anti-vivisectionists, pacifists, Theosophists, Tolstoyans, and Christian reformers. The anti-imperialism of London counter-culture introduced Gandhi to a different kind of subject that also demanded freedom from imperial rule – the subject of the personal consciousness or psyche.³³

The emphasis on consciousness and spirit is fully documented in the concerns of Gandhi's most important monograph, *Hind Swaraj*, completed in 1908. It is not legal personhood that forms his main focus, nor the subject of legal enfranchisement, but the subject of the spirit. Significantly, he penned the text on a trip back from the law courts of London, returning to a South Africa still crippled by the belligerencies of the Anglo-Boer war, including what Gandhi characterized as "concentration camps [for Boer insurgents]" and "indescribable suffering."³⁴ *Hind Swaraj* presented anti-imperial struggle as a cultural war against English civilization, and as a spiritual war against greed, machinery, and industrialism. What was needed, Gandhi proposed, is a retrieval of India's native values based on the great indigenous traditions of Hinduism, Islam, Sikhism, Zoroastrianism, and Christianity. He called for a return to "homespun" fabric instead of factory-made cotton cloth, and to the simplicity of the Indian village. Gandhi argued in *Hind Swaraj* for a cultural and spiritual shift among Indians struggling against empire, so that eventual

---

31 Law 3 of 1884, Article 3. Quoted in Gandhi to Chamberlain, May 16, 1899, in *The Collected Works of Mahatma Gandhi*, 100 vols. (New Delhi: Publications Division, Government of India, 1958), vol. III, 72.
32 Mohandas K. Gandhi, "The Indian Question in South Africa," Durban, July 12, 1899, *Collected Works Works of Mahatma Gandhi*, 100 vols. (New Delhi: Publications Division, Government of India, 1958), vol. III, 96.
33 Leela Gandhi, *Affective Communities: Anticolonial Thought, fin-de-siècle Radicalism, and the Politics of Friendship* (Durham: Duke University Press, 2006).
34 Mohandas K. Gandhi, "Gandhi to Ashram Women," in *The Collected Works of Mahatma Gandhi*, 100 vols. (New Delhi: Publications Division, Government of India, 1958), vol. XXXIV, 18 and 63.

independence would not result in "English rule without the Englishman."[35] A resonant argument about cultural resistance to Western values and norms, and about a worlded freedom outside Western universalism, was expressed by both Rabindranath Tagore and Mohammad Iqbal.[36]

Gandhi argued in *Hind Swaraj* that freedom cannot merely be defined as "self-government," since self-government was the prize cynically dangled before the colonized by the British imperial overlords in order to assure their allegiance.[37] For Gandhi, *swaraj*, or "rule by self," was needed, not "self-government."[38] This rule by Indians themselves would constitute a wholly different cultural and political space in which supposedly Indic values, namely non-industrial values of duty, *ahimsa* (non-violence), *satya* (truthfulness), *dharma* (religious responsibility), and filial coexistence between different religious communities, would lead to a conversion of Indians away from the acquisitive, vulgar, and vain values of empire. Gandhi's program aimed at the "invention of tradition"[39] not just for short-term tactical ends of nation formation, but for the long-term strategic pursuit of political, cultural, and psycho-affective transformation. Swaraj, in Gandhi's 1908 treatise, addressed not only the legal person, but also the culture of a colonized people, their aspirations, and their psychic needs.

Gandhi first began developing civil disobedience as a way of pleading for rights from the imperial state, inspired by the writings of Leo Tolstoy and Henry David Thoreau.[40] But as he experienced severe and repeated disappointment before the imperial system, he developed a cultural stance called "satyagraha" or "standing in truth." Satyagraha required a cultural and personal reorientation away from Western values. Freedom could not just be legal or jurisprudential. Freedom had to address the consciousness and the spirit, and required more than what the imperial state could grant. This accords with Partha Chatterjee's important argument that Gandhi engendered a crucial shift

---

35 Mohandas K. Gandhi, *Hind Swaraj and Other Writings* (Cambridge: Cambridge University Press, 1997), 45.
36 Sugata Bose, "Different Universalisms, Colorful Cosmopolitanisms: The Global Imagination of the Colonized," in *Cosmopolitan Thought Zones: South Asia and the Global Circulation of Ideas*, ed. Sugata Bose and Kris Manjapra (Houndmills: Palgrave Macmillan, 2010), 97–111; and Iqbal Singh Sevia, *The Political Philosophy of Muhammad Iqbal: Islam and Nationalism in Late Colonial India* (Cambridge: Cambridge University Press, 2012).
37 Gandhi, *Hind Swaraj and Other Writings*, 26.
38 Gandhi, *Hind Swaraj and Other Writings*, 70.
39 Eric Hobsbawm and Terence Ranger (eds.), *The Invention of Tradition* (Cambridge: Cambridge University Press, 1983).
40 Domenico Losurdo, *Non-Violence: A History beyond the Myth* (Lanham: Lexington Books, 2015), 22–23.

in Indian nationalism, as it turned away from the outer realm of petitions before imperial magistrates, toward an inner realm of vernacular language and cultural practice. This accorded with a "moment of maneuver," in Chatterjee's discussion, a major and incontrovertible shift in the trajectory of the Indian freedom struggle under the guidance of the Mahatma when a new "problematic" of anti-imperialism was introduced.[41] Satyagraha emerged as a way for Gandhi to conceptualize and advance a program to demand the freedom of the spirit. He narrates how he arrived at "satyagraha," "non-violent struggle," and "soul force" in his 1927 *Autobiography*.

But we must also note yet another, third, subject that soon became of great importance to Gandhi's anti-imperialism, even while he was still in South Africa. This was the laboring subject, the toiling body. Gandhi's preoccupation with freedom for the laboring subject developed through his increasing involvement in the plight of Indian indentured servants. "Labourers," he wrote, "are not the least important among the citizens of India. Indeed, if we include the peasantry, they form by far the vast majority ... There is only one occasion to be given in asking the labourers to understand and recognize that they, after all, are the predominant power and the predominant partners and they should recognize their strength."[42] Fond of articulating political engagement through dietary choices, Gandhi even banned sugar from his home since its production depended on the exploitation of indentured workers.[43]

From 1910 onwards, Gandhi applied intense criticism to the indentured labor system, and soon segued to address the condition of peasant labor in India. Indentured laborers were lynchpin workers for imperial capitalism, Gandhi believed. They were among the most disenfranchised of India's rural poor, mobilized through long-distance migration networks to work on exploitative short-term contracts to build railroads, excavate mines, and harvest plantations. From 1910 to the time when the indenture system was finally abolished in 1917, the indentured laborer, indigo farmer, plantation worker, and toiling peasant became the representative subjects of Gandhi's anti-imperialist struggle.

Gandhi's struggle in the name of labor began assuming its full form by 1913. He led his most important South African satyagraha that year, and modeled it on the tactics of the general strike. General strikes, *hartals, bandhs*, and work-

---

41 Partha Chatterjee, *Nationalist Thought and the Colonial World* (London: Zed Books, 1986).
42 Mohandas K. Gandhi, "Speech on Capital and Labour and Rowlatt Bills, Nagapatam," March 29, 1919, in *The Collected Works Works of Mahatma Gandhi*, 100 vols. (New Delhi: Publications Division, Government of India, 1958), vol. XV, 162.
43 Guha, *Gandhi before India*, 199.

stoppage campaigns had long been used across both the industrializing and the colonial world.[44] Gandhi, for example, took a great first-hand interest in the strategies and tactics of the London dock strike of 1889, as well as the suffragette movement.[45] And in 1913, he helped instigate a strike of indentured coal-mine workers in Natal, which quickly spread beyond collieries to include Indian servants, sweepers, and menial workers of all kinds. It also included workers on sugar estates, street cleaners, railway workers, and boatmen.[46] Soon, Gandhi combined the tactic of the general strike, as it spread from Newcastle to Durban, with the tactic of courting arrest. He urged miners to march off their compounds and across the Transvaal border, an illegal act, and this prompted the colonial government to place hundreds of Indian non-violent protestors in jail. At this very time, Gandhi also changed the way he dressed. He donned the simple clothes of the indentured, and no longer dressed in lawyer's suits. Gandhi's last satyagraha in South Africa was a labor strike of massive scale, focused on the poorest of poor Indians who had the most intimate material understanding of the brutality of imperial labor exploitation.

From 1910 onwards, Gandhi wrote incessantly about the plight of indentured laborers in South Africa, just as he wrote about the conditions of indenture in Fiji and Ceylon.[47] Protesting the £3 head tax on laborers, Gandhi spoke of "iniquity," and described indenture as a "remnant of slavery." In his campaign, he followed the lead of his mentor, Gopal Krishna Gokhale, for whom indentured labor was anathema.[48]

After his return to India in 1915, Gandhi was ready to begin his first mass anti-imperialist agitation in 1917. Unsurprisingly, he focused on the plight of peasant indigo farmers in Champaran, rural Bihar, before soon inaugurating the most important mass nationalist mobilization in India before the Salt

---

44 W. E. B. Du Bois, *Black Reconstruction in America* (New York: The Free Press, 1998), 381–430; "The light of the sublime message of truth and nonviolence will shine forever," wrote Roy late in life, "The end does not justify the means ... [is] the core of the Mahatma's [M. K. Gandhi's] message. The Mahatma wanted to purify politics; that can be done only by raising political practice above the vulgar level of a scramble for power."
45 Stanley Wolpert, *Gandhi's Passion* (New York: Oxford University Press, 2001), 25.
46 Joseph Lelyveld, *Great Soul* (New York: Vintage, 2011), 111–113.
47 Mohandas K. Gandhi, "The 3 Pound Tax," *Indian Opinion*, November 11, 1911, in *The Collected Works of Mahatma Gandhi*, 100 vols. (New Delhi: Publications Division, Government of India, 1958), vol. XII, 88; and Mohandas K. Gandhi, "Significance of Fiji Struggle," September 7, 1919, *Navajivan*, in *The Collected Works of Mahatma Gandhi*, 100 vols. (New Delhi: Publications Division, Government of India, 1958), vol. XVI, 109.
48 Mohandas K. Gandhi, "The Indenture Resolution," *Indian Opinion*, March 16, 1912, in *The Collected Works of Mahatma Gandhi*, 100 vols. (New Delhi: Publications Division, Government of India, 1958), vol. XII, 172.

March of 1930. This was the Khilafat/Non-Cooperation movement of 1919–1922, organized and executed in collaboration with the eminent Muslim leaders Shaukat and Muhammad Ali. Gandhi was no longer concerned about sueing for legal personhood within empire. He now demanded "Swaraj within a year," or the complete end of imperial rule. As far as he and his followers were concerned, the British empire in India was already dead. It now merely exerted domination, not hegemony.[49] And the chilling manifestations of its munitions, police forces, and armories, its military men, jails, and magistrates, no longer induced fear and trembling. It could break the bones of Indians but not their resolve. Gandhi's new tactic of non-cooperation, or active withdrawal from or boycott of imperial institutions, was a way of demonstrating this ultimatum. In the Khilafat/Non-Cooperation movement, the concern for the psycho-affective (the sociogenic principle) was combined with a concern for the material conditions of labor (the socio-economic principle). "We must first come in living touch with them [the laboring poor] by working for them and in their midst. We must share their sorrows, understand their difficulties and anticipate their wants ... We must identify ourselves with the villagers who toil under the hot sun beating on their bent backs and see how [we] would like to drink water from the pool in which the villagers bathe, wash their clothes and pots and in which their cattle drink and roll ... I do claim that some of us at least will have to go through the agony and out of it only will a nation full, vigorous and free be born."[50] He sought in this struggle to form a coalition between Hindus and Muslims, and among toilers, workers, and laborers across region and caste divides.

This politics of severe disruption through non-violent means, and of disregard for the imperial monopoly on martial force, represented not only a practical program for insurrection but also a mobilization of spirit. Through it, Gandhi hoped to kick-start an "Indianization" program that transcended community, religious, and ritual divides between Hindus and Muslim, as well as the caste chasm separating high-caste Hindus from the vast majority of Indians deemed either "low" or "untouchable."

In some ways, Gandhi even anticipated and foreshadowed the rise of Indian communism, which developed in 1920. Some Indian communists, such as

---

49 Ranajit Guha, *Domination without Hegemony* (Cambridge: Harvard University Press, 1998).
50 Mohandas K. Gandhi, "The Realities," September 11, 1924, in *The Collected Works of Mahatma Gandhi*, 100 vols. (New Delhi: Publications Division, Government of India, 1958), vol. XXV, 121–122.

Shripad Amrit Dange, immediately foregrounded similarities between Gandhi's thought and Marxism, writing *Gandhi vs. Lenin* in 1921. Dange described both Gandhi and Lenin as pursuing the enfranchisement of laborers and the destruction of bourgeois values of "acquisitiveness, vanity, rivalry and love of power."[51] For Dange, "Gandhism" was an Indian form of historical materialism, and was potentially even more radical than Marxism itself since it "attacks the very foundations of modern social arrangements and divisions introduced by modern industrialization." By insisting on the return to village and craft production, Gandhi's prescriptions differed starkly from the Marxist embrace of modernization. Dange was one among a large number of Gandhian Marxists who emerged in the middle of the twentieth century, including Kamala Chattopadhyaya, Natesa Aiyer, and Ram Manohar Lohia.[52]

But at the same time as some Indian Marxist thinkers found accommodations with Gandhi's approaches, many others saw him as their foil. In the 1920s and 1930s, young thinkers concerned with the social deformations caused both by caste domination and by capitalist accumulation in India found much wanting in Gandhi's leadership. M. N. Roy sounded a relentless *ostinato* to the Gandhian leitmotif of cultural–spiritual uplift in the 1920s and 1930s. Roy argued that Gandhi's politics relied on a "weak and watery reformism, which shrinks at every turn from the realities of the struggle for freedom."[53] Gandhi, for Roy, was the quintessence of the anti-colonial leader who lacked a program, substituting "spiritual patriotism" for true revolutionary thought.[54] E. V. Ramaswamy, popularly known as Periyar, was a great Dalit intellectual-activist from Tamil Nadu. He stringently criticized Gandhi for tying his agenda so closely to the high-caste Hindu religious stricture: "The day when Gandhi said God alone guides him, that Varnashramadharma (the system of the four castes) is [a] superior system fit to govern the affairs of the world and that everything happens according to God's will, we came to the conclusion that there is no difference between Gandhism and Brahminism."[55] Meanwhile, the Muslim Marxist thinker Muzaffar Ahmad, writing in 1926 in the wake of the failed

---

51 Shripad Amrit Dange, *Gandhi vs. Lenin* (Bombay: Lokseka Press, 1921), 1.
52 Subrata Mukherjee, *Gandhian Thought, Marxist Interpretation* (New Delhi: Deep & Deep Publications, 1991); see Akeel Bilgrami, "Gandhi (and Marx)," in Akeel Bilgrami, *Secularism, Identity, and Enchantment* (Cambridge: Harvard University Press, 2014), 122–174; and Ram Manohar Lohia, *Marx, Gandhi, and Socialism* (Hyderabad: Navahind, 1963).
53 Manabendra Nath Roy and Evelyn Roy, *One Year of Non-Cooperation from Ahmedabad to Gaya* (Calcutta: Communist Party of India, 1923), 56–58.
54 Manabendra Nath Roy, "The Political Situation," *Vanguard*, October 15, 1922, 7.
55 Periyar, "On the Execution of Bhagat Singh," March 29, 1931, republished in *The Modern Rationalist* (November 2006), www.revolutionarydemocracy.org/archive/periyar.htm.

Khilafat/Non-Cooperation movement and the rise of violent conflicts between Hindu and Muslim communities across northern India, observed that "selfish people are using workers and peasants in the name of religion. Communism is one thing that can save India from destroying itself. Because it looks after humanity, it is not communalist."[56] One must observe what seems a flaw in Gandhi's enterprise, as his stance for inclusiveness seemed often to be rooted in a sense of disciplined, even prim, high-case Hindu identity, and in an off-putting sense of moral superiority. A mode of inclusivity that presumed high-caste Hindu majoritarianism could push large segments of the diverse Indian society to the margins, or seek to yoke them to an unwelcome system of patronage.[57]

In framing M. K. Gandhi as an "interregnal thinker," I suggest that Gandhi's thought and action were on the way to a destination that was never reached. In other words, we recognize flux, not a steady state, in Gandhi's work. We should also not forget the motivating intention underlying Gandhi's turn to culture, identity, and religion. It is evident from his many lectures, writings, and statements about the mixed cultural heritages of South Asia that he was not motivated by the pursuit of Hindu cultural or ethnic purification.[58] Rather, his intention was to address the racial colonial sociogenesis of Indians, which alienated the colonized from their native contexts and from one another. Gandhi was not motivated by a wish to retrieve the mythic origins of a supposedly Hindu nation, but wished to establish the horizon for a new kind of "conscious experience" among Indians that might rehabilitate their psyches and prepare them for a proximate future after British empire. M. K. Gandhi's insistence on the importance of Indic civilization was constructive and creative, not atavistic. Yet, the resulting applications and implications of his thought, often toward Hindu majoritarian ends, have made Gandhi into an unwitting sorcerer's apprentice.[59]

In the 1920s, Gandhi's politics was very much a labor politics *and* a cultural politics in one, while never relinquishing its demand for the legal rights of sovereign rule by the self. In his magazine, *Young India*, during the 1920s, Gandhi strove to reinvent anti-imperialism along productivist lines, with an emphasis on socio-economic principles of self-sufficiency, the homespun,

---

56 Muzaffar Ahmad, *Langol*, 14 Magh 1332 (January 1926), translated by Neilesh Bose.
57 Shubnam Tejani, *Indian Secularism: A Social and Intellectual History, 1850–1950* (Bloomington: Indiana University Press, 2008).
58 Guha, *Gandhi before India*, 181–183.
59 See Faisal Devji's discussion of Gandhi's strenuous efforts to quell the outbreak of violence between Hindus and Muslims at the time of partition, which finally resulted in his assassination. Faisal Devji, *The Impossible Indian: Gandhi and the Temptation of Violence* (London: Hurst & Company, 2012), 151–184.

and the *swadeshi* boycott of foreign goods. The focus on the working body and the recuperated cultural spirit moved Gandhi to emphasize, even fetishize, the *charka*, or the traditional cotton spinning wheel, as a symbol for Indian anti-imperial nationalism across the Hindu and Muslim religious lines, but also as an ethic of daily work.

Between 1906 and 1922, Gandhi went from lawyer, to cultural leader, to labor organizer. These roles were not played out sequentially. Rather, they were combined in his developing politics. Anti-imperialism came to address the freedom needs of three different kinds of subject simultaneously: the legal person, the spirit, and the laboring body. His last great march, the Salt March of 1930, combined all three elements: It was a march of the legal person to demand the right to harvest salt from the sea; a march of the cultural self, or "spirit," to stand up against British imperial racial domination; and a march of the laboring body to protest the dispossession of the peasants of the product of their own labor.

M. K. Gandhi stands out for his work in reorientating and redefining "anti-imperialism" during the early twentieth century, during a time when redefinition was accelerating. He reprised anti-imperialism in a way that expanded and multiplied its meanings, in a manner resonant with a larger shift taking place in the thought of many colonial thinkers across different regions as we shall see next. Anti-imperialism was no longer focused solely on the critique of militarism and industry. The keyword anti-imperialism now included and combined legal, sociogenic, and socio-economic problematics. This redefinition permitted anti-imperialism in India to become a mass affair, commanding the imagination and the actions of diverse millions of South Asians.

Gandhian Influences Abroad

Gandhi's impact was felt across different colonial situations worldwide. It received one of its most powerful receptions within the world of Black thought. Pan-African Congresses took place in 1919, 1921, and 1923, at the very peak of the Non-Cooperation Movement in India led by Gandhi and the Ali brothers. W. E. B. Du Bois, the African American philosopher and convener of the Pan-African Congresses, reproduced in the pages of his journal, *The Crisis*, a public letter written by Gandhi to the personified British empire in August 1921:

> I know you would not mind if we could fight and wrest the scepter from your hands. You know that we are powerless to do that, for you have ensured our incapacity to fight in open and honorable battle. Bravery on the battlefield is

thus impossible for us. Bravery of the soul still remains open to us ... I know you will respond to that also. I am engaged in evoking that bravery.[60]

Du Bois identified Gandhi's "declaration of Indian independence" as one of the most important events of his times. And Marcus Garvey, the Jamaican Pan-African leader, spoke of Gandhi in 1922 as "one of the noblest characters of the day."[61] Later on, Martin Luther King, in the context of the Civil Rights struggle in the 1950s and 1960s, famously looked toward Gandhi's civil-disobedience campaigns for direct inspiration.[62]

Léopold Senghor, poet, theorist, and the first president of Senegal, drew inspiration from Gandhi's focus on freeing the collective spirit of a people. If Gandhi wished to "Indianize" people in South Asia regardless of religious community, then Senghor argued for "Negritude" as an inclusive identity of African-descended peoples.[63] And Kwame Nkrumah, trained as a theologian and one day to become the first prime minister of Ghana, also appealed to the authority of M. K. Gandhi in articulating his "positive action" campaign of anti-colonial nationalism in the 1950s. "The weapons were legitimate political agitation, newspaper and educational campaigns and, as a last resort, the constitutional application of strikes, boycotts and non-cooperation based on the principle of absolute non-violence, as used by Gandhi in India," Nkrumah wrote.[64] Gandhian anti-imperialist idioms reverberated through Black and Pan-Africanist thought from the 1920s, through the Civil Rights Movement, and on to the South African freedom struggle led by Nelson Mandela.[65]

Changing the Subject

Gandhi's approaches hailed from a patently twentieth-century, colony-centric, perspective, and a concern to define oppression and freedom in new ways. We might think of the new anti-imperialism that emerged during this interregnum, 1898–1930, as a fundamental change of subject. If metropolitan thinkers (e.g., Hobson, Schumpeter, and Lenin) launched a socio-economic critique of

---

60 Mohandas K. Gandhi, "An Open Letter from Gandhi," *Young India*, October 10, 1920, in *The Collected Works of Mahatma Gandhi*, 100 vols. (New Delhi: Publications Division, Government of India, 1958), vol. XXI, 385–387.
61 Nico Slate, *Colored Cosmopolitanism: The Shared Struggle for Freedom in the United States and India* (Cambridge: Harvard University Press, 2012), 51.
62 Sudarshan Kapur, *Raising Up a Prophet: The African-American Encounter with Gandhi* (Boston: Beacon Press, 1992), 41–71.
63 Léopold Sédar Senghor, *Négritude et humanisme* (Paris: Éditions du Seuil, 1964).
64 Kwame Nkrumah, *The Autobiography of Kwame Nkrumah* (London: Thomas Nelson and Sons, 1957), 112.
65 Ramin Jahanbegloo, *The Gandhian Moment* (Cambridge: Harvard University Press, 2013).

imperialism from socialist, liberal, and communist vantage points at the turn of the twentieth century, there also was a distinctive *colonial* vantage point that changed the very subjects at issue in anti-imperialist discourse. Instead of focusing on the motives of the imperial lords, new anti-imperialist thinkers such as M. K. Gandhi emphasized what it was like to be a racialized and colonized subject, and the tactics and strategies needed to free colonized people from the interlinked psychic, cultural, and material effects of imperial oppression. Instead of believing that legal petitions and pleas alone would suffice, Gandhi combined them with campaigns concerning culture and labor, namely the psycho-affective and the materialist-productive. Like the other anti-imperialist theorists from across the colonial world of the same generation such as the Ali brothers, Kamaladevi Chattopadhyay, Muhammad Iqbal, W. E. B. Du Bois, Zora Neale Hurston, Martin Luther King, and Kwame Nkrumah, he pursued a practical theory of freedom in which person, body, and spirit were addressed.

A key outcome of this new 'anti-imperialism' was to make the colonized the subjects of their own history; intelligible historical agents for themselves. Gandhi positioned Indians in the narrative of the end of empire. Instead of being spoken for, Gandhi instead insisted that colonized subjects speak out about the meaning of freedom; and express their culturally situated vision of what it's like to be free. Anti-imperialism, for the colonized during the global interregnum, was primarily a struggle to become fully-fledged subjects of history, agents in the ending of their own oppression.

A change in historical epochs is marked by a break in the way historical actors speak about their worlds – a break in the use of keywords. We study the interregnums of history to glimpse the kinetic social and intellectual energy that they unleash, before a steady state solidifies under the pressure of a new hegemonic order. Gandhi's anti-colonial praxis represents the discharge and freeing up of kinetic energy in the history of twentieth-century ideas, in a turbulent moment of transition.

12

Late Modern Feminist Subversions: Sex, Subjectivity, and Embodiment

SANDRINE SANOS

The story of late modern feminist thought is not a story of waves or turns that succeed one another. Feminist thought does not follow a simple linear temporality, even if we often tend to tell the story that way. Building on intellectual feminist traditions as well as engaging with their historical moment, feminist thinkers follow a more complicated periodization. As the incarnation of a long feminist tradition, post-1968 feminism holds an especially important place in the story of late modern Europe and its intellectual and political revolutions, though that place is often seen to be historically past, even antiquated. It has been conventionally named as belonging to the "second wave," making claims to demands beyond the right to vote. A more fruitful framework, however, would be to think of late-twentieth-century feminist thought emerging out of overlaps, echoes, and legacies that often coexisted in the same moment. It both reflected and subverted the conventions and norms of its time, while maintaining its transgressive and utopian orientation. At the heart of feminist projects lay the imperative to theorize and wrestle with the category of "woman" and how it had been given meaning through time and in culture.

Whatever the temporality assigned to feminist thought, one name that immediately comes to mind in these histories is that of Simone de Beauvoir. She was already known as both author and philosopher when she received the prestigious French Goncourt literary prize for her 1954 novel *The Mandarins*. Six years earlier, she had published a two-volume philosophical analysis of female consciousness and of the social world that always marked women as other, titled *The Second Sex*. It caused uproar, shocking many. Though considered a pioneer, Beauvoir was far from alone in writing then about women, sex, and female subjectivity. In 1957, Assia Djebar published her first novel, *The Mischief*, while the Algerian War of Independence was raging. Djebar had been the first Algerian woman to be admitted at the prestigious École Nationale Supérieure in Sèvres. Just as

Beauvoir had subverted philosophy from within, Djebar challenged the French canon. In her novels, she turned the language of the colonizer, French, against itself to tell the story of women's subjective experiences and imaginaries. Ten years later, Djebar wrote about the generation of the Algerian revolution in *The Naïve Larks*. The aspirations and failures of politics were at the heart of many of these writers' works.

In 1968, another female novelist caused a scandal with a novel fictionalizing the perils of oppression and conformity inflicted upon female minds and bodies. East German author Christa Wolf published *The Quest for Christa T.*, the story of a young woman whose utopian egalitarian yearnings floundered in socialist East Germany. There was no happy ending. Her protagonist ultimately dies of cancer. Like Beauvoir in *The Woman Destroyed* two years earlier, Wolf wrote about women dissatisfied with their lives whose bodies failed them. Such novels mattered because, as Wolf wrote, these were stories of lives that might otherwise go unnoticed. She wrote "against [them] being forgotten."[1] Djebar, too, wrote about women whose voices had been forgotten and whose lives had been erased from history. In her 1980 *Women of Algiers in Their Apartment*, Djebar turned to Eugène Delacroix's famous orientalist painting to tell tales of Algerian women as subjects rather than objects of (western) desire. In 1983, Wolf published *Kassandra*, a feminist parable. Djebar's 1985 *Fantasia, an Algerian Cavalcade*, rewrote Algerian history, revealing the temporal, spatial, and bodily dislocation unleashed by French imperialism. Both Wolf and Djebar subverted literary form in the service of their feminist writing.

Despite their chronological overlaps over two decades, these three authors did not cross paths. They nonetheless had one thing in common: Their works offered a relentless exploration of the realities of the female subject in the world, her embodied experience, and the ways society held women to be different, inferior, and other. They did not always name themselves as feminist, although all three have become iconic references in feminist thought since. Their place in this canon illustrates the complicated ways in which late modern feminism has structured itself in a tension between individual and collective voice and in experiments with the ways to theorize the experience of subjection, subordination, and oppression. For these authors, feminist politics meant engaging with the idea, experience, and

---

[1] Christa Wolf, *The Quest for Christa T.*, trans. Christopher Middleton (New York: Farrar, Strauss & Giroux, 1979).

politics of writing. Sex, the body, language, and lived experience have been at the heart of modern feminist thought's preoccupations.

Genealogies of Modern Feminisms

Modern feminism is hardly a homogeneous, "continuous," and linear intellectual tradition, even if it has relied on the "retrospective identification" of feminist ancestry.[2] Its origins have been traced to a variety of 'pioneering' works conceived as a response to a masculine tradition that erased women. Its authors wrote themselves into the genre that had shaped the intellectual canon, echoing, mirroring, and subverting the language of politics and history. One early example is that of the late medieval author Christine de Pisan whose 1405 *Book of the City of Ladies* imagined a city where women were both prominent and celebrated. Her work clearly offered an alternative to Plutarch's *Lives*, this time written from a female perspective. Pisan used allegory to argue against the prejudices erasing women and to praise the honorable and virtuous women who should be remembered.

Searching for origins has led others to eighteenth-century figures who wrote treatises, essays, and polemics of the kinds that came to mark the Enlightenment era. In *A Vindication of the Rights of Women*, published in 1792, the British political author Mary Wollstonecraft wrote her own political and philosophical treatise on the "Woman Question." She denounced the widely shared belief that reduced women to emotion and irrationality. Instead, they were "rational creatures" debased by lack of freedom and education.[3] In fact, "Many are the causes that, in the present corrupt state of society, contribute to enslave women by cramping their understandings and sharpening their senses."[4] She explained that, "if women are to be excluded, without having a voice, from a participation of the natural rights of mankind," this would mean only "tyranny" that would "ever undermine morality."[5]

Like Wollstonecraft, the French author Olympe de Gouges criticized philosopher Jean-Jacques Rousseau whose political theory relied upon the firmly held conviction that only men must be educated (to become citizens) since women were emotional creatures best suited for the domestic and the

---

2 Joan W. Scott, "Fantasy Echo: History and the Construction of Identity," *Critical Inquiry*, 27(2) (Winter 2001), 284–304, pp. 286 and 287.
3 Mary Wollstonecraft, *A Vindication of the Rights of Woman*, ed. Eileen Hunt Bottig (New Haven: Yale University Press, 2014), 31.
4 Wollstonecraft, *A Vindication of the Rights of Woman*, 48.
5 Wollstonecraft, *A Vindication of the Rights of Woman*, 23.

familial. In 1791, as a slave revolution engulfed the French colony of Saint-Domingue, de Gouges denounced tyranny, just as she had denounced slavery. Now, she wrote the *Declaration of the Rights of Woman and the (Female) Citizen*, a clear subversion of the foundational document of the 1789 French Revolution. She revealed its universalism to be an illusion and called for women's rights to education and citizenship. For her, "A woman has the right to mount the scaffold. She must equally possess the right to mount the speaker's platform."[6]

Modern feminists called for emancipation and equality in political and social action as well as in their writing. Their efforts were both individual and collective. In an age of anxiety in the face of rapid social change, modernization, and imperialism, reform became the order of the day. Suffrage was paramount for most European feminists in the nineteenth century and early twentieth century. French republican Hubertine Auclert argued that gender was irrelevant to citizenship, while British leader of the women's suffrage movement Emmeline Pankhurst believed only activism would force the state to recognize women's rights. They called for an end to their disenfranchisement. They also called for access to education. Reform was never just political but always also "moral reform."

These campaigns were shaped by the politics of sex in the age of capitalism. Marriage-law reform and prostitution were urgent issues. Sex was on people's minds as it spoke to the very nature of the relation between self and social. In the age of sexology, psychoanalysis, eugenics, and Social Darwinism, feminists turned sex into a political and sometimes ethical question. Swedish activist Ellen Kay published a manifesto in 1905, *Love and Marriage*, that called for the "deregulation of sexual relations as the key to a human future," since reformers should recognize the "life-enhancing use of the sexual powers both for the individual and for the race."[7] She was not alone. Her work was translated into German and eagerly debated by German reformers who came to recognize that "sexuality was somehow constitutive of the moral subject."[8] A prolific writer and one of the first German women to receive a doctorate, Helene Stöcker argued for "sexual liberation." She founded the *League for the Protection of Mothers* in 1905, which called for

---

6 Cited in Joan W. Scott, *Only Paradoxes to Offer: French Feminists and the Rights of Man* (Cambridge: Harvard University Press, 1996), 42.
7 Tracie Matysik, *Reforming the Moral Subject: Ethics and Sexuality in Central Europe, 1890–1930* (Ithaca: Cornell University Press, 2008), 1.
8 Matysik, *Reforming the Moral Subject*, 6.

reproductive and sexual rights for women.⁹ Like the writer and politician Lily Braun, she advocated for the autonomy of the female subject

Sexual emancipation, however, could have different meanings. For the German writer and activist Bertha Pappenheim, founder of the remarkably successful League of Jewish Women, equality and emancipation should prevail. She had translated Wollstonecraft's *Vindication* into German and wrote her own play, *Women's Rights*, in 1899. But, at the same time, she "believed in the sacredness of the family and insisted that every woman fulfill her responsibilities as wife and mother first."¹⁰ For these thinkers, motherhood posed the question of sexuality, reproduction, morality, and bodily and political autonomy. French utopian socialist feminist Jeanne Deroin argued in the late 1840s that women's capacity for motherhood meant that "childbearers are rights-bearers according to prevailing moral and political criteria."¹¹ German socialist Lily Braun believed "feminine sexuality" to be synonymous with "maternity."¹² Socialist and Marxist feminists, such as German theorist Clara Zetkin, especially criticized the ways the family, property, and work enslaved women.

Feminists also negotiated multiple contexts bearing upon women's experience and looked beyond their national borders. Pappenheim was keenly aware of the constraints placed upon her as a German Jewish woman, simultaneously, "urg[ing] German-Jewish women to mobilize their womanly virtues in the service of the Gemeinde and apply[ing] German feminism to the situation of Jewish women."¹³ She wrote about the fate of Jewish girls in Eastern Europe, especially "prostitution and white slavery in Eastern Europe and the Middle East."¹⁴ That "turn to the East" characterized many feminists, who were often convinced that "woman [was the] savior of the nation, race, and empire."¹⁵ Eager to "save" their "Eastern" and African sisters, British and French feminists claimed that imperial work would prove the necessity of female emancipation.

While most European feminist movements floundered after the end of World War I (feminist activists turned to pacifism and suffrage was granted in most European nations), others began exploring the ways sex and gender

---

9 Matysik, *Reforming the Moral Subject*, 55–91.
10 Marion Kaplan, *The Jewish Feminist Movement in Germany: The Campaigns of the Jüdischer Frauenbund, 1904–1938* (Westport: Connecticut Press, 1979), 40.
11 Scott, *Only Paradoxes to Offer*, 71.   12 Matysik, *Reforming the Moral Subject*, 209.
13 Kaplan, *The Jewish Feminist Movement in Germany*, 12.
14 Kaplan, *The Jewish Feminist Movement in Germany*, 43.
15 Antoinette Burton, *Burdens of History: British Feminists, Indian Women, and Imperial Culture, 1865–1915* (Chapel Hill: University of North Carolina Press, 1994), 3.

shaped the self and its relation to the social. The politics of sex inspired a sustained interrogation and reflection on the nature of femininity. Psychoanalysis proved especially productive for thinking about the nature of female sexuality, consciousness, and femininity. While Lou Andreas-Salomé theorized narcissism and "objectless love," Karen Horney challenged Freud's elaboration of a feminine development harnessed to the masculine. She refuted that masochism characterized the female psyche and insisted upon "look[ing] not for biological reasons but cultural" and historical reasons for women's sense of inferiority.[16] She called for the recognition of female sexual pleasure, though, like others before her, she ultimately equated femininity with maternity. These discussions over sex, embodiment, and freedom continued throughout the century.

But to look for modern feminist thought requires exploring the ways in which the experience and practice of writing constituted a means of mapping out a (feminist) self and remaking the world. Whether it meant reinventing the very nature of language, the imaginative translation of lived experience, or the exploration of female subjectivity, feminist thought took many different forms. Experiments in genre especially characterized twentieth-century feminist thought. Virginia Woolf explored these themes both in essay form (such as her 1929 *A Room of One's Own*) and in fiction. She published her last novel, *The Years*, in 1937. This exploration of temporality, family, and place focused on the ways in which the social arrangement of the sexes shaped these individual characters' lives. Fiction was a privileged site for feminist theorization. Literature especially allowed the imaginative and utopian force of such thought, in ways that philosophy and political essay did not always permit. As Beauvoir wrote years later, "literature emerges when something in life has become unhinged ... The first condition is to realize that reality is not a self-evident and transparent thing, only then are we able to perceive it and bring it to life for others to see."[17]

In contrast to earlier in the twentieth century, late-modern feminist authors did not just seek reform or emancipation, nor did they just respond to the canon of political and intellectual thought. They refused the very terms according to which the modern Western canon of philosophy, literature, and knowledge had been made. This task appeared especially urgent since most European thinkers had found themselves challenged by the devastating

---

16 Karen Horney, "Feminine Psychology," in Karen Horney, *New Ways in Psychoanalysis* (New York: W. A. Norton, 1939), 113. On the "femininity debates," see Matysik, *Reforming the Moral Subject*, 218–252.
17 Simone de Beauvoir, *The Prime of Life* (New York: World, 1962), 290.

experience of World War II and the decolonization movements that came in its wake. Post-1945 feminist thought focused especially on the feminist subversions of (social, cultural, and even epistemological) norms, analyzing how oppression took different (systemic) forms, and revealing how "common sense" often obscured the work of subordination. It no longer took the category of "women" to be a self-evident one.[18] It questioned what it meant to be a (female) subject, recoding the very ways in which language provided meaning to culture and society. It shaped and coexisted with one of the largest political movements of the late twentieth century, though it was not always synonymous with it. Unlike some of the activists and thinkers of the early twentieth century, its framework was secular. The paradox that had structured feminist thought – the need to both accept and refuse "sexual difference" to make claims on the behalf of "women" – continued haunting these late-modern thinkers.[19]

Within this European history, French feminist thought holds an important place. Because it was shaped in the crucible of a political culture firmly rooted in a universalist ideology of inalienable rights and individual freedom, it has been especially influential. Beauvoir's *Second Sex* inspired many radical feminist writers and activists around the world. In the decades after May '68, other French writers were widely read (and translated) beyond French borders. (Though that has led, at times, to a truncated vision of "French feminism" from afar.[20]) At the same time, it was a body of thought that emerged in transnational and transatlantic conversations, irrigated by other political modes of thinking over questions of race, power, and inequality.[21] Strikingly, a number of these thinkers – beginning with Beauvoir herself – had found inspiration in writings about racism, colonialism, and critiques of capitalism elsewhere. These conversations and exchanges proved a fertile ground for a feminist thought that aimed to go beyond the political as the realm of rights, law, and citizenship.

---

18 On this, see Denise Riley, *Am I That Name? Feminism and the Category of "Women" in History* (Minneapolis: University of Minnesota Press, 1994).
19 Scott, *Only Paradoxes to Offer*, 3–4.
20 As is the case for the Anglo-American vision of "French feminism." On this, see Claire Moses Goldberg, "Made in America: 'French Feminism' in Academia," *Feminist Studies*, 24(2) (Summer 1998), 241–274; and Anne Emmanuelle Berger and Éric Fassin (eds.), special issue "Transatlantic Gender Crossings," *Differences: A Journal of Feminist Cultural Studies*, 27(2) (September 2016).
21 Feminist thought has always been transnational as it emphasized theorizing the (universalist) female subject across imperial and post-imperial borders. See, for instance, Lucy Delap, *The Feminist Avant-Garde: Transatlantic Encounters of the Early Twentieth Century* (New York: Cambridge University Press, 2007).

Postwar Writings: Beauvoir and *The Second Sex*

In the story of late-modern feminism, Beauvoir's work looms large (even if her iconic presence often obscures as much as it reveals).[22] The paradox of the public's identification of Beauvoir with feminism is that she claimed the name only when she joined the political movement that emerged in the wake of May '68. Beauvoir had tackled many of these feminist issues throughout her entire work as philosopher and novelist. Her 1949 two-volume *The Second Sex* was, in fact, the culmination of a long philosophical exploration of the question of being, subjectivity, autonomy, and freedom. Beauvoir's existential phenomenology shaped her reflections on the question of women, a topic that she had disingenuously said she had not thought much about.[23] Beauvoir's first collection of stories, which was rejected by publishers, focused on young female characters and how they were trapped and oppressed by the confining strictures of bourgeois Catholic France. In this early work and her subsequent fiction, she explored the meaning of living one's life in "bad faith," in relation to oneself and to others, and of one's embodied experience.

Beauvoir's works asked how one could emancipate oneself and achieve freedom beyond mere political rights – a question many feminists had posed before her. These were not merely abstract considerations for her and her philosophical companion, Jean-Paul Sartre. Both sought to devise a political and philosophical thought that refused, on the one hand, Marxism and its materialist emphasis and, on the other, Christianity and its theological framework. Instead, Sartre declared in 1945 that "existence comes before essence" because "man is nothing other than what he makes of himself."[24] As Beauvoir explained, existentialism "defined man through his or her actions."[25] This, however, was not solely an individual endeavor since human beings lived in the world with one another. Individuals were therefore bound by their responsibility to one another. Beauvoir conceived of that relationship as a secular one in contrast to a Christian vision of the social. The experience of World War II and of the Nazi occupation had convinced Beauvoir and

---

22 For a brief overview, see Nathalie Debrauwere-Miller, "Parcours historique des féminismes intellectuels en France depuis Beauvoir," *Contemporary French Civilization*, 38(1) (2013), 23–46.
23 On this, see Wendy O'Brien and Lester Embree (eds.), *The Existential Phenomenology of Simone de Beauvoir* (Boston: Kluwer Academic Publishers, 2001).
24 Jean-Paul Sartre, *Existentialism Is a Humanism* (New Haven: Yale University Press, 2007), 20 and 22.
25 Simone de Beauvoir, *The Force of Circumstance* (New York: Putnam's, 1964), 8. For an overview of existentialism, see Edward Baring's Chapter 5 on existentialism.

Sartre of the necessity of such a philosophical and political project. Beauvoir dramatized these insights in a 1945 novel, *The Blood of Others*, whose female protagonist freed herself from the conformism of her selfish life in wartime France by turning herself outward. That realization and her acting upon it led, in the novel, to her death.

Freedom was not easily achieved. If one's existence was necessarily bound up with that of others, how did each individual realize their freedom against the pressure imposed by society and the world? That dilemma had been the focus of her 1947 essay *The Ethics of Ambiguity*. Beauvoir examined childhood in order to theorize the conditions for (true) freedom. How does one choose to act if so much is beyond one's control? Overcoming one's "situated" freedom was necessary yet demanded abandoning all illusions regarding one's experience and alienation. One's experience of the world was always embodied and therefore shaped one's consciousness. Ultimately, freedom was ambiguous because it required struggle to attain it. (Her emphasis on the ambiguity of one's life and the ambivalence of one's condition unsurprisingly echoed the reflections of interwar thinkers.) These considerations came together when Beauvoir began *The Second Sex*.

Beauvoir began by asking why women had always been made secondary, anecdotal, and invisible in the social, political, and cultural world. She insisted there was something particular about the condition of women and set out to distinguish women's experience from that of "blacks, Jews, and workers," who, like women, were deemed different and inferior and subject to "myths": the "myth of an eternal feminine, of a black soul, and a Jewish character."[26] Women, however, Beauvoir explained, were neither a minority (numerically) nor a separate group with its own "past, history, religion." Instead, women were both invisible and always "the Other" in a world where "man" was a "subject."[27] How did that epistemological construction come about, and how had that shaped the experience and consciousness of female beings? Such was the question that Beauvoir posed at the outset of her philosophical treatise. She answered it in the opening of her second volume with the now canonical phrase: "one is not a woman, one becomes a woman."[28]

Beauvoir set out to undo the familiar opposition between nature and culture that haunted much of philosophy. She pointed out that "Man seeks the Other in woman as Nature and as his peer. But Nature inspires

---

26 Simone de Beauvoir, *The Second Sex* (New York: Alfred A. Knopf, 2010), 4.
27 Beauvoir, *The Second Sex*, 8 and 10.   28 Beauvoir, *The Second Sex*, 283.

ambivalent feelings in man" even as he needs definition through "the Other."[29] She demonstrated instead that there was nothing 'natural' about sexual difference, femininity, and gender roles (though she did not use the now familiar distinction between sex and gender, or the term 'gender'). Indeed, "No biological, psychic, or economic destiny defines the figure that the human female takes on in society; it is civilization as a whole that elaborates this intermediary product between the male and the eunuch that is called feminine."[30] She examined biology and anatomy to illuminate how cells and bodies were not gendered but ultimately given a sex through culture and history. After all, the human "body is not a thing but a situation," that is "subjected to taboos" and "laws."[31] The body did not exist outside of the social. Laws and cultural beliefs were made by societies and had been solidified through history. Sexual difference had no pre-existing meaning but had been turned into a hierarchical relationship between men, who were Subject, and women, who were Other. She explained that "history had shown that men have always held all the concrete powers" and had organized women's dependence.[32] That dependence and secondary status had been naturalized through "myths" expressed in culture and literature. These myths (of women as mysterious, dangerous, incapable of reason, emotional) relied on a series of impossible choices for women (irrational or all-knowing, motherly or narcissistic, whore or virgin). Women could never exist independently of men.

Beauvoir's phenomenological orientation allowed her to highlight how the "myths of femininity" shaped women's own experience of their bodies and their sexuality. Menstruating bodies were shameful, sex was a source of anxiety for teenage girls and young women, and women existed only as objects of desire for men. Female sexual pleasure was always somewhat forbidden because, while men have a "right to relieve [their] sexual desire," women were confined to chastity or to conjugal sex.[33] It was also always to be feared for it meant uncontrollable reproduction – except, Beauvoir pointed out, for lesbians.[34] Out of these myths, only marriage and motherhood were available for women, making autonomy and emancipation difficult, even impossible. Domestic conjugality implied invisible and unpaid labor naturalized as women's destiny. Motherhood was expected and imposed, essentialized as "instinct."[35] Most troublingly, Beauvoir showed, women

---

29 Beauvoir, *The Second Sex*, 163. 30 Beauvoir, *The Second Sex*, 283.
31 Beauvoir, *The Second Sex*, 46, 47. 32 Beauvoir, *The Second Sex*, 159.
33 Beauvoir, *The Second Sex*, 386. 34 Beauvoir, *The Second Sex*, 417–436.
35 Beauvoir, *The Second Sex*, 533 and 539.

themselves were complicit and participated in their own subordination, as she had dramatized in her own novels.

The publication of *The Second Sex* did not signal the end of Beauvoir's analysis of the centrality of sexual difference and gender to the organization of the world and to the ways in which women were still the "Other." In the following decades, she denounced the gendered nature of state violence against bodies during the Algerian War of Independence and looked to socialist regimes for the eradication of the sexed division of labor and the end of the regime of domesticity that trapped women. She refused to call her own existential phenomenology a feminist philosophy until the early 1970s when, she explained, she realized only feminism, as a political movement, could translate and bring to life the insights of feminist thought.

In many ways, Beauvoir's intellectual legacy endured in the work of feminists who came of age during the 1968 revolutions. A series of common themes characterized their work: the interrogation of the relation between the self and the social, how the meaning given to sexual difference organized power and marked bodies, and how women as embodied subjects were relegated to a secondary position in a system that organizes these relations and identities. These theorists and writers have traditionally been identified as *equality* ("universalist" or "materialist") or *difference* ("differentialist") feminists. (Although this binary opposition has erased the echoes and commonalities that existed between them.) While their aim was the same – to denounce the manner in which patriarchy constituted the world, and demonstrate that it needed to be undone – their modes of analysis of the social tackled the question of gender, sex, and sexuality differently and disagreed "about what difference is and what difference makes."[36] Their analyses fell into two main conceptual orientations: one was rooted in explaining and undoing the production of female subordination and domination to map out the conditions of true emancipation; the other was intent on rescuing sexual difference from its hierarchical meaning in order to reinvent female subjectivity.

Materialist Feminism: Power, Subjection, and Freedom

While political action inaugurated their feminist work, materialist feminists sought to bring about, in the words of Monique Wittig, an "epistemological

---

[36] Kelly Oliver "French Feminism in an American Context," in Kelly Oliver (ed.), *French Feminism Reader* (Oxford: Rowman & Littlefield, 2000), ix.

revolution."[37] They offered an analysis of the operations of patriarchy, focusing on the ideological work of sex, race, and class in radical and new ways. For them, scholarly knowledge production could best denaturalize the world around them. Most were academically trained. Both Christine Delphy and Colette Guillaumin were sociologists, while Nicole-Claude Mathieu was an anthropologist. (Despite their theoretical importance, Guillaumin and Mathieu have been neglected in Anglo-American scholarship.) This was not surprising, as sociology in late-1960s and early-1970s France was one of the most subversive academic and scientific fields, with its practitioners interrogating power.[38] Delphy, Guillaumin, Mathieu, and a few others therefore founded the academic and political journal *Feminist Questions* in 1977. Beauvoir was chief editor (in practice, she only lent her name), signaling her commitment and the journal's orientation. The journal offered rigorous, academically oriented analyses of the present. While neither polemical or activist, it was clearly committed to a thought that was both political and theoretical, and it became the platform for materialist feminist thought.[39]

Like Beauvoir, Christine Delphy was critical of Marxist historical materialism and, instead, sought to reinvent it.[40] A feminist analysis required taking seriously the "materiality of ideology" while subverting the common sense of Marxist politics.[41] Because Marxism saw class as the fundamental category of alienation, the working class remained an ungendered category. For Delphy, however, capitalism and patriarchy were imbricated systems of domination. She called for a focus on the ideological and material operations of patriarchy, understood to be an autonomous system of exploitation and domination of women by men. Beginning from "the postulate that the way in which life is materially produced and reproduced is the basis for the organization of all societies," Delphy argued that the family was not a "private" and natural social form but an "economic system" participating in relations of production.[42] The sexual division of labor was not a natural fact later

---

37 Monique Wittig, *The Straight Mind* (Boston: Beacon Press, 1992), xvii.
38 See Judith Surkis, *Sexing the Citizen: Morality and Masculinity in France* (Ithaca: Cornell University Press, 2006).
39 The *Questions Féministes* collective split in 1980. It inspired the American journal *Feminist Questions* (in which Wittig was involved) and re-emerged under the name *Nouvelles Questions Féministes*, lasting to this day.
40 In her, now classic, "The Main Enemy" ("L'ennemi principal"), published in 1970 in the French *Partisans* magazine and later translated into English by the British Women's Research and Resources Centre in 1977.
41 Christine Delphy, "A Materialist Feminism Is Possible," trans. Diana Leonard, *Feminist Review*, 4(1) (1980), 79–105, p. 97.
42 Delphy, "A Materialist Feminism Is Possible," 87.

appropriated by capitalism. Despite being rendered invisible by Marxist theory and politics, the "domestic mode of production" was central to capitalism.[43]

This materialist feminist thought emerged in part out of the American context of the post-slavery civil rights movement: Delphy had spent a year at UC-Berkeley and worked with the civil rights movement, Wittig was in conversation with American feminists, and Guillaumin turned to American sociology in the service of her own thinking.[44] In many of these works, as had been the case in eighteenth-century feminist writings, slavery was the most commonly cited comparison and historical antecedent these thinkers invoked. Already Beauvoir, influenced by the work of her friend, novelist Richard Wright, on race and racism, had looked to the United States to reflect upon the ways certain categories of people were marked as different in their bodies. This was not mere analogy, however. For these feminists, analyzing patriarchy, capitalism, and oppression was made possible by thinking about the ways in which the social facts of race and sex/gender were naturalized and ideologically organized.

The "idea of race" structured Colette Guillaumin's thinking about the work of difference on bodies and of the ideological effects of subordination upon individuals.[45] She extended Delphy's analysis by examining how the organization of labor required the organization of bodies and the naturalization of division into a hierarchy. Moving beyond Beauvoir's analogy between "women, black, and Jews," she analyzed how these categories of meaning were made and how they structured the social. As she explained, "The invention of the idea of nature cannot be separated from domination and the appropriation of human beings."[46] Guillaumin refused to distinguish between the material and mental forms the operation of power took. She examined the ways in which "race" was a "heterogeneous intellectual formulation" that was more than a "material phenomenon." Its aim was to

---

43 For a summary of Delphy's work, see Doris Rita Alphonso, "Christine Delphy: Sex and Gender; Introduction," in Kelly Oliver (ed.), *French Feminism Reader* (Oxford: Rowman & Littlefield, 2000), 59–60.

44 For instance, Delphy debated British feminist thinkers such as sociologist Ann Oakley, writer Juliet Mitchell, and other feminist socialists. This was a Western-oriented transnational thought that, before the late 1990s, did not engage with the aftereffects of colonialism or with non-Western feminist theorizing.

45 Guillaumin's first book theorized the work of racism, Colette Guillaumin, *L'idéologie raciste* (La Haye: Mouton, 1972); while her second was a collection of essays written between 1970 and 1980, Colette Guillaumin, *Sexe, race et pratique du pouvoir* (Paris: Côté-femmes, 1992).

46 Colette Guillaumin, "Race and Nature: The System of Marks," (1977) in Kelly Oliver (ed.), *French Feminism Reader* (Oxford: Rowman & Littlefield, 2000), 97.

produce "a group perceived as natural, a group of people considered as materially specific to their bodies."[47] This is how, she argued, racism "produced the category of race," which was then essentialized just as sex and gender were: "Colonization by appropriation of people (traffic in slaves, later in laborers)" and "territories" was identical to the "appropriation of the bodies of women."[48] The production of individuals through the mark of difference was always a system of hierarchical meaning and power. Ultimately, for Guillaumin, this led to *sexage*. She coined this term in reference both to slavery (*esclavage*) and to serfdom (*servage*) to capture this historical and totalizing system of appropriation of women's bodies that constituted them as individuals and as a subordinated group.

Guillaumin was not alone in denaturalizing the categories of sex and race and how they marked bodies. Working at the intersection of sociology and anthropology, theorist Nicole-Claude Mathieu shared the belief that embodiment is always political.[49] She offered an equally rigorous and theoretically ambitious analysis of the ways "sex" structured social relations and organized women into an essentialized class of subordinated individuals.[50] Mathieu took inspiration from Hegel, and especially turned to Marcel Mauss's analysis of the ways the social shaped consciousness and the self to reflect upon the role of sexual difference in societies.[51] Like Beauvoir before them, Mathieu began by positing that "the invisibility of male social actors as a gendered group (that is defined within and by the economic, legal, reproductive relations they have with another gendered group: women) has depended (and still depends) upon the invisibility of

47 Guillaumin, "Race and Nature," 81–82.
48 Doris Rita Alphonso, "Introduction: Colette Guillaumin," in Kelly Oliver (ed.), *French Feminism Reader* (Oxford: Rowman & Littlefield, 2000), 77; and Guillaumin, "Race and Nature," 84.
49 Nicole-Claude Mathieu, *L'anatomie politique: Catégorisations et idéologies de sexe* (Paris: Côté-femmes, 1991). My translation. Although Mathieu was a foundational figure of materialist feminist thought and one of its most committed theoreticians, her work has not been translated and is usually left out of French and other feminist readers and collections.
50 Materialist feminists did not use the term "gender" that came into common use in the Anglo-American world in the 1980s. Their use of "sex" denotes both sex and gender. Their radically anti-essentialist position means that they refused to use "gender" since they held that it carried within it an artificial difference between anatomical sex and socially constructed gender. On this, see Delphy, "Rethinking Sex and Gender," in Kelly Oliver (ed.), *French Feminism Reader* (Oxford: Rowman & Littlefield, 2000), 63–76.
51 For an overview of Mathieu's work, see Natacha Chetcuti-Osorovitz and Martine Gestin, "La notion de personne sexuée dans l'œuvre de Nicole-Claude Mathieu," in *Penser "L'arraisonnement des femmes," vivre en résistance, Nicole-Claude Mathieu (1937–2014)*, ed. Dominique Bourque and Johanne Coulomb (Montreal: Les éditions sans fin, 2017), 119–134.

women as social actors."[52] Revealing that women were imagined as a gendered "class" of individuals only in relation to another – men – required that gender relations should be understood for what they were, namely a relationship of domination and subordination. She explained that any theorization should analyze the affiliation of "the thought of sex" (*sexe pensé*), which concerns representations and myths, with the "agency of sex" (*sexe agi*), which concerns social relations of genders. Because of this, women's identity emerged as the result of the imbrication of (individual) "sexual identity" (*identité sexuelle*), (collective) "sexed identity" (*identité sexuée*), and the "identity of sex" (*identité de sexe*), which spoke to the fact that women existed as a "class."[53]

Undoing subordination meant understanding how those who belong to an oppressed group negotiate the constraints and paradoxical injunctions they were subjected to. She explained that "to surrender is not to consent" (*céder n'est pas consentir*) – which became a widely shared feminist slogan. She insisted that nonetheless oppression did not preclude the possibility of resistance.[54] Disentangling these configurations was, for Mathieu, at the heart of any epistemological challenge to relations of power and the essentialist ordering of bodies in a society. In turn, "imagination and knowledge" were needed. As Delphy summed up, "To construct another future we obviously need an analysis of the present, but what is less recognized is that having an Utopian vision is one of the indispensable staging posts in the scientific process – in *all* scientific work."[55]

Psychoanalytic Feminism: Language, Sex, and Subjectivity

In contrast to materialist feminism, the authors who became associated with the intellectual group Psychanalyse et Politique led by Antoinette Fouque gave a different explanation of the operations of patriarchy. They agreed with Delphy, Mathieu, and others that women were constrained and shaped by a patriarchal world. But, they argued, the phallocentric and hierarchical binary system of meaning in which women existed was more than a material and ideological system. For them, a radical revolution required interrogating the work of sexual difference as totalizing mechanism and undoing the subordination of women and of the feminine in culture,

---

52 Mathieu, *L'anatomie politique*, 81. The translations are my own.
53 Mathieu, *L'anatomie politique*, 209–244.   54 Mathieu, *L'anatomie politique*, 121–207.
55 Delphy, "Rethinking Sex and Gender," 74.

language, and signification. Authors such as Luce Irigaray, Julia Kristeva, Hélène Cixous, and Catherine Clément found in psychoanalysis a philosophy of the subject that allowed them to subvert the very foundations of language and subjectivity. Their aim was different than that of the previous generation of female psychoanalysts such as Karen Horney and Joan Riviere, who had theorized the female subject in Freudian and post-Freudian ways. By the mid to late 1960s, the structuralism that had dominated and informed anthropology, linguistics, and philosophy was being radically revised. This intellectual ferment shaped the thought of Irigaray, Kristeva, and Cixous. Like materialist feminists, they sought no less than another epistemological revolution, which they materialized in the very form of their writings. Theirs, however, drew from linguistics, literature, and psychoanalysis.

Turning to Freud, Lacan, and metaphysics rather than Hegel or Marx, these theorists refused both the name and the politics of feminism because, for them, claims to equality did not escape the social world, accepting its assumptions rather than undoing them. Rather than looking at how the body and consciousness were social constructions, they explored how language provided meaning to the facts of nature. For, as philosopher and psychoanalyst Luce Irigaray insisted, "Deconstructing the patriarchal tradition is certainly indispensable but it is hardly enough. It is necessary to define new values directly or indirectly suitable to feminine subjectivity or feminine identity."[56] Irigaray's epistemological project therefore explored the meaning and reinvention of feminine subjectivity. It was an extension to Beauvoir's initial mapping out of 'Woman' as Other in society, discourse, and history. In order to do this, she argued, "we must reinterpret the whole relationship between the subject and discourse, the subject and the world, ... and this subject had always been written in the masculine form."[57] In her 1974 work, *Speculum and the Other Woman*, she explained that the subject was conceptualized through the logic of sameness: "Categories construct the symbolic division between male and female."[58] As a result, women could only be secondary, derivative; and they existed outside of the realm of representation. Irigaray further insisted that, in this "male imaginary," not only was female sexuality "inert" and passive, but

---

56 Luce Irigaray, *Why Different? A Culture of Two Subjects. Interviews with Luce Irigaray* (New York: Semiotext(e), 2000), 10.
57 In Toril Moi, *Sexual/Textual Politics: Feminist Literary Theory* (New York: Routledge, 1985), 119.
58 Margaret Whitford, *Luce Irigaray: Philosophy in the Feminine* (New York: Routledge, 1991), 152.

female subjectivity could not emerge fully and autonomously: "the articulation of my sex is impossible in discourse."[59]

While Beauvoir had offered a form of existentialist feminism, Irigaray aimed to disrupt the very foundations of the philosophical canon and discourse and to challenge Cartesian metaphysics.[60] Rather than eradicate the symbolic division of male and female, Irigaray called for the recognition of "sexual difference [that] would constitute the horizon of worlds more fecund than any known to date – at least in the West – and without reducing fecundity to the reproduction of bodies."[61] Irigaray therefore suggested the reinvention of femininity and the "reuniting" of masculine and feminine, "such that the sexual encounter would be a festive celebration and not a disguised or polemical form of the master–slave relationship."[62] For a "Copernican revolution" to take place, Irigaray argued that binary oppositions should be abandoned in favor of a concept of being that recognized the porosity of the body's borders and reimagined subjectivity from the point of view of the "female sex," focusing on that which lay in between (mucus, membrane) and the "threshold of *the lips*, which are strangers to dichotomies and oppositions."[63] Only then will "each one discover the self in that experience which is inexpressible yet forms the supple grounding of life and language."[64]

Irigaray's poetic evocation of the reinvention of sexual difference echoed Julia Kristeva's psychoanalytic reinterpretation of language and subjectivity. Kristeva's involvement in the *Tel Quel* avant-garde literary movement framed her theoretical interests. She sought to subvert the authoritarian, masculine, and oppressive nature of language, that is to enact a *Revolution in Poetic Language*, as she titled her 1984 work. This revolution required the undoing of the Symbolic realm (structured by the Law of the Father). Refusing the Oedipal structure of the subject-in-making that Freud had theorized and which repressed maternal authority, she argued that the signifying process was fundamentally heterogeneous.[65] Kristeva argued that individuation was

---

59 Luce Irigaray, "This Sex which Is Not One" (1977), in Kelly Oliver (ed.), *French Feminism Reader* (Oxford: Rowman & Littlefield, 2000), 206.
60 Irigaray has been active in feminist campaigns for reproductive rights, and her work is influential in Italy.
61 Luce Irigaray, "The Ethics of Sexual Difference" (1984), in Kelly Oliver (ed.), *French Feminism Reader* (Oxford: Rowman & Littlefield, 2000), 226.
62 Irigaray, "The Ethics of Sexual Difference," 234.
63 Irigaray, "The Ethics of Sexual Difference," 235.
64 Irigaray, "The Ethics of Sexual Difference," 235.
65 Julia Kristeva, "From One Identity to an Other," in Kelly Oliver (ed.), *French Feminism Reader* (Oxford: Rowman & Littlefield, 2000), 158.

a process that required separation, the process of abjection (from the maternal body) that produced the subject. To overcome the "Fear of the archaic mother [which] turns out to be essentially fear of her generative power," signification (and subjectivity) should be anchored in the realm of the pre-Oedipal (prior to castration, that is the Law of the Father): This was the site of the maternal – which she named the *chora*.[66] She called for the restoration of the maternal out of repression. That operation could be best grasped in the realm of the aesthetic (and in certain forms of literary modernism).[67] Kristeva argued for the maternal as the foundation of the social and for the revolutionary possibilities of aesthetics.

Literature provided both the site and the practice of resignification that Hélène Cixous imagined – a project sustained by the creation of the publishing house *Des Femmes* by Antoinette Fouque, for whom publishing meant to "pro-create, give birth to beings of language and life."[68] Like Monique Wittig before her, Cixous had been awarded the prestigious Médicis literary prize, for her first autobiographical novel, *Inside*, in 1969. In 1975, she published, with Catherine Clément, an essay, *The Newly Born*. While Clément put forth the usually derided and marginalized figures of the "hysteric" and the "sorceress" as sites of contradiction replete with potentialities, Cixous pointed to the ways "Thought has always worked through oppositions" that are complementary and hierarchically organized.[69] This "organization by hierarchy makes all conceptual organization subject to man."[70] This is how the question of sexual difference was translated in language. Now, "it has become rather urgent to question this solidarity between logocentrism and phallocentrism" and undo the enduring association of woman with passivity in knowledge.[71] History had been coded masculine, and philosophy has been "constructed on the premise of woman's abasement."[72] This subordination at the level of meaning and language meant that 'woman' "had not been able to live in her 'own' house, her very body." This was an impossible proposition for her especially: as an "Algerian French girl" who

---

66 Julia Kristeva, "From Filth to Defilement," in Kelly Oliver (ed.), *French Feminism Reader* (Oxford: Rowman & Littlefield, 2000), 174.
67 Kristeva's theorization of the aesthetics is exemplified by Julia Kristeva, *The Powers of Horror: An Essay on Abjection* (New York: Columbia University Press, 1982); and Julia Kristeva, *Black Sun: Depression and Melancholy* (New York: Columbia University Press, 1989).
68 Antoinette Fouque (April 1983), in the anniversary brochure *Des Femmes: 1974–1994* (Paris, Des Femmes, 1994), 7.
69 Hélène Cixous, "Sorties: Out and Out: Attacks/Ways Out/Forays," in *The Newly-Born Woman* (Minneapolis: University of Minnesota Press, 2001), 63.
70 Cixous, "Sorties," 64.   71 Cixous, "Sorties," 65.   72 Cixous, "Sorties," 65.

was also Jewish, she had "come, biographically, from a rebellion, from a violent and anguished direct refusal to accept what is happening on the stage on whose edge [she] find[s] [she is] placed."[73] That experience had shown her how "the world is divided in half, organized hierarchically, and that it maintains this distribution through violence."[74] Instead, she called for the undoing of the unified (masculine) subject of Western thought.

Two years after she had founded the Centre de recherches en Études féminines at the newly created university of Paris VIII in Vincennes, Cixous published "The Laugh of the Medusa" (1976), one of her most famous essays. She explained that "Woman must write her self: must write about women and bring women to writing, from which they have been driven away as violently as from their bodies – for the same reasons, by the same law, with the same fatal goal. Woman must put herself into the text – as into the world and into history – by her own movement."[75] To write oneself as woman required recognizing and undoing the hierarchical binaries that structured consciousness and language: "When I say 'woman,' I'm speaking of woman in her inevitable struggle against conventional man; and of a universal woman subject who must bring women to their senses and to their meaning in history."[76] To enact this, Cixous experimented with narrative form, refusing the theoretical and scientific (unlike materialist feminists), privileging the metaphoric, and emphasizing "feminine writing" (*écriture féminine*). Only "feminine writing" would "exceed the discourse governing the phallocentric system."[77] Cixous did as much in her fiction, essays, dialogues, theater, and other literary texts, moving between genres, disciplines, and literary traditions beyond France. Writing was her politics.

Reimaginings and Revolutions

Revolution required imagination and reinvention. Monique Wittig called for a feminist revolution and, like the Psychanalyse et Politique authors, explored subjectivity, language, and female desire, but followed the conceptual frameworks and utopian aims of materialist feminists. Four years after her first prize-winning novel *L'Opoponax*, she translated philosopher Herbert

---

73 Cixous, "Sorties," 70.   74 Cixous, "Sorties," 70.
75 This is the most often cited of her essays, first published in English in Isabelle de Courtivron and Elaine Marks (eds.), *New French Feminisms* (New York: Schocken, 1980). Hélène Cixous, "The Laugh of the Medusa," in Kelly Oliver (ed.), *French Feminism Reader* (Oxford: Rowman & Littlefield, 2000), 257. See also Hélène Cixous, *Le Rire de la Méduse et autres ironies* (Paris: Éditions Galilée, 2010).
76 Cixous, "The Laugh of the Medusa," 258.   77 Cixous, "Sorties," 92.

Marcuse's critique of the forms of social repression that characterized both capitalism and communism, *One-Dimensional Man*. In his essay, Marcuse had explained that the "technological rationality of the totalitarian universe was but the most recent manifestation of the idea of Reason," a historical "evolution" that had shaped the very foundations of the philosophical enterprise.[78] The Marcusian denunciation of the "closed universe" of industrialized civilization and call for "radical refusal" fit perfectly with the May '68 moment.[79] Marcuse and Beauvoir had opened the way for Wittig to begin crafting her revolutionary theories in literature and in theoretical essays.

Like Delphy, Wittig believed that Marxism had failed as a political theory of emancipation. (She had been a member of the original *Feminist Questions* collective.) Because it refused to consider the "subject," it could never recognize the specificity of women's oppression, instead "leaving the relation women/men outside of the social order," naturalizing their alienation and their reproductive role.[80] She was also critical of (Lacanian) psychoanalysis, which, by the 1950s, dominated the French intellectual world.[81] For her, the Structural unconscious also did the work of naturalization, turning "the concept of difference between the sexes" into an ontological operation that "constitute[d] women" as "different/other."[82] In this, she echoed Simone de Beauvoir (who had argued that Marxism had failed because it excluded sex from the social, as had psychoanalysis because it theorized sex without the social), from whom she borrowed the title of her 1981 essay "One Is Not Born a Woman." Like Irigaray and Cixous, she noted that "The primacy of difference so constitutes our thought that it prevents turning inward on itself to question itself," to become "the thought of domination" that kept women enslaved.[83] "Just as there are no slaves without masters, there are no women without men," she stated at the outset of the 1976 article "The Category of Sex." But, for Wittig, the aim was not to reimagine (sexual) difference. She

---

78 Herbert Marcuse, *L'homme unidimensionnel*, trans. Monique Wittig with Herbert Marcuse (Paris: Éditions de Minuit, 1968), 148. My translation.
79 Marcuse, *L'homme unidimensionnel*, 271–281.
80 Monique Wittig, "One Is Not Born a Woman," in Monique Wittig, *The Straight Mind* (Boston: Beacon Press, 1992), 18.
81 See Camille Robcis, *The Law of Kinship: Anthropology, Psychoanalysis, and the Family in France* (Ithaca: Cornell University Press, 2013); and Élisabeth Roudinesco, *Jacques Lacan & Co.: A History of Psychoanalysis in France, 1925–1985* (Chicago: University of Chicago Press, 1990).
82 Monique Wittig, "The Straight Mind," in Monique Wittig, *The Straight Mind* (Boston: Beacon Press, 1992), 29.
83 Monique Wittig, "The Category of Sex," in Monique Wittig, *The Straight Mind* (Boston: Beacon Press, 1992), 2.

wanted to undo the ways sex, gender, and sexuality functioned as political regimes ordering the world and individuals within it.

Wittig showed how "The ideology of sexual difference functions as censorship in our culture by masking on the ground of nature, the social opposition between men and women."[84] That relation created men and women and established the political regime that organized the social and ensured that women were alienated, appropriated, always othered, and trapped by the demands of reproduction, production, and the marriage contract. Wittig's famous pronouncement allowed her to argue that women were an ideological creation – a point Beauvoir had also insisted upon. Unlike Beauvoir, however, who never contested the "naturalness" of heterosexuality and whose chapter on the figure of the lesbian portrayed her as a tragic figure, Wittig argued that women were "heterosexualized." This was a "totalitarian" ideological operation, for "The category of sex is the political category that founds society as heterosexual."[85] She concluded that "There is no escape (for there is no territory, no other side of the Mississippi, no Palestine, no Liberia for women)."[86] Like Beauvoir before her, the analogy that she drew was with (American) slavery – a comparison that recurred in her writings – but Wittig was not interested in remaking the theoretical, philosophical, and ideological canon. She explained that the only way out of this system for women was to "choose" to become an "escapee, a fugitive slave, a lesbian."[87] Only lesbians (and sometimes nuns, she conceded) undid this naturalized oppression. That is why she declared, "lesbians [we]re not women."[88]

Wittig envisaged an "epistemological revolution" that demanded more than the undoing of the "myth" of "Woman."[89] That revolution meant interrogating the very ways language produced sex and naturalized difference and oppression: Language bore the "Mark of Gender."[90] This diagnosis was fundamental to her work because, as she explained, "To destroy the categories of sex in politics and in philosophy, to restore language (at least to modify its use)" was "part of [her] work in writing, as a writer."[91] Since "Language casts sheaves of reality upon the social body, stamping it and violently shaping it," remaking the social body required the reinvention of

---

[84] Wittig, "The Category of Sex," 2.   [85] Wittig, "The Category of Sex," 5.
[86] Wittig, "The Category of Sex," 8 and xvii.   [87] Wittig, "The Category of Sex," 8 and xvii.
[88] Wittig, "One Is Not Born a Woman," 13.   [89] Wittig, *The Straight Mind*, xvii.
[90] Wittig, "The Mark of Gender," in Monique Wittig, *The Straight Mind* (Boston: Beacon Press, 1992), 76.
[91] Wittig, "The Mark of Gender," 81.

language, as she did in her fiction. Her 1964 novel *L'Opoponax* had fictionalized the experience of childhood in order to "restore an undivided 'I,' to universalize the point of view of a group condemned to being particular, relegated in language to a subhuman category."[92] It was the novel published one year after May '68, *Les Guérillères*, which embodied her revolutionary project. The narrative structure of this fiction of a brutal but successful Amazonian war against men resignified the ways gender was embedded in language. Against the tradition of the generic (singular or plural) masculine that organized the French language, Wittig wrote exclusively in the feminine collective plural ("elles") whose "sovereign presence" "dictated the form of the book."[93] In other writings, she tried to materialize "the lesbian body" and undo the heterosexual regime she had denounced.

Wittig forged a unique mode of thought. The same can be said of Sarah Kofman, one of the most formidable and eclectic late-twentieth-century feminist philosophers. Kofman first began writing about aesthetics and Freud, and the role of metaphor in Nietzsche, two thinkers she returned to throughout her entire life. As she explained later, she did not claim the self-designation of feminist nor speak to a feminist politics since her "feminist position [could] be found in these kinds of readings" and in the manner she engaged with the philosophical canon.[94] It was the very themes she explored, the history of philosophy she unraveled, and the symptomatic reading to which she subjected these authors that have marked her as a feminist philosopher.

Kofman explored how the figures of woman and femininity haunt and structure philosophy and psychoanalysis, from Aristotle and Kant to Freud. In doing so, she showed how "the great masculine masters [and philosophers] were governed by the irrational domain of their sexual economy," which allowed them to claim transcendence "at women's expense."[95] That textual undoing of philosophy's "libidinal economy" emerged out of a sustained engagement with the ways "figures of femininity serve[d] as blindspots" in philosophy.[96] In *The Enigma of Woman*, published in 1980, Kofman analyzed how the question of femininity constituted an "exciting enigma" in Freud's work, fueled by the "anxiety" that traversed his thought: namely the "discovery of the radical otherness of woman, which threatens to bring about

---

92 Wittig, "The Mark of Gender," 82.   93 Wittig, "The Mark of Gender," 85.
94 Cited in Penelope Deutscher and Kelly Oliver, "Sarah Kofman's Skirts," in *Enigmas: Essays on Sarah Kofman*, ed. Penelope Deutscher and Kelly Oliver (Ithaca: Cornell University Press, 1999), 3.
95 Deutscher and Oliver, "Sarah Kofman's Skirts," 4.
96 Deutscher and Oliver, "Sarah Kofman's Skirts," 5.

a thoroughgoing upheaval in psychoanalysis."[97] Kofman was not interested in revealing Freud as "phallocentric" (or Nietzsche as "misogynist"): For her, Freudian writings were always traversed by a double movement that undoes the supposed naturalness of sexual difference, unmooring it from anatomy, while reinserting a binary opposition that haunted Freudian psychoanalysis. Because the figure of "the enigmatic woman" could not be done away with, "the psychoanalytic solution restores speech to woman only the better to rob her of it, the better to subordinate it to that of the master."[98]

Kofman's turn to psychoanalysis differed from Irigaray's, Kristeva's, and Cixous's. She refused the idea of a "feminine writing," and of "a writing that's proper to women."[99] Nor did she want to restore or reinvent femininity. Her exploration of the question of 'woman' in philosophy did not spring from a belief in irreducible (sexual) difference, but was rooted in an investigation of the ways in which that difference was given meaning and structured thought. She turned to Freud to show how his work troubled "the immediate certainty of difference."[100] For Freud, she explained, "the opposition between masculine and feminine is thus not a primary one."[101] In fact, her encounter with the philosophical canon echoed Beauvoir's own philosophical project. While Beauvoir had developed an "existential phenomenology," Kofman interrogated metaphysics through the subversive deployment of philosophy against itself. In her 1982 essay "The Economy of Respect," Kofman tackled Kant's moral philosophy, opening with the following question: "To respect women, is this simply to obey the categorical imperative that requires respect with respect to the other as a moral personage?" She continued: "Are women solely and simply special cases, models, or examples of the moral law, which they present and make visible, acquiring by that same law, as all moral persons do, an unalienable dignity that puts them above all price?"[102] She showed how, in the Kantian world of sentiment and morality, "thanks to respect, in spite of her weakness, woman dominates, like a queen. But at the same time, she, who represents feeling, does not govern. It is man, the minister, who governs through his understanding."[103]

---

97 Sarah Kofman, *The Enigma of Woman: Woman in Freud's Writings* (Ithaca: Cornell University Press, 1985), 36 and 33.
98 Kofman, *The Enigma of Woman*, 41 and 48.
99 Cited in Deutscher and Oliver, "Sarah Kofman's Skirts," 3.
100 Kofman, *The Enigma of Woman*, 106.   101 Kofman, *The Enigma of Woman*, 108.
102 Sarah Kofman, "The Economy of Respect: Kant and Respect for Women," in *Selected Writings: Sarah Kofman*, ed. Thomas Albrecht with Georgia Albert and Elizabeth G. Rottenberg (Stanford: Stanford University Press, 2007), 187.
103 Kofman, "The Economy of Respect," 191.

Like other feminist thinkers such as Cixous and Wittig, she also found in the aesthetic and literature a privileged mode of thinking through questions of knowledge, subjectivity, and meaning. She, too, turned to autobiography even as she had warned of the perils and the "illusion" of the biographical. After all, she mused, "every text is tissue that masks at the same time that it reveals."[104] When she wrote of her own childhood (as a little girl whose father had been sent to Auschwitz and who had had to live as a hidden child torn between her Jewish mother and a Catholic foster-mother), she offered readers the keys to thinking about her words, her psyche, and the erasure of her own body. She had to write in order to materialize those "suffocated words" (*paroles suffoquées*), which had irrigated her first works on aesthetics and psychoanalysis.[105] Again, she turned the canon against itself to write of her own self.

Autobiographies, the Self, and the World

These thinkers were Beauvoirian in different ways, revealing how her work and figure shaped generations. They reinvented the canon. In 2001, Assia Djebar was inducted into the highest French institution of (canonical) knowledge, the Académie Française. Hélène Cixous has continued writing, reinventing the terms of French literature, arts, and philosophy.[106] She had explained in 1975 that, "When '*the* repressed' of their culture and their society come back, it is an explosive return, which is *absolutely* shattering, staggering, overturning, with a force never let loose before."[107] These shatterings and overturnings have not abated in the early twenty-first century.

The Beauvoirian themes of sex, embodiment, culture, and lived experience are still urgent concerns for feminist theorists who interrogate their new configurations. They have explored these legacies in a variety of genres and forms. Some have written manifestos, such as author and filmmaker Virginie Despentes, who published *King Kong Theory*, where she discussed pornography, sexual violence, and "what remained of the sexual revolution in the

---

[104] Sarah Kofman, "The Double Reading," in *Selected Writings: Sarah Kofman*, ed. Thomas Albrecht with Georgia Albert and Elizabeth G. Rottenberg (Stanford: Stanford University Press, 2007), 44.

[105] Sarah Kofman, *Paroles suffoquées* (Paris: Éditions Galilée, 1987); and Sarah Kofman, *Rue Ordener, rue Labat* (Paris: Éditions Galilée, 1994).

[106] See for instance Jacques Derrida, *Genèses, Généalogies, Genres et le génie: Le secret de l'archive* (Paris: Éditions Galilée, 2003).

[107] Cixous, *The Newly-Born Woman*, ix.

twenty-first century."[108] Queer theorists have invoked Wittig. In 2016, Moroccan author Leila Slimani was awarded the prestigious Goncourt prize for her novel about the oppressive nature of domesticity, the perversity of capitalist-induced intimacy, and the transgression of female infanticide.[109] Building on a lineage of subversive feminist filmmakers, the 2017 documentary film *Speak Up/Make Your Way* from "Afro-descendant" writer and filmmaker Amandine Gay has been one of these explosive texts. It features black Francophone women reflecting on their lived experience of racism, misogyny, and homophobia. Many of these self-proclaimed "afro-feminists" invoked the intellectual legacies not of late-modern French feminist thought but of African-American poet Audre Lorde, activist and writer Angela Davis, theorist bell hooks, as well as Martiniquan philosopher Frantz Fanon and others excluded from the French canon. The film denaturalized the ways sex, race, and embodiment still operated in culture and language, revealing how the category of "woman" was always both a lived experience and a fictive, contingent, historical construction.

108 Virginie Despentes, *King Kong théorie* (Paris: Grasset, 2006).
109 Leila Slimani, *Chanson douce* (Paris: Gallimard, 2016).

13

Modernist Theologies: The Many Paths between God and World

PETER E. GORDON

Introduction

On November 7, 1917 Max Weber offered his comments on "Science as a Vocation" before an assembly of students and faculty at the University of Munich, declaring that "disenchantment" was an "inescapable condition" and "the fate of our times."[1] But history tells us that nothing is truly inevitable. Although modern European intellectual history is replete with narratives of disenchantment and religious decline, the fact remains that religious speculation and formal discourses of theology survived well through the end of the twentieth century. For intellectuals who have shed the last remnants of personal faith, the endurance of theology in late modernity may seem perplexing, a symptom of what Nietzsche called *Unzeitgemäßigkeit*, or a decalibration in time. Already in 1882 Nietzsche's madman declared that "God is dead. God remains dead. And we have killed him." But even the madman recognized that he had come "too early." What he called the "tremendous event" of God's death was "still on its way"; it had "not yet reached the ears of men." Critics who harken to the madman's prophesy may likewise insist that European religious thought is a remnant of an earlier and more pious age.

It is hard to contest the fact that over the course of the twentieth century Western Europe (along with much of Eastern and East-Central Europe) has experienced a gradual decline in religious belief: Today sociologists often speak of "Eurosecularity" as an established fact.[2] But

---

[*] I would like to express my sincere gratitude to Francis Fiorenza and Sarah Shortall for their many suggestions on this chapter.
[1] Max Weber, "Science as a Vocation," in *From Max Weber: Essays in Sociology*, ed. H. H. Gerth and C. Wright Mills (New York: Oxford University Press, 1946), 129–156.
[2] See, for example, the opening essay by Peter Berger, "Religious America, Secular Europe?," in *Religious America, Secular Europe?: A Theme and Variations*, ed. Peter Berger, Grace Davie, and Effie Fokas (New York: Routledge, 2008), 9–22.

this was not always the case. In 1916, the novelist James Joyce could still capture in startling prose the personal terror of Stephen Daedalus, the fictional hero of *A Portrait of the Artist as a Young Man*, who emerges from a priest's sermon gripped with the fear that any wrong step may plunge him through the floor into hell. But such views are increasingly uncommon, and it can hardly be denied that throughout most of Europe faith has suffered a marked decline, especially since the end of World War II. In regions historically marked by Catholicism, such as Poland and Ireland, religious institutions remain strong even as individual reports of belief suggest an overall retreat. But in countries such as Great Britain, France, Germany, and Spain pronounced religiosity is now unusual, while in Scandinavia and the Balkan lands once under communist control, secularism has become more or less the norm. Notwithstanding such statistical evidence, however, theology and religious thought remain alive, even within the otherwise secular discourses of modern European elites. Nietzsche knew that secularization happens slowly; like thunder, its message is heard long after the lightning strikes. For some intellectuals, however, the challenge of secular consciousness itself has awakened a new energy for theological innovation. Because religion no longer serves as the presumptive horizon of common discussion, its philosophical articulation assumes a more heightened urgency. Nietzsche announced the decline of the gods, but a divine thunder still answers back.

This chapter provides a survey and guide of major themes and thinkers in European religious thought, with an emphasis on noteworthy innovators whose work serves as counter-evidence against the Weberian thesis of world-disenchantment. Although differences of doctrine are considerable, one may detect in nearly all of these movements a similar attempt to negotiate between the demands of the world and the exigencies of faith. The late-modern era has brought unprecedented challenges to religious consciousness: Totalitarian governments have exercised censorious and sometimes violently oppressive policies on faith-communities, international conflict and mass immigration have increased the ethno-religious diversity of European communities and tested the tolerance threshold among host populations, and new discourses of multiculturalism and feminism have prompted a reconsideration of longstanding traditions of belief. Such challenges have imposed on theologians a special burden, compelling them to re-examine old but enduring questions concerning the relation between nature and grace, person and community, revelation and humanity.

PETER E. GORDON

The Barthian Revolt

A new chapter in twentieth-century theology began with the appearance of *The Epistle to the Romans* (*Der Römerbrief*), originally published in 1918, revised in a second edition in 1922, by the Swiss Reformed pastor Karl Barth (1886–1968). The transformative significance of this explosive work is best understood if we see it as a reaction to the conventional national-bourgeois synthesis of Christianity that reigned in later-nineteenth- and early-twentieth-century Germany under the name of *Kulturprotestantismus* and was associated with venerable theologians such as Albrecht Ritschl, Wilhelm Hermann, and Adolf von Harnack. This "Culture-Protestantism" tended to see Protestant Christianity and German national culture as a harmonious whole grounded in the achievements of the educated bourgeoisie. For Barth this illusory synthesis between religion and national culture came to a catastrophic end in the violence of World War I, when leading theologians such as Hermann signed a manifesto to declare their support for Germany's military ambitions.

Barth considered this readiness to conflate religion with national-cultural values an outrage. In *The Epistle to the Romans* he insisted on the chasm between God and humanity, between the absolute transcendence of the divine and the utterly mundane character of all merely human national-cultural ambitions. Although the book is structured as a line-by-line commentary on Paul's epistle to the Romans in the New Testament, it offers a bold new statement of theological priorities. For Barth the guiding theme of Paul's Epistle, as indeed of all theology, is the simple proposition that God surpasses all human values and categories: "God is God."[3] In elaborating this idea Barth built upon arguments from theologians such as Johannes Weiß (1863–1914), whose *Jesus's Proclamation of the Kingdom of God* (1892) dealt a first blow to the harmonistic teachings of Cultural Protestantism by insisting on the eschatological message of the Gospels and the otherness of God's kingdom. More importantly, however, Barth also appealed to the writings of Søren Kierkegaard, whose works were then enjoying a major revival across Central Europe, captivating the attention not only of theologians but also of philosophers (such as Martin Heidegger, Georg Lukács, and Theodor Adorno) and novelists (such as Franz Kafka). Citing Kierkegaard, Barth characterized the divide between humanity and God as an "infinite

---

3 Karl Barth, "Vorwort zur zweiten Auflage," of *Der Römerbrief*, Zweiter Fassung (1922), in *Gesamtausgabe*, ed. Cornelis van der Kooi and Katja Tolstaja (Zurich: Theologischer Verlag, 2010), 18.

qualitative distinction" between time and eternity.[4] For Barth it is just this divide (or *"krisis"* in Greek) and the relation across it that should be acknowledged as the essential theme of the Bible and of philosophy.

It would be difficult to exaggerate the transformative impact of Barth's "crisis-theology" on twentieth-century religious and philosophical discourse. Its ardent affirmation of divine transcendence injected new passion into the discipline of Protestant theology that many had considered conformist or moribund; and its muscular rejection of historicist methods of biblical interpretation helped to fuel what the liberal Protestant scholar Ernst Troeltsch (1865–1923) called "the crisis of historicism."[5] By the end of the 1920s Barth's anti-historicist conception of God as infinitely distinct from humanity had become a commonplace theme for philosophical speculation, leaving its imprint on Jewish as well as Christian thinkers.[6] Friedrich Gogarten (1887–1967) was among the earliest Protestant theologians to ally himself with Barth. Already in his 1917 book *Religion from Afar* Gogarten had begun to develop the Kierkegaardian ideas and a specific interest in the "I–Thou" relation that would remain among his most characteristic themes, also informing the work of the Jewish thinker Martin Buber. Gogarten's 1920 essay "Between the Times" amplified Barthian complaints against the culture-Protestant synthesis: "We have all entered so deeply in the human that we have lost God," he complained. "We can no longer deceive ourselves and mistake the human for the divine." Historicist confidence in the future as continuous with the present had been shattered. "The times have fallen apart," Gogarten wrote. "*We* stand between the times."[7]

Under the name of "dialectical theology," Barth and his many followers transformed the landscape of interwar German religious thought. The Swiss Reformed theologian Emil Brunner (1989–1966) was an early ally to Barth, but also an independent thinker of enormous consequence for twentieth-century Protestantism not only in Europe but also in North America. During his long tenure as a professor of theology in Zurich Brunner authored numerous works, including *God and Man* (1930), a collection of four essays in which Brunner expressed his famous challenge to Barth's theme of radical

---

4 Barth, "Vorwort zur zweiten Auflage," 17.
5 Charles R. Bambach, *Heidegger, Dilthey, and the Crisis of Historicism* (Ithaca: Cornell University Press, 1995).
6 For Barth's impact on Emmanuel Lévinas, see Samuel Moyn, *Origins of the Other: Emmanuel Levinas between Revelation and Ethics* (Ithaca: Cornell University Press, 2005).
7 Friedrich Gogarten, "Zwischen den Zeiten," *Die Christliche Welt*, no. 34 (1920), 374–378, p. 375; translated as "Between the Times," in *The Beginnings of Dialectical Theology*, ed. James M. Robinson (Richmond: John Knox Press, 1968), 277–282.

transcendence.[8] Where Barth saw a radical chasm between God and humanity, Brunner insisted on the possibility of human knowledge, however imperfect, as an opening step in humanity's relation with the divine. As he explained in *Nature and Grace* (1934), "What the natural man knows of God, of the Law and of his own dependence upon God, may be very confused and distorted. But even so it is the necessary, indispensable point of contact for divine grace."[9] Barth responded to Brunner in 1934 with a harsh essay, "No!" in which he warned that Brunner's accommodation to human knowledge would descend into a "natural theology" that would rob divine revelation of its ultimacy.[10]

Among the many Protestant theologians who associated with Barth was the Lutheran pastor Dietrich Bonhoeffer (1906–1945), a founding member alongside Barth and Martin Niemöller of the anti-Nazi dissident group known as the "Confessing Church." From prison Bonhoeffer wrote that "Barth was the first theologian to begin the criticism of religion, and that remains his great merit." Like many other theologians, however, Bonhoeffer expressed some misgivings about the radicalism of Barth's theological claims, as they tended to absolutize revelation beyond all interpretation or appeal. Barth's model of revelation, Bonhoeffer observed, was supposed to stand as the "law of faith," but in its incorrigibility it assumed a "positivist" character.[11] Bonhoeffer is best known for his 1937 work, *Nachfolge* (known in English as *The Cost of Discipleship*) in which he distinguished between "cheap" and "costly" grace. "Cheap grace means grace as a doctrine, a principle, a system. It means forgiveness of sins proclaimed as a general truth, the love of God taught as the Christian 'conception' of God. An intellectual assent to that idea is held to be of itself sufficient to secure remission of sins." Cheap grace allows for "the justification of sin without the justification of the sinner." It preaches forgiveness but does not require repentance. "Grace does everything, they say, and so everything can remain as it was before." By contrast, costly grace is "the treasure hidden in the field; for the sake of it a man will gladly go and sell all that he has." It is costly because "it calls us to

---

8 Emil Brunner, *God and Man*, trans. David Cairns (London: SCM Press, 1956 [1930]).
9 Emil Brunner, "Nature and Grace," in *Natural Theology: Comprising "Nature and Grace" by Professor Dr. Emil Brunner and the Reply "No!" by Dr. Karl Barth*, trans. Peter Fraenkel (London: Geoffrey Bles, 1946), 32–33.
10 For an excellent summary of Brunner's debate with Barth, see Gary Dorrien, *The Barthian Revolt* (Louisville: Westminster John Knox Press, 2000), 120–124.
11 Bonhoeffer to Eberhard Bethge (4 May, 1944), in Dietrich Bonhoeffer, *Letters and Papers from Prison: The Enlarged Edition*, English edn. ed. Eberhard Bethge (New York: Macmillan, 1971), 286.

follow, and it is *grace* because it calls us to follow *Jesus Christ*. It is costly because it costs many his life, and it is grace because it gives a man his only true life."[12] Imprisoned by the Nazi regime for his participation in the Confessing Church, Bonhoeffer was executed at the Flössenburg concentration camp in April 1945.

Modern Jewish Thought

Rabbinic orthodoxy in Europe developed patterns of textual and legal interpretation with roots that span the centuries back to the medieval era and to late antiquity. The mid-century destruction of major centers of traditional Jewish learning in Eastern Europe during the Holocaust brought to an end the institutional settings for rabbinic interpretation on the Continent, shifting the major centers of rabbinic education elsewhere on the globe. But the early twentieth century also saw an expansion of original and diverse trends in Jewish philosophy and history. Within the predominantly Christian cultures of Europe Jewish thinkers have often felt the need to defend Judaism's religious legitimacy. This is undoubtedly true of the German Reform rabbi Leo Baeck (1873–1956), who published *The Essence of Judaism* (1905) in part as an apologetic response to the Protestant theologian Adolf von Harnack's *The Essence of Christianity*. Whereas the latter upholds a conventional "supersessionism" (celebrating Christianity's "deliverance" from the strictures of Jewish law), Baeck made a case for the continued legitimacy and independence of Judaism as a dynamic union between "mystery" and "command." Baeck also reconfirmed the nineteenth-century view of Judaism as "ethical monotheism."[13]

Modern Jewish philosophy in the twentieth century is traceable most of all to the formidable writings of Hermann Cohen (1842–1918), a German-Jewish professor who devoted most of his career to the promotion of neo-Kantian philosophy at the university in Marburg. Late in life, however, he assumed a post at the Academy of Jewish Sciences in Berlin, where he produced his final and most distinctively Jewish philosophical work, *Religion of Reason out of the Sources of Judaism* (1919). A bracing affirmation of rationalist and prophetic themes, Cohen's *opus postumum* became an object of both fascination and

---

12 Dietrich Bonhoeffer, *Nachfolge* (Munich: Christian Kaiser Verlag, 1937); English translation *The Cost of Discipleship*, rev. Irmgard Booth (New York: Touchstone, 1995), 43–45.
13 See Michael A. Meyer, "The Thought of Leo Baeck: A Religious Philosophy for a Time of Adversity," in *Modern Judaism*, 19(2) (1999), 107–117; also see Albert H. Friedlander, *Leo Baeck: Teacher of Theresienstadt* (New York: Holt, Rinehart and Winston, 1968).

criticism for the younger generation of Jewish thinkers who followed. The German-Jewish philosopher Franz Rosenzweig (1886–1929) drew some inspiration from Cohen but also synthesized themes from the European philosophical tradition (Kierkegaard, Schelling, Hegel) to create a remarkably original and systematic work of religious philosophy, *The Star of Redemption* (1921), in which he responded to the apparent crisis of religion's historical decline with a new vision of religious experience that aligned him with ascendant trends in existentialism. During the 1920s Rosenzweig also devoted himself to the creation of the Jüdisches Lehrhaus, an institute for adult Jewish education in Frankfurt.[14]

Rosenzweig also cooperated with Martin Buber (1878–1965) on a new translation of the Hebrew Bible into German, a project that Buber completed on his own after Rosenzweig's death. Buber himself ranks among the best-known Jewish thinkers of the entire twentieth century. In his early years he worked for Jewish cultural and national renewal, and became an ardent spokesman for the Zionist dream of restoring the Jewish people to a homeland in Palestine. His early translations of Hasidic tales about the Baal Shem Tov helped to inspire the romantic rediscovery of Eastern European Hasidism among the more assimilated Jewish communities in Western Europe. Buber's earlier, more mystical phase came to an end with the 1923 publication of *Ich und Du* (*I and Thou*), a foundational text in "dialogical" philosophy that extolled the immediacy of personal encounter and communication.

The historical rediscovery of the Jewish mystical tradition, or 'Kabbalah,' has played a powerful role in reshaping both perceptions of the Jewish past and the agenda for Jewish thought in the present. The historian Gershom Scholem (1897–1982) deserves singular credit for this achievement, beginning with his *Major Trends in Jewish Mysticism* (1941) and reaching its zenith with *Sabbatai Zevi, the Mystical Messiah* (1973). A committed socialist-Zionist with an anarchistic temperament, Scholem portrayed the Kabbalah as an ancient and subterranean tradition of messianic energy that periodically burst out from the constraints of rabbinic Judaism to effect dramatic changes in Jewish history, culminating in the early-modern heretical movement of the false-messiah Sabbatai Zevi, whose antinomian spirit Scholem interpreted as a harbinger of revolutionary change both in the Jewish world and in the non-Jewish world.[15] His fascination with the mystical dimension of religion brought him into contact with other

---

14 On Rosenzweig see Peter E. Gordon, *Rosenzweig and Heidegger: Between Judaism and German Philosophy* (Berkeley: University of California Press, 2003).

15 The classic study of Scholem's theory of history is David Biale, *Gershom Scholem: Kabbalah and Counter-history* (Cambridge: Harvard University Press, 1982).

noteworthy historians of religion, including the German-Jewish historian Hans Jonas (1903–1993), whose ground-breaking work on the Gnostic religion influenced his understanding of the Kabbalah. He also associated with the Swiss psychiatrist and theorist of archetypes Carl Jung (1875–1961) and the Romanian-born Mircea Eleade (1907–1986); all three were occasional visitors at the Eranos meetings for the history of religion in Switzerland.

Perhaps the most noteworthy European contributor to modern Jewish philosophy in the later twentieth century was the Lithuanian-born Emmanuel Lévinas (1906–1995), a student of Husserlian and Heideggerian phenomenology who spent his mature years as a professor in France. Imprisoned in Germany during the war and deeply marked by the Holocaust (in which members of his immediate family were murdered) Lévinas went on to develop a philosophy that placed primary emphasis on the ethical responsibility for the "other." Noteworthy philosophical works include *Time and the Other* (1948), *Totality and Infinity* (1961), and *Otherwise than Being, or, Beyond Essence* (1974). Although his strictly philosophical writings typically make little mention of Judaism, it is clear that for Lévinas the metaphysical bond between human being and God as the "infinitely other" served as a template for his conception of "ethics as first philosophy." Alongside his philosophical writings, Lévinas also authored many interpretations of the Talmud as well as essays on the modern Jewish experience.[16] His philosophy of alterity also served as a powerful inspiration for the later, more explicitly "ethical" writings by Jacques Derrida, who spoke at Lévinas's funeral.[17]

Mid-Century Catholicism

For the first half of the twentieth century the Catholic Church retained the strong imprint of the neo-Thomist revival that had begun the century before. The revival of Thomism remained strong even through the middle decades of the twentieth century, especially in France, thanks in part to the masterful historical and exegetical studies of Aquinas and medieval Christian philosophy by the philosopher and historian Étienne Gilson (1884–1978).[18]

---

16 See, for example, Emmanuel Lévinas, *Nine Talmudic Readings*, trans. Annette Aronowicz (Bloomington: Indiana University Press, 1990). An excellent contextual study is Samuel Moyn, *Origins of the Other: Emmanuel Levinas between Revelation and Ethics* (Ithaca: Cornell University Press, 2005).

17 Jacques Derrida, *Adieu to Emmanuel Lévinas*, trans. Pascale-Anne Brault and Michael Naas (Stanford: Stanford University Press, 1999).

18 See, inter alia, Étienne Gilson, *Le Thomisme, introduction au système de saint Thomas* (Paris: J. Vrin, 1919); in English as *The Christian Philosophy of St. Thomas Aquinas* (New York: Random House, 1956).

The revival also gained support from Jacques Maritain (1882–1973), the French Catholic thinker and prolific author whose popular works ranged from studies of natural law to reflections on personalism. Best known for promoting the idea of an "integral Christian humanism," Maritain opposed individualism on the one hand and socialism on the other, arguing instead for the "dignity" of the person as a "whole."[19] His Christian personalism played a noteworthy role in the philosophical deliberations that led to the drafting of the United Nations' "Declaration of Human Rights."[20]

From the end of World War II to the debates that contributed to the Second Vatican Council in the early 1960s, European Catholicism underwent a dramatic period of innovation. Church theologians were plunged into a maelstrom of modern controversies (concerning the meaning of grace, to take only one example) and confronted the twin challenges of religious diversity and rising secularism. Arguably the greatest and most original thinker in this era was Henri de Lubac (1896–1991), a French Jesuit who spent most of his life as a teacher and expositor of patristic texts, first in Lyons and then in Paris. De Lubac, who was an active member of the French Resistance, was doctrinally heterodox and regarded with some suspicion by Church authorities, but ultimately exerted a major impact on other Catholic theologians even long after the era of Vatican II.

De Lubac's first major work, *Catholicisme*, published in 1938 but readily available in a revised edition only after the war, enjoyed a major impact on many theologians as a remedy for what Cardinal Ratzinger later called the "narrow-minded individualistic Christianity" of the times.[21] Presented as an anthology of passages chiefly from medieval and patristic texts, its introductory summary of major themes reinforces a holistic vision of the relation between revelation and redemption, recognizing the human desire for grace as a crucial element within the collaborative drama of salvation. In a strong rejoinder to individualistic interpretations of Catholicism, de Lubac sought to restore a proper balance between person and collective, with special emphasis on the *corpus mysticum* as Christ's mystical body as present in the Eucharist (rather than the body of the Church). God did not come, de Lubac observes,

---

19 Jacques Maritain, *Les droits de l'homme et la loi naturelle* (New York: Éditions de la Maison française, 1942), 84.
20 Jacques Maritain, *Humanisme intégral: Problèmes temporels et spirituels d'une nouvelle chrétienté* (Paris: Fernand Aubier, 1936). See Samuel Moyn, *Christian Human Rights* (Philadelphia: University of Pennsylvania Press, 2015).
21 Joseph Cardinal Ratzinger, "Foreword" to Henri de Lubac, *Catholicism: Christ and the Common Destiny of Man* (San Francisco: Ignatius Press, 1988), 12.

"to win for us an external pardon," for salvation was fundamentally "ours from all eternity and is presupposed by the Incarnation itself."[22]

In his 1946 book *Surnaturel: Études historiques*, de Lubac extended this doctrine, using what seemed *prima facie* to be merely a reconstruction of Thomist theological debate as an occasion to set forth a dramatically new account of the central role of grace in human nature. Against conventional readings of Thomas Aquinas and the Church fathers, de Lubac argued that human destiny should not be conceived as purely natural, since this would entail that grace itself appear as a distinctively *supernatural* intervention from beyond the human being's natural condition. According to de Lubac, however, the idea of a purely natural existence was only injected into Thomism by commentators such as Cajetan, whose naturalist interpretation reinforced a false dualism that, ironically, served as the conceptual opening toward individualism, deism, and even secularist atheism. Against this dualistic interpretation de Lubac discerned in Church teachings a species of holism, insisting on the "finality" or internal relation between nature and grace. Contemporary critics disparaged de Lubac's views as "nouvelle théologie," a term that originally implied unwarranted deviation but later became a generic and even affirmative name for a broad trend of modern innovation. In 1960 de Lubac was appointed as a consultant to a commission preparing for the Second Vatican Council, which issued several statements that reflect his influence.

No less influential than de Lubac, and equally formidable in his thinking, was the German Jesuit Karl Rahner (1904–1984), a tremendously prolific and controversial theologian whose philosophically sophisticated thinking would play a major role in Vatican II. Especially important in this regard is Rahner's idea of "anonymous Christianity," which extends possible salvation to those who may have never encountered Christianity in its doctrinal form. In an essay on "Christianity and the Non-Christian Religions," Rahner wrote that the Church "will not so much regard herself today as the exclusive community of those who have a claim to salvation but rather as the historically tangible vanguard and the historically and socially constituted explicit expression of what the Christian hopes is present as a hidden reality *even outside the visible Church*."[23] Much like de Lubac, Rahner also contested the dualistic

---

22 Henri de Lubac, *Catholicism: Christ and the Common Destiny of Man* (San Francisco: Ignatius Press, 1988), 226. See Sarah Shortall, *Soldiers of God in a Secular World: The Politics of Catholic Theology in Twentieth-Century France* (Cambridge: Harvard University Press, forthcoming).
23 Karl Rahner, "Christianity and the Non-Christian Religions," in Karl Rahner, *Theological Investigations*, 23 vols. (Baltimore: Helicon Press, 1966), vol. V, 115–134; p. 133.

distinction between "pure nature" and a state of grace; he thus saw in the Eucharist not an incidental joining between the sacred and profane but rather a manifestation of their ongoing and necessary union. "We are always in spiritual communion with Christ (or we could be)," Rahner observed, "whether we kneel in church or walk the dusty streets of everyday life."[24] It followed that the sacraments for Rahner were "the historical manifestations of the grace which is always and everywhere present in the world."[25] Rahner's affirmation of a this-worldly communion offered a bold rejoinder to theories of religious decline.

Also prominent was the Swiss Jesuit theologian Hans Urs von Balthasar (1905–1988), who drew inspiration both from de Lubac and from the Jesuit Erich Przywara, and also developed a strong interest in the Protestant teachings of Karl Barth. Balthasar was generally supportive of Vatican II though not a participant in its deliberations. But he was nonetheless in some respects a theological conservative, insisting, for example, that the Christian alone "remains the guardian of that metaphysical wonderment which is at the point of origin for philosophy and the continuation of which is the basis for its further existence."[26] Finally, it is also worth mentioning Romano Guardini (1885–1968), the Italian-born priest who taught theology in Germany and whose early work *The Spirit of the Liturgy* (1918) helped to inspire the movement for liturgical reform that culminated in Vatican II.[27] His postwar address *The End of the Modern Age* (1950) extolls the sacrality of the person and condemns the modern era of totalitarianism and utilitarianism in which power obscures revelation.[28]

Toward Vatican II

Many theologians contributed to the era of self-scrutiny and innovation that informed the Second Vatican Council (which first convened in October 1962 under Pope John XXIII and reached its conclusion in December 1965 under

24 Karl Rahner, *Meditations on the Sacraments* (New York: Seabury Press, 1977), 36.
25 Karl Rahner, "Thoughts about the Sacraments in General," in *Karl Rahner: Theologian of the Graced Search for Meaning*, ed. Geffrey B. Kelly (Minneapolis: Fortress Press, 1992), 288.
26 Hans Urs von Balthasar, *The Glory of the Lord: A Theological Aesthetics, Volume V: The Realm of Metaphysics in the Modern Age* (San Francisco: Ignatius Press, 2011), 646. For more on Balthasar, see David L. Schindler, *Hans Urs von Balthasar: His Life and Work* (San Francisco: Ignatius Press, 1991); and Edward T. Oakes SJ and David Moss (eds.), *The Cambridge Companion to Hans Urs von Balthasar* (Cambridge: Cambridge University Press, 2004).
27 Romano Guardini, *Vom Geist der Liturgie* (Freiburg im Breisgau: Herder & Co., 1921); translated as *The Spirit of the Liturgy* (New York: Herder & Herder/Crossroad, 1998).
28 Romano Guardini, *Das Ende der Neuzeit* (Basel: Hess Verlag, 1950).

Pope Paul VI). Vatican II marked a watershed in the history of Catholic teaching. Among other modifications in religious practice, it relaxed the Latin-only stricture, allowing vernacular language for the Mass. It also strengthened ecumenical policy toward other Christian denominations and modified Church teaching on non-Christian religions, including Judaism and Islam, as set forth in *Nostra Aetate*, the "Declaration of the Relation of the Church to Non-Christian Religions."

Between the wars theologians such as the German Catholic Karl Adam (1876–1966) sometimes presented a violent contrast between Judaism and Jesus Christ. In a 1935 lecture Adam asked, "How could there have emerged from ... a world of ossified belief in the letter, of a narrow-minded caste spirit and materialistic piety, ... a human nature so incomparably pure, so God-united and holy and gracious, so inwardly free and genuine as his?"[29] In the wake of the Holocaust, however, many considered a reappraisal of such disparaging theological doctrines a moral necessity. Alongside Henri de Lubac, Yves Congar (1904–1995), and Joseph Ratzinger (1927–) several other theologians and religious thinkers, both Christian and non-Christian, played a prominent role in encouraging the Church to revise its traditional attitude toward Jews and Judaism. It is interesting to note that much of the theological inspiration for the doctrinal innovations of *Nostra Aetate* came from two converts: Johannes Oesterreicher (1904–1993), the Moravian-born Jewish convert to Catholicism, and Karl Thieme (1902–1963), a Lutheran convert to Catholicism.[30] Their efforts were preceded by the British Anglican James Parkes (1896–1981), author of *The Conflict of the Church and the Synagogue* (1934) and one of the first Christian thinkers in the twentieth century to call for a revision in traditional Christian teaching about Judaism.[31]

No less important in promoting such a reappraisal was the historian Jules Isaac (1877–1963), the French-Jewish author of several works on the history of Christian teaching about Judaism, including *Jésus et Israël* (1948) and *L'enseignement du mépris* (*The Teaching of Contempt*, 1962), which Isaac wrote on the eve of the Second Vatican Council. Isaac called upon Christians to abandon the "mythical and unhappy tradition of the 'deicide people'" and to achieve an "atonement" that would have "infinitely beneficial consequences

---

29 Karl Adam, *Jesus Christus und der Geist unserer Zeit: Ein Vortrag* (Augsburg: Haas und Grabherr, 1935); translated as *The Son of God*, trans. Philip Hereford (London: Sheed & Ward, 1935), 183.
30 On the general history of *Nostra Aetate*, with particular attention to the roles of Oesterreicher and Thieme, see John Connelly, *From Enemy to Brother: The Revolution in Catholic Teaching on the Jews, 1933–1965* (Cambridge: Harvard University Press, 2012).
31 James Parkes, *The Conflict of the Church and the Synagogue* (London: Sonco Press, 1934).

for Christianity as well as for Judaism."[32] In the aftermath of Vatican II most Catholics have come to accept it as a legitimate reconciliation between essential points of Church doctrine and undeniable facts of modern life. Though some conservative voices in the Church still regret its innovations as an illicit concession to modernity that can only weaken Catholicism's standing, the greater share of prominent theologians and Catholic intellectuals have come to feel that the Second Vatican Council helped to assure the endurance of the Church in an age of growing secularization and religious diversity. In 1972, on the tenth anniversary of the inaugural meeting of the Council, then-Cardinal Karol Wojtyła (later Pope John Paul II) published a commentary on its significance, taking special care to extol the Conciliar teachings as an "enrichment of faith" and a "mature expression, adapted to the reality of our times."[33]

Voices of Islam

It could be argued that Muslim scholars have been present in European society for more than a millennium, especially if one were to embrace a more expansive notion of Europe that includes the portions of the Ottoman Empire and the Islamic culture of the Iberian peninsula before the *Reconquista*. But within the circumference of Western Europe in the modern era, Muslim voices were often marginalized or seen as illegitimate. Meanwhile, the vigorous program of modernization promoted by the modern state of Turkey since its founding in 1923 under the leadership of Kemal Atatürk also included a state-funded effort to translate the Qu'ran into Turkish. The fact remains, however, that until the most recent years the distinctive contribution of Muslim intellectuals in modern Europe has remained difficult to hear. This situation has changed markedly with the growth of Muslim populations in Western Europe since World War II, especially with the emergence of distinctive Muslim subcultures that represent diverse ethno-national origins (primarily Middle-Eastern, North-African, Sub-Saharan African, and Turkish) in major urban centers of Europe such as London, Paris, Marseilles, and Berlin.

---

32 Jules Isaac, *Jésus et Israël* (Paris: A. Michel, 1948); and Jules Isaac, *The Teaching of Contempt: Christian Roots of Anti-Semitism*, trans. Helen Weaver (New York: Holt, Rinehart and Winston, 1964), 146–147.
33 Originally published in Polish as Kardynal Karol Wojtyła, *U podstaw odnowy: Studium o realizacji Vaticanum II* (Kraków: Polskie Towarzystwo Teologiczne, 1972); English translation *Sources of Renewal: The Implementation of the Second Vatican Council*, trans. P. S. Falla (San Francisco: Harper & Row, 1980), 422.

Arguably the best known representative of Islamic thought in the European sphere is Tariq Ramadan (1962–), a professor of contemporary Islamic Studies at Oxford. Born in Switzerland into a family of Egyptian Muslims, Ramadan was educated both in French literature and in Islamic studies at the University of Geneva and has published widely on contemporary Islam, while also playing a prominent role in the media as a contributor to debates over multicultural and multi-religious dialogue in Europe. He is best known for accessible books such as *Western Muslims and the Future of Islam* (2005) and more detailed calls for innovation in the Islamic religion such as *Radical Reform: Islamic Ethics and Liberation* (2008). Another noteworthy scholar of Islam is Shaykh Abdal Hakim Murad (also known as Timothy John Winter; 1960–) a Sunni-Muslim who is Shaykh Zayed Lecturer in Islamic Studies at Cambridge University. A specialist in classical Islamic theology, Winter also contributes to ongoing discussion concerning Muslim–Christian relations.[34] Like all scholars and intellectuals of Europe's non-Christian minority religions, these figures are often expected to play a representative role when in fact Islam is no more unified than Christianity or Judaism (and is arguably less so, especially when compared with the institutionally reinforced doctrines of the Catholic Church).

Muslim intellectuals in Europe today face considerable challenges in part due to continued prejudice and misunderstanding harbored by many toward Islam. At the end of the twentieth century and into the new millennium, fears of an Islamist insurgency within Western Europe have become commonplace, as evidenced in alarmist manifestos such as Thilo Sarrazin's *Deutschland schafft sich ab* (2010); and in the controversial French novelist Michel Houellebecq's dystopian political fantasy *Soumission* (2015), a book which the Dutch-Moroccan novelist Fouad Laroui has criticized as contributing to the climate of racism and intolerance in Europe.[35]

Philosophies of Religion

Beyond the sphere of official theology, the twentieth century has also seen the flourishing of various philosophical movements that drew upon religion or sustain an alliance with official religious doctrine. Of these movements the

---

34 See, for example, Norman Solomon, Richard Harries, and Tim Winter (eds.), *Abraham's Children: Jews, Muslims and Christians in Conversation* (London: Continuum, 2006).
35 Fouad Laroui, "«Soumission» de Houellebecq? Bon roman, très mauvaise action ...," *Jeune Afrique* (January 2015), www.jeuneafrique.com/34812/culture/soumission-de-houellebecq-bon-roman-tr-s-mauvaise-action/.

most significant is Christian existentialism, a term that should be used with care since it embraces such a wide variety of creeds and tendencies. Much of what we call Christian existentialism drew inspiration from the early-nineteenth-century Danish philosopher Søren Kierkegaard, whose many works, often published pseudonymously and steeped in irony, meditated upon the paradoxical relation between public conformity and inward belief, and also from the later-nineteenth-century Russian novelist Fyodor Dostoevsky, whose final masterpiece, *The Brothers Karamazov* (1880), explores universal themes of goodness and the drama of faith.

The philosopher Nikolai Berdyaev (1874–1948) ranks among the most significant contributors to Christian existentialism in the tradition of Russian Orthodoxy. A professor of philosophy at the University of Moscow following the Bolshevik Revolution, Berdyaev was eventually expelled by the Soviet state for his criticism of its authoritarianism, and he lived his later years in Germany and then France. Berdyaev harshly criticized the Russian Orthodox Church for supporting Tsarist absolutism. "Orthodoxy," he wrote in 1907, "gave away the earth into the hands of the state because of its own non-belief in man and mankind, because of its nihilistic attitude towards the world. Orthodoxy does not believe in the religious ordering of human life upon the earth, and it compensates for its own hopeless pessimism by a call for the forceful ordering of it by state authority." Against what he called the "nihilism" of the orthodox Church, Berdyaev called for a "new religious consciousness" and a "religious rebirth" that would involve both the "declaration of the will of God" and "a declaration of the rights of man." He affirmed the "objective, the cosmic might of the truth of God" along with God's guidance for "the earthly destiny of mankind."[36] In later writings such as *The Fate of Man in the Modern World* (1934), Berdyaev observed that Christianity is vulnerable to the same forces of routinization and objectivication as all mundane things. "Objectivized in history, Christianity becomes a social phenomenon, it is subject to the socially prosaic. Christianity accepts history, operates within it, even battles against it, and its spirit would be unrecognizable in an historic objectivization. In a certain sense, every single soul has more

---

36 Nikolai Berdyaev, "Nigilizm na religioznoi pochve" (1907), in Nikolai Berdyaev, *Dukhovnyi krizis intelligentsii* (1910), Section II, 1; reprinted in *Tipy religioznoi mysli v Rossii* (Paris: YMCA Press, 1989), vol. III, 197–204; English translation "Nihilism on a Religious Soil," trans. Fr. S. Janos, wwwberdyaev.com/berdiaev/berd_lib/1907_135_4.html.

meaning and value than the whole of history with its empires, its wars and revolutions, its blossoming and fading civilizations."[37]

The Russian-Jewish philosopher Lev Shestov (1866–1938) belonged to the same circle of Russian intellectuals as Berdyaev but developed a doctrinally non-specific variety of religious existentialism strongly influenced by Nietzsche and Kierkegaard. Beginning with his first published work, *The Apotheosis of Groundlessness* (1905), he expressed a strong reaction against rationalism and foundationalism: "We know nothing of the ultimate realities of our existence, nor shall we ever know anything," he wrote. "The business of philosophy is to teach man to live in uncertainty." Following his disputes with the Bolsheviks, Shestov and his family fled westward, to Switzerland and eventually to Paris, where he lived until his death. His magnum opus, *Athens and Jerusalem* (1937), is an extended and eclectic mediation – invoking a great many thinkers such as Socrates, Tertullian, and Kierkegaard – on the conflict between rationalism and religion, knowledge and morality, philosophy and belief. The "Judeo-Christian philosophy," Shestov writes, rejects both the problem and the techniques of the rationalist tradition. When Athens proclaims *urbi et orbi*, "If you wish to subject everything to yourself, subject yourself to reason," Jerusalem hears through these words, "All these things will I give thee if thou wilt fall down and worship me."[38]

The revolt against philosophical rationalism in both religious and non-religious existentialism became most pronounced in the 1920s and 1930s among the diverse philosophers and theologians who drew upon the legacy of Kierkegaard, Nietzsche, and Dostoyevsky. Although many of these thinkers participated in the Barthian movement of dialectical theology, not all of them were Barthians in the strict sense. Hardest to categorize is Rudolf Otto (1869–1937), the German professor of religion best known for his philosophical inquiry *The Holy: On the Irrational in the Idea of the Divine and its Relationship to the Rational* (1917). Using careful techniques of Kantian analysis and borrowing, in subtle ways, from the nineteenth-century theologian Friedrich Schleiermacher's experientialism, Otto sought to define the distinctive religious (as opposed to ethical or doctrinal) element in religious experience as an awe-filled and mysterious encounter with the "numinous." For the proponents of dialectical theology, however, Otto's efforts fell short precisely because his emphasis on religious feeling betrayed a greater interest in

---

37 Nicholai Berdyaev, *The Fate of Man in the Modern World*, trans. Donald Lowrie (Ann Arbor: University of Michigan Press, 1961).
38 Lev Shestov, *Athens and Jerusalem*, ed. and trans. Bernard Martin (Athens: Ohio University Press, 1966), 224.

human experience rather than a devotion to the event of divine revelation itself. "Even in the numinous," wrote one critic, "man does not become aware of God, but only of himself. And he is deceived if he interprets the numinous as the divine, even when his frightful shuddering is a blessed experience. For then he always asked only about himself and not really about something that lies beyond him."[39]

Christian existentialism in the true sense of the term is most associated with a handful of early- and mid-twentieth-century thinkers such as Rudolf Bultmann, Paul Tillich, and Gabriel Marcel.[40] Rudolf Bultmann (1884–1976) is best known for developing a strategy of biblical criticism that stripped away the merely historical surface of the New Testament from its authentic and existential core: Only via such a "demythologization" could one redeem the genuine *kerygma* of Christ's teaching from the biblical *mythos* of ancient metaphors and themes.[41] In Bultmann's interpretation Christianity was essentially a revelation to humanity of its own finitude: "To know about revelation," he wrote, "means to know about our own authenticity – and, at the same time, thereby to know of our own limitation."[42] It should perhaps not surprise us that the genuine lessons of Christianity in this interpretation bore a noteworthy resemblance to the phenomenological and "formal-indicative" interpretation of religious texts as developed by the philosopher Martin Heidegger, Bultmann's colleague at the university in Marburg in the early 1920s.[43] Although Heidegger was Catholic by origin and had studied for the Jesuit priesthood, he later abjured the explicitly Catholic-doctrinal character of his own work. When he delivered his public lecture "Phenomenology and Theology" in 1928 he openly declared that *"faith,* as a specific possibility of existence, is in its innermost core the mortal enemy of the *form of existence* that is an essential part of *philosophy."*[44] Such statements make it difficult, though not impossible, to place Heidegger among the ranks

---

39 Todd Gooch, *The Numinous and Modernity: An Interpretation of Rudolf Otto's Philosophy of Religion* (Berlin: Walter de Gruyter, 2000), 68.
40 For a general survey see Andreas Grossmann, "Existential Theology," in *Phenomenology: Responses and Developments*, ed. Leonard Lawlor (New York: Routledge, 2014), 177–194.
41 Rudolf Bultmann, "New Testament and Mythology," in *Kerygma and Myth*, ed. Hans Werner Bartsch (New York: Harper & Row, 1961), 1–44.
42 Rudolf Bultmann, "The Concept of Revelation in the New Testament," in *Existence and Faith: Shorter Writings of Rudolf Bultmann*, trans. Schubert M. Ogden (New York: Meridian Books, 1960), 58–91, p. 62.
43 For more on Heidegger's readings of theological texts, see John van Buren, *The Young Heidegger: Rumor of the Hidden King* (Bloomington: Indiana University Press, 1994).
44 Martin Heidegger, "Phenomenology and Theology," in *Pathmarks*, ed. William McNeill (New York: Cambridge University Press, 1998), 39–62, p. 52.

of the Christian existentialists, notwithstanding his later quasi-religious statement that questioning itself is "the piety of thinking."[45]

One of the most enduring voices in the tradition of Christian existentialism is Paul Tillich (1886–1965), the son of a Lutheran pastor whose experience as an army chaplain in World War I turned him into a dedicated socialist. During his time as a professor at Marburg he came to know both Bultmann and Heidegger, and drew some inspiration from the rebellious spirit of dialectical theology, though he mistrusted the strain of asocial quietism and the "one-sided" affirmation of absolute transcendence that he detected in the Barthian movement. Like the Barthians, Tillich resisted any attempt to efface the qualitative distinction between God and humanity, and he embraced Christian revelation as "the breaking-in of the unconditioned."[46] In *The Present-Day Religious Situation* Tillich blamed capitalism for obscuring the possibility of "self-transcendence" and the "hallowing of existence."[47] In 1932 Tillich published *The Socialist Decision*, a strong condemnation of the Nazis, which eventually led to his dismissal from his chair at the University of Frankfurt. Tillich had once served as the advisor to the young Theodor W. Adorno's habilitation on Kierkegaard; during his later years in the United States he sustained his association with members of the Institute for Social Research (the "Frankfurt School").[48] During those years in the United States, Tillich composed his three-volume *Systematic Theology*, which explores the "correlation" between humanity and God and, using the language of existentialism, defines God as "the Ground of Being."[49]

Among the earliest and most influential exponents of Christian existentialism in France was Gabriel Marcel (1889–1973), whose "Friday evenings" gathered many intellectuals such as Emmanuel Lévinas, Simone de Beauvoir, Nikolai Berdyaev, and Paul Ricœur. Beginning with his *Journal métaphysique*, written between 1913 and 1923, Marcel developed a largely anti-systematic approach to philosophical and religious problems with strong undertones of existential pathos.[50] Beyond the human being lies "the transcendent," which

---

45 Martin Heidegger, "The Question Concerning Technology," in *The Question Concerning Technology and Other Essays*, trans. William Lovitt (New York: Harper Perennial, 1982), 35.
46 Paul Tillich, "Kairos," in *Main Works/Hauptwerke*, ed. Carl H. Ratschow, 6 vols. (New York: de Gruyter, 1987), vol. IV, 55–57.
47 Paul Tillich, *Die religiöse Lage der Gegenwart* (Berlin: Ullstein, 1926).
48 On Tillich and Adorno's study of Kierkegaard, see Peter E. Gordon, *Adorno and Existence* (Cambridge: Harvard University Press, 2016).
49 Paul Tillich, *Systematic Theology*, 3 vols. (Chicago: University of Chicago Press, 1951), vol. I.
50 Paul A. Schilp and Lewis E. Hahn (eds.), *The Philosophy of Gabriel Marcel* (La Salle: Open Court, 1984).

is separated from us by "an absolute, unbridgeable chasm."[51] But we live in a "broken world," that "ignores the tragic and denies the transcendent"[52] The child of a Jewish mother and a self-described atheist father, Marcel converted to Catholicism in 1929 and played an important role in the renewal of Catholic thought in the postwar era. Reluctant to embrace fixed doctrines and more interested in questioning than arriving at certain conclusions, Marcel accepted the term "Neo-Socratism" as a characterization of his method.[53] The best-known student of Marcel was Paul Ricœur (1913–2005), a highly esteemed French philosopher of the Protestant faith who taught for many years in France before joining the faculty of the Divinity School at the University of Chicago. Best known for his wide-ranging contributions to phenomenology and hermeneutics, Ricœur retained in much of his work a strong interest in questions that were conventionally understood as theological (such as human fallibility and evil), though he rarely thematized their religious nature.[54]

Throughout the twentieth century it was not uncommon for European thinkers to develop lines of affinity between theology and phenomenology, beginning as early as Max Scheler (1874–1928), a student of Edmund Husserl and an important interlocutor for Martin Heidegger, whose call for Christian renewal in works such as *On the Eternal in Man* (a series of essays written during the years 1916–1920) helped to inspire a host of later thinkers.[55] Among the most prominent contributors to the expressly Christian stream of phenomenology were Edith Stein (1891–1942), a Jewish-born convert to Catholicism and Carmelite nun who was murdered in Auschwitz for her statements against Nazism. She was later beatified by Pope John Paul II (Karol Wojtyła, 1920–2005), who earned his own doctorate in theology from the Jagiellonian University in Kraków with a thesis on Scheler's philosophy. The strong tradition of Catholic phenomenology has continued up to the end of the twentieth century, as represented by a host of philosophers and theologians, most notably Jean-Luc Marion (1946–). Born in France and

---

51 Gabriel Marcel, *Tragic Wisdom and Beyond*, ed. John Wild, trans. Stephen Jolin and Peter McCormick (Evanston: Northwestern University Press, 1973), 193.
52 Gabriel Marcel, *The Philosophy of Existentialism*, trans. Manya Harari (New York: Carol Publishing Group, 1995), 15.
53 "Conversations between Paul Ricœur and Gabriel Marcel," in Gabriel Marcel, *Tragic Wisdom and Beyond*, ed. John Wild, trans. Stephen Jolin and Peter McCormick (Evanston: Northwestern University Press, 1973), 251.
54 Paul Ricœur, *Fallible Man*, rev. trans. Charles A. Kelbley (New York: Fordham University Press, 1986 [1960]); and Paul Ricœur, *The Symbolism of Evil*, trans. Emerson Buchanan (New York: Harper & Row, 1967 [1960]).
55 For a comprehensive study, see Edward Baring, *Converts to the Real: Catholicism and the Making of Continental Philosophy* (Cambridge: Harvard University Press, 2019).

educated in philosophy under the direction of Jacques Derrida, but also strongly influenced by thinkers as diverse as Louis Althusser, Lévinas, Gilson, and von Balthasar, Marion eventually assumed a professorial appointment at the University of Chicago Divinity School, where he has contributed to a wide variety of themes in the philosophy of religion. Beginning with his work on Husserl and Heidegger, Marion continues to work at the interstices of phenomenology and Christianity, best exemplified by his book *Dieu sans l'être* (originally 1982; translated into English as *God without Being*).[56] Drawing upon insights from Heidegger and Derrida regarding the history of metaphysics, Marion has aligned himself with the thought of "postmodernity," namely, its challenge to conventional ontologies. Marion argues that "Being" should not stand as the highest determination of the divine. In claiming that "God loves before being," Marion does not mean to dispute that God exists; rather, in homage to the ancient critique of idolatry, he aims to show that the "absolute freedom" of God means that we should not conceive of Being as "the first and highest of the divine names."[57] This argument clearly involves a subtle reconsideration of Thomist principles, and Marion has readily acknowledged that some critics fault him for disputing the Thomist foundations that have remained authoritative in modern Catholic theology.[58]

Religion, Revolution, and Global Responsibility

The last third of the twentieth century brought to the fore emancipatory trends in Catholic theology that occasionally tested or even broke the bonds of official Church doctrine. Johann Baptist Metz (1928–) is a German-born Catholic theologian strongly influenced by Karl Rahner but best known for developing a "new" political theology (wholly unlike the authoritarian political theology associated with Carl Schmitt) with progressive strains that helped to inspire Gustavo Gutiérrez and the broader movement of liberation theology in Latin America.[59] Drawing chiefly on the New Testament concept

---

56 Jean-Luc Marion, *God without Being* (Chicago: University of Chicago Press, 1991). For an overview of the trend in Christian phenomenology, see Dominique Janicaud, Jean-François Courtine, Jean-Louis Chrétien, Michel Henry, Jean-Luc Marion, and Paul Ricœur, *Phenomenology and the "Theological Turn": The French Debate* (New York: Fordham University Press, 2000).
57 Jean-Luc Marion, "Preface to the English Edition" of *God without Being*, 2nd edn. (Chicago: University of Chicago Press, 2012), xxii.
58 Marion, *God without Being*, 235 and xxiv.
59 For an excellent summary of the postwar German rebirth of Christian theology in relation to liberation theology, see Dagmar Herzog, "The Death of God in West Germany: Between Secularization, Postfascism, and the Rise of Liberation Theology," in *Die*

of *anamnesis* in combination with Marxian themes from Walter Benjamin and the Frankfurt School, Metz has articulated a theory of "dangerous memory" as a critical point of leverage against bourgeois and conformist forms of the Christian faith. Christianity, especially in its memory of Christ's passion, preserves "non-contemporaneous elements" that awaken a "capacity for resistance" and make "radical claims" on humanity.[60] "Every rebellion against suffering," he argues, "is fed by the subversive power of remembered suffering."[61]

Jürgen Moltmann (1926–) is a German-born Protestant theologian who took his major inspiration from Barth and Bonhoeffer but also drew considerable instruction from Ernst Bloch's multi-volume study from the 1950s, *The Principle of Hope*.[62] In his first major work, *Theology of Hope* (first published in 1964), Moltmann argues that "Expectation makes life good, for in expectation man can accept his whole present and find joy not only in its joy but also in its sorrow, happiness not only in its happiness but also in its pain. Thus hope goes on its way through the midst of happiness and pain, because in the promises of God it can see a future also for the transient, the dying and the dead." Thus "living without hope is no longer living."[63]

In *The Crucified God* (1972) Moltmann turned his attention to the paradoxical event of divine crucifixion as the heart of Christian doctrine. "If faith in the crucified Christ is in contradiction to all conceptions of the righteousness, beauty and morality of man, faith in the 'crucified God' is also a contradiction – of everything men have ever conceived, desired, and sought to be assured of by the term 'God.' That 'God,' the 'supreme being' and the 'supreme good,' should be revealed and present in the abandonment of Jesus by God on the cross, is something that it is difficult to desire." For Moltmann, however, it was not the supremacy of God but rather the event of divine debasement that distinguishes the "irreligious" and "revolutionary" moment in Christianity. "In spite of all the 'roses' which the needs of religion and theological interpretation have

---

Gegenwart Gottes in der modernen Gesellschaft: Transzendenz und religiöse Vergemeinschaftung in Deutschland/The Presence of God in Modern Society: Transcendence and Religious Community in Germany, ed. Michael Geyer and Lucian Hölscher (Göttingen: Wallstein, 2006), 431–466.

60 Johann Baptist Metz, "Productive Noncontemporaneity," in *Observations on "The Spiritual Situation of the Age*," ed. Jürgen Habermas, trans. Andrew Buchwalter (Cambridge: MIT Press, 1985), 169–177, p. 176.

61 Johann Baptist Metz and Jürgen Moltmann, *Faith and the Future: Essays on Theology, Solidarity, and Modernity* (Maryknoll: Orbis Books, 1995), 8.

62 Ernst Bloch, *Das Prinzip Hoffnung*, 3 vols. (Frankfurt am Main: Suhrkamp, 1985 [1954–1959]).

63 Jürgen Moltmann, *Theologie der Hoffnung: Untersuchungen zur Begründung und zu den Konsequenzen einer christlichen Eschatologie* (Gütersloh: Gütersloher Verlagshaus, 1997); English translation *Theology of Hope*, trans. James W. Leitch (Minneapolis: Fortress Press, 1993), 32.

draped round the cross," he argued, "the cross is the really irreligious thing in Christian faith. It is the suffering of God in Christ, rejected and killed in the absence of God, which qualifies Christian faith as faith, and as something different from the projection of man's desire."[64] In his lecture "God and Revolution" (first presented in the summer of 1968 at the World Student Christian Federation Conference in Finland), Moltmann emphasized the emancipatory meaning of Christianity. "The Church," he declared, *"is not a heavenly arbiter in the world's strifes. In the present struggles for freedom and justice, Christians must side with the humanity of the oppressed."*[65]

Hans Küng (1928–), born in Switzerland and employed in Tübingen as a professor on the Catholic faculty until his 1996 retirement, ranks among the most original and heterodox theologians in the Catholic tradition. His work is distinctive among Catholic theologians for its readiness to engage with Protestant thought, especially with the work of Karl Barth, the topic of Küng's 1957 doctoral dissertation.[66] He is perhaps best known for his 1967 work *The Church*, which appeared in the wake of the Second Vatican Council. *The Church* heralded his increasingly critical attitude toward the hierarchical character of the Roman Catholic Church, and even suggested that in the past the Church had occasionally departed from the truth of Christianity. "In all ages," he wrote, "the Church has been partly responsible for the rise of great heresies, and nearly always by neglecting or even by obscuring and distorting the Gospel."[67] Even more controversial was Küng's 1970 book *Infallible*, in which he rejected the doctrine of papal infallibility, as he did also in other, related works on the same theme.[68] Among the more troublesome instances of papal infallibility in Küng's view was *Humanae Vitae*, Pope Paul VI's encyclical which prohibits Catholic use of contraception. His argument against infallibility involves an appeal to the modern ideal of truthfulness. "Today – very differently from former times," he wrote,

> we do not take it badly if anyone says he has changed his opinion, that he has revised, corrected his view, that today he would see it differently, better, or in the opposite way. We respect a person for saying this. We take it badly

---

64 Jürgen Moltmann, *The Crucified God: The Cross of Christ as the Foundation and Criticism of Christian Theology*, trans. R. A. Wilson and J. Bowden (Minneapolis: Fortress Press, 1993), 37.
65 Jürgen Moltmann, "God in Revolution," in *Religion, Revolution and the Future*, trans. M. Douglas Meeks (New York: Charles Scribner's Sons, 1969).
66 Hans Küng, *Justification: The Doctrine of Karl Barth and a Catholic Reflection* (London: Burns and Oates, 1964 [1957]). Originally in German.
67 Hans Küng, *The Church* (London: Burns & Oates, 1967), 247.
68 Hans Küng, *Unfehlbar?: Eine Anfrage* (Zurich: Benziger, 1970).

only if someone changes his mind but does not admit it; when a person says the opposite of what he said before, but now asserts that he has always said it. For modern man it is not the revision of a position but the negations of a revision which offend against truthfulness.[69]

As a consequence of his challenge to the doctrine of infallibility, Küng was stripped by Church authorities of his license to teach as a Catholic, though he continued as a professor of ecumenical theology. Since the early 1990s he has directed his attention primarily toward the question of a "global ethics" shared in common by the world's diverse religions. As the head of the "Foundation for a Global Ethics," Küng drafted the "Declaration of a Global Ethics" at the 1993 Parliament of the World's Religions. Its mission is summarized in his book *Global Responsibility*, in which he declared that "There will be peace on earth when there is peace among the world religions."[70]

A no less formidable challenge to the conventional understanding of Christianity has come from the feminist theologian Elisabeth Schüssler Fiorenza (1938–), a Romanian-born Roman Catholic who studied in Germany before moving to the United States, where she taught at Notre Dame before assuming a post at Harvard Divinity School. A cofounder of the *Journal of Feminist Studies in Religion*, Schüssler Fiorenza has played a major role in transforming received notions concerning women in early Christianity, most notably in her book *In Memory of Her: A Feminist Theological Reconstruction of Christian Origins* (1983), a work that explores the prominent missionary work of women in early Christianity. It has been translated into no fewer than thirteen languages.[71]

Among the many controversies that have roiled Christian theology over the course of the last century, perhaps the most prominent is that which concerns the divinity of Christ. It was not only Moltmann who discerned something "irreligious" in the doctrine of divine incarnation. Already the Church father Tertullian (155–240 C.E.) had announced in his *De Carne Christi* (203–206) that this "absurdity" was not an obstacle to belief but its precondition: "*prorsus credibile est, quia ineptum est* [it is by all means to be believed, because it is absurd]." In the nineteenth century, Søren Kierkegaard identified this as a distinguishing paradox of Christian faith, while the left-Hegelian

---

69 Hans Küng, *Truthfulness: The Future of the Church* (New York: Sheed & Ward, 1968), 130.
70 Hans Küng, *Global Responsibility: In Search of a New World Ethic* (Eugene: Wipf and Stock, 1991), 76. Originally published in German as *Projekt Weltethos*.
71 Elisabeth Schüssler Fiorenza, *In Memory of Her: A Feminist Theological Reconstruction of Christian Origins*, new edn. (New York: Crossroad Publishing, 1995).

David Friedrich Strauss (1808–1874) tried to overcome this paradox in his historical study, *The Life of Jesus* (1835), in which he interpreted Christ as a purely human being. It is perhaps unsurprising that the idea of Christ's this-worldly appearance as a human being has taken on a special and more poignant meaning in an era of European secularization. The Greek novelist Nikos Kazantzakis (1883–1957) made this idea the central conceit in his postwar novel *The Last Temptation of Christ* (1955), a work which was condemned as blasphemous by the Greek Orthodox Church, but which the author, himself a Christian believer, defended as a sincere theological inquiry: "In order to mount to the Cross, the summit of sacrifice, and to God, the summit of materiality, Christ passed through all the stages which the man who struggles passes through. That is why his suffering is so familiar to us," Kazantzakis explained. "That part of Christ's nature which was profoundly human helps us to understand him and love him and to pursue his Passion as though it were our own. If he had not within him this warm human element, he would never be able to touch our hearts with such assurance and tenderness; he would not be able to become a model for our lives."[72] More recently, the Italian philosopher Gianni Vattimo (1936–) has extended this idea by claiming that secularization is not the denial of religion but rather signals a final extension of the religious (specifically Christian) event of divine *kenosis*, that is, the "self-emptying" or worldly debasement by which God becomes incarnate in a human being.[73] A striking, if seemingly paradoxical, consequence of this argument is that it redescribes even the rejection of religion *as a religious event*. It thereby reclaims modern secularization not as a challenge to Christianity but as a further confirmation of Christianity's validity and longevity in the modern era.

Conclusion

By the end of the twentieth century, the combined forces of immigration and international conflict had transformed Europe from a region with an overwhelmingly Christian majority population into a multicultural landscape rich with representatives of the world's many ethno-religious groups. In a speech in Frankfurt in 2001, the German social theorist Jürgen Habermas observed that this "post-secular" condition presents a challenge especially to adherents

---

72 Nikos Kazantzakis, *The Last Temptation of Christ*, trans. P. A. Bien (New York: Simon & Schuster, 1960 [1955]); quotation from the author's prologue, 1–3. Originally in Greek.
73 Gianni Vattimo, *After Christianity*, trans. Luca D'Isanto (New York: Columbia University Press, 2002), 24.

of faith-traditions who must "come to terms with the cognitive dissonance of encountering other denominations and religions."[74] If they do not take upon themselves the "thrust of reflection," he warned, "monotheisms in relentlessly modernized societies unleash a destructive potential." But, as Habermas acknowledged, the new era places demands on *both* religious *and* irreligious citizens alike, qualifying all absolutistic worldviews and increasing the need for self-scrutiny and the readiness to learn from others. What one might call the "deep pluralism" of Europe today demands a willingness to abstain from grounding one's politics in metaphysical schemes that would exclude other forms of life. Secularism need not be secularist; those who do not adhere to faith-traditions must make room for their religious co-citizens as equal partners in dialogue within the framework of the secular-democratic state. The transformation of theology and religious consciousness belongs to this same process, an ongoing and cooperative effort from which no religion can abstain. "All paths, Arjuna, lead to Me."[75]

---

74 Jürgen Habermas, "Faith and Knowledge," reprinted in *The Frankfurt School on Religion: Key Writings of the Major Thinkers*, ed. Eduardo Mendieta (London: Routledge, 2005), 329.
75 *Bhagavad Gita* 4.11.

14

Modern Economic Thought and the "Good Society"

HAGEN SCHULZ-FORBERG

Liberalism and the "Good Society"

In liberal economic thought, debating the "good society" was particularly prominent in the middle decades of the twentieth century, a period in which, as John Maynard Keynes (1883–1946) put it, people were "unusually expectant of a more fundamental diagnosis."[1] Good society here describes a normative horizon against which arguments are legitimized and toward which societies should strive. The term itself is mentioned rarely by economists. Mostly, they shared the notion that what is "good" cannot be defined in detail beyond the fact that it entails more than individual happiness and thus more than the hedonistic utilitarianism attached to the liberal tradition of the eighteenth and nineteenth centuries.[2] The economists and philosophers who, like Keynes, engaged in "a more fundamental diagnosis" of the link between economics and the "good society" conversed in a number of languages and argued in an institutional landscape that had been erected by and attached to the League of Nations in the 1920s and 1930s. Its funding mainly came from the League, governments, and private foundations. It was the first generation of internationally linked universities, foreign policy institutions, international affairs institutes, think-tanks, international organizations, and national

---

1 John Maynard Keynes, *The General Theory of Employment, Interest, and Money* (London: Macmillan, 1936), 383.
2 Debates about the good society included reflections on the role of givens and values in liberalism. Fundamental for Keynes in particular and representative of a general discussion is the work of G. E. Moore, *Principia Ethica* (Cambridge: Cambridge University Press, 1903); and G. E. Moore, *Ethics* (London: Williams & Norgate, 1912). When thinking about society (and not only about the individual as its constituent) economists often made the point that they were not merely utilitarians. See particularly the discussion "Liberalism and Christianity" at the Mont Pèlerin Society's first conference, April 1–10, 1947, held on April 4, in Liberaal Archief, Ghent, Belgium, Folder 01-1-08–14-01.

governments.[3] During the 1930s, economists were engaged in rethinking a liberal doctrine that would both provide a socially more balanced polity within the framework of a strong, independent state based on the rule of law and at the same time help create a peaceful international order. Some economists called their new agenda "neoliberalism."

The nascent neoliberalism of this period might best be called 'early neoliberalism,' to distinguish it from the more contemporary neoliberalism that emerged in the 1970s and 1980s. While, today, neoliberalism is virtually never self-declared but a critical term describing others or, rather, describes a free market ideology that excludes the state as much as possible and imagines the market as a self-propelling machine that is best left to private citizens as its only contractors, early neoliberalism was not only self-declared, but economists identified with the concept, its agenda foregrounded a concern about the concept of the human person in connection with a concern about the social, and it attached quite comprehensive responsibilities for society to the state.[4]

3 Daniel Laqua, "Transnational Intellectual Cooperation, the League of Nations, and the Problem of Order," *Journal of Global History*, 6(2) (2011), 223–247; Michael Riemens, "International Academic Cooperation on International Relations in the Interwar Period: The International Studies Conference," *Review of International Studies*, 37(2) (2011), 911–928; Katharina Rietzler, "Experts for Peace: Structures and Motivations of Philanthropic Internationalism in the Interwar Years," in *Internationalism Reconfigured: Transnational Ideas and Movements between the World Wars*, ed. Daniel Laqua (London: I. B. Tauris, 2011), 45–65; Katharina Rietzler, "Expertenwissen, Internationalismus und Idealismus: Amerikanische Stiftungen als Förderer der Disziplin der Internationalen Beziehungen in der Zwischenkriegszeit," in *Jenseits der Anarchie: Weltordnungsentwürfe im frühen 20. Jahrhundert*, ed. Jens Steffek and Leonie Holthaus (Frankfurt am Main: Campus Verlag, 2014), 255–279; Jo-Anne Pemberton, "The Changing Shape of Intellectual Cooperation: From the League of Nations to UNESCO," *Australian Journal of Politics and History*, 58(1) (2012), 34–50; and Hagen Schulz-Forberg, "Laying the Groundwork: The Semantics of Neoliberalism in the 1930s," in *Re-Inventing Western Civilisation. Transnational Reconstructions of Liberalism in Europe in the Twentieth Century*, ed. Hagen Schulz-Forberg and Niklas Olsen (Newcastle upon Tyne: Cambridge Scholars Press, 2014), 13–39.

4 The semantics of the concept of the human person are not free from power relations. The concept of the human person, which has inspired international lawyers as well as Christian thinkers, can be interpreted as fertile ground for the emergence of human rights, which semantically (partly) build on Christian interpretations of the human person; see S. Moyn, *Christian Human Rights* (Philadelphia: Pennsylvania University Press, 2015). Yet the concept entails even racist undertones, when interpreted in a way that would put each human person in his or her supposed place within a hierarchy among different humans (and thus secure white leadership). See Mark Mazower, *No Enchanted Palace: The End of Empire and the Ideological Origins of the United Nations* (Princeton: Princeton University Press, 2009), particularly the chapter on the South African prime minister Jan Smuts, and his vision and role related to the UN, pp. 28–65. For colonialist and racist undertones in early neoliberal thought see also Quinn Slobodian, "The World Economy and the Color Line: Wilhelm Röpke, Apartheid, and the White Atlantic," *German Historical Institute Bulletin Supplement*, no. 10 (2014), 61–87.

Modern Economic Thought and the "Good Society"

Furthermore, early neoliberalism strongly argued for two more key conditions for a sustainable free (and, thus, "good") society, namely the price mechanism and the rule of law. The price mechanism describes a market in which the cost and the number of goods traded are not predefined. Prices are not tagged on products, but emerge freely through the interplay of supply and demand. Conscious of the need to support national labor and production to sustain social peace, early neoliberals did not insist on one global free market, however. They insisted on the international compatibility of national markets and polities. As long as the price mechanism could unfold without inhibition, national markets' labor supply could be influenced by decisions on working conditions and working hours, for example. Tariffs could be imposed.[5] Similarly, currency exchange rates could be used to support national economies without infringing on the making of prices inside markets. The latter were among the accepted forms of state intervention from a liberal point of view.[6] Generally speaking, the state could intervene in manifold ways as long as whatever it did would not infringe on the price mechanism. Any social policy and state intervention needed to take place in a transparent manner and within a balanced budget.[7] The red line never to be crossed was conscious making of prices in a top-down manner by defining the quantity and cost of a product. The price mechanism's function or dysfunction was the benchmark for any form of state action characterizing so-called liberal interventionism.

While the price mechanism served as a way to ward off top-down tendencies of an economically active state, the rule of law, in the arguments of early neoliberals, served as insulation against a notion of politics that finds source and reference for legitimate rule solely within the boundaries of the nation-state. The rule of law served as the normative framework of the state. Politics may unfold freely, but within its limits, and, what is more, in a way that allows international cooperation. This, for early neoliberals, was essential to avoid a form of politics that merely pleases populist tendencies, which might quickly turn into a state-led economy. To avoid any deviations from the liberal core, economics needed to be joined with law at the constitutional level of the liberal society. An economic order that considered social needs and guaranteed free markets simultaneously (termed a "competitive order"

---

5 See one of the most well-known and outspoken experts on state intervention, Jacques Rueff, *Épître aux dirigistes* (Paris: Gallimard, 1949), 52–60.
6 Friedrich Hayek, "The Economic Condition of Inter-State Federalism," *New Commonwealth Quarterly*, 5(2) (1939), 131–149.
7 Jacques Rueff, *L'ordre social* (Paris: Librairie de Médicis, 1948), esp. 556–567. See also Rueff's interventions at the Walter Lippmann Colloquium in Louis Rougier, *Compte-rendu des séances du Colloque Walter Lippmann* (Paris: Librairie de Médicis, 1939).

by early neoliberals[8]) had to be erected from its legal source and not by politics alone to keep both laissez-faire and illiberal tendencies at bay. Questions related to the segments of society and the economy in which the price mechanism should reign led to constant discussion, tensions, and redefinitions. The contestation of early neoliberalism's core concepts – the human person, the price mechanism, and the rule of law – is a defining element of modern economic thought's grappling with the ways in which the "good society" might be achieved. At the same time, this contestation reconfirmed the fundamental importance of the concepts.

Among the early neoliberal economists prominently engaged in debating the good society in Europe during the middle decades of the twentieth century were (here listed alphabetically) Louis Baudin (1887–1964), Constantino Bresciani-Turroni (1882–1963), Luigi Einaudi (1874–1961), Walter Eucken (1891–1950), Friedrich August von Hayek (1899–1992), Robert Marjolin (1911–1986), Louis Marlio (1878–1952), Alfred Müller-Armack (1901–1978), Lionel Robbins (1898–1984), Wilhelm Röpke (1899–1966), Jacques Rueff (1896–1978), and Alexander Rüstow (1885–1963). They engaged prominently with fellow economists and philosophers (and fellow neoliberals) like Raymond Aron (1905–1983), Michael Polanyi (1891–1976), Karl Popper (1902–1994), and Louis Rougier (1889–1982), the Dutch humanist Johan Huizinga (1872–1945), fascist economists such as Luigi Amoroso (1886–1965), legal philosophers like Bruno Leoni (1913–1967), Hans Kelsen (1881–1973) and his anti-liberal counterpart Carl Schmitt (1888–1985), and their American colleagues Aaron Director (1901–2004), Milton Friedman (1912–2006), Frank Knight (1885–1972), Walter Lippmann (1889–1974), and Henry Simons (1899–1946). All of them debated the ideas of Keynes and Keynesianism.

Early neoliberalism was formulated more precisely by the participants at the Walter Lippmann Colloquium (WLC) held in Paris at the International Institute for Intellectual Cooperation (IIIC) in late August 1938.[9]

---

8 See the discussion following Hayek's introductory paper at the Mont Pèlerin Society, April 1, 1947, Liberaal Archief, Folder 01-1-08-14-01, particularly the intervention by Aaron Director. Furthermore, see an already edited and slightly changed version: Friedrich Hayek, "'Free' Enterprise and Competitive Order," in Friedrich Hayek, *Individualism and Economic Order* (Chicago: Chicago University Press, 1948), 107–118.

9 François Denord, *Néo-libéralisme version française: Histoire d'une idéologie politique* (Paris: Demopolis, 2007), esp. 112–125; Serge Audier, *Néo-libéralisme(s): Une archéologie intellectuelle* (Paris: Grasset, 2012), esp. 59–164; and Serge Audier, *Le Colloque Lippmann: Aux origines de néo-libéralisme* (Lormont: Éditions Bord de l'Eau, 2008). In these books neither Denord nor Audier includes the decisive institutional element of the transnational intellectual and institutional landscape shaped by the IIIC. For this see Schulz-Forberg, "Laying the Groundwork."

The influence of the American public intellectual and political consultant Walter Lippmann and his programmatically titled 1937 book *An Inquiry into the Principles of the Good Society*[10] was particularly marked among European interlocutors. This eloquently written book amplified many of the positions shared among liberal economists in Europe. The early neoliberal agenda is forcefully outlined in the book; the concept of the human person is central, as is the rule of law and the necessity to allow prices and markets to develop on their own, though within certain limits necessary for keeping the social peace and for making liberalism not only more social, but also more sustainable. It was also written at a time in which not many key books with a similar focus and depth existed,[11] yet the general questions it addressed were pondered within extensive transnational networks. How can a national social and political order be reconciled with an international one to secure peace? How can peaceful change be achieved? Can a common value system be achieved internationally?

The role of economics within all these larger questions was fundamental, and the economists mentioned above were not only connected with each other, but also connected to the policy-making institutions informing international institutions and carving out the language for international order. Lippmann's book provided a uniting and succinct synthesis for a liberal way to actively create a good society. As one of the most influential and internationally known scholars from the German ordoliberal variety of early neoliberalism, Wilhelm Röpke, illustrated in his introduction to the German translation of Lippmann's treatise, the book "had an overwhelming impact on both sides of the Ocean that was amplified by translations and it gave the discussion about possibilities and forms of 'neoliberalism' the most numerous and fertile inspirations."[12]

Finally, Lippmann was highly prolific at the time, well known for his work for President Woodrow Wilson, his publications on public opinion, and his

10 Walter Lippmann, *An Inquiry into the Principles of the Good Society* (Boston: Little, Brown & Co., 1937).
11 The works available and renowned among liberal economists were few. Among the most circulated and translated was Ludwig von Mises, *Die Gemeinwirtschaft: Untersuchungen über den Sozialismus* (Jena: Gustav Fischer Verlag, 1922), which was translated into Swedish (1930), English (1936), and French (1938) during the 1930s. Further points of orientation were Lionel Robbins, *Economic Planning and International Order* (London: Macmillan, 1937), translated into French in 1938; Louis Rougier, *Les mystiques économiques: Comment l'on passe des démocraties libérales aux états totalitaires* (Paris: Librairie de Médicis, 1938); and Jacques Rueff, *La crise du capitalisme* (Paris: Éditions de la Revue bleue, 1935).
12 Wilhelm Röpke, "Einführung," to Walter Lippmann, *Die Gesellschaft freier Menschen* (Bern: A. Francke Verlag, 1945), 25–33, p. 28.

frequent interventions in public debate.[13] His standing certainly helped European economists to get heard.[14] When the French publishing house Librairie des Médicis provided its translation in 1938 (calling it *La cité libre*), the IIIC tasked Louis Rougier with organizing the colloquium. This philosopher and key intellectual within the French group of thinkers engaged in reshaping liberalism had gained prominence following his publications on the fragility of liberal democracies and economies.[15]

According to the "Agenda of Liberalism" developed at the WLC, the "good society" comprised five key elements. Beside the price mechanism, the state must, second, put in place and guarantee a legal order to safeguard the market's development and to legally justify any intervention. Third, political liberalism must embrace the law as the ultimate cornerstone of legitimacy, and the process of codifying law must be based on representative debates and capable of establishing general norms. Fourth, such a legal regime constitutes the liberal method to "control the social." Fifth, a liberal state is responsible for continuously providing society with five essential elements, to which end taxes may be imposed: national defense, social insurance, social services, education, and scientific research.[16]

The proponents of and contributors to a re-emergent liberalism did not develop this agenda for a new kind of liberalism in isolation and within closed circles, quite the contrary. Within the transnational landscape of actors and institutions emerging in the 1920s they built their ideas in conversation with and in contestation of different viewpoints, particularly fascism and socialism; and Keynes as well as Keynesianism. They were also not confined to careers in the closet of scholarship. The new landscape allowed international mobility between both countries and roles. For example, Alfred Müller-Armack, the German economist who coined the concept of a social market economy in the postwar period (and who argued in support of fascist corporatism before the war[17]), was a university professor, but also

---

13 See Walter Lippmann, *Public Opinion* (New York: Harcourt, Brace and Co., 1922); and Walter Lipmmann, *The Method of Freedom* (New York: Macmillan, 1934).
14 For information on how the relationship between Lippmann and Hayek developed and what Hayek expected from the link see Ben Jackson, "Freedom, the Common Good, and the Rule of Law: Lippmann and Hayek on Economic Planning," *Journal of the History of Ideas*, 73(1) (2012), 47–68.
15 Rougier, *Les mystiques économiques*; François Denord, "Aux origines du néo-libéralisme en France: Louis Rougier et le Colloque Walter Lippmann de 1938," *Le Mouvement Social*, no. 195 (April–June 2001), 9–34; and Schulz-Forberg, "Laying the Groundwork."
16 Paper given by Walter Lippmann at the WLC, see Rougier, *Colloque Walter Lippmann*, reprinted in Audier, *Le Colloque Lippmann*, 485–486.
17 Alfred Müller-Armack, *Staatsidee und Wirtschaftsordnung im neuen Reich* (Berlin: Junker and Dünnhaupt, 1933).

a member of the government administration and close collaborator of the German Minister of Economics, Ludwig Erhard; Robert Marjolin was a researcher for a think-tank, a member of the government, the secretary-general of an international organization (the Organisation for European Economic Co-operation, OEEC), and a member of the European Commission. In the 1920s, before taking up his role as general manager for the Bank for International Settlements from 1938 to 1959, Roger Auboin had been actively involved in founding the journal *L'Europe Nouvelle*, to which other early neoliberals also contributed. As well as being French President de Gaulle's postwar specialist on money and gold, the internationally recognized expert on currencies and liberal state intervention Jacques Rueff was also secretary for financial matters at the League of Nations and first president of the International Council for Philosophy and Humanistic Studies at UNESCO after the war from the late 1940s until 1955. These leading economists were attached to the same transnational networks as other scholars concerned with international relations. In fact, the International Studies Conference, a permanent organization run by the IIIC in the interwar period, was a very important platform for economists as well as political theorists, philosophers, and other academics and intellectuals concerned with recasting the global order.[18] And while, in 1948, the German émigré theorist of international relations Hans Morgenthau (1904–1980), who moved within the same networks as, and was inspired by, both Carl Schmitt (with whom he broke after a personal meeting)[19] and Hans Kelsen (with whom he worked in Geneva), coined the realist dictum that "nations meet under an empty sky from which the Gods have departed,"[20] values mattered for early neoliberals (not necessarily Gods, which mattered only for some) when it came to constructing the state and its economy within an international order. As the responsibility of the state and with it its administrative bodies grew increasingly comprehensive, normative ideas of statehood actively populated the skies above nations in the liberal imagination.[21]

---

18 Riemens, "International Academic Cooperation on International Relations in the Interwar Period."
19 For a critical reading of Morgenthau putting him closer to both Schmitt and Hayek, see Philip Mirowski, "Realism and Neoliberalism: From Reactionary Modernism to Conservatism," in *The Invention of International Relations Theory*, ed. Nicolas Guilhot (New York: Columbia University Press, 2011), 210–237.
20 Hans Morgenthau, *Politics among Nations* (New York: Alfred A. Knopf, 1948), 249.
21 In relation to liberal international thought, see particularly Susan Pedersen, "Getting out of Iraq – in 1932: The League of Nations and the Road to Normative Statehood," *The American Historical Review*, 115(4) (2010), 975–1000.

Yet, how social could any state's market economy be before it lost its liberal identity? From the late nineteenth century until the interwar period, social functions of the state increased in Europe, from Bismarck's social security bills in Prussia to the origins of the welfare state in the England of, particularly, Lloyd George before World War I when the concept of 'new liberalism' emerged.[22] Reworkings of liberal economic thought through the inclusion of welfare emerged in Sweden and England, and had a lasting European impact on liberal economic thought.[23] In England, particularly Leonard Trelawny Hobhouse (1864–1929) and John Atkinson Hobson (1858–1940) worked on ideas concerning a social liberalism. William Beveridge (1879–1963) and Keynes further developed their thought. Beveridge was one of the most important and politically influential academics of his time, beginning his career as the research assistant of Beatrice and Sidney Webb and having a stellar career at the London School of Economics (LSE, which was founded by the Webbs in 1894 on the template

22 For the origins of the Prussian social reforms see Hermann Beck, *Origins of the Authoritarian Welfare State in Prussia: Conservatives, Bureaucracy, and the Social Question, 1815–70* (Ann Arbor: University of Michigan Press, 1995); and Reinhart Koselleck, *Preußen zwischen Reform und Revolution: Allgemeines Landrecht, Verwaltung und soziale Bewegung von 1791 bis 1848* (Stuttgart: Klett-Cotta, 1967). For an interpretation of the impact of the Prussian model, see Wolfgang Streeck and Kozo Yamamura (eds.), *The Origins of Nonliberal Capitalism: Germany and Japan in Comparison* (Ithaca and London: Cornell University Press, 2001). The social question, which was prominent behind the Prussian social reforms, sparked the foundation of one of the most influential social-scientific organizations, the Verein für Socialpolitik (Social Policy Association), in 1872, where economists began a policy-conscious reflection connecting economics and concrete politics regarding ways to the good society (and of which both Hayek and von Mises were members). The critique of the Prussian reforms as something close to the original sin of the erroneously intervening state and the demise of the free-trade paradigm was also vividly discussed among early neoliberals in the 1930s and onwards as a root cause for the liberal crisis of the interwar years. See Lippmann, *An Inquiry into the Principles of the Good Society*, 135, for example. For the British case, key works of L. T. Hobhouse are *Liberalism* (London: Williams and Norgate, 1911); *Social Evolution and Political Theory* (New York: Columbia University Press, 1911); and *The Elements of Social Justice* (New York: H. Holt and Company, 1922). J. A. Hobson's work from the 1890s to the 1930s was extremely voluminous. In the context of this chapter the following publications may be highlighted: *The Problem of the Unemployed: An Enquiry and an Economic Policy* (London: Methuen & Co., 1896); *The Economics of Distribution* (New York and London: Macmillan, 1900); *The Crisis of Liberalism* (London: P. S. King & Son, 1909); *Towards International Government* (New York and London: Macmillan, 1915); *The Morals of Economic Internationalism* (Boston: Houghton Mifflin, 1920); and *Rationalism and Humanism* (London: Watts, 1933). For a discussion of the relation between socialism and new liberalism see Ben Jackson, "Socialism and the New Liberalism," in *Liberalism as Ideology: Essays in Honour of Michael Freeden*, ed. Ben Jackson and Marc Stears (Oxford: Oxford University Press, 2012), 34–52.
23 Roger E. Backhouse, Bradley W. Bateman, Tamotsu Nishizawa, and Dieter Plehwe (eds.), *Liberalism and the Welfare State: Economists and Arguments for the Welfare State* (Oxford: Oxford University Press, 2017).

of Paris's École Libre des Sciences Politiques, Sciences Po, founded in 1872 to serve as a private, independent source of elite formation) as its director from 1919 to 1937, when he moved to Oxford University and became Master of University College. His biggest legacy clearly is the Beveridge Report from 1942, which laid the foundations for the postwar welfare state in the United Kingdom and is the basis for his book *Full Employment in a Free Society*.[24] Additionally, Beveridge was a sought-after political consultant and during his years at the LSE among the most important figures not only nationally, but also internationally, when the LSE was probably the most important center of expertise catering for the provision of scientific input to the IIIC's global policy network. Similarly to Beveridge, Keynes was also very active both as a highly prolific academic and during spells within government, for example when he represented the United Kingdom at the Bretton Woods conference in 1944, and when one looks at the impact of those of his writings which were more accessible to the general public.[25] A brilliant economist at Cambridge University, he was also a member of the influential intellectual circle known as the Bloomsbury Group during the first half of the twentieth century. Both Beveridge and Keynes were members of the Liberal Party, yet, as Keynes said, pure capitalism was objectionable. "[W]isely managed," however, it "can probably be made more efficient for attaining economic ends than any alternative system yet in sight … Our problem is to work out a social organisation which shall be as efficient as possible without offending our notions of a satisfactory way of life."[26] This relationship between as much market as possible and as much state as necessary, to paraphrase Karl Schiller,[27] draws the lines of the field within which economic thought in the twentieth century debated the "good society."

---

24 William Beveridge, *Full Employment in a Free Society* (London: Allen and Unwin, 1944).
25 Keynes's competences are probably most vividly illustrated in Lionel Robbins's *Bretton Woods Diary* in the LSE Archives, folder: ROBBINS/6/1/2. See also Benn Steil, *The Battle of Bretton Woods: John Maynard Keynes, Harry Dexter White, and the Making of a New World Order* (Princeton: Princeton University Press, 2013); on Keynes's early years see Robert Skidelsky, *John Maynard Keynes: Hopes Betrayed, 1883–1920* (London: Penguin, 1994); how deeply disappointed Keynes was can be traced in John Maynard Keynes, *The Economic Consequences of the Peace* (London: Macmillan, 1919).
26 John Maynard Keynes, "The End of Laissez-Faire," in John Maynard Keynes, *Essays in Persuasion* (London: Palgrave Macmillan, 2010), 272–294, p. 294.
27 Schiller represents the social democratic side of early neoliberalism. He was a member of the Social Democratic Party, Minister of Economic Affairs from 1966 to 1972, and member of the Mont Pèlerin Society; he was also on good terms with Ludwig Erhard. His famous quote sums up the position German social democrats had developed toward the market economy in their Godesberg Program from 1959, which Schiller had influenced. See Erich Egner, *Studien über Haushalt und Verbrauch* (Berlin: Duncker & Humblot, 1963), 267, who attributes the quote to Schiller.

In their effort at welding a social element to liberalism in the 1930s and 1940s, French economists, for example, proposed a variety of terms ranging from "libéralisme social"[28] to "libéral-socialisme,"[29] "socialisme individualiste,"[30] "socialisme libéral,"[31] "libéralisme constructeur,"[32] and "néo-capitalisme" as well as "néo-socialisme,"[33] while in Germany Alexander Rüstow, a participant at the WLC and outspoken critic of laissez-faire liberalism, a friend of Walter Eucken and one of the foundational thinkers (together with Eucken) of Western Germany's ordoliberalism and its model of a social market economy alongside Wilhelm Röpke and Alfred Müller-Armack, talked of a "neue[r] Liberalismus."[34]

Ever since World War II, the Mont Pèlerin Society (MPS), which was founded in April 1947 on the initiative of Friedrich August von Hayek, has continued the discussion of fundamental questions of liberalism's economy and society. The MPS was not the only institution in which early neoliberals from the 1930s continued their effort, however, as members of the WLC can be found in a string of national and international institutions. Unlike his fellow Austrian mentor and colleague Ludwig von Mises, who remained a staunch old-school liberal wary of any function of the state beyond implementing the law, Hayek, who is today often portrayed as the anti-Keynes of the twentieth century and almost exclusively associated with contemporary neoliberalism's free-market ideology, was a colleague of Beveridge at the LSE in the 1930s and in fact agreed with some of the points made in the Beveridge Report. The practice of the welfare state in the 1950s led him to become increasingly disenchanted with the concept, however, and his position against state interventions took shape in his (at the time of its publication utterly ignored) *The Constitution of Liberty* (1960), which later inspired British prime minister Margaret Thatcher.[35] To his mind, it had turned into a top-down,

---

28 Louis Marlio, *Le sort du capitalisme* (Paris: Flammarion, 1938).
29 Alfred S. Jacquier-Bruère, *Refaire la France: L'Effort d'une génération* (Paris: Plon, 1945).
30 Roger E. Lacombe, *Déclin de l'individualisme?* (Paris: Les Éditions Denoël, 1937).
31 Carlo Rosselli, *Socialisme libéral* (Paris: Librairie Valois, 1930). Rosselli was Italian, but his work was first published in French. He was at that time living in Parisian exile.
32 Rougier, *Les mystiques économiques*.
33 Gaëtan Pirou, *Les doctrines économiques en France depuis 1870* (Paris: Armand Colin, 1934).
34 Alexander Rüstow, "Freie Wirtschaft, starker Staat. Die staatspolitischen Voraussetzungen des wirtschaftspolitischen Liberalismus," in *Deutschland und die Weltkrise*, ed. Franz Böse (Munich: Duncker & Humblot, 1932), 62–69.
35 Friedrich Hayek, *The Constitution of Liberty* (Chicago: Chicago University Press, 1960); Richard Vinen, *Thatcher's Britain: The Politics and Social Upheaval of the Thatcher Era* (London: Simon & Schuster, 2009); and Florence Sutcliffe-Braithwaite, "Neo-Liberalism and Morality in the Making of Thatcherite Social Policy," *The History Journal*, 55(2) (2012), 497–520.

planned economy, arbitrarily excuted by politics.[36] Today's scholarship often uses Hayek's think-tank as a point of access to the discussions about neoliberalism.[37] While the MPS was (and still is) an important actor in the field of economic thought and liberal philosophy, and while most of the economists mentioned in this chapter were members, it was never the only one and never represented ideological homogeneity. It was a place of broad discussion on the basis of shared concerns.[38] Particularly during its early decades, the various contestations about key liberal ideas and their operationalization are enlightening from a 'good society' perspective. The discussions of the early MPS meetings perpetuated the agenda laid out by the IIIC in the interwar years and the issues discussed within the newly emerging international organizations after 1945 and the whole international relations' diplomatic and intellectual landscape. Among the topics under discussion were liberalism's role within different policy fields, the task and the limits of state intervention, the role of history, the relation to former European colonies and the concept of development, the fundamental social presuppositions of liberalism, its relationship to Christianity, and its proper organization as a competitive order.[39] The discussion of European integration continued those on federalism within the IIIC landscape and the pro-European Federal Union

36 George Peden, "Liberal Economists and the British Welfare State: From Beveridge to the New Right," in *Liberalism and the Welfare State. Economists and Arguments for the Welfare State*, ed. Roger E. Backhouse, Bradley W. Bateman, Tamotsu Nishizawa, and Dieter Plehwe (Oxford: Oxford University Press, 2017), 39–56.
37 Most importantly Philip Mirowski and Dieter Plehwe (eds.), *The Road from Mont Pèlerin: The Making of the Neoliberal Thought Collective* (Cambridge: Harvard University Press, 2009). More contextualized interpretations of the history of neoliberalism both before and after World War II are provided by Angus Burgin, *The Great Persuasion: Reinventing Free Markets since the Depression* (Cambridge: Harvard University Press, 2012); and Daniel Stedman Jones, *Masters of the Universe: Hayek, Friedman, and the Birth of Neoliberal Politics* (Princeton: Princeton University Press, 2012), who, similarly to Jamie Peck, *Constructions of Neoliberal Reason* (Oxford: Oxford University Press, 2010) focus mostly on Hayek and Friedman on the one hand (Burgin and Stedman Jones) and on a very broad critical understanding of the term "neoliberalism" as shorthand for an individualist and minimal state ideology on the other hand (Peck).
38 For an overview on the history of the IMF and the Bretton Woods insitutions see Harold James, *International Monetary Cooperation since Bretton Woods* (Oxford: Oxford University Press, 1996); on the role of exchange rates in neoliberal thought see Matthias Schmelzer, *Freiheit für Wechselkurse und Kapital: Die Ursprünge neoliberaler Währungspolitik und die Mont Pèlerin Gesellschaft* (Marburg: Metropolis, 2010); and Matthias Schmelzer, "What Comes after Bretton Woods? Neoliberals Debate and Fight for a New Monetary Order," in *The Nine Lives of Neoliberalism*, ed. Philip Mirowski, Dieter Plehwe, and Quinn Slobodian (London: Verso, forthcoming 2019).
39 See the first MPS conference's agenda, April 1–10, 1947, Liberaal Archief, Folder 01-1-08-14-01.

from the late 1930s and early 1940s.[40] The MPS was an echo chamber for economists coming to terms with the pressing issues of their times.

European economic thought after 1945 continued to ponder the same questions as in the 1930s, albeit within a new global political and economic setting. Increasingly, since the 1940s, European integration was included as a real possibility in conceptualizations of the good society. The Marshall Plan meant a massive reconstruction program that was hardly confined to market forces alone. Its institutional implementer, the OEEC – directed by WLC participant Robert Marjolin – became a transnational nodal point for data generation, policy recommendations, and a new kind of policy science aiming at the harmonization of national economies and ensuring continuous growth.[41] Furthermore, the Bretton Woods institutions reorganized the financial system of the West, and the Cold War military and ideological entrenchment unfolded. Within this new institutional setup, economics redefined its position as a science of both fundamental academic and practical expertise, able to generate policy solutions conducive to peace and prosperity based on a liberal script, even though there were disagreements within the discipline about the best way to enact such a liberal script, and early neoliberals, for example, strongly argued against the fixed-exchange-rates mechanism of the Bretton Woods institutions.[42]

Already by the 1930s, the increasingly comprehensive approach to economics had grown into econometrics with the foundation of the Econometric Society and the journal *Econometrica*. Ragnar Frisch (1895–1973), the Norwegian economist and first recipient of the Nobel Memorial Prize in Economics, founded the Econometric Society in December 1930 together with Joseph Schumpeter (1883–1950) and Irving Fisher (1867–1947). It was Frisch who had introduced the distinction

---

40 See Tommaso Milani, "From Laissez-Faire to Supranational Planning: The Economic Debate within Federal Union (1938–1945)," *European Review of History / Revue européenne d'histoire*, 23(4) (2016), 664–685; Or Rosenboim, "Barbara Wooton, Friedrich Hayek and the debate on democratic federalism in the 1940s," *The International History Review* 36(5) (2014), 894–918; and further developing on the role of federalism among efforts at building a global order see Or Rosenboim, *The Emergence of Globalism. Visions of World Order in Britain and the United States, 1939–1950* (Princeton: Princeton University Press, 2017); and archival information at the LSE Archives, BEVERIDGE-ADDENDA 6–11. Economists involved with the IIIC and present at the WLC also participated at Federal Union activities related to Anglo-French cooperation, for example. Here, Hayek, Robbins, and Beveridge met again with Baudin, Bourgeois, Marlio, Rougier, and Rueff (see LSE Archives, BEVERIDGE-ADDENDA 9).
41 Matthias Schmelzer, *The Hegemony of Growth: The OECD and the Making of the Economic Growth Paradigm* (Cambridge: Cambridge University Press, 2016).
42 Schmelzer, *Freiheit für Wechselkurse und Kapital*.

between "macro" and "micro" economics to distinguish a comprehensive approach from contained, smaller questions, and the discipline of economics increasingly gathered data, mathematized its methodology, and began building "models."[43] The breakthrough for macroeconomics was Keynes's *General Theory*, which, just like early neoliberalism, strove simultaneously to save liberal capitalism and be conducive to peaceful relations, both inside and between nation-states.[44]

One of the central elements of macroeconomics is business cycle theory. It combines an understanding of economic expansion and contraction with a reflection on adequate policies for both phases and thus informs the actual construction of the "good society." It is also a field on which Keynes and the early as well as the contemporary neoliberals strongly disagree. The League of Nations (together with one of the largest funders for economic research at the time, the Rockefeller Foundation) was a nodal point for the developments in business cycle research.[45] Von Mises and Hayek stepped forward with their Austrian version, which built on the two Austrian economists Carl Menger (1840–1921) and Eugen von Böhm-Bawerk (1851–1914) and the works of Knut Wicksell (1852–1926) from Sweden.[46] What von Mises and particularly Hayek stressed was that the roots of the bust are to be found in an erroneously steered boom.[47] Ultimately, and until today, this logic allows neoliberals to claim that the reason for an economic crisis lies in earlier mismanagement, calling for more reform of the market rather than

---

[43] Frisch called it "macro-dynamic analysis" in Ragnar Frisch, *Propagation Problems and Impulse Problems in Dynamic Economics* (Oslo: University Institute of Economics, 1933), 2.

[44] Keynes, *The General Theory of Employment, Interest, and Money*, 382: "I have mentioned in passing that the new system might be more favourable to peace than the old has been. It is worthwhile to repeat and emphasise that aspect."

[45] Important contributions to business cycle theory were Joseph Kitchin, "Cycles and Trends in Economic Factors," *Review of Economics and Statistics*, 5(1) (1923), 10–16; N. D. Kondratieff and W. F. Stolper, "The Long Waves in Economic Life," *Review of Economics and Statistics*, 17(6) (1935), 105–115; and Gustav Cassel, *The Theory of Social Economy* (London: Fisher Unwin, 1923). Joseph Schumpeter, *Business Cycles. A Theoretical, Historical and Statistical Analysis of the Capitalist Process* (New York: McGraw-Hill, 1939) was recognized only after the war due to the overpowering influence of Keynes at the time (and because of the war).

[46] Foundational were Carl Menger, *Grundsätze der Volkswirtschaftslehre* (Vienna: Braumüller, 1871); and Eugen von Böhm-Bawerk, *Kapital und Kapitalzins* (Innsbruck: Wagner, 1884). Wicksell's important works were also published in German early on. See Knut Wicksell, *Geld und Güterpreise: Eine Studie über die den Tauschwert des Geldes bestimmenden Ursachen* (Jena: Gustav Fischer, 1898), which was translated into English only in 1936; and Knut Wicksell, *Föreläsningar i nationalekonomi, Del I: Teoretisk nationalekonomi* (Lund: Berlingska Boktryckeriet, 1906), translated into English with an introduction by Lionel Robbins in 1934.

[47] Friedrich Hayek, *Prices and Production* (London: Routledge, 1931).

intervening with a social or moral political impetus.[48] Austrian business cycle theory was cutting-edge in the 1930s, and before it increasingly embraced Keynes's ideas (still far from any 'ism' at the time) by the end of the decade[49] the League built on it to tackle the economic problems in Central Europe after the unraveling of the Russian, Austro-Hungarian, German, and Ottoman empires. It initiated the Danubian Economic Study (co-funded by the Rockefeller Foundation), one of the first attempts in Europe to manage crisis and build nation-states through global governance,[50] and the Austrian Business Cycle Institute, founded by von Mises and Hayek (and funded by Rockefeller as well), was tasked with providing the scientific tools for data generation and policy recommendation.[51]

Like early neoliberalism, macroeconomics found fruitful soil within the League of Nations' institutional landscape since the early 1930s and was professed by, among others, the Swedish economists Gustav Cassel (1866–1945) and Wicksell, who (beside the Austrians) influenced not only von Mises and Hayek, but also Gottfried Haberler (1900–1995) and Wilhelm Röpke, who each presented business cycle theories as well. Haberler worked on a theory particularly for the League and, like Hayek, focused on the relation between boom and bust. He found that a disconfigured market expansion could be regarded as the main reason for economic crisis.[52] Röpke developed his theory throughout the 1920s, when he became a renowned economist in Germany at a very young age. In a report to the German government on the solutions to the economic crisis from 1931, he came to conclusions similar to those of Keynes, whose *Treatise on Money* (1930) he endorsed. His business cycle theory has been regarded as being somewhere between Hayek and Keynes, and indeed Röpke discusses the two intensely. Crucially, however, Röpke remains in the paradigm of his time and looked for the causes of the bust in the maladjusted boom. His major English-language contribution to the field was *Cycles and Crises* (1936). The German original (1931) was first translated into Swedish (1934), reflecting the important

---

48 Philip Mirowski, *Never Let a Serious Crisis Go to Waste: How Neoliberalism Survived the Financial Meltdown* (London: Verso, 2014).
49 Patricia Clavin, *Securing the World Economy: The Reinvention of the League of Nations, 1920–1946* (Oxford: Oxford University Press, 2013), 198.
50 See the archival folders in the Rockefeller Foundation Archive, RF-RG1-S100, Box 110.
51 See RF-RG1-S100. By then, the institute was directed by Oskar Morgenstern (1902–1977), who himself left Austria in 1938 and joined Princeton University, where his major academic contribution lay in the development of game theory together with John von Neumann, *Theory of Games and Economic Behavior* (Princeton: Princeton University Press, 1944).
52 Gottfried Haberler, *Prosperity and Depression* (Geneva: League of Nations, 1937).

position of Swedish economic thought at the time, and only then into English on the initiative of Ragnar Nurkse from the Financial and Economic Section at the League of Nations.[53] Röpke did not have the time to incorporate a detailed critique of the *General Theory* into his manuscript, but signaled in his foreword that he strongly differed from Keynes's "bold views."[54] Indeed, the dividing line between early neoliberals and Keynes was connected to the latter's rethinking of business cycles. He moved from the focus on maladjustments during boom periods to the very reasons for unemployment (inadequate demand) and an emphasis on counter-cyclical intervention. His solutions may strike us today as rather conventional, but at the time of their initial appearance they sent the world of economics into intense dispute.

The *General Theory* changed the setup of macroeconomics completely, and from the 1940s to the 1970s, the neoclassical synthesis[55] built on Keynes's groundbreaking work and added early neoliberal elements. It considered involuntary unemployment and provided arguments for government spending when fiscal and monetary policies were not delivering effects on recovery fast enough after a decrease of demand. The background assumption supporting these policies was that a liberal good society is likely to emerge and sustain itself in conditions of full employment. The birth of a political economy focusing on the origins of unemployment through social-scientific tools remains one of Keynes's biggest legacies.

Pinpointing certain conceptions of neoliberalism against certain readings of Keynes and Keynesianism is a tendency in contemporary scholarship, but, like the division of economics into 'schools,' is less illuminating when the question of the good society in European economic thought of the twentieth century is of interest. For early neoliberals and Keynesians, the goal was the same – to unite capitalism with social responsibility – and while the means were sometimes different, they often also overlapped. Röpke was convinced by much of Keynes's economics but rejected his business cycle approach and his pragmatism when it came to values. Michael Polanyi, participant at the WLC, lifelong friend of Hayek, member of the MPS, and affiliate of the

---

53 Wilhelm Röpke, *Cycles and Crises* (London: W. Hodge, 1936).
54 Röpke, *Cycles and Crises*, vi.
55 The neoclassical synthesis, as a matter of fact, was a merger of Keynes's ideas and neoliberal ones, swiftly after the *General Theory* had been published. See J. R. Hicks, "Mr Keynes and the 'Classics': A Suggested Interpretation," *Econometrica*, 5(2) (1937), 147–159. Further important actors in merging Keynes with neoliberal thought were Maurice Allais and Paul Samuelson. See Maurice Allais, *Économie pure et rendement social: Contribution de la science économique modern à la construction d'une économie du bien-être* (Paris: Receuil Sirey, 1945); and Paul Samuelson, *Foundations of Economic Analysis* (Cambridge: Harvard University Press, 1947).

Christian think-tank The Moot from 1946 to 1948,[56] was a convinced (albeit unorthodox) Keynesian,[57] and Lionel Robbins, inspired by von Mises and the Austrian School in the interwar period, turned into a Keynesian during the 1940s.[58] And Roger Auboin (1891–1974) and Robert Marjolin, participants of the WLC, implemented one of the most Keynesian policies in postwar Europe. As general manager of the Bank for International Settlements (Auboin) and director of the OEEC (Marjolin) they inaugurated and successfully completed the European Payments Union (EPU) from 1950 to 1958. The EPU was based on Keynes's ideas for an international clearing union which he had developed for the Bretton Woods conference in 1944. The system then in operation globally until 1973 was not based on Keynes's plan, however, but on the US position represented by Harry Dexter White. Keynes's idea was to replace the gold standard and the exchange rate between national currencies with an International Clearing Union based on an accounting unit Keynes had called bancor. Quite precisely, this plan was put into operation by the early neoliberal WLC participants Auboin and Marjolin in Western Europe, except that the bancor became the Ecu.[59]

Beyond methodological discussions and beside fixing imminent social needs, something deeper was at stake for early neoliberals: the very nature of the good society. They broadly agreed on core concepts necessary for such a renovated liberal order. These concepts, reinterpreted and reconnected during the 1930s, functioned like a basic tonality, a common key for variations of liberal economies and societies. The basic chord of early neoliberalism's good society was built on three elements. The root note, the ultimate point

---

56 Keith Clements (ed.), *The Moot Papers: Faith, Freedom and Society, 1938–1944* (London: Bloomsbury, 2010), 11.
57 See Struan Jacobs and Phil Mullins, "Friedrich Hayek and Michael Polanyi in Correspondence," *History of European Ideas*, 42(1) (2016), 107–130.
58 Both Robbins and Keynes traveled to Bretton Woods to represent the United Kingdom. In his diary, Robbins speaks very favorably about Keynes, and during the foundational meeting of the Mont Pèlerin Society he defends Keynes and admits his shift toward some Keynesian positions. See Robbins, *Bretton Woods Diary*, and the MPS files in the Liberaal Archief, Folder 01-1-08-14-01.
59 See already in 1950, at the inauguration of the EPU, P. B. (full name not specified in the original), "The European Payments Union: A Step towards Economic Integration," *The World Today*, 6 (1950), 490–498, p. 491: "The mechanism which has been chosen to achieve this objective borrows all that was good, and all the experience of technical administration, from the previous Intra-European Payments Scheme as administered for the Bank for International Settlements in Basle. It also bears distinct traces of inspiration from the late Lord Keynes's war-time proposals for an International Clearing Union." Marjolin found his way to Keynes during his doctoral dissertation years after reading Wicksell, Hayek, Myrdal, and Hicks. See Robert Marjolin, *Le travail d'une vie: Mémoires 1911–1986* (Paris: Robert Laffont), 52.

of reference and source of legitimation, was the concept of the human person and its dignity and inviolability; the major third was the theory and policy of the price mechanism; the perfect fifth was the rule of law.

Values, Prices, and the Rule of Law in Early Neoliberalism

"If we are liberals, it is because we think that liberty should allow the realization of certain values,"[60] Marjolin exclaimed at the WLC in 1938 in the discussion following Lippmann's presentation of the Agenda of Liberalism. The greater share of the colloquium's participants agreed to call their new agenda "neoliberalism."[61] The term was rarely used enthusiastically by its proponents, however. Rüstow and Baudin were probably among its most engaged champions.[62] Others, like von Mises and Hayek, refrained from using it, and some applied it rather grudgingly, mainly to identify an agenda that was, while broad, a list of givens for building a good society with a liberal heartbeat.

That political systems would organize their societies by a conscious choice of economic policies was the consensus view at least by the 1930s.[63] A strong state positioned above politics needed to be guaranteed, as Rüstow, for example, exclaimed: "The new liberalism in any case, which can be defended today, and which I defend together with my friends, demands a strong state, a state above the economy, above interested people, there, where it belongs."[64] Early neoliberal economic thought was deeply concerned with

---

60 Marjolin in Rougier, *Colloque Walter Lippmann*, 486.
61 They literally took a majority vote on the term that should identify the new agenda for liberalism. L. Marlio illustrates this in the opening discussion of the Centre International pour la Reconstruction du Libéralisme (CIRL) in Paris, in 1939, following talks by himself, by L. Rougier, and by J. Rueff. See "Centre International d'études pour la rénovation du libéralisme, Le néo-libéralisme," Inaugural discussion on March 8, 1939, reprinted in *Les Essais. Cahiers bimestriels* (Nancy: Didry et Varcollier, 1961), 86–108, p. 94.
62 See as late as 1961, Alexander Rüstow, "Paläoliberalismus, Kommunismus und Neoliberalismus," in *Wirtschaft, Gesellschaft und Kultur: Festgabe für Alfred Müller-Armack*, ed. Franz Greiß and Fritz W. Meyer (Berlin: Duncker & Humblot, 1961), 61–70; and Louis Baudin, *L'Aube d'un nouveau libéralisme* (Paris: Librairie de Médicis, 1953), particularly "Le Néo-libéralisme," 142–169.
63 See Moritz J. Bonn, *Wealth, Welfare or War: The Changing Role of Economics in National Policy* (Paris: International Institute of Intellectual Co-operation, 1939), 48; and Hagen Schulz-Forberg, "Rejuvenating Liberalism: Economic Thought, Social Imagination and the Invention of Neoliberalism in the 1930s," in Hagen Schulz-Forberg (ed.), *Zero Hours: Conceptual Insecurities and New Beginnings in the Interwar Period* (Brussels: P.I.E.–Peter Lang, 2013), 233–268.
64 Rüstow, "Freie Wirtschaft, starker Staat," 69.

the state and with the values that inform its basic norms. Indeed, the concept of the basic norm, stemming from the work of the legal theorist Hans Kelsen[65] (professor at the Geneva Institute of International Studies at the same time as von Mises) comes quite close to the function of values in early neoliberal thought.

It is instructive to see how neoliberalism developed in contestation with fascist thought, which was in its internationally recognized prime in the early 1930s.[66] By the mid to late 1930s, it had become clear to many that national-socialist Germany was not a social vision after all, but the "completest development of the nation in arms."[67] During the Great Depression, however, Italy's fascism was studied with some curiosity. Making a similar claim on the individual's rights, risks, and responsibilites as its economic basis, fascism proposed to protect the market actor within its economic theories.

Among the internationally most recognized fascist economists was Luigi Amoroso (a foundational fellow of the Econometric Society like Keynes and Rueff [68]). He was part of the general trend to mathematize economics, and his work on price development and elasticity was influential for measuring market power in order to see whether any tendencies toward monopoly are virulent.[69] Amoroso described three main failures of laissez-faire during the IIIC's conference on "State and Economic Life," held in London in the spring of 1933 and bringing together liberal, fascist, and national-socialist perspectives in a debate about the philosophical aspects of state intervention (among other things). At the conference, many of Europe's leading economists were present. Keynes was invited as well, yet, since he was busily working on the *General Theory*, he declined the invitation because he had to "make it a rule to cut out almost entirely occasions for expounding or discussing orally the sort of questions about which I write."[70]

65 Hans Kelsen, *General Theory of Law and State* (Cambridge: Harvard University Press, 1949), 110–122; and Hans Kelsen, *Pure Theory of Law* (Berkeley: University of California Press, 1969 [1934]).
66 A. James Gregor, *Mussolini's Intellectuals: Fascist Social and Political Thought* (Princeton: Princeton University Press, 2005); and Jens Steffek, "Fascist Internationalism," *Journal of International Studies*, 44(1) (2015), 3–22.
67 Lippmann, *An Inquiry into the Principles of the Good Society*, 66.
68 "Memorandum in re: the Econometric Society," 3. Document retrieved from the website of the Econometric Society: www.dev.econometricsociety.org/sites/default/files/historical/Schumpeter-Frisch%20memo%20Sept%201931.pdf.
69 His work has left a trace within economics as part of the so-called Amoroso–Robinson relation, which describes the relation between price, marginal revenue, and the elasticity of demand. It is not without irony that this relation is named after a fascist theoretician and one of the most well-known post-Keynesian economic thinkers, Jean Robinson, who increasingly moved toward Marxist and collectivist views.
70 Keynes to H. Bowen, May 3, 1933, LSE Archives, BAILEY/2.

The first flaw of liberalism, Amoroso argued, was the naïve liberal belief that a free market automatically generates the best possible society. "We see every day that that is not true."[71] Second, liberalism claimed to be an ahistorical body of thought, a system capable of being understood without its history. Third, liberalism was both materialistic and deterministic. "According to determinism, man is powerless in the presence of social difficulties, and liberal agnosticism is based on the fundamental conception of that philosophic system, according to which man is the plaything of forces immeasurably greater than himself."[72]

Fascism, instead, extolled the man-made nature of economies and societies and placed "the political," as Carl Schmitt termed it, at their center. Nothing is above the political: No moral ground higher than politics gives birth to legitimacy. Rather, the state and its citizens, which during liberalism were in critical opposition to each other, would unite in a dialectical synthesis and provide identity to a political regime.[73] For fascists, the ultimate root of any political legitimacy was thus found not to reside in a basic norm that presupposed a universal value seen as valid, as Kelsen might have put it.[74] Rather, the nation and its state represented a closed system. Along similar lines, Schmitt argued that the many problematic assumptions of liberalism were rooted in its claim to apolitical progress. In his *The Concept of the Political* (1932),[75] he contends that "one of the few truly un-discussable, not to be doubted dogmas of the liberal age" was the conviction that economics forms an autonomous entity untouched by ethics or aesthetics, religion, or least of all by politics.[76]

---

71 Luigi Amoroso, speech at the League of Nations Sixth International Studies Conference, a Second Study Conference on "The State and Economic Life," London, May 29 to June 2, 1933, in *The State and Economic Life* (Paris: International Institute of Intellectual Co-operation, 1934), 183–184.
72 Amoroso, speech at the League of Nations Sixth International Studies Conference, 184.
73 Amoroso, speech at the League of Nations Sixth International Studies Conference, 184.
74 Kelsen, *General Theory of Law and State*, 116: "The basic norm is not created in a legal procedure by a law-creating organ. It is not – as a positive legal norm is – valid because it is created in a certain way by a legal act, but it is valid because it is presupposed to be valid; and it is presupposed to be valid because without this presupposition no human act could be interpreted as a legal, especially as a norm-creating, act."
75 Carl Schmitt, *Der Begriff des Politischen* (Berlin: Duncker & Humblot, 1932). Schmitt based his 1932 book on an article published under the same title five years earlier, Carl Schmitt, "Der Begriff des Politischen," *Archiv für Sozialwissenschaft und Sozialpolitik*, 58 (1927), 1–33, and on a lecture given at the Deutsche Hochschule für Politik in 1928. The latter was the German variation of the international affairs institutes modeled on Chatham House after World War I and a key nodal point in Germany for the IIIC network beside Heidelberg University.
76 Schmitt, *Der Begriff des Politischen*, 66–67.

While early neoliberals shared the critique of laissez-faire, they were not inclined to give up "the very strong faith of liberalism" which does not only entail the human person in isolation but implies "responsibility for other people's suffering."[77] United in agreement about basics despite there being some disagreement about details and practices, early neoliberals attempted to carve out the basic concepts of a rebooted liberal state conscious of its social tasks, relying on social science, and endowed with the responsibility not only for building a good society nationally, but also for saving a certain idea of civilization globally and thus contributing to a peaceful organization of international relations. As Louis Rougier exclaimed at the WLC, "It is to descend into the fray in order to fight with the arms of the spirit; it is political action, it is fighting for the protection and the renovation of the only economic and political regime compatible with spiritual life, human dignity, the common good, peace among peoples and the progress of civilization: liberalism."[78] To do this, a basic norm needed to be established firmly in position above the realm of politics. Neoliberalism's "basic idea," Louis Baudin explained in 1953, "is the rescue of the human person."[79]

Early neoliberals all agreed that the good society needed to be based on values – what Röpke called the "ultimate foundations"[80] – defined by man and expressing universal beliefs. State institutions were not to be built for their own sake: They were not an end in themselves, but were needed to build an order in the light of the basic value. Again, Lippmann's *Good Society* provided early neoliberals with a blueprint. He had argued that the historical achievement of civilization was that "[t]he inviolability of the human person was declared. Toward this conviction men have fought their way in the long ascent out of the morass of barbarism. Upon this rock, they have built the rude foundations of the Good Society."[81]

States and their economies needed to be erected in the image of the true interpretation of this "rock," they argued. To build this adequate order, neoliberals from Lippmann to Hayek and Rueff exclaimed,[82] it was vital to

---

77 Karl Popper, discussion statement, MPS "Liberalism and Christianity."
78 Rougier, *Colloque Walter Lippmann*, 418.
79 Baudin, *L'Aube d'un nouveau libéralisme*, 146.   80 Röpke, "Einführung," 28.
81 Lippmann, *An Inquiry into the Principles of the Good Society*, 378.
82 Lippmann, *An Inquiry into the Principles of the Good Society*, 359: "The ultimate concern of the liberal is with the enhancement of real values." The whole article by F. Hayek "Individualism True and False" revolves around this division. Finally, J. Rueff, *L'ordre social*, 568–582, includes the possibility of non-democratic states having "true" rights if they follow a rule of law, allow the individual to act in the market and if there is a guarantee of the price mechanism.

attain clarity over the difference between so-called true and false values. "Real values" rather than "pseudo-values" must be put in their correct place, argued Edith Eucken-Erdsieck (1896–1985) in the first edition of the ORDO yearbook from 1948.[83] In times of conceptual and political turmoil, when formerly self-evident ideas erode, reconfirmation is needed. "It is just here," Lippmann contended, "that the ultimate issue is joined, on the question whether men shall be treated as inviolable persons or as things to be disposed of . . ."[84] In early April 1948, Röpke declared, "As an economist, I believe we have to say that the economy follows at second rank. This is the conclusion at which we arrived a year ago [at the foundational meeting of the MPS]."[85]

Schmitt, on the other hand, accused liberalism of using apolitical arguments to hide its ideological convictions. In particular, he contested Kelsen's pure theory of law, whose definition of the basic norm, Schmitt claimed, was more political than anything else, all the more so because it pretended to be apolitical.[86]

For Kelsen, such a norm, while man-made, represented the essence of what societies regard as valid (not as true in the sense that physics is true and not as "good" in the sense of an unquestioned universal morality, but as something one agrees on consciously as a presupposition).[87] Echoing this basic difference between neoliberalism and anti-liberal thought, Alexander Rüstow, in a letter to Carl Schmitt from July 4, 1930, remarked on the relation between value-based rule of law and "the political":

> It seems to me that the idea of a democratic state based on the concept of humanity represents not only a possible, but in a certain way an unavoidable utopia . . . I am deeply convinced that on the level of the political, nation and the national state do not represent anything final, but that, rather, the more one is in favor of nation and the national state, the more one needs to admit the nature of its composite character.[88]

---

83 Edith Eucken-Erdsieck, "Chaos und Stagnation," ORDO, 1 (1948), 3–15.
84 Lippmann, An Inquiry into the Principles of the Good Society, 375.
85 "Le Colloque d'Avignon," Rougier Papers, Chateau de Lourmarin, Box R3, Annex.
86 Schmitt, Der Begriff des Politischen, 20, footnote 2.
87 Kelsen, General Theory of Law and State, 111: "The ground of truth of an 'is' statement is its conformity to the reality of our experience; the reason for the validity of a norm is not – like the quest for the cause of an effect – a *regressus ad infinitum*; it is terminated by the highest norm which is the last reason of validity within the normative system." And it is "presupposed to be valid."
88 Letter from Rüstow to Schmitt, July 4, 1930, Carl Schmitt Papers, Federal State Archive of North Rhine-Wesphalia, Duisburg, RW 265-11879/3.

The relation of law to politics is a key figure of thought for early neoliberals in the middle of the twentieth century.[89] Accordingly, economics and law needed to be welded together to safeguard them from too much politics. To achieve a sustainable and ideal result when rebuilding liberal society and to avoid any bias, one would need to go to the ultimate norms and values of a state. The economy had to be in line with a liberal constitutionalism; and liberal constitutionalism, in turn, had to be in line with a particular understanding of economics.

In German *ordoliberalism*, the term used to capture this economy-based constitutionalism was *Wirtschaftsordnung*[90] (which was translated in the writings of Hayek, for example, as "competitive order"[91]) or *Wirtschaftsverfassung*[92] (economic constitution). Across the transnational network generally, at the hotspots of economic thought such as Chicago (where Henry Simons pioneered the new essential link[93]) the conviction spread that law and economics must speak from the same source. Constitutions could become truly market-conducive (and thus able to sustain a good society) only if lawyers either understand economics or collaborate with economists.[94] Confirming the need to reconcile economics and law, Lippmann had argued in his *Good Society* that "the progress of liberalism was ... halted by the wholly false assumption that there was a realm of freedom in which the exchange economy operated and, apart from it, a realm of law where the state had jurisdiction."[95]

If it is liberal, Rueff exclaimed when expanding on Lippmann's argument, a civilization needed to be based not on any kind of law, but on "true law":

89　Friedrich Hayek, *The Road to Serfdom* (Chicago: University of Chicago Press, 1944), for example, constructs already basic legal philosophical arguments in favor of a rule of law. See also his Italian friend and colleague, Bruno Leoni, "Verso una nuova teoria 'pura' del diritto," *Il Politico*, 19(1) (1954), 80–84.

90　See Franz Böhm, *Die Ordnung der Wirtschaft als geschichtliche Aufgabe und rechtsschöpferische Leistung* (Stuttgart and Berlin: Kohlhammer, 1937); Fritz W. Meyer and Hans Otto Lenel, "Vorwort," *ORDO*, 1 (1948), vii–xi; and importantly Alfred Müller-Armack, "Die Wirtschaftsordnung sozial gesehen," *ORDO*, 1 (1948), 125–154.

91　Hayek, "'Free' Enterprise and Competitive Order."

92　Franz Böhm, Walter Eucken, and Hans Großmann-Doerth, "Unsere Aufgabe," preface by the series editors to the book series *Ordnung der Wirtschaft*, in Friedrich A. Lutz, *Das Grundproblem der Geldverfassung* (Stuttgart: Kohlhammer, 1936), vii–xxi, pp. xx–xxi.

93　Simons was appointed director of the law department at Chicago University, where he hired, among others, Aaron Director, a founding member of the MPS. See William Davies, *The Limits of Neoliberalism: Authority, Sovereignty and the Logic of Competition* (London: Sage, 2017), esp. Chapter 3, "The Liberal Spirit of Economics: Competition, Anti-trust and the Chicago Critique of Law."

94　Böhm, Eucken, and Großmann-Doerth, "Unsere Aufgabe," viii.

95　Lippmann, *An Inquiry into the Principles of the Good Society*, 191.

> Liberalism will never escape from the state of nature, the "rule of the jungle," if it is not completed by the authoritative constraints necessary to impose a morality onto man. But, far from neglecting them, it spells out these constraints as the necessary aide-de-camp of its constitution. The liberal order requires the support of a morality, divine or human. Without such support, it will remain a social order, but an uncivilized one.[96]

By placing human dignity and a fundamental morality at the ultimate point of reference for its economics, early neoliberalism inevitably engaged with Christian thought, and vice versa.[97] In 1949, Alfred Müller-Armack explained that economics in his day

> cannot live without the inclusion of values into its observations. [Science's] task can only be to avoid value deceit and to strive for the acknowledgement of true orders of value as opposed to purely subjective interpretations of values. Such an order of values, for us, originates in Christian values.[98]

While stating a clear wariness toward organized religion, formulations placing Christian and humanitarian convictions side by side were commonplace among early neoliberals, and debates about the relation with Christianity emphasized the common root in the concept of the human person. The relation between liberalism and Christianity was on the agenda at the very first meeting of the MPS in 1947. The founder of the Chicago School, Frank Knight, a former Christian who had become an atheist, started the discussion and stressed the historical differences between a secular liberalism and the Church as well as generally illiberal tendencies within any religion. But, in theory, he conceded, liberalism and Christianity could lead a common life. In this context, Hayek asked, "Does liberalism presuppose some set of values which are commonly accepted as a faith and in themselves not capable of rational demonstration?" He goes on to strategize, saying that "there is no chance of any extensive support for a liberal programme unless the opposition between liberals and Christians can somehow be bridged. This antagonism is an accidental accretion of liberalism, rather than one of the essentials to liberalism."[99] For Christians among early

---

96 Rueff, *L'ordre social*, 563.
97 For the German debate, in which neoliberalism's social claims were taken as merely skin deep by Church-related authors, see, for example, Helmut Paul Becker, *Die soziale Frage im Neoliberalismus: Analyse und Kritik* (Heidelberg: F. H. Kerle, 1965); E. E. Nawroth, *Die Sozial- und Wirtschaftsphilosophie des Neoliberalismus* (Heidelberg: F. H. Kerle, 1961); and Hans Peter, *Freiheit der Wirtschaft: Kritik des Neoliberalismus* (Cologne: Bund Verlag, 1953).
98 Alfred Müller-Armack, *Diagnose unserer Gegenwart: Zur Bestimmung unseres geistesgeschichtlichen Standorts* (Bern and Stuttgart: Haupt, 1949), 224.
99 Hayek, discussion statement, MPS "Liberalism and Christianity."

neoliberals, the social order emerging on the tonality of the human person's dignity, the price mechanism, and the rule of law was acceptable, indeed necessary. As Eucken stressed, "I am a Christian, and I want to say that from a purely Christian point of view I regard the competitive order as essential." Christians without "any formal dogma, but agreeing on man having an eternal life" would be the ones who are both liberals and Christian, he concluded.[100]

Thus recognizing the importance of a consciously constructed moral order, economists embedded legal and philosophical elements in their thought. Here lies one of the crucial differences between the laissez-faire liberalism of the eighteenth and nineteenth centuries and the strain of neoliberalism that flourished in the middle of the twentieth century, or, as Hayek put it, the difference between earlier understandings of free enterprise and the now consciously constructed "competitive order."[101] For the early neoliberals, free enterprise was supposed to take place within this competitive order, which was not unrestrained by any framework but rather based on a "social humanism"[102] and not on a pure laissez-faire individualism with social Darwinian qualities. Milton Friedman illustrated Hayek's distinction, explaining that "Neo-liberalism would accept the nineteenth-century liberal emphasis on the fundamental importance of the individual, but it would substitute for the nineteenth-century goal of laissez-faire as a means to this end, the goal of the competitive order."[103]

The crucial element linking the value base with practical politics was the concept of the price mechanism. Jacques Rueff compressed the early neoliberal perspective into the following formula: "If we wish to save civilization we need to reconstitute the price mechanism."[104] With the price mechanism, Röpke explained, "we are on the right track when our intention is to find the watershed between market economy and collectivism."[105] Societies leave the market economy and step into the realm of collectivism, he continued, when "allocation, that is the What and the How Much of production in all its branches, is not anymore determined by the price mechanism but by the order of an administrative

---

100 Eucken, discussion statement, MPS "Liberalism and Christianity."
101 Hayek, MPS 1947, opening speech.
102 Müller-Armack, *Diagnose unserer Gegenwart*, 277–280.
103 Milton Friedman, "Neo-Liberalism and Its Prospects," *Farmand* (February 1951), 1–4, p. 3.
104 J. Rueff, in "Le Colloque d'Avignon," April 1, 1948.
105 Wilhelm Röpke, *Maß und Mitte* (Zurich: Eugen Rentsch, 1950), 148.

body."[106] Tariffs as well as fiscal stimuli were in conformity with a liberal doctrine only as long as the price mechanism was guaranteed.[107] Within a market, prices must be able to form freely; and the citizen, conceptualized as a consumer who sustains his own sovereignty through the act of consumption, accordingly must be able to buy what he or she has reason to desire.[108] Political contestation about the sectors of society in which the price mechanism might run its course, where consumption ended and the state's obligation to provide the common good more directly began, accordingly ensued and is still flaring. At the same time, some early neoliberals also accepted that under certain circumstances the price mechanism might be shut down temporarily until conditions in which markets can be reintroduced are reached, as has happened in a number of cases during the postwar years in Western Europe, particularly in France.

Beside the *conditio sine qua non* of the price mechanism and the rule of law as necessary support systems for the 'truly' good society in which the human person's inviolabilty was guaranteed, neoliberals invoked the role of science as a guardian for the liberal order. One of the most fundamental epistemological convictions they shared was that knowledge could never be absolute. Hayek's formula of the "pretence of knowledge" sums this up vividly,[109] and Popper, among others, shares this basic critique of an epistemology claiming a holistic totality of data, when, 'truly,' neither a full possession nor a complete understanding of data allowing a full-blown, science-led construction of the social is possible.[110] Any claims on a total scope of human knowledge were merely pseudo-rationalist, evidence of the "hubris of ratio," as Röpke called it.[111] This argument is deployed against "scientism,"[112] a false belief in human rationality, which was detected by early neoliberals in older liberalism's belief in the *ratio* of nature and seen by them as surviving in contemporary socialist economic thought,[113] and later against so-perceived blind faith in the use of data within

---

106 Röpke, *Maß und Mitte*, 148.   107 Baudin, *L'Aube d'un nouveau libéralisme*, 157.
108 Rueff, *L'ordre social*, 95–102.
109 Hayek, Lecture to the Memory of Alfred Nobel, December 11, 1974, www.nobelprize.org/nobel_prizes/economic-sciences/laureates/1974/hayek-lecture.htm l.
110 Maybe most poignantly in Karl Popper, *The Poverty of Historicism* (London: Routledge, 1957).
111 Wilhelm Röpke, *Civitas Humana: Grundfragen der Gesellschafts- und Wirtschaftsreform* (Zurich: Eugen Rentsch, 1944), 107–112.
112 Röpke, *Civitas Humana*, 119–123.
113 This debate on the role of science and knowledge in constructing society, which has been raging since the late nineteenth century, is usually called the socialist calculation debate. For a prism about this debate see the exchange between Otto Neurath and Friedrich von Hayek on the epistemology of economics in John O'Neill, "Knowledge,

Keynesianist macroeconomics (as opposed to neoliberal macroeconomics based on Hayek and von Mises). Hayek had in 1947 called these claims expressions of "fierce rationalism," which in the nineteenth century "exercised its influence mainly through the twin movements of Positivism and Hegelianism in an expression of intellectual hubris."[114]

Positivism and "historicism" (to use Popper's term)[115] were particularly criticized. Both ways of approaching knowledge were seen as flawed: Positivism suggested that knowledge is gained on the basis of assumptions deduced from imaginations of a purely natural order; historicism falsely implied that the study of history could lead to an understanding of historical progress and thus entailed the ability to uncover historical laws. A rift between earlier liberalism and any new liberalism needed to take this into account, Hayek argued in his opening speech at the Mont Pèlerin Society in April 1947, for indeed, he said, "the popular liberal creed ... had antagonised many who shared the basic value of individual freedom but who were repelled by the aggressive rationalism which would recognise no values except those whose utility could be demonstrated by individual reason and which presumes science was competent to tell us not only what is but also what ought to be."[116] Since science was among the main sources of information for any society, doing it "right" was essential for the good society.[117] Forceful critiques of the "historicists" Hegel, Comte, and Marx (whom

Planning and Markets: A Missing Chapter in the Socialist Calculation Debates," *Economics & Philosophy*, 22(1) (2006), 55–78.

114 Hayek, Opening Speech at MPS, April 1, 1947, document 47_1.1, p. 16. Concerning Hegel's and Marx's (and others') 'philosophies of history' criticized as prophecy by neoliberals, see also Louis Rougier, *Génie de l'Occident* (Paris: Robert Laffont, 1969), 217–222.

115 For common arguments across languages see the very influential humanist and board member of the International Committee of Intellectual Co-operation in Geneva in the 1920s and 1930s, Johan Huizinga, *In the Shadow of Tomorrow: A Diagnosis of the Spiritual Distemper of our Time* (London and Toronto: Heinemann, 1936). Among neoliberals (in reference to Huizinga) see in particular Luigi Einaudi, "Ipotesi astratte ed ipotesi storiche e dei giudizi di valore nelle scienze economiche," *Atti della Reale Accademia delle Scienze di Torino*, 78(2) (1942–1943), 57–119; Röpke, *Civitas Humana*, 119–123; and Popper, *The Poverty of Historicism*. On value positions within early neoliberalism see H.-J. Seraphim, "Kritische Bemerkungen zur Begriffs- und Wesensbestimmung der Sozialen Marktwirtschaft," in *Wirtschaft, Gesellschaft und Kultur: Festgabe für Alfred Müller-Armack*, ed. Franz Greiß and Fritz W. Meyer (Berlin: Duncker & Humblot, 1961), 184–196.

116 Hayek, Opening Speech at MPS, April 1, 1947, document 47_1.1, pp. 15–16.

117 On science's assumed role, see for example Karl Popper, *The Open Society and Its Enemies* (London: Routledge 2002 [1945]), xxxi: "If in this book harsh words are spoken about some of the greatest among the intellectual leaders of mankind, my motive is not, I hope, the wish to belittle them. It springs from my conviction that, if our civilization is to survive, we must break with the habit of deference to great men. Great men make great mistakes ... Their influence, too rarely challenged, continues to mislead those on whose defence civilization depends."

Popper criticized for "economic historicism"[118]) fill the pages of early neoliberals' reasoning. History has neither direction nor any inherent meaning of its own, Popper "contend[s]. But this contention does not imply that all we can do about it is to look aghast at the history of political power . . . [W]e can . . . fight for the open society, for a rule of reason, for justice, freedom, equality."[119] While history has no meaning other than that we give to it, liberals should stop "posing as prophets" and instead "become the makers of our own fate."[120] History and values needed to be connected consciously in order to save and sustain Western civilization.

Overall, early neoliberalism was flexible, within limits, when it came to the political shape of the good society. Fundamentally shared values could take the shape of very different political realities. From the French presidential system to German ordoliberalism and social-democratic Sweden, postwar liberal reconstruction was built on the same values, and its various political forms were merely improvisations on the same basic chord. As Marjolin, then still director of the OEEC, explained in 1950, the differences between the various European countries might seem large, but when compared with regimes outside Europe, similarities become clear. Countries like Norway and Great Britain might be "dirigiste," but the different European methods were all "founded on the same essential philosophy."[121]

The basic chord of early neoliberalism was not exclusively welded to democracy alone, however. Lippmann rooted liberalism in democracy and Rüstow complained about the WLC's new agenda's lack of democratic commitment.[122] Others were more wary toward democracy, which was seen as a possibly populist system, where "the masses" took over (or could do so easily) and in which the state is under pressure to serve the interest of the many. Very soon, the neoliberal chord could become out of tune, the impartiality of the rule of law threatened by the amalgamation of the state with politics in the absence of an impartial legal regime, and the price mechanism quickly muddied when the state tries to please those same "masses."[123] The best check on too much popular will would be a federal

---

118 Popper, *The Open Society and Its Enemies*, 311–320.
119 Popper, *The Open Society and Its Enemies*, 482.
120 Popper, *The Open Society and Its Enemies*, 484.
121 Marjolin, talk given at the Society for Political Economy of Belgium, March 14, 1950, Robert Marjolin Papers, Fondation Jean Monnet, ARM 6/3/3.
122 Rüstow during discussion following Lippmann's presentation of the Agenda for Liberalism at the WLC, see Audier, *Le Colloque Lippmann*, 487.
123 Röpke, *Civitas Humana*, 186–188; also, for a similar argument, see L. Robbins, Discussion at MPS on "Counter-cyclical measures, full employment and monetary reform," April 7, 1947, who warned that public spending, to keep full employment at all

system in which shared elements of sovereignty keep nations within liberal limits and unable to change into populist variants of democracies.[124]

On the other end of the political spectrum, authoritarian states could have a liberal basic grid in the eyes of some early neoliberals. Fascism as such was mostly seen as an anti-liberal closed and nationalist system. Ludwig von Mises was among the few who thought it was "full of good intentions" and granted it an important position as a transitory political formation between a crisis of liberalism and a reconstructed liberalism.[125] In 1933, Alfred Müller-Armack even thought that fascist means were better suited to bring about liberalism's ends.[126] With the clear definition of basic values above politics as a necessary condition for a liberal state, however, any collective system or any purely nationalist system was ruled out as an alternative by the 1940s as both would lead along the "road to serfdom," as Hayek wrote, defying promises of social peace and prosperity.[127]

However, when the elements of the liberal chord of basic values, the price mechanism, and the rule of law are given, even authoritarian regimes could be run on a liberal script. Rueff's "true laws" could take shape in democracies, but non-democratic systems could just as well erect a "true" social order.[128] In the early 1950s, Baudin accordingly expanded his list of neoliberal successes in Europe (where he had enumerated West Germany, Belgium, Sweden, England, and Italy as neoliberal countries) and included Portugal's *Estado Novo* under its military dictator Antonio de Oliveira Salazar, which he perceived as a society rooted in individualist values and Christianity, run by a leader bound by law and morality and implementing a corporatist economy that allowed scope for private initiative. This qualified the country as neoliberal.[129] Indeed, Baudin was not the only one to include Portugal's military dictatorship.

cost, could easily get out of hand and "if pushed too far, may change the type of society in which we live." Public spending should, accordingly, be guarded closely because the "state tends to go the same way as the herd."
124 Wilhelm Röpke, *Internationale Ordnung* (Zurich: Eugen Rentsch, 1945), 55: "It is the federal structure that allows one to distribute political power among smaller and larger units within the state as well as among states." See also Lionel Robbins, "Economic Aspects of Federation," in *Federal Union: A Symposium*, ed. M. Chaning-Pearce (London: Jonathan Cape, 1940), 167–186; and F. Hayek, "Inter-State Federalism" and the discussion at the first MPS meeting on April 3, 1947, "The Problems and Chances of European Federation."
125 Ludwig von Mises, *Liberalismus* (Jena: Gustav Fischer, 1927), 45.
126 Müller-Armack, *Staatsidee und Wirtschaftsordnung im neuen Reich*, 40–41.
127 Hayek, *The Road to Serfdom*.   128 Rueff, *L'ordre social*, 583–587.
129 Baudin, *L'Aube d'un nouveau libéralisme*, 169.

The country was a beneficiary of the Marshall Plan, a founding member of NATO, a member of the European Payments Union, and firmly integrated into the postwar Western institutional framework from the start (as opposed to the Spain of General Franco).

From the 1970s onward, macroeconomic steering on Keynesian premises, along with the ideal of full employment as the central concept guiding economic thought and policy-making, were both receding. The basic chord began to be interpreted along more classical liberal lines when liberalism's social responsibilities lost their primary position and so did the concept of full employment. The state, until the 1970s, was seen as able to interfere in the market effectively on the basis of the neoclassical synthesis. It was now increasingly written off as the exact opposite, namely as being ineffective, and welfare turned from being a guarantor of the good society through full employment and social peace to being a threat to the good society, supposedly quenching dynamics and growth as the economic basis for this same good society to develop and sustain itself.[130]

European integration increasingly merged national markets, capped nation-state sovereignty, introduced elements of shared sovereignty, and erected a strict rule of law nationally as a condition of membership and transnationally as a way to build a common European free market and society, making the European Court of Justice an important (and today increasingly criticized) agent of European integration.[131] It is clearly a liberal project, and much of its original design echoes with the thought of early neoliberals and Keynes. Since the 1980s, however, it has followed a more contemporary neoliberal idea in that the market forces are expected to create the best possible society in their wake and the concept of full employment has lost its unquestioned key position. Today, after the financial crisis of 2008, a crisis of globalization's liberal narrative, and facing populist challenges that reclaim the identity of state and nation on the basis of "the political" rather than participating in the effort to realize basic values larger than the nation, liberal economists face a task similar to that of the 1930s. In all likelihood, a new social compromise will be on the European agenda in the years to come and a new kind of neoliberalism will be honed

---

130 For a reflection on shifting economic narratives see Bo Stråth and Lars Magnusson, *A Brief History of Political Economy: Tales of Marx, Keynes and Hayek* (Cheltenham: Edward Elgar, 2016).

131 See, for example, Jürgen Habermas, *The Crisis of the European Union: A Response*, trans. Ciaran Cronin (Cambridge: Polity Press, 2012).

within the (still thriving, though strongly criticized) transnational networks of policy-shaping, in which economics and the "good society" are again more openly and more deeply discussed, albeit within a global context wholly different from the interwar as well as the postwar years. The alternative, quite clearly, is the unraveling of the European Union.

15
Conservatism and Its Discontents

STEVEN B. SMITH

> That every boy and every gal
> That's born into the world alive
> Is either a little Liberal
> Or else a little Conservative
>
> Gilbert and Sullivan, *Iolanthe*

Conservatism and modernity are both terms that suffer from considerable ambiguity and both are in need of considerable refinement. In common parlance, conservatism is opposed to liberalism, even though in practice as well as in theory, the distinction is not so easy to maintain. Conservatism and liberalism are both the products of modernity and could not exist elsewhere. The distinction between conservatism and liberalism is even more difficult to maintain in continental Europe. The term "conservatism" was coined by René de Chateaubriand whose journal *Le Conservateur* was issued to propagate the cause of the clerical and political restoration in France.[1] On the continent, conservatism was frequently associated with reaction to the legacy of the French Revolution. From Joseph de Maistre to Juan Donoso Cortes and Carl Schmitt, these radicals of the Right saw themselves as engaged in a wholesale struggle against the Revolution and the intellectual tradition of the Enlightenment that helped to inspire it. They were not conservatives attempting to restore the *status quo ante*, but political messianists who imagined a Counter-Revolution, a mirror image of the very Revolution they sought to overthrow.[2]

---

[*] I thank Daniel Mahoney, Joshua Cherniss, Aurelian Craiutu, Mark Somos, Martin Jay, and the editors of this volume for some very useful comments on an earlier version of this chapter.
[1] Noël K. O'Sullivan, *Conservatism* (New York: St. Martin's Press, 1976), 9–10.
[2] For a brilliant analysis of the reactionary mind, see Albert O. Hirschman, *The Rhetoric of Reaction: Perversity, Futility, Jeopardy* (Cambridge: Harvard University Press, 1991); see also Mark Lilla, *The Shipwrecked Mind: On Political Reaction* (New York: New York Review Books, 2016).

Conservatism, by contrast – the habitual attitude of a ruling class whose loyalty is wholly to constitutional government rather than any specific body of legislation – has been largely an Anglo-American disposition whose heroes have been Halifax, Edmund Burke, John Adams, T. B. Macaulay, and Churchill. The emergence of modern European conservatism was a product of the Cold War. It developed as a defensive posture against Soviet Marxism and the progressive liberalism that had become the unofficial ideology of the Western democracies. Under these circumstances, conservatism came to regard itself as the guardian of a constitutional order whose very existence was seen as endangered often by tendencies internal to liberalism itself. Instead of attempting to reverse the wheel of history, modern conservatives concentrated on the more limited task of trying to save liberalism from itself by establishing safeguards that would ensure the rule of law, limited government, and moderation. European conservatism had become the voice of an older liberalism.

There is not a single conservative critique of modernity or a unifying vision about what kind of society conservatism wants to bring about, but rather a variety of conservatisms that share a number of "family resemblances." Conservatives have typically nourished a deep skepticism about the wisdom of large-scale social reform and an appreciation of the role of fate, chance, and unintended consequences to undercut the best laid plans. The motto of conservatism could be "the best is the enemy of the good." They have advocated for a wide degree of individual liberty, often combined with market incentives, as the best way to attain social order. And they have generally expressed a preference for the nation-state, with the different and competing moral and religious traditions of each country, as the basic unit of political life in opposition to plans for a United States of Europe and other multinational forms of organization. I will consider each of these points in turn.

Conservatism and Skepticism about Reason

No one has challenged the central premises of twentieth-century progressivism more profoundly than the English political philosopher Michael Oakeshott (1901–1990).[3] Indeed, he was the only twentieth-century thinker of the first rank to self-consciously describe himself as a conservative.

---

3 For an excellent biography, see Paul Franco, *Michael Oakeshott: An Introduction* (New Haven: Yale University Press, 2004); see also Efraim Podoksik (ed.), *The Cambridge Companion to Oakeshott* (New York: Cambridge University Press, 2012).

Oakeshott was appointed to the Chair of Politics at the London School of Economics (LSE) in 1951 during the height of the postwar construction of the British welfare state. His inaugural lecture titled "Political Education" signaled a radical departure from the tradition of Fabian socialism upon which the LSE had been founded. Although Oakeshott paid tribute to his predecessors, Graham Wallas and Harold Laski, he noted the irony that they should be followed by a skeptic "who would do better if only he knew how."[4] In the most memorable image from the lecture, Oakeshott declared that,

> In political activity, then, men sail a boundless and bottomless sea; there is neither harbor for shelter nor floor for anchorage, neither starting-place nor appointed destination. The enterprise is to keep afloat on an even keel; the sea is both friend and enemy; and the seamanship consists in using the resources of a traditional manner of behavior in order to make a friend of every hostile occasion.[5]

Oakeshott's use of the occasion to reject the idea that politics consists in the application of rational principles to public affairs and his self-conscious embrace of "a traditional manner of behavior" was nothing less than a fire bell in the night.

Oakeshott saw the dominant form of political progressivism as being of a piece with a larger trend in European thought that he designated as Rationalism.[6] By Rationalism, he meant a specifically modern disposition, associated with Bacon and Descartes, according to which all knowledge is a form of technique, reducible to rules and susceptible to expression in propositional form. What cannot stand up to this kind of methodological rigor is no longer to count as knowledge. Although Oakeshott's critique of Rationalism bore a resemblance to a certain strain of mid-century European criticism of science and technology – as found, for example, in Max Horkheimer and Theodor Adorno's *Dialectic of Enlightenment* – he was unique in basing his critique on a thoroughgoing skepticism.

At the core of Oakeshott's critique of Rationalism stands a distinction between two kinds of knowledge that he calls practical and technical.[7] Practical knowledge is knowledge acquired through doing; it is the kind

---

[4] Michael Oakeshott, "Political Education," in *Rationalism in Politics and Other Essays* (Indianapolis: Liberty Press, 1991), 44.
[5] Oakeshott, "Political Education," 60.
[6] Michael Oakeshott, "Rationalism in Politics," in *Rationalism in Politics and Other Essays* (Indianapolis: Liberty Press, 1991), 5–11.
[7] Oakeshott, "Rationalism in Politics," 11–17.

of knowledge involved in riding a bicycle, driving a car, or hitting a baseball. Technical knowledge, by contrast, is knowledge of rules, rules that can be read in a book or manual, memorized by heart, and applied by rote. Technical knowledge is based on an abstraction from the concrete practices and activities that make up human experience. Technical knowledge is to practical knowledge what knowing the traffic code is to driving a car or what knowledge of a legal textbook is to the practice of law. These two forms of knowledge may be inseparable from one another, but in every instance, Oakeshott wants to say, it is practical knowledge that forms the ground from which a tradition of thought and practice arises.

The triumph of Rationalism has created a new kind of politics, "the politics of the book," that Oakeshott associates with the rise of ideology.[8] Oakeshott traces the emergence of ideology to writers like Machiavelli and Locke whose works were intended as "cribs" for a new politically inexperienced class of rulers. Over time, these manuals of reform came to substitute for the painstakingly acquired knowledge gained through long experience of political life. Ideological politics – associated with liberalism, progressivism, socialism, fascism, and communism – are all attempts to replace traditional political knowledge with intellectual shortcuts that can be condensed into doctrines and put into book form. Ideology is the antithesis of tradition. Ideological politics are "abstractions" from political experience in which all the complexities and subtleties have been squeezed out.

Oakeshott's critique of Rationalism has often been taken as a rejection of reason *per se* and, therefore, as an endorsement of anti-rationalism in politics.[9] His description of a tradition as a "flow of sympathy" and as "the pursuit of intimations" invited the charge that he was rejecting rational standards for decision-making. But Oakeshott pushed back with the argument that reason is not something that stands apart from tradition but is embedded within it. He was not attacking reason but an ideological misuse of reason. The correct way to make an omelet is embedded in the tradition of cookery, just as the correct way of rendering a legal decision is embedded in the tradition of

---

8 Oakeshott, "Rationalism in Politics," 25–35.
9 For some examples of the angry response to Oakeshott, see Richard Crossman, "Political Realities," *Times Literary Supplement*, September 28, 1962, 753–754; Bernard Crick, "The World of Michael Oakeshott or the Lonely Nihilist," *Encounter*, 20 (June 1963), 65–74; and Hanna Fenichel Pitkin, "The Roots of Conservatism and the Denial of Politics," *Dissent* (Fall 1973), 496–525.

jurisprudence. A rational course of action is not the result of a premeditated plan, but is expressed in fidelity to an existing practice.[10]

To be sure, Oakeshott's defense of a moral and political tradition needs to be distinguished from two other kinds of conservatism. Most commonly, Oakeshott is associated with Burkean conservatism for their similar critiques of rationalism and defense of prejudice, custom, and circumstance as the most reliable guides to action. Burke's prescient reading of the direction of the French Revolution has been seen as the template for Oakeshott's warnings against the danger of the modern welfare state with its belief in the guiding role of intellectuals in using social policy to remake society. Yet it is surprising that Oakeshott rarely cites Burke's writings, and when he does, it is more often to criticize than to endorse him. What is the difference?

On Oakeshott's reading, Burke was a kind of metaphysical conservative. Burke had described English constitutional government as a providential gift patterned after a correspondence with nature. Oakeshott found in Burke's defense of tradition the same kind of ideological thinking that he had deplored in the revolutionary doctrines of the rights of man. Oakeshott's defense of tradition was also combined with a more robust individualism than Burkean traditionalism. It is revealing that Oakeshott wrote a scathing review of Russell Kirk's *The Conservative Mind* and deplored that it was Burke rather than Hume who became the father of American conservatism.[11]

Oakeshott's conservatism needs to be further distinguished from another that has been called "the politics of imperfection."[12] On this account, conservatism embraces a particular conception of human nature, sometimes described as "Augustinian," that is deeply, perhaps metaphysically, flawed. It is because evil cannot be eradicated that our expectations from politics must be limited. The primary task of politics is, accordingly, negative, being not the moral improvement of humankind, but the preservation of order and of the distinction between the public and the private world.

Oakeshott would not necessarily disagree with the practical proposals of this kind of conservatism, but would take exception to its premises. His conservatism is of the epistemological rather than the metaphysical or theological kind. It is not rooted in a conception of human nature as

---

10 This argument is developed at length in Michael Oakeshott, "The Tower of Babel," in *Rationalism in Politics and Other Essays* (Indianapolis: Liberty Press, 1991), 465–487.
11 See Michael Oakeshott, "Review of Russell Kirk, 'The Conservative Mind,'" in *The Vocabulary of a Modern European State*, ed. Luke O'Sullivan (Thorverton: Imprint Academic, 2008), 81–84.
12 Anthony Quinton, *The Politics of Imperfection: The Religious and Secular Traditions of Conservative Thought in England from Hooker to Oakeshott* (London: Faber & Faber, 1978).

irretrievably fallen, corrupt, or sinful. This is simply the reverse side of Rationalist perfectionism. Oakeshott's heroes are typically drawn from the list of philosophic skeptics like Montaigne, Pascal, Hobbes, and Hume, all of whom stress the limits of what we can know. His description of the conservative disposition displays a cheerful embrace of human nature as it is, warts and all, without longing to restore a world that is lost or to bring about an imaginary future:

> The general characteristics of this disposition are not difficult to discern, although they have often been mistaken. They center upon a propensity to use and to enjoy what is available rather than to wish for or to look for something else; to delight in what is present rather than what was or what may be ... To be conservative, then, is to prefer the familiar to the unknown, to prefer the tried to the untried, fact to mystery, the actual to the possible, the limited to the unbounded, the near to the distant, the sufficient to the superabundant, the convenient to the perfect, present laughter to utopian bliss.[13]

Although Oakeshott was conservative in his thinking, he was not politically *engagé*. The principles of his philosophy discouraged any direct form of political engagement. Philosophy was philosophy, practice was practice, and never the twain shall meet. Oakeshott feared that a philosophy that attempted to become practical, to offer itself as a guide for life or a roadmap for the future, was in danger of overstepping its limits. The intrusion of philosophy in the public sphere could not only lead to the corruption of society by the attempt to replace practical knowledge with technical know-how, but would lead to the corruption of philosophy, whose task is to understand the world, not to change it.[14]

Oakeshott's self-denying strictures did not discourage some of his students from engaging more directly with the politics of the present era. Interestingly, his three greatest disciples all came from abroad. Elie Kedourie (1926–1992), an Iraqi Jew who joined Oakeshott at the LSE, wrote powerfully against the forces of nationalism and so-called national liberation movements especially in the Middle East in his books on *Nationalism* and *Nationalism in Asia and Africa*.[15] In *The Servile Mind*,

---

13 Michael Oakeshott, "On Being Conservative," in *Rationalism in Politics and Other Essays* (Indianapolis: Liberty Press, 1991), 408.
14 See Steven B. Smith, "Practical Life and the Critique of Rationalism," in *The Cambridge Companion to Oakeshott*, ed. Efraim Podoksik (New York: Cambridge University Press, 2012), 131–152; see also Steven B. Smith, "Oakeshott on the Theory–Practice Problem: A Reply to Terry Nardin," *Global Discourse*, 5(2) (2015), 323–325.
15 Elie Kedourie, *Nationalism* (New York: Praeger, 1961); and Elie Kedourie, *Nationalism in Asia and Africa* (New York: World Publishing, 1970).

Kenneth Minogue (1930–2013), an Australian émigré also at the LSE, deplored the way modern democracy erodes the culture of individuality and moral responsibility.[16] And Shirley Robin Letwin (1924–1993), an American expat and mother of the Tory MP Oliver Letwin, defended the English tradition of gentlemanship in her book *The Gentleman in Trollope* and praised Margaret Thatcher for reinvigorating a moral tradition of the "vigorous virtues" in *The Anatomy of Thatcherism*.[17]

Conservatism and Liberty

No aspect of twentieth-century conservative thought is more deeply ingrained than the idea of liberty. To be sure, things have not always been this way. Reactionaries like Maistre saw the principle of individual liberty – "political Protestantism" – as creating deep social fragmentation and division. Hegel associated "subjectivity" with the experience of *Zerrissenheit* (tornness) or the destructiveness of the social order during the French Revolution. Even Burke feared that without the restraining effects of tradition and authority men would become "flies of a summer." Liberty was always the rallying cry of classical liberalism from Locke to the *Federalist Papers* to John Stuart Mill.

In the twentieth century, however, classical liberalism morphed into progressivism. Progressivism was the product of the idealist philosophy of Kant, Hegel, T. H. Green, and John Dewey. Its goal was not to protect a zone of liberty for individuals to pursue their wants and desires, but to progressively eliminate obstacles to the achievement of their wants and desires. The right to the pursuit of happiness became the right to happiness. Progressivism introduced an undeniably collectivist component to liberalism. Accordingly, the older liberal doctrine of individual rights to such formal goods as life, liberty, and property became entitlements to substantive goods such as the right to employment, health care, family leave, and a paid vacation. Individual rights had become group entitlements. Under these circumstances, it became the duty of conservatism to defend classical liberalism from its progressivist stepchild.

---

16 Kenneth Minogue, *The Servile Mind: How Democracy Erodes the Moral Life* (New York: Encounter, 2010); see also Kenneth Minogue, *Alien Powers: The Pure Theory of Ideology* (New York: St. Martin's Press, 1985).
17 Shirley Robin Letwin, *The Gentleman in Trollope: Individuality and Moral Conduct* (Cambridge: Harvard University Press, 1982); and Shirley Robin Letwin,*The Anatomy of Thatcherism* (New Brunswick: Transaction, 1993).

The most eloquent defender of the classical doctrine of liberty was undoubtedly Isaiah Berlin (1909–1997).[18] His famous essay *Two Concepts of Liberty* given as an inaugural lecture at Oxford University in 1958 was an intellectual landmark in the history of the Cold War.[19] Berlin often supported moderately leftist political positions while advocating conservative philosophical stances. He once wittily described himself as occupying "the extreme Right Wing of the Left Wing movement, both philosophically and politically."[20] Berlin's essay began with an attack on the progressivist vision of society in which all fundamental conflict had been eliminated. In such a society – a society of the kind dreamt of by anarchists, socialists, and Marxists – political disputes would be replaced by a technical science of public administration. Disputes over the ends of political life – the kinds of disputes on which philosophy thrives – would be replaced by disputes over means. Against the allures of progressivism and determinism, Berlin warned his readers to remain alive to the power of ideas and, above all, their role in shaping the ideological conflicts of the present age.

The core of Berlin's lecture turns on two different kinds of liberty that he refers to as negative and positive liberty, respectively. What is this controversial distinction intended to signify? Negative liberty is in the first instance freedom from external impediments or controls. We are free when we are left alone or unattended, that is, when we are not interfered with by other persons, institutions, or agencies. Negative liberty concerns itself with the space within which persons are free to act without being coerced by others. It is described as negative because it represents freedom from external hindrances to action. At the essence of this conception of freedom stands a theory of choice or will. We are free to the extent that we can exercise our wills not just to *do* this rather than that, but to *become* this rather than that. Negative liberty presupposes that persons are malleable and underdetermined, that we not only choose between values and ways of life, but are the active makers and shapers of these values and ways of life, or, in one of Berlin's striking images, that we are the driver and not the horse.[21]

The theory of positive liberty, on the other hand, is ultimately less about will or choice than about human rationality. On the positive theory of liberty,

---

18 For a useful biography, see Michael Ignatieff, *Isaiah Berlin: A Life* (New York: Henry Holt, 1998); see also Joshua L. Cherniss, *A Mind and Its Time: The Development of Isaiah Berlin's Political Thought* (Oxford: Oxford University Press, 2013).
19 Isaiah Berlin, "Two Concepts of Liberty," in *The Proper Study of Mankind*, ed. Henry Hardy and Roger Hausheer (New York: Farrar, Straus, and Giroux, 2000).
20 Cited in Cherniss, *A Mind and Its Time*, 80.
21 Berlin, "Two Concepts of Liberty," 194–203.

we are said to be free only when we exercise control over our choices. The classic theorists of positive liberty understood correctly, Berlin believed, that our choices may be constrained or even determined by a range of variables over which we may have no control, such as upbringing, education, social conditioning, and the like. We are not free unless and until we exercise control over those determinants that condition our choices. Berlin associates this kind of liberty with a conception of self-mastery or self-determination. We are free not just by virtue of the choices we make, but when we live our lives according to a plan or a set of rules that we have made for ourselves and that we find worth living for. Freedom consists here not just in the act of choice, but in choosing what most fully realizes our humanity.[22]

Berlin is not simply a neutral in the debate over negative and positive liberty. He associates negative liberty with the tradition of political liberalism and positive liberty with the vast networks of tyranny and social control. He believes that positive liberty contains a coercive component that leads to tyranny. Berlin does not mean to say that there is a necessary or logical entailment between ideas of positive liberty and social coercion; nor does he claim (as he sometimes appears to do) that there is an invariable historical association between the two.[23] He even admits that negative liberty is not the "necessary condition for the growth of human genius" and that "Integrity, love of truth, and fiery individualism grow at least as often in severely disciplined communities or under military discipline, as in more tolerant or indifferent societies."[24]

For Berlin, there is a kind of psychological affiliation – an "elective affinity" to use a different vocabulary – leading from positive liberty to political extremism. Positive liberty contains a dogmatic belief – one that Berlin calls "demonstrably false" – that it is possible to know what human beings ought to be or what is the best way of life; those who fall short of this ideal are deemed ignorant, corrupt, or sinful. In its effort to make us more rational, enlightened, or virtuous, proponents of positive liberty are bound to violate the autonomy of the individual. Positive libertarians are necessarily led to treat individuals as means to the promotion of their goals, however worthy those goals might be. And when such people feel called upon to use the state or other institutional means of coercion to achieve those ends, the result can only be despotism masquerading as freedom.

---

22 Berlin, "Two Concepts of Liberty," 203–206.
23 Berlin, "Two Concepts of Liberty," 216–226.   24 Berlin, "Two Concepts of Liberty," 200.

The great heroes of the tradition of negative liberty are thinkers like Montesquieu, the authors of the *Federalist Papers*, Constant, and Mill, all of whom defended the maximum space for human choice and action. By contrast, it was the tradition of positive liberty championed by Rousseau and his epigones (Fichte, Hegel, and Marx) which was responsible for the creation of some of the worst experiments in social control known to history. The paradox that Berlin never ceased to explore is how political ideas that aimed to liberate us from tyranny could be at the root of even more extensive forms of coercion, all in the name of political freedom. Not inaccurately, *Two Concepts* has been described by one reader as an "anti-communist manifesto."[25]

Perhaps the most famous of the mid-century critics of totalitarianism was Friedrich von Hayek (1899–1992).[26] Hayek was an Austrian-born economist who taught at the LSE in the years just prior to Oakeshott and later at the University of Chicago. Along with Chicago economists Frank Knight and George Stigler, Hayek was one of the founders of the Mount Pelerin Society devoted to libertarian ideas and free market economics.[27] Hayek did not consider himself a conservative. Conservatism, he thought, could not offer an alternative to the existing direction of society. It remained an oppositional ideology.[28] Only the tradition of classical liberalism from Mandeville, to Smith, to Tocqueville could provide the resources for a principled commitment to liberty and resistance to unlimited government.

Hayek's principal concern is with a corruption of the language of liberty.[29] Like Berlin, Hayek associates liberty or freedom with the absence of coercion or not being under the arbitrary will of another. This needs to be distinguished from two misuses of the term. One associates liberty with power, by which is meant the ability to satisfy our wishes. The second is the confusion of liberty with democracy, or the participation in government or in the process of legislation. Both of these, Hayek insisted, were derivative from and conceptually different from the primary conception of liberty as individual choice and non-interference. The misuse of liberty was not merely

---

25 Leo Strauss, "Relativism," in *The Rebirth of Classical Political Rationalism*, ed. Thomas Pangle (Chicago: University of Chicago Press, 1989), 16.
26 On Hayek, see John Gray, *Hayek on Liberty* (New York: Routledge, 1998); and Norman P. Barry, *Hayek's Social and Economic Philosophy* (London: Macmillan, 1979).
27 For an excellent history of the movement, see Angus Burgin, *The Great Persuasion: Reinventing Free Markets since the Depression* (Cambridge: Harvard University Press, 2012).
28 Friedrich Hayek, *The Constitution of Liberty* (Chicago: University of Chicago Press, 1978), 397–414.
29 Hayek, *The Constitution of Liberty*, 11–21.

a conceptual confusion; it was used by collectivists of both the Left and the Right to justify large increases in state power. Even here, Hayek did not oppose all encroachments on liberty, but rather the *arbitrary* use of power to do so. Interference that takes the form of law is not a violation of liberty, something that suggests the Kantian character of Hayek's thought.

Like Oakeshott, Hayek associates the misuses of liberty with the "rationalist" liberalism of Descartes, Voltaire, and Rousseau. Rationalism or "constructivism" are terms associated with the attempt to build society in accordance with a blueprint or a plan. This is contrasted to what Hayek regards as the "spontaneous" growth of society or the idea that accident over a long period of time ensures good results. Unlike a constructed order – consider Stalin's Five-Year Plans – that requires the presence of a guiding intelligence, the spontaneous order is the creation of the sum total of human minds working together to satisfy human ends. Unlike the advocates of intentional social planning, Hayek expressed a Burkean belief that traditions and practices that have evolved over centuries embody the collective wisdom of generations that we ignore at our peril. Given the limitations of what any one person or even generation can know, it is preferable to allow social institutions to develop spontaneously as the best means of avoiding coercion. The spontaneous order functions like a market guided by an invisible hand that leaves its members freer than any created by centralized direction.[30]

Hayek's attack on central planning in *The Road to Serfdom* (1944) has been a mainstay of the conservative critique of the post-World War II welfare state. As the title of the book suggests, experiments in planning are simply the first step toward tyranny. As an epigraph for the book he chose a passage from Hume: "It is seldom that liberty of any kind is lost all at once." What Hayek valued was above all human liberty and not simply market freedom. It is important to distinguish Hayekean freedom from any form of "economism." He denied that the market is the panacea for all social ills, claiming only that the very impersonality of the market provides more general freedom for all. "Probably nothing has done so much harm to the liberal cause," he wrote, "as the wooden insistence of some liberals on certain rough rules of thumb, above all the principle of *laissez-faire*."[31] And elsewhere he complained that opposition to planning should not be confused with "a dogmatic

---

30 For the contrast between "constructed" and "spontaneous" order, see Friedrich Hayek, "Kinds of Order in Society," in *The Politicization of Society*, ed. Kenneth Templeton (Indianapolis: Liberty Press, 1975), 501–523; see also Gray, *Hayek on Liberty*, 26–53.
31 Friedrich Hayek, *The Road to Serfdom* (London: Routledge, 2001), 18.

laissez-faire attitude."[32] Although Hayek supported a minimal state, the powers he believed the state could legitimately exercise include the provision of health care, safety regulations in the workplace, and environmental protection.

There remained an ambiguity in Hayek's thought between spontaneity and planning. Hayek's spontaneous social order is very close to Oakeshott's conception of a civil association held together by procedural ("adverbial") rules that are purely instrumental to the purposes of its citizens. These rules impose no substantive plan or purpose other than allowing citizens the maximum liberty to pursue their own ends and purposes. But while Oakeshott saw these conditions as embedded in longstanding European traditions and practices, he criticized – perhaps unfairly – Hayek's spontaneous order as participating in the very rationalism he had so eloquently denounced:

> How deeply the rationalist disposition of mind has invaded our political thought and practice is illustrated by the extent to which traditions of behavior have given place to ideologies ... This is perhaps the main significance of Hayek's *Road to Serfdom* – not the cogency of the doctrine, but the fact that it is a doctrine. A plan to resist all planning may be better than its opposite, but it belongs to the same style of politics.[33]

Another figure in the postwar conservative revival was Karl Popper (1902–1994). Like Hayek, Popper was a Viennese refugee who fled first to New Zealand in 1937 and later to London, where he attracted a formidable following including the Hungarian philosopher Imre Lakatos and the Israeli philosopher Joseph Agassi. Unlike Hayek, who came from a background in classical economics, Popper's interest was in the philosophy and methodology of science. It was during the war that he turned to the philosophy of history and political theory in works like *The Open Society and Its Enemies* (1945) and *The Poverty of Historicism* (1957).

The main focus of Popper's attack was the doctrine of historical inevitability. He dedicated *The Poverty of Historicism* to "the countless men and women of all creeds or nations or races who fell victims to the fascist and communist belief in Inexorable Laws of Historical Destiny." It was not rationalism or planning *per se* as Oakeshott believed, but a particular theory

---

32 Hayek, *The Road to Serfdom*, 36.
33 Oakeshott, "Rationalism in Politics," 26; for some useful comparisons between Hayek and Oakeshott, see Robert Devigne, *Recasting Conservatism: Oakeshott, Strauss, and the Response to Postmodernism* (New Haven: Yale University Press, 1994), 14–23.

of history that Popper called "historicism" that is at the basis of the twentieth-century experiments in totalitarianism. By historicism, Popper means "an approach to the social sciences which assumes that *historical prediction* is their principal aim, and which assumes that this aim is attainable by discovering the 'rhythms' or the 'patterns,' the 'laws' or the 'trends' that underlie the evolution of history."[34] According to this doctrine, the roots of which Popper believed could be found in Plato, Hegel, and Marx, history is governed by general laws that can be known and predicted with scientific certainty. When applied to society, this leads to the authoritarian or totalitarian belief that the direction of history can be predicted and controlled by an intellectual elite or vanguard.

The basic flaw with all systems of historicism is an overconfidence in the scope of knowledge. Popper's refutation of historicism can be summed up in the form of a syllogism: Major Premise: the course of history is shaped by the development of knowledge; Minor Premise: we cannot predict where the future course of knowledge may lead; Conclusion: we cannot predict the future direction of history.[35]

Popper incongruously claimed to trace historicism back to Plato.[36] Basing his critique on the cycle of regimes in book eight of the *Republic*, he argued that one can find here the beginnings of a theory of historical determinism. The basic fallacy with Platonic thought derived from a theory of knowledge that Popper called "essentialism" or "holism" that attempts to immunize itself from self-correction and development. It was Hegel and Marx, however, who produced a fully fledged theory of historicism. Hegel especially is singled out for offering a metaphysical theory of the state that led directly to Hitler and Nazism.[37] Popper is on stronger ground when alleging the influence of Marx on Soviet Communism or even that Marx was an incipient totalitarian. The Leninist theory of the "dictatorship of the proletariat" is simply the logical conclusion of the Marxian theory of history.

Popper's preference for "open societies" – a concept that has been endorsed both by libertarians and by billionaire investor George Soros – is based principally on his conception of critical rationality. On this view, knowledge and science advance through a negative process of falsification

---

34 Karl Popper, *The Poverty of Historicism* (New York: Harper, 1964), 3.
35 Popper, *The Poverty of Historicism*, vi–vii.
36 Karl Popper, *The Open Society and Its Enemies, Volume One: The Spell of Plato* (London: Routledge & Kegan Paul, 1957), 5–28.
37 For a sustained attack on Popper's use of Hegel, see Walter Kaufmann, "The Hegel Myth and Its Method," in *Hegel's Political Philosophy*, ed. Walter Kaufmann (New York: Atherton, 1970), 137–171.

applied to previously held beliefs. Only what can stand up to the rigorous test of empirical refutation can count as knowledge. For Popper, our knowledge of the world is always provisional due to human fallibility. Open societies, just like ideal scientific communities, are those that embody this kind of fallibilism based on a continuous process of trial and error. The basic tenet of fallibilism remains "I may be wrong and you may be right, and by an effort, we may get nearer to the truth."[38]

Popper's critique of historical determinism was very similar to Berlin's, yet, while he valued the importance of individual liberty against all forms of collectivism, he held none of the veneration of tradition that one finds in Oakeshott or faith in the spontaneous social order associated with Hayek. Yet Berlin, as we shall see shortly, praised German romanticism for its appreciation of cultural diversity, something that Popper would see simply as a misguided form of irrationalism. In Popper's work, one finds not the slightest trace of interest in moral diversity for its own sake. There are only open and closed societies. Popper opposed "utopian social engineering," but was not against "piecemeal" engineering that respected the limits of human knowledge and accepted the fallibility of all experiments in social reform.[39] Like Hayek, he remained a Rationalist in Oakeshott's sense of the term, not that he believed in wholesale social change, but that he assumed an ultimate harmony between the methods of science and the methods of society. A free society is one that is the most open to scientific inquiry, and in turn scientific inquiry is the best support of a free society.

The most pungent Cold War critic of Marxist totalitarianism was the French philosopher and sociologist Raymond Aron (1905–1983).[40] Like Berlin, Aron was scarcely a conservative in the strict sense, unless judged from the standpoint of the extreme progressivism of his contemporaries. He took a firm stand in favor of the democratic capitalist nations, in opposition to most French intellectuals, who either favored the Soviet bloc or hoped for some "third way" between capitalism and communism. Aron was a qualified supporter of de Gaulle and a firm Atlanticist who preferred to write for the conservative *Le Figaro* rather than the progressive *Le Monde* or the Marxist-

---

38 Karl Popper, *The Open Society and Its Enemies, Volume Two: Hegel and Marx* (London: Routledge & Kegan Paul, 1957), 225.
39 Popper, *The Poverty of Historicism*, 64–70.
40 See Daniel Mahoney, *The Liberal Political Science of Raymond Aron* (Lanham: Rowman & Littlefield, 1992); see also Tony Judt, *The Burden of Responsibility: Blum, Camus, Aron, and the French Twentieth Century* (Chicago: University of Chicago Press, 1998), 137–182; and Pierre Manent, "Raymond Aron," in *European Liberty* (The Hague: Martinus Nijhoff, 1983), 1–23.

inspired *Les Temps Modernes*. In *The Opium of the Intellectuals* (1955), he accused his *marxisant* contemporaries like Sartre and Merleau-Ponty of abrogating their critical rationality and adopting Marxism as a form of "secular religion."[41] Here he reprised the role played a generation before by Julien Benda, who accused his contemporaries of a *trahison des clercs*, or putting ideological partisanship before the role of independent judgment and responsibility.[42]

Aron was unique – perhaps characteristically French – in the importance he attributed to the "intellectuals" in the struggle between freedom and its enemies. "The revolutions of the twentieth century," he wrote in an especially arresting sentence, "have not been proletarian revolutions; they have been thought up and carried out by intellectuals."[43] Aron regards the intelligentsia as something akin to a new priesthood, but one that has put the worldly goals of the relief of man's estate in place of the transcendent aim of heavenly salvation. The archetypal intellectuals were the *philosophes* of the French Enlightenment, but nowhere have the missionary or redemptive aspirations of this class been given greater prominence than in Marxism. "The Marxist prophetism," Aron writes, "conforms to the typical pattern on the Judeo-Christian prophetism ... The classless society which will bring social progress without political revolution is comparable to the dreams of the millennium. The misery of the proletariat proves its vocation and the Communist Party becomes the Church."[44]

Aron's critique was in many ways similar to that of other Cold War intellectuals who sought to debunk the "scientific" pretensions of Marxism by showing it to be the heir of a theological worldview. "Faith in the proletariat and in history," he writes, "charity for those who suffer today and who tomorrow will inherit the earth, hope that the future will bring the advent of the classless society – the theological virtues reappear in a new guise."[45] Nevertheless, Aron wondered whether Marxism was the heir to the Judeo-Christian tradition of "prophetism" or simply to the revolutionary cults of the French Revolution. "It is the psychology of the sect rather than of a universal Church," he concludes.[46]

Marxist ideology remains incorrigibly deformed by its commitment to the concept of "totality," that is, the aspiration to unite all aspects of human

---

41 Raymond Aron, *The Opium of the Intellectuals*, trans. Terence Kilmartin (New Brunswick: Transaction, 2009), 267–270 and 293–294.
42 See Judt, *The Burden of Responsibility*, 10–11.   43 Aron, *The Opium of the Intellectuals*, 312.
44 Aron, *The Opium of the Intellectuals*, 267.   45 Aron, *The Opium of the Intellectuals*, 269.
46 Aron, *The Opium of the Intellectuals*, 269.

experience in a single coherent whole. It is characteristic of totalitarian thought to exaggerate the dependence of fact on interpretation. Aron, like Berlin, is at heart a methodological pluralist who denied that history could be grasped from a single, all-encompassing perspective. "Marxists who imagine that the 'economic factor' is the unifying force are mixing up a causal primacy and a primacy of interest."[47] Aron offered instead a multi-layered, overdetermined conception of history. History consists of a plurality of values that can never be reduced to a single interest and, while each of these values may be intelligible, they preclude arriving at the meaning of the whole. "In a certain sense," Aron writes, "each and every fragment of history is inexhaustible ... one never plumbs the mystery even of one's nearest and dearest."[48]

Does the almost infinite complexity of history result in a relativism that precludes the possibility of moral assessment? Aron certainly denied this implication. He distinguished between three different forms of criticism. Technical criticism consists of putting oneself in the place of those who govern or administer and asking what actions might be appropriate given the restraints of the situation. Moral criticism denounces the way things are in the light of an image of how things ought to be irrespective of the consequences or practicability of the critique. Finally, ideological or historical criticism consists of attacking the current state of affairs in the name of a future society that will emerge in the course of time to remedy all the injustice of the present.[49]

Aron's own practice of social criticism does not quite fall under any of these descriptions. Clearly, he distances himself from the moral and ideological critic. Moral criticism ("the original source of all criticism") suffers from a fundamental lack of responsibility. It can denounce existing evils but evades responsibility for the inevitably unpleasant consequences of correcting them. Ideological criticism – the kind closest to Marxism – is even worse. It stands condemned for playing the cynical game of opposing the status quo for its putative injustices while providing moral justification for the enormities of violence and terror when committed in the name of the revolutionary Party. Merleau-Ponty's *Humanism and Terror* with its defense of the Moscow show

---

47 Aron, *The Opium of the Intellectuals*, 149.
48 Aron, *The Opium of the Intellectuals*, 138–139.
49 Aron, *The Opium of the Intellectuals*, 210–211; see also Raymond Aron, "The Social Responsibility of the Philosopher," in *Politics and History*, trans. Miriam Bernheim Conant (New York: Free Press, 1978), 249–259.

trials was the most blatant instance of this hypocrisy. It is a classic example of an idealism of ends combined with a Machiavellianism of means.

On its surface, Aron would seem closest to the technical form of criticism that always thinks within the limits of the possible. Even if this is broadly correct, it does not do justice to the scope of the Aronian vision. The true intellectual is one who understands the limits of his situation but is prepared to accept moral responsibility for his actions. To act is to take risks and these risks are inseparable from the historical situation in which we act. Above all, it is necessary to "try never to forget the arguments of the adversary, or the uncertainty of the future, or the faults of [one's] own side, or the underlying fraternity of ordinary men everywhere."[50] These are hardly the sentiments of a technocrat.

Aron was an empiricist and realist in the best sense. This is characterized vividly in a story that he recalled in his *Memoirs*. In 1932, after returning to Paris from a year spent in Berlin as a young doctoral student from the École Normale Supérieure, he arranged through an intermediary a meeting at the French Foreign Ministry to inform the minister about the threat represented by Hitler's rise to power. When asked to give his opinion about the current state of affairs, he delivered a brilliant lecture "in the pure style of a student from the ENS." After listening politely, the minister's aide asked, "You have spoken so well about Germany and the dangers appearing on the horizon, what would you do if you were in his place?"[51] Aron admits that he had no idea what to say but took away a life-long lesson always to ask himself the question, "What would I do?" Aron's practical orientation served as a prophylactic against both revolutionary romanticism and reactionary nostalgia.

It was fashionable in leftist circles to declare, "better wrong with Sartre than right with Aron."[52] Yet by the end of his life, it was Aron who triumphed over his *petit comrade*. His steady advocacy for moderate and conservative thinkers like Montesquieu, Tocqueville, and Weber seemed to offer a sane and responsible alternative to the illusions of *la pensée '68*. A new generation of post-1968 thinkers was coming to see the wisdom in Aron's defense of a "decadent Europe" against the forces of radicalism and nihilism emanating

---

50 Aron, *The Opium of the Intellectuals*, 313.
51 Raymond Aron, *Memoirs: Fifty Years of Political Reflection*, trans. George Holoch (New York: Holmes & Meier, 1990), 41–42; I had the honor of hearing Aron tell this story once in the apartment of Allan Bloom. His humor and self-effacement made an impression on all who were there.
52 Cited in Mark Lilla, "The Legitimacy of the Liberal Age," in *New French Thought: Political Philosophy*, ed. Mark Lilla (Princeton: Princeton University Press, 1994), 12.

from the Rue d'Ulm.[53] Aron was the guiding force behind a new journal, *Commentaire*, that brought together some of the most impressive figures in France, including international relations scholar Pierre Hassner (1933–2018), economist Jean-Claude Casanova (1934–), historian Alain Besançon (1932–), sociologist Jean Baechler (1937–), and philosopher Pierre Manent (1949–).

The Universal and the Particular

Conservatism in European thought has traditionally been the voice of moral pluralism over the liberal tendency toward moral universalism. Pluralism tends to respect tradition, that is always a particular tradition, as opposed to universalism, that is guided by the idea of a single moral code applicable for all time and place. In political terms, this has meant a preference for the individual sovereign state as the basic unit of political life as opposed to the liberal preference for internationalist political organizations as embodied in institutions like the United Nations and the European Union. This is not to say that conservatives frown on all forms of international association – NATO, for example – but they tend to see these differently from liberals. Liberals increasingly reject the sovereignty of the nation-state, while conservatives are not embarrassed to speak of "national greatness" and think of Europe as something other (and higher) than a trading partnership or a common currency.[54]

The defense of moral pluralism was given its most articulate expression in the writings of Isaiah Berlin. He first put this thesis about value pluralism forward in the eighth and final section of *Two Concepts* titled "The One and the Many."[55] It is his view that values – the ideals and aspirations that we care most deeply about – are in a condition of permanent and ineradicable conflict. At the core of Berlin's vision is not just a teaching of negative liberty, but a defense of what he calls "value pluralism." It is the belief that this is not a peaceful convergence on ultimate ends, but rather a spirited agonistic struggle between these ends, that gives Berlinian philosophy a tragic, even heroic, dimension.

The doctrine of value pluralism, along with his defense of negative liberty, has become Berlin's most important legacy. It is a claim about the objective

---

53 See Raymond Aron, *In Defense of Decadent Europe*, trans. Stephen Cox (Chicago: Regnery, 1979).
54 See Daniel J. Mahoney, *De Gaulle: Statesmanship, Grandeur, and Modern Democracy* (New Brunswick: Transaction, 2000), 147–149.
55 Berlin, "Two Concepts of Liberty," 237–242.

structure of the moral universe. There *are* real moral goods – justice, liberty, mercy, the pursuit of excellence, the need for social cohesion – that stand in a relation of radical tension with one another. What is more, these goods cannot be rank ordered with one representing the highest and the others seen simply as means to the achievement of this end. Rather there is no common metric in terms of which these goods can be judged. The result for Berlin is that life is choice, and choice not between absolute good and evil, but between competing and rival sets of goods.[56]

Berlin's insight into the inherently pluralistic quality of moral life breaks down into competing liberal and more conservative interpretations. Liberals regard value pluralism as a more complete means of recognizing individual autonomy. On this account, the incommensurability of basic values leads to an enhanced awareness of the role of individual choice. The free or autonomous person's life is a product of his own making. We are free not simply in the economic sense of "free to choose," but free in a much more radical sense to choose to become the kinds of persons we want to be. Life is here based on a free and self-conscious struggle to create our own identities.

But there is a more conservative reading of value pluralism found in Berlin's writings on nationalism.[57] Far more than most liberals, Berlin found not only strength but dignity in the claims for national identity. Nationalism was a product of the European Counter-Enlightenment, the Romantic movement, that grew up in opposition to the individualism and universalism of the French Enlightenment. Nationalism was given its most coherent expression by the eighteenth-century German philosopher of history Johann Gottfried Herder, who regarded it as a fundamental need of human beings to belong to or be a part of a people with a continuous tradition of language and culture. More than most liberals of his era, Berlin appreciated the affective and non-rational sources of political life stemming from the need for membership in a community. The need to belong has always been a conservative impulse. Just like such biological imperatives as the need for food, clothing, and shelter, the need to belong expressed a genuine human desire that cannot be permanently overlooked. Nations or cultures express over time a people's act of collective self-creation. They

---

56 John Gray, *Isaiah Berlin* (Princeton: Princeton University Press, 1996), 38–75.
57 See Isaiah Berlin, "Nationalism," in *Against the Current: Essays in the History of Ideas*, ed. Henry Hardy (Harmondsworth: Penguin, 1979), 333–355; see also Isaiah Berlin, "The Bent Twig," in *The Crooked Timber of Humanity*, ed. Henry Hardy (Princeton: Princeton University Press, 1990), 238–261.

are not the products of individual choice, but set the terms in which self-creation can take place.[58]

Like Elie Kedourie, Berlin certainly understood the dangers of nationalism in its collectivist and racialist forms. But Berlin tended to view these as perversions of the original impulse rather than its logical or necessary expression. From Berlin's Herderian point of view, distinct national cultures are an expression of the pleasing variety of human arrangements that resist homogenization or reduction to a universal set of rules generally set by the "dominant" cultures. What Berlin resisted was the idea that the recognition of cultural plurality must necessarily lead to a kind of war of all against all or a parsing of humanity into irreconcilable groupings of friend and enemy. Although he was deeply attuned to the later Fascist and National Socialist appeals to nationalism, Berlin saw the true form of nationalism as compatible with his commitments to value pluralism that allowed for the diversity of a vast variety of peoples, traditions, and cultures all within a common horizon of humanity.

For Berlin, the type of nationalism that most clearly fit his model was Zionism. A Russian Jew by birth and an Englishman by adoption, Berlin saw Zionism as a legitimate expression of the need for Jewish survival in a hostile Gentile world. Berlin's heroes were not the archetypal "non-Jewish Jews" (to use Isaac Deutscher's phrase) such as Disraeli or Marx, who found surrogates for their own identities by looking outside their tradition, but more modest figures like Moses Hess and Chaim Weizmann who looked to political Zionism as a means of responding to the experience of humiliation and exclusion. Although Berlin was by no means uncritical of the state of Israel, he never doubted the essential justice of the case for Israel to take its place among the nations of the world.[59]

Berlin was not a religious thinker by any means, and even reveals a certain tone deafness to the music of religious belief, but he regarded Zionism as a legitimate response to the European persecution of the Jews. While

---

[58] For a discussion of some of the tensions between Berlin's stress on individual freedom and his embrace of nationalism and other forms of social embeddedness, see Steven B. Smith, "Isaiah Berlin's Enlightenment and Counter-Enlightenment," in *The Cambridge Companion to Isaiah Berlin*, ed. Joshua L. Cherniss and Steven B. Smith (New York: Cambridge University Press, 2018).

[59] Berlin's most extensive statements on Zionism can be found in Isaiah Berlin, "The Origins of Israel" and "Jewish Slavery and Emancipation," in *The Power of Ideas*, ed. Henry Hardy (Princeton: Princeton University Press, 2000), 143–161 and 162–185; for a recent study on Berlin's lifelong concern with Zionsm, see Arie Dubnov, *Between Zionism and Liberalism: Isaiah Berlin and the Dilemma of the Jewish Liberal* (New York: Palgrave Macmillan, 2012).

assimilation may be possible in individual cases, it has proven to be unworkable as a collective response to the problem of anti-Semitism. The nineteenth century – the great age of assimilationism – also produced the emergence of anti-Semitism on a hitherto unprecedented scale. There is a wonderful story that Berlin recounted about a conversation with the Russo-French philosopher Alexandre Kojève, who had his own doubts about Zionism. "You're a Jew," Kojève said to him. "The Jewish people probably have the most interesting history of any people that ever lived. And now you want to be Albania?" "Yes, we do," was Berlin's reply. "For our purposes, for Jews, Albania is a step forward."[60]

Berlin's defense of Zionism bears comparison with that of another European émigré, Leo Strauss (1899–1973).[61] Strauss is more conventionally considered a conservative or "neo-conservative" than Berlin, although it was a title he never accepted. Strauss entered the conservative canon for his defense of "natural right" in opposition to the prevailing doctrines of relativism and historicism. He singled out the influence of Friedrich Nietzsche and Max Weber in particular for having introduced these doctrines, thus weakening the moral defenses of the West against the extremisms of both the left and the right. Having witnessed the destruction of constitutional government in Weimar Germany, Strauss thought he saw the same processes afoot in America. Writing in the years immediately after World War II, he warned that "It would not be the first time that a nation, defeated on the battlefield, and, as it were, annihilated as a political being, has deprived its conquerors of the most sublime fruit of victory by imposing on them the yoke of its own thought."[62]

Strauss regarded the rise of historicism as responsible for a "crisis of the West" whose most obvious manifestations were Nazi Germany and Soviet Russia. The deeper meaning of this crisis can be traced back to the roots of modern philosophy. Modernity, Strauss believed, was constituted by a specific purpose or project, namely the creation of a universal society of free and equal nations living peacefully under the rule of international law. This purpose was given theoretical expression in the philosophies of the Enlightenment and received political endorsement in such official (or unofficial) documents as Woodrow Wilson's Fourteen Points and Franklin

---

60 Ramin Jahanbegloo, *Conversations with Isaiah Berlin* (London: Pater Halban, 1992), 86.
61 For useful studies, see Steven B. Smith, *Reading Leo Strauss: Politics, Philosophy, Judaism* (Chicago: University of Chicago Press, 2006); and Steven B. Smith (ed.), *The Cambridge Companion to Leo Strauss* (New York: Cambridge University Press, 2009).
62 Leo Strauss, *Natural Right and History* (Chicago: University of Chicago Press, 1971), 2.

Roosevelt's Four Freedoms. Today, however, the West has become uncertain of its purpose. This uncertainty has arisen in part from doubts about the fundamental principles that once governed this project, which are increasingly thought to be merely subjective preferences or "values," or are regarded as historical artifacts of our time. In either case, we no longer seem to be fortified by the clarity that animated earlier generations, and this lack of purpose, even despair about the future, explains many contemporary forms of Western degeneration. Strauss singled out Berlin's doctrine of value pluralism as symptomatic of the "crisis of liberalism" for its abandonment of a belief in natural right and its attempt to become entirely relativistic.[63]

More to the point, Strauss emphasized what he termed the "theologico-political problem" as the fundamental theme of his life's work.[64] Like Berlin, he rejected the Enlightenment's facile claim that the progressive development of reason would put religion on the path of ultimate extinction. Strauss regarded this claim as superficial at best and dishonest at worst. The fact that the Enlightenment had to resort to mockery and polemic – consider Voltaire's *écrasez l'infâme* – indicated the weakness of the critique.

More than Berlin or Popper, Strauss took seriously the theological critique of the Enlightenment. The Enlightenment had attempted to solve the theologico-political problem by cordoning religion off into its own private sphere in civil society. Even defenders of theology accepted this strategy of "internalization," by coming to regard religion as nothing more than a form of personal experience, but, influenced by the revival of theology in the twentieth century (as represented by thinkers such as the Protestant theologian Karl Barth and the Jewish philosopher Franz Rosenzweig), Strauss began to entertain serious doubts about whether the Enlightenment's "Napoleonic" assault on the citadel of orthodoxy had truly been successful. He saw instead that reason and revelation – what he sometimes metaphorically referred to as Athens and Jerusalem – represented two incommensurable sources of knowledge, that is, neither can definitively refute the other without resorting to arbitrary premises.[65]

---

63 Strauss, "Relativism," 17; see also Leo Strauss, *The City and Man* (Chicago: University of Chicago Press, 1977), 3–4; and Leo Strauss, "The Crisis of Our Time," in *The Predicament of Modern Politics*, ed. Harold Spaeth (Detroit: University of Detroit Press, 1964), 41–45.

64 Leo Strauss, "Preface to Spinoza's Critique of Religion," in Leo Strauss, *Liberalism Ancient and Modern* (New York: Basic Books, 1968), 224; see also Leora Batnitzky, "Leo Strauss and the 'Theologico-political Predicament,'" in *The Cambridge Companion to Leo Strauss*, 41–62.

65 See Steven B. Smith, "How Jewish was Leo Strauss?," in Steven B. Smith, *Reading Leo Strauss: Politics, Philosophy, Judaism* (Chicago: University of Chicago Press, 2006), 23–42.

Strauss traced Zionism back to Spinoza's defense of a revived Jewish sovereignty in his *Theologico-political Treatise*.[66] Spinoza was the profound source of the purely secular or political Zionism of later thinkers like Moses Hess, Leo Pinsker, and Theodor Herzl. But Strauss was aware of the inadequacy of a Zionism that was disconnected from its roots in Jewish culture and tradition. He spoke favorably of the cultural Zionism of Ahad Ha'am for recognizing that a Jewish state without a Jewish culture would be an empty shell. Yet Strauss saw that even cultural Zionism was a compromise with modernity. Culture is a modern term that presupposes the secular point of view. Zionism, to be worthy of its own name, cannot subsist on folk music, dance, and pottery. Judaism is based not on culture but on revelation. If it is to be true to itself, cultural Zionism must necessarily morph into religious Zionism.[67]

Strauss did not definitively state which of the three forms of Zionism – political, cultural, religious (if any) – best suited his definition, but in a public letter to the *National Review* written in 1957, he made the conservative case for a purely political Zionism.[68] Strauss began the letter by questioning the "anti-Jewish animus" that seemed to run through the magazine in that period. A conservative, he chided the editors, is supposedly someone who believes that "everything good is heritage," so in Israel the Hebrew Bible absolutely predominates in the public schools. The spirit of the country can be described as "heroic austerity supported by the nearness of biblical antiquity." Perhaps, Strauss goes on, the conservative criticism of Israel stems from the fact that the country is run by a socialist government. He counters by suggesting that the founders of Israel are better understood as pioneers than as labor unionists. They are looked upon as the "natural aristocracy" of the country in much the way Americans look at the Pilgrim Fathers. Finally, Strauss praises Herzl as a conservative who attempted to save the "moral spine" of Judaism at the time when it was threatened by the emancipation and complete dissolution. "Political Zionism," he concluded, "was the attempt to restore that inner freedom, that simple dignity, of which only people who remember their heritage and are loyal to their fate are capable."[69]

---

66 For Spinoza's role in the rise of Zionism, see Steven B. Smith, *Spinoza, Liberalism, and the Question of Jewish Identity* (New Haven: Yale University Press, 1997), 101–103 and 204–205.

67 Strauss, "Preface to Spinoza's Critique of Religion," 228–230.

68 Leo Strauss, "Letter to the Editor: The State of Israel," in *Jewish Philosophy and the Crisis of Modernity*, ed. Kenneth Hart Green (Albany: SUNY Press, 1997), 413–414. See also Steven B. Smith, "Leo Strauss's Forgotten Letter," *Commentary*, October, 2016, 17–19.

69 Strauss, "Letter to the Editor," 414.

The defense of the nation-state as an antidote to the new wave of transnational cosmopolitanism has been powerfully restated by Pierre Manent.[70] A student of Aron who is also deeply indebted to the work of Strauss, Manent has increasingly focused his attention on the emergence of the new Europe since the Maastricht Treaty of 1992. In a series of works with titles like *Democracy without Nations?*, *A World beyond Politics?*, and *Metamorphoses of the City*, Manent explored the history of European political forms – the city, the empire, the church, and the nation – and the growing tension between the nation and democracy in contemporary Europe.

Manent's early work followed Strauss's genealogy of modernity, beginning with Machiavelli's break with classical thought that gave rise in turn to Hobbes's scientific approach to the modern state, but the central figure in Manent's account of modernity to whom he has recurred time and again is Tocqueville. Tocqueville, he wrote, "formulated the problem of liberal societies in the most extensive and profound way."[71] More than any other thinker, Tocqueville unveiled the driving force of modern history, namely, the passion for equality, but this passion has cut in two directions. He saw that modern liberty and equality were the legitimate offspring of early modernity's aspiration to a kind of Promethean self-creation, yet the very desire for equality threatened to create new forms of "soft despotism" under the guise of the administrative state. Manent emphasizes how the restless desire for equality tends over time to destabilize all existing arrangements, but without offering its own answer to the problem of democratic legitimacy.

The ambiguities to which Tocqueville pointed have allowed Manent in his more recent work to explore the increasing "formlessness" of contemporary Europe. Democracy, he notes, grew up in the nation-state and is inconceivable in any other form, but today the democratic principle of equality has attempted to slough off the nation which was its original form. "One might say," he observes, "that the democratic principle, after having used the nation as an instrument or vehicle, abandons it by the wayside."[72] The result has been the depoliticization of Europe. The collective life of Europeans is now dispersed among the organs of "civil society," while governance is centralized in

---

70 For an overall evaluation, see Giulio De Ligio, Jean-Vincent Holeindre, and Daniel J. Mahoney, *La politique et l'âme: Autour de Pierre Manent* (Paris: CNRS, 2014).
71 Pierre Manent, *The Intellectual History of Liberalism*, trans. Rebecca Balinski (Princeton: Princeton University Press, 1994), 114.
72 Pierre Manent, *Democracy without Nations? The Fate of Self-Government in Europe*, trans. Paul Seaton (Wilmington: ISI, 2007), 77.

supranational legislatures far removed from public accountability. The idea of the nation as the locus of political life has been systematically undermined by the dream of a new European "humanity" that stands at the forefront of civilizational change.

Manent has described contemporary Europe as inhabiting a "Ciceronian moment" for the very uncertainty of its future political form. He speaks of the European Union as a "vacation" from history for its attempt to sever itself from its roots in the individual nation-states that were its foundation. The idea of the nation has been replaced by that of a humanitarian democracy shorn of tradition, religion, and everything connected to the "old West." The new Europe has become "a veil over our eyes and a down comforter to our hearts" for its attempt to substitute the illusions of a pacified humanity living under international law for the concrete realities of states and their political responsibilities.[73] The task facing Europe today will be either the creation of a new political form to take the place of the national state or, more likely, the return to an older order of nation-states closer to the Christian democracies of Adenauer and de Gaulle.[74] To a greater degree than the other authors considered in this chapter, Manent has a deep appreciation for the Christian, and especially the Catholic, roots of democracy.

Manent's call to reinvigorate the nation is not quite the same as Berlin's defense of moral pluralism. It is less a moral and aesthetic stance and has more to do with recapturing some sense of the political from the tendencies of a global civil society without borders ("the kiss of two telephone numbers on a computer screen") and a European superstate that is similarly disconnected from a national language, territory, and mores.[75] Manent is one of the few Europeans not ashamed to speak of national greatness or to call de Gaulle a "hero."[76] Far from rejecting the doctrine of the universal in the name of the particular, Manent sees particular nations with their own traditions as bearers of a profound message of universality. One figure who expressed this message is the now largely forgotten poet Charles Péguy (1873–1914), whose work Manent has sought to rehabilitate. One can find in Manent's description of Péguy something of his own attempt to crystallize

---

73 Pierre Manent, *Seeing Things Politically*, trans. Ralph C. Hancock (South Bend: St. Augustine's Press, 2015), 147.
74 Manent, *Democracy without Nations?*, 81.   75 Manent, *Democracy without Nations*, 79–80.
76 Pierre Manent, "De Gaulle as Hero," in Pierre Manent, *Modern Liberty and Its Discontents*, trans. Daniel J. Mahoney and Paul Seaton (Lanham: Rowman & Littlefield, 1998), 173–184.

the "concrete universal" that alone bestows meaning and dignity on political life:

> Some works seem to belong more particularly to the nation which gave birth to them. The foreigner who approaches them sees them more often as a curious monument than as the exponents of thoughts of interest to the whole of humanity. Nevertheless, when these writings are profound, the national specificity is but one means of access to the universal. The fiercely French character of Charles Péguy's personality and of his writings should not conceal from us the fact that his thought is important for all who are concerned with the destinies of Europe.[77]

Conservatism is, as it always has been, an endangered species in Europe. It is squeezed between the universalism and cosmopolitanism of the multicultural left and the nationalism and nativism of the reactionary right. Conservatism is concerned today with the survival of constitutional democracy, where this means a kind of *Europe des patries* that is both based on the political unity of a common civilization but also contains distinct and competing national and religious traditions. The core of this conservatism is above all a sense of restraint and moderation. Only moderation, Strauss warned, will protect us against "the twin dangers of visionary expectations from politics and unmanly contempt for politics."[78] It is the basis not only for a decent constitution but for the cause of constitutional government.

---

77 Pierre Manent, "Charles Péguy: Between Political Faith and Faith," in Pierre Manent, *Modern Liberty and Its Discontents*, trans. Daniel J. Mahoney and Paul Seaton (Lanham: Rowman & Littlefield, 1998), 94.
78 Leo Strauss, "Liberal Education and Responsibility," in Leo Strauss, *Liberalism Ancient and Modern* (New York: Basic Books, 1968), 24.

16
Modernity and the Specter of Totalitarianism

SAMUEL MOYN

It often happens in the history of thought that philosophers come belatedly to a popular theme and attempt to make it serve new purposes. They volunteer to articulate intuitive sentiment and to make implicit dilemmas explicit. And they take what emerged as partisan slogans and determine whether to raise them to the level of philosophical claim. Just as regularly, however, the discourse that stimulated the thinkers proves stronger than their innovations. It is not, after all, as if the public noise around concepts, especially new ones, is stilled when the philosophers turn to canonize them. Hannah Arendt and Claude Lefort, the most serious theoreticians of what appeared to so many as a novel and unprecedented phenomenon of "totalitarianism" in the last century, attempted to make an extant discourse rigorous. They developed proprietary approaches that reshaped a popular intellectual discourse. To an impressive extent, however, their interventions did more to amplify the impact and to extend the longevity of the popular theories of "totalitarianism" they dearly hoped to reorient.

Before their largely independent efforts, which themselves were quite different, totalitarianism primarily implied a theory of the commonalities of two new regimes, Nazi and Soviet. For all the word implied that a new form of rule beyond old typologies, unknown to the annals of political science back to Plato and Aristotle, had emerged. In particular, the tyrannies of ancient and modern history that had attracted theorists for decades were said to be different than what the twentieth century oversaw. In agreeing with this contention and attempting to give it substance, Arendt and Lefort each began with one of the two regimes, largely ignoring the other. And each moved away from defining an aberrant regime for the sake of ratifying a liberal democratic norm and of stigmatizing the "totalitarian enemy." Instead, both reassessed the entirety of the modern experience in the light of its extreme forms of rule and argued that, just as there is no way to understand twentieth-century horror except as an outcome of earlier commitments, so a theory of modernity demands an account of how totalitarianism can arise out of it.

Nothing about how Arendt and Lefort proceeded, however, is intelligible apart from a baseline of discourse about "totalitarianism" that they inherited from fascists such as Giovanni Gentile, Catholic publicists such as Waldemar Gurian, and Cold War liberals from Raymond Aron to Jacob Talmon, and may have done little to transform even today. In spite of the efforts of Arendt and Lefort, totalitarianism mainly survived as an attack on enemies, just as it does in contemporary discourse, rather than the sort of rich and rigorous theory they envisioned in their radically distinctive fashions. Since the end of the Cold War, parties as distinctive as Muslims, populists, and neoliberals have been denounced as totalitarians, but virtually no one has pursued the more incisive and specific investigations that Arendt and Lefort undertook. For these reasons, this chapter combines portraits of these two master thinkers typically lost or omitted in surveys of theories of totalitarianism against the backdrop of the discourse they inherited and its fate in spite of their efforts.[1]

The notion of the "totalitarian" state began on the political right – as a way of praising the new postliberal governance of the era between the world wars, and especially the early novelty of Italian fascism in the 1920s. Postliberal and "planned" governance seemed, indeed, to be in the vanguard of history, the next step after the failures of more limited political authority. The adjective, later turned into the noun "totalitarianism," described a state with new reach, vastly beyond that of the nineteenth-century state that came before. And nearly all, in the interwar age, agreed that the state must now penetrate to an unprecedented extent into social life, to counteract the disaster of economic liberalism and the dithering of political democracy.

But after its original honorific uses, the concept of totalitarianism became famous among those who insisted that there had to be *limits* to the expansion of states of the period: Now critics arose to insist that the twentieth-century statist revolution could indeed go too far. Interestingly, in this new, critical

---

[1] The best surveys remain Abbott Gleason, *Totalitarianism: The Inner History of the Cold War* (New York: Oxford University Press, 1995); and Anson Rabinbach, *Begriffe aus dem Kalten Krieg: Totalitarismus, Antifaschismus, Genozid* (Göttingen: Wallstein, 2009). Aside from neglecting the right-wing origins of the discourse, these rich surveys do not deal with Arendt as a thinker, and do not or barely mention Lefort, hence the emphases in what follows. See also such works as Bernard Bruneteau, *Totalitarisme: Origine d'un concept, genèse d'un débat, 1930–1942* (Paris: Éditions du Cerf, 2010); Philippe de Lara (ed.), *Naissances du totalitarisme* (Paris: Éditions du Cerf, 2011); and Enzo Traverso (ed.), *Le Totalitarisme: Le XXe siècle en débat* (Paris: Éditions du Seuil, 2001).

sense, the notion of totalitarianism also gained earliest traction on the right. For the political left, the critique of fascism, not that of totalitarianism, prevailed as the rubric for thinking about political extremism for a long time, in part because it was critical to distinguish *what purpose* the statist revolution might have. It was important, as well, to protect the fledgling Soviet experiment in postliberal governance (in contrast to fascist evil) by distinguishing the maximal state sponsored by communists as utterly different from its fascist *Doppelgänger*. As Marxist theory dictated, communism sponsored an expansion of the state that would then lead to its own contraction or "withering" once freedom and equality had been institutionalized. The analysis of a totalitarianism in which communism and fascism were tokens of the same type therefore found its earliest home on the political right as World War II approached, and especially among Christian thinkers who diagnosed the same pox in both houses of secular evil. Both communism and fascism, they said, were the outcomes of the modern hypertrophy not simply of the state, but also of politics itself.

The earliest critics of totalitarianism were hardly friends of liberal regimes. But in the fires of World War II, the concept eventually became central to liberal thinking. The pact between Adolf Hitler and Josef Stalin in 1939, so disconcerting to antifascism, provided disturbing vindication for antitotalitarianism, even though a popular front against fascism through the war undercut it soon after. Thereafter, the fragmentation of the alliance that had banded together to defeat the Axis gave the concept a massive new lease on life. Indeed, had the original formulations of the nature of totalitarianism not been routinized in the invention of Cold War liberalism, it is doubtful that the notion would have survived. The most fateful event in the trajectory of the notion of totalitarianism, therefore, was its endurance after World War II, when one half of the equation it set up between communism and fascism disappeared as a living political endeavor, a few old and new redoubts aside, and antitotalitarianism was repurposed for Cold War politics. With its interwar roots on the right, Cold War liberalism breathed new spirit into the concept, even as some idiosyncratic renditions were offered, Hannah Arendt's towering above them all in contemporary prominence.

The concept has been in decline ever since its Cold War apogee in the 1950s. On the French left, however, Claude Lefort also engaged in a critique of totalitarianism – originally to theorize the Soviet Union, with the original fascist component of the totalitarian equation an increasingly distant memory. Eventually, the same was true among Eastern European dissidents such as Václav Havel, for whom the concept mattered when saving Marxist "humanism" from Marxist regimes became implausible. The 1970s took the French critique of totalitarianism, which had previously trailed the Anglo-American and German, far beyond either, thanks to dissident interventions and the so-called "new philosophy" propagating them, not to mention the interventions of old hands at the genre like Lefort and new ones such as Michel Foucault. To understand the attempts of Arendt and Lefort to make "totalitarianism" their own, in their distinctive ways, requires a survey of the baseline of discourse from which they attempt to depart so creatively.

The Total State, the Antifascist Alternative, and the Catholic Invention

It was Italian fascists celebrating their early victory in 1922 who first called their state "totalitarian." More exactly, after Giovanni Amendola, an antifascist journalist, compared Benito Mussolini's "*sistema totalitaria*" (totalitarian system) with governments ruled by majorities or minorities, fascists took the word over as a term of praise. In June 1923, Mussolini himself embraced "what has been called our fierce totalitarian will."[2] Fascism's best-known house philosopher, idealist Giovanni Gentile (1875–1944), was most associated with the honorific "totalitarian" in the middle of the 1920s. Even so, the term, and especially its conversion into a noun, did not enter widespread usage until the 1930s, apparently in reaction to the argument by reactionary legal theorist Carl Schmitt (1888–1985) late in the Weimar Republic that Chancellor Heinrich Brüning should aim for expansive control over the German economy, not respecting any limits between state and civil society.[3]

Yet most critics of both the fascist state and the Nazi state, for a long time, did not seek any general account of the totalitarian state that would embrace the Soviet state. It would not have occurred to fascists and Nazis themselves to do so, for they considered Bolshevism their most implacable foe. And, more importantly, the invention of the theory of totalitarianism analogizing two disparate regimes occurred only against the backdrop of an earlier and much more popular approach known as antifascism. The critique of totalitarianism long outlives the critique of fascism, but the origins of the one are

---

2 Both citations from Gleason, *Totalitarianism*, 16–17.
3 Carl Schmitt, "Die Wendung zum totalen Staat," *Europäische Revue*, 7 (1931), 241–250, republished in Carl Schmitt, *Positionen und Begriffe im Kampf mit Weimar–Genf–Versailles, 1923–1939* (Berlin: Duncker & Humblot, 1940), 167–179; in English as "The Way to the Total State," trans. Simona Draghici, *Counter-Currents*, www.counter-currents.com/2013/07/the-way-to-the-total-state.

unintelligible apart from the other. It was a response and alternative to an earlier critique of "fascism" alone that started first and long predominated in twentieth-century thought.[4]

Antifascism had had the chance to crystallize earlier, and in the era of the Popular Front it was pervasive, when few yet conceived of the Nazi and Soviet states as sharing fundamental characteristics, let alone propounded a theory of a novel kind of regime unknown to earlier typologies. And even though the period of the later 1930s saw the invention of antitotalitarianism, World War II was still fought in some sense as an antifascist war, with the Soviets and the Western Allies joining to defeat the Axis powers, transforming ideological forces that were considered strange bedfellows more and more into common-sense and eventually victorious allies. It was only thereafter that antitotalitarianism was reasserted in its classic Cold War form.

Originating as a transnational ideology through Comintern organization in the years immediately following Hitler's seizure of power in 1933, and crystallizing in the era of the Popular Front as the rationale for unity with "bourgeois" forces, antifascism survived the confusing years of 1939–1941 when Stalin reached his famous accommodation with Hitler. Many intellectuals, notably literary and visual artists, had been swept up in the mid-1930s apogee of transnational antifascism, which then provided the central ideology justifying engagement in the Spanish Civil War and later what resistance and partisan activity there was in occupied and collaborationist Europe during World War II, as well as being adopted by many exiles abroad. In these years, no one was interested in grouping the totalitarian powers together, for it was up to one of them to bring the other to its knees, as eventually occurred at Stalingrad and after.[5]

In comparison with antifascism, antitotalitarianism has proved much more durable as an optic, not least in recent admiration for those intellectuals who resisted or at least later stigmatized Nazism while also unsparingly criticizing the new Soviet foe. However, far from forming a coherent tradition,

---

4 For more on the opposition, see my "Intellectuals and Nazism," in *The Oxford Handbook of Postwar European History*, ed. Dan Stone (New York: Oxford University Press, 2012), 671–691.

5 See, for example, Leonid Luks, *Entstehung der kommunistischen Faschismustheorie: Die Auseinandersetzung der Komintern mit Faschismus und Nationalsozialismus, 1921–1935* (Stuttgart: Deutsche Verlags-Anstalt, 1984); and Anson Rabinbach, "Paris, Capital of Anti-fascism," in *The Modernist Imagination: Intellectual History and Critical Theory*, ed. Warren Breckman, Peter E. Gordon, A. Dirk Moses, Samuel Moyn, and Elliott Neaman (New York: Berghahn, 2009), 183–209.

antitotalitarian interpretations of Nazism were quite diverse, and got a slower start.

The honorific adjective "totalitarian" from the 1920s became the critical noun "totalitarianism" first among right-wing Catholics – Schmitt's former intellectual community – interested not in expanding the state, but in finally marking its limits. The pivotal figure was Waldemar Gurian (1902–1954), who did most to publicize the theory in his study *Bolshevism* (1931), which appeared in multiple languages almost simultaneously.[6] Joined by such Roman Catholic thinkers as Dietrich von Hildebrand and Jacques Maritain, Gurian (who had been born a Russian Jew and migrated to Germany before leaving for the United States) originally did so in the name of the very allergy to liberal democratic politics on which Schmitt drew.[7] Antitotalitarianism as a theory grouping Bolshevism and Nazism under the same rubric surged in the mid 1930s in direct response to the crystallization of the Popular Front under antifascist auspices. Perhaps the most interesting fact about the surging popularity of antitotalitarian perspectives is its dependence on events. After Gurian's breakthrough in the early 1930s, the discourse enjoyed a breakthrough on the Christian right only later in the decade. And for ten years, even when a few on the democratic left turned to the rubric because it served them to indict fascism in the same breath as Stalinism, it took the end of the war to create the possibility of truly widespread use of "totalitarianism." By the postwar epoch, the term "totalitarianism" functioned, thanks at first to these Catholics, to stigmatize Nazi Germany as a disaster much more like the Soviet Union than like the original Italian avatar of the syndrome.

In the first version of the theory, which Gurian spelled out further the next year and world-renowned intellectual Maritain made even more famous, Nazism and Stalinism were equally "statist" results of a disastrous modern turn that could be traced to various sources, but especially to secularism.[8] Even in America, it was Roman Catholic Columbia University historian Carlton J. H. Hayes who adopted the category earliest and as a label for civilizational pathology.[9] Nazism was not a "stage" in modernity that had

---

6 Waldemar Gurian, *Der Bolschewismus: Einführung in Geschichte und Lehre* (Freiburg im Breisgau: Herder, 1931); Waldemar Gurian, *Bolshevism: Theory and Practice* (London: Macmillan, 1932).
7 James Chappel, "The Catholic Origins of Totalitarianism Theory," *Modern Intellectual History*, 8(3) (2011), 561–590.
8 Walter Gerhart [Waldemar Gurian], *Um des Reiches Zukunft: Nationale Wiedergeburt oder politische Reaktion?* (Freiburg im Breisgau: Herder, 1931).
9 Carlton J. H. Hayes, "The Novelty of Totalitarianism in the History of Western Civilization," *Proceedings of the American Philosophical Society*, 82(1) (1940), 98–102.

become inevitable as monopoly capitalism reached a crisis, promising some brighter future, but the inevitable outcome of modern delusions about human self-sufficiency. Such theories indeed sometimes insisted that, by deifying race or state, totalitarianism's atheism or paganism masked its true status as heresy: The totalitarianisms were political or "secular" religions. In the beginning, in the hands of ideological pioneers such as Gurian and Maritain, liberal democracy was by no means either the necessary basis or the necessary outcome of the antitotalitarian perspective. In fact, liberalism with its atomistic individualism and democracy with its slavery-prone masses were themselves part of the syndrome that had led to totalitarianism. But if the original, typically Catholic antitotalitarians were most likely to recommend corporatist solutions against the Nazi state (including so-called "Austro-fascism") or pine for some personalist-cum-communitarian utopia, World War II left the theorization of Nazism as part of a totalitarian syndrome open for appropriation by a wider range of analysts.

If antifascists confused by the Hitler–Stalin pact faced the problem of explaining it away ever after, antitotalitarians who had treated that event as a welcome vindication of their theory of Nazism were then forced to downplay the brute fact of the wartime alliance between Stalin's Soviet Union and the Anglo-American democracies. After all, one "totalitarian" power had now proved most crucial for putting down the other. The Cold War – which antitotalitarians earnestly promoted as an alternative to nerve-wracking antifascist compromises during the war – saved them. Its Christian antecedents helped make antitotalitarianism the ideological backbone not least for transatlantic Christianity and the usually Catholic-led Christian Democracy in Western European countries, as well as for the first versions of so-called federalist thought regionally – all three of which had many intellectual defenders. But alongside a huge set of Cold War liberals in Western Europe such as Raymond Aron, Isaiah Berlin, Friedrich Hayek, and Karl Popper, antitotalitarianism also beckoned the unclassifiable Arendt.[10]

Hannah Arendt and Cold War Liberalism

A thinker who came to attention during the Cold War, Arendt (1906–1975) was too idiosyncratic to fall under any label, and her theory of totalitarianism

---

10 See Jan-Werner Müller, "Fear and Freedom: On 'Cold War Liberalism,'" *European Journal of Political Theory*, 7(1) (2008), 45–64.

is likewise unclassifiable and unique. Arendt's case raises the fascinating irony that the thinker most enduringly associated with a concept engaged with it accidentally and instrumentally. But it is clear that when Arendt, a German Jewish émigré with a background in philosophy and Jewish political journalism, embarked in the United States on a soon classic book around 1946, it was solely intended as an archaeology of Nazi rule. It was intended to illustrate the sources of Nazism not solely in anti-Semitism but also in imperialism, the topics of the first two-thirds of *The Origins of Totalitarianism* that Arendt composed in a first stage.

Her plans changed after she wrote the first two parts on anti-Semitism and imperialism, coinciding with the crystallization of the Cold War in 1947–1948. Shortly before the book's appearance in 1951, she wrote a new third part of the book on "totalitarianism," but its relation not only to the prior sections of her book but also to earlier discourse on the subject remained unclear. She did not care to explain it, and readers have long suspected that her relation to "totalitarianism" was largely opportunistic, attempting to change the subject in the guise of contributing to its discussion. "Although Arendt is known as one of the foremost proponents of the 'totalitarian' thesis," Margaret Canovan observes, "totalitarianism in this sense [of theorizing the two regimes] was not in fact the original subject of her book, and [its] last and most influential section was largely an afterthought."[11] Revealingly, for the English version of her book she altered its famous American title to *The Burden of Our Time*, while the German one referred to "total domination" (*totale Herrschaft*) rather than "totalitarianism."

By virtue of her early timing in 1951 and American location, Arendt was commonly read in order to establish a descriptive and typological theory of the distinctive features that totalitarian regimes share as a matter of definition, as was later sought by numerous political scientists. Her deepest agenda, however, was *explanation*, in particular grasping the radicalism of the totalitarian experiment in effacing or transforming human nature. Troublingly, in retrospect, Arendt gave little centrality to the Holocaust understood as the intentional destruction of millions of Jews on grounds of their "race" – not because she understated the rise of modern racism, but rather because she overstated the relation of the Jewish fate to the system of concentration camps through a version of which she had herself transited and which were famous in the postwar world. As historians have tirelessly emphasized, most

---

[11] Margaret Canovan, *Hannah Arendt: A Reinterpretation of Her Political Thought* (Cambridge: Cambridge University Press, 1992), 18.

Jews who died did so as victims of shooting or in death facilities where they did not stay the night. Inspired by concentration camp survivors such as David Rousset, the non-Jewish survivor of Buchenwald whom Arendt made her privileged witness to the extremity of Nazi horror, however, she focused almost exclusively on those sites where the Nazis interned people indefinitely on various grounds. There, according to Arendt, they engaged in the signature totalitarian process, which was to alter and if possible negate human nature. The defining feature of totalitarianism was the attempt to eliminate "spontaneity itself."[12]

One way to put Arendt's argument is that she was attempting to supplement Aristotle's ancient typology of regimes by showing that totalitarian ones went so far as to extinguish the basis of politics altogether. Aristotle had claimed that humans were distinctively political animals, and Arendt famously developed the theory that this meant that they engage in their highest activity (contemplation possibly aside) in action in concert demonstrating their spontaneity. Authors of prior typologies of regimes from Aristotle onward organized their thinking around who emerged to rule and whether they ruled for the sake of all or for themselves. Totalitarianism sought to deprive human beings of their humanity, which is to say their distinctive capacity for action that made any form of politics possible. If this was a regime typology in the tradition of classical political science applied to a new modern form, as other Cold War thinkers were to believe, one must hasten to add that Arendt thought it was a regime made distinctive by its elimination of the grounds of politics itself.

Whatever the formal structure of her book, Arendt relied most substantially in plotting the origins of totalitarianism not on the antecedents of Jew-hatred and imperialism, but on the decomposition of the bourgeoisie into atomized individuals who prepared the ground for totalitarianism. It was not just that, denuded of any collective endeavors, individuals were already increasingly superfluous before totalitarians stripped them of their legal rights (and sometimes life itself). Rather, modernity involved the destruction of the distinction between public and private that both protected the latter from the invasions of the former and allowed grandeur in politics a "world" in which to shine forth. Once the liberal bourgeoisie in the nineteenth century had erected public power as a mere façade for the advancement and protection of the individual private interests of its members, Arendt wrote, the die was cast for totalitarianism. "In this sense, the bourgeoisie's

---

12 Hannah Arendt, *The Origins of Totalitarianism*, 2nd edn. (New York: Meridian, 1958), 438.

political philosophy was always 'totalitarian.'" And in the midst of great crisis, it was possible to make them quick converts into servants to demagogic leaders; not the mob but the philistine, on Arendt's account, drove totalitarian rule. It was possible to make everything public and the state total because the bourgeoisie had made everything private. "Nothing proved easier to destroy," Arendt explained, "than the privacy and private morality of people who thought of nothing but safeguarding their private lives."[13]

Of course, Arendt nestled her account of this ultimate goal within a broader set of discussions of the nature of totalitarian politics that led to the camps, with especially interesting passages on propaganda in totalitarian countries. Nearly ten years later, at the height of the Cold War, she added new chapters for a new edition of *The Origins of Totalitarianism* that vastly extended her engagement with Soviet politics, which had barely figured before. It was also here that she took most seriously the need for an argument for the distinctive character of Nazi and Soviet rule, which distinguished them from age-old tyranny. It was not, she averred, the use of law for the sake of mere despotism but to allow the terrifying laws of history and nature to rule unimpeded. Totalitarianism was the opposite of freedom not because government enforced repression but because human agency was made the instrument of compulsive forces that did not brook its spontaneity. While Arendt had otherwise dropped comparative inquiry, she reinvented the extant theory of totalitarian rule as an outgrowth of modernity. In this sense alone, the Christian origins of antitotalitarianism left an enduring legacy. Even the secular-minded among Cold War antitotalitarians inherited a worry that Nazism might have followed from "modernity" run amok.

Arendt did not promote the concept of totalitarianism either before or after her book – though she did dutifully attend a famous conference on the subject focused on a comparison between regimes and maintained friendships with both Gurian and perhaps the leading political scientist theorizing the concept in the Cold War, fellow German émigré and Harvard professor Carl Joachim Friedrich (1901–1984). The latter had worked with the concept of totalitarianism for a decade, but only in the depths of the Cold War did he organize the conference called by the American Academy of Arts and Sciences in 1953 on the topic. Soon after this he collaborated with his younger colleague, Polish exile (and future US national security adviser) Zbigniew Brzezinski (1928–2017), to offer the most mainstream attempt to describe

---

13 Arendt, *The Origins of Totalitarianism*, 336 and 338. For a book written in an Arendtian spirit, see also Michael Halberstam, *Totalitarianism and the Modern Conception of Politics* (New Haven: Yale University Press, 2000).

totalitarian regimes as a "model." Crucially, both Friedrich and Brzezinski were committed to the novelty of the phenomenon but did not venture to go beyond describing its general characteristics – which is to say, they explicitly presented themselves as carrying out a prior, and "humbler," task than Arendt had in venturing a theory of modernity. The approach did "not seek to explain why this dictatorship came into being, for the authors are convinced that such an explanation is not feasible at the present time ... Some brilliant efforts have been made in this field, but they have remained speculative and controversial."[14]

This descriptive typological inquiry – widely regarded as misguided by later generations of analysts – paled beside the endurance of the concept of totalitarianism in the intellectual discourse of Cold War liberals largely interested in stigmatizing the communist project. Perhaps the most subtle of these was the French sociologist and international relations theorist Raymond Aron (1905–1983), who for all his liberalism remained a student of classical social theorists such as Karl Marx, Vilfredo Pareto, and Max Weber. Accordingly, he took it as self-evident that democratic societies with capitalist economies established class rule and elite domination, and he became controversial both among liberals and among leftists for proposing that as industrializing welfare states the democratic and totalitarian experiments might well converge in the same place. Friends of the welfare state, such as Friedrich, grappled with how to square the democratic planning they championed with the totalitarian planning of the economy that had done much to set an example for state intervention in "private" affairs. Far simpler and ultimately more influential was the antitotalitarian critique of a classical liberal such as Friedrich Hayek, for whom any sort of planning was close enough to what totalitarians were doing to require a staunch defense of freedom in a moment of crisis.

Where antifascism as an alternative to Nazism had featured a strong democratic, emancipatory, and even populist streak, antitotalitarians concurred in ranking the hypertrophic modern state first among all evils, especially when it promised collective liberation and social protection. Unlike in Arendt's theory, to some Cold War antitotalitarians democracy itself seemed

---

14 Carl Joachim Friedrich (ed.), *Totalitarianism* (Cambridge: Harvard University Press, 1954); Carl Joachim Friedrich and Zbigniew Brzezinski, *Totalitarian Dictatorship and Autocracy* (Cambridge: Harvard University Press, 1956), vii; see also the concurrent volume Zbigniew Brzezinski, *The Permanent Purge: Politics in Soviet Totalitarianism* (Cambridge: Harvard University Press, 1956). See also David C. Engerman, *Know Your Enemy: The Rise and Fall of America's Soviet Experts* (New York: Oxford University Press, 2009).

to be the source of the trouble, unless hemmed in by liberalism. Jacob Talmon (1916–1980), a Central European Jew who ended up in Israel, developed these views during a sojourn in England, whose "indigenous" liberalism he found attractive. Other émigrés who stayed, such as Berlin (1909–1997) and Popper (1902–1994), did too, and contributed to the sense of stark division between its social freedoms and Continental totalitarianism.[15] And the secular liberals found it possible to replace the Christian thesis that totalitarianism was a modern version of age-old sin with their own psychology emphasizing the hubris that drove emancipation to turn into its opposite and the anxiety and fear that they counseled in response. As American political theorist and Friedrich student Judith Shklar (1928–1992), a one-time critic of Cold War liberalism before becoming one of its representatives herself, put it at the time, antitotalitarianism "is only another expression of social fatalism, not an answer to it. To those who ... find it difficult to accept formal Christianity, conservative liberalism offers the opportunity to despair in a secular and social fashion."[16]

For obvious reasons, antitotalitarian intellectuals tended to be much more pro-American than antifascists were, with the United States – sometimes explicitly viewed as Britain's heir in mastering democracy through liberalism – providing the true or at least necessary historical alternative to Nazi and Stalinist barbarity. Such antitotalitarians founded and promoted the agenda of the American-sponsored cultural Cold War, notably the Congress for Cultural Freedom.[17] Nevertheless, before and during the Cold War, antitotalitarianism accommodated left-wing and dissident visions. Even Marxists could join the chorus, as for example in Leon Trotsky's memorable claim when closing his biography of his mortal enemy Stalin, a book that remained unfinished because of Trotsky's Mexico City assassination, that the Soviet Union had become a species of totalitarian personal rule. Unlike Louis XIV, however, Stalin in effect went beyond embodiment of the state to claim "la société, c'est moi."[18] More regularly, dissident leftists who were critical of communism could adopt antitotalitarian rhetoric. Albert Camus's later

---

15 On Cold War conservative liberalism, see also Chapter 15 by Steven B. Smith.
16 Judith N. Shklar, *After Utopia: The Decline of Political Faith* (Princeton: Princeton University Press, 1957), 235.
17 See, for example, Pierre Grémion, *Intelligence de l'anticommunisme: Le Congrès pour la liberté de la culture à Paris (1950–1975)* (Paris: Fayard, 1995); or Giles Scott-Smith, *The Politics of Apolitical Culture: The Congress for Cultural Freedom, the CIA, and Post-war American Hegemony* (London and New York: Routledge, 2002).
18 Leon Trotsky, *Stalin: An Appraisal of the Man and His Influence* (New York: Stein and Day, 1967), 421.

novels and essays unforgettably staged the antitotalitarian fear that the threat of despotism – especially when driven by the temptations to rebellion of the modern age – remained ever present. Just as with its Roman Catholic originators, the common rejection of Nazism and communism by no means entailed political liberalism. But it led there frequently enough in the Cold War as antifascism receded and antitotalitarianism took its place that it is striking that its other major theorist besides Arendt was not a liberal either. In spite of Arendt's intervention, then, the theory of totalitarianism in the early Cold War either retreated to a project of typological description, or found a home as a discourse of fear and stigma, now most frequently with the explicit alternative of the United States as the exemplary free society.[19]

Claude Lefort and the Antitotalitarian Moment East and West

Hannah Arendt's opposite number was Claude Lefort (1924–2010). He independently forged his totalitarianism theory in the 1950s on the example of the Soviet Union, belatedly and never fully engaging with Nazi Germany, in a reversal of Arendt's priorities. And, far from offering a brief and opportunistic engagement with totalitarianism theory, he struggled for decades to promote his version of it, across radically different historical moments. Arendt rarely returned to totalitarianism after she had published her famous study, in spite of devoting some thinking to Karl Marx before turning to other things; Lefort rarely strayed from the topic.

His classic early version of totalitarianism theory sprang up just a few years after Arendt's, prompted by Stalin's death in 1953 and even more by the so-called "secret speech" delivered by subsequent Soviet leader Nikita Khrushchev denouncing his predecessor.[20] A student of phenomenologist Maurice Merleau-Ponty and a Trotskyist during and after World War II, Lefort preceded his teacher in breaking with Stalinism, before Merleau-Ponty was led to abandon not only Trotskyism but Marxism itself. Yet Lefort's early theory of totalitarianism came from his phase after he had given up on Trotskyist politics but before he relinquished Marxism. During that time,

---

19 Benjamin L. Alpers, *Dictators, Democracy, and American Public Culture: Envisioning the Totalitarian Enemy, 1920s–1950s* (Chapel Hill: University of North Carolina Press, 2003).
20 See Claude Lefort, "Le totalitarisme sans Staline: L'URSS dans une nouvelle phase," *Socialisme ou Barbarie*, no. 19 (July–September 1956), 1–72; in English as "Totalitarianism without Stalin," in Claude Lefort, *The Political Forms of Modern Society: Bureaucracy, Democracy, Totalitarianism*, ed. and trans. John B. Thompson (Cambridge: MIT Press, 1986), 52–88.

Lefort's hopes still reposed in the class he still considered the subject, following the inherited teaching, of modern world history: the proletariat. The abandonment of Trotskyism, and the attempt to discover the principle of a democratic radicalism that would avoid devolving into bureaucracy, encouraged him to begin the difficult search for a proletariat that did not need to be led. Many of the reflections he published in *Socialisme ou Barbarie*, the journal of the eponymous militant group he co-founded with Cornelius Castoriadis in 1946 (and left in 1958), are devoted to the theoretical problem of the source and formation of such a historical agent.

Lefort's belief in the availability of a proletariat that would ultimately self-organize not simply to overthrow the old society but to create a lasting new order is the major position that he defended throughout his tenure in *Socialisme ou Barbarie*, in diverse essays. This stance pitted him against Jean-Paul Sartre in a once-prominent exchange, since the famed existentialist insisted not simply on the necessity of a vanguard party, but also on the indispensability of Soviet leadership of the left. Elaborating a non-vanguardist vision of workers' self-organization and criticizing Sartre's deference to Soviet control over progressive politics, Lefort presented himself as the more authentic Marxist, faithful to Marx's text and vision against the "pseudo-Marxism" of those who could not admit that the Stalinist and post-Stalinist bureaucracy had established itself on a permanent basis. In a new phase in history, the self-styled workers' state dominated the workers. Sartre, in turn, ridiculed a position that conceived of the working class as if it could blossom like a flower or fruit by itself, or grow up like a gifted child who can learn from experience and no teacher.

It was to press the point, after Stalin's death, that bureaucratic socialism was not going away that Lefort published his first work of totalitarianism theory, "Totalitarianism after Stalin" (1956). The essential purpose of the essay, written in response to the Soviet Twentieth Party Congress where Khrushchev delivered his speech, was to show how class rule obtained in communist as much as in capitalist societies. The former had come to host an even more perverse form of bureaucratic domination than the latter. Stalin's monstrous role merely epitomized this systemic fact after "capitalism expelled the capitalists." In such arguments, Lefort was especially indebted to Castoriadis's immediate postwar depiction of Russian society as a picture of class rule no less than that capitalist societies presented. It followed that Stalin was the carapace of the organism of totalitarian domination. "The bureaucracy cannot hope to escape its own essence," Lefort wrote,

"It may bury its dead skin in the Kremlin crypt and cover its body with alluring finery, but totalitarian it was and totalitarian it remains."[21]

At this point Lefort was really offering a theory of bureaucracy, referring to "totalitarianism" mainly to arrogate a central Cold War concept for intra-Marxist debates. Interestingly, while apparently ignorant of Arendt, Lefort well knew that the theory of totalitarianism came not from the non-communist left or from the liberal center but from the political right. "Socialists and liberals who denounced the regimes of Hitler and Mussolini," Lefort later observed, "saw their struggle in terms of antifascism [and] the totalitarian theme... was not... an important aspect of their work. [But] one must admit that this theme inspired right-wing ideologists." Nonetheless, Lefort made it his own. Where Arendt had barely referred to the Soviet Union in her original depiction, Lefort referred to Nazi Germany not once in his own debut as a theorist of totalitarianism. The same was true of Lefort's mature totalitarianism theory, which emerged only two decades later, after Merleau-Ponty had led him beyond Marxism.[22]

In his autopsy of Marxism, *Adventures of the Dialectic* (1955), and before his own death soon after, Merleau-Ponty suggested that Lefort's own argument effectively required a post-Marxist theory of totalitarianism. Lefort had argued that one could not, like Trotsky, simply "restart bolshevism outside bolshevism," but then it was also true that one could not do the same with "Marxism outside Stalinism." Lefort, Merleau-Ponty wrote, still hoped to "restart Marxism outside the ambit of the U.S.S.R., but also, and yet further, outside that of Trotsky himself." A response to the failure of revolution that blamed the rise of bureaucracy and simply called for a purer revolution would always repeat the difficulty it was meant to solve. Hence Merleau-Ponty's conclusion: "Lefort makes the deviation begin with bolshevism, ... but he leaves uncontested the proletarian philosophy of history ... Lefort, too, proceeds *minimo sumptu*. He is Trotsky's Trotsky."[23] Could one really critique not simply Stalinist but Soviet totalitarianism from the perspective of Marxist theory? Merleau-Ponty answered the question in the negative.

---

21 Lefort, "Totalitarianism without Stalin," 75. See Anon. [Cornelius Castoriadis], "Les rapports de production en Russie," *Socialisme ou Barbarie*, no. 2 (May–June 1949), 1–66; in English as "The Relations of Production in Russia," in Cornelius Castoriadis, *Political and Social Writings*, ed. and trans. David Ames Curtis, 3 vols. (Minneapolis: University of Minnesota Press, 1988–1993), vol. I, 107–158.
22 Claude Lefort, "The Logic of Totalitarianism," in Claude Lefort, *The Political Forms of Modern Society: Bureaucracy, Democracy, Totalitarianism*, ed. and trans. John B. Thompson (Cambridge: MIT Press, 1986), 273.
23 Maurice Merleau-Ponty, *Les aventures de la dialectique* (Paris: Gallimard, 1955), 125–126 and 134.

It meant that political theory had to be saved not simply from bolshevism, but from Marxism, and rooted somewhere else.

Lefort never responded directly to this critique, at the time or later. But his outlook transformed, taking a quantum leap when, not long after his exit from Socialisme ou Barbarie, Merleau-Ponty died in 1961. Now Lefort radicalized an opposition between democracy and totalitarianism dear to Cold War liberals, such as his own thesis advisor Raymond Aron. Before his Cold War liberalism, Aron had pioneered the opposition between totalitarianism and democracy already in 1939, in a now famous lecture before the Société Française de Philosophie, which was published only in 1946. Yet at this early date Aron did not even consider the Soviet Union a totalitarian country, and was not hard at work, like later figures and his later self, on a comparative understanding of totalitarianism.[24] Talmon had made democracy central to his own theory of totalitarianism, faulting Jean-Jacques Rousseau's voluntarism for twentieth-century horror. Likewise, Lefort reinvented Aron's distinction between democracy and totalitarianism to try to see in the first the source of the second under specific circumstances. He insisted in particular, against his old advisor, that the distinction between democracy and totalitarianism was not "sociological," based for example on the contrast of a multiparty versus a monopoly party system for realizing comparable ideals of freedom and equality.[25]

For Lefort, there was no way to grasp the distinction between democracy and totalitarianism without the further distinction between the representational and the real in politics. "The critique of totalitarianism," Lefort observed, characterizing most social-science work in the Cold War era, "most frequently projected the image of a flawless system of oppression, capable of effectively crushing all opposition, against which only heroic personalities – the dissidents – could protest."[26] No society, however, was

---

24 Raymond Aron, "États démocratiques et états totalitaires: Exposé," *Bulletin de la Société Française de Philosophie*, 40(2) (1946), 41–55; in English as "Democratic and Totalitarian States," in Raymond Aron, *The Dawn of Universal History: Selected Essays from a Witness to the Twentieth Century*, trans. Barbara Bray (New York: Basic Books, 2002), 163–176; and Raymond Aron, *Democracy and Totalitarianism*, trans. V. Ionescu (London: Weidenfeld and Nicholson, 1968), esp. Chapter 15.

25 Claude Lefort, "Reflections on the Present," in Claude Lefort, *Writing: The Political Test*, trans. David Ames Curtis (Durham: Duke University Press, 2000), 266. For his lengthiest criticisms, see Claude Lefort, *Complications: Communism and the Dilemmas of Democracy*, trans. Julian Bourg (New York: Columbia University Press, 2007), Chapter 8; and a lecture from a Hungarian conference on Aron in 2000, Claude Lefort, "Raymond Aron et le phénomène totalitaire" (2000), in Claude Lefort, *Le temps présent: Écrits 1945–2005* (Paris: Belin, 2007), 993–999.

26 Claude Lefort, "Pushing Back the Limits of the Possible," in Claude Lefort, *The Political Forms of Modern Society*, 314.

without division and all featured a usually obfuscating further division between that division and society's representation of itself. Lefort therefore proposed that what is unique to totalitarianism is the paradoxical attempt to make a reality the representation of democracy as a regime in which the people rule. Insofar as no society exists without division, it was an impossible project, but this does not mean that totalitarian societies and their leaders standing for an ultimately democratic aspiration did not try to unify them beyond that division – and even beyond the division between the real and representative itself. According to Lefort, there was no way to interpret the usual themes of the totalitarianism literature – the charismatic leader, the single party, propaganda and lies, and violent terror – outside this framework.[27]

Lefort did not read Arendt seriously until the 1970s after he had developed his theory. (*The Origins of Totalitarianism* in particular was not translated into French in integral form until 1984, with the section on anti-Semitism appearing separately in 1973, and the crucial last part on the nature of totalitarian government only along with the entirety of the book.) Despite his being an enthusiast like Arendt for the Hungarian uprising in 1956 and its device of worker's councils, and an admirer and promoter of Arendt's pioneering interest in totalitarianism, Lefort offered numerous biting criticisms of her theory of it. In an essay originally published in 1985, he agreed that the unprecedented regimes of the twentieth century revealed something essential about modern times, but differed from Arendt in a series of other respects. But "the most disturbing thing about Hannah Arendt," argued Lefort, "is that, while she rightly criticizes capitalism and bourgeois individualism, she never shows any interest in democracy as such, in modern democracy."[28]

It was because Lefort made his approach to representation so central to his theory of totalitarianism that he correspondingly found the theme lacking in Arendt's rendition, a claim to which he returned frequently. Talmon had argued that the fantastic Enlightenment desire for direct democracy fed the messianism of modern politics that refused compromise with merely representative democracy and ultimately led to Stalin. Arendt, by contrast, was herself a votary of ancient politics, rejecting representative democracy and

---

27 See further Bernard Flynn, *The Philosophy of Claude Lefort: Interpreting the Political* (Evanston: Northwestern University Press, 2005), Part IV.
28 Claude Lefort, "Hannah Arendt and the Question of the Political," in Claude Lefort, *Democracy and Political Theory*, trans. David Macey (Minneapolis: University of Minnesota Press, 1988), 55.

struggling for other ways to find the greatness of participatory democracy resuscitated in modern circumstances. For Lefort, it was only because of the representational claims to give voice to the whole people – on which so-called "representative democracy" also depended in offering devices for voters to elect politicians for deliberation and decision-making – that totalitarianism had become possible. Where Talmon celebrated representation as an alternative to "totalitarian democracy," Lefort considered the one the condition of possibility of the other. Where Arendt rejected representation out of nostalgia for ancient politics, Lefort claimed that she did not follow through on her own promise to root totalitarianism in a fully fledged theory of modernity. Of course, Arendt did not know of Lefort, and while he pursued similar criticisms of her thereafter – among other things, in an unpublished lecture engaging with her account of Nazism that forced him to take it more seriously than the communism on which he always focused – it is unknown how she would have answered.[29]

Lefort's approach to totalitarianism did not find many takers in its 1950s form, but enjoyed a breakthrough in its 1970s form. His most significant disciple, political theorist Marcel Gauchet (1946–), wrote a much noticed interpretation of democracy and totalitarianism vulgarizing Lefort's sometimes more opaque writings in 1976. Forty years later, he completed his own philosophy of history that pivoted on the totalitarian experience, understood as a moment in the modern attempt to leave premodern religiosity behind. Drawing substantially on his teacher (with whom he nevertheless personally broke), Gauchet is probably the most significant self-styled theorist of totalitarianism in the tradition of Arendt and Lefort. Equally a follower of Aron, however, Gauchet took more seriously than either Arendt or Lefort the need to do justice to both Nazi and Stalinist regimes, rather than forging an interpretation privileging one or the other.[30]

---

29 Claude Lefort, "Hannah Arendt: Antisémitisme et génocide des juifs," a lecture originally prepared for a pivotal 1982 conference on Nazism and the Holocaust in Paris, ultimately appeared in Claude Lefort, *Le temps présent: Écrits 1945–2005* (Paris: Belin, 2007), 505–528. For his criticisms of Arendt on the law in totalitarianism, see Claude Lefort, "Thinking with and against Arendt," *Social Research*, 69 (2002), 447–459; and Claude Lefort, *Complications*, Chapter 14. Perhaps his most accessible statement both of his theory and of his critique of Arendt is a lecture from 1995, Claude Lefort, "Le concept de totalitarisme," in Claude Lefort, *Le temps présent: Écrits 1945–2005* (Paris: Belin, 2007), 869–891.

30 Marcel Gauchet, "L'expérience totalitaire et la pensée de la politique," *Esprit*, no. 459 (July–August 1976), 3–28; republished in Marcel Gauchet, *La condition politique* (Paris: Gallimard, 2005), 433–464; and Marcel Gauchet, *À l'épreuve des totalitarismes (1914–1974)* (Paris: Gallimard, 2010).

Just as with Arendt and Cold War liberalism, however, Lefort's enterprise enjoyed its greatest prominence only to suffer a much more powerful wave of antitotalitarian sloganeering that overwhelmed it. After 1968, as historian Michael Christofferson has shown, a generation in revolt clashed with a strong communist party in France. Socialists such as the French president François Mitterrand (in power from 1981 to 1995) added insult to injury by joining the communist party in a campaign to power, a strategy which elicited a massive denunciation of "totalitarianism" in France, a country that had – unlike other North Atlantic settings – bypassed much popular engagement with the idiom. It was in this cauldron that Soviet dissident Alexandr Solzhenitsyn, though bringing less novel information than sometimes thought, was made a tool to dissent above all from an alliance with local communists that horrified many young activists. What came to be known as "the antitotalitarian moment" was born.[31] As Lefort and others warned, a popular left-wing movement that had veered in the direction of Trotskyism and even Maoism now careered toward the tragic wisdom of Cold War liberalism that had once been viewed as a nest of apologetics for crimes around the world and class domination at home. In the form of the "new philosophy," associated with publicists such as André Glucksmann (1937–2015) and Bernard-Henri Lévy (1948–), antitotalitarianism found itself vulgarized for a large audience, sometimes drawing directly on Castoriadis and Lefort, in spite of their attempts to disavow their progeny. In an early phase of this development, increasingly widespread antitotalitarianism made room for some claims of popular justice – for example, in Glucksmann's sympathy for the "plebs" whose historical fate was to suffer subjugation.[32] But with their own liberal and religious turns, it soon became increasingly difficult to distinguish France's new philosophers from Cold War liberals of old.

It helped that, after their own attempts to save Marxism from their own states, East European dissidents both in exile, such as Leszek Kołakowski (1927–2009), and at home turned to the critique of totalitarianism. Easily the most influential writer in this vein, famed for his membership in the Czechoslovak dissident group Charter 77, was Václav Havel (1936–2011). In his classic long essay "Power of the Powerless," Havel actually worked with the description of "post-totalitarianism," in recognition of the

---

[31] Michael Scott Christofferson, *French Intellectuals against the Left: The Anti-totalitarian Moment of the 1970s* (New York: Berghahn, 2004).
[32] André Glucksmann, *La cuisinière et le mangeur d'hommes: Essai sur les rapports entre l'État, le marxisme et les camps de concentration* (Paris: Éditions du Seuil, 1975).

adjustment of regimes after Stalin's death, even when they still engaged in brutal crackdowns, as had occurred in Havel's own Prague in 1968. Notwithstanding this terminological difference, Havel depicted totalitarian society as one in which the willing deference of ordinary people to the power and propaganda of a state that had all the cards left no hope of political change. Only morality, what Havel called "living in truth," could possibly make a difference, albeit mostly as a stance of principled non-affiliation.[33] The effects were tremendous, albeit less in communist societies that mostly weathered the storm of a critique they had experienced for decades from abroad than for Western audiences. Outside the communist world, on the right dissidents were seen as belated ratification of a long-since confirmed propriety of liberal democratic capitalism, whatever its faults – though it was far more likely for dissidents themselves to be influenced by such European schools as Marxism and phenomenology than by the central texts of Cold War liberal antitotalitarianism. As for the left, in France as elsewhere, dissident activism unleashed enormous concern, blandishments of evil regimes were ruled out, Marxism was increasingly abandoned, and even welfare states once castigated as sham compromises in need of socialist correction were increasingly abandoned as a neoliberal age began. It was unsurprising that, alongside more traditional categories such as "empire" and "tyranny," communist states in their last decade attracted the last major era of denunciation of "totalitarianism."

Concluding Thoughts

For historians and social scientists in the Cold War, following the Roman Catholic founders, the whole purpose of a theory of totalitarianism was to identify common features in apparently opposed regimes. For most experts, that endeavor is now dead; the most recent attempt to engage in the comparative enterprise of Nazism and Stalinism is explicitly entitled "beyond totalitarianism."[34] Yet the two central figures of twentieth-century totalitarianism theory among philosophers, Hannah Arendt and Claude Lefort, were barely interested in comparison. They based their approaches and conclusions almost exclusively on a single regime, interested in the fate and future of

---

33 Václav Havel, "The Power of the Powerless," in Václav Havel, *Open Letters: Selected Writings, 1965–1990* (New York: Vintage, 1992), 125–214.
34 Michael Geyer and Sheila Fitzpatrick (eds.), *Beyond Totalitarianism: Stalinism and Nazism Compared* (Cambridge: Cambridge University Press, 2009); and John Connelly, "Totalitarianism: Defunct Theory, Useful Word," *Kritika*, 11(4) (2010), 819–835.

a new form of twentieth-century rule that, they believed, revealed most about modernity as a whole rather than in saving liberal regimes from scrutiny. Their reflections on totalitarianism have borne fruit, but perhaps more as overall interpretations of the modern experience than as typological arguments about a novel regime, let alone as lasting portraits of the specific historical regimes Arendt and Lefort undertook to analyze. Not only on the left, for example in the denunciations of the concept by Slovenian thinker Slavoj Žižek (1949–), but across the board the concept of totalitarianism has come to have a bad odor, even as, in the trenches of stigmatizing the latest enemy, the label has proved open to recycling after the Cold War's end.[35] In spite of certain subtle revivals, such as the work of Bulgarian-turned-French literary critic Tzvetan Todorov (1939–2017), the pertinence of a theory of a novel form of government called "totalitarian" may have passed. As Anson Rabinbach observes, "More often than not over the years, historical precision was sacrificed to the political gains of invoking the word." To which one might add that so was theoretical clarity.[36]

The risks incurred by volunteering to theorize a popular discourse may have been greater than the rewards. No state has ever been or ever could be "total." Much as recent historians of "total war" have observed, the most that can be said is that some states are more totalizing than others – but all enact and experience limits on a continuum. Most states are limited because of their failures of capacity, a syndrome that has interfered with freedom and justice to date much more than the opposite, in part because from the beginning of their history states were mostly weak. The mid-twentieth-century era of the apogee of states was, in spite of the regrettable excesses of some, also a period in which other states provided a maximum of freedom and justice to their citizens. A neoliberal age characterized by repetitious fears of menacing totalitarianism suggests that intellectuals require just as much justification of state capacity and expansion as warnings about state domination and terror, especially if they believe in modernity as an inherently democratic age.

---

35 Slavoj Žižek, *Did Somebody Say Totalitarianism?* (London, 2001).
36 Anson Rabinbach, "Totalitarianism Revisited," *Dissent*, 53(3) (2006), 77–84, p. 78. See also Tzvetan Todorov, *Hope and Memory: Lessons from the Twentieth Century*, trans. David Bellos (Princeton: Princeton University Press, 2003); Anson Rabinbach, "Moments of Totalitarianism," *History and Theory*, 45(1) (2006), 72–100; and my "The Ghosts of Totalitarianism," *Ethics and International Affairs*, 18(2) (2004), 93–98.

17

Decolonization Terminable and Interminable

JUDITH SURKIS

> It seems that those who come from a small island always think of a revolution in very wide terms. That is the only way they could come out of it. You can't begin to think of a little revolution in a small island.
>
> C. L. R. James

Decolonization, understood as the achievement of national independence for formerly colonized peoples, was hardly pre-ordained. Its conception and concretization depended on transformations in political imagination as well as activism. The possibility of decolonization as an aspirational idea of liberation from colonial oppression thus exceeds the narrow temporal boundary of a discrete era. It both preceded the postwar decades in which many colonized nations acceded to formal political independence and continues to resonate beyond that period, not least because the achievement of national sovereignty did not necessarily bring about social and psychic emancipation. Decolonization thus remains subject to a perpetual questioning, and it is hard to determine whether and where it might end. To this day, postcolonial critics continue to revisit the question, to paraphrase Freud, of decolonization as "terminable or interminable."

By placing both the legitimacy and the fate of colonial empires into question, World War II is nonetheless widely understood to have ushered in a global "era of decolonization." The Atlantic Charter jointly signed by Winston Churchill and Franklin Roosevelt in 1941 committed the Allied Powers to principles of self-government, promising to restore sovereignty to those peoples who had been "forcibly deprived" of it. Despite European imperial powers' resistance to extending these rights to the colonized world, anti-colonial intellectuals and activists seized on the new possibilities of this moment to reimagine alternative political, social, economic, and psychic futures. As historians have recently underscored, the concrete form of these alternatives was not fixed in advance.[1]

In this chapter, I frame the intellectual history of the era of decolonization through the lens of an event that both inspired twentieth-century anti-colonial intellectuals and served as a cautionary lesson of postcolonial sovereignty's limits: the Haitian Revolution. "Independence or death," proclaimed the formerly enslaved people who liberated themselves from French rule on January 1, 1804. And yet, as the new nation's Declaration underscored, the weighty "memories of the cruelties of this barbarous people" remained after independence. Exorcizing that psychic and material legacy was a perpetual project, not least because the French, and other major imperial powers, refused to recognize Haitian independence. Over the course of the nineteenth century, European countries endeavored to crush the new nation under crippling debt, while repressing the events of the revolution from European memory.[2] Because Haitian sovereignty challenged the totalizing fantasy of European empire, Haiti's persistent struggle for recognition sparked the political imagination of anti-colonial thinkers in the twentieth century, and it continues to preoccupy postcolonial thinkers today.

Feeling Revolution in Haiti's Decolonization

The Trinidadian author and activist C. L. R. James (1901–1989) published his magisterial history of the Haitian Revolution *The Black Jacobins* in 1938. As James made clear in his original preface, the events of the Haitian Revolution assumed new meaning and currency in the tumultuous decade of the 1930s. The first edition of *Black Jacobins* resonated with more recent revolutionary struggles from Trotsky's exile by Stalin to Pan-African responses to Mussolini's invasion of Ethiopia to the Spanish civil war. In the previous year, James's *World Revolution: The Rise and Fall of the Communist International, 1917–1936* took stock of this contemporary crisis. A committed Trotskyist, James maintained a deep commitment to internationalism and the combined powers of antifascism and anti-imperialism.

---

1 Frederick Cooper, *Citizenship between Empire and Nation: Remaking France and French Africa, 1945–1960* (Princeton: Princeton University Press, 2014); Gary Wilder, *Freedom Time: Negritude, Decolonization, and the Future of the World* (Durham: Duke University Press, 2015); and Todd Shepard, *The Invention of Decolonization: the Algerian War and the Remaking of France* (Ithaca: Cornell University Press, 2006).
2 Michel-Rolph Trouillot, *Silencing the Past: Power and the Production of History* (Boston: Beacon Press, 1995); and Laurent Dubois, *Haiti: The Aftershocks of History*, 1st edn. (New York: Metropolitan Books, 2012).

Heralding the future promise of a Fourth International, he hoped that "the working-class movement and the colonial peoples will safeguard the precious beginning in Russia, put an end to imperialist barbarity, and once more give some hope in living to all overshadowed humanity."[3]

Upon arriving in England in 1932, James, who had received a classical education at Queen's Royal College in Trinidad, started reading revolutionary histories, including Trotsky's 1930 account of the Russian Revolution. He also proceeded to make his way through the writings of Stalin, Lenin, Marx, and Engels, and began to frequent a small, cosmopolitan group of Trotskyist militants. Joining theory with praxis, he engaged in nascent anti-colonial projects and wrote on West Indian self-government. At this time, he began to collect material on the history of the revolution in Saint-Domingue, taking a research trip to Paris in winter 1933 and spring 1934. While there, he was guided by the French Guyanese poet Léon-Gontran Damas (1912–1978), who, along with Aimé Césaire (1913–2008) and Léopold Senghor (1906–2001), was a leading light of *négritude*.[4]

When Mussolini invaded Ethiopia in 1935, James and fellow West Indian activists Amy Ashwood Garvey (the ex-wife of Marcus Garvey) and Sam Manning together founded the International African Friends of Abyssinia (IAFA). They were soon joined by his childhood friend and the future Prime Minister of Trinidad, George Padmore (1902–1959), T. Ras Makonnen, the Barbadian seamen's organizer Chris Braithwaite, and Johnstone (soon to be Jomo) Kenyatta. In their public protests in London and in their journal, they participated in a transcontinental wave of black nationalist and anti-colonial resistance to the invasion – and the League of Nations' failure to react to it.[5] James described the situation's galvanizing impact at one of the group's demonstrations in Trafalgar Square: "the question of Ethiopia has brought about a union of sentiment between black men in Africa, America, the West Indies, and all over the world. Ethiopia's cause is our cause and we will

---

3 C. L. R. James and Christian Høgsbjerg, *World Revolution, 1917–1936: The Rise and Fall of the Communist International* (Durham: Duke University Press, 2017), 400; and Kent Worcester, *C. L. R. James: A Political Biography* (Albany: SUNY Press, 1996), 40–51.
4 Charles Forsdick and Christian Høgsbjerg, *The Black Jacobins Reader* (Durham: Duke University Press, 2017), 5.
5 Joseph Fronczak, "Local People's Global Politics: A Transnational History of the Hands Off Ethiopia Movement of 1935," *Diplomatic History*, 39(2) (2014), 245–274; Robert G. Weisbord, "British West Indian Reaction to the Italian–Ethiopian War: An Episode in Pan-Africanism," *Caribbean Studies*, 10(1) (1970), 35–38; William R. Scott, "Black Nationalism and the Italo-Ethiopian Conflict 1934–1936," *The Journal of Negro History*, 63(2) (1978), 118–134; and Cedric J. Robinson, "The African Diaspora and the Italo-Ethiopian crisis," *Race and Class*, 27(2) (1985), 51–65.

defend it by every means in our power."[6] Among others, Toussaint L'Ouverture's militant example inspired the founders of the IAFA, including James. In homage to his legacy, they read William Wordsworth's 1803 poem dedicated to the slain revolutionary leader aloud at their rally on July 28, 1935.[7]

It was in this militantly anti-imperialist context that James wrote his play on the life of Toussaint and arranged for it to be staged at London's Westminster Theatre in 1936, with Paul Robeson in the lead role. The revolutionary hero's life continued to resonate for James in the wake of the disappointments of the Ethiopia crisis. The momentary defeat spurred further organizing. As Padmore later explained, "With the realization of their utter defenselessness against the new aggression from Europeans in Africa, the blacks felt it necessary to look to themselves."[8] By 1937, the IAFA had reorganized itself into the International African Service Bureau for the Defence of Africans and People of African Descent (IASB). Their journal, *International African Opinion*, edited by James, presented the group's aim as "mobilizing whatever assistance there is to be found in Europe for the cause of African emancipation."[9] The IASB and its journal exemplified what Brent Hayes Edwards has described as the "practice of diaspora." Emblematized by the masthead's image of an African woman whose torch lights up the globe, the journal confirmed and created a diasporic community.

During his time in London, James contributed to this community of African and Afro-Caribbean writers and intellectuals who engaged with pressing questions – of socialism and Pan-Africanism; anti-fascism and anti-colonialism – in their publications and public activism. The new publishing house Secker and Warburg provided a crucial venue for their work, including Padmore's *How Britain Rules Africa* (1936), Kenyatta's landmark ethnography *Facing Mount Kenya* (1938), and James's own twin publications, *A History of Negro Revolt* and *The Black Jacobins* in 1938. The books reflected how a local intellectual milieu in the imperial metropolis gave rise to a collective and collaborative anti-colonial project. James himself understood his writing as indebted to this simultaneously local and global context. As he later explained, *The Black Jacobins*, while "historical in form," expressed the

---

6 Cited in Christian Høgsbjerg, *C. L. R. James in Imperial Britain* (Durham: Duke University Press, 2014), 96.
7 Cited in Høgsbjerg, *C. L. R. James in Imperial Britain*, 97.
8 George Padmore, *Pan-Africanism or Communism* (Garden City: Anchor Books, 1972), 124.
9 Cited in Brent Hayes Edwards, *The Practice of Diaspora: Literature, Translation, and the Rise of Black Internationalism* (Cambridge: Harvard University Press, 2003), 301.

political and intellectual dynamism of the moment, drawing "its contemporaneousness ... from the living struggles around us, and particularly from the daily activity that centered around Padmore and the African Bureau. It represented in a specific form the general ideas that we held at that time."[10]

The *History of Negro Revolt* captured this sense of urgency. Commissioned by James's publisher Frederic Warburg, it linked the political significance of the past to an anti-colonial present. The revolution in Saint-Domingue was a point of departure for a global story of black anti-colonial struggle. As later explained, it was "preparation for the revolution that Padmore and all of us were interested in, that is, the revolution in Africa."[11] Emerging out of longer histories of oppression, revolution nonetheless required preliminary political and intellectual organization.

For James, the revolution in Saint-Domingue was illustrative. Although it was prepared by more than a century of resistance to the violently extractive regime of plantation slavery, the victorious slave rebellion required the French Revolution's spark. As he explained at the beginning of his *History*, "The only successful Negro revolt, the only successful slave revolt in history, had its roots in the French Revolution, and without the French Revolution its success would have been impossible."[12] Effective revolutions, both past and future, also depended on the enlistment of "colored" men. As James explained, "The part played by blacks in the success of the great French Revolution has never received adequate recognition. As Franco's Moors have once more proved, the revolution in Europe will neglect colored workers at its peril."[13] For James, as for the African American poet Langston Hughes, the enlistment of Moroccan soldiers to fight on the side of the Falangists in Spain was demonstrative of this historical truth.[14] In their view, the revolution would be international and anti-colonial or it would not be at all.

This was an intellectual as well as a political argument. James presented the thought and action of the ex-slaves in Saint-Domingue as a genuine expression of the ideas of "the great French revolution," whose doctrine

---

10 C. L. R. James, "The Revolution in Theory," *The Black Jacobins Reader*, ed. Charles Forsdick and Christian Høgsbjerg (Durham: Duke University Press, 2017), 356.
11 C. L. R. James, "Lectures on *The Black Jacobins*," *Small Axe*, no. 8 (September 2000), 65–82, p. 72.
12 C. L. R. James, *A History of Negro Revolt* (New York: Haskell House Publishers, 1969), 6.
13 James, *A History of Negro Revolt*, 13.
14 On the critical insights offered by "Franco's Moors," see Langston Hughes, *I Wonder as I Wander: An Autobiographical Journey* (New York: Rinehart & Co., 1956), 353; and Brent Hayes Edwards, "Langston Hughes and the Futures of Diaspora," *American Literary History*, 19(3) (2007), 689–711.

"they embraced." Despite their wretched status, "lacking education, half-savage, and degraded," the black revolutionaries of Saint-Domingue achieved, in his view, "a liberality in social aspiration and an elevation of political thought equivalent to anything similar that took place in France."[15] In retrospect, he seems to have set a European standard against which to measure the rebellious slaves' achievements. But for James, who remained a committed Marxist, this was not a demerit, only an historical derivation. What ultimately mattered to him was where history was going.

To that end, *The Black Jacobins* offered up an "anatomy of revolution" markedly different from the one published by the historian Crane Brinton that same year. In his original preface, James thus explained how "the violent conflicts of our age enable our practiced vision to see into the very bones of previous revolutions more easily than before." Present-day events sharpened and deepened James's sense of the past, both its structures and its affects. Indeed, as he continued, "it is impossible to recollect historical emotions in that tranquility which a great English writer, too narrowly, associated with poetry alone." He wrote his work "with something of the fever and the fret" of his age.[16]

Invoking Keats's "Ode to a Nightingale," James highlighted the impossibility of conjuring away the worldly struggles of the present day, either poetically or historically. This opening allusion to romantic poetry also recalled Wordsworth's 1803 "To Toussaint Louverture," written on the occasion of the general's arrest and imprisonment by Bonaparte. Elegiac in tone, the poet metaphorized the revolutionary leader's liberatory legacy as natural forces that would bring about a future freedom: "Thou hast left behind / Powers that will work for thee; air, earth, and skies." For James, the contemporary moment demanded more than poetic palliatives and hopeful dreams endlessly deferred. As critic David Scott suggests, James "could not but have noticed the transcendental complacency of the poet's regard." Rather than burying Toussaint and the powerful emotions he stirred among his revolutionary followers in Saint-Domingue, James brought them back to life.[17]

---

15 James, *A History of Negro Revolt*, 18.
16 C. L. R. James, *The Black Jacobins: Toussaint L'Ouverture and the San Domingo Revolution*, 2nd edn. (New York: Vintage Books, 1963), xi.
17 David Scott, *Conscripts of Modernity: The Tragedy of Colonial Enlightenment* (Durham: Duke University Press, 2004), 62. For more on Wordsworth and Toussaint, see Cora Kaplan, "Black Heroes/White Writers: Toussaint L'Ouverture and the Literary Imagination," *History Workshop Journal*, no. 46 (Autumn 1998), 32–62, p. 41.

James saw Toussaint as an effective embodiment of the formerly enslaved masses' revolutionary will. In James's account, it was not military genius alone that shaped his success. It was also his political imagination, powerfully stirred by Enlightenment figures of abolition, including the image of a "Black Spartacus" evoked by Abbé Raynal and Denis Diderot in a famous passage from their *Histoire des deux indes* (1774) that read as follows: "Everywhere people will bless the name of the hero who shall have re-established the rights of the human race, everywhere will they raise trophies in his honor." According to James, "Over and over again Toussaint read this passage: 'A courageous chief only is wanted. Where is he?'"[18]

Historians have repeatedly questioned the veracity and significance of the intellectual encounter between the literate freed slave and the pronouncements of the *philosophes*. For Michel-Rolph Trouillot, the conventional rhetorical figure of the Black Spartacus was not intended to inspire slave revolt.[19] In representing the Haitian Revolution as an extension of the French revolutionary project, this origin story recapitulated Eurocentric historical presumptions. It assigned agency to the European idea, rather than representing the uprising in Saint-Domingue as a project of self-emancipation. As a movement "from below," the revolution's political imagination also drew on indigenous African religious beliefs and ideologies, most notably from the Kingdom of the Kongo.[20] James did not, however, share this anxiety regarding European influence. He saw Toussaint's ability to appropriate and actualize heroic French revolutionary ideals on behalf of the masses as an expression of his genius and power.

James placed Toussaint in a pantheon of revolutionary thinkers – Pericles, Paine, Marx, and Engels – whose writings "moved men and will always move them" because they were able to "strike chords and awaken aspirations that sleep in the hearts of the majority of every age." James commented thus on the letter written by Toussaint to the Directory on November 5, 1797, urging

---

18 James, *The Black Jacobins*, 25.
19 Most notably, see Trouillot, *Silencing the Past*, 85. See also David Geggus, "Print Culture and the Haitian Revolution: The Written and the Spoken Word," *Proceedings of the American Antiquarian Society*, 116(2) (2007), 299–316, p. 305; and Laurent Dubois, "An Enslaved Enlightenment: Rethinking the Intellectual History of the French Atlantic," *Social History*, 31(1) (2006), 1–14, p. 7.
20 Alyssa Goldstein Sepinwall, "Beyond *The Black Jacobins*: Haitian Revolutionary Historiography Comes of Age," *Journal of Haitian Studies*, 23(1) (2017), 4–34, p. 17; Carolyn E. Fick, *The Making of Haiti: The Saint Domingue Revolution from Below* (Knoxville: University of Tennessee Press, 1990); and John K. Thornton, "'I Am the Subject of the King of Congo': African Political Ideology and the Haitian Revolution," *Journal of World History*, 4(2) (1993), 181–214.

"France" not to betray its liberatory principles: "But no, the same hand which has broken our chains will not enslave us anew. France will not revoke her principles, she will not withdraw from us the greatest of her benefits . . . *But if, to re-establish slavery in San Domingo, this was done, then I declare to you it would be to attempt the impossible: we have known how to face dangers to obtain our liberty, we shall know how to brave death to maintain it.*"[21] In declaring stalwart resistance to the re-imposition of slavery, a resistance that would ultimately lead to independence, Toussaint "incarnated the determination of his people never, never to be slaves again." For James, "uninstructed as he was," Toussaint "could find the language and accent of Diderot, Rousseau, and Raynal, of Mirabeau, Robespierre, and Danton." Indeed, in the "strength and singlemindedness" of his defense of black freedom, "he excelled them all."[22]

Speaking several decades later, James reconfirmed the proximate historical relationship between the French revolution and the slave uprising in Saint-Domingue. Answering those "who are very concerned that I say that the revolution in San Domingo owed so much to the French Revolution," he asserted that it had to be "studied in close relationship with the Revolution in France." In his view, blacks in Saint-Domingue watched events in France and elaborated their own "theory," which they then put into practice: "They got the idea that they are doing what we are doing, and let us go further with it here. They couldn't read but they could make a revolution."[23] James's account of this revolutionary project was not framed in the individualizing, liberal language of "human rights."[24] Its universalist promise was in no way exclusively "French" or European, either in origin or in end. The ultimate outcome of the revolution in Saint-Domingue – the declaration of independence and the creation of a new nation – made this clear. It rather pointed to an immanent contradiction within the purported universalism of the French revolutionary project – and signaled the advent of revolutions to come.[25]

As recent analysis by David Scott and Gary Wilder has underscored, Toussaint himself did not envision full independence. He remained torn between an idealized vision of a more capacious "France" and Bonaparte's brutal threat of re-enslavement. Ultimately, it was Dessalines who would

---

21 James, *The Black Jacobins*, 196–197.   22 James, *The Black Jacobins*, 198.
23 James, "Lectures on *The Black Jacobins*," 76.
24 Adom Getachew, "Universalism after the Post-colonial Turn: Interpreting the Haitian Revolution," *Political Theory*, 44(6) (2016), 821–845. See also Nick Nesbitt, *Universal Emancipation: The Haitian Revolution and the Radical Enlightenment* (Charlottesville: University of Virginia Press, 2008); and Robin Blackburn, *The American Crucible: Slavery, Emancipation and Human Rights* (London: Verso, 2011).
25 James, *A History of Negro Revolt*, 20.

pronounce the word, while "the black revolution had passed [Toussaint] by."[26] The General's persistent fealty to France represented something of a tragic dilemma even in James's romantic revolutionary epic of 1938. The revelatory significance of that tragedy – the "impossibility" of Toussaint's federated vision – took on even greater significance in the "era of decolonization."[27]

James was deeply aware of the violent cost and historical limitations of the national independence that Dessalines ultimately pursued. The Haitian Declaration clearly indicated that colonial history was not easily dispatched despite claims to formal political sovereignty. As James noted, "That the new nation survived at all is forever to its credit for if the Haitians thought that imperialism was finished with them, they were mistaken."[28] This skepticism did not prevent James from imagining an alternative future. But it also meant that he, along with others of his generation, realized that, because events might fail to live up to revolutionary expectations, political theory – and tactics – were likewise contingent and subject to change. James's later writing on anti-colonial revolutions, from Fidel Castro's Cuba to Kwame Nkrumah's Ghana, emphasized how and why the idea and ideal of decolonization instantiated by the radical event of Haitian independence remained subject to change.

Crossing Empires

Much like interwar London, Paris in the 1930s was a center of anti-imperial activism, where new associations, new journals, and novel conceptions of political and artistic subjectivity flourished.[29] On his research trips to the city, James encountered this cosmopolitan colonial metropole and made two important contacts, the negritude poet Damas and the Trotskyist intellectual Pierre Naville (1903–1993). James continued to reflect on the significance of negritude as an important current of West Indian thought and politics in the decades to come. Naville, meanwhile, remained a crucial bridge figure for

---

26 James, *A History of Negro Revolt*, 321.
27 Scott, *Conscripts of Modernity*, 132; and Wilder, *Freedom Time*.
28 James, *A History of Negro Revolt*, 374.
29 Edwards, *The Practice of Diaspora*; Gary Wilder, *The French Imperial Nation-State: Negritude and Colonial Humanism between the Two World Wars* (Chicago: University of Chicago Press, 2005); Jennifer Anne Boittin, *Colonial Metropolis: The Urban Grounds of Anti-imperialism and Feminism in Interwar Paris* (Lincoln: University of Nebraska Press, 2010); and Michael Goebel, *Anti-Imperial Metropolis: Interwar Paris and the Seeds of Third World Nationalism* (New York: Cambridge University Press, 2015).

James, publishing his translation of *The Black Jacobins* in 1949. These continental contacts illustrate points of connection and disjuncture, deferred action and reaction, in the imaginary of decolonization across the twentieth century in the British and French Empires.

The overlaps and intersections between James's London milieu and that of the writers of "negritude," especially Césaire and Damas, are evident. Their shared trajectories as Caribbean-born writers who made their way to the metropole in the 1930s established strong parallels between their works. Steeped in the colonizer's language and culture, they worked to critically displace the exclusionary assumptions of assimilationism and the European civilizing mission. Similarly to James, Césaire attended elite French schools. After his secondary education at the Lycée Victor Schoelcher alongside Damas in Fort-de-France in Martinique, he traveled to Paris to study at the École Normale Supérieure.[30] While pursuing this formal education, Césaire also became a student of Marxism and associated with other black intellectuals, from the United States, the Antilles, and Africa, including Senagalese-born Senghor. Césaire's experiments in anti-imperial politics alongside Senghor and Damas as well as the Nardal sisters, Paulette, Jane, and Andrée, led to their collaboration on the journal *L'étudiant noir* in 1935. Césaire first articulated his conception of an "immediate blackness" or "negritude" in the shared discursive and social space of this black public sphere.

Césaire's writing also registered the "fever and fret" of the moment. In a 1935 article on "Racial Consciousness and Social Revolution" he too worked to reconcile "racial consciousness" with a universalist revolutionary project. "Before making the Revolution and in order to make the revolution – the true one," he proclaimed, it was necessary to "tear up superficial values, apprehend in ourselves the immanent Negro, plant our negritude."[31] Much like James in *A History of Negro Revolt*, Césaire foregrounded the contributions of black political consciousness to "Revolution" – and, eventually, to decolonization.

These authors drew on a shared Caribbean heritage, casting Haiti's revolutionary decolonization as the site of negritude's historical emergence and as a touchstone for a decolonial future. James drew these parallels in his 1963 afterward to *The Black Jacobins*, citing extensively from Aimé Césaire's monumental surrealist poem *Notebook of a Return to the Native Land*,

30 Wilder, *The French Imperial Nation-State*, 153.
31 Christopher L. Miller, "The (Revised) Birth of Negritude: Communist Revolution and 'the Immanent Negro' in 1935," *PMLA*, 125(3) (2010), 743–749, p. 747.

published in 1939 – the year after James originally published his own text. In this afterward, he hailed the Martiniquan-born writer for making "the forward step of resurrecting not the decadence but the grandeur of the West Indian people."[32] Both James and Césaire viewed the Caribbean as a crucible of anti-colonial politics and subjectivity. Césaire, in contrast to Senegalese-born poet and politician Léopold Senghor, imagined negritude as an invention of the Caribbean, where his "island, [his] non-enclosure" lay alongside "Haïti where negritude rose to its feet for the first time and said it believed in its own humanity." He laid claim not to a mythologized and timeless African authenticity, but rather to a lived history of colonial violence and anti-colonial revolt that gave rise to "negritude." For Césaire as for James, Toussaint's heroic ascent and fall was an inspiring historical resource for the anti-colonial future. In the poem, he reclaimed Toussaint's heroic suffering ("Mine too, a small cell in the Jura") and the legacy of the Haitian Revolution as his own.

Damas similarly embraced Toussaint's revolutionary inheritance as an immanent critique of French republicanism's assimilationist mythology. In "89 and Us, the Blacks," a text published in a special issue of the journal *Europe* on the 150th anniversary of the French Revolution, Damas retold the event's history from the perspective of Saint-Domingue. Like James, whose work he cites, Damas described Toussaint as "a true son of the French Revolution" who "knew how to apply its teaching in order to liberate his brothers in race and poverty, first from the physical constraint of slavery, and later, from the yoke of colonial imperialism." As "a revolutionary for all times," Toussaint's "work, which survived him up until our times" represented a "very important stage in the realization of the emancipation of people of color from 'the white man's burden.'"[33] Like James, Damas aligned the French Revolutionary legacy with a liberatory anti-imperialism.

Anti-colonial writing and activism of the late 1930s were marked by the menace of impending military conflict. For many, the prospect of fighting on the side of imperial powers against the fascist menace provoked an acute dilemma, captured powerfully in Damas's 1937 poem, *Et caetera*, which he addressed to once and future conscripts in the colonial corps of the *tirailleurs sénégalais*. Damas urged them to lay down their arms rather than fight on the side of the French empire. Indeed, he implored them to "leave 'the Krauts'

---

32 James, *A History of Negro Revolt*, 402.
33 Léon Damas, "89 et nous, les noirs," *Europe*, no. 139 (1939), 511–516, pp. 515–516.

[les Boches] alone."[34] As the poem anticipated, the war brought the allied imperial powers' contradictory intentions and ideologies to the fore.

Anti-colonial thinkers pursued their critical projects after dispersing from imperial city centers. After leaving for the United States to pursue work with the Socialist Workers Party on the "Negro Question," James published his serial article "Why Negroes Should Oppose the war," which denounced the claim that the allies were fighting against "aggression" and for "democracy."[35] Padmore, who remained in London as head of the IASB, expressed similar skepticism regarding Allied war aims, writing regular columns for African American newspapers such as the *Chicago Defender*, the *Pittsburgh Courier*, and W. E. B. Du Bois's *The Crisis*.[36] Césaire, meanwhile, returned to Martinique to teach at the Lycée Victor Schoelcher and to found the journal *Tropiques*, with his wife Suzanne. He also wrote the first version of the play *Les chiens se taisaient*, which featured a rebel hero based on the life of Toussaint. Damas, meanwhile, despite having penned anti-militarist poems (which were eventually censored by the government in 1939), was conscripted. Pursuing an internal exile during France's dark years, he published a collection of African folktales from Guyana, *Veillées noires*, in 1943. Senghor, who also served in the army, spent two years as a German prisoner of war. These exiles and returns created new opportunities for anti-colonial connection and collaboration in the face of the violent crisis of the war. Its aftermath radically called into question the legitimacy of imperialism and its racialized structures of oppression.

Promising Self-determination

"The Atlantic Charter" of war and peace aims signed by Roosevelt and Churchill in August 1941 anticipated and contributed to debates over the war's implications for the fate of empire. The initial anti-colonial optimism that it fostered was soon followed by disappointment. The document, which was drawn up before the entry of the United States into hostilities, announced "hopes for a better future for the world." The signatories promoted a vision of

---

[34] Léon-Gontran Damas, *Et caetera*, in *Pigments* (Paris: Présence Africaine, 1972 [1937]), 79–80.
[35] C. L. R. James [under the pseudonym J. R. Johnson], "The Negroes and the War," *Socialist Appeal* (September 6–October 3, 1939); reprinted as J. R. Johnson, *Why Negroes Should Oppose the War* (New York: Pioneer Publishers, 1939); and Worcester, *C. L. R. James*, 50.
[36] Penny M. Von Eschen, *Race against Empire: Black Americans and Anticolonialism, 1937–1957* (Ithaca: Cornell University Press, 1997).

postwar peace and security, including a joint renunciation of territorial expansion, in an effort to distinguish Anglo-American values from the bellicose imperialism of their fascist opponents. Article 3 expressed their commitment to "respect the right of all peoples to choose the form of government under which they will live" and a "wish to see sovereign rights and self-government restored to those who have been forcibly deprived of them." Neither Winston Churchill nor Charles de Gaulle understood these clauses as applicable to their empires. But the Charter nonetheless inspired British and French imperial subjects to call out the hypocrisy of Allied war aims and to denounce their subordinated status within the existing structure of empire.

Deputy Prime Minister Clement Attlee initially upheld the liberatory promise of the Charter, declaring to the West African Students' Union that "we are fighting this war not just for ourselves but for all peoples." The Labour Party's *Daily Herald* likewise affirmed that "coloured peoples, as well as white, will share the benefits of the Roosevelt–Churchill Atlantic Charter." As Padmore explained in his 1942 report for the *Chicago Defender*, "for the colonies this was the best piece of news since the war, and aroused tremendous enthusiasm among the 500 million colored peoples in the empire, who believed that the principle of equality of races had been accepted as a fundamental principle of the United Nations."[37] These hopes were dashed, however, when Churchill averred that, in contrast to the "nations of Europe now under the Nazi yoke," the "regions and people who owe allegiance to the British Crown" were "quite a separate problem." Efforts to scale back the Charter's scope drew a swift and emphatic response. As Padmore and others made clear, the British position was increasingly untenable once the Japanese had invaded Hong Kong, Malaya, and Burma. Activists and intellectuals from India to South Africa seized on the language of self-determination in order to press new claims for political reform.[38]

---

37 George Padmore, "The Atlantic Charter and the British Colonies," *Chicago Defender*, September 26, 1942.
38 George Padmore, "Nigeria Questions Intent of Atlantic Charter," *Chicago Defender*, January 31, 1942; George Padmore, "Britain Informs World: 'We'll Hold Our Colonies,'" *Chicago Defender*, March 13, 1943; and Nancy Cunard and Maureen Anne Moynagh, *Essays on Race and Empire* (Orchard Park: Broadview Press, 2002). For the African American response, see The Committee on Africa, the War, and Peace Aims, *The Atlantic Charter and Africa from an American Standpoint* (New York, 1942). On the ambivalent intentions and effects of the Atlantic Charter, see also Elizabeth Borgwardt, *A New Deal for the World: America's Vision for Human Rights* (Cambridge: Belknap Press, 2005); Fabian Klose, *Human Rights in the Shadow of Colonial Violence: The Wars of Independence in Kenya and Algeria* (Philadelphia: University of Pennsylvania Press, 2013); Samuel Moyn, *The Last Utopia: Human Rights in History* (Cambridge: Belknap Press, 2010); and Brad Simpson, "The United States and the Curious History of Self-determination," *Diplomatic History*, 36(4) (2012), 675–694.

The language of the Charter resonated beyond the British colonies, not least after the Allied landings in North Africa in November 1942. In the February 1943 "Manifesto of the Algerian People," Ferhat Abbas explicitly named Roosevelt, who "in his declaration made in the name of the Allies, gave assurances that, in the organization of a new world, the rights of all peoples, small and large, would be respected." "Empowered by this declaration," Abbas and his fellow signatories announced a series of Algerian demands for basic freedoms and a constitution, in order to establish "a government of the people and acting in the interest of the people." In exchange, the Muslim Algerians pledged their support for the "triumph of Right and Liberty."

Assimilationist "young Algerians" like Abbas had learned the lesson of World War I. In light of past disappointment, anti-colonial thinkers and activists now vowed to seize the political and ideological opportunity created by this war.[39] Ho Chi Minh, a veteran of the Wilsonian moment who became the communist leader of Vietnamese resistance to the Japanese occupation, understood these wartime stakes well. Imperial collapse made the assertion of Vietnamese national autonomy possible. In his 1945 Declaration of Independence of the Democratic Republic of Vietnam, Ho boldly invoked American precedent and example, citing the 1776 Declaration directly. Like its model, the Vietnamese Declaration catalogued the hypocrisy and betrayals of the deposed French imperial power, whose reassertion of sovereignty in the wake of Japanese defeat the Vietnamese people boldly refused. Noting the Allied meetings at Yalta and Tehran, as well as the recent United Nations Assembly in San Francisco, the Declaration affirmed "the principles of self-determination and the equality of nations."[40]

The Charter of the United Nations, which had been adopted several months earlier, indeed purported to guarantee the interests of those who remained under imperial rule and promised "to develop self-government, to take due account of the political aspirations of peoples, and to assist them in the progressive development of free political institutions, according to the particular circumstances of each territory and its peoples and their varying stages of advancement."[41] Despite the lofty language of the Charter's

---

[39] Erez Manela, *The Wilsonian Moment: Self-determination and the International Origins of Anticolonial Nationalism* (Oxford: Oxford University Press, 2007).

[40] Ho Chi Minh, "Declaration of Independence of the Democratic Republic of Vietnam," September 2, 1945, in Todd Shepard, *Voices of Decolonization: A Brief History with Documents* (Boston: St. Martin's Press, 2015), 49–52. On the anti-colonial genealogy of Declarations of Independence, see David Armitage, *The Declaration of Independence: A Global History* (Cambridge: Harvard University Press, 2007).

[41] United Nations Charter, cited in Shepard, *Voices of Decolonization*, 48.

preamble, written by the South African segregationist and British imperial thinker Jan Smuts, the ability of this updated League of Nations to honor bids for territorial independence was constrained by British and French continued resistance to the dismantling of their empires.[42]

Contemporary critical observers such as Padmore and W. E. B. Du Bois (1868–1963) had few illusions about the promises held forth by the new institution that upheld "faith in human rights, in the dignity and worth of the human person, in the equal rights of men and women, and of nations large and small." Padmore made this abundantly clear in the article he penned for the *Defender*, on the occasion of the UN's San Francisco meeting. The title alone announced his skepticism: "Future Gloomy for African Natives: Europe Wants Status Quo," he somberly declared.[43]

Ever the activist, however, Padmore refused to be discouraged. After leaving the Communist party in the 1930s, he remained committed to a Pan-Africanist socialist idea of colonial independence.[44] In the fall of 1945, he worked to organize a Pan-African Congress in Manchester, alongside many members of his interwar anti-colonialist circles, such as Amy Garvey; a number of these figures went on to become leading African politicians, including Kenyatta, Makonnen, and Nkrumah (to whom Padmore was introduced by James). Elected the Congress's International President, W. E. B. Du Bois also played a crucial role. Modeled on previous Congresses convened between 1900 and 1927, the meeting brought together trade unionists, intellectuals, and future leaders of independence in order to answer colonial authorities and issue memoranda of their own, including to the United Nations Organization. For Du Bois, their Pan-Africanism stood in stark contrast to Smuts, who represented "a union of the white rulers of Kenya, Rhodesia, and Union of South Africa." In response to their exploitative model of "trusteeship," Du Bois and other participants envisioned building "a new world, which includes black Africa." Calling for the inclusion of black voices in the United Nations, they demanded "autonomy and independence, so far and no further than it is possible in this 'One World'

---

42 Mark Mazower, *No Enchanted Palace: The End of Empire and the Ideological Origins of the United Nations* (Princeton: Princeton University Press, 2009).

43 Shepard, *Voices of Decolonization*, 48; and George Padmore, "Future Gloomy for African Natives: Europe Wants Status Quo," *Chicago Defender*, April 28, 1945. On the limitations of the UN's rhetoric, see Samuel Moyn, "Imperialism, Self-determination, and the Rise of Human Rights," in *The Human Rights Revolution: An International History*, ed. Akira Iriye, Petra Goedde, and William I. Hitchcock (Oxford: Oxford University Press, 2012).

44 Theo Williams, "George Padmore and the Soviet Model of the British Commonwealth," *Modern Intellectual History* (2018), 1–29.

for groups and peoples to rule themselves subject to inevitable world unity and federation."[45]

Subjects of the French Empire were similarly wary of official promises about the improved postwar order. In his famous speech at the Brazzaville Conference of Free French leaders in January 1944, de Gaulle acknowledged the empire's role in sustaining Free France, "its honor and independence." Noting the necessity of reform, he deployed soaring rhetoric about the "nation whose immortal genius" would lead men "toward the heights of dignity and fraternity where, one day, all would be united." As a corollary to this renewed civilizing mission, de Gaulle affirmed French imperial sovereignty, declaring that "for the world of tomorrow, autarky would not be for anyone desirable, or even possible." He nonetheless granted that inhabitants of territories under the French flag would be allowed to "participate in the management of their own affairs."[46] The final declaration of the conference meanwhile ruled out the prospect for autonomy outside the framework of the "French imperial bloc." Claims about French national genius and France's ongoing civilizing mission underwrote this model of a "French Union" that was legally elaborated in the Constitution of 1946.

This vision for the Union remained both developmentalist and horizontal; it was, hence, also open to reimagination and debate. Whether the new Union was simply the empire in new clothes or a genuinely federalist reorientation of "France" had yet to be determined.[47]

Cycles of Colonial Violence

The situation in Vietnam immediately tested promises about the French Union. Despite efforts to reach compromise and settlement, the conflict between the communist Viet Minh in the North and the French army in the South continued to escalate over the course of the late 1940s. Events elsewhere in the empire gave further lie to the official rhetoric of dignity, fraternity, and civilization that underwrote France's postwar imperial reorganization. Evidence of the serious disconnect between promises of reform and the persistence of imperial repression quickly mounted. An estimated 45,000

---

45 Hakim Adi, Marika Sherwood, and George Padmore, *The 1945 Manchester Pan-African Congress Revisited* (London: New Beacon Books, 1995), 55; and W. E. B. Du Bois, *Color and Democracy: Colonies and Peace* (New York: Harcourt, 1945). On the Congress, see Von Eschen, *Race against Empire*.
46 Charles de Gaulle, "Discours de Brazzaville, 30 janvier 1944," www.charles-de-gaulle.org/wp-content/uploads/2017/03/Discours-de-Brazzaville.pdf.
47 Wilder, *Freedom Time*, 137–140.

Algerians were massacred in northeastern Algeria, in response to the killing of several hundred French colonists in demonstrations at Sétif on May 8, 1945. In March 1947, the French army responded with unspeakable brutality to a political uprising in Madagascar, killing some 80,000 Malagasy. The French army's repression and reprisal against colonial subjects weakened claims to moral and political capital garnered by the French resistance to Nazism.

Among the more prominent intellectuals to seize upon this contradiction was the French Algerian writer and prominent resistor Albert Camus (1913–1960). In the journal *Combat*, whose editorship he assumed in 1944, Camus responded to events in Sétif by calling for a radical reorientation of French policy, one that moved beyond promissory discourses: "Let us be clear," he proclaimed, "that we will save nothing of what is French in Algeria or anywhere else if we do not save justice."[48] Two years later, the brutality of extra-legal repression in Madagascar further underscored the hypocrisy and racism of French official policy. Camus vociferously denounced this "contagion": "Three years after being subject to a policy of terror themselves, Frenchmen are reacting to this latest news with the indifference of people who have seen too much. Yet the facts are there, the clear and hideous truth: we are doing what we reproached the Germans for doing." For Camus, this manifest contradiction proved that French racism stood in the way of justice and the universalist principles to which the nation laid claim: "If we French revolted against [German] terror, it was because we believed that all Europeans were equal in rights and dignity. But if Frenchmen can now hear of the methods used in some instances by other Frenchmen against Algerians and Malagasies and not react, it is because they are unconsciously certain that we are in some way superior to those people." Only by vanquishing the deep "flaw" of racism, Camus asserted, would France "win the right to denounce the spirit of tyranny and violence wherever it arises."[49] Camus's allegorical fictions, from *The Stranger* (1942) to *The Plague* (1947) to *The Fall* (1956), were much more circumspect in their overt denunciation of the "contagion" of French racism and the depredations of colonialism. His journalistic writing, especially in the immediate postwar period, directly took the authorities to task for failing to address the prejudice standing in the way of genuine reform.[50]

48 *Combat*, June 15, 1945, in Albert Camus, *Camus at Combat: Writing 1944–1947*, trans. Arthur Goldhammer (Princeton: Princeton University Press, 2006), 227.
49 Albert Camus, "Contagion," May 10, 1947, in Camus, *Camus at* Combat, 291–292.
50 For further discussion, see David Carroll, *Albert Camus, the Algerian: Colonialism, Terrorism, Justice* (New York: Columbia University Press, 2007); and Debarati Sanyal, *Memory and Complicity: Migrations of Holocaust Remembrance* (New York: Fordham University Press, 2015).

A 1947 law extending full citizenship to Algerians with Muslim law status while consigning them to political representation in a second Chamber went some way toward achieving equality. Substantive economic and social reform nonetheless remained severely wanting. For years afterwards, Camus remained committed to a liberal vision of how French Algeria might be "saved" by a commitment to justice. He continued to regret the French government's failure to fully reckon with the errors of Sétif and to formally declare an end to colonial domination. Long after many other intellectuals, including his erstwhile friend Jean-Paul Sartre (1905–1980) had endorsed the cause of Algerian national independence, Camus continued to promote a federalist vision for Algeria as the only viable one. Like his associate the ethnologist Germaine Tillion (1907–2008), Camus was convinced that "a purely Arab Algeria will never accede to economic independence, without which political independence is a pure fantasy."[51]

The French military's use of repressive force to maintain the "French Union" provoked skepticism about the break with the colonial past. Pierre Naville was one such skeptic. He registered this deep ambivalence in his preface to the translation of *The Black Jacobins*, published in 1949. 150 years after the outbreak of the French Revolution, the message of *Les Jacobins noirs* remained timely, and it found resonance among anti-colonial intellectuals associated with postwar négritude. A brief excerpt of Naville's translation appeared, alongside an excerpt from Sartre's preface to the volume of African poetry *L'Orphée noire*, in the journal *La Presence Africaine* which had newly been founded by the Senegalese philosopher Alioune Diop (1910–1980).[52] That same year, the prominent publishing house Gallimard issued the full translation with Naville's preface. Sartre also wrote a preface in which he celebrated "la nouvelle poésie nègre et malgache" as the "only great revolutionary poetry today."[53] Naville, like Sartre, looked to the historical and

---

[51] Albert Camus, "Algérie, 1958," in Albert Camus, *Chroniques algériennes 1939–1958* (Paris: Gallimard, 2002), 202. See also Germaine Tillion, *France and Algeria: Complementary Enemies*, trans. Richard Howard (New York: Knopf, 1961).

[52] Pierre Naville, "L'abolition de l'esclavage et la révolution française," *Présence Africaine*, no. 6 (1949), 22–25. Both authors had hailed the journal's inaugural publication in 1947, see especially Pierre Naville, "Présence africaine," *Présence Africaine*, no. 1 (1947), 44–46. On the inaugural issues of the journal, see Salah D. Hassan, "Inaugural Issues: The Cultural Politics of the Early 'Présence Africaine,' 1947–55," *Research in African Literatures*, 30(2) (1999), 194–221; and Bernard Mouralis, "'Présence Africaine': The Geography of an 'Ideology,'" in *The Surreptitious Speech: "Présence africaine" and the Politics of Otherness, 1947–1987*, ed. Valentine Y. Mudimbe (Chicago: University of Chicago Press, 1992).

[53] Jean-Paul Sartre, "L'Orphée noir," *Présence Africaine*, no. 6 (1949), 11. The original was published in 1948 in *Les Temps Modernes*.

literary resources of anti-colonialism to inspire the future of revolution not just abroad, but also at home.

For the Trotskyist Naville, James's work was a "history lesson" that provided a "means of reflecting thoughtfully on the very evident current crisis in the French colonial system now dubbed (with this appellation perhaps adopted too late) the 'French Union.'"[54] Rejecting the piecemeal and partial solutions pursued in the name of the Union as woefully inadequate, Naville called for a far more revolutionary federation: "reform can only be durable if it abandons the ways of capitalism and leads to a federation based on genuine equality. In this case, it is of course linked to a social revolution in the metropolitan center itself. But it needs to be recognized that, until now, colonized peoples seem to have had a much clearer awareness of these requirements than socialist movements in France itself."[55] While the Haitian Revolution had taken a "national turn," Naville continued to invest in ideas of a socialist federation. He viewed James's text as carrying this revolutionary lesson, not only for the new citizens of the French Union, but for French socialists in the metropole. Beyond the legal framework offered by the 1946 Constitution, there was much still to be done.

Postwar disappointment also shaped Césaire's political vision. In 1945, he had joined the Communist Party (he would leave in 1956) and embarked on a career in politics, while still publishing poetry and plays. In advocating for Martinique's status as a fully fledged department in 1946, he aimed to transform formal political equality into a more substantive economic and racial equality. He continued to be a fierce critic of the French Union's failures, while remaining invested in an alternative political future. That project also entailed a reckoning with France's – and Europe's – deep history of colonial violence.

In the wake of the egregious episodes of violence in Algeria, Indochina, Madagascar, and Côte d'Ivoire, Césaire's *Discourse on Colonialism* (1950) took aim at European humanism's persistent pretensions. His poetic essay inverted the familiar colonialist opposition between civilization and barbarism, demonstrating instead how "colonization works to *decivilize* the colonizer, to brutalize him in the true sense of the word." For Césaire, the advent of Nazism was no exception; it extended a long colonial history. A symptom of a far deeper "poison" and "gangrene," Nazism was best

---

54 Pierre Naville, "Preface" to *Les Jacobins noirs*, in *The Black Jacobins Reader*, ed. Charles Forsdick and Christian Høgsbjerg (Durham: Duke University Press, 2017), 368. It was also published in *Présence Africaine* in 1951.
55 Naville, "Preface," 375–376.

understood as a "boomerang effect" that visited historical violence back on the imperial metropole itself. By denouncing these crimes only when they were committed against "the white man," European "humanism" revealed itself to be a "pseudo-humanism." Césaire saw many reasons to condemn this faux-universalism: "that for too long it has diminished the rights of man, that its concept of those rights has been – and still is – narrow and fragmentary, incomplete and biased, and, all things considered sordidly racist."[56] Still a member of the French Communist Party (PCF), he concluded with the hope that a proletarian revolution would overcome the destructive history of colonialism in order to save "Europe."

When Césaire joined the Communist Party, he had believed that it held out the best hope for the future of the colonized world. His faith in that promise, alongside that of Martiniquan departmentalization, shifted substantially in the 1950s.[57] In 1955, he issued a new edition of the *Discourse on Colonialism* with *Présence Africaine*, which reflected this new politico-cultural position. Recent events, from the explosion of war in Algeria to the increasing political visibility of newly independent states across Asia and Africa, reoriented both Césaire's perspective and that of the journal. In 1955, Diop's review published the addresses of African leaders at the meeting of newly independent nations in Bandung. And, in the winter of 1956, it printed the Communiqué of the Comité d'Action contre la Poursuite de la Guerre en Afrique du Nord, whose meeting featured Diop and Césaire alongside many other intellectuals – Jean Amrouche, André Mandouze, and Jean-Paul Sartre. Vehemently denouncing the French military's recourse to extra-legal violence and torture, these engaged intellectuals sought, in Sartre's words, "to deliver both the Algerians *and* the French from colonial tyranny."[58]

The shift in Césaire's perspective became evident in his contribution to the major conference of Negro writers and artists organized by *Présence Africaine* in 1956. Bridging the Anglophone and Francophone worlds, it featured American and Caribbean as well as African writers. Césaire's intervention condemned the persistence of colonialism, including the "semi-colonialism" of nominally independent nations like Haiti as well as the legacy of

---

56 Aimé Césaire, *Discourse on Colonialism*, trans. Joan Pinkham (New York: Monthly Review Press, 2000), 35–37.
57 Brent Hayes Edwards, "Introduction: Césaire in 1956," *Social Text*, 28(2) (103) (2010), 115–125; and Wilder, *Freedom Time*, 267–272.
58 Jean-Paul Sartre, "Colonialism as a System," in Jean-Paul Sartre, *Colonialism and Neocolonialism* (London: Routledge, 2001), 47. On the meeting, see James D. Le Sueur, *Uncivil War: Intellectuals and Identity Politics during the Decolonization of Algeria* (Lincoln: University of Nebraska Press, 2005), 32–61.

colonialism for African Americans. His speech highlighted how political and economic dispossession produced and perpetuated colonialism's cultural and psychological effects. And he hailed Bandung not only as a "political event," but also as a "cultural event of the first order." Césaire, by contrast, was increasingly skeptical about the genuine "birth of an Anglo- or Franco-African or an Anglo- or Franco-Asiatic civilization," as a route beyond the devastating history of colonialism. While he did not refuse the prospect of cultural *métissage*, he believed that further historical transformation was needed before arriving at such a "synthesis." His speech thus urged, "Let the black peoples come onto the great stage of history."[59]

Later that year Césaire broke with the PCF. Though still a committed Marxist, he repudiated the PCF's incomplete de-Stalinization, its support for the war in Algeria, and its failure to bring about true transformation in the Caribbean.[60] Césaire was not alone in this judgment. The delegitimation of the Communist Party had broad implications for the global reorientation of the left. In turning away from Moscow, dissident Marxists increasingly identified revolution with anti-colonial revolt. The political future lay not in "old Europe," but in what the French demographer Alfred Sauvy had recently described as "le troisième monde," between the West and the Communist Bloc. In Africanist Georges Balandier's suggestive 1956 rephrasing, it became "le tiers monde" or Third World.[61] Not all anti-colonial thinkers were Marxists – some were Catholics, like François Mauriac, and others were liberals, like Raymond Aron. But intellectual defection from the Communist Party buoyed "Third Worldism" at the very moment when the Algerian War was entering its most heated and violent phase.

The Pitfalls of National Consciousness

The Martiniquan-born psychiatrist and powerful advocate of Algerian national liberation Frantz Fanon (1925–1961) emerged as a global intellectual spokesperson of this nascent Third Worldism. A student of Césaire's at the Lycée Victor Schoelcher in Martinique, Fanon enlisted to fight on the side of the Free French in 1943 and eventually traveled to the metropole, where he studied literature and psychiatry in Lyon. A student of Maurice Merleau-Ponty, Fanon's account of colonial racism's pernicious effects was

---

59 Aimé Césaire, "Culture and Colonization," *Social Text*, 28(2) (103) (2010), 127–144, p. 142.
60 Aimé Césaire, "Letter to Maurice Thorez," *Social Text*, 28(2) (103) (2010), 145–152.
61 Christoph Kalter, "From Global to Local and Back: The 'Third World' Concept and the New Radical Left in France," *Journal of Global History*, 12(1) (2017), 115–136.

phenomenological as well as psychological, as his work *Black Skin, White Masks* (1952) made clear. In 1953, he took up a position at a clinic in Blida, a city outside of Algiers. After the outbreak of the Algerian war, he treated both its perpetrators and its victims. His increasingly politically engaged writing reflected on the cultural and psychic effects of colonial domination and violence. Fanon outlined his position on Algerian independence clearly at the 1956 Conference on Negro writers, where his talk on "Racism and Culture" flatly rejected appeals "to assimilation, then to integration, then to community." He framed the battle to overcome cultural and racial domination in Hegelian terms. The confrontation between master and slave under colonialism rendered recognition impossible. He thus concluded that "the logical end of this will to struggle is the total liberation of the national territory."[62] By 1957, he had resigned from his post as a French state employee and was soon forced into exile in newly independent Tunisia, the seat of the Provisional Government of the Algerian Republic. The powerful articles he wrote in favor of the Front de Libération Nationale (FLN) outlined a vision of a newly liberated, decolonized "Man," and assured him a prestigious role as spokesperson for the "Third World."[63] In his preface to Fanon's influential 1961 collection of essays *The Wretched of the Earth*, Sartre proclaimed that "the Third World finds *itself* and speaks to *itself* through his voice."[64]

In his signature essay "Concerning Violence," Fanon asserted that "decolonization is the veritable creation of a new man" – above and beyond the recognition of a "new nation" and its acquisition of formal political sovereignty.[65] Deeply attuned to the psychic dynamics of colonial violence, he envisioned "decolonization" as extending beyond the political form of national independence. In his analysis, overcoming the "alienation" and "compartmentalization" produced by the colonial system entailed violence – or, rather, "counter-violence" – which contributed to the making of "new men" and "new nations." Violence, for Fanon, was psychically "purifying." It promised to free the native from his "inferiority complex and from his despair and inaction," making him "fearless" and restoring his "self-respect."[66]

---

62 Frantz Fanon, *Toward the African Revolution* (New York: Grove Press, 1988), 43.
63 David Macey, *Frantz Fanon: A Biography* (London: Verso, 2012).
64 Jean-Paul Sartre, "Preface" to Frantz Fanon, *The Wretched of the Earth* (New York: Grove Press, 1965), 10.
65 Frantz Fanon, "Concerning Violence," in Frantz Fanon, *The Wretched of the Earth* (New York: Grove Press, 1965), 35.
66 Fanon, "Concerning Violence," 94.

Sartre's preface to the volume further emphasized the sacrificial character of violence. For the French philosopher, the Third World man's emergence had deep implications for European "man," as well. He, too, would be "decolonized," forcibly confronted, most viscerally in Algeria, with what Sartre, echoing Césaire, described as colonial violence's "boomerang" effect. The result was a profoundly subjective as well as political transformation, as the "settler which is in all of us is being savagely rooted out." In this historical inversion, the "Third World" became the true subject of history: "in the past we made history, now it is being made of us."[67] While the Algerians became new men, Sartre and numerous other critics pointed to how the French military perverted *French* men by conscripting young soldiers to maim and torture in the nation's name. In advocating for the "Third World," they refused that devirilizing guilt and humiliation, identifying with the Algerian revolutionary as a new and radically free Man.[68] In endorsing the purifying effect of Algerian violence, Sartre sought to answer anti-colonial critics, such as Jean Daniel of *France Observateur* and Jean-Marie Domenach of the Catholic left journal *Esprit*, who condemned the FLN's recourse to terror.

These political as well as psychic claims countered charges of treason against those who refused to fight for France. The 1960 Manifesto of 121 intellectuals drew on this logic to uphold men's right to insubordination. Drafted by the writers Maurice Blanchot and Dionys Mascolo, and signed by, among many others, Sartre and de Beauvoir, novelists Alain Robbe-Grillet and Nathalie Sarraute, Michel Leiris, Pierre Vidal-Naquet, and Vercors (Jean Bruller), the Manifesto, published on September 6, accused the French army of "betraying the ends confided in it by the whole country" and hence of "perverting the nation." In this way, "French militarism" repeated the crimes of the "Hitlerite order." As the leaders of a network in support of the FLN, Sartre's associate Francis Jeanson and his wife Colette were put on trial; the Manifesto reversed the valence of loyalty and treason, drawing a direct link between the French resistance in World War II and the Algerian one. The Manifesto hailed the universalist import of the Algerian struggle, asserting that "the cause of the Algerian people, which contributes decisively to the ruin of the colonial system, is the cause of all free men."[69] For signatories of

---

67 Sartre, "Preface," 20, 24, and 27.
68 Emma Kuby, "From the Torture Chamber to the Bedchamber: French Soldiers, Antiwar Activists, and the Discourse of Sexual Deviancy in the Algerian War (1954–1962)," *Contemporary French Civilization*, 38(2) (2013), 131–153; and Todd Shepard, *Sex, France, and Arab Men, 1962–1979* (Chicago: University of Chicago Press, 2018), 11–12.
69 "Déclaration sur le droit à l'insoumission dans la guerre d'Algérie. Manifeste dit des '121,'" *Lignes*, 1(33) (1998), 84–87, p. 86.

the Manifesto and Sartre, Algerian decolonization meant more than one country's political independence; it promised to revitalize the European left.

While Sartre's preface valorized violent regeneration, Fanon's collected essays recognized the traumatic and not only the redemptive aspect of decolonizing violence.[70] Fanon had few illusions that the promise of formal political sovereignty at the behest of former colonizers could bring the cycle of violence to an end. He dismissed the rapid accession of African nations to political independence in 1960 as nothing more than a neo-colonial ruse, mockingly imitating European powers: "quick, quick, let's decolonize." Their aim, in his view, was "a strategy of encirclement – based on the respect of the sovereignty of states." Without a significant achievement of economic redistribution, for Fanon, "the apotheosis of independence is transformed into the curse of independence." The result in other words would be a continuation of violence, through neo-colonial economic exploitation and the chronic suffering of "underdevelopment." Responding to the feeble promise of an illusory sovereignty in the international state system, Fanon emphasized that "colonialism and imperialism have not paid their dues when they withdraw their flags and police forces from our territories."[71] Seen from this vantage, Fanon's essay foresaw not heroic and redemptive triumph, but ongoing and uncertain struggle. Substantive "decolonization" was far from being achieved.

Fanon famously left Martinique and the Caribbean behind, to seek the prospect of a decolonial future in Algeria. He nonetheless (re)turned to Césaire in "Concerning Violence" to represent the paradigmatic figure of the revolutionary. Describing Césaire's voice as "prophetic," Fanon included an extended citation from the 1946 tragedy, roughly based on Toussaint's life, *Les chiens se taisaient*. In dialogue with his mother, the "Rebel," who is destined to die, asserts his rebirth – his "baptism" – in and through the bloody act of killing his master. His mother begged for his deliverance from violence, but the rebel rejects her pacifist pleas: "My heart, thou wilt not deliver me from all that I remember." The rebel, while "reborn" in his revolutionary act, did not transcend the cycle of violence. Nor would independent Algeria, even as it became the "mecca of revolution" and a beacon for liberation movements around the world.[72]

---

70 Emma Kuby, "'Our Actions Never Cease to Haunt Us': Frantz Fanon, Jean-Paul Sartre, and the Violence of the Algerian War," *Historical Reflections/Réflexions Historiques*, 41(3) (2015), 59–78.
71 Fanon, "Concerning Violence," 70, 97, and 101.
72 Robert Malley, *The Call from Algeria: Third Worldism, Revolution, and the Turn to Islam* (Berkeley: University of California Press, 1996); and Jeffrey James Byrne, *Mecca of*

Conclusion

When seventeen African countries acceded to independence in 1960, politicians and journalists across the world hailed it as the "Year of Africa." Marking this significant historical moment, the French historian of colonialism Henri Brunschwig published a short note in the *Cahier d'Études Africaines* that reflected on the emergent meanings of "decolonization." "Nothing is so apparently simple as decolonization," he wrote. "It is the abandonment by the metropole of political sovereignty over its colony." But, as Brunschwig foresaw, the apparently straightforward process of political transfer by former colonial powers raised new historical questions. Any return to a *status quo ante* was impossible. Brunschwig nonetheless underscored how newly independent nations would remain economically dependent on their former metropoles. He thus raised a note of caution, emphasizing that "complete independence no longer exists today ... the sole reality is an interdependence that requires abandoning sovereignty."[73]

Thirteen years later, Brunschwig wrote a revealing addendum that traced the advent of a new neologism: "neo-colonialism." At the "All-African People's Conference" in March 1961, newly independent nations gathered together in Cairo adopted a "resolution on neo-colonialism." The document denounced "the survival of the colonial system in spite of formal recognition of political independence in emerging countries which become the victims of an indirect and subtle form of domination by political, economic, social, military or technical means."[74] Subsequent meetings of the Non-Aligned Movement issued analogous declarations, and in 1965, Nkrumah devoted a book-length study to *Neo-colonialism, the Last Stage of Capitalism*. The founder and president of independent Ghana denounced the fiction of political sovereignty in the context of neo-colonial dependence: "The essence of neo-colonialism," he explained, "is that the State which is subject to it is, in theory, independent and has all the outward trappings of international sovereignty. In reality its economic system and thus its political policy is directed from outside."[75] As Brunschwig and many contemporaries

---

Revolution: Algeria, Decolonization, and the Third World Order (Oxford: Oxford University Press, 2016).

73 Henri Brunschwig, "Colonisation–Décolonisation. Essai sur le vocabulaire usuel de la politique coloniale," *Cahiers d'Études Africaines*, 1(1) (1960), 44–54, pp. 52–54.

74 Guy Martin, "Africa and the Ideology of Eurafrica: Neo-colonialism or Pan-Africanism?," *The Journal of Modern African Studies*, 20(2) (1982), 221–238, p. 227.

75 Kwame Nkrumah, *Neo-colonialism, the Last Stage of Imperialism* (London: Nelson, 1965).

recognized, true decolonization required *economic* as well as political independence. The problem was how to attain it.

In the decade to come, many newly independent, non-aligned states sought to establish greater control over their own national resources and to achieve a "New International Economic Order." The role of Mohammed Bedjaoui, a leading theorist of Algeria's legal sovereignty in these efforts, speaks directly to the limits of postcolonial independence.[76] The revolutionary achievement of political sovereignty could not and did not offer sufficient conditions for self-determination. For many contemporary critics of the postcolonial condition, this is the lesson of James's *Black Jacobins* and its "far-off horizon of an imagined sovereignty."[77] The idea of decolonization no longer furnishes the romance of revolution that it once did. But its history nonetheless continues to inspire present-day intellectuals to imagine alternative futures.

---

76 Mohammed Bedjaoui and Algeria (Provisional Government 1958–1962), *La révolution algérienne et le droit* (Brussels: Éditions de l'Association Internationale des Juristes Démocrates, 1961); Umut Özsu, "'In the Interests of Mankind as a Whole': Mohammed Bedjaoui's New International Economic Order," *Humanity: An International Journal of Human Rights, Humanitarianism, and Development*, 6(1) (2015), 129–143; and Samuel Moyn, *Not Enough: Human Rights in an Unequal World* (Cambridge: Harvard University Press, 2018), Chapter 4.

77 Scott, *Conscripts of Modernity*, 22; and Adom Getachew, *Worldmaking after Empire: The Rise and Full of Self-Determination* (Princeton: Princeton University Press, 2019).

18
Structuralism and the Return of the Symbolic

CAMILLE ROBCIS

There is an intrinsic difficulty in attempting to pin down a definition of structuralism, either as a conceptual enterprise or as a label applied to thinkers as diverse as Claude Lévi-Strauss, Roland Barthes, Jacques Lacan, Louis Althusser, or Michel Foucault. Although these scholars read and often discussed each other's works, they remained politically, intellectually, and disciplinarily extremely different. Furthermore, ever since its development in the postwar period, structuralism seems to have been attacked more than it was actually defined. Critics have accused structuralism of being apolitical in a time of great *engagement*; of being complicit with Gaullism, capitalism, or managerialism; of contributing to the death of history and historical analysis; of evacuating agency and destroying the subject; of championing positivism, relativism, anti-humanism, and presentism; and, most importantly, of lacking normative foundations. At various times, structuralism has been conflated with deconstruction, postmodernism, new criticism, formalism, and post-structuralism. While some of the authors associated with structuralism eagerly embraced the term to characterize their intellectual project (as was the case for Barthes and Lévi-Strauss), others (such as Althusser and Foucault) refused the designation. Similarly, while some of these thinkers showed a strong interest in reflecting on their methodological innovations, others shied away from theoretical manifestoes. Structuralism, in sum, appears as one of the most misunderstood movements in the history of modern European thought.

Part of the challenge of defining structuralism is that unlike surrealism, existentialism, situationism and many other intellectual movements in the twentieth century, structuralism was never a belief-system, a philosophy, or a school that one could adhere to. Structuralism was primarily a method – not a method in the sense of a fixed program or grid that could be applied, but rather a mode of reading and interpreting texts and social facts. Anchored in linguistics, and more precisely in the work of Ferdinand de Saussure, structuralism, despite its diversity, insisted on two points. First, texts, things, events, and behaviors had meaning: They *signified*. They were necessarily mediated by language and representation, and hence they could be apprehended only through language. It is in this sense that Saussure referred to structuralism as a semiology, a "science that studies the life of signs within society," a science that examines "what constituted signs, what laws govern them."[1] Second, the meaning of these signs was never intrinsic to the signs themselves: It was not pre-given but rather determined by the network of relations and significations in which the sign was inscribed. Meaning was thus contingent, historical, and arbitrary. Structuralism historicized and denaturalized culture and conventions, and thus it defied all models of conceptual fixity, rigidity, or transcendence. This process of de-essentialization of both object and method made the task of identifying a "structuralist agenda" complex.

Linguistics

It was a Swiss linguist, Ferdinand de Saussure (1857–1913), who laid the foundation for what would later be called structuralism. Saussure gave a series of lectures at the University of Geneva between 1906 and 1911 which were published posthumously, in 1916, as *Course on General Linguistics*. In these lectures, Saussure's intervention was as much theoretical as it was disciplinary. Indeed, structuralism offered an entirely new conception of language but it also presented a radical departure from how linguistics had been taught, studied, and practised since ancient times. The *Course on General Linguistics* thus begins with a lengthy discussion of the history of linguistics, which Saussure divides into three stages. First were the early grammarians (the Greeks and later the French) who relied on logic to study language. As Saussure puts it, their work "lacked a scientific approach and was detached from language itself. Its only aim was to give rules for distinguishing between correct and incorrect forms; it was a normative discipline, far removed from actual observation, and its scope was limited."[2] The grammarians were followed in the late eighteenth century by the philologists, who sought to "correct, interpret and comment upon written texts." In their case, the main problem was that they "follow[ed] the written language too slavishly and neglect[ed] the living language."[3] The third stage,

---

1 Ferdinand de Saussure, *Course in General Linguistics* (New York: McGraw-Hill, 1966), 16.
2 Saussure, *Course in General Linguistics*, 1.   3 Saussure, *Course in General Linguistics*, 2.

known as "comparative philology," began in the early nineteenth century when scholars determined that languages could be compared with one another, especially after the discovery of Sanskrit as a third point of comparison in addition to Latin and Greek. While comparative philology "had the indisputable merit of opening up a new and fruitful field, [it] did not succeed in setting up the true science of linguistics."[4] Indeed, as Saussure writes, comparative philologists "never asked themselves the *meaning* of their comparisons or the *significance* of the relations they had discovered. Their method was exclusively comparative, not historical."[5] It was not until the 1870s that scholars began to look for general principles and that linguistics could become a science as such. "Thanks to them," Saussure explains, "language [was] no longer looked upon as an organism that develops independently but as the product of the collective mind of linguistic groups."[6]

By highlighting the strengths and weaknesses of the history of linguistics, Saussure positions his work both in line with these theories and as a clear break since, in his words, "the fundamental problems of general linguistics still await a solution."[7] In order to reach this "solution," Saussure argues that modern linguistics should have three goals: "(a) to describe and trace the history of all observable languages ... (b) to determine the forces that are permanently and universally at work in all languages and to deduce the general laws to which all specific phenomena can be reduced; and (c) to delimit and define itself."[8] As this statement makes clear, linguistics according to Saussure should be solidly grounded in science, attuned to historical developments as well as to universal patterns, and methodologically self-aware. Close to and yet separate from ethnology, anthropology, sociology, psychology, the physiology of sounds, and philology, linguistics deserves to be its own discipline with its own goal: the study of language as Saussure understands it.

Language [*langue*], Saussure insists, should not be confused with speech [*parole*], the individual act of expression. While speech lacks unity and remains heterogeneous (that is to say, composed of unrelated parts), language is coherent, orderly, and analyzable as a whole. As Saussure defines it, language is the "social product of the faculty of speech and a collection of necessary conventions that have been adopted by a social body to permit individuals to exercise that faculty."[9] Language is thus the "social institution"

---

4 Saussure, *Course in General Linguistics*, 3.
5 Saussure, *Course in General Linguistics*, 4 (my emphasis).
6 Saussure, *Course in General Linguistics*, 5.   7 Saussure, *Course in General Linguistics*, 5.
8 Saussure, *Course in General Linguistics*, 6.   9 Saussure, *Course in General Linguistics*, 9.

created by a collectivity that gives unity to speech. It is what allows a speaker to understand others and to be understood.[10] In separating language from speaking, Saussure explains, we are at the same time separating "(1) what is social from what is individual; and (2) what is essential from what is accessory and more or less accidental."[11] With this vision of language as a social phenomenon, it is easy to see why linguistics would provide a model for semiology, the study of signs and of the laws that govern them. This also explains why linguistics would share a conceptual basis with social-scientific disciplines such as anthropology.

As Saussure thus suggests, the object of linguistics is language understood as a semiology, as a system of signs. Indeed, sounds and noises are considered language only if they signify, if they can communicate ideas. In Saussure's famous definition, a sign is the union of a concept – which Saussure calls a signified (*signifié*) – and a sound-image – a signifier (*signifiant*).[12] Language is the process that links a particular signifier to particular signified. Furthermore, Saussure argues, that bond, the linguistic sign, is entirely arbitrary.[13] This does not mean that the sign is entirely "left to the speaker" but rather that there is no *natural* connection with the signified, no intrinsic rapport with the concept.[14] Language, in other words, is conventional, social, and contingent. Because the sign has no essence or core, it can be understood only as a relational entity; its meaning established only in comparison with other signs. Saussure refers to this as the synchronic study of language: "synchronic linguistics will be concerned with the logical and psychological relations that bind together coexisting terms and form a system in the collective mind of the speakers." In contrast, diachronic linguistics "will study relations that bind together successive terms not perceived by the collective mind but substituted for each other without forming a system."[15] Whereas linguistics prior to Saussure had focused on diachronic analysis, on tracing the historical evolution of words, Saussure makes clear that the future of linguistics lies in a synchronic approach, one that will examine contrasts, combinations, and distinctions, one that will treat the system as a functional whole, as a structure.

Saussure's definition of the sign as arbitrary and his push toward synchronic analysis entail several consequences, concerning not only the study of

---

10 Saussure, *Course in General Linguistics*, 15 and 11.
11 Saussure, *Course in General Linguistics*, 14.
12 Saussure, *Course in General Linguistics*, 66–67.
13 Saussure, *Course in General Linguistics*, 67.   14 Saussure, *Course in General Linguistics*, 69.
15 Saussure, *Course in General Linguistics*, 99–100.

signification but also the definition of the human subject whose specificity is to speak, to possess language. As Jonathan Culler puts it,

> What the study of language reveals about mind is not a set of primitive conceptions or natural ideas but the general structuring and differentiating operations by which things are made to signify. When Saussure argues that meaning is "diacritical" or differential, based on differences between terms and not on intrinsic properties of terms themselves, his claim concerns not only language but the general human process in which the mind creates meaning by distinguishing.[16]

Language is thus not the product of a rational, conscious, and autonomous subject but rather "a system of forms that are governed by their own law, that possess an autonomous formal pattern."[17] From this perspective, one can see how, later in the twentieth century, structuralism was often opposed to humanism, ego psychology, communicative rationality, and analytic philosophy. In the field of criticism, Saussure's analysis also suggests that it is futile to search for general laws of history, for teleologies. Rather, criticism should focus on determining the formal and structural parameters of texts – understood largely as literature, film, art, subjects, events. This hypothesis will lead Jacques Derrida, many years later, to posit that "there is nothing outside of the text" (*il n'y a pas de hors-texte*).[18] As we can see, structuralism as devised by Saussure shook some of the most engrained suppositions of modern European thought.

Literature

One thinker who was especially influenced by Saussure, and was responsible for coining the term structuralism, was the Moscow-born linguist and literary critic Roman Jakobson (1896–1982). Jakobson became an avid reader of Saussure when he was studying linguistics at the University of Moscow at the beginning of the twentieth century. Like Saussure, Jakobson felt constrained by the neo-grammarian control of linguistics in the early twentieth century. Within the orbit of Russian linguistics, the only acceptable scientific study of language was historical and genetic. In 1915, Jakobson participated in the foundation of the Moscow Linguistic Circle for the study of language, poetics, metrics, and folklore, which called for the immanent analysis of

---

16 Jonathan D. Culler, *Ferdinand de Saussure* (Ithaca: Cornell University Press, 1986), 71.
17 Culler, *Ferdinand de Saussure*, 73.
18 Jacques Derrida, *Of Grammatology*, trans. Gayatri Chakravorty Spivak (Baltimore: Johns Hopkins University Press, 1997), 158.

literary works. In 1920, Jakobson left Russia for Prague, where he enrolled in a doctoral program. In Prague, he continued to read Saussure but also immersed himself in Husserl's phenomenology, Gestalt psychology, and formalist literary criticism. Eventually, he helped establish the Prague Linguistic Circle dedicated to the study of general linguistics, poetics, and the history of Slavic languages, literatures, and cultures, in which he was active from 1926 to 1938. It is in the context of this "Prague school" that Jakobson met Nikolai Trubetzkoy, with whom he collaborated extensively in the study of sound-patterns. According to these scholars, because sounds had no intrinsic meaning, linguistics needed to take on a strictly relational approach to explore the functions of sound differences. Phonological systems were thus structural wholes and the "basic task [of the linguist was] to reveal the inner, whether static or developmental, laws of this system."[19] The work of Jakobson and Trubetzkoy launched what Claude Lévi-Strauss would later call a "phonological revolution."

In 1939, Jakobson fled to Scandinavia after the Nazi invasion of Czechoslovakia. In Denmark, he joined the Copenhagen Linguistic Circle through which he collaborated with Louis Hjelmslev. In Sweden, he taught at the University of Uppsala, before emigrating to New York City in 1941. From 1942 to 1946, Jakobson taught, along with various other European émigrés, at the École Libre des Hautes Études, housed in the New School for Social Research and funded by the Rockefeller Foundation. Eventually he moved to Columbia and later to Harvard and MIT. It was in this context that Jakobson met Claude Lévi-Strauss, also exiled at the École Libre des Hautes Études, a meeting that Lévi-Strauss describes as decisive in his intellectual trajectory: "At the time, I was a sort of naïve structuralist. I did structuralism without knowing it. Jakobson revealed to me the existence of a theoretical corpus already constituted within a discipline: linguistics, which I had never practiced. For me, it was an illumination."[20] It was Jakobson who encouraged Lévi-Strauss to write *The Elementary Structures of Kinship*, and it was through Lévi-Strauss that Jakobson eventually met the psychoanalytic theorist Jacques Lacan. Structuralism was traveling from linguistics to the most innovative frontiers of literary criticism, anthropology, and psychoanalysis.

While Jakobson turned to some of these early structuralist theories for the study of literature, it was Roland Barthes (1915–1980) who systematized this practice in order to promote a new type of literary criticism – which

---

19 Roman Jakobson, *On Language*, ed. Linda R. Waugh and Monique Monville-Burston (Cambridge: Harvard University Press, 1990), 6.
20 Didier Eribon and Claude Lévi-Strauss, *De près et de loin* (Paris: Odile Jacob, 1988), 63.

eventually came to be known as *la nouvelle critique* – and a new science of signs: semiology. Barthes studied classical literature at the Sorbonne and was introduced to modern linguistics by Julien Greimas. At the beginning of the 1950s, literary criticism – *la critique universitaire* to use Barthes's term – focused primarily on the study of how authorship and socio-historical context shaped a particular work. Despite the efforts of figures such as Jean-Paul Sartre and Maurice Blanchot to revitalize this field, literary criticism remained remarkably closed. In this context, Barthes's first two books, *Writing Degree Zero* in 1953 and his study of the historian Jules Michelet from 1954, appeared quite revolutionary in their celebration of self-conscious and modernist literary projects. As Barthes suggested, writing (*écriture*) was never a transparent, direct, or literal exercise as existentialism hoped it could be. Rather, writing was the product of unique and creative choices. The goal of literary criticism was thus neither to force a text into a pre-determined model nor to uncover an author's hidden intentions but instead to analyze the proliferation of meanings in a particular text, to study a text's "textuality."

Barthes perfected his theory of literary criticism throughout his life. In 1968, he published one of his best-known essays, "The Death of the Author." As writers such as Mallarmé and Proust had made clear, writing was the "destruction of every voice, every origin."[21] In this sense, the claim to "decipher" or "explain" a text was entirely futile.[22] Indeed, according to Barthes, texts "consist of multiple writings, proceeding from several cultures and entering into dialogue, into parody, into contestation."[23] The "site where this multiplicity is collected" is not the author but the reader. As Barthes famously declared, "the birth of the reader must be requited by the death of the Author."[24] Barthes put into practice this mode of synchronic analysis that seeks to bring out the intertextual construct of a particular text and its different narrative techniques (or "narratology") in 1970, in *S/Z*, a commentary on Honoré de Balzac's novella *Sarrasine*. Literary criticism, Barthes made clear, should not strive to be objective, positivist, or free of ideology but should instead embrace this new exciting vision of the reader as critic.

Barthes's semiology, however, did not simply take as its object literature. In his short essays collected under the title of *Mythologies* (published in 1957), Barthes proposed to consider myth as a type of speech, a form of *écriture*, "a

21 Roland Barthes, *The Rustle of Language* (Berkeley: University of California Press, 1989), 49.
22 Barthes, *The Rustle of Language*, 53. 23 Barthes, *The Rustle of Language*, 54.
24 Barthes, *The Rustle of Language*, 55.

system of communication ... a message."[25] From this perspective, there was no fixed or intrinsic relation between the form and the meaning of a myth but rather a "constant game of hide-and-seek" in which mythic concepts "can come into being, alter, disintegrate, disappear completely."[26] In redefining the myth as a sign, Barthes was also explicit about the political consequences that structuralist analysis could have. "Semiology," Barthes suggested "has taught us that myth has the task of giving an historical intention a natural justification, and making contingency appear eternal. Now this process is exactly that of bourgeois ideology."[27] Myth is "depoliticized speech" because it naturalizes the relationship between signifier and signified: "Myth does not deny things, on the contrary, its function is to talk about them; simply, it purifies them, it makes them innocent, it gives them a natural and eternal justification, it gives them a clarity which is not that of an explanation but that of a statement of fact."[28] The task of the critic is thus to bring to light this political dimension, to demystify, and to reveal the arbitrariness and the contingency of cultural codes. As Barthes put it in 1953, analyzing myths was "the only effective way for an intellectual to take political action."[29] In 1977, Barthes was elected to the Chair of Literary Semiology at the Collège de France. In his inaugural lecture, Barthes declared that the goal of semiology was to "stimulate social criticism": "Sartre, Brecht, and Saussure," he declared, "could join forces in this project."[30] By revealing how language articulates our lived reality, structuralism was indeed a deeply political project.

Anthropology

The encounter of Claude Lévi-Strauss (1908–2009) with structural linguistics was foundational both from a disciplinary and from a theoretical perspective. Anthropology was vibrant in France throughout the nineteenth century, in the context of the Société d'Anthropologie, the École d'Anthropologie, the Musée d'Histoire de l'Homme, and the Musée d'Ethnographie. The members of these early anthropological associations were mainly physicians, archeologists, and scientist, many of whom had participated in France's extensive colonial missions. Even though these anthropologists aspired to objectively study human "races" in all their forms and variations, their work often posited a correlation

---

25 Roland Barthes, *Mythologies* (New York: Hill and Wang, 1972), 107.
26 Barthes, *Mythologies*, 117–119.   27 Barthes, *Mythologies*, 142.   28 Barthes, *Mythologies*, 143.
29 Cited in Jonathan D. Culler, *Roland Barthes* (New York: Oxford University Press, 1983), 29.
30 Cited in Culler, *Roland Barthes*, 57.

between physical type and the degree of development of a specific race. The extreme right celebrated this racist vision of anthropology and, by 1940, several of these anthropologists had welcomed the arrival of the Vichy regime while others – such as Georges Montanton – accepted institutional positions in the new government.[31] In other words, by the time of World War II, anthropology in France referred primarily to this racist version of physical anthropology.

It was partly in opposition to this conservative scholarship that sociology also emerged during the Third Republic as the privileged discipline for social and cultural analysis. In particular, French sociology found a new impetus in the work of Émile Durkheim and his students. For Durkheim, the goal of sociology was to discern the specificity of the social, its totalizing and autonomous nature, the whole that was irreducible to the sum of its parts. Marcel Mauss, Durkheim's nephew and disciple, encouraged sociologists to study "total social facts" as he had in his 1925 essay, *The Gift*. To demarcate himself from the École d'Anthropologie's increasingly conservative positions, Mauss, who was strongly identified with the left, preferred to describe his work as "ethnology" rather than "anthropology." Mauss's efforts to build a different kind of anthropology were also institutional as he helped develop the Institut d'Ethnologie and the Musée d'Ethnographie du Trocadéro, which would later become the Musée de l'Homme.

Lévi-Strauss, who was born in 1908, was personally and intellectually close to many of the members of the Institut d'Ethnologie from his student days. Mauss's influence was particularly evident in *The Elementary Structures of Kinship*, in which Lévi-Strauss characterized the incest prohibition as a total social fact and as the "supreme rule of the gift."[32] Lévi-Strauss admired the French sociological school for trying to discern the specificity of the social, and he affiliated himself with this tradition in many ways. Yet, he often found the empirical research of these French ethnologists – many of whom had barely ventured abroad – disappointingly thin. Thus, Lévi-Strauss's encounter with the much more empirically grounded American anthropology during his exile in New York was crucial. During these years, he established close ties with the most prominent American anthropologists, in particular Franz Boas and many of his students, including Ralph Linton, Ruth Benedict, Alfred

---

31 Herman Lebovics, "Le conservatisme en anthropologie et la fin de la Troisième République," *Gradhiva*, no. 4 (1988), 3–16; and Alice L. Conklin, *In the Museum of Man: Race, Anthropology, and Empire in France, 1850–1950* (Ithaca: Cornell University Press, 2013).
32 Claude Lévi-Strauss, *The Elementary Structures of Kinship* (Boston: Beacon Press, 1969), 480.

Kroeber, and Robert Lowie. Furthermore, Lévi-Strauss greatly benefited from the wide collection of English-language sources at the New York Public Library, where he wrote most of the *Elementary Structures*. In this sense, *The Elementary Structures of Kinship* was the product of this double heritage. In the exhaustiveness of his research, the range of scholarship he engaged with, and the sheer quantity of ethnographic data he had assembled, Lévi-Strauss inscribed himself within this "Anglo-Saxon" tradition of empirically driven social and cultural anthropology that he so admired. However, by considering the social as a whole, as a universal and as a total social fact, he remained committed to the theoretical enterprise of the French school of sociology. Lévi-Strauss thus located *The Elementary Structures of Kinship* at the crossroads of these two genealogies, but he also envisioned it as a solution to the impasses facing each one – a solution founded in structural linguistics. For Lévi-Strauss, *The Elementary Structures* was to serve as the prototype for a new kind of anthropology, and one that would also overcome the tainted politics of French anthropology during the Vichy years, a discipline that would take the name of "structuralist anthropology."

Indeed, *The Elementary Structures of Kinship* was not merely innovative in disciplinary terms; it was also theoretically extremely ambitious. As Lévi-Strauss stated in the first pages of his book, his goal was to propose a definitive theory of how the social related to the biological, to determine, once and for all, where "nature ends and culture begins."[33] Is human identity (physical and behavioral) determined by biologically innate and instinctual attributes, or is it the product of a complex interaction of our social, educational, and familial contexts? This question, Lévi-Strauss tells us, has puzzled sociologists, biologists, and anthropologists for years. Given the inherent difficulty in isolating humans from any social interaction, social scientists had opted for a functionalist model that juxtaposed culture to biology or vice versa, or simply abandoned the question altogether. Similarly, social scientists had attempted to discern traces of culture in animal life, particularly among great apes. Chimpanzees, for instance, are able to "articulate several monosyllables and disyllables but they never attach any meaning to them."[34] Although monkeys can utter sounds, these are never *signs* in the sense that a particular signified is attached to a particular signifier. To use one of Lévi-Strauss's most important concepts, animals are incapable of "symbolic thought." Most significantly, Lévi-Strauss argues, "the social life of monkeys

---

[33] Lévi-Strauss, *The Elementary Structures of Kinship*, 4.
[34] Lévi-Strauss, *The Elementary Structures of Kinship*, 6.

does not lend itself to the formulation of any norm ... Not only is the behavior of the single subject inconsistent, but there is no regular pattern to be discerned in collective behavior."[35] This lack of norms and regularity is particularly striking in the chimps' sexual activity, where "monogamy and polygamy exist side by side."[36] Thus, Lévi-Strauss claims, it is "this absence of rules [that] seems to provide the surest criterion for distinguishing a natural from a cultural process."[37] "Let us suppose," Lévi-Strauss famously concludes, "that everything universal in man relates to the natural order, and is characterized by spontaneity, and that everything subject to a norm is cultural and is both relative and particular."[38]

It is through the prohibition of incest that Lévi-Strauss links his discussion of nature and culture to his analysis of kinship. Indeed, after defining nature by universality and culture by the existence of relative and particular norms, Lévi-Strauss writes that we are confronted with a "scandal": the prohibition of incest which "presents, without the slightest ambiguity, and inseparably combines, the two characteristics in which we recognize the conflicting features of two mutually exclusive orders. It constitutes a rule, but a rule which alone among all the social rules, possesses at the same time a universal character."[39] Just as sociologists have failed to give a definitive explanation of the distinction between nature and culture, they have been unable to determine the precise origin of this incest prohibition and to account for its sacredness, in all times and all cultures. Specifically, Lévi-Strauss contends, sociologists who have tried to understand the incest taboo have fallen into one of the three methodological "traps," all resulting from an inadequate conceptualization of nature and culture.

The first "trap" is to argue that the prohibition was imposed by societies which had become aware of the hazardous biological effects of consanguinity. Genetic foreshadowing, however, cannot justify the existence of the incest taboo, since the medical ramifications of incest have been fully grasped only recently and since biology alone cannot account for the arbitrariness regarding which unions are considered incestuous and which are not. A second "trap" is to claim that the prohibition is merely the formal expression of a universal, deep-rooted instinct of natural repugnance toward incest. Again, Lévi-Strauss dismisses this "universal disgust" theory by claiming not

---

35 Lévi-Strauss, *The Elementary Structures of Kinship*, 6.
36 Lévi-Strauss, *The Elementary Structures of Kinship*, 7.
37 Lévi-Strauss, *The Elementary Structures of Kinship*, 8.
38 Lévi-Strauss, *The Elementary Structures of Kinship*, 8.
39 Lévi-Strauss, *The Elementary Structures of Kinship*, 8–9.

Structuralism and the Return of the Symbolic

only that incestuous relations exist but, as psychoanalysis has shown, that incest is in fact generally desired at an unconscious level, as the Oedipus complex suggests. Finally, a third "trap" has treated the prohibition as a purely social or historical phenomenon, one imposed by particular cultures at particular times. These explanations all "attempt to establish a universal phenomenon on an historical sequence, which is by no means inconceivable in some particular case but whose episodes are so contingent that the possibility of this sequence being repeated unchanged in every human society must be wholly excluded."[40] To summarize, for Lévi-Strauss, natural explanations of the incest taboo can account for universality but not for the rule, whereas historical/sociological accounts can account for the rule but not for its universality.

It is in opposition to these two options that Lévi-Strauss sets up his own model of interpretation of the incest prohibition, which, he suggests, moves beyond the biological and historical accounts, beyond the nature/culture paradigm. "The problem of the incest prohibition," Lévi-Strauss writes, "is not so much to seek the different historical configurations for each group as to explain the particular form of the institution in each particular society. The problem is to discover what profound and omnipresent causes could account for the *regulation* of the relationships between the sexes in every society and age."[41] To pinpoint this problem of regulation, Lévi-Strauss makes the now-famous argument that we must understand the incest prohibition as situated at the *transition* from nature to culture and as such, that it is, by definition, both nature *and* culture: "The prohibition of incest is in its origin neither purely cultural nor purely natural, nor is it a composite mixture of elements from both nature and culture. It is the fundamental step because of which, by which, but above all in which, the transition from nature to culture is accomplished."[42] The prohibition of incest, Lévi-Strauss concludes, is the link between man's biological existence and his social existence.[43] It is, we could say, the necessary condition for the social contract, the structure that brings men from the scattered state of nature into an integrated social framework.

The implications of Lévi-Strauss's concepts of nature, culture, and the incest prohibition become apparent in the last chapter of *The Elementary Structures*. Lévi-Strauss begins this section by clarifying his critique of history

---

40 Lévi-Strauss, *The Elementary Structures of Kinship*, 22.
41 Lévi-Strauss, *The Elementary Structures of Kinship*, 23 (my emphasis).
42 Lévi-Strauss, *The Elementary Structures of Kinship*, 24.
43 Lévi-Strauss, *The Elementary Structures of Kinship*, 24–25.

through an analysis of Freud's 1913 work, *Totem and Taboo*. In Freud's narrative, the brothers' murder of the Father and the sacrificial meal that follows mark the institution of the super-ego. Out of the brothers' guilt emerges the rule of law, morality, and religion, but also exogamy, since the Father can no longer keep all of the women for himself. The prohibition of incest thus inaugurates the birth of culture, of the symbolic: "the beginnings of religion, morals, society, and art converge in the Oedipus complex."[44] Lévi-Strauss focuses on Freud's analogy between individual psyche and social formation to maintain the uniqueness and specificity of the incest taboo:

> Freud's work is an example and a lesson. The moment the claim was made that certain extant features of the human mind could be explained by an historically certain and logically necessary event, it was permissible, and even prescribed, to attempt a scrupulous restoration of the sequence. The failure of *Totem and Taboo*, far from being inherent to the author's proposed design, results rather from his hesitation to avail himself to the ultimate consequences implied in his premises. He ought to have seen that phenomena involving the most fundamental structure of the human mind could not have appeared once and for all. They are repeated in their entirety within each consciousness, and the relevant explanation falls within an order which transcends both historical successions and contemporary correlations.[45]

Thus, while Lévi-Strauss credits Freud for thinking the individual and the social together, he criticizes him for remaining caught in historical explanations that Freud himself constantly put into question. Freud's methodological "timidity," Lévi-Strauss continues, leads him to a "strange and double paradox": "Freud successfully accounts, not for the beginning of civilization but for its present state; and setting out to explain the origin of a prohibition, he succeeds in explaining, certainly not why incest is consciously condemned, but how it happens to be unconsciously desired."[46]

Hence, for Lévi-Strauss, the main problem with *Totem and Taboo* was not the actual event of patricide that preoccupied Freud, but rather the fact that Freud still thought of this event and its prohibition in historical terms. Freud's inability to abandon history was paradoxical, Lévi-Strauss tells us, since in his other writings he had often suggested that "certain basic phenomena," such as anxiety and sublimation, "find their explanation in the permanent

---

44 Sigmund Freud, *Totem and Taboo: Some Points of Agreement between the Mental Lives of Savages and Neurotics* (New York: Norton, 1989), 194.
45 Lévi-Strauss, *The Elementary Structures of Kinship*, 491.
46 Lévi-Strauss, *The Elementary Structures of Kinship*, 491.

structure of the human mind, rather than in its history."[47] Hence, Lévi-Strauss concludes, Freud's "hesitations" in *Totem and Taboo* were revealing: "They show a social science like psychoanalysis ... still wavering between the tradition of an historical sociology ... and a more modern and scientifically more solid attitude, which expects a knowledge of its future and past from an analysis of the present."[48] This "more modern and scientifically more solid attitude" will be structuralism. Only structuralism, Lévi-Strauss concludes, will be able to avoid the methodological impasses of biology and history, of the natural and social sciences, and only structuralism will rescue anthropology as a discipline from the political polarization of the pre-war period: "Only one science has reached the point at which synchronic and diachronic explanation have merged ... This social science is linguistics. When we consider its methods, and even more its object, we may ask ourselves whether the sociology of the family, as conceived of in this work, involves as different a reality as might be believed, and consequently whether it has not the same possibilities at its disposal."[49]

The analogy between kinship and structural linguistics that Lévi-Strauss establishes at the end of his book has several crucial consequences. First, Lévi-Strauss makes clear that his structuralist social contract is also a linguistic contract: It assumes that signifiers and signified are attached to one another in a particular way. Language, kinship, symbolic thought, sociality, and psychic adjustment are now structurally equivalent on the side of culture, whereas sounds (with no signifier attached to them), mating, isolation, and psychic trouble are on the other side, that of nature. Being outside the social contract means not being able to "signify" to others. It is in this sense that we should understand Lévi-Strauss's assertions "the relations between the sexes can be conceived as one of the modalities of a great 'communication function' which also includes language"[50] and "language and exogamy represent two solutions to one and the same situation"[51] – the situation of social exchange. In opposition to the Tower of Babel, a kind of state of nature "when words were still the essential property of each particular group," words have now "become common property" and, as such, they function as vehicles of solidarity:

---

47 Lévi-Strauss, *The Elementary Structures of Kinship*, 491.
48 Lévi-Strauss, *The Elementary Structures of Kinship*, 492.
49 Lévi-Strauss, *The Elementary Structures of Kinship*, 492–93.
50 Lévi-Strauss, *The Elementary Structures of Kinship*, 494.
51 Lévi-Strauss, *The Elementary Structures of Kinship*, 496.

If the incest prohibition and exogamy have an essentially positive function, if the reason for their existence is to establish a tie between men which the latter cannot do without if they are to raise themselves from a biological to a social organization, it must be recognized that linguists and sociologists do not merely apply the same methods but are studying the same thing. Indeed, from this point of view, "exogamy and language . . . have fundamentally the same function – communication and integration with others."[52]

Exogamy (and thus, heterosexual exchange) leads to kinship, integration, sociality, psychic cohesion, a common language, and culture. Faced with the theoretical difficulty presented by his concepts of nature and society, Lévi-Strauss contends that the incest taboo is neither cultural nor social, but rather *structural* like language, universal, and, in many ways, inevitable. In this sense, Lévi-Strauss can argue that it is not "symbolic thought" or culture that produces the prohibition of incest. This would be a socio-historical explanation. Rather, the prohibition, and its correlation, exogamy and the family, are coextensive with the symbolic: They are the "general condition of culture."[53]

The conclusions that Lévi-Strauss put forth in *The Elementary Structures of Kinship* resonated with the more theoretically oriented texts that he wrote throughout the 1940s and 1950s and that were eventually collected in the first volume of *Structural Anthropology*, which was published in 1958. More specifically, Levi-Strauss called for a synchronic analytic framework that would be able to detect systems and account for patterns. The main difference between anthropology and history, Lévi-Strauss explained, was not

> one of subject, of goal, or of method. They share the same subject which is social life; the same goal, which is a better understanding of man; and, in fact, the same method, in which only the proportion of research techniques varies. They differ, principally, in their choice of complementary perspectives: History organizes its data in relation to conscious expressions of social life, while anthropology proceeds by examining its unconscious foundations.[54]

History and anthropology were thus not mutually exclusive, but, as Lévi-Strauss made clear, linguistics was, by far, the most stimulating field in the social sciences. In their previous historical configuration, linguistics could offer some interesting insights to the social sciences, but "nothing foretold

---

52 Lévi-Strauss, *The Elementary Structures of Kinship*, 493.
53 Lévi-Strauss, *The Elementary Structures of Kinship*, 24.
54 Claude Lévi-Strauss, *Structural Anthropology* (New York: Basic Books, 1963), 18.

a revelation. The advent of structural linguistics completely changed this situation."⁵⁵

In this context, Lévi-Strauss stresses his debt to Jakobson and to Trubetzkoy, who shifted the focus of study from conscious linguistic phenomena to their unconscious infrastructure. Furthermore, these linguists introduced the concept of system, sought to discover its general laws, and analyzed relations between terms instead of treating them as independent entities. "Like phonemes," Lévi-Strauss argued,

> kinship terms are elements of meaning; like phonemes, they acquire meaning only if they are integrated into systems. "Kinship systems," like "phonemic systems," are built by the mind on the level of unconscious thought. Finally, the recurrence of kinship patterns, marriage rules, similar prescribed attitudes between certain types of relatives . . . lead us to believe that, in the case of kinship as well as linguistics, the observable phenomena result from the action of laws which are general but implicit.⁵⁶

Just as Trubetzkoy and Jakobson had freed linguistics from discontinuity and singularity, anthropology needed to work toward the establishment of these general rules, toward the understanding of the arbitrary systems of representation that governed our social world:

> Each detail of terminology and each special marriage rule is associated with a specific custom as either its consequence or its survival. We thus meet with a chaos of discontinuity. No one asks how kinship systems, regarded as synchronic wholes, could be the arbitrary product of a convergence of several heterogeneous institutions (most of which are hypothetical), yet nevertheless function with some sort of regularity and effectiveness.⁵⁷

In both anthropological and linguistic research, Lévi-Strauss proclaimed, "we are dealing strictly with symbolism."⁵⁸

Psychoanalysis

By the time he encountered the works of Jakobson and Lévi-Strauss in the 1950s, Jacques Lacan (1901–1981) had already been thinking about structures for quite some time. Born into a Parisian bourgeois Catholic family, Lacan studied medicine before choosing to specialize in psychiatry in 1927. As a medical intern at the Sainte-Anne Hospital, he discovered German

---

55 Lévi-Strauss, *Structural Anthropology*, 33.   56 Lévi-Strauss, *Structural Anthropology*, 34.
57 Lévi-Strauss, *Structural Anthropology*, 35.   58 Lévi-Strauss, *Structural Anthropology*, 51.

philosophy, phenomenology, and Surrealism, which led him to the work of Freud. Frustrated with the biological essentialism of much of French mainstream psychiatry at the time, the young Lacan read extensively in these various fields, and he incorporated many psychoanalytic insights into his 1932 doctoral thesis *On Paranoid Psychosis and Its Relations to the Personality*. Lacan's thesis focused on the origins of paranoid psychosis, and asked whether it was the result of the "development of a personality, and thus does it correspond to a constitutive anomaly or to a reactionary deformation? Or was psychosis an autonomous illness, that reshapes the personality by breaking the course of its development?"[59] Did madness, in other words, stem from the brain as many neuroscientists believed, from the body as an acquired disease, or from the patient's social and familial worlds? Lacan's answer was clear: "It is absurd to attribute these phenomena to a specifically neurological *automatism*."[60] Rather than focusing on a single origin, Lacan argued, psychosis needed to be studied in relation to the formation of a specific structure, a "personality." If psychosis also had a social "origin, exercise, and meaning,"[61] it was important to consider at least three factors: "the childhood history of the patient, the conceptual structures of his delirium, and the drives and intentions behind his social behavior."[62] Psychiatric clinical work thus needed to remain open to sociological inquiry, medical exams, and, most importantly, psychoanalytic treatment.

Indeed, psychoanalysis was, according to Lacan, the only discipline able to provide a coherent theory of subjectivity. For Lacan, the subject was never an isolated atom as many psychiatrists assumed. It was neither the autonomous Cartesian ego nor the transcendental Kantian mind. Rather, Lacan drew his theory of subjectivity from Hegel, whose thought Lacan studied in depth throughout the 1930s in the context of Alexandre Kojève's seminar on the *Phenomenology of the Spirit*.[63] The Hegelian subject, just like the Lacanian subject, was constructed in relation to others who were both the objects and the agents of desire. Psychiatry, Lacan thus argued, ought to abandon its focus on the brain or the will (central in Philippe Pinel's "moral treatment") to embrace instead the study of the unconscious. The influence of Hegel on Lacan was also evident in his theory of the "mirror stage," first presented at

---

59 Jacques Lacan, *De la psychose paranoïaque dans ses rapports avec la personnalité, suivi de Premiers écrits sur la paranoïa* (Paris: Éditions du Seuil, 1975), 15.
60 Lacan, *De la psychose paranoïaque dans ses rapports avec la personnalité*, 346.
61 Lacan, *De la psychose paranoïaque dans ses rapports avec la personnalité*, 311.
62 Lacan, *De la psychose paranoïaque dans ses rapports avec la personnalité*, 323.
63 On Lacan, Kojève, and Hegel, see Carolyn J. Dean, *The Self and Its Pleasures: Bataille, Lacan, and the History of the Decentered Subject* (Ithaca: Cornell University Press, 1992).

an International Psychoanalytic Association (IPA) congress in 1936 and which Lacan refined throughout his career. The mirror stage describes the reaction of a baby from age six to eighteen months, who, despite his lack of physical coordination, recognizes himself in a mirror. The child, who is carried by his parent, experiences his body as fragmented. Yet, the image he perceives is whole, integrated, and contained. This contrast produces a feeling of conflict and aggression, which the child attempts to overcome by identifying with the image, which in itself leads to a sense of jubilation. For Lacan, the mirror stage describes the structure of subjectivity more generally: The unconscious, self-defined by the free play of the drives, identifies with an ideal I, the ego, or the social self. This constitutive ambiguity in identity formation, this sense of fundamental alienation, is absolutely central to Lacan's work: Identifications are based on self-recognitions that are always already misrecognitions. The mirror stage, as Lacan will later argue, also marks the subject's entry into language. There is an imaginary dimension to this double process of language acquisition and identity formation, resulting from the sense of mastery, autonomy, and wholeness.

Lacan reworked his concepts of the Imaginary, the Symbolic, and the Real in his 1953 IPA paper "The Function and Field of Speech and Language in Psychoanalysis," also known as the Rome Discourse. A few months before his presentation, Lacan had – along with other French psychoanalysts – resigned from the Société Psychanalytique de Paris to found the Société Française de Psychanalyse. The relationship between Lacan and the IPA had been contentious for several years, particularly because of his practice of variable-length sessions, which could last from a few minutes to several hours. In this context, the Rome Discourse represented for Lacan a sort of theoretical manifesto for a new psychoanalysis: a new practice, a new discipline, and a new theory, one increasingly influenced by structuralism. Language was the starting point of Lacan's "return to Freud," because language, the patient's word, or *parole*, was the only medium available to psychoanalysis. Lacan opposed his notion of language to that of the ego psychologists or the behaviorist school interested in establishing "communication" with the patient. Psychoanalysis, he argued, ought to focus on the gaps in language, silences, paradoxes, symptoms, and dreams, even if they did not appear to communicate anything. The idea behind the variable-length sessions was precisely to revive the "talking cure" along Freud's guidelines, to set up a forum in which the unconscious, as opposed to the ego, could speak.

According to Lacan, contemporary psychoanalysts had overlooked Freud's two most important innovations: his invention of the unconscious and the crucial role of sexuality in all psychic formation and development. Both the unconscious and sexuality had a linguistic expression and could be studied only in relation to language. Thus, linguistics appeared as an essential complement to psychoanalysis. Lacan also borrowed from *The Elementary Structures of Kinship*. In particular, Lacan returned to Lévi-Strauss's system of structural equivalences between subjectivity, the social, and language, all of which were mediated by the prohibition of incest. Lacan's notion of castration operated similarly: No object could ever fully satisfy desire, not even the mother or the child, but other "small objects" (*objets petit a* as opposed to the big "Other") could come into being. Although these *objets a* generated desire, they also remained unobtainable. The structural lack of the object – the impossibility of having the full thing, *das Ding* – was once again analogous to the structural inability to ever have a full, transparent, immediate language. Just as Lévi-Strauss suggested that man could never return to a state of nature – which was by definition always already foreclosed – Lacan indicated that humans could never lead a purely instinctual existence.

The Imaginary, the Symbolic, and the Real, the three orders that Lacan would eventually represent in a "Borromean knot" to illustrate the mutual implication of the terms, were also defined in relation to castration and to language. The Imaginary, illustrated in the mirror stage, describes the identification of the ego and the specular image, the reflection of one's own body. The Imaginary is the realm not only of synthesis, plenitude, and duality, but also of alienation and illusion. The Symbolic is always already implicated in the Imaginary as the image of the parent holding the child suggests. If the Imaginary is the realm of the signified, the Symbolic is the realm of the signifier, of the "Other," and of radical alterity. The law that regulates desire in the Oedipus complex or that mandates the prohibition of incest is also located in the Symbolic. In this context, Lacan developed the notion of the *nom-du-père* ("name of the father"), based on the homophony *nom* as "name" and *non* as "no," to expand the role of the biological father in the Oedipus complex as the one who breaks the dual identificatory relation between mother and child and to designate broader structures of authority (other people, but also institutions such as the school, the army, and the law). Finally, the Real designates what escapes from both the Imaginary and the Symbolic, the undifferentiated, the traumatic, the impossible, that which cannot be expressed in language but always returns.

In 1963, the Société Française de Psychanalyse finally received from the IPA the official recognition that it had sought for years, but under the condition of

Lacan's exclusion. Following his "excommunication" from the IPA and the Société Française de Psychanalyse, Lacan founded yet another school, the École Freudienne de Paris, where he continued to imagine new, unorthodox practices to prevent the reification of the psychoanalytic theory and experience. In 1966, Lacan published his only collection of written texts, *Écrits*. His main teaching during those years was oral, in the form of his seminar, held first at the Sainte-Anne Hospital from 1953 to 1964, then at the École Normale Supérieure from 1964 to 1969, and finally at the Faculté de Droit until his death in 1981. After the 1970s, Lacan was increasingly attracted to mathematics, logic, and formalization as a way to represent certain psychoanalytic concepts differently and to avoid impasses of the written word.

Aside from his attention to language, Lacan's interest in structuralism was especially evident in two domains that preoccupied him throughout his life: in his understanding of neurosis, perversion, and psychosis; and in his analysis of sexual difference. While Freud conceived of neurosis, perversion, and psychosis as phenomenological categories, Lacan treated them as structures in which symptoms and behaviors may or may not always be present. Furthermore, he defined all three subjective structures around the modalities of avoiding or refusing castration, avoiding or refusing to live as decentered subjects who must contend with an inadequate language and with a lack of objects to fulfill their desire. In neurosis, the solution to this dilemma takes the form of seduction. Perversion is the "demonstration" or repetitive staging of a scenario directed toward the production of a specific *jouissance*, an unbearable pleasure. In psychosis, it expresses itself in the delusion. Lacan was particularly interested in the structure of psychosis, which resulted, he argued, from the foreclosure of the signifier, a "hole" in the Symbolic due to the absence of the *nom-du-père*. The psychotic is unable to function in the social just as he is unable to "signify" linguistically, to be understood. Psychosis, in this sense, represents the "outside" to the structuralist social contract that Lévi-Strauss had described in *The Elementary Structures*. As a psychic structure, sexual difference is reducible neither to sex (biological) nor to gender (social). Rather, sexual difference escapes representation. In this sense, Lacan claimed the concept of the phallus, a symbol of desire that was discursive rather than anatomical (as the penis functioned in Freud's work). Similarly, in 1972–1973, he devoted a seminar to feminine sexuality (Seminar XX: *Encore*) in which he made the famous declaration that "Woman does not exist" and that woman "is not-whole." Lacan, here again, should not be read literally: Women as biological and social creatures of course exist but not "The Woman" as the perfect fulfillment of desire. Throughout his career, Lacan worked and reworked his structuralist paradigm, his theory of the self, a theory of what it meant to be human, to be governed by desire, by language, and to have the ability to symbolize.

Marxism

One of the most consistent supporters of Lacan throughout his tumultuous career was Louis Althusser (1918–1990), who, in 1964, invited Lacan to hold his seminar at the École Normale Supérieure (ENS) where he acquired some of his most faithful disciples. Althusser was also responsible for popularizing structuralism throughout the 1960s within the ENS – one of France's most prestigious institutions of higher learning – and for developing a structuralist rereading of Marx. Althusser spent most of his life at the ENS, first as a student in philosophy and then, after the war, as *caïman*, the professor responsible for preparing students for the *agrégation*, a highly selective exam for future teachers. The *agrégation* program in philosophy included several canonical authors such as Hobbes, Spinoza, Locke, Montesquieu, Rousseau, Hegel, and Feuerbach, but Althusser also insisted on familiarizing his students with what he perceived as the most innovative philosophical currents of his time: structuralist linguistics, anthropology, and psychoanalysis.

Althusser's interest in structuralism coincided with his renewed interest in Marx's work. Although he had been a member of the French Communist Party (PCF) since 1948, Althusser began teaching and writing on Marx only after translating Ludwig Feuerbach's *Philosophical Manifestoes* in 1960. In 1961–1962, several of Althusser's students – a group which at various times included Pierre Macherey, Roger Establet, Étienne Balibar, Christian Baudelot, Jacques Rancière, Régis Debray, Jacques-Alain Miller, Alain Badiou, Robert Linhart, Jean-Claude Milner, Jacques Broyelle, and Benny Lévy – asked him to organize a seminar devoted to Marx's thought. In the heated political environment of the 1960s, many of these students were gravitating toward communism, and many would eventually join the Maoist organization Union des Jeunesses Communistes Marxistes–Léninistes (UJCml) after 1966. In this context, the correct reading and interpretation of Marx seemed imperative.

As Althusser told them, however, reading Marx by himself was not enough. Thus, from 1962 to 1963, the Marx seminar focused on "The Origins of Structuralism," and it included the works of Lévi-Strauss, Lacan, and Foucault. In 1963–1964, Althusser and his students deepened their knowledge of psychoanalysis in a seminar titled "Lacan and Psychoanalysis." Several of the students in that seminar would eventually participate in the creation of the *Cahiers pour l'Analyse*, a journal published between 1966 and 1969 that tried to push psychoanalysis toward a more abstract form of structuralism, one premised on logical and mathematic formalization.[64] Finally, from 1963 to 1964, the seminar centered on *Capital*. There, Althusser developed some of his most important theories on Marx, including the notions of symptomatic reading, epistemological break, overdetermination, structural causality, science, and ideology. In 1965, he published his two best-known works, the culmination of these years of reflection interweaving structuralism, psychoanalysis, and Marxist theory: *For Marx* and *Reading Capital* (co-authored with Étienne Balibar, Roger Establet, Pierre Macherey, and Jacques Rancière). Both of these texts established the foundation for a new "structuralist Marxism."[65]

Althusser's attraction to structuralism was the product of a particular political and intellectual conjuncture brought about by the death of Stalin in 1953. This conjuncture, as Althusser put it, was dominated by two "great events: the critique of the 'cult of personality' by the Twentieth Congress, and the rupture that has occurred between the Chinese Communist Party and the Soviet Communist Party."[66] The Twentieth Congress of the Communist Party of the Soviet Union (CPSU) in February 1956 did indeed profoundly shake the Communist world. In his famous "secret speech" to a closed session of the Congress, Nikita Khrushchev, who had taken over the Party's direction in 1953, condemned the cult of personality around the figure of Stalin and explicitly denounced Stalin's crimes and abuses of power. The "secret speech" sent shock waves throughout the Eastern bloc, especially in Poland, Yugoslavia, and Hungary, where dissident movements flourished and were immediately crushed. The CPSU was also at the origin of the Sino-Soviet split since the attack on the cult of personality had obvious implications for Mao, and since Khrushchev's behavior struck Beijing as particularly irresponsible. For many Communist intellectuals in Western Europe, these events also indicated that the "eastern wind" which would eventually prevail over the "western wind" was arriving not from the Soviet Union, but from the Far East, and, more specifically, from the Third World. If the working classes in the West appeared to have lost their revolutionary spark, the left needed to look elsewhere, in the Third World: in Africa, in Latin America, and in Asia. For many *gauchistes* who considered themselves on the left of the

---

64 See Peter Hallward and Knox Peden (eds.), *Concept and Form*, 2 vols. (London: Verso, 2012).
65 Étienne Balibar, "Althusser and the Rue d'Ulm," *New Left Review*, no. 58 (2009), 91–107, p. 95.
66 Louis Althusser, *For Marx* (London: Allen Lane, 1969), 9–10.

Communist Party – including many of Althusser's students – the Third World was now leading the way.

Althusser's "return to Marx" was thus "indispensable if we were to escape from the theoretical impasse in which history had put us."[67] As Althusser suggested, the correct interpretation of Marxist theory could determine the fate of the socialist revolution itself. More specifically, Althusser's endeavor was to rescue Marx from several misreadings that had produced this theoretical impasse: subjectivism, economism, historicism, and humanism. Structuralism offered an alternative to all these models at once. Humanism had become the rallying cry for Soviet Marxism after 1961 when Khrushchev declared during the Twenty-Second Congress of the CPSU that the dictatorship of the proletariat had been "superseded" in the Soviet Union and that his country was no longer a class State but a "State of the Whole People."[68] Humanism could justify the new Soviet policies of peaceful coexistence (since the fight between imperialism and communism was no longer perceived as inevitable), and of a potentially peaceful transition to communism (since class warfare was no longer a precondition). As Althusser summarized it in his 1964 essay "Marxism and Humanism," "the Soviet Union has proclaimed the slogan: All for Man, and introduced new themes: the freedom of the individual, respect for legality, the dignity of the person."[69] In parallel to this Soviet revival, the concept of "humanism" was also popular within French leftist circles during the 1960s. In 1962, the PCF had agreed to join a coalition of left-wing parties in the hope of winning the 1965 presidential elections. "Humanism" appeared as a consensual theme and political platform around which these various parties could gather. Furthermore, humanism appeared to be "in the air," as it featured centrally in the existentialist philosophies of Jean-Paul Sartre and Maurice Merleau-Ponty and as it was also championed by Catholic thinkers such as Teilhard de Chardin.

For Althusser, however, humanism was an *ideological* concept (*concept idéologique*), as opposed to a scientific one (*concept scientifique*): "When I say that the concept of humanism is an ideological concept (not a scientific one), I mean that while it really does designate a set of existing relations, unlike a scientific concept, it does not provide us with a means of knowing them. In a particular (ideological) mode, it designates some existents, but it does not

---

67 Althusser, *For Marx*, 21.   68 Althusser, *For Marx*, 11.
69 Althusser, *For Marx*, 221. See also Althusser, *For Marx*, 10–11.

give us their essences."[70] To clarify these terms, Althusser turned to Marx and proceeded to famously "periodize" his work. According to Althusser, the "Young Marx," closer to Kant and Fichte than to Hegel, still clung to a "philosophy of man" and to Enlightenment principles. However, in a second stage, from 1842 to 1845, Marx, who was increasingly disillusioned by the Prussian State's failures to reform, no longer appealed to the "reason of the State." Nonetheless, he was still unable to abandon the concepts of alienation and of human essence which would supposedly be fulfilled with the advent of the revolution. Marx's "epistemological break" (*coupure épistémologique*) (a term that Althusser borrowed from the philosopher of science Gaston Bachelard) came in 1845 as he sought to understand the logic of the capitalist system in history. The point of Marx's "science of history" was not to isolate a single cause (whether it be society, the economy, or ideology) but rather, to understand how the mode of production operates through a multiplicity of practices. According to Althusser, Marx's realization that humanism was an ideology and his subsequent radical anti-humanism became the condition for scientific knowledge and, consequently, for a real transformation of the politics.[71]

Althusser's structuralism also had significant consequences for his theory of subjectivity. One of the main challenges facing Marxist theory in the 1960s was understanding not only production but the "reproduction of the conditions of production." Althusser explored this question further in his 1970 essay "Ideology and Ideological State Apparatuses," in which he put forth his definition of ideology as the "imaginary relationship of individuals to their real conditions of existence."[72] Ideology was the unconscious mechanism through which individuals were coerced, but also the way individuals were produced, "interpellated" *as* subjects through ideological state apparatuses (ISAs) such as the school, the Church, the law, the family, and the political party. In this sense, ideology was not an illusion that could be escaped but rather a constitutive feature of subjectivity, similar to the incest prohibition for Lévi-Strauss and castration for Lacan. "Recognizing" ideology, Althusser explained, meant recognizing its necessity: "for the knowledge of this ideology, as the knowledge of its conditions of possibility, its structure, of its specific logic and its practical role, within a given society, is simultaneously knowledge of the conditions of its necessity."[73]

70 Althusser, *For Marx*, 223.   71 Althusser, *For Marx*, 227.
72 Louis Althusser, *Lenin and Philosophy, and Other Essays* (New York: Monthly Review Press, 2001), 109.
73 Althusser, *For Marx*, 230.

Post-structuralism

Many of the features attributed to post-structuralism were already prominent in structuralism, in particular the suspicion of ideology, humanism, meta-narratives, metaphysics, closed and stable meanings, and origins. Both structuralism and post-structuralism insisted on the mediating role of history and language in the construction of social and cultural artifacts. Post-structuralism is in this sense as difficult to define as structuralism, since most of the thinkers associated with this current – such as Michel Foucault (1926–1984) and Jacques Derrida (1930–2004) – remained ambivalent regarding the label. Furthermore, Foucault's and Derrida's works shared many explicitly structuralist sensibilities. Foucault's notion of governmentality, for example, resonated in many ways with Althusser's analysis of ideology. Both authors stressed how particular institutions (such as the asylum, the prison, the family, the school) and specific discourses of power–knowledge (around madness, crime, pedagogy, sexuality, the economy) produced different forms of subjectivities while at the same time coercing these into molds. For Foucault and Althusser, power and ideology are thus inescapable since they are the condition of subject production: There is no human core, no subject prior to power or to ideology. In this sense, Foucault locates political agency not in a form of liberation or escape from power but rather in the act of demystification, historicization, and critique – something he tried to do in his various works, from *Madness and Civilization* (1960), *The Order of Things* (1966), and *Discipline and Punish* (1975) to the *History of Sexuality* (1976) and the courses at the Collège de France.

Foucault's prediction in the conclusion to *The Order of Things* that man would disappear "like a face drawn in the sand at the edge of the sea" also corroborated Barthes's theories concerning the death of the author and the importance of immanent criticism. Barthes was especially important for Jacques Derrida, who shared his interest in textuality, *écriture*, reading, and synchronic analysis, all of which were central in Derrida's notion of *différance*, play, and deconstruction more generally. But while structuralism played a foundational role in Derrida's philosophy, Derrida was also responsible for elaborating one of the most important critiques of structuralism, first in a lecture entitled "Structure, Sign, and Play in the Human Sciences" delivered at Johns Hopkins University in 1966 and later expanded in his 1967 book *Of Grammatology*. Specifically, Derrida accused structuralism, and in particular Claude Lévi-Strauss, of remaining caught in the binary oppositions and the "metaphysics of presence" of Western philosophy. In the case of

Lévi-Strauss, these "metaphysics of presence" were especially obvious, Derrida argued, in the opposition between nature and culture in the *Elementary Structures of Kinship*, the opposition that allows Lévi-Strauss to present the prohibition of incest as a "scandal." As Derrida puts it,

> Obviously there is no scandal except within a system of concepts which accredits the difference between nature and culture. By commencing his work with the *factum* of the incest-prohibition, Lévi-Strauss thus places himself at the point in which this difference, which has always been assumed to be self-evident, finds itself erased or questioned. For from the moment when the incest-prohibition can no longer be conceived within the nature/culture opposition, it can no longer be said that it is a scandalous fact, a nucleus of opacity within a network of transparent significations. The incest prohibition is no longer a scandal one meets with or comes up against in the domain of traditional concepts; it is something which escapes these concepts and certainly precedes them – probably as the condition of their possibility. It could perhaps be said that the whole of philosophical conceptualization, which is systematic with the nature/culture opposition, is designed to leave in the domain of the unthinkable the very thing that makes this conceptualization possible: the origin of the prohibition of incest.[74]

For Derrida, Lévi-Strauss's inability to give up transcendental signifiers is symptomatic of structuralism's complicity with metaphysics, a philosophy dreaming of deciphering origins, of discovering reassuring foundations and asserting full presence. It is in contrast to this philosophical project that Derrida proposed another mode of reading, "one no longer turned toward the origin, [which] affirms play and tries to bypass man and humanism,"[75] a mode of reading sometimes called "post-structuralism."

---

74 Jacques Derrida, *Writing and Difference*, trans. Alan Bass (Chicago: University of Chicago Press, 1978), 283.
75 Derrida, *Writing and Difference*, 293.

19
Post-structuralism: From Deconstruction to the Genealogy of Power

JULIAN BOURG AND ETHAN KLEINBERG

Summarizing post-structuralism faces an initial challenge since as a style and a form of thought it submits to self-reflexive criticism the identity, clarity, and fixedness of delineation itself. By definition it problematizes definition in ways that take issue with the task of concise historical appraisal. Still, we can distinguish two generative scenes: French thought in the 1960s and 1970s, and its global reception. Reflecting complex similarities to and differences from structuralism, post-structuralist styles of thought came to be associated with diverse figures such as Louis Althusser, Roland Barthes, Jean Baudrillard, Hélène Cixous, Guy Debord, Gilles Deleuze, Jacques Derrida, Michel Foucault, Félix Guattari, Luce Irigaray, Julia Kristeva, Jacques Lacan, and Jean-François Lyotard. The term post-structuralism, however, never resonated a great deal in France itself. More than a tendency but less than a school, post-structuralism became a truly global, late-twentieth-century intellectual phenomenon from the 1970s through the 1990s. Its incalculable influence was felt first in fields such as literary criticism, film studies, and feminism, then in cultural and postcolonial studies, history, the social sciences, art history and musicology, professional studies, in the arts, and even extended to popular culture. But how did this tremendous movement come about? How did structuralism come to be untied from its post?

Forming a heterogeneous field, supposed post-structuralists seldom agreed among themselves: Derrida and Foucault famously fought over the meaning of madness and Descartes; Deleuze and Foucault parted company over the emancipatory potential of desire; Baudrillard said to forget both Foucault and Deleuze because resistance in the era of simulation was futile. Seen from afar, however, such differences tended to be overlooked, especially insofar as various French thinkers were often lumped together. The notion that post-structuralism shared common traits was thus largely a function of extrinsic reception and historical retrospection, coherence emerging at a distance and after the fact. The qualities of what became known as neo-structuralism, superstructuralism, French theory, deconstruction (a particular approach sometimes conflated with the whole), or postmodernism (a more general phenomenon) appeared in the aggregate. To some extent, post-structuralism was a diffuse "assemblage" (Deleuze and Guattari) characterized first of all by what it opposed: humanism, metaphysics, the state, etc., what Irigaray called "the economy of the Same." In another way, the formal conditions of post-structuralism's development and its substantive claims could be seen to converge: Texts could not be contained by contexts, frameworks, and disciplines; systems depended on exclusions and exceptions possessing disruptive capacity (wherein the obligatory gesture of saying that reducing post-structuralism to a chapter in the history of European thought is in some sense to betray it). Bywords such as textual effect, margin, and difference could apply both to a conceptual repertoire and to the circumstances that gave rise to it. Post-structuralism involved productive reception of texts beyond authorial intent; it derived from an original center – France – but flourished outside its boundaries; and the closer one looks the more differences gather. Its interpretive appropriations paradoxically collapsed distinctions among thinkers in favor of a projective identity while treating theory as a potentially limitless mobile procedure or space of critique dissociated from particular authors, a meta-language and move away from traditional philosophy and the human sciences.

Notwithstanding the fact that there was never any self-proclaimed post-structuralist movement with a programmatic core, by the 1980s outside of France this constellation of thought was nevertheless understood as sharing common characteristics related to language, subjectivity, desire, history, and politics:

- akin to other expressions of the twentieth-century "linguistic turn," the treatment of language less as a transparent means of communication than as opaque codes or discourses in need of critical explication;
- a general celebration of margins and the marginal, difference, disjunction, alterity, absence, instability, indeterminacy, play, heterogeneity, and pluralism – together with (1) a concomitant deprecation of metaphysics, essentialism, homogeneity, foundationalism, universalism, and rationalism, and (2) the disruption of simplistic either–or thinking drawing facile contrasts between center and margin, same and different, self and other, etc.;
- strong suspicions about the humanist unified self as well as the restoration of the problems of subjectivity and embodiment against methods such as structuralism that had downplayed them;

- a celebration of unfettered desire but also worries about the promises of free-for-all emancipation;
- a critique of totalizing, teleological, and progressive views of history coupled with renewed attention to temporality, becoming, process, open-endedness, rupture, and events;
- a rejection of politics centered on the state or other "molar" (Deleuze and Guattari) formations in favor of analyses of power's diffuse operations and of culture's role in domination; an emphasis on tactics of antinomian resistance, local performance, and the prioritization of gender, race, and sexuality in ways that asserted the emancipatory potential of anti-essentialism, anti-humanism, and the critique of Western ratiocination.

While no alleged post-structuralist thinker ascribed to all of these qualities, post-structuralism as a global style of thought has had a life of its own. Like earlier modes of immanent criticism, it sought to expose unreflective or naturalized positions. Yet it often minimized or concealed the criteria that enabled its denuding moves, dissecting as well the various authoritative metaphors, structures, and binary oppositions on which Western thought has long relied (such as surface/depth, darkness/light, truth/falsehood, and philosophy/poetry). Neologisms devised to express non-traditional positions could be seen to yield original, sometimes abstruse positions, and breaking down genre distinctions contributed productively to the rise of interdisciplinarity. The view that stability itself was constraining and imperious, together with an embrace of salutary instability, made an intellectual virtue of modest provisionality. The notion of a substantial self consistent over time (the soul, ego, etc.) was treated as a philosophical conceit and historical artifact and contrasted to versions of a decentered, minimalist subject, as in Deleuze and Guattari's schizoanalysis or Lyotard's view of subjectivity as a nodal point at the intersection of different language games. Self-consciousness about stylistics, sometimes to the point of deliberately cultivated opacity, intended to curb the tendency of thought toward tyrannical identity and homogeneity, came to be recognized as one of post-structuralism's principal characteristics. It prioritized peripheries in ways that challenged various kinds of centers – perspectival truths against Truth, minor literatures against the canon, local mobilizations against state power, and multiple, differential, and marginalized histories against monolithic History.[1]

---

[1] On "core" and "limit" see James Williams, *Understanding Poststructuralism* (London: Routledge, 2005), 1–24.

Post-structuralism

Many qualities of post-structuralism were not without precedent. Precursors variously included the Comte de Lautréamont, Stéphane Mallarmé, Antonin Artaud, André Breton, Mikhail Bakhtin, Pavel Medvedev, Martin Heidegger, Georges Bataille, Maurice Blanchot, Emmanuel Lévinas, Jean Cavaillès, and Georges Canguilhem. The master thinkers of a "hermeneutics of suspicion" – Karl Marx, Friedrich Nietzsche, and Sigmund Freud – already pointed to the path of post-structuralism, most especially Nietzsche whose critique of truth and emphases on interpretation, power, and style in philosophy were often cited explicitly and with admiration by post-structuralists themselves.[2] Even Jean-Paul Sartre could be taken as a forerunner insofar as his notion of *nothingness* suggested "the foundationless-ness of foundations."[3] Yet, as we will see below, it was post-structuralism's similarities to and differences from structuralism that mattered most. With the exception of Claude Lévi-Strauss, who was never counted among the post-structuralists, most thinkers associated with structuralism contested that label, and such contestation helped open fissures through which post-structuralism would emerge. Foucault's disavowal that he was a structuralist, for instance, contributed to the perception that a rupture had developed. Lacan and perhaps Althusser could be read as bridging the divide, and some have distinguished between Barthes's early structuralist and later post-structuralist phases. Deleuze's treatment of structuralism, emphasizing the themes of symbol, system, difference, singularity, series, and empty place, was framed by his own non-structuralist projects.[4]

As a kind of immanent criticism, post-structuralism "took on" structuralism in the dual senses of continuing and opposing.[5] It shared with its antecedent an appreciation for the impersonality of languages and systems, the anti-humanist implications of which it often extended. Similarly, both forms of thought criticized monolithic, teleological, and progressive philosophies of History. Differences appeared in part through the intensification of structuralist techniques, yet the structuralist pursuit of comprehensive or totalizing systems seemed flawed since certain elements always escaped attempts to contain and control them. Structures, it turned out, depended on their parts

---

[2] Paul Ricœur, *Freud and Philosophy: An Essay in Interpretation*, trans. Denis Savage (New Haven: Yale University Press, 1970), 32.

[3] Michael Ryan, "Marxism and Poststructuralism," in *The Cambridge History of Literary Criticism, Volume IX, Twentieth-Century Historical, Philosophical and Psychological Perspectives*, ed. Christa Knellwolf and Christopher Norris (Cambridge: Cambridge University Press, 2001), 102.

[4] Gilles Deleuze, "How Do We Recognize Structuralism?" (1967), in *Desert Islands and Other Texts, 1953–1974* (Los Angeles: Semiotext(e), 2004), 170–192.

[5] Simon Choat, *Marx through Post-structuralism: Lyotard, Derrida, Foucault, Deleuze* (London: Continuum, 2010), 13.

and margins. Likewise, temporality eluded efforts at synchronic mastery. Whereas structuralism had flattened and spatialized history, post-structuralism reintroduced contingency, variability, and open-endedness. Against synchronic structures, it asserted the irruptive, uncontrolled quality of diachronic historicity and events. In contrast, structuralist aspirations to general or universal laws could seem idealist. Alan Schrift sees post-structuralism as a "distinctly philosophical response" to structuralist human science, yet it also broke down genre distinctions, for example, between philosophy and literature.[6] Beyond unpacking the immanent logic of texts, it attended to the productive exchanges between texts and readers – how texts were used. And if the so-called death of the author, *à la* Barthes and others, drew on structuralist anti-humanism, by the same token post-structuralism began to revive the subject as a problem and question to consider. José Guilherme Merquior contrasted structuralism's "kaleidoscopic" approach to holism and universality to post-structuralism's "mantic outlook": "pointing at the place of meaning without naming it."[7]

After Structuralism

In order to fully discern the cause and moment of post-structuralism's separation from structuralism, we must begin by examining the ways in which post-structuralism derived from, and maintained affinities with, its predecessor. While the figures of Marx, Nietzsche, and Freud are "more commonly associated with French philosophy *after* structuralism, it was really the structuralists' desire to locate the underlying structures of kinship, society, or the unconscious" that led them to these thinkers in an attempt to "decipher the superstructural world in terms of underlying infrastructural relations of economic forces and class struggle, relations of normative forces and wills to power, and relations of psychic forces and unconscious libidinal desires respectively."[8] As we have seen, what was at work in thinkers like Althusser, Lacan, and Lévi-Strauss was an attempt to develop a more

---

6 Alan D. Schrift, "Introduction" to Alan D. Schrift (ed.), *The History of Continental Philosophy, Volume 6: Poststructuralism and Critical Theory's Second Generation* (Chicago: University of Chicago Press, 2010), 2 and 5.
7 In Merquior's view, with the exception of Lacan, many post-structuralists were often non- or anti-structuralist. Derrida and Foucault shared an adherence to a "Nietzschean formalism" that denied objective, disinterested knowledge. José Guilherme Merquior, *From Prague to Paris: A Critique of Structuralist and Post-structuralist Thought* (London: Verso, 1987), 190–199.
8 Alan D. Schrift, *Twentieth-Century French Philosophy: Key Themes and Thinkers* (Malden: Blackwell Publishing, 2006), 42.

rigorous, more modern, and more solid science of man based on the structures that form our world and society. Hence, following Camille Robcis's analysis in the previous chapter, Lévi-Strauss concludes that Freud's "hesitations" in *Totem and Taboo* are revealing: "They show a social science like psychoanalysis ... still wavering between the tradition of an historical sociology ... and a more modern and scientifically more solid attitude, which expects a knowledge of its future and past from an analysis of the present."[9] This "more modern and scientifically more solid attitude" is structuralism.

We want to linger on two factors that can be drawn from the quotation above and from the structuralist project. First, paramount to this new "science of man" was an emphasis on linguistics: This was the main area of convergence between the structuralists and the post-structuralists. The influence of Ferdinand de Saussure, Roman Jakobson, and Lévi-Strauss as well as Lacan, Althusser, and Barthes led younger intellectuals such as Derrida, Foucault, Kristeva, and Pierre Bourdieu to engage with the emphasis on language and its structure. But it also led them to question the efficacy and underlying principles of traditional philosophy and history. Phenomenology, hermeneutics, Marxist humanism, and existentialism became obvious targets because of the way in which the structuralist paradigm sought to demote the significance of the individual subject while emphasizing the general relations that govern social practices. At this level it can be said that structuralists were united by their commitment to Saussurean linguistics and thus a series of methodological rather than philosophical assumptions. Like the structuralists before them, post-structuralist thinkers were also keen to embrace the turn to language, which had promised a more rigorous scientific approach, along with a radical critique of humanism, philosophy, and history. But unlike their predecessors, post-structuralists were unwilling to dispel or dismiss philosophy or history wholesale, nor thinkers such as Immanuel Kant, G. W. F. Hegel, Edmund Husserl, and Martin Heidegger, notwithstanding the merits of the structuralist critique.

The second factor from the quotation above is the emphasis on a knowledge of the future and the past that is based on an analysis of the present. This is a synchronic approach to the human and social sciences where, as Lévi-Strauss puts it, we find "explanation in the permanent structure of the human mind, rather than in its history."[10] This synchronic

---

9 Claude Lévi-Strauss, *The Elementary Structures of Kinship* (Boston: Beacon Press, 1969), 492.
10 Lévi-Strauss, *The Elementary Structures of Kinship*, 491.

approach marked a decisive shift away from the emphasis on either origin or telos that had long informed traditional philosophy or history. Indeed, the emphasis on the permanence of signifying structure and synchronic investigation rendered diachronic history superfluous to, and symptomatic of, the network of signification under investigation. The novelty of the approach and the emphasis on the structure of language proved attractive to younger thinkers, but for the figures most often associated with post-structuralism, the seemingly static, ahistoric nature of the permanently available structure appeared inadequate to the task of accounting for change over time.

We see both the points of agreement and the areas of dissent if we recall the 1966 symposium on "The Languages of Criticism and the Sciences of Man" held at the Johns Hopkins University Humanities Center in Baltimore, Maryland and specifically in Derrida's contribution, "Structure, Sign, and Play in the Discourse of the Human Sciences." The symposium marked both the apogee of structuralism and the birth of post-structuralism, announcing structuralism's decline in the same breath as its ascension. Organized by Eugenio Donato, Richard Macksey, and René Girard, the symposium was the inaugural installment in a two-year program of seminars and colloquia whose goal was to explore the impact of contemporary 'structuralist' thought on critical methods in humanistic and social studies.[11] Several issues can be gleaned from the event of the conference. The first is that the organizers, and the Ford Foundation which sponsored the endeavor, deemed structuralism a sufficiently promising advance in scholarship to warrant such an investment. Second, there was significant interest in the Gallic variant of structuralism among academics in the United States. But it is also worth noting that, while the organizers were keen to bring French proponents of structuralism to the United States, they also sought to balance the structural contingency by inviting some key figures affiliated with the more traditional variants of philosophy, such as Jean Hyppolite, to provide alternative arguments to the structuralist paradigm. This indicates the way that the organizers believed they had recruited a block of structuralist thinkers without fully realizing the internal divisions among them, which were exacerbated by the presence of Hyppolite.

By 1971, the organizers could see clearly the rifts between the participants, and the edited volume based on the conference took as its name *The Structuralist Controversy*. In the 1971 edition, Macksey and Donato state

---

[11] Richard Macksey and Eugenio Donato (eds.), *The Structuralist Controversy: The Languages of Criticism and the Sciences of Man* (Baltimore: Johns Hopkins University Press, 1970), xv–xvi.

that "Today we may question the very existence of structuralism as a meaningful concept ... With the exception of Lévi-Strauss, all those whose names have come to be associated with structural theory – Foucault, Lacan, Derrida – have felt obliged programmatically to take their distance with relation to the term."[12] Here we see that the symposium intended to announce structuralism's arrival actually called its very existence into question. And while it is true that "evidence was already available in the Johns Hopkins symposium of the ensuing moment of theoretical deconstruction," such an evaluation was by no means obvious in the years leading up to the symposium, when a different understanding seemed warranted.[13] In his 1963 essay *Force et signification*, Derrida (1930–2004) characterized the "structuralist invasion" as "an adventure of vision, a conversion of the way of putting questions to any object posed before us, to historical objects – his own – in particular."[14] Derrida's enthusiasm at the possibilities offered by structuralism is evident in his prose: "since we take our nourishment from the fecundity of structuralism, it is too soon to dispel our dream."[15] Thus there were compelling reasons to align Derrida with the structuralist project, though it is important to note that Derrida's sustained interest in phenomenology, hermeneutics, and the question of history in philosophy places him at odds with structuralism, and this makes him a particularly instructive figure through which to illustrate the general similarities and differences between structuralism and post-structuralism.

The full force of the tension between structuralism and what came after is apparent in Derrida's presentation at the symposium: It illustrates the differences between structuralism and its post, but also some of the key concerns that run through the thinkers of post-structuralism even given their diverse strategies. It is significant that at a symposium devoted to the structuralist paradigm, Derrida began "Structure, Sign, and Play" with an appeal to history: "Perhaps something has occurred in the history of the concept of structure that could be called an 'event,' if this loaded word did not entail a meaning which it is precisely the function of structural – or structuralist – thought to reduce or to suspect."[16] What follows is a history of the concept of structure – a history of structuralism – that seeks to place the concept in

12 Macksey and Donato, *The Structuralist Controversy*, ix.
13 Macksey and Donato, *The Structuralist Controversy*, ix.
14 Jacques Derrida, *Writing and Difference*, trans. Alan Bass (Chicago: University of Chicago Press, 1978), 3. Originally published as *Force et signification*, *Critique*, nos. 193–194 (June–July 1963).
15 Derrida, *Writing and Difference*, 4.
16 Macksey and Donato, *The Structuralist Controversy*, 247.

a longer history of philosophy. The strategy deployed by Derrida is, at its most basic level, antagonistic to the axioms of structuralism.

Derrida begins by combing through the history, asserting that structure has long been at work in intellectual production as its organizing principle, even in the time before the structuralist paradigm came into play. "Nevertheless, up until the event which I wish to mark out and define, structure – or rather the structurality of structure – although it has always been involved, has always been neutralized or reduced, and this by a process of giving it a center or referring it to a fixed point of presence, a fixed origin."[17] Something or someone has always provided the structure with coherence, and this organizing principle is then located as a "center." By organizing coherence, the center allows for play or movement but within the confines of a total form: "The concept of centered structure is in fact the concept of a freeplay based on a fundamental ground, a freeplay which is constituted upon a fundamental immobility and a reassuring certitude, which is itself beyond the reach of the freeplay."[18] But, Derrida tells us, the function of structurality was rendered invisible by the emphasis on the particular mode of structuring at work in any given time or place. Thus, in Derrida's account, the whole history of the concept of structure before the rise of structuralism was a series of substitutions of center for center over time as each paradigm of understanding yielded to its successor.[19] But, on Derrida's reading, at a certain point the organizing structure itself became visible to its investigators and from that moment on it became necessary to investigate the question as to why proponents of the previous systems of thought felt compelled to posit such a center as well as the rules or laws proffered to account for such a center.[20] From this point on the organizing principle was seen no longer as an attribute of the center which holds the system, but as a function that is external to the system and serves as an explanatory cipher of how the system works. Here we see a shift from the concept of a fixed locus to that of a function.

Derrida locates the impetus for this shift or rupture in the space opened up by the work of Nietzsche, Freud, and Heidegger, and specifically the Nietzschean critique of metaphysics, the Freudian critique of self-presence, and the Heideggerean destruction of metaphysics.[21] In Derrida's history of the concepts of structure, it is the radical critique of traditional philosophy

---

17 Macksey and Donato, *The Structuralist Controversy*, 247.
18 Macksey and Donato, *The Structuralist Controversy*, 248.
19 Macksey and Donato, *The Structuralist Controversy*, 249.
20 Macksey and Donato, *The Structuralist Controversy*, 249.
21 Macksey and Donato, *The Structuralist Controversy*, 250.

and history provided by Nietzsche, Freud, and Heidegger that opens the space for structuralism. "One can in fact assume that ethnology could have been born as a science only at a moment when a de-centering had come about: at the moment when European culture – and, in consequence, the history of metaphysics and of its concepts – had been *dislocated*, driven from its locus, and forced to stop considering itself as the culture of reference."[22] The turn to the study of other cultures and their systems of meaning was possible only after the demotion of European "history" and "philosophy" from their perch as the arbiters of truth and understanding. Thus the "ethnologist accepts into his discourse the premises of ethnocentrism at the very moment when he is employed in denouncing them."[23] But by appealing to Nietzsche, Freud, and Heidegger as the source of the initial critique, and thus the progenitors of structuralism, Derrida also opens the possibility of a return to these thinkers and their respective investigative strategies to revisit the questions they interrogated in light of structuralism. Most notable is Derrida's own use of phenomenology to expose the limitations of structuralism. Leaving aside Derrida's deconstruction of the appropriation of "nature" and "culture" in Lévi-Strauss, where Derrida demonstrates that, rather than moving beyond the metaphysics of presence inherent in Western philosophy, Lévi-Strauss actually remains caught in its snares, we will turn to Derrida's assessment of the methodology by which Lévi-Strauss makes this move as well as Derrida's presentation of the ramifications.

Derrida explains the shift in methodology and epistemology by using the metaphors of the "engineer" and the "bricoleur." Derrida argues that in earlier understandings of thought a strong and autonomous subject was imagined to be the center or "engineer" of systems of thought. This subject would be the absolute origin of his own discourse and would construct it "out of nothing," "out of whole cloth."[24] Here the subject is the center of order, and Derrida tells us that the model is ultimately a theological one. By contrast, Derrida presents the structuralist paradigm as best understood by the *bricoleur*, who is willing to appropriate any and all methodologies or tools in the service of their endeavor. This is how Derrida describes the work of Lévi-Strauss, who conserves "in the field of empirical discovery all the old concepts, while at the same time exposing here and there their limits, treating them as tools which can still be of use."[25] Unlike the engineer, who is invested

---

22 Macksey and Donato, *The Structuralist Controversy*, 251.
23 Macksey and Donato, *The Structuralist Controversy*, 251.
24 Macksey and Donato, *The Structuralist Controversy*, 256.
25 Macksey and Donato, *The Structuralist Controversy*, 254.

in the truth-claims of his/her particular approach, the *bricoleur* conserves these methods only so long as they are of use, but is willing to abandon them if something more useful comes along. In doing so, the *bricoleur* exposes the privileged position of the engineer as a myth. The demotion of the engineer has far-reaching consequences according to Derrida because, and not without irony, central to this "critical search for a new status of the discourse is the stated abandonment of all reference to a *center*, to a *subject*, to a privileged *reference*, to an origin, or to an absolute *archè*."[26] Thus at the center of the structuralist exile of the center and abandonment of the subject is the mythopoetic function that exposes the function of the center as a myth.

Derrida goes further, arguing that a structural analysis no longer requires an understanding of origins in the past or goals for the future. One need not study the history of a myth to understand it. Derrida quotes Lévi-Strauss instructing us that just as linguists need not investigate the totality of words that have been uttered to perform an analysis of a given sentence, the structural anthropologist has no need for a historical analysis of a myth to perform their analysis.[27]

For Derrida, the structuralist event had decided benefits but also limitations. On the one hand, it exposed the limits of "history" and traditional metaphysics, but on the other hand, by forsaking history, it remained beholden to the history of traditional metaphysics. Derrida first explained the benefit of the structuralist critique which "by reducing history ... has treated as it deserves a concept which has always been in complicity with a teleological and eschatological metaphysics, in other words, paradoxically, in complicity with that philosophy of presence to which it was believed history could be opposed."[28] Here, Derrida was interested in the merits of a critique that exposed the ways "history" is complicit with the program of traditional metaphysics and the privileging of presence. But Derrida also indicated that, while it is legitimate to criticize this concept of history, there is also a risk, if it is reduced without confronting the problem, "of falling into an ahistoricism of a classical type ... More concretely, in the work of Lévi-Strauss it must be recognized that the respect for structurality, for the internal originality of the structure, compels a neutralization of time and history."[29] For Derrida, this is the blind spot of structuralism and the vantage point of post-structuralism. In François Dosse's account, "Derrida should be

---

26 Macksey and Donato, *The Structuralist Controversy*, 256.
27 Macksey and Donato, *The Structuralist Controversy*, 260.
28 Macksey and Donato, *The Structuralist Controversy*, 262.
29 Macksey and Donato, *The Structuralist Controversy*, 263.

considered the person who pushed the structuralist logic to its limits and toward an even more radical interrogation of all substantification of founding essence, in the sense of eliminating the signified."[30] From the start to the finish, Derrida injected his paper with his concerns about history and temporality to substantiate his critique of structuralism's own lack of history. In the end, for Derrida, "one can only describe what is peculiar to the very structural organization only by not taking into account, in the very moment of this description, its past conditions: *by failing to pose the problem of the passage from one structure to another, by putting history into parentheses.*"

Thus one unifying feature of post-structuralist thought is the desire to take history out of parentheses to reintroduce the problems of temporality and change, each a key component of "difference." This, of course, was by no means a return to the traditional understanding or methodologies of history or philosophy but one that sought to revisit the concerns of these fields from the other side of the structuralist critique. Here the return to thinkers like Nietzsche, Freud, Husserl, and Heidegger served the purpose of crafting a structuralism that moved beyond structuralism by reintroducing the problem of time and of the subject. Derrida makes this last part clear in his response to a question during the discussion portion of the symposium: "The subject is absolutely indispensable. I don't destroy the subject; I situate it. That is to say, I believe that at a certain level both of experience and of philosophical and scientific discourse one cannot get along without the notion of subject."[31] This emphasis on the questioned and questionable subject in time, what Kristeva calls "le sujet en procès," meaning "in process" and "on trial," is also a part of the post-structuralist legacy.

The Subject after Structuralism

The early work of Kristeva (1941–) gives us purchase on the ways in which post-structuralist thinkers sought to re-evaluate the "subject" after structuralism. Like Derrida and Foucault, Kristeva recognized the limitations of structuralism but came to her assessment of this movement with a different set of intellectual tools than her French counterparts. Kristeva was born in Bulgaria, where she attended a francophone school and then the University of Sofia. Her life in an Eastern Bloc country gave her a decidedly

---

30 François Dosse, *History of Structuralism, Volume 2: The Sign Sets, 1967–Present*, trans. Deborah Glassman (Minneapolis: University of Minnesota Press, 1997), 19.
31 Macksey and Donato, *The Structuralist Controversy: The Languages of Criticism and the Sciences of Man* (Baltimore: Johns Hopkins University Press, 1970), 271.

different perspective and education. Kristeva was fluent in Russian and developed an advanced understanding of Marxist theory and also Russian Formalism. In addition, she was deeply influenced by the work of Mikhail Bakhtin and instrumental in introducing his work to France. At the end of 1965 Kristeva was awarded a research fellowship to study in Paris and in so doing brought her unique constellation of influences to bear on structuralist thought as it had developed in France.

Kristeva's mastery of Marxist and Formalist theory allowed her to enter seamlessly into the intellectual conversations around structuralist thought, but her deployment of the works of Bakhtin and also Hegel enabled her to engage with this thought as critic and innovator. But there are two other factors to consider. In Σημειωτιϰὴ Kristeva asks whether "to work on language, to labor in the *materiality* of that which society regards as a means of contact and understanding, isn't that at one stroke to declare oneself a foreigner to language?"[32] Later, in her preface to *Desire in Language* Kristeva states that "It was perhaps also necessary to be a *woman* to attempt to take up that exorbitant wager of carrying the rational project to the outer borders of the signifying ventures of men."[33] While her particular training provided her with the tools to immediately engage with the French intellectual scene in the 1960s, her status as a foreigner among the French and a woman among men served as the crucible in which her critical innovations were forged.[34]

Soon after beginning her studies in Paris, Kristeva recognized structuralism's emphasis on synchrony and thus its historical limitations, and sought to use the work of Bakhtin to provide an account of dynamism that she believed structuralist work lacked.[35] As with Derrida, this led Kristeva to reconsider the position and functions of the subject in light of the structuralist critique of traditional philosophy while accounting for historical dynamism. Kristeva wanted to follow the structuralist move toward a systematic engagement with language and the production of discourse but by means of an investigation into the subject who emits and receives language. Thus Kristeva was critical of Cartesian philosophy and Husserlian phenomenology because of

---

32 Julia Kristeva, Σημειωτιϰὴ: *Recherches pour une sémanalyse* (Paris: Éditions du Seuil, 1969), 11.
33 Julia Kristeva, *Desire in Language* (New York: Columbia University Press, 1980), x.
34 See Toril Moi's insightful "Introduction" to *The Kristeva Reader*, ed. Toril Moi (New York: Columbia University Press, 1986), 1–19.
35 See Julia Kristeva, "Le mot, le dialogue et le roman," in Σημειωτιϰὴ: *Recherches pour une sémanalyse* (Paris: Éditions du Seuil, 1969); also see François Dosse, *History of Structuralism, Volume 2*, 55.

what she considered to be the overreliance on a rigid or ideal subject through which all meaning was supposed to flow, be it the Cartesian cogito or Husserl's transcendental ego. But she was equally critical of the structuralist attempt to remove such a subject in pursuit of systematic structures of meaning. Perhaps most importantly, she came to the conclusion that these seemingly opposite approaches were two sides of the same coin. In "Desire in Language," Kristeva argues that "structural linguistics and the ensuing structural movement seem to explore this epistemological space by removing the speaking subject. But on a closer look, we see that the subject that they legitimately do without is nothing but the subject (individual or collective) of historico-philosophical discourse."[36] Thus because "linguistics since Saussure adheres to the same presuppositions" as traditional philosophies of the ideal subject, "implicit within the structuralist current" are the same tendencies that "can be found in the philosophy of Husserl."[37]

For Kristeva, structuralism still bears the imprint of Husserl's transcendental ego and thus structuralists cannot get around Husserl's presentation of a sanitized and ideal subject. Even absent the subject itself, what is at stake in both cases is a model of pure unmediated meaning. But, for Kristeva, this understanding of both meaning and the subject is predicated on a static snapshot of any given moment in time that renders meaning as homogeneous and the subject as stable. On this reading, the Cartesian cogito and the Husserlian transcendental ego are each indicative of moments of stability that are fleeting but mistaken to be permanent. To return to the two sides of our one coin, phenomenology freezes the subject to render meaning stable, while structuralism silences the subject entirely to let meaning speak for itself. In both cases, according to Kristeva, what is lost is the role and place of the dynamic body as a constitutional aspect of the subject and meaning. The poverty of traditional philosophy was not the dominance of the subject as the structuralists supposed, but the underlying assumption that the subject and language are each the site of unified, homogeneous, and ultimately disembodied intellectual meaning, an assumption that Kristeva claimed the structuralists similarly maintained.

By contrast, Kristeva's investigation into the subject and language begins with the body and those aspects of bodily functions that ostensibly lie outside or beyond language and "meaning." Kristeva readily accepts that meaning-making and signification are essential aspects of language and self-

---

36 Julia Kristeva, "Desire in Language," in *The Portable Kristeva*, ed. Kelly Oliver (New York: Columbia University Press, 2002), 96.
37 Kristeva, "Desire in Language," 97.

understanding but is equally interested in exploring the role and place of the body in language acquisition as well as the places where language fails to make sense. Thus Kristeva is interested not only in the ways in which the subject is constituted via language but also in the places where the subject and language break down and what this can tell us. Here, Kristeva seeks to investigate the bodily drives, desires, and workings that are excluded from the Cartesian, phenomenological, and structuralist accounts. It is in this sense that Kristeva deploys the term "semiotic" to designate an investigation that seeks to account for the relation of bodily drives, instincts, incorporation, and excretions, and "clearly designates that we are dealing with a disposition that is definitely heterogeneous to meaning but always in sight of it or in either a negative or surplus relationship to it."[38] Kristeva seeks to differentiate what she calls the semiotic from more traditional fields of investigation which she refers to as the "symbolic." While the two are related, it has been the "symbolic," which Kristeva associates with scientific language, that has been dominant, while the "semiotic," which Kristeva relates to poetic language, has been marginalized. But, according to Kristeva, "it is poetic language that awakens our attention to this undecidable character of any so-called natural language, a feature that univocal, rational, scientific discourse tends to hide – and this implies considerable consequences for the subject."[39] Chief among these consequences is the ways in which this scientific or symbolic approach has served to "repress instinctual drive and continuous relation to the mother" and fostered a patriarchal order of logic wherein the rational subject or enduring structure is always coded as male. Here Kristeva is deploying the theory of instinctual drives and desires (Freud) and the formation of language as the Symbolic (Lacan), but she is also challenging Freud and Lacan's respective reliance on the figure of the father. For Freud this occurs through the Oedipal complex and the fear of castration; in Lacan this occurs through the "no" of the father which ushers the child into language and into law.

Kristeva follows the work of Freud and Lacan in asserting that the unconscious allows access, or at least insight, into the heterogeneity of the subject. But she posits our entrance into language and discourse as prior to the moment of symbolic understanding and inextricably related to our relationship with the maternal:

> The semiotic activity, which introduces wandering or fuzziness into language and, a fortiori, into poetic language is, from a synchronic point of

[38] Kristeva, "Desire in Language," 97.   [39] Kristeva, "Desire in Language," 103.

view, a mark of the working of drives (appropriation/rejection, orality/anality, love/hate, life/death) and, from a diachronic point of view, stems from the archaisms of the semiotic body. Before recognizing itself as identical in a mirror and, consequently, as signifying, this body is dependent vis-à-vis the mother. At the same time instinctual and maternal, the semiotic processes prepare the future speaker for entrance into meaning and signification (the symbolic).[40]

The workings of language and meaning are initially derived from bodily drives and a rhythmic relation with the mother (within whom one is incorporated and from whom one is then separated), but once differentiation occurs the wandering or fuzzy nature of the operation is displaced and repressed by the singular clarity of meaning. But the "unsettled and questionable subject of poetic language (for whom the word is never uniquely sign) maintains itself at the cost of reactivating this repressed instinctual, maternal element."[41] And it is thus to poetic language that Kristeva turns to investigate the moments of crisis, the unsettling process of meaning and subject that places into question the coherence of identity of either one or a multiplicity of structures.

For Kristeva, poetic language resists systematization or regulation and exists as a site of transgression and struggle. "Meaning and signification do not exhaust the poetic function" because the "poetic function departs from the signified and the transcendental ego and makes of what is known as 'literature' something other than knowledge: the very place where social code is destroyed and renewed."[42] It is in poetic language that one can discern what Kristeva refers to as the "questionable subject-in-process" referencing the temporal dimension of an ever-changing subject but also the way in which this subject is heterogeneous and non-coincident to itself and thus must be put on trial.

As a result, for Kristeva, the semiotician (in her sense of the word) is caught in the paradox of metalanguage, language about language, and thus is forced to reflectively analyze her own discursive position to avoid reifying and freezing the understanding of subject and meaning. This interminable self-reflective analysis keeps the semiotician in contact with the heterogeneous forces of language and the dynamic, unstable, subject-in-process.[43] The "pro" of such an approach is that it provides a sophisticated analysis of the subject positon in relation to language that accounts for unreason as well as reason

---

40 Kristeva, "Desire in Language," 104.   41 Kristeva, "Desire in Language," 104.
42 Kristeva, "Desire in Language," 101.
43 See Toril Moi, "Introduction" to *The Kristeva Reader*, 24.

but also the possibility of change over time. The "con" is that such an interminable investigation based on self-reflection can devolve into an endless self-obsessed exercise itself open to the charges of solipsism or "navel-gazing."

For our purposes, Kristeva's engagement with the subject demonstrates the movement beyond the intellectual parameters of structuralism and its predecessors insofar as this kind of heterogeneous economy of meaning and questionable subject-in-process called for a revision of linguistics "capable, within its language object, of accounting for a nonetheless articulated instinctual drive, across and through the constitutive and insurmountable frontier of meaning."[44] Thus it is the result of her particular historical moment that she comes to account for the subject after structuralism and can state that "It is only now, and only on the basis of a theory of the speaking subject as subject of a heterogeneous process, that semiotics can show that what lies outside its metalinguistic mode of operation – the 'remained,' the 'waste' – is what, in the process of the speaking subject, represents the moment in which it is set in action, put on trial, put to death: a heterogeneity with respect to system, operating within a practice and which is liable, if not seen for what it is, to be reified into a transcendence."[45]

Kristeva's treatment of the subject is particular to her own approach and impact on the field but also indicative of the larger trend among post-structuralist thinkers who sought to explore the subject as a limited but nevertheless dynamic agent within the context of a larger discursive web or network of signification.

History after Structuralism

Michel Foucault (1926–1984) powerfully illustrated the unwillingness to give up on history and subjectivity while at the same time, too, revisiting those themes from the other side of structuralist critique. From his earliest work on psychology in the 1950s through his engagement in the early 1980s with "practices of the self" in Antiquity and Patristic Christianity, he extended and overcame synchronic structuralist analysis rooted in linguistics. Foucault identified chiefly as a historian. He examined various discursive practices, institutions, power relationships, and models of subjectivity in historically identifiable circumstances. In spite of criticisms that he failed to explain *why*

---

44 Kristeva, "Desire in Language," 113.
45 Julia Kristeva, "The System and the Speaking Subject," in *The Kristeva Reader*, ed. Toril Moi (New York: Columbia University Press, 1986), 30–31.

change occurred and that his treatment of discourse and power was one-sidedly deterministic (the latter, an ultimately spurious charge), his various studies of madness, medicine, epistemology, prisons, and sexuality demonstrated historicist difference and the historical constitution of subjectivity. It has been customary to divide his intellectual career into three phases: archeology, genealogy, and "subjectivation" (*assujettissement*). In works of the first moment Foucault pursued the question of how human subjects came to see themselves and be seen by others as objects of knowledge. In *Madness and Civilization* (1961), for instance, he followed different configurations of "the mad" from medieval religiosity to Renaissance ironic wisdom to "the Great Confinement" of the 1600s to modern attempts to "cure" insanity. And in *The Order of Things* (1966) he traced epistemic shifts from Renaissance resemblance to Classical representation to the modern human sciences. These works led others to associate him with structuralism, an identification he immediately rejected.

The essay "Nietzsche, Genealogy, History" (1971) marked a new direction in his investigations of discourses, institutions, and subjects. The main publication of the genealogical phase, *Discipline and Punish* (1975), examined how modern institutions, notably prisons but also factories, schools, hospitals, asylums, and the military, produced selves through diffuse "microphysics of power" and mechanisms such as the all-seeing panopticon. Disciplinary knowledge and power acted on consciousnesses and consciences – "the soul is the prison of the body," he famously remarked. The pursuit of a notion of power beyond the model of sovereign states and autonomous individuals led next to the concept of biopower, the power to make live and let die, introduced in the first volume of his *History of Sexuality* (1976). There, he challenged the view that Victorians had repressed sexuality whereas in fact they had endlessly talked about it in efforts to segregate and contain it. Foucault's analyses of biopower in his mid-to-late-1970s lectures at the Collège de France led him in his final years to explore ethical and aesthetic models of self-formation in ancient Greece and Rome and early Christianity. Throughout his mature career from the early 1960s through the early 1980s, his research consistently circled back to historically embedded and thus contingent forms of reason and subjectivity: how different subjects are formed in time, how they form themselves, and the costs they pay for being obliged to tell the truth about themselves.

With increasing regularity after the late 1960s, Foucault denied any affiliation with the methods of structuralism, which, like phenomenology and Marxism, he described as forms of thought to be surpassed. By the same token, when eventually pressed in 1983, he said that he was unable to tell "what kind of problem is common to the people we call post-modern or post-structuralist."[46] Two poignant occasions when he attempted to differentiate his own projects from structuralism were the Conclusion to *The Archaeology of Knowledge* and the 1976 interview "Truth and Power" – the former marked the transition from archeology to genealogy and the latter that from genealogy to the problem of "subjectivation." *The Archaeology of Knowledge* offered a retrospective methodological statement on Foucault's three main early works: *Madness and Civilization, The Birth of the Clinic* (1963), and *The Order of Things*. In it, he introduced a topographic analysis of discourse, theorized the notion of the archival "statement," and distinguished the method of archeology from the history of ideas. This agenda, in its seemingly synoptic freeze-frame of the historical field, lent itself to a structuralist reading – a possibility to which Foucault replied in the Conclusion. The text took the form of an imagined dialogue between himself and a phenomenological critic who nonetheless admitted the value of structuralism. The critic began by observing that although Foucault had been "at great pains to dissociate" himself from structuralist thinking, the very categories he used in the book (formations, positivities, knowledge, discursive practices) seemed to rely on "fundamental themes of structuralism." Three structuralist inheritances appeared at work: closing the "openness" of language, discarding "the speaking subject," and reducing events to spatialized "simultaneity." Responding in his authorial voice, Foucault insisted on the "density" and differences *internal* to particular discursive systems: multiple enunciations, "discursive practices," and temporal accumulations, connections, successions, and so forth. The position approached Derrida's notion of "freeplay" discussed above. Remarking that uninteresting "polemics about 'structuralism'" were best left to "mimes and tumblers," Foucault seemed to share with Derrida the abandonment of an anchoring center.[47]

The imagined critic then complained that analysis of reason without subjectivity or without a sense of historical origin was unacceptable. Foucault acknowledged that he had wanted "to cleanse" history of "all transcendental narcissism" contained in the notions of "a continuous history" and "a constituent consciousness." Since Kant, he observed, "transcendental reflection" had

---

46 Michel Foucault, interview with Gérard Raulet, "Critical Theory/Intellectual History," in *Politics, Philosophy, Culture: Interviews and Other Writings, 1977–1984*, ed. Lawrence D. Kritzman (New York: Routledge, 1984), 34.
47 Michel Foucault, *The Archaeology of Knowledge*, trans. A. M. Sheridan Smith (New York: Pantheon, 1972), 199–201.

already been in crisis: The notion of origin obscured the "difference of our present" and the notion of the subject "allows us to avoid an analysis of practice."[48] Foucault was attempting to articulate a position from which both phenomenological and structuralist approaches could be questioned. However, the critic then challenged the legitimation of Foucault's own discourse: "Where does it come from and from where does it derive its right to speak?" Without epistemological foundations, was his work then merely descriptive? While conceding that "this question embarrasses me more than your earlier objections," Foucault replied that he had nevertheless sought to avoid a "ground," "a hidden law, a concealed origin," or a "general theory." Instead, building on the above notion of internal variation, the point was "to *make* differences" through "dispersion," "scattering," and "decentering." Neither traditional philosophy, nor conventional history, nor a plan for a future epistemology, his project involved "mapping" discursive practices.[49] Finally, to the charge that he himself had made "curious use of a freedom that you question in others," Foucault denied that his approach was deterministic. Simply because "determinations" were "conditions" of practices and "positivities" established a "field" of articulation did not mean that change was not possible. "I have not denied – far from it – the possibility of changing discourses: I have deprived the sovereignty of the subject of the exclusive and instantaneous right to it."[50] For Foucault as for Derrida, the task was not to expound a holistic systematic logic but rather to provide a map of differences so as to free up possibly multiple interpretations and explanations. Foucault insisted on the historicist dimensions of this procedure, considering events, discontinuities, ruptures, and non-deterministic openness. If suspicions of the phenomenological subject remained at the forefront, the stage was also set for Foucault's post-1968 focus on the theme of power, a focus accompanied by increasing attention paid to the subject in a reconstructive mode.

In the interview "Truth and Power" (1976), Foucault made clear how the category of power differentiated his methods from structuralism. The theme of power had emerged after the events of May–June 1968 through the "political opening created during those years" and his activist and scholarly work on prisons.[51] He declared his anti-structuralist esteem for the notion of

---

48 Foucault, *The Archaeology of Knowledge*, 203–204.
49 Foucault, *The Archaeology of Knowledge*, 205–208.
50 Foucault, *The Archaeology of Knowledge*, 208–209.
51 Michel Foucault, "Truth and Power," in *The Foucault Reader*, ed. Paul Rabinow (New York: Pantheon, 1984), 53.

event, on the condition that events were understood as always plural and comprised of different networks, levels, and connections. To the archeological analysis of enunciations and discursive practices was now added the "question of what *governs* statements, and the way in which they *govern* each other ... a problem of the regime, the politics of the scientific statement."[52] Foucault rejected the notion that power and discourse were easily separable and thus the view that some pre-existing force called power simply imposed itself on, or used, discourses to its own ends; rather, power and discourse were mutually constitutive and emerged together in what he called knowledge–power complexes. He thus sought to nuance the density and differences within discourses we saw above: "what effects of power circulate among scientific statements, what constitutes as it were, their internal regime of power, and how and why at certain moments that regime undergoes a global modification."[53] New in the 1970s were the metaphors through which such immanent politics and regimes operated: war and battle. Conflict and contestation impeded any synoptic or totalizing grasp of systems. What might have been implicit in early work on madness, medicine, and knowledge had become plain in *Discipline and Punish* (1975): the techniques, technologies, tactics, strategies, mechanics, and networks through which knowledge/power concretely operated – the different terms mattered because they referred to distinctive and mutually reinforcing operations. Foucault's question was *how?* not *why?* did power operate. The analysis was conjunctive, involving sovereign state power ("I don't want to say that the state isn't important"), disciplinary institutional power, and biopower (populations, sexuality, etc.).[54] How were truth and power related? "'Truth,'" he concluded, "is linked in circular relation with systems of power which produce and sustain it, and to effects of power which it induces and which extend it."[55] The political task was to pursue "the possibility of constituting a new politics of truth."[56] This approach also enabled a more explicit confrontation with the notion of the subject. "One has to dispense with the constituent subject, to get rid of the subject itself," Foucault said, "to arrive at an analysis which can account for the constitution of the subject within a historical framework."[57] The earlier rejection of the phenomenological subject, which Foucault, like Derrida, shared with structuralists such as Lévi-Strauss and Lacan, was now understood as a preliminary to freshly revisiting the issue of historical subjectivity. This undertaking was pursued in the late

[52] Foucault, "Truth and Power," 54.
[53] Foucault, "Truth and Power," 55.
[54] Foucault, "Truth and Power," 64.
[55] Foucault, "Truth and Power," 74.
[56] Foucault, "Truth and Power," 74.
[57] Foucault, "Truth and Power," 59.

lecture courses at the Collège de France and in the posthumously published second, third, and eventually fourth volumes of the history of sexuality project: The historical excavation of models of subjectivity in other times and places provided critical vantage points from which to reconsider what it meant to be a subject in our own time.

Philosophy after Structuralism

In his most influential work, *The Postmodern Condition* (1979), Jean-François Lyotard (1924–1998) asserted that the subject was "always located at 'nodal points' of specific communication circuits."[58] Drawing on systems and cybernetic theory and on Ludwig Wittgenstein's concept of "language games," he proposed a highly qualified, minimalist version of subjectivity that was characterized by difference ("the differend" in his terminology), interacted agonistically, and proved capable of ethics and justice. However, history, insofar as it provided legitimating stories of political emancipation and advancing knowledge, seemed a dead letter. Such "metanarratives" no longer successfully garnered widespread assent. Thought itself had to adjust to a new scene of plurality: Multiple local knowledges and discrete visions of emancipation had taken the place of the grand political and epistemological visions of the Enlightenment: reasons instead of Reason, dissensus in lieu of consensus, and incommensurability over universality. As we will see below, the situation offered possibilities as well as dangers.

The Postmodern Condition marked a transition from Lyotard's early to late contributions to the post-structuralist field: from explicitly anti-structuralist texts in the post-1968 moment – for instance, *Discourse, Figure* (1971) and *Libidinal Economy* (1974) – to writings on differential justice, aesthetics, and postmodernity – including *Just Gaming* (1979), *The Differend* (1983), and *Postmodern Fables* (1993). Lyotard's advantage vis-à-vis structuralism was that he had never been influenced by or associated with it. His first book, a 1954 introduction to phenomenology, was republished a dozen times before he died, and his early career had been spent teaching philosophy in Algeria and, until 1964, writing for the independent left publication *Socialisme ou Barbarie*. Lyotard settled accounts with structuralism in the wake of the events of May 1968. In *Discourse, Figure* he followed the tensions between two kinds of difference: on the one hand, distinctions based on conceptual

---

58 Jean-François Lyotard, *The Postmodern Condition: A Report on Knowledge*, trans. Geoff Bennington and Brian Massumi (Minneapolis: University of Minnesota Press, 1984), 15.

negation such as Ferdinand de Saussure's structural linguistics; and on the other hand, rendering found, for example, with visual aesthetics, embodiment, and gestures toward the non-representable. Rather than simply prioritize the figural over the discursive, Lyotard suggested instead that attempts to collapse the distinction between these two kinds of difference led to metaphysics. In *Libidinal Economy* he cut the final tie with his earlier Marxist commitments and with psychoanalysis by attacking Marx's and Freud's systematic repression of libidinal intensities; they had wrongly postponed the expression of desire by trapping it in rigid structures. The rejection of totalizing systematic logics, the concern to preserve difference as difference, and the sense of untamed mobility all found more ambitious articulation in *The Postmodern Condition*, originally commissioned by the government of Quebec as a report on the state of contemporary knowledge.

Beginning with the judgment that science had since the 1950s been treated as a discourse or commodity in relation to power, Lyotard observed that the central epistemological problem of the day concerned the legitimation of knowledge. The method of language games enabled him to revisit a foundational contrast between narrative and scientific knowledge. Modern science's commitment to procedures of verification and falsification was understood to have broken with traditional ways of knowing based in narrative (myths, religion). In recent years, Lyotard said, there had been growing recognition that science itself was a kind of narrative knowledge analogous to politics. "The hero of knowledge" and "the hero of liberty" were two sides of modern legitimation narratives: Knowledge and emancipation both improved over time. Yet, in the postwar era, such "grand narrative has lost its credibility" and was being replaced by the "computerization of society."[59] It had become increasingly difficult to grasp the social as a functional whole or as simplistically divisible, say, between the bourgeoisie and proletariat; rather society itself could be considered "flexible networks of language games."[60] In such a postmodern condition, access to information was key. Lyotard's final judgment was measured. On the one hand, the imperative of "performativity" threatened to reduce language games to instrumental, technically efficient inputs and outputs. It also raised the specter of dominating powers monopolizing information. On the other hand, a new postmodern science capable of conceptualizing undecidables, conflicts, fractals, catastrophes, and paradoxes offered other ways forward. "Paralogy" – suggesting both thinking beyond reason and biological

59 Lyotard, *The Postmodern Condition*, 37 and 47.   60 Lyotard, *The Postmodern Condition*, 17.

divergence – could be an antidote to performativity. As in science so too in politics, the challenge of the postmodern condition was to conceive of justice beyond "universal consensus" by embracing local differences and temporary agreements. For all to become polyglots of multiple language games might lead to "a politics that would respect both the desire for justice and the desire for the unknown."[61]

Conclusion

As an ideal type, post-structuralism could be understood politically as subversive, democratic, or quietistic. The celebration of differences and the marginal could be seen to hold unlimited transformational potential. The American intellectual historian Mark Poster referred to its embrace of open-endedness as its "utopian epistemological vantage point."[62] The freedom of the particular was asserted against the tyrannical authority of the universal, opening a potentially limitless range of expansive applications to feminism, post-colonialism, disability studies, and so forth. Some could see emancipatory or democratic possibility in play in its attention to alterity and anti-authoritarian thinking. Post-structuralism also seemed to offer a form of chastened realism in the sense that systems are never entirely determinative and that agency is never entirely free. Or at times the attractions of resistance, transgression, and anarchic subversion against social control seemed to predominate. For some critics, post-structuralism's slippery prevarications meant that its politics were inscrutable and even irresponsible, since it downplayed the significance of states, parties, and the law.

Originality was an issue for post-structuralism. Many of its advocates and detractors in the 1980s and 1990s emphasized its distinctive and supposedly unprecedented challenge to Western humanism. Hyperbolic worries about totalizing linguistic determination or the disappearance of the subject were widespread, if exaggerated. Like some of the postmodernist discourse to which it contributed, however, suggestions of novelty were tempered by a sense of exhaustion. Was post-structuralism merely the latest fashion, yet another in a succession of intellectual movements, or was it a welcome way of seeing that opened up seemingly limitless insight (e.g., the early modern decentered self, postcolonial margins, etc.)? The temporalities of the post

---

61 Lyotard, *The Postmodern Condition*, 67.
62 Mark Poster, *Critical Theory and Poststructuralism: In Search of a Context* (Ithaca: Cornell University Press, 1989), 9.

were not straightforward, and the issue of originality raised questions about origins and continuities.

Although critics of post-structuralism were never any more unified than its alleged progenitors, certain patterns could nonetheless also be identified. Together with charges of relativism and nihilism, accusations of turgid opacity and pantextualism came early and persisted. For all the self-reflexive appeals to openness, there could be something about post-structuralist discourse that seemed authoritatively impervious to criticism since its own confident assertions about language, power, desire, subjectivity, etc. were themselves seldom submitted to the kind of rigorous dismantling to which logocentrism, humanism, metaphysics, and so forth were subjected. In other words, the tendency to analyze other times and places seemed to forestall post-structuralists' scrutiny of the present conditions of possibility of their own thought. Two representative critics can be mentioned. The German philosopher Manfred Frank preferred hermeneutics to post-structuralism. Observing in 1983 that the latter designation seemed "too neutral," he acknowledged that the label "neo-structuralism" was also "somewhat misleading" since the field had preserved aspects of structuralism while radicalizing them. In his view, a break with "ethno-linguistic structuralism" had occurred around 1968, and neo-structuralism's overcoming of metaphysics linked it to a more general postmodern condition. The field was characterized by its emphasis on open and decentralized structures, the view that meaning took shape through the differential play of the non-meaningful (Derrida), misgivings about consensus (Lyotard) and about the universal theoretical subject, vitalistic desire (Deleuze), and a troubling foreclosure of "truly feasible alternatives."[63]

In step with Jürgen Habermas's contention that post-structuralism could not account for its own critical positions, Peter Dews argued that post-structuralism failed to detect one of its own significant blind spots: "the internal relation between subjective disintegration and the restoration of a featureless presubjective totality." In other words, the "diffuse heterogeneity of the exploded subject" lay in tension with "endless, objectified process," whether power, desire, or textual play. The Frankfurt School critical theorist Theodor W. Adorno had earlier diagnosed this dynamic as "the logics of disintegration," forswearing "the magical assumption that the fragmentation of knowledge will somehow break the grip of the object of knowledge." Without a clearly

---

[63] Manfred Frank, *What Is Neostructuralism?*, Foreword by Martin Schwab, trans. Sabine Wilke and Richard Gray (Minneapolis: University of Minnesota Press, 1989), 18–22, 76–77, and 86.

expressed view of the relation between identity and non-identity, post-structuralism was more a symptom of "an overbearing totality" than "a means to escape from it." Its characterization of Western subjectivity was something of a straw man and its political consequences remained unclear.[64]

Whatever they may have missed or mischaracterized, the many critics of post-structuralism were correct in observing that it represented a worldwide phenomenon of considerable significance. As both an explicit articulation and a symptom, its ideas related to *fin-de-siècle* fragmentary pluralization. Symbolically, it could be linked to the turbulent Sixties and the signature year of 1968; notions of difference, alterity, multiplicity, and anti-foundationalism resonated with contestation and new social movements.[65] Post-structuralism could furthermore be tied to social digitization and the shift to post-industrialization. For instance, Mark Poster saw it as arising from and providing critical purchase on "new language situations characterized by electronic mediation": a new "mode of information."[66] Part of the success of post-structuralism in, say, the United States stemmed from the fact that French structuralism had never been firmly rooted there. Through that American reception some thinkers known as structuralists in France were recast as post-structuralists.[67] The way post-structuralism arrived in the United States – for instance, different French authors published by the same American publishing houses – contributed to its apparently "timeless" quality.[68] The very success of post-structuralist theories and strategies led to the waning of an identifiable movement but also to seemingly infinite varieties, extensions, and elaborations.

One such elaboration reveled in Nietzschean excess and an increased attention to the playfulness of language and the use of playful prose. The emphasis on play at the expense of structure ultimately led to what one might call a post-structuralist fatigue, and it is certainly the case that in some quarters attention to rhetorical style came to outweigh attention to

---

[64] Peter Dews, *Logics of Disintegration: Post-structuralist Thought and the Claims of Critical Theory* (London: Verso, 1987), 229–231; and Jürgen Habermas, *The Philosophical Discourse of Modernity: Twelve Lectures*, trans. Frederick Lawrence (Cambridge: MIT Press, 1987).

[65] Luc Ferry and Alain Renault, *French Philosophy of the Sixties: An Essay on Antihumanism*, trans. Mary Schnackenberg Cattani (Amherst: University of Massachusetts Press, 1990).

[66] Poster, *Critical Theory and Poststructuralism*, 5 and 32.

[67] François Cusset, *French Theory: How Foucault, Derrida, Deleuze, & Co. Transformed the Intellectual Life of the United States*, trans. Jeff Fort (Minneapolis: University of Minnesota Press, 2008).

[68] Johannes Angermuller, *Why There Is No Poststructuralism in France: The Making of an Intellectual Generation* (London: Bloomsbury, 2015), 20, 71, and 74.

substance. Once the emphasis had come to focus solely on "play" absent the productive tension with the "structures" that both generated and constrained such "play," the "post" was untied from the "structure," leaving only a chain of free-floating signifiers. The backlash against what was seen as an excessive emphasis on language removed attention from the critical and self-critical post-structuralist agenda and gave rise to a returned emphasis on empiricism, materiality, and experience.

We would, however, be remiss to overlook the lasting legacy of the loose-knit phenomenon known as post-structuralism or the thinkers associated with it. One place to look is the continued interest in the role and place of language which, despite calls to immediacy, has become ingrained in the humanities and most social sciences. But the most important points are the sustained critique of the "subject" as a necessary but problematic focus of scholarly work and also the interminable relation between the synchronic analysis of structure and the diachronic analysis of change. This post-structuralist legacy was central to the work of influential feminist thinkers such as Luce Irigaray and Hélène Cixous. Here, as we saw in the work of Kristeva, the cultural and epistemological matrix that assumes the subject to be gendered male and then effaces this assumption under a claim of neutral objectivity is placed in permanent question. A similar strategic move is achieved by scholars of postcolonialism and subaltern studies, where the analysis seeks to expose the structures of power that enable the colonial endeavor but also the privileged position of the European or Western subject in traditional historical accounts. Most recently, this point of entry has been important for the field of animal studies, where the logic of human superiority or mastery is interrogated to re-examine the relationship between human and non-human animals. These fields are each far reaching and beyond the scope of this conclusion, but all involve a concerted interest in and engagement with questions of ethics. This, too, is a part of the post-structuralist legacy.

In the end, the phenomenon of post-structuralism is irreducible to either its critics or its seemingly paradoxical explanatory contextualization. It is a movement whose very origin lies in contesting the possibility of an origin but that nonetheless is deeply attuned to what a history without origins or ends might look like. Suspended between the structuralist paradigm it sought to contest and the previous models it hoped to re-deploy by means of the structualist critique, it embodies the hyphen of *post-structuralism*.

20

Contesting the Public Sphere: Within and against Critical Theory

DAVID INGRAM

This chapter examines how European thinkers working from within and without the Frankfurt School of critical theory have understood the public sphere as a distinctive political category. First-generation members of the school rejected institutional democracy and mass politics as ideologies that mask domination. The succeeding generation, whose most important representative is Jürgen Habermas, rejected that diagnosis. Habermas's more optimistic assessment of the emancipatory potential of the public sphere as a medium of rational learning sought a middle ground between critics and defenders of liberal democracy. This ambivalence provoked strong counter-reactions from systems theorists, such as Niklas Luhmann, and from adherents of theories of agonal democracy descended from Carl Schmitt, on the right, and Hannah Arendt, on the Left. As we shall see, these reactions are amplified by those who seek to extend the public sphere beyond the boundaries of the nation state. Because of its contested interpretation as a descriptive and normative category, the public sphere presents us with ambivalent possibilities for legitimating regional governing bodies, such as the EU, as well as the global legal institutions of the United Nations.

Early Frankfurt School Dismissal of the Public Sphere

The public sphere as we know it today was not a central category of first-generation critical theory except in the sense that it epitomized a symptom of modern administered society. It was mass democracy and the propagandistic manipulation of public opinion, after all, that gave rise to the totalitarian political movements of the twentieth century.

Although first-generation critical theorists recalled the bourgeois ideal of liberal democracy as a high point of the European Enlightenment, they believed that the economic and political conditions sustaining it had long been surpassed by the rise of industrial capitalism. In their opinion, even if the ideal was more than an ideology, given its utopian potential for realizing emancipatory, egalitarian, and communitarian aspirations, it clashed with the factual description of democratic politics they inherited from Marx and Weber and so was never taken seriously by them as a moral ideal that could ever have real purchase in modern political life.

As intellectuals who were committed to the Marxist critique of the state, first-generation critical theorists believed that politics passively mirrored economic class struggles. According to this interpretation, political interaction is fiercely partisan, non-consensual, and strategic. Here formal rights constitutive of liberal democracy, such as freedom of speech and freedom of association, appear not as universal norms serving the common interests of humanity but as false ideologies that conceal the true nature of the state as an instrument of bourgeois domination. Revolutionary politics thus reduces to a power struggle for hegemonic control of the state. In Antonio Gramsci's view, leaders of revolutionary movements (with the aid of "organic intellectuals") should mold their propaganda around the overlapping interests of diverse social groups in forming an oppositional united front. Compromises and strategic alliances between competing groups appear here as temporary weddings of convenience, nodal points in a precarious balance of power (*modus vivendi*) that serve the revolutionary struggle – hence Gramsci's Machiavellian disdain for moral scruples about fair play.[1]

The bourgeois ideal of the public sphere finds just as little purpose in the Marxist vision of post-revolutionary communist society. For Marx, the overcoming of class domination that would accompany the advent of communism would usher in a "dictatorship of the proletariat," which, in turn, would gradually terminate in the "withering away of the state" as a coercive legal order once social conflicts were pacified. Over time, the rational administration of productive machinery under the democratic control of producers would ostensibly give rise to material abundance and a reduction of the workday, so that individuals could spend their non-laboring hours developing their aesthetic, social, and intellectual capacities. Discussions about economic planning and culture, however mentally stimulating, fall short of that vibrant political life involving clashing institutional values and partisan interests.

The second factor inclining first-generation critical theorists to dismiss the public sphere was their reception of Max Weber's science of organizational

---

[1] Antonio Gramsci, *The Modern Prince and Other Writings* (New York: International Publishers, 1959).

rationality. Although Weber's starkly pessimistic view of modern, rationalized societies led them to reject the orthodox Marxist understanding of communist society as a domination-free society, it also entrenched their dismissal of the public sphere as a counter-model of enlightened freedom. Especially seminal for their thinking was Georg Lukács's *History and Class Consciousness* (1923), which represented one of the earliest attempts to translate Marx's theory of "commodity fetishism" into a Weberian register. Linking the commodity form (the exchange of equivalents) to analytic reasoning, he argued that the orthodox Marxist scientific understanding of society as a law-governed system, which he believed correctly captured the mechanical nature of capitalism, nonetheless concealed a more revolutionary, dialectical understanding of society as a contradictory totality.

Weber had described modern capitalism in similar terms, as a regime that placed on the individual not just a light cloak of easily discarded material comfort but a hard shell (*stahlhartes Gehäuse*) of rationally efficient consumption and production in which sub-rational impulses for moral autonomy were crushed between the oscillating hedonism and bureaucratic discipline dictated by the system. First-generation critical theorists expanded this diagnosis further by noting that the drive toward logical coherence and instrumental efficiency governing rational society inevitably leads to government administration of a crisis-prone economic system (the thesis of state capitalism). The "totalitarian" image of a managed society wherein bureaucratic social engineers, government insiders, and elite party cadre join forces to manufacture popular consent around a policy of stable growth under conditions of class compromise found its most memorable depiction in the diagnosis of the "culture industry" advanced in Adorno and Horkheimer's wartime classic *Dialectic of Enlightenment*.[2] Adorno and Horkheimer not only dissected the "identity thinking" underlying the manipulation of public opinion from above, but also showed how mass culture generally reinforces conformism. From their perspective, the mass-culture-mediated public sphere was thoroughly permeated by the unspontaneous responses of pre-programmed ("scripted") actors mechanically playing out their pre-assigned roles.

Critical reflection that resists the objectifying effects of the system, they concluded, can thus arise only by withdrawing from the public and its political spectacles and cultivating solitary meditation on literature and

---

2 Theodor W. Adorno and Max Horkheimer, *Dialectic of Enlightenment* (London: Continuum, 1973).

other "non-affirmative" art forms that bespeak internal psychological conflicts in the face of conformist social demands. In the words of Herbert Marcuse, true enlightenment and emancipation must begin with the "Great Refusal": "dropping out" of society and reconnecting with repressed erotic instincts which aim toward utopian fulfillment in a domination-free reconciliation of reason and sensibility, individual and society.[3] This aesthetic pathway toward enlightenment – satirized by Lukács as a "retreat to the grand hotel Abyss" – would eventually clash with the student political movements that were celebrated by Marcuse for their erotic counter-cultural imaginary.[4] True to Marcuse's philosophy, these movements combined political protest with civilly disobedient carnival-like displays, thereby constituting an anarchic, plebeian counterpart to the government-manipulated, mass-mediated bourgeois public sphere.

Habermas's Reappraisal of the Early Modern Public Sphere

Habermas's reappraisal of the public sphere is typically understood from the vantage point of his mature thought. The theory of communicative action and the discourse theory of law and democracy inaugurated a paradigm shift in the way critical theorists conceived reason in general and practical reason in particular. The elevation of democratic debate rather than scientific calculation as the essence of practical reason enabled Habermas to circumvent many of the pessimistic implications of the "dialectic of enlightenment." But Habermas did not develop his theory of communicative rationality – let alone his discourse theory of the public sphere – until long after he had resurrected a category of political life that had chiefly described middle-class society in eighteenth-century Europe and North America. Today, "critical theory" and "public sphere" have become indelibly linked in contemporary thought thanks to the original publication of his second dissertation, *The Structural Transformation of the Public Sphere* (1962), and its momentous translation into English in 1989.[5]

Indeed, this book might be understood as foreshadowing Habermas's later involvement in the Sixties student movement. This is only partly true.

---

3 Herbert Marcuse, *One-Dimensional Man: Studies in the Ideology of Advanced Industrial Society* (Boston: Beacon Press, 1964).
4 Herbert Marcuse, *Counter-revolution and Revolt* (Boston: Beacon Press, 1972).
5 Jürgen Habermas, *The Structural Transformation of the Public Sphere: An Inquiry into a Category of Bourgeois Society* (Cambridge: MIT Press, 1989).

Habermas's entry into public life as well as his theoretical elaboration of the public sphere did valorize liberal bourgeois sensibilities, but these were not the *plebeian* sensibilities associated with late-eighteenth-century revolutionary mass movements that foreshadowed the rise of the proletariat and contemporary student protest movements. That said, it is important to bear in mind that in Habermas's account even the plebeian public sphere, with its "pre-literary" populist and anarchist undertones, "remain[ed] oriented toward the intentions of the bourgeois public sphere."[6] In this respect both plebeian and bourgeois public spheres stand opposed to another mass political type of public sphere: the "plebiscitary-acclamatory form of regimented public sphere characterizing dictatorships in highly developed industrial societies." For Habermas, then, the plebeian public sphere is an outgrowth of the Enlightenment and its critical sensibilities, and is thus to be distinguished from the conservative, counter-Enlightenment public sphere associated with authoritarian rule as well as from the desiccated, depoliticized and manipulated, public sphere associated with the modern welfare state.

The critical sensibilities of the plebeian public sphere could not have been cultivated independently of the bourgeois public sphere, because these sensibilities drew their nourishment from a literate and educated class composed of students, writers, and artists that had the time and the freedom to engage in solitary reflection. Conversely – and contrary to the dominant strand of Frankfurt School thinking, with the possible exception of Walter Benjamin – Habermas insisted that such solitary literary reflections be linked to a public sphere, which in the twentieth century would include mass-mediated venues of communication, such as television, radio, film, and the internet.[7] In any event, by the end of the eighteenth century the bourgeois public would begin to awaken to the cries emanating from the plebeian public, with both complementing the other in attacking injustices associated with class privilege.

As we shall see, Habermas's most mature thinking about the public sphere realigns the bourgeois public sphere and the plebeian public sphere with different but complementary political functions within liberal democracy. Whereas the informal public sphere of civil society gives voice to discontent and protest, the formal public sphere institutionalized in parliamentary

---

6 Habermas, *The Structural Transformation of the Public Sphere*, xviii.
7 Walter Benjamin, "The Work of Art in the Age of Mechanical Reproduction," in Walter Benjamin, *Illuminations*, ed. Hannah Arendt (London: Fontana, 1969); and Jürgen Habermas, *The Theory of Communicative Action, Volume Two. Lifeworld and System: A Critique of Functionalist Reason* (Boston: Beacon Press, 1987), 387–391.

bodies obeys the logic of public-spirited argumentation oriented toward reaching consensus (or compromise) for purposes of decision-making. In between these informal and formal public spheres is the quasi-formal public sphere constituted by mass media, which, when properly regulated, transform expressions of discontent into reasoned opinions carrying varying degrees of weight that government officials should take into account when formulating their agendas. At issue is whether this two-track division of political communication does not reflect an unstable marriage between fundamentally opposed conceptions of political action that fall short of Habermas's ideal of rational discourse: agonal contestation on one side versus system-managed communication on the other.

Habermas and the Structural Transformation of the Public Sphere

The earliest and most seminal of Habermas's writings on the public sphere was his second dissertation, published in 1962 under the title *Strukturwandel der Öffentlichkeit. Untersuchungen zu einer Kategorie der bürgerlichen Gesellschaft* (*The Structural Transformation of the Public Sphere: An Inquiry into a Category of Bourgeois Society*). The timing of its publication was prescient, as the West German government was engaging in draconian suppression of free speech; in October of 1962 the offices of one of the most critical and respected news journals, *Der Spiegel*, were raided by the police, and several of its editors were arrested, imprisoned, and charged with treason for allegedly disclosing classified defense "secrets" in the journal's critical exposé of the FRG's defense policies. Cold War hysteria had already forced the German Social Democratic Party to renounce the Marxist language in its platform during its 1959 conference in Bad Godesberg. Habermas was among those professors who officially protested the suppression of *Der Spiegel*; he and his second-dissertation supervisor, Wolfgang Abendroth, helped co-found an academic support group for the radical student wing of the Social Democratic Party, the SDS, whose expulsion from its increasingly reactionary parent organization would eventually propel the SDS (and Habermas) into the maelstrom of the student movement.

Structural Transformation chronicles the rise and fall of the bourgeois public sphere in Northern Europe during the eighteenth century. It philosophically interprets this sphere as a space encompassing face-to-face discussions in public gatherings (such as coffee shops and town squares), informed by a public of letters (such as newspaper and journal readership), and facilitating the generation and dissemination of public opinion as a critical check on government.

The emergence of the public sphere is here portrayed as paralleling the rise of pre-industrial capitalism and the decline of feudalism, in which state and society, public and private, were undifferentiated. According to Habermas, most decisive in this regard was the public appearance of "civil society." Paraphrasing Hannah Arendt, Habermas attributes this appearance to "[a] private sphere that has become publicly relevant."[8] Ancient Greek society had consigned economic concerns to the unfree, private dominion of the household (*oikos*), far from the agora, the assembly, and other public venues where political issues were openly discussed among a very small minority of free male citizens. In the Middle Ages, economic concerns migrated out of the household only to the extent that they came under the private dominion of church and state. With few exceptions (such as carnivals), these institutions monopolized public spaces for their own benefit, aimed at representing their exclusive dominion over all things public and private.[9] This form of "representative publicity" gradually lost its exclusive hold with the ascendance of city life and a burgeoning commercial trade among independent artisans and merchants.[10] Now economic life, partly emancipated from church and state, became a matter of social concern and public discussion, much of it increasingly directed against official censorship and tax policy.[11]

The gradual expansion of a market economy composed of independent property owners who increasingly sought to broaden their economic freedom *vis-à-vis* government led to correlative demands for broader civil and political freedom. The middle class (the Third Estate) pressured their representatives to hold government accountable to their interests, which they came to regard as inherently rational, and to rule by their consent. The public's right to know everything that affected it demanded an end to government secrecy. In addition to challenging the legitimacy of the state, members of the middle class organized themselves as political parties in informal gatherings which took place in coffee houses, domestic salons, and semi-secret "table societies" (*Tischgesellschaften*). By the end of the eighteenth century the presumed fairness of a *laissez-faire* market economy based on contractual exchanges between free and equals would find its supreme philosophical defense in Immanuel Kant's

---

8 Habermas, *The Structural Transformation of the Public Sphere*, 19; and Hannah Arendt, *The Human Condition* (Chicago: University of Chicago Press, 1958), 46.
9 Habermas, *The Structural Transformation of the Public Sphere*, 8.
10 Habermas, *The Structural Transformation of the Public Sphere*, 18.
11 Habermas, *The Structural Transformation of the Public Sphere*, 27.

1784 essay "What Is Enlightenment?," which defended the "public use of reason" in transforming politics into morality.[12] For Kant, the critical force of rational suasion in polite conversation among intellectuals, businessmen, and women could effect a harmonization of conflicting economic and political interests in conformity with Rousseau's moral ideal of a General Will, thereby revealing the cosmopolitan unity of humanity necessary for universally binding citizens to *legitimate* legal coercion.[13] The rational overcoming of what appeared to be an underlying contradiction between *bourgeois*, *citoyen*, and *homme*, however, presumed that private property ownership and contractual exchange between free and equals rested on a natural foundation.[14]

The reverse side of the bourgeois public sphere was the bourgeois private sphere, centered on the nuclear family. Middle-class domiciles were divided into private and public spaces; libraries and bedrooms provided room for reading and solitary reflection; parlors and salons provided furnishings for intimate discussions between friends, neighbors, and other members of the community. The consumption of popular literature and culture generally was seen as indispensable to forming good taste in morals, but the public's right to judge what it read, heard, and saw had to be informed by the philosophical arguments of essayists. At stake were social mores, which writers and painters often depicted as hypocritical and counter to natural common sense. Importantly, it was the cultivation of empathy in the arts and letters that stimulated reflection on ordinary life and a common humanity that would later galvanize the political struggle for equal rights.[15] Here, as in the public sphere, the illusion of universal culture – and later, of universal rights – was premised on masking over the contradiction that the bourgeois nuclear family, as a space of intimate equality and humanity, presupposed ownership of private property under the supreme authority of an independent patriarch.[16]

Although Habermas observes that the bourgeois public sphere was an elite network composed mainly of *men* of education and/or property, it was in principle open to all regardless of status (hence the crucial role played by women in the salons). The equality among participants was further supported by their common economic independence (whether aristocratic or middle class), which, in turn, encouraged trust and openness among the

---

12 Habermas, *The Structural Transformation of the Public Sphere*, 104–106.
13 Habermas, *The Structural Transformation of the Public Sphere*, 54.
14 Habermas, *The Structural Transformation of the Public Sphere*, 115.
15 Habermas, *The Structural Transformation of the Public Sphere*, 48–51.
16 Habermas, *The Structural Transformation of the Public Sphere*, 55.

interlocutors. Rational suasion, rather than the status of the speaker, ideally governed the outcome of discussion; and, in principle, anything that had formerly been viewed as falling under the exclusive purview of church and state was now open to question.[17] The equality, freedom, openness, and public-mindedness of the public sphere in turn informed the liberal and democratic ethos of the enlightenment. But mass democracy – driven by the emergence of industrial capitalism – coupled with the corresponding decline of independent shop owners and small farmers, would lead to the demise of the public sphere by the late nineteenth century.

Much of Habermas's history of the structural transformation of the public sphere in the nineteenth and twentieth centuries recalls familiar themes previously adumbrated by the political theorist Hannah Arendt, concerning the corrosive effect that socio-economic inequalities, instrumental thinking, and the welfare state had on political action as a medium for the plural expression of free personality, and by Adorno and other first-generation critical theorists, concerning the degradation of a critical literary culture in the era of mass consumerism. The impetus for this transformation is a dialectic pitting the implicit universality of the public sphere, which presages the advent of mass democracy, against its foundation on private property and commerce, whose inherent naturalness came under attack by the other class seeking a political voice: the proletariat. This contradiction undermined the idea of the public sphere as an arena in which rational agreement on common interests was possible. Carl Schmitt, whose analysis of the crisis of parliamentary democracy Habermas approvingly cites,[18] portrayed this crisis as a contradiction between liberalism's Enlightenment faith in rational discourse and the democratic ideal of majority rule. Unlike the former, the latter could be configured only as a Hobbesian war between friend and foe culminating in the sovereign imposition of a single will. To a certain extent, Schmitt was echoing Hegel's own suspicions about the irrationality of public opinion as an expression of civil society's competing interests.[19] However, whereas Hegel and Schmitt looked to a strong bureaucracy and executive authority to restore rational order, Marx sought a more populist solution. Rather than abandon the Enlightenment ideals underwriting the public sphere, he predicated their realization on the revolutionary

---

17 Habermas, *The Structural Transformation of the Public Sphere*, 36.
18 Habermas, *The Structural Transformation of the Public Sphere*, 81 and 205; and Carl Schmitt, *The Crisis of Parliamentary Democracy*, trans. E. Kennedy (Cambridge: MIT Press, 1988), 3–6.
19 Habermas, *The Structural Transformation of the Public Sphere*, 122.

abolishment of bourgeois civil society and its constitutional institutionalization of class domination, coupled with the reabsorption of a tyrannical state bureaucracy into a now democratized proletarian civil society. John Stuart Mill, by contrast, took the side of liberalism in his critique of majoritarian tyranny and conformism. Defending the free and open marketplace of ideas as the *via regia* toward reason and truth, he defended the importance of educated and reasoned dissent in maintaining a politically vital public sphere. However, because he rejected the postulate of a natural unity of interests that still informed Marx's vision of communist society, his faith in the epistemological virtues of the marketplace of ideas proved to be ill-founded.[20]

As Habermas observed, echoing Schmitt, once the social question concerning inequality entered the expanded public sphere, the purpose of parliamentary discussion shifted from reaching rational consensus on common interests to negotiating compromises between differently weighted and irreconcilably opposed interests.[21] Given the importance of securing popular support in leveraging political demands, politicians came to rely on the less-compromising rhetoric of class warfare in their popular political propaganda. After the political debacles of the first half of the twentieth century, Europe's efforts at seeking class compromise finally succeeded in the form of the welfare state. Government management of an industrial corporate economy dissolved the distinction between state and civil society, on one side, and public and private spheres, on the other, that had been foundational for the bourgeois public sphere. The resulting "refeudalization" of society saw the return of the older representational form of publicity, with staged spectacles featuring political stars who exploit the cult of personality in attracting a loyal following. Mass democracy here amounts to passively acclaiming this or that slate of techno-political elites,[22] who in turn negotiate back-room deals between the special interest groups that elected them, in a manner reminiscent of older forms of privatized corporatist decision-making.[23] Once elected, these elites follow the dictates of their respective parties, whose administrative practices, if not campaign platforms, converge toward the political center in managing economic growth conducive to sustaining class compromise.

Accompanying this privatization of political decision-making is an "externalization" of private domestic life.[24] The mass-media invasion of the

20 Habermas, *The Structural Transformation of the Public Sphere*, 135.
21 Habermas, *The Structural Transformation of the Public Sphere*, 178.
22 Habermas, *The Structural Transformation of the Public Sphere*, 176 and 231.
23 Habermas, *The Structural Transformation of the Public Sphere*, 203–204.
24 Habermas, *The Structural Transformation of the Public Sphere*, 159.

household in the form of radio and television transfers thinking from the inward and solitary experience of reading to an outward immersion in mass culture and advertising, where "consent" to social norms is manufactured by government and commercial propaganda.[25] Accompanying this depoliticization of consumers and clients, we find the intelligentsia receding into their ivory towers, taking with them their specialized focus on serious culture and leaving the masses bereft of public reason.[26]

Habermas's Transition to His Mature Theory of the Public Sphere

By 1973 these sentiments would find but a distant echo in Habermas's work. Reversing course in the wake of the turbulent sixties, Habermas argued that a re-politicized public of students, political activists, and denizens of counter-cultural venues had provoked a legitimation crisis.[27] Aside from changing events, what led to Habermas's more optimistic appraisal of the critical potential of mass democracy was a change in his thinking about the public sphere. *The Structural Transformation of the Public Sphere* could not have envisaged even the conceptual possibility for a reinvigorated politics because in theory it provided no way for the modern welfare state to recover the ideals that had formerly underwritten the bourgeois public sphere. Habermas's concluding recommendation in that earlier book – that political parties and special interest groups adopt more transparent, inclusive, and rationally accountable forms of communication – only democratized organizational decision-making and did not address the intransigency of inter-group conflict that had proven so fatal to a moral form of politics.[28] His hope that future development of the welfare state might transform conflict into consensus recalled a familiar theme among socialists.[29] Three decades later Habermas himself remarked[30] that the book's implicit hope that a state-administered political economy could be totally democratized from within, conformable to Marx's own belief in radical democratic socialism, grossly underestimated the degree to which modern social alienation could be overcome, first with regard to conflicting values and interests and second

---

25 Habermas, *The Structural Transformation of the Public Sphere*, 172.
26 Habermas, *The Structural Transformation of the Public Sphere*, 175.
27 Jürgen Habermas, *Legitimation Crisis* (Boston: Beacon Press, 1975).
28 Habermas, *The Structural Transformation of the Public Sphere*, 248–250.
29 Habermas, *The Structural Transformation of the Public Sphere*, 250.
30 Jürgen Habermas, "Further Reflections on the Public Sphere," in *Habermas and the Public Sphere*, ed. Craig Calhoun (Cambridge: MIT Press, 1992), 431–436 and 442–444.

with regard to a functional split between a technically administered legal–economic system and a communicatively mediated lifeworld.

To a large extent, Habermas blamed the book's confusion of normative idealization and empirical description – which provoked criticism from historians as well as from feminists and other critics writing on behalf of marginalized groups and their counter-publics – on the Hegelian Marxist method of ideology critique it deployed.[31] This approach depended on selectively reducing a complex historical institution to an ideal type, whose underlying values pointed beyond their partial, contradictory constellation toward a more complete realization. The idea of a complete democratization of society undervalued not only efficiencies associated with bureaucratic administration and market economy, but also the difficulties of including domestic caregivers (chiefly women), overworked employees, and less educated persons as equal participants in what were supposed to be informed and impartial political discussions.[32]

Rejecting the Hegelian idealization of the public sphere, Habermas also rejected his countervailing Marxist tendency to misrepresent the civil society in which it was anchored as a quasi-economic category. By linking the structural transformation of the public sphere to the structural transformation of capitalism, Habermas's account in *Structural Transformation* displayed the defects of an economic determinism that undervalued that sphere's enduring capacity to function in a critical capacity despite distortions wrought by the economic–administrative system.

Habermas's subsequent effort to ground public sphere and civil society on a non-economic foundation, specifically with reference to universal normative presuppositions of communicative action, removed the central contradiction that prevented his understanding of the bourgeois public sphere from being reduced to either utopian wish fantasy or uncritical appendage of the system. By the late sixties Habermas had begun exploring several Kantian approaches that sharply distinguished instrumental–economic and moral–practical domains of action, learning, and social development.[33] By the early seventies this line of thought had led him to reconstruct the universal pragmatic presuppositions underlying everyday speech action oriented toward facilitating open and transparent cooperation.[34] Unlike

---

31 Habermas, "Further Reflections on the Public Sphere," 435–436.
32 Habermas, "Further Reflections on the Public Sphere," 426–428.
33 Jürgen Habermas, *Knowledge and Human Interests* (Boston: Beacon Press, 1971); and Jürgen Habermas, *Toward a Rational Society* (Boston: Beacon Press, 1970).
34 Jürgen Habermas, *Communication and the Evolution of Society* (Boston: Beacon Press, 1979).

strategic or otherwise manipulative uses of language, communicative action presupposes mutual agreement between the agent proposing cooperation and the recipient of the proposal. More precisely, communicative action presupposes that the recipient understands and accepts, among other things, the proposer's understanding of the factual background and rightness of the proposed interaction, an understanding that the proposer tacitly claims to be valid (true or right). Most importantly, in claiming this about her action, the proposer also commits herself to justifying these claims.

Crucially, Habermas reconstructs how speaker and listener must imagine the way justification should unfold as a critical dialogue ("discourse") wherein skeptical doubts are overcome and consensus restored by the "unforced force" of the better argument alone, a force that gains strength only to the extent that the interlocutors are presumed to have equal opportunities to present the fullest range of reasons without any mental or physical constraints.[35] This counterfactual ideal perfectly captures the moral point of view – that each person must be accountable to others, so that their reasonable (justifiable) dissent is respected. When transferred to the legal sphere, the discourse principle retains this reference to morality but with an important twist.[36] The basic equal rights to free speech, association, and personal liberty that it stipulates do not impose a reciprocal moral duty to justify one's actions but instead open up a range of permissible action to which the individual rights holder need be accountable to no one. Such liberal rights, however, are but empty principles of freedom unless politically qualified by another application of the discourse principle, this one involving a procedure of democratic consent.[37]

Thus, contrary to the Schmittian analysis of modern liberal democracy Habermas had once partly endorsed, the discourse-theoretic conception of democracy logically entails liberal features – basic individual freedoms, equal protection from discrimination, separation of powers, and the rule of law. However, elements of Schmitt's analysis are retained in Habermas's two-track model of political deliberation. For example, while discourse in so-called *weak* publics is largely contestatory and agonal – aimed at interminable protestation of injustice rather than timely resolution on positive courses of

---

35 Jürgen Habermas, "Discourse Ethics: Notes on a Program of Philosophical Justification," in Jürgen Habermas, *Moral Consciousness and Communicative Action* (Cambridge: MIT Press, 1990), 43–115.
36 Jürgen Habermas, *Between Facts and Norms: Contributions to a Discourse Theory of Law and Morality* (Cambridge: MIT Press, 1996).
37 Habermas, *Between Facts and Norms*, 123.

action – discourse in *strong* publics oriented to institutional decision-making terminates in reaching some kind of agreement. Although the legitimation of law remains conceptually linked to the regulative ideal of attempted rational consensus on generalizable interests, deliberation that terminates in political compromise – which Habermas regards as the normal outcome of policy debates – conforms to this ideal insofar as all parties undertake to modify their irreducibly competing interests for the sake of achieving a fair and mutually acceptable balance of power.[38]

Habermas's Analysis of the Public Sphere in Later Writings

Suffice it to say that Habermas's discourse theory has implications for the way in which the abstract features of a procedurally just liberal democracy are concretely interpreted and institutionalized. The constitutional flow of institutional power – from legislative deliberation and enactment to executive and judicial application – should be entirely responsive to public opinion undistorted by excessive influence emanating from government elites and private interests.[39]

In a more recent essay on normative democratic theory and empirical mass media studies, Habermas formulates the supposition that rational discourse can legitimate democratic decision-making as an assumption

- that relevant issues and controversial answers, requisite information, and appropriate arguments for and against will be mobilized;
- that the alternatives which emerge will be subjected to examination in argumentation and will be evaluated accordingly; and
- that rationally motivated 'yes' and 'no' positions on procedurally correct decisions will be a deciding factor.[40]

These three suppositions are satisfied differently depending on what arena of the public sphere they occur within: (1) the *formal institutional debates* that occur within the *political system*; (2) the *informal, everyday communications* that occur within *civil society*; or (3) the *passive reception* and *reflective consideration* of *abstract information and public opinion that occur in mass media*.[41] Beginning with the peripheral sphere of political life that is furthest removed from political decision-making proper, Habermas identifies *civil society*, composed

---

38 Habermas, *Between Facts and Norms*, 166.   39 Habermas, *Between Facts and Norms*, 193.
40 Jürgen Habermas, *Europe: The Faltering Project* (Cambridge: Polity Press, 2009), 162.
41 Habermas, *Europe*, 159.

of "citizen groups, advocates, churches, and intellectuals," as well as the social movements and social networks around which they organize themselves, as responsible for communicating social injustices.[42] The political communication generated through physical encounter and social media contains a large quantity of non-discursive expressions of social discontent, involving the use of "story-telling and images, facial and bodily expressions in general, testimonies, appeals, and the like."[43] The "wild" (spontaneous and unregulated) nature of political expression within civil society, ranging from loud plebeian demonstrations of civil disobedience to dispassionate arguments in academic forums, stands in sharp contrast to the highly regulated arguments that occur within the center of political life, the *political system*, which is charged with responding sensitively to the most vocal concerns circulating in civil society as well as those emanating from lobbyists representing "industry and the labor market, health care, traffic, energy, research and development, education" and other "functional subsystems."[44] Less inclusive and free, but procedurally fairer, arguments conducted by government officials within institutional settings, Habermas notes, abide by strict courtroom and parliamentary procedures that are designed to ensure that all participating parties have an equal voice in debating policies. But these rules impose rational orderliness by subjecting speakers to severe time limits, legal constraints, and rules of civil decorum that restrict freedom to argue and exclude less mainstream points of view. Intermediary between civil society and the political system is the *mass-mediated sphere of communication*, which is charged with condensing, refining, weighing, and selecting public opinions emanating from civil advocacy groups, special interest lobbyists, and politicians. When properly instituted, with appropriate government regulation ensuring independent, fully representative, and roughly equal access, this arena of the public sphere can counteract shortfalls in discursive rationality that dominate in civil society and government by disseminating opinions more widely and by subjecting already filtered arguments to a second level of public reflection.

Any possibility of democratic process producing rational, viz., legitimate, decisions thus depends on the proper institution of the mass media. Assuming that rational argumentation can have an impact on cooperative learning and political problem-solving, the question arises whether mass media can function as well as face-to-face focus-group discussion in generating rational public-opinion formation conducive to reaching consensus.

42 Habermas, *Europe*, 163.   43 Habermas, *Europe*, 154.   44 Habermas, *Europe*, 163.

Mass Media in the Age of Digital Communication

A new structural transformation of the public sphere driven above all by digital technological revolutions has accelerated and intensified the diversity of information flows. It may seem that the resulting "communicative liquefaction of politics" has made it difficult for any entity to monopolize political communication.[45] Yet Habermas cites several factors that speak against the prospect that this upsurge in political communication tracks an increase in rational deliberation.

> [T]wo deficits in particular immediately stand out: the lack of straightforward, face-to-face interactions, between really (or virtually) present participants, in a shared practice of collective decision-making; and the lack of reciprocity between the roles of speakers and addressees in an egalitarian exchange of opinions and claims. In addition, the dynamics of mass communication betrays relations of power which make a mockery of the presumption of a free play of arguments. The power of the media to select messages and to shape their presentation is as much an intrinsic feature of mass communication as the fact that other actors use their power to influence the agenda, content, and presentation of public issues is typical of the public sphere.[46]

To begin with, mass communication "remains 'abstract' insofar as it disregards the actual presence of the more or less passive recipients and ignores the immediateness of the concrete glances, gestures, thoughts, and reactions of those who are present and addressed."[47] By not being "open to the game of direct question and answer, the exchange of affirmation and negation, assertion and contradiction," mass communication detaches the propositional content of opinions from the validity-claim structure of everyday communicative interaction, in which opinions are linked to a process of argumentative challenge and redemption. In this respect it is more like a "price regulated network of transactions between producers and consumers."[48]

Second, mass communication possesses an "asymmetrical structure," insofar as it reduces addressees to the status of passive spectators and consumers. Journalists and politicians are like actors on a stage vying for the public's applause. It is true, of course, that the Internet has provided a censure-free mechanism for political communication in authoritarian regimes that has led to remarkable (if short-lived) democratic victories (as

---

45 Habermas, *Europe*, 154–155.   46 Habermas, *Europe*, 154.   47 Habermas, *Europe*, 156.
48 Habermas, *Europe*, 156.

witnessed, for example, in the Arab Spring). But in liberal democracies the "chat rooms" that seem to have "revived the historically submerged phenomenon of an egalitarian public of reading and writing conversational partners and correspondents" have largely crystalized around partisan or otherwise parochial niche audiences, thereby belying the globalizing and decentering potential of the Internet and, Habermas adds, fragmenting the public sphere further into entrenched and closed interest groups.[49]

That said, Habermas insists that these structural deviations from rational discourse do not necessarily mean that mass media fail to contribute to rational deliberation . They contribute by *filtering* inputs from elites within civil society, government, and functional subsystems in the form of *published opinions*, and then reflectively generating *public opinions* ("clusters of controversial issues and inputs to which the parties concerned intuitively attach weights in accordance with their perceptions of the cumulative 'yes' and 'no' stances of the wider public" as conveyed by a "representative spectrum of pooled opinions reflected in survey data").[50] Beyond this, mass media also enable a secondary stage of reflection on public opinion, which generates *considered public opinion*, by which Habermas understands "a pair of contrary, more or less coherent opinions, weighted in accordance with agreement and disagreement, which refer to a relevant issue and express what appears at the time, in light of available information, to be the most plausible or reasoned interpretations of a sufficiently relevant – though generally controversial – issue."[51] Considered opinions "fix the parameters for the range of possible decisions [made by political elites] which the public of voters would accept as legitimate." In this way, properly functioning mass media perform two invaluable tasks in democratic deliberation: They return to civil society its own messages of discontent, now reflectively worked up in the form of considered public opinion; and they place such opinion before institutional deliberative bodies, commenting and observing how well such bodies incorporate said opinion into their agendas and debates.[52]

However, mass media function properly only if the power structures of the public sphere and the dynamics of mass communication permit it. The public sphere is influenced by *political power*, which shapes the legal regulations that constitute the diversity and independence of the mass media. It is influenced by *social power* (especially economic power), which must be exercised in a relatively transparent manner; and it is influenced by *media*

---

49 Habermas, *Europe*, 158.　50 Habermas, *Europe*, 165.　51 Habermas, *Europe*, 166.
52 Habermas, *Europe*, 162.

power, which shapes the content and formating of public opinion according to its own professional code of integrity (fairness and independence). Although Habermas concedes that sectorial and government elites have a financial and organizational advantage in shaping public opinion according to their preferences relative to the "weak" and "dispersed" publics that form civil society, he thinks that their strategic interventions can be checked by the reflective counter-responses of well-regulated mass media. Whether this actually happens depends not only on the independence of the media, but also – most importantly – on the "motivational dispositions and cognitive abilities" of average citizens. Citizens, Habermas contends, need not possess a large body of knowledge about politics in order to be knowledgeable in their reasoning about political choices.[53]

Habermas expresses considerable skepticism about whether these two conditions are in fact met. In addressing the problem of independence, he notes that mass media may be "incompletely differentiated" from their social and government environments. This was the case with the Italian government's postwar monopoly over the broadcasting system, when each of the three major political parties recruited media personnel from its own ranks. A potentially more sinister instance occurred when the United States' National Security Agency enlisted such telecommunications and Internet giants as Verizon, Telstra, Google, and Facebook in tracking user data. Lack of independence may also take the form of a "temporary dedifferentiation," as when media and government collude for mutual advantage (favorable news coverage in exchange for access).[54]

A second pathology manifests itself in citizens' overly passive and uncritical consumption of public opinion. Consumption is unequally partitioned among the various sectors of society depending on educational achievement, social class, and cultural marginalization.[55] Apathy, powerlessness, and cynicism, largely in response to the devolution of political campaigns into image-making spectacles and the debasement of news to "infotainment" (the blending of news and entertainment in easily consumed soundbites), also reinforce the passive-consumer mentality of citizens.[56]

---

53 Habermas, *Europe*, 172–173.   54 Habermas, *Europe*, 174–176.
55 David Ingram and Asaf Bar-Tura, "The Public Sphere as Site of Emancipation and Enlightenment: A Discourse Theoretic Critique of Digital Communication," in *Re-Imagining Public Space: The Frankfurt School in the 21st Century*, ed. Diana Boros and James M. Glass (New York: Palgrave, 2014), 65–85.
56 Habermas, *Europe*, 178–189.

Counterbalancing this gloomy diagnosis, Habermas cites studies showing that citizens' "ascriptive ties between political behavior and social and cultural backgrounds have increasingly loosened." Such loosening suggests a growing "independence of political attitudes from determinants such as place of residence, social class, or religious affiliation." From this Habermas infers that public reason may be gaining the upper hand over parochial prejudice when it comes to thinking about particular issues. The new media-generated interest in participating in multiple "issue publics" centered on immediate (short-term), non-economic concerns has "pluralized" participation in distinct but overlapping publics, thereby weakening monolithic partisan loyalties, ideological antagonisms, and narrow group- and identity-based patterns of political association.[57]

Alternatives to the Deliberative Model of the Public Sphere

Habermas's discourse-theoretic understanding of the public sphere has been challenged from a variety of fronts too numerous to catalog here. I shall focus on three of them that have influenced Habermas's thinking from the very beginning: Luhmann's systems theory, Arendt's phenomenology of spontaneous grass-roots political activism, and Left-Schmittian realism. Although traces of these approaches still remain in his mature philosophy, each taken separately contradicts core tenets of his discourse theory of deliberative democracy.

The Systems-Theoretic Alternative: Niklas Luhmann

Niklas Luhmann (1927–1998) developed a non-normative theory of society whose cybernetic and biological modeling of self-contained and self-creative communication *systems* is important to us because it represents the exact antithesis of a society theorized as *primarily* integrated by personal communication *actions* regulated by universal egalitarian and consensual norms. Luhmann's debate with Habermas in the early seventies and Habermas's ongoing efforts to grapple with the implications of Luhmann's evolving theory of society for legal and political theory were made all the more significant given that both thinkers drew inspiration from Talcott Parsons (Luhmann's former mentor at Harvard) and specifically incorporated into their own theories his mature account of differentiated social systems, which

---

57 Habermas, *Europe*, 178–189.

substitute generalized strategic media (such as money, in the case of the economic system, and power in the case of the legal system) for consensual communication in integrating (or coordinating) social behavior.[58]

In Habermas's socal theory, consensual communication normatively anchors the system. By contrast, Luhmann's theory of society (*Gesellschaftstheorie*) makes the continuation of systems-mediated communication the anchor for normative integration. Indeed, his theory demotes individual social agents to relatively insignificant systems of personal meaning ("consciousness") in comparison with the interactive communicative systems which connect them (Luhmann's dismissal of the theory of consciousness as an ontological starting point is one of the very few points on which he and Habermas agree). 'Communication' here is described in the non-normative language of cybernetics: Systems – be they persons, organizations, or functional orders – observe each other as environments whose complex effects they process into information (reduce to 'meaning') for purposes of selection, pursuant to the re-establishment of successful adaptation and internal stability. The successful functional adaptation of a system's social structure to its outer environment along with the subsequent restabilization of its inner identity reinforces a conservative tendency toward maintaining continuity.

Luhmann's theory of society is more than just a theory of social systems.[59] Like Parsons's (and Habermas's) social theory, it also contains a theory of social evolution and a theory of functional social differentiation.[60] Over time pre-modern societies develop organizational systems that culminate in an administrative state as supreme coordinator of otherwise chaotic networks of communicative interaction; but, pressured by problems of growth, the unified, hierarchical community (*Gemeinschaft*) such stratified state-centered societies normatively integrate will evolve into a functionally differentiated, decentralized, non-normatively integrated communication network coupling distinct economic, legal, political, familial, educational, and religious subsystems. These functional systems are "autopoietic," or self-contained in their internal generation of meaning; each processes what it has observed from its environment into information using its own unique binary code for selecting inputs. For example, events in the legal system are coded in terms of

---

58 Jürgen Habermas (with Niklas Luhmann), *Theorie der Gesellschaft oder Sozialtechnologie – Was leistet die Systemforschung?* (Frankfurt: Suhrkamp, 1971); Niklas Luhmann, *A Sociological Theory of Law*, ed. Martin Albrow, trans. Elizabeth King-Utz and Martin Albrow (London: Routledge, 1985); and Habermas, *Between Facts and Norms*.
59 Niklas Luhmann, *Theory of Society*, trans. Rhodes Barrett, 2 vols. (Stanford: Stanford University Press, 2012–2013).
60 See Habermas, *The Theory of Communicative Action, Volume Two*.

whether they are lawful or unlawful, whereas events in the political system are coded in terms of whether they are legitimate or illegitimate; that is to say, whether or not they successfully motivate public compliance with government decision-making.

Here we see how the background interaction systems that populate the public sphere and generate public opinion play a potentially ambivalent – and by no means critical – role in Luhmann's analysis of the political system.[61] The political system in the modern welfare state understands itself (paradoxically) as a *universal* decision procedure for solving problems that arise from within other functional subsystems. But in reality its power to steer these other systems is limited because it communicates with them in its own language, the 'effects' of which are processed very differently by these other systems in terms of their languages. The possibility of synchronized structural coupling linking different functional systems is thus utterly contingent, leading Luhmann himself to doubt whether inter-systemic integration (e.g., revolutionary political change of the constitutional legal order) is possible (*Steuerungsskeptizismus*). To take an iconic example drawn from the public sphere, a judge cannot but regard a peaceful act of civil disobedience as a form of law-breaking that should be suppressed. For a state that needs law to resolve its own paradox of self-authorizing power, maintenance of constitutional procedure would seem to demand the same course of action. However, from the perspective of the democratic political system which motivates compliance with state authority, elected officials cannot but regard this same event as one – potentially necessary – reflection on (or observation of) the political system's current state of instability. Because the state organizational system must communicate with both legal and political subsystems in order to function successfully, it must unhappily choose between two horns of a dilemma, both of which are guaranteed to produce systemic crisis: tolerate law breaking or suppress politics.

In sum, Luhmann's reduction of the public sphere to a network of cybernetically conceived interactive subsystems that are subsumed under more hegemonic functional systems renders, by his own admission, democracy, representation, and sovereignty inherently paradoxical as meaningful political categories. Equally paradoxical, on his account, is the successful functioning of public opinion as a critical check on organizational and functional political power. Indeed, the political, understood as a distinctive

---

61 Niklas Luhmann, *Political Theory in the Welfare State* (Berlin: de Gruyter, 1990); and Niklas Luhmann, *Die Politik der Gesellschaft* (Frankfurt: Suhrkamp, 2000).

category of communicative action, appears to have been all but effaced by the technical, understood as a general feature of social administration.

The Neo-anarchist Alternative: Hannah Arendt

Diametrically opposed to techno-scientific descriptions proffered by systems theory are those neo-anarchist interpretations of the public sphere that descend from Hannah Arendt (1906–1975), an existential phenomenologist who, as we saw above, has influenced Habermas's thought from the very beginning. As a former student of Heidegger, Arendt was concerned about rescuing an archaic mode of existence from the oblivion of modern technology. In keeping with the communication-centered *Existenzphilosophie* elaborated by her dissertation supervisor, Karl Jaspers, the mode of existence she sought to recover was not poetic thinking about being as such but political action as a distinctive form of manifesting a world of meaning and individual identity that first – and Arendt seems to suggest, most authentically – appeared in the ancient Greek *polis*.[62]

Like Habermas, Arendt closely ties political action to the legitimation of power, with some of her accounts of political action resonating with the social-contractarian language favored by Habermas. In discussing the spontaneous act of constituting a shared political space through mutual promising, Arendt seems to postulate voluntary consent as a universal norm of legitimation.[63] Her contrast between the 'communicative power' (*Macht*) of public opinion and the 'violence' (*Gewalt*) of coercive legal imposition is later taken up by Habermas in explaining how legitimate exercises of the latter depend upon the former.[64] Again, in her discussion of Kant's political understanding of judgment (1982), she draws attention to the importance of communication in generating an "enlarged thought" that takes into account the opinions of others.[65]

But some of Arendt's other descriptions of political action deviate so markedly from Habermas's as to constitute a counter-theory to his own. For Arendt, the essence of political action is essentially non-instrumental, not the achievement of this or that end but the public revelation of each actor's

---

62 Arendt, *The Human Condition*.
63 Hannah Arendt, *On Revolution* (New York: Viking, 1973), 173 and 192–268; and David Ingram, "Novus Ordo Seclorum: The Trial of (Post)Modernity or the Tale of Two Revolutions," in *Hannah Arendt: Twenty Years Later*, ed. Larry May and Jerome Kohn (Cambridge: MIT Press, 1997), 221–250.
64 Habermas, *Between Facts and Norms*, 196.
65 Hannah Arendt, *Lectures on Kant's Political Philosophy*, ed. and trans. Ronald Beiner (Chicago, University of Chicago Press, 1982).

individuality in an agonal exchange of opinions. In keeping with this dramaturgic notion of political action, Arendt introduces the public space as the cultural arena where public spectators memorialize the fleeting deeds and words of political actors by judging them and, in so doing, narrate their own shared political identity. All of this, Habermas observes, suggests an aesthetic – rather than cognitive–practical – understanding of the public.[66]

The Realist Left-Schmittian Alternative: Chantal Mouffe

Given Habermas's hostility to Carl Schmitt (1888–1985) and his political theology, it may seem strange to claim him as anything more than a passing influence on Habermas's early theorizing of the structural transformation of the public sphere. Stranger still is the very idea that an unrepentant Nazi jurist could find a receptive home in any contemporary left-wing political theory, until we recall the antipathy toward liberalism that many on the left (including his former students Otto Kirchheimer and Franz Neumann, who later affiliated with the Frankfurt School) shared with Schmitt. More recent left-wing revivals of Schmitt's thought have appropriated his incisive observations regarding the impotence of law in relation to its decisive application by executive authority, the theological genealogy of political categories such as sovereignty, the opportunistic manipulation of humanitarian law as subterfuge for imperial aggression, and the need to define politics in terms of implacable partisan opposition rather than compromise.

No other contemporary theorist has done more to revive Schmitt's reputation in this regard than Chantal Mouffe, who, joining with many leftists in the eighties and nineties, felt betrayed by the willingness of socialist parties to compromise their militant platforms for the sake of collaborating with big business in pursuing liberal and neoliberal administrative policies. Like Schmitt, Mouffe objects to liberalism because it privileges individuals as the central actors in political life, which liberalism incoherently conceives as a domain dominated by the pursuit of both rational self-interest and universal morality. More precisely, liberalism overlooks individuals' passionate identification with identity groups such as labor unions, whose very identities are necessarily shaped in an agonal struggle for hegemony in opposition to other identity groups, such as business associations.[67] The reference to hegemony

---

66 Jürgen Habermas and Thomas McCarthy, "Hannah Arendt's Communications Concept of Power," *Social Research*, 44(1) (1977), 3–24.
67 Chantal Mouffe, *Agonistics: Thinking the World Politically* (London: Verso, 2013), 4–5 and 137.

underscores Mouffe's disagreement with Arendt and her debt to Gramsci, for whom the acquisition of power serves as the principal aim of politics.[68]

Mouffe parses the theoretical implications of hegemonic power by referencing Schmitt's equation of democracy and unrestricted majoritarian dictatorship. For Schmitt the general will inscribed in democratic rule cannot be universal; it cannot reflect the common interests of humanity, as liberalism claims. An abstract norm such as human rights lacks sufficient concreteness to be the basis for a ruling will. Indeed, this and every other general norm lacks prescriptive force until its precise meaning has been decided. But decision, as an act of will, must be particular and exclusive. If we say, as Schmitt does, that the specific meaning of a general law ultimately depends on the sole discretion of the supreme executive power enforcing it, then we go no further than asserting a Hobbesian identification of legal order with absolute sovereign authority. However, if we insist that sovereign power must be authorized democratically, then we assert something more, namely, that an adversarial struggle must identify the holder of that power as a majority that possesses an exclusive right to decide for a minority.[69]

The exclusive exercise of sovereign political power dictates the adversarial nature of democratic politics. Although Mouffe disagrees with Schmitt's characterization of democratic politics as an antagonistic war uniting friends against foes, she agrees that any such politics will involve partisan groups that view each other as adversaries.[70] Adversaries respect the legitimacy of each party's right to advance its political agenda. To that extent they can be said to agree on an abstract constitutional framework of equal rights and toleration. But this consensus is grounded not in common reason, but in overlapping comprehensive belief systems (as Rawls puts it) that are irreducibly particular, if not incommensurable. Because these comprehensive belief systems are embedded in emotionally imbued group identities that are maintained only in opposition to other such identities, this consensus will itself take the form of contestation and struggle (what Mouffe calls conflictual consensus and what Rawls would call a *modus vivendi*). Indeed, the very constitutional framework constraining this struggle will also be a site of political contestation.[71]

The fault lines separating Mouffe and Habermas are not as clearly demarcated as those separating Schmitt and Habermas, but they are sharp nonetheless. Both Habermas and Mouffe identify the public space of democratic

---

68 Mouffe, *Agonistics*, 9–11 and 73–75.   69 Mouffe, *Agonistics*, 5–6.
70 Mouffe, *Agonistics*, 7 and 137–139.   71 Mouffe, *Agonistics*, 8–9.

political life with a plurality of voices that are free to criticize and contest. But their understanding of the mutual respect that constrains political opponents is different. For Habermas respect for someone implies a willingness to offer her reasons that she could in principle accept. If we now follow Mouffe in discarding the rational premises underlying Habermas's notion of consent, then respect for the other resides in acknowledging that the adversary is like oneself in her passionate attachment to an emotionally compelling political worldview and, as such, should be given the freedom to contest, if not the freedom to share in political rule. But this weak legitimation of democratic order – that all are free to contest – is qualified by the fact that the composition of the 'all' is itself a political issue that those in power must decide. Should all groups – no matter how threatening to the hegemonic order (as seen by those in power) be free to contest as respected adversaries? Where do we (the dominant majority) draw the line between 'enemies of the state' and adversaries whose worldviews strike us as deeply corrosive of society? For Mouffe, there is no way to decide this question rationally.

Habermas and Mouffe both view the public sphere as fitting into a circulation of power that culminates in a decision to exercise legal coercion, and in this respect their understanding of the political differs from Arendt's. But Habermas sees the primary function of politics as deliberation centered around collaborative and *rational* problem-solving, whereas Mouffe sees it as a *non-rational*, agonistic struggle oriented toward achieving hegemonic power for one's group. In essence, they depart from conflicting phenomenologies of political experience that have distinctive affinities with social class. Habermas does not deny the emotional identification underlying group loyalty, but he can point to empirical evidence showing that more educated citizens who are guided by enlightened self-interest identify less strongly with ideological groups and show more independence in their political preferences than do their less educated counterparts.

Globalizing the Public Sphere

Since the late nineties globalization has overwhelmed the state's capacity to manage its borders, defend against internal and external security risks, regulate its economy, and guarantee public services. Meanwhile, the parallel expansion of transnational systems of governance has increasingly limited what states can do to advance their subjects' well-being.

If society must be conceived as *world* society, as Luhmann argues, then we would naturally expect to find it structured by various functional systems, including a global political system, that would supersede and connect its state-centered segments. Luhmann's surprising silence on this possibility – and his neglect of international relations in general – is only now drawing a response from systems theorists, such as Günther Teubner (1944–), who, using Luhmann's model of autopoietic systems, has argued that globalization has effectively detached constitutional law from public law and from the nation state.[72] International law has increasingly migrated from the domain of public law (dealing with humanitarian crimes, for example) to the plural domains of private law. International law has become fragmented into heterogeneous, autopoietic (self-constituting), transnational legal subsystems (of copyright, trade, and so on) that compete with international public law. Neoliberal trade regulations effectively prohibit states from performing welfare functions that institutionalize human rights. Accordingly, social movements have now switched from criticizing states to protesting against non-state organizations, such as the World Trade Organization (WTO) and the various systems of private law within which it operates. But as the targets of protest constantly shift and fragment, so do the protesting publics. The self-referential paradoxes of self-creating systems diagnosed by Luhmann at the level of the welfare state become more intense globally, as legal and political systems become increasingly decoupled and fragmented.

Habermas and other critical theorists express ambivalence regarding this development, at once bemoaning the decline of *local* democratic control while remaining guardedly hopeful that *global* democratic control can reassert itself against legal and political fragmentation and steer supranational government toward more effective and fair cosmopolitan humanitarian policies aimed at mitigating civil conflict, human rights violations, poverty, inequality, and climate change. Here they look to an emerging global public sphere, anchored largely by NGOs, popular social movements, and similar "players" within a global civil society. The public opinion generated by these voices is leveraged against outlaw states and other human rights violators as well as democratically unaccountable global economic multilaterals, such as the WTO and the World Bank, whose trade and lending policies are widely believed to benefit richer nations (and richer individuals) to the detriment of the poor.[73]

---

[72] Günther Teubner and Peter Korth, "Two Kinds of Legal Pluralism: Collision of Transnational Regimes in the Double Fragmentation of World Society," in *Regime Interaction in International Law: Facing Fragmentation*, ed. Margaret A. Young (Cambridge: Cambridge University Press, 2010), 23–54.

[73] Habermas, *Europe*, 125.

Contemporary political theorists in the European tradition by no means agree on whether this emerging site of global public *opinion* constitutes a global public *sphere*. If we depart from critical theory's standard understanding of the public sphere as essentially connected to the legitimation of political power as distinct from occasional protestation of its exercise, then any talk of a global public sphere would seem to presuppose the existence of a relatively unified global opinion capable of influencing the deliberation and decision-making of international agencies possessing global legislative powers. It is far from clear whether such agencies currently exist (or even could exist) and what form they might possibly take in the future. What is clear is that without them it would make no sense to talk about a global public sphere functioning in a way analogous to a domestic public sphere. Furthermore, the existence of such international legislative bodies tells us little about the possibility of a global public opinion that might direct their deliberation and decision-making. Absent global legislative agencies that are susceptible to democratic structuration and a global civil society capable of generating global opinions influencing their deliberation and decision-making, one might at best speak of a global public sphere whose functioning would be very different from the domestic model.

The possibility of a global public sphere analogous in functioning to a domestic public sphere depends on the coherence of democratic global governance. No critical theorist believes that such a system of global governance currently exists, but Habermas and other theorists such as Brunkhorst and Benhabib, who interpret the post-World War II development of humanitarian law as a process of constitutionalization, see it as an emerging fact, centered on a reformed UN.[74] Such a government would not replace nation states, which would still be responsible for enforcing and interpreting international and cosmopolitan law. But its laws and regulations, to the degree that they were coercively enforced, would require democratic legitimation. *International* legislation could be legitimated through national and regional public spheres as is now the case, but *cosmopolitan* legislation affecting human rights and other forms of humanitarianism would likely be carried out by a constitutionally re-founded General Assembly whose legitimate functioning would depend on public opinion generated by a global public sphere.

---

74 Seyla Benhabib, *Another Cosmopolitanism: Hospitality, Sovereignty and Democratic Iterations*, ed. Robert Post (Oxford: Oxford University Press, 2006); and Hauke Brunkhorst, *Critical Theory of Legal Revolutions: Evolutionary Perspectives* (London: Bloomsbury, 2014).

Many critical theorists have questioned the legitimacy of the current state system that anchors international law. If discourse ethics demands that all who are affected by governance have some say in shaping it, then no municipal policy possessing global impact can rely on national public opinion alone for its legitimation. The determination of whose voice should count in shaping national immigration, energy, and trade policy cannot be determined by simple appeal to a nationally bounded public sphere. The determination of this matter would instead lie with some supranational (but not necessarily global) public.[75]

If international treaty law cannot rely on the bounded publics of its constituent parties for democratic legitimation without begging the meta-political question regarding the legitimacy of those very publics, then its true scope will have to be reconceived as transnational, if not cosmopolitan. Some critical theorists challenge the idea of such a transnational (or cosmopolitan) public sphere.[76] The scope and diversity of such a public would likely undermine any possibility of generating a relatively unified global opinion capable of guiding global legislators. However, in the absence of a centralized, hierarchically structured global government – whose monopoly over the creation and interpretation of cosmopolitan law many critical theorists fear – the need for such a global sphere analogous to the domestic type seems rather superfluous. If we then continue to speak of a global public sphere, it would be in terms of a structurally transformed public sphere. The kind of global public sphere appropriate to a decentered system of global governance linking overlapping *demoi* would be neither strong nor weak but distributive, enhancing deliberation across *demoi*. Whether this decentered model of global governance, with its modest conditions for democratic legitimation, can compel hegemonic superpowers to effectively and fairly address our current humanitarian crises remains to be seen.

---

[75] Nancy Fraser, *Scales of Justice: Reimagining Political Space in a Globalizing World* (New York: Columbia University Press, 2009).

[76] James Bohman, "Democracy, Solidarity and Global Exclusion," *Philosophy and Social Criticism*, 32(7) (2006), 809–817.

21

Restructuring Democracy and the Idea of Europe

SEYLA BENHABIB AND STEFAN EICH

In March 1994, Václav Havel, then President of the Czech Republic, stepped in front of the European Parliament in Strasbourg and issued a passionate plea for opening up the European Union (EU) toward the East. Nothing less was expected. What captured his audience, however, was his unexpectedly harsh criticism of the emotional poverty of European integration. In his speech, Havel called for an urgently needed "Charter of European Identity" that would clearly set out the ideas and values Europe was intended to embody. The Maastricht Treaty, which then had been in force for only three months, may have been a ground-breaking constitutional document setting out a daring institutional path toward integration. But it lacked an ethical dimension. The Treaty, Havel explained, had engaged his brain, but failed to address his heart.[1] The single most important task facing the EU now was to reflect on what it might mean to speak of a European identity and to "impress upon millions of European souls an idea, a historical mission and a momentum."[2]

Debates about European identity rose to public prominence in the wake of the Maastricht Treaty. But the issue had been on the minds of the architects of the European Economic Community (EEC) at least since the 1970s. In December 1973, representatives of the then nine member states met in Copenhagen to issue a first "Declaration on European Identity" that formally introduced the concept of European identity and sought to turn it into a cornerstone of future relations of the member states with one another

---

[1] Václav Havel, "Speech in the European Parliament (March 8, 1994)," in Václav Havel, *Toward a Civil Society: Selected Speeches and Writings 1990–1994*, trans. Paul Robert Wilson and Rostislav Vaněk (Prague: Lidové Noviny, 1995), 291–303, p. 296. For an account of cosmopolitan solidarity drawing on Havel's diagnosis of the ethical, cultural, symbolic, and spiritual poverty of European integration, see Paul Linden-Retek, "Cosmopolitan Law and Time: Toward a Theory of Constitutionalism and Solidarity in Transition," *Global Constitutionalism*, 4(2) (2015), 158–194.
[2] Havel, "Speech in the European Parliament (March 8, 1994)," 301.

but even more so with the rest of the world.[3] The time had come, the Nine explained, to develop a coherent European identity that would not only guide the path toward "the construction of a United Europe" but also improve member states' understanding of their changing place in the global affairs of a decolonized world. Embracing European identity meant looking back at a common heritage to acknowledge how much member countries already acted in concert. But it also meant developing common interests and pursuing the "special obligation" of European unification. This path, the Declaration emphatically concluded, was in principle open to any other European nation that shared the same ideals and objectives.

The very fact that the 1973 summit met in Copenhagen itself reflected the first wave of enlargement earlier that year. In January 1973 the EEC had grown from its six founding nations to nine member states by admitting Ireland, the United Kingdom, and Denmark. Norway had narrowly rejected membership when a referendum overturned a previous parliamentary majority for joining. Over the next decades the radical promise of open-ended enlargement gradually transformed what began as an elite economic club of wealthy Western European nations into one of the most ambitious regional political experiments of the twentieth and twenty-first centuries. Where the admission of the UK, Ireland, and Denmark had merely extended the existing club to three additional Northern European democracies, the Community followed up on its more explicitly political intentions during the second half of the 1970s when it guided a recently democratized Greece to its eventual admission in 1981. Five years later, in 1986, Spain and Portugal joined after their own transitions to democracy.[4] Almost to its own surprise, the EEC had become a major player in Cold War efforts at stabilizing Europe's periphery.[5]

Nonetheless, few would have dared to foresee the radical enlargement toward the East and the internal transformation that swept over the continent in the following two decades. The unexpected rupture of 1989 and the end of the Cold War not only made possible a reunified Germany and triggered closer economic integration, but also paved the way for three waves of enlargement. After admitting the three formerly neutral countries

---

3 *Declaration on European Identity* (Copenhagen, 14 December 1973), *Bulletin of the European Communities*, no. 12 (Luxembourg: Office for Official Publications of the European Communities, 1973), 118–122.
4 The previous year, Greenland had voted to leave the EC in a referendum after being granted home rule by Denmark.
5 Barry Eichengreen and Jeffry A. Frieden (eds.), *Forging an Integrated Europe* (Ann Arbor: University of Michigan Press, 1998).

of Austria, Finland, and Sweden in 1995, the EU embarked on its most transformative and daring experiment by admitting thirteen additional member states, eleven of which were post-Communist countries. By the summer of 2013, with the admission of Croatia, the EU counted twenty-eight member states. Alongside enlargement, meanwhile, European constitutional jurisprudence in the hands of the European Court of Justice (ECJ) worked ceaselessly to create a European single market. Since 1999 a single European currency has stretched from Portugal to Finland. Enlargement and economic integration radically remade the continent.

This recasting of the European project inevitably raised a triplet of questions: *What* was Europe? *Where* was Europe? *Who* was European? During the 1990s and 2000s, renewed attempts to give Europe normative meaning and to form a genuinely public debate about European identity and the nature of the European political experiment competed with skeptical narratives stressing distinctively national cultural legacies and democratic achievements. Was the EU a regionalist stepping-stone toward cosmopolitan internationalism and global economic governance, European intellectuals asked, or instead a hegemonic project of market liberalization? Did it pave the way for transnational citizenship or merely replicate an exclusionary identity logic on a continental scale? As this chapter will argue, these debates reflect a threefold struggle over unstable and contested identity categories that oscillate between universalistic and particularistic understandings. These contestations touch on, first, the external boundaries of the EU; second, the nature of the European project; and third, the reconfiguration of citizenship and belonging in Europe.

This chapter constitutes an early attempt at writing the history of post-1989 European integration from the inevitably disillusioned vantage point of crisis offered by the experience of politicized austerity in response to the Eurocrisis, fraught inhospitality toward asylum seekers, and the British referendum decision to leave the EU.

Any attempt to evaluate these developments requires an unflinching look back onto the European identity debates of the 1990s and the way in which Europe was remade after 1989. Thus, the chapter combines a history of debates over European identity since the end of the Cold War with a history of European integration and, ultimately, its current crisis.

Writing the history of European integration and expansion from the vantage point of crisis means confronting a period too recent to have accumulated layers of historiography. But it also brings us face to face more generally with the EU as a political experiment whose contested nature and uncertain future inevitably shape any assessment.[6] The crisis only underscored the treacherous difficulty involved in writing about European integration from a vantage point that is still too close to the events. Acknowledging today's sense of crisis and disappointment cannot but shape our account of integration, but by itself it cannot be a warrant to dismiss real achievements. Nor, more subtly, can it license the erasure of once-real hopes that have since been disappointed. While the current crisis must lead to a more unflinching assessment of integration, it would be a mistake to conclude that disappointment was inevitable or that the current crisis merely revealed the EU as what it always had been. Instead, particularly in moments of uncertainty, it is important to insist on the openness of past futures. This means acknowledging present disillusionment without erasing that the path to a different union was at times within reach even though it was ultimately not taken. Looking back from a moment of crisis forces us to take stock unsentimentally. But it cannot unduly license us either to project the current sense of crisis back in time as an inevitability or to fatalistically extrapolate from it an insurmountable impasse.

Creating a Common Market

While the 1970s indicated a first willingness to create a more political union of European states, the first decisive change occurred in the course of the 1980s.[7] Under the aegis of a German–French axis between German Chancellor Helmut Kohl and French President François Mitterrand, overseen by Jacques Delors as President of the European Commission from 1985 until 1995, the European project received a new impetus. Behind the new momentum stood less Delors's high-flying rhetoric than the earlier reversal of economic policy under François Mitterrand. Elected in 1981 as the first socialist President of the Fifth Republic, Mitterrand's government struggled for two years against humiliating turmoil in the currency markets. It capitulated in March 1983 when Delors, then Mitterrand's finance minister,

---

6 For an overview of theoretical accounts of European integration and identity, see Jeffrey T. Checkel and Peter J. Katzenstein (eds.), *European Identity* (Cambridge: Cambridge University Press, 2009); Neil Fligstein, *Euroclash: The EU, European Identity, and the Future of Europe* (Oxford: Oxford University Press, 2008); and Christopher J. Bickerton, *European Integration: From Nation-States to Member States* (Oxford: Oxford University Press, 2012).

7 The successive waves of enlargement and integration that followed both built on older notions of collective memory and also altered them in turn. See Peter J. Verovšek, "Expanding Europe through Memory: The Shifting Content of the Ever-Salient Past," *Millennium: Journal of International Studies*, 43(2) (2015), 531–550; and Peter J. Verovšek, *Memory and the Future of Europe* (Manchester: Manchester University Press, forthcoming).

won the internal struggle for austerity and monetary stabilization. Within a matter of months France turned from Europe's last socialist experiment to the leading architect of capital mobility.[8]

Only in the wake of the French turn toward economic discipline could the formation of a single European market become a point of convergence – not least because it allowed, at least initially, the projection of wildly divergent political visions. As France and West Germany sought to remake the continent in the image of their new alliance, capital mobility quickly emerged as a key catalyst. By the mid 1980s, four of the largest economies in the world – the United States, the UK, Japan, and crucially West Germany – had largely liberalized their capital accounts after the collapse of the Bretton Woods monetary system. With France's longstanding veto removed after 1983, the path was now open for a new Europe of freely flowing capital. The new doctrine was soon enshrined in a European directive (1988/361/EEC) that required all member states to remove restrictions on the movement of capital, including short-term hot money and not just among member states but also toward all non-member states. "Brussels," Rawi Abdelal explains, "became the source of the most liberal set of multilateral rules of international finance ever written. The financial integration of Europe entailed, as a matter of European law, Europe's embrace of the internationalization of finance."[9] Within only a few years capital controls became heretical. The Maastricht Treaty, negotiated in 1991, gave this liberalization a constitutional character.

But with their capital accounts open, Western European countries were now fully exposed to the policies of the Bundesbank. The question soon arose in France whether the country might not be better served within a European monetary union than by the informal dominance of the Bundesbank.[10] From the corresponding German perspective, monetary union was the price to be paid for the long-sought European flow of capital that would allow German savings to flow into Europe's periphery and discipline macroeconomic policy. With the capital liberalization directive passed in 1988, Helmut Kohl and François Mitterrand agreed to form a committee to explore monetary union. Although most observers and even many committee members did not expect the report to leave much of a mark, it proved remarkably resilient.

---

8 Rawi Abdelal, *Capital Rules. The Construction of Global Finance* (Cambridge: Harvard University Press, 2007).
9 Abdelal, *Capital Rules*, 11.
10 As Jacques Delors, architect of the *tournant* as Mitterrand's Finance Minister, put it retrospectively, "[we] decided that it would be better to live in an EMU zone than in a Deutsche mark zone." As cited in Abdelal, *Capital Rules*, 10.

The sudden end of the Cold War and the prospect of German reunification clinched the underlying calculations and the resulting settlement was soon codified in the Maastricht Treaty.[11]

In retrospect, the monetary union that emerged cannot but appear as the result of an odd overlap between two fundamentally different visions. For some, monetary union constituted an ingenious stepping-stone to further political integration and European economic government. The political path forward had to rely on economic trailblazing. A European polity would come about in response to the challenges of governing a monetary union. For others, the creation of a single market and monetary union meant the depoliticization of the economy through the creation of a liberalized European market beyond statist interventions, devaluations, or inflation. Now the Bundesbank's anti-inflationist policy would be exported to the entire Euro-area while flexible labor markets would improve productivity and allow the real-wage reductions previously achieved by devaluations.

Far more than a roadmap toward integration, the Maastricht Treaty thus fundamentally reconfigured domestic democratic politics and curtailed states' ability to intervene in the economy. The new consensus of a low-inflation European monetary system combined with capital mobility, Kathleen McNamara has noted, "redefined state interests in cooperation ... and induced political leaders to accept the domestic policy adjustments needed to stay within the system."[12] The new rules of financial liberalization exerted their most profound effect in negotiations with prospective members.[13] With EU membership contingent on meeting the new rules, countries pursuing membership during the 1990s and 2000s comprehensively moved toward more flexible labor markets and rapidly liberalized both financial markets and international capital flows. Tied to a geopolitical logic of democratization and market liberalization, the EU shepherded post-Communist Central and Eastern Europe into the new global market order.

What is most striking in retrospect is not merely how assessments of the Maastricht Treaty could diverge, but how these starkly different visions of the EU's future could exist alongside each other. During the 1990s the single

---

11 Martin Sandbu, *Europe's Orphan: The Future of the Euro and the Politics of Debt* (Princeton: Princeton University Press, 2015), 12–14. See also Harold James, *Making the European Monetary Union* (Cambridge: Harvard University Press, 2012), 214–215.
12 Kathleen R. McNamara, *The Currency of Ideas: Monetary Politics in the European Union* (Ithaca: Cornell University Press, 1998), 62–65; and Eric Helleiner, *States and the Reemergence of Global Finance: From Bretton Woods to the 1990s* (Ithaca: Cornell University Press, 1994), 161–163.
13 Abdelal, *Capital Rules*, 12.

market became the shared fetish both of neoliberals and of European federalists. The legal trailblazing of the ECJ and the European Court of Human Rights, as well as the supranational quality of European treaties, were from this perspective celebrated as paving the transformation of the EU from a mere supranational economic organization to a distinct political entity, either as a stepping stone toward cosmopolitanism or at least as a guarantee for a pluralist post-Cold War order.

Admittedly, while member states grew together economically, democratic processes remained constituted at the level of the nation-state. The European Parliament remained largely powerless against the intergovernmental brokering in the Council of Ministers. As the constitutional lawyer Dieter Grimm asked in this context, if the EU proceeded on its path of gradual transformation from a supranational institution grounded in intergovernmental treaties toward a postnational state, how would the resulting entity be able to meet democratic requirements of legitimation, not least a European-wide political public sphere and a common political culture?[14] Conceding Grimm's diagnosis while countering its political conclusion, the critical theorist Jürgen Habermas responded by pointing to the mounting challenges of democratic legitimation that equally faced the nation-state. European federalists, like Habermas, detected from this perspective in the gradual development of European political structures the promise of an eventual counter to unregulated global market expansion. As Habermas put it, democratic processes and economic government simply "lagged behind" economic integration.[15] Adapting an argument from the political economist Karl Polanyi's 1944 *Great Transformation*, Habermas suggested in 1998 that just as the economic liberalism of the nineteenth century had triggered the formation of the postwar welfare state, so would the transnational economic liberalization of the late twentieth century culminate in new forms of economic governance and democracy beyond the state, such as the EU.[16]

In an era of globalized capital flows and integrated supply chains, nation states' ability to regulate capitalism had become severely constrained. With states

---

14 Dieter Grimm, "Does Europe Need a Constitution?," *European Law Journal*, 303(1) (November 1995), 298–302.
15 Jürgen Habermas, "Appendix II: Citizenship and National Identity (1990)," in Jürgen Habermas, *Between Facts and Norms: Contributions to a Discourse Theory of Law and Democracy*, trans. William Rehg (Cambridge: MIT Press, 1996), 491.
16 Jürgen Habermas, "The Postnational Constellation and the Future of Democracy" (1998), in Jürgen Habermas, *The Postnational Constellation*, trans. Max Pensky (Cambridge: MIT Press, 2001), 84. For a critical argument on how such narratives relied on an unspoken commitment to a fixed vision of historical development, see John McCormick, *Weber, Habermas and Transformations of the European State: Constitutional, Social, and Supranational Democracy* (Cambridge: Cambridge University Press, 2007).

locked into a struggle over national economic competitiveness, Habermas argued, the survival of a meaningful welfare state depended on the formation of institutions "capable of acting supranationally."[17] To be sure, building a supranational democracy was a political gamble with uncertain consequences. But the dystopian alternative in the case of failure was not the old cocoon of the national welfare state. Instead, what loomed was a hyperglobalized economic modernity in which corporations could pit states against one another to shed welfare programs and labor laws. The result would be a pool of increasingly alienated losers from globalization – what Habermas dubbed "the Third world within the First" – living in the nostalgic shadow of past democratic agency.

> The decisive elements of this future scenario would be the postindustrial misery of the 'surplus' population produced by the surplus society – the Third world within the First – and an accompanying moral erosion of community. This future-present would in retrospect view itself as the future of a past illusion – the democratic illusion according to which societies could still determine their own destinies through political will and consciousness.[18]

Such a narrative did not deny worries about Europe's democratic deficit. Nor did its suggested developmental path provide guarantees that deeper political integration would ultimately succeed in overcoming the democratic deficit. But it set out a stark view of the grim realities that awaited those who did not try. Building new political institutions on a European level was by contrast a constructive, if admittedly uncertain, path toward a democratic deepening of the Union and a supranational model of economic governance. The only possible solution to the democratic deficits of integration was more integration.

Where Habermas portrayed the underlying process of integration as a gradual approximation of the ideal of postnational citizenship, the philosopher Étienne Balibar framed the EU as neither on its way toward a supranational state, nor a postnational cosmopolitical society. Instead, the EU reflected a "transnationalization of the political" that had taken politics across borders without fully erasing those borders.[19] Unlike in the postnational cosmopolitan narrative, for Balibar the EU embodied the difficulties and aporias of reinventing democratic politics in a transnational context that had not erased the old ties of belonging but

---

17 Jürgen Habermas, "Remarks on Dieter Grimm's 'Does Europe Need a Constitution?,'" *European Law Journal*, 1(3) (November 1995), 305.
18 Habermas, "Remarks on Dieter Grimm's 'Does Europe Need a Constitution?,'" 305.
19 Étienne Balibar, *Nous, citoyens d'Europe?: Les frontières, l'État, le people* (Paris: Éditions La Découverte, 2001). Translated as Étienne Balibar, *We, the People of Europe?: Reflections on Transnational Citizenship*, trans. James Swenson (Princeton: Princeton University Press, 2004).

complicated them through the transnational movements of goods, capital, and people. This meant that the EU was hardly a stepping-stone toward cosmopolitan citizenship as an experiment in the construction of "transnational citizenship" and the democratization of borders. Balibar embraced in this context instead the prospect of disruptive, confrontational, and radically participatory forms of democracy, ranging from "counter-democracy" (Pierre Rosanvallon) to the construction of a new "commons" (Antonio Negri).[20] The insertion of democracy into the European project, according to Balibar, cannot be a developmental process but requires a radical "jump."

Despite their divergent conceptions of European democracy, Habermas and Balibar nonetheless agreed in seeing in the EU a possible bulwark for the future governance of globalized capitalism. But such hopes have to be contrasted with the vision that motivated many of the political architects of one of the most far-reaching dimensions of European integration – the single market. For them, the construction of a European single market served neither as a step toward an incipient moral cosmopolitanism, nor as a blueprint for supranational state structures. Instead, the single market functioned as an embodiment of precisely the kind of liberalized economic hyperglobalization that Habermas and Balibar had hoped the EU would come to counter. The constitutional character of European law, this practitioners' view celebrated, was attractive because it would place incontestable constraints upon states' ability to meddle in the economy. After all, many of the rights and freedoms enforced by the ECJ were primarily economic in nature.[21] The single market's four freedoms – freedom of movement for goods, services, persons, and capital – could thereby be instituted above the heads of national legislatures and without attracting direct political opposition.

A European Constitution?

What allowed such divergent assessments of the EU to exist alongside each other throughout the 1990s and 2000s was precisely the project's seemingly indeterminate, fluid, and contested shape. As late as 1998, even an observer as

---

20 Étienne Balibar, "Quelle Europe démocratique? Réponse à Jürgen Habermas," *Libération* (September 3, 2012).
21 For a theoretical account of Europe's functional constitutionalism, see Turkuler Isiksel, *Europe's Functional Constitution: A Theory of Constitutionalism beyond the State* (Oxford: Oxford University Press, 2016). See also the discussion in Class Offe and Ulrich K. Preuß, *Citizens in Europe: Essays on Democracy, Constitutionalism and European Integration* (Colchester: ECPR Press, 2016).

critical as the historian Perry Anderson could entertain the possibility that "with a modicum of luck" the EU could be turned into an engine of European socialism.[22] Anderson pointed specifically to three critical issues facing the EU: the single currency, the role of Germany, and the multiplication of member states.[23] All three were harbingers of "radical indeterminacy." But if Europe's future would have to be built on unpredictable political quicksands, this constituted as much an opportunity as a challenge.

Part of the EU's fluid character was of course always fueled by intentional mystification. As long as the EU could be described as an "unidentified political object," as Delors famously quipped, its shape remained conveniently hazy.[24] But to present the EU as *sui generis*, without precedents or comparisons, became in this context a fig leaf that could disguise mounting tensions between radically divergent visions of Europe's future. The shibboleth of European identity was intimately bound up with these contradictory institutional assessments. Proliferating invocations of European identity proved notoriously, and intentionally, elusive not despite, but because of, the rapid construction of an enlarged European single market.

One attempt to harness these divergent forces into a coherent narrative emerged toward the end of the 1990s in the form of calls for a European Constitution. In February 2000, almost six years after his first speech in Strasbourg, Havel returned to the European Parliament, still president of the Czech Republic but with his country now on a firm path toward membership.[25] Turning once more to the question of how Europe could be endowed with a political and ethical identity, Havel joined the emerging chorus of those calling for a European Constitution, not least Habermas. When Joschka Fischer, then Germany's Foreign Minister, used a speech at Humboldt University in Berlin in May 2000 to call for a codified European Constitution as the basis for an accelerated integration of a European core, he immediately drew attention from across the continent.[26] At the turn of the

22 Perry Anderson, "A Reply to Norberto Bobbio," *New Left Review*, I/231 (September–October 1998), 91–93. Cited in Mark Mazower, "Anderson's Amphibologies," *The Nation* (April 8, 2010), www.thenation.com/article/andersons-amphibologies-perry-anderson/.
23 Perry Anderson, "The Europe to Come," in *The Question of Europe*, eds. Perry Anderson and Peter Gowan (London: Verso, 1997), 144.
24 Speech by Jacques Delors in Luxembourg (September 9, 1985), *Bulletin of the European Communities*, no. 9.
25 Václav Havel, "Address to the European Parliament (February 16, 2000), www.europarl.europa.eu/sides/getDoc.do?pubRef=-//EP//TEXT+CRE+20000216+ITEM-012+DOC+XML+V0//EN.
26 Joschka Fischer, "From Confederacy to Federation – Thoughts on the Finality of European Integration," Speech at Humboldt University, Berlin (May 12, 2000), http://ec.europa.eu/dorie/fileDownload.do?docId=192161&cardId=192161.

millennium Europe seemed to be experiencing its Philadelphia moment and widespread optimism about the prospects of European unification reigned supreme. As Havel echoed in his speech, "I welcome with satisfaction the fact that our Europeanism is starting to emerge clearly today."[27]

In one sense, calls for a European Constitution only acknowledged what had already become a reality. Since the 1980s the ECJ had repeatedly stressed that Community law was no longer a mere matter of treaties but had acquired a constitutional character. In 1986 the Court thus referred to the Community's founding treaties as its "Basic Constitutional Charter."[28] But while the EU's pursuit of a single market had acquired constitutional character, its lack of a popular basis and a political statement of values had become increasingly apparent. Europe may have been operating according to constitutional norms, but it lacked a political constitution.[29] The leap to a genuine European Constitution offered in this context the promise of endowing the EU with the necessary spirit to hold it together as a political entity.

Such aspirations for a European postnational constitutional order during the late 1990s also formed part of a broader turn toward universalism and human rights. The explicit background to debates about European values at the time was the genocidal war in Kosovo and NATO's intervention in response in the spring of 1999. As participants such as Havel and Fischer stressed, for the first time human rights had risen above the rights of the state. "[W]hile the state is a human creation, human beings are the creation of God," Havel explained to the Canadian Parliament in April 1999, during week six of NATO's bombing campaign and a mere month after the Czech Republic had joined the alliance alongside Poland and Hungary.[30] But oddly, such appeals to universalism were not meant to pave the way to a global civil society. Instead, as Havel stressed in the same speech, they pointed to distinct "spheres of culture and civilizations" that would require an awareness of their respective identity.

Despite the initial optimism, the idea of building a European identity on a constitutional foundation ultimately proved at once too anemic and

---

27 Havel, "Address to the European Parliament (February 16, 2000)."
28 Parti écologiste "Les Verts" v European Parliament, Case 294/83. As quoted in Jan-Werner Müller, "‹Our Philadelphia›? On the Political and Intellectual History of the ‹European Constitution›," *Journal of Modern European History*, 6(1) (2008), 137–154, p. 143.
29 J. H. H. Weiler, *The Constitution of Europe: "Do the New Clothes Have an Emperor?" and Other Essays on European Integration* (Cambridge: Cambridge University Press, 1999), 8.
30 Václav Havel, "Kosovo and the End of the Nation-State," *New York Review of Books* (June 10, 1999), 4–6. Originally given in Ottawa on April 29, 1999 as a speech to the Canadian Senate and House of Commons.

too far-reaching. The European constitutional patriotism that Habermas had envisaged as a solution to the dilemma of European identity failed to strike roots. When French President Jacques Chirac echoed Fischer's proposal in a speech to the German Parliament in June 2000, he immediately incurred the wrath of his own government back in Paris.[31] In 2004, less than four years after he had first floated the idea of a fast-track European core (the so-called *Kerneuropa*), Fischer had to concede that instead of paving the way for a strengthened European identity his speech had only succeeded in solidifying Eurosceptical sentiment across the continent. "I would give parts of the Humboldt speech differently today," he admitted.[32] When Dutch and French voters rejected the new European Constitutional Treaty in two referenda in 2005, they fatally smashed with it any hope for imminent political unification of a European core. The prospective Constitution was silently withdrawn and replaced by the unwieldy Lisbon Treaty, which was conveniently passed on the intergovernmental level without democratic consultation. Instead of a quotable pocket constitution that would have described Europe as "an area of special hope" the result was a textual monstrosity. The democratic attempt to give Europe a political identity had failed.

European Identity and Citizenship between Universalism and Particularism

Tellingly, already the Treaty of Rome, which had stipulated that only a European state could acquire membership, nowhere defined what exactly this meant.[33] The 1973 Declaration similarly spoke of a diversity of national cultures embedded within the common framework of a single "European civilization" but failed to define the values or delineate the contours of such a civilization. Instead, it merely concluded evasively that "the European identity will evolve as a function of the dynamic construction of a United Europe."[34] This dynamic construction of Europe soon threw up significant forks in the road. In 1987 Morocco's application was rejected on the grounds that it was quite simply not a European

---

31 Jacques Chirac, "Our Europe. Address to the German Bundestag," June 27, 2000.
32 Damir Fras and Bettina Vestring, "Interview mit Joschka Fischer," *Berliner Zeitung* (February 28, 2004).
33 Peo Hanssen and Stefan Jonsson, *Eurafrica. The Untold History of European Integration and Colonialism* (London: Bloomsbury, 2014), 2.
34 1973 EEC Declaration on European Identity, 122.

country.³⁵ But again no definition was given of what it would mean to be a European country. Marked by the awkward rejection of Morocco's bid for membership and conscious of the fraught status of Turkey's application the same year, Brussels sought to steer away from definitions of cultural identity and instead set out formalized institutional conditions that it presented as culturally agnostic.

The resulting Copenhagen criteria for EU membership, pinned down in June 1993 with the question of Eastern enlargement already on the horizon, set out adherence to four constitutive values: democracy, the rule of law, the protection of human rights, and a market economy (which now included, crucially, the free movement of capital). Instead of cultural markers, legal criteria now specified conditions for membership. While this seemingly freed questions of enlargement from contentious cultural baggage, it inevitably and intentionally obscured and impoverished the question of Europe's normative purpose and identity. It was precisely this ethical poverty that Havel lamented when he addressed the European Parliament in 1994. Placing the EU in a row of "large empires, complex supranational entities or confederations of states that we know from history," Havel insisted that the only such entities to succeed had been "buoyed by a spirit, an idea, an ethos."³⁶ The nightmarish alternative, Havel implied, was dissolution and with it a return of violence, as the genocidal war in the former Yugoslavia illustrated.

But while the attempt to rest European integration and enlargement on thin liberal-democratic institutional criteria intentionally avoided debates about identity, at the same time it only thinly veiled the undiminished reliance on cultural markers of identity. Attempts to spell out European specificity remained either excessively abstract or suspiciously essentialist, or occasionally even both.³⁷ The challenge was, as Balibar put it, how to give Europe a fictive identity that was at once strong enough to guide its institutions and become part of individuals' imaginations while at the same time resisting the seductive closure characteristic of national identities.³⁸ But this meant that the quest for a European identity involved nothing less than the invention of "a new image of a people" that could negotiate anew the relation between membership in historical communities of fate and the

---

35 Council Decision of October 1, 1987, in *Europe Archives*, Z 207. See also Iver B. Neumann, *Uses of the Other: "The East" in European Identity Formation* (Minneapolis: University of Minnesota Press, 1998).
36 Havel, "Speech in the European Parliament (March 8, 1994)," 297.
37 Jan-Werner Müller, *Constitutional Patriotism* (Princeton: Princeton University Press, 2007), 97.
38 Balibar, *We, the People of Europe?*, 9.

lived experience of democratic citizenship. Instead of such a leap forward, debates about European identity continued to be stuck in an oscillation between liberal cosmopolitanism on the one hand and a belief in a Judeo-Christian European civilization on the other – the term "Judeo-Christian" being a pious nod to a history of European intolerance, expulsion, and eventual extermination of the Jews of Europe. The project of European integration remained constitutively beset by a dualism between universalism and particularism.

The question of Turkish membership is illustrative in this regard.[39] When Turkey applied to join in 1987, its application was not immediately rejected. Instead, in the context of the Cold War the country was declared to be in theory admissible, on the basis of a 1963 Association Agreement. This led observers to conclude that the term "European State" need not be interpreted in a strictly geographical sense and was subject to political assessments. But this did not, of course, preclude that such political assessments would unfold along geographical or indeed confessional lines. Eligibility in principle thus did not prevent Turkey's bid for membership from lingering in a seemingly endless holding pattern. Turkey received formal candidate status only in 1999. Not least thanks to Germany's strong opposition, the EU's relation to Turkey is still no more than a mere "special partnership." Its membership negotiations, which officially opened in 2005, are formally still pending but look, as of 2019, more doubtful than ever. While the EU has today come to rely on Turkey to prevent refugees from crossing the Aegean, President Erdoğan's crackdown in the wake of the failed military coup of July 2016 has rendered any discussion of Turkish membership moot for the foreseeable future. This cannot hide that Turkey's failure to fulfill the conditions of the *Acquis Communautaire* and the Copenhagen criteria, as well as its increasingly egregious flouting of European human rights norms, conveniently converged with only rarely articulated fears of adding seventy million Muslims to the EU.

Debates about European identity are bound to bring to the fore Europe's Christian dimension, then as now. Widespread Islamophobia and suspicion dominates European public discourse. Most recently this sentiment found expression in the refusal of several Eastern European governments to accept Muslim refugees. Miloš Zeman, Havel's successor as President of the Czech Republic, has declared Islam incompatible with Europe and ruled out that his

---

39 For an extended discussion, see Seyla Benhabib and Türküler Isiksel, "Ancient Battles, New Prejudices, and Future Perspectives: Turkey and the EU," *Constellations* 13(2) (June 2006), 218–233.

country would welcome any Muslim refugees.[40] It is furthermore not only the openly xenophobic governments of the Visegrád states that unapologetically press the image of a Christian Europe. Earlier conservative thinkers of European unity, such as the Christian theologian Jacques Maritain, had long stressed a shared Christian heritage from which common rules and rights could be derived.[41] It had after all been a generation of mainly Christian-Democratic politicians who forged the European Coal and Steel Community and the Rome Treaty in the postwar decades with a clear sense of ecumenical Christian purpose in the context of the Cold War.[42] Against such essentialist visions of Europe as a common Christian civilization, alternative proposals for European unity have instead embraced the other side of the dualism.[43] The tentative emergence of signs of a European identity appeared from this perspective not so much as a uniquely European achievement but rather as reflecting a wider global trend that witnessed a reconfiguration of national identities within a post-Westphalian world – be it toward postnational cosmopolitanism or the transnationalization of the political.

While citizenship in Europe had traditionally been predicated upon an individual's status as citizen of a particular nation-state, European integration has challenged this model culturally, politically, and administratively. The category of EU citizenship transcends national distinctions of belonging and designates a legal identity that is granted to nationals of all EU member countries.[44] Migration within the EU, it was expected, would over time

40 "Integrating Muslims into Europe is 'impossible,' says Czech president," *The Guardian* (January 17, 2016). Refugees arriving on Europe's shores, Zeman had explained earlier, constituted "an organized invasion."
41 Samuel Moyn, *Christian Human Rights* (Philadelphia: University of Pennsylvania Press, 2015). Müller, "Our Philadelphia," 139. For the longer historical arc, see Mary Anne Perkins, *Christendom and European Identity: The Legacy of a Grand Narrative since 1789* (Berlin: De Gruyter, 2004).
42 On the role of Christian-Democratic parties in the making of the European Union, see Wolfram Kaiser, *Christian Democracy and the Origins of the European Union* (Cambridge: Cambridge University Press, 2007); Martin Conway and Kiran Klaus Patel, *Europeanization in the Twentieth Century* (London: Palgrave Macmillan, 2011); Dieter Gosewinkel (ed.), *Anti-liberal Europe: A Neglected Story of Europeanization* (New York: Berghahn Books, 2014); and Lucian Leustean, *The Ecumenical Movements and the Making of the European Community* (Oxford: Oxford University Press, 2014).
43 Jürgen Habermas, "Citizenship and National Identity: Some Reflections on the Future of Europe," *Praxis International*, 12(1) (1992), 1–19; and Balibar, *We, the People of Europe?* See also Kalypso Nicolaïdis, "Our European Demoi-cracy: Is This Constitution a Third Way for Europe?," in *Whose Europe? National Models and the Constitution of the European Union*, ed. Kalypso Nicolaïdis and Stephen Weatherill (Oxford: Oxford University Press, 2003), 137–152.
44 Less visible, but perhaps just as important, has been the attendant regionalization of identity as forms of belonging are becoming rooted in regional or urban identities again, be they Catalonia or Tuscany, Berlin, or Amsterdam.

further level traditional distinctions between EU citizens. But while pan-European labor mobility has shot up during the Eurocrisis, it remains low in comparative terms, in particular when compared with the United States.[45] Young Europeans value their freedom of travel and residency within Europe, but neither European citizenship nor the Erasmus student exchange program, launched in 1987, have so far led to the emergence of a widespread pan-European political identity. Even where social movements have begun to conceive of themselves as acting in European networks, as is the case with anti-austerity parties in Greece and Spain, their concrete struggles for electoral representation continue to play out largely on a domestic stage.

The obverse side of Union citizenship has meanwhile meant that citizenship became delineated ever more sharply against non-members. The result has been a distinct two-tiered status of foreignness throughout Europe. While Europe's internal borders within the Schengen zone have become porous, its external borders have hardened. Moreover, different groups of residents are entitled to different packages of rights and benefits depending on the status of their residency – whether citizens, resident aliens, asylum seekers, or so-called third-country nationals.[46] This has become particularly visible for refugees and asylum seekers who find themselves confronted with "Fortress Europe," policed since 2004 by the EU's border management agency Frontex, as well as a treacherous patchwork of immigration rules. Where Union citizenship extends the benefits of membership to all EU nationals, the principles on which European countries accept (and eventually naturalize) asylum seekers continue to differ markedly among member states. The Dublin regulations, originally signed in 1990 and in force since 1997, harmonized the processing of asylum applications by granting member states the right to decide where an application is examined (usually in the first country of entry) and preventing asylum seekers from applying in another European country until the first application has been resolved. The agreement furthermore instituted an implicitly asymmetric regime whereby an asylum rejection by one member state is valid for all member states, whereas a positive decision applies only to the member state

---

45 Europe's mobility rate – the percentage of people moving to another country each year – of around 0.5 percent pales in comparison with the approximately 3 percent annually moving across state lines in the United States. Furthermore, a significant share of European mobility derives from naturalized immigrants from third countries. Julia Jauer, Thomas Liebig, John P. Martin, and Patrick A. Puhani, "Migration as an Adjustment Mechanism in the Crisis? A Comparison of Europe and the United States," *OECD Working Papers*, no. 155 (January 2014).

46 Seyla Benhabib, *The Claims of Culture. Equality and Diversity in the Global Era* (Princeton: Princeton University Press, 2002); and Seyla Benhabib, *The Rights of Others: Aliens, Residents, and Citizens* (Cambridge: Cambridge University Press, 2004).

where the decision was made. This has made it harder to receive refugee status in Europe. As the handling of refugees in the summer of 2015 showed, immigration and asylum policies continue to straddle the sovereign jurisdiction of individual member states and discretionary intergovernmental agreements of cooperation, making it easy for those in power to evade their responsibilities and allowing a convenient apportioning of blame.[47]

The underlying tension recalls the refugee crisis of the early 1990s when similar numbers of refugees and immigrants arrived from former Soviet Republics and the Balkans. Already in the course of the 1980s the number of asylum seekers had steadily risen. But with the end of the Cold War, borders in Eastern Europe were suddenly open, just as violence erupted in the Balkans. As a result, the number of asylum seekers spiked in 1991–1993. This triggered fierce debates across Europe about the required extent of hospitality. While many countries accepted asylum seekers, violence against refugees soon flared up throughout the continent, in particular in Germany where anti-foreigner attacks and riots took place in several East German cities. Official statistics of racially motivated attacks in Germany shot up from 2,426 in 1991 to 6,336 in 1992.[48] Indeed, the European Council meeting in June 1993 that produced the Copenhagen criteria culminated in the assembled heads of states being forced to condemn rampant attacks on immigrants and refugees across Europe.[49]

At the same time as the European Council publicly condemned violent attacks on immigrants, the same European governments passed legislation that directly targeted migrants. In France, Interior Minister Jean-Louis Debré proposed a further tightening of the already severe immigration laws that curtailed the rights of immigrants and made it a "crime of hospitality" to shelter undocumented immigrants (*les sans-papiers*).[50] It was in this context that Jacques Derrida turned his attention to the *sans-papiers*.[51] Addressing a demonstration against the Debré law in Nanterre in December 1996,

---

47 While Germany temporarily suspended the enforcement of the country-of-entry rule in 2015, it has since denied asylum applications on this ground again.
48 Triadafilos Triadafilopoulos, *Becoming Multicultural: Immigration and the Politics of Membership in Canada and Germany* (Vancouver: UBC Press, 2012), 137–139.
49 The Council expressed "its deep sympathy with the innocent victims of such aggressions," pledging "to protect everybody, including immigrants and refugees, against violations of fundamental rights and freedoms." Press Release, European Council Meeting in Copenhagen, June 1993.
50 Patrick Weil, *Qu'est-ce qu'un Français? Histoire de la nationalité française de la Révolution à nos jours* (Paris: Grasset, 2002), 165–181.
51 Jacques Derrida, "Derelictions of the Right to Justice" (1996), in *Negotiations: Interventions and Interviews, 1971–2001*, ed., trans., and with an Introduction by Elizabeth Rottenberg (Stanford: Stanford University Press, 2002), 133–144.

Derrida declared that in the eyes of the law "the *sans-papiers* are without dignity because they are unworthy of our hospitality."[52] As he elaborated in his essay "On Cosmopolitanism," originally an address to the International Parliament of Writers in Strasbourg in 1996, the French treatment of the undocumented revealed the extent of French hypocrisy. France paid lip service to the ideal of cosmopolitanism but at the same time passed exclusionary immigration laws.[53] Building on the observation that the Latin words *hospis* (host) and *hostes* (enemy) have common roots, Derrida highlighted the historical and phenomenological entanglement of hospitality and hostility.[54] Europe was caught in the politics of *hostipitality*.

The oscillation between reluctant hospitality and violent inhospitality mirrors the larger contested dualism between universalistic understandings of citizenship and opposing particularistic claims to traditional life forms. Throughout the second half of the twentieth century former colonial populations and new guest workers had increased the share of foreign-born inhabitants of most Western European countries. In 1950, foreigners made up barely 1 percent of the Dutch and West German population, and little more than 4 percent in France and Belgium. By 2016, the share of foreign-born inhabitants had increased to around 12 percent in France and Spain, 15 percent in Germany and Norway, and 18 percent in Sweden and Austria.[55] Despite their substantial share of immigrant populations, many European countries nonetheless struggled against seeing themselves as immigrant nations. Earlier promises of European multiculturalism have since been gradually eroded or entirely retracted. The status of Muslims in particular remains a fraught one as culture wars continue to be fought over Islam's place in Europe. Widespread Islamophobia exists alongside a small but growing number of young European Muslims who feel little allegiance to the countries in which they were born and grew up. Europe remains stuck between the challenges of integrating Muslim populations and containing frequent nationalist backlashes against them.

---

52 Derrida, "Derelictions of the Right to Justice," 137.
53 Jacques Derrida, "On Cosmopolitanism," in *On Cosmopolitanism and Forgiveness*, trans. Mark Dooley and Michael Hughes (London: Routledge, 2001), 1–24.
54 Jacques Derrida, "Hostipitalité," *Cogito*, no. 85 (1999), 17–44. Translated as Jacques Derrida, "Hostipitality," *Angelaki: Journal of Theoretical Humanities*, 5(3) (December 2000), 3–18. See also Seyla Benhabib, *Another Cosmopolitanism: The Berkeley Tanner Lectures* (Oxford: Oxford University Press, 2006).
55 Pew Research Center estimates based on UN and Eurostat data (June 2016), Phillip Connor and Jens Manuel Krogstad, "Immigrant Share of Population Jumps in Some European Countries," www.pewresearch.org/fact-tank/2016/06/15/immigrant-share-of-population-jumps-in-some-european-countries/.

Political Fragmentation

Concrete contestations over European identity have periodically brought to the fore this unresolved institutional dualism between universalism and particularism. But instead of a teleology of economic integration spurring European political union, what has emerged is a disaggregation of rights and a sense of political fragmentation. Not only did the different dimensions of integration not proceed at the same pace, they did not even proceed in the same direction. Economic integration spelled not unity but political backlash. Just as global integration has proceeded alongside socio-cultural disintegration and the resurgence of ethnic, nationalistic, religious, and linguistic separatism, economic and monetary integration in Europe has been similarly accompanied by ethnic and cultural disintegration. This has left politics ambiguously torn between the contradictory pressures of economic integration and political fragmentation.

As the political economist Dani Rodrik pointed out on the eve of the Asian financial crisis in 1997, globalization and economic integration expose and widen social fissures between those able to take advantage of liberalized international markets, thanks to their mobility and education, and those unable to do so.[56] Rodrik concluded from this that there was a need for extensive social programs that could buffer some of the inequalities caused by increased trade in goods and services. But the EU has proven itself to be distinctly ill-equipped and unwilling to engage in what the German political economist Fritz Scharpf has called "positive integration."[57] Instead of constructing a European social safety net or issuing European public debt, the EU has largely restricted itself to the pursuit of "negative integration" in the form of tearing down internal market barriers.[58] Driven by technocratic imperative and judicial fiat, the Commission and the ECJ could autonomously pursue negative integration behind the back of elected politicians. Positive integration, by contrast, would have had to take the form of treaty changes and therefore require difficult, politically visible bargains on an intergovernmental level. Even after qualified majority voting replaced unanimity in many policy areas, in practice this has meant increasingly complex backroom dealings in the Council of Ministers, not a path toward positive integration.

---

56 Dani Rodrik, *Has Globalization Gone Too Far?* (Washington: Institute for International Economics, 1997), 38.
57 Fritz W. Scharpf, "Negative and Positive Integration," in *Governing in Europe: Effective and Democratic?* (Oxford: Oxford University Press, 1999), 43–83.
58 Scharpf, "Negative and Positive Integration," 56.

While European integration, like economic globalization, has undoubtedly contributed to a greater fluidity and instability of identity categories, this has resulted neither in a "flat world" (to borrow a phrase from the *New York Times* columnist Thomas Friedman), nor in a European republic. Instead, economic inequalities and unstable identity categories have reinvigorated struggles over distribution and recognition. While these pressures are far from peculiar to Europe, it was the EU that was long thought to be uniquely able to respond to them.[59] What could during the 1990s and 2000s still be read as the nascent promises of a postnational cosmopolitanism has with the Eurocrisis lost much of its ambiguity, shed its normative rhetoric, and hardened into an austerity-driven economic frame guided by an interplay of increasingly asymmetric intergovernmentalism and a technocratic European executive. Clashing national democratic wills are adjudicated not in the European Parliament but behind closed doors, where the hierarchies of economic and political might inevitably structure outcomes. Even previously sympathetic and enthusiastic supporters of the European project, such as Habermas, have since denounced the maneuverings of the European Council as a disturbing form of "post-democratic executive federalism."[60] In light of the EU's handling of the Eurocrisis, observers have been forced to wonder how to uphold the vision of European unity without becoming, in Immanuel Kant's words, "sorry comforters."[61]

Already before the crisis much of the federalist sentiment of the 1990s had gradually been deflated. "Future historians," Andrew Moravcsik predicted in 2002, "may someday look back on the 1990s as the decade when Europeans began to view the European Union without illusions."[62] While this was meant to clear the way for a sober embrace of the EU, shedding illusions could flip over all too easily into "Euroskepticism."[63] There had of course long been conservative and nationalist intellectuals skeptical of European integration, especially in Britain. But it was during the 1990s that these voices

---

59 Dani Rodrik, *The Globalization Paradox* (New York: W. W. Norton, 2011).
60 Jürgen Habermas, *The Crisis of the European Union: A Response*, trans. Ciaran Cronin (Cambridge: Polity Press, 2012), 12.
61 Immanuel Kant, "Zum ewigen Frieden. Ein philosophischer Entwurf" (1795), in *Werkausgabe*, 12 vols. (Frankfurt am Main: Suhrkamp, 1992), vol. XI, 210. Translated as "Perpetual Peace. A Philosophical Sketch," in *Kant: Political Writings*, ed. Hans Reiss, trans. H. B. Nisbet (Cambridge: Cambridge University Press, 1991), 103.
62 Andrew Moravcsik, *Europe without Illusions: The Paul Henri Spaak Lectures, 1994–1999* (Lanham: University Press of America, 2005), 3.
63 The concept of Euroskepticism, popularized in the wake of the Maastricht Treaty, originated in the 1970s, just as Eurobarometer surveys began to measure the identification of Europeans with their Community.

self-consciously embraced the label. Mirroring them on the left were "sovereigntist" socialist critics of the EU, ranging from Régis Debray and Didier Motchane in France to Perry Anderson and Susan Watkins in Britain. The Eurocrisis has since deepened these factions and thrown into limelight a new inflection of left Euroskeptics, such as Frédéric Lordon, Stathis Kouvelakis, and Costas Lapavitsas, as well as the sociologist Wolfgang Streeck, who emerged as the most influential critic of the Euro on the German left.[64]

As the Eurocrisis revealed, the rapid combination of deepening integration and Eastern enlargement did not prepare the way for a *finalité politique* but solidified a functional constitution of executive intergovernmentalism and technocratic governance dedicated to the creation of a liberalized common market.[65] For those who have always seen the EU as little more than a rather successful intergovernmental forum of nation states, this was hardly a surprise. The European states that emerged from World War II were after all democracies with consciously neutered and constrained forms.[66] An ingrained habit of delegation to unelected bodies was from this perspective a constitutive feature of the postwar European state system, rather than a bug specific to the EU.[67] But, unsurprisingly, a supranational structure based on the promise of economic integration and prosperity has proven particularly vulnerable to the disappointment of precisely such promises during the crisis. In the decade 2010–2020, youth unemployment in many regions of Southern Europe continues to hover at almost 50 percent and the EU's favorability ratings have sunk to unprecedented lows.[68]

Where they continue to exist at all, calls for a European political union beyond market integration find themselves embattled by left and right

---

64 See Wolfgang Streeck, "Why the Euro Divides Europe," *New Left Review*, no. 95 (September–October 2015), 5–26; and Wolfgang Streeck, "Small-State Nostalgia? The Currency Union, Germany, and Europe: A Reply to Jürgen Habermas," *Constellations*, 21(2) (2014), 213–221.
65 Isiksel, *Europe's Functional Constitution*, 1–30.
66 Jan-Werner Müller, *Contesting Democracy: Political Ideas in Twentieth-Century Europe* (New Haven: Yale University Press, 2011), 128 and 149. See also Isiksel, *Europe's Functional Constitution*, 221.
67 Instead of detecting in the reliance on intergovernmentalism and technocratic fiat the root cause of the EU's "democratic deficit," some have suggested that it is precisely the additional layer of European constraints that added legitimacy. See Andrew Moravcsik, "Reassessing Legitimacy in the European Union," *Journal of Common Market Studies*, 40(4) (2002), 603–624; and Giandomenico Majone, *Dilemmas of European Integration: The Ambiguities and Pitfalls of Integration by Stealth* (Oxford: Oxford University Press, 2005).
68 Since the onset of the crisis, approval for the EU has fallen in every single member of the Eurozone. *February 2016 Eurobarometer Report*.

Euroskepticism. In response, calls for further integration have become self-consciously utopian.[69] Rejecting both a withdrawal into the shell of the nation-state as well as the EU's current market fundamentalism beyond the state, they instead hope for the creation of democratic state structures on a European level. Rather than regarding the EU as a stepping-stone, today's advocates of political union are more likely to pit themselves against currently existing European institutions.

Provincializing a Special Area for Hope

When Havel, in his second address to the European Parliament in 2000, turned once more to the question of European identity, he opened with a confession. Embarrassingly, it had only been in response to the demands of his political office that he had first asked himself whether he felt European and what, if anything, bound him to Europe. No doubt, he explained, this had primarily to do with the fact that "everything with which I have always identified myself was so naturally European that it never occurred to me to consider it as such."[70] But there was a second reason. "[I]f Europe has thought so little about its own identity in the past, that is no doubt because it considered itself, wrongly, to be the entire world; or at least it considered itself to be better than the rest of the world, because it did not feel the need to define itself in relation to others."[71]

From this perspective, it was European dominance that had long rendered the question of European identity mute. In turn this meant that it was precisely Europe's ultimate loss of global pre-eminence with the end of the Cold War that structured its searching quest for identity during the 1990s. This may appear counter-intuitive. After all, Francis Fukuyama's contemporary vision had ended with a distinctly European twist. The end of history was supposed to spell the universalization not of Cold War America but of the European Community as a post-ideological common market.[72] From a European perspective, however, the supposed end of history turned out

---

69 Ulrike Guérot, *Warum Europa eine Republik werden muss! Eine politische Utopie* (Bonn: Dietz Verlag, 2016); and *Manifesto of DiEM25: Democracy in Europe Movement 2025* (2015), https://diem25.org.
70 Havel, "Address to the European Parliament (February 16, 2000)."
71 Havel, "Address to the European Parliament (February 16, 2000)."
72 Francis Fukuyama, "The End of History," *The National Interest* (Summer 1989). This was not meant as an untroubled compliment as Fukuyama's later references to Nietzsche's "last man" made clear. See also Lutz Niethammer, *Posthistoire: Has History Come to an End?* (London: Verso, 1994); and Müller, *Contesting Democracy*, 239.

to mean first and foremost the continent's accelerated provincialization. In the course of the twentieth century, the modern age of European influence had gradually given way to other regional and global configurations in the form of America's rise to global power and decolonization. Rather than heralding Fukuyama's last universalism, for Europe the end of the Cold War reflected a further deepening of this process of European provincialization.[73]

But as the historian Dipesh Chakrabarty has explained, while the region of the world we call "Europe" has been provincialized by history itself, European *thought* is still in need of provincialization.[74] How are we then to reconcile the political facts of Europe's provincialization with the remains of its universalistic intellectual aspirations and self-understanding? Was the European project's cosmopolitan universalism of the 1990s just a "last refuge of Eurocentrism," a "bandage" to disguise irrevocable provincialization?[75] Or might it be worth pondering, in Chakrabarty's spirit, what it would mean to hold onto Europe as more than a geographic designator while at the same time provincializing it as an ideal? Like Chakrabarty's pithy characterization of European thought as simultaneously indispensable and inadequate, it is tempting to see Europe's conflicted universalism as similarly indispensable but inadequate.[76] Crucially, it is inadequate because in order to escape its violent oscillations between appeals to empty universalism and exclusionary particularism, a provincialized European identity would require an awareness that its universalism does not derive from a normative core but stands in need of constant renewal from the margins.

Even in today's environment of profound disillusionment, Europe remains the site of one of the most important political and economic experiments of our time, animated by rich intellectual and cultural traditions. But Europe's future will depend on its ability to embrace renewal from the margins in order to live up to its universalism by provincializing it. As the intellectual historian

---

73 François Hartog, *Régimes d'historicité: Présentisme et expériences du temps* (Paris: Éditions du Seuil, 2003).
74 Dipesh Chakrabarty, *Provincializing Europe: Postcolonial Thought and Historical Difference* (Princeton: Princeton University Press, 2000), 3.
75 Stefan-Ludwig Hoffmann, "Human Rights and History," *Past & Present*, 232(1) (August 2016), 279–310, p. 306. Hoffman addresses this question to the universalism of the 1990s more generally, in particular Euro-Atlantic human rights discourse.
76 Chakrabarty illustrated his claim about the indispensability of European thought by developing his own argument out of a reading of Martin Heidegger and Hans-Georg Gadamer. In his work on the Anthropocene, he has similarly relied on a productive engagement with the thought of Karl Jaspers. See Dipesh Chakrabarty, "The Climate of History: Four Theses," *Critical Inquiry*, 35(2) (Winter 2009), 197–222.

J. G. A. Pocock already pointed out during the 1990s, this would also imply a related ability to forge a historical narrative fit for Europe's peculiar contradictions, experiences, and hopes that can undergird such a provincialized universalism.[77] Europe's haphazard handling of the eurocrisis and the arrival of refugees on the continent's shores continue to test the EU's self-image as a bastion of humanitarian reason and a beacon of democracy. In light of managed inhospitability and perennial austerity, European appeals to moral leadership can easily ring hollow today.[78] The EU's "thin cosmopolitanism" appears increasingly all too content with integrating markets and merely fulfilling minimalist human rights norms. In a painful twist of irony, the only ones who still appear to take seriously the preamble of the failed European Constitution that would have described Europe as "a special area of human hope" are the refugees landing on Europe's shores or, all too often, drowning in the Mediterranean. While Europe's politicians are working hard to discourage potential asylum seekers and appear determined to prove that Europe is not a special area of human hope, refugees are voting with their feet for a life in Europe.

[77] J. G. A. Pocock, "Deconstructing Europe," in *The Question of Europe*, ed. Perry Anderson and Peter Gowan (London: Verso, 1997).
[78] These two pithy terms are borrowed from "Europe at a Crossroads," *Near Futures Online*, ed. Wendy Brown and Michel Feher, http://nearfuturesonline.org.

Index

Abbas, Ferhat, 451
Abendroth, Wolfgang, 522
Aberastury, Arminda, 63
Adam, Karl, 347
Adams, John, 204, 206, 392
Addams, Jane, 211, 217, 220, 231
Adler, Alfred, 56–57
Adorno, Theodor W., 14, 17, 25, 68, 274–280, 514, 525
African Americans, 228–230
Agnoli, Johannes, 258
Algeria, 454–455
Ali, Muhammad, 305
alienation, 267
Althusser, Louis, 13, 66, 284, 464, 484–488, 490, 493, 494–495
Amendola, Giovanni, 420
America. *See* United States
  Europe and, 201
Amoroso, Luigi, 364, 378–379
Amrouche, Jean, 457
analytic philosophy *See* philosophy, analytic
Anderson, Perry, 260, 283, 554, 565
Anscombe, Elizabeth, 197
anthropologists, 224
anthropology, 159, 471, 479
  structuralist, 471–479
  US and European mutual influence, 220, 224
anti-communism, 11
antifascism, 421, 427
anti-imperialism, 289, 291–292, 295, 296, 309–310, 439
  major figures
    Gandhi, 299–308
    James, 439–446
  sociogeny, 297–299
anti-Semitism, 91, 149, 254–256, 411, 424, 433

Heidegger, 134
Husserl and, 113
physics and, 90–92
antitotalitarianism, 421–423, 427–428, 429, 435
anxiety, 133, 141
Aquinas, Thomas, 345
Aragon, Louis, 68
Archaeology of Knowledge, The, 508
Arendt, Hannah, 8, 201, 517, 523, 538–539, 540
  public sphere and, 538–539, 541
  totalitarianism and, 9, 417–418, 419–420, 423–427, 431, 433–434, 436
Argentina, psychoanalysis, 63–64, 66
Argentine Psychoanalytic Association (APA), 63, 66
arithmetic, 176–177, 181–182, 184–186, 191
Aron, Raymond, 11, 22, 143, 219, 225, 404–408, 432, 434, 458
Arrow, Kenneth, 226
astronomy, 6
  general relativity and, 78
Atatürk, Kemal, 348
Atlantic Charter, 438, 449–451
Attlee, Clement, 450
atomic bomb, 98
Auboin, Roger, 367, 376
Austin, J. L., 196, 198
Azaldúa, Gloria, 231

Bachelard, Gaston, 99
Badiou, Alain, 484
Baeck, Leo, 341
Baeumler, Alfred, 254
Bakhtin, Mikhail, 493, 502
Baldwin, James, 229–230
Balibar, Étienne, 485, 552–553, 557
Balzac, Honoré de, 21, 470
Barnes, Hazel, 151
Barth, Karl, 5, 130, 338–340, 346, 356–357

569

Barthes, Roland, 13, 99, 208, 464, 469–471, 488, 490, 493–495
Barthian Revolt, 341
Bassiri, Nima, 70
Bataille, Georges, 4, 493
Baudelaire, Charles, 18–19, 21–22, 25, 29, 39, 41–43
Baudin, Louis, 364, 377, 380, 388
Baudrillard, Jean, 490
Beaney, Michael, 178
Beauvoir, Simone de, 12, 129, 257, 312, 316, 322, 323, 330–331, 333, 353
  othering, 151, 326
  Sartre and, 143, 151
  Second Sex, The, 12, 151, 229, 311, 318–321
Bebel, Isaac, 263
Beckett, Samuel, 10, 17
Becquerel, Henri, 84
Bedjaoui, Mohammed, 463
being-in-itself, 140
Bell, Daniel, 219
Bellah, Robert, 231
Benda, Julien, 10
Benedict, Ruth, 216, 221, 472
Benhabib, Seyla, 287, 543
Benjamin, Walter, 9, 21, 22, 29, 39, 40, 41, 165, 281–282, 521
Bentley, Eric, 23–24, 39
Berdyaev, Nikolai, 138, 350–351, 353
Berger, Peter, 125–126
Bergman, Gustav, 190
Bergson, Henri, 4, 87, 92–93, 95, 99, 158, 164, 167, 172–174
  Einstein and, 92–93
Berlin, Isaiah, 9, 196, 398, 408, 423
Berman, Marshall, 22
Bernheim, Hippolyte, 48
Bernstein, Richard J., 212, 214
Berthelot, René, 173
Beveridge, William, 368–370
Beyond the Pleasure Principle, 3, 53–54
Bhabha, Homi K., 67
Big Bang theory, 6
Binet, Alfred, 93
Binswanger, Ludwig, 171
Biologismus-Streit, 160
biology, 155
Black Jacobins, The, 439, 441, 443, 447, 455
Black Panther Party, 230
Blanchot, Maurice, 470, 493
Bloch, Ernst, 262, 281, 356
Bloomsbury Group, 6, 10, 369
bohemia, 10

Bohm, David, 96
Bohr, Niels, 74, 96
Bolshevik Revolution, 5
Bonaparte, Marie, 60
Booth, Charles, 217
Born, Max, 75
Boulanger, Georges, 28
Bourdieu, Pierre, 223, 495
Boutroux, Émile, 157
Brand, Stewart, 231
Brandom, Robert, 214
Brasillach, Robert, 234
Braun, Lily, 315
Brecht, Berthold, 8, 18, 471
Brentano, Franz, 103–104
  Husserl and, 104
Breuer, Josef, 46, 47–48, 52, 56
Britain, 229
British Empire, 296
British Psychoanalytical Society, 61–62
Broyelle, Jacques, 484
Bruller, Jean, 460
Brunner, Emil, 339–340
Brunschwig, Henri, 462
Buber, Martin, 5, 130, 342
Buckley, William, 227
Bultmann, Rudolf, 352–353
Burke, Edmund, 392, 395, 397
Burlingham, Dorothy, 60
Butler, Judith, 231

Callois, Roger, 4
Calvinism, 32, 43
Camus, Albert, 10, 12, 129, 147, 150–151, 428, 454
  anti-imperialism, 454–455
  communism and, 146–148
  early life, 146
Canguilhem, Georges, 172–173, 493
Canovan, Margaret, 424
Carlyle, Thomas, 23, 26, 206
Carman, Taylor, 115
Carnap, Rudolf, 89, 172, 178, 190–191, 193–194, 195
Carson, Rachel, 231
Cassirer, Ernst, 172
Castoriadis, Cornelius, 430, 435
Catholicism, 337, 343, 357
  existentialism and, 139
  Second Vatican Council, 344, 345, 346, 347, 348, 357
  theology, 343–348, 355, 357–358
  Thomism, 5

Cavaillès, Jean, 493
Céline, Louis-Ferdinand, 9, 234
Césaire, Aimé, 228, 298–299, 310
Charcot, Jean-Martin, 46
Chicago School (economics), 226
Chodorow, Nancy, 69, 231
Chomsky, Noam, 222–223
Christian Democracy, 11
Christian existentialism, 136, 140, 354
Christianity, neoliberal economics and, 383–384
Christians, 384
Christology, 358–359
Churchill, Winston, 392, 438, 449–450
citizenship, 559–561
civil disobedience, 300
Civil Rights movement, 150
Cixous, Hélène, 12, 69, 326, 328–330, 333–334, 490, 516
class consciousness, 267
Claus, Carl, 45
Clément, Catherine, 12, 326, 328
Clifford, James, 223
Collège de Sociologie, 10, 30
colonialism, 149
Commons, John, 226
communism
  existentialism and, 140–148
  Stalinist, 144
Communist parties, 142, 260
Comte de Lautréamont, 493
Comte, Auguste, 26, 157, 158, 217, 386
Congar, Yves, 347
consciousness, Freudian, 47
conservatism, 233, 281, 391–392, 395, 400, 416
  liberty and relation to economic and social liberalism, 397–408
  major figures
    Aron, 404–407
    Berlin, 398–400, 408–411
    Hayek, 400–402
    Manent, 414–416
    Oakeshott, 392–396
    Popper, 402–404
    Strauss, 411–413
  moral particularism, 408–416
  reason and, 392–397
conventionalism, 83, 87
Cooley, Charles, 218
Copenhagen criteria, 558
correlationism, 106
  Heidegger, 118
  Merleau-Ponty, 118

critical theory, 15, 262, 271–288
Dialectic of Enlightenment, The, 69, 276–280, 393, 519
dialectical epistemology, 273
major figures
  first generation, 274–284
  Habermas, 520–531
  second generation, 284–286
  third generation, 286–288
  Weber and, 519–520
postcolonial theory and, 287
public sphere and, 517–520
  Habermas, 520–531
  Luhmann, 535–538
  mass media, 532–535
Croly, Herbert, 224
Cuadernos Sigmund Freud, 66
cubism, 72, 211
Culler, Jonathan, 468
cultural pessimism, 236–240
culture, Freud on, 55
Culture-Protestantism, 338

Daily Herald, 450
Dalí, Salvador, 68
Damas, Léon-Gontran, 228, 447, 448–449
Daniel, Jean, 460
Darwin, Charles, 160
Daubert, Johannes, 104
Davis, Angela Y., 230
Debray, Régis, 484
Debré, Jean-Louis, 561
decolonization, 438–439
  Algeria, 454–455
  Haiti, 292, 296, 439–446, 457
  national consciousness and, 458–461
  self-determination, 449–453
  Vietnam, 451, 453
  violence associated with, 453–458
Defert, Daniel, 230
Deledalle, Gérard, 212
Deleuze, Gilles, 99, 173–174, 490–492, g514
Delors, Jacques, 548, 554
Delphy, Christine, 322–323, 325, 330
Derrida, Jacques, 14, 468, 490, 498, 499, 500, 501, 502, 508–509, 510, 514, 561–562
  ethical writing, 16, 343
  psychoanalysis and, 70
  structuralism and, 488–489, 497–498
Deutsche Physik movement, 91
Deutscher, Isaac, 410

Dewey, John, 209, 211–213, 214, 215, 224–225, 227, 397
Dews, Peter, 514
Dialectic of Enlightenment, 69, 276–280, 393, 519
Dickens, Charles, 205
Diderot, Denis, 444–445
Dilthey, Wilhelm, 162
Dinnerstein, Dorothy, 69
Dirac, Paul, 75
Director, Aaron, 364
Djebar, Assia, 311–312, 334
Donato, Eugenio, 496
Dos Passos, John, 200
Douglass, Frederick, 207
Driesch, Hans, 163–164, 167, 169, 171–172, 173
Du Bois, W. E. B., 298, 308–310, 449, 452
Duhem, Pierre, 83, 100
Durkheim, Émile, 2, 4, 22, 26–30, 33, 42, 93, 221
Dussel, Enrique, 287
Dworkin, Andrea, 231
Dyson, Frank Watson, 78

economics, 226, 368, 372–373, 375, 382–383, 390, 393
　Keynesian, 361
　macroeconomics, 374–375
　neoliberal *See* neoliberal economics.
　US–European mutual influence, 224–227
Eddington, Arthur, 78, 81
ego psychology, 61, 69, 468
Einstein, Albert, 6, 72–73, 75, 78–88, 90–99
　influence and peers
　　Bergson, 92–93
　　Husserl, 93
　　Merleau-Ponty, 98
　personal views
　　philosophy of science, 87–88
　　political views, 90
　popular acclaim, 79, 82
　publications
　　"Foundation of the General Theory of Relativity, The," 80
　　"Internationalism and Science," 91
　quantum mechanics and, 96
　relativity theory
　　field equations, 78
Ellison, Ralph, 151, 230
Ely, Richard T., 226
émigrés, 201
Enlightenment, lost ideals, 1
epoché, 107, 108–109

EPU (European Payments Union), 376
Erdoğan, Recep Tayyip, 558
Ernst, Max, 68
Escuela Freudiana de Buenos Aires, 66
Establet, Roger, 484–485
Eucken, Rudolf, 160, 162
Eucken, Walter, 364
Eucken-Erdsieck, Edith, 381
Europe, identity, 545–553
European Council, 561
European Court of Human Rights, 551
European Court of Justice, 389, 547
European Economic Community (EEC), 545–546
European Payments Union (EPU), 376
European Union, 16, 545
　economic integration, 548–551
　expansion and enlargement, 545–547
　　membership criteria, 557–558
　　Turkey and, 558
　institutional identity and purpose, 553–556, 557
　political integration, 551–553
　reversal and resistance, 563–566, 568
　refugees and immigration, 561–562
　treaties and legislation
　　Treaty of Rome, 556
evolutionary theory, 161
existentialism, 4–5, 128–130, 135–140, 142–143, 145, 150–152, 257–258, 464, 470
　Communism and, 140–148
　major figures
　　Heidegger and Jaspers, 131–136
　　Kierkegaard and, 130–131
　　Sartre, 140–146
existentialism, Christian, 136–140, 352–354
existentialism, othering, 148–151, 321, 343, 482

Fabian Society, 270
Fanon, Frantz, 11, 67, 149–150, 299, 458–461
fascism, 9, 234–235, 275, 378–379, 388, 420
Faulkner, William, 200
Fechner, Gustav Theodor, 161, 215
feminism, 311–313, 318
　autobiographies, 334–335
　French, 317
　literary fiction, 6, 316
　materialist, 321–325
　origins and pre-twentieth-century history, 313–314
　psychoanalytic, 325–329
　reinvention and reimagination, 329–334

subversion of norms, 317
Ferenczi, Sándor, 49, 58
Fischer, Emil, 91, 555–556
Fisher, Irving, 372
Foot, Philippa, 197
Forsthoff, Ernst, 244
Forsythe, William, 201
Foucault, Michel, 13–14, 18–20, 21, 42–43, 229–230, 464, 488, 490, 506–510
   Baudelaire and, 21
   ideas
      governmentality, 488
      structuralism, 488
   publications
      Archaeology of Knowledge, The, 508
      Discipline and Punish, 229
      Nietzsche, Genealogy, History, 507
      Order of Things, The, 13, 155, 175, 488, 507, 508
      Truth and Power, 508, 509–510
Fouillé, Alfred, 158
Fouque, Antoinette, 325
fragmentation, political, 568
France
   communism, 142
   crisis of science movement, 75
   phenomenology, 126
   secularism, 2
   separation of church and state, 2
Frankfurt Psychoanalytic Institute, 68
Frankfurt School (of critical theory), 14–15, 68, 97, 262, 271–288
   critique (as concept), 273–274
   social and political theory, 517–520
Fraser, Nancy, 287
free association, 48
Frege, Gottlob, 176–178, 181–186, 187, 188, 190–191, 192–194
French Empire, 453
Freud, Anna, 59–62
   Klein and, 62–64
Freud, Sigmund, 2, 44
   early scientific work, 45–47
   ideas
      art theory, 68
      death drive, 3, 53–54
      ego, 53–55, 56, 59–61, 64–68, 481–482, 492
      id, 53–55, 58–59, 67
      libido, 3, 52–53, 59, 280, 512
      Oedipus complex, 52
      psychosexual development, 52, 59, 61
      sexuality, 52–55, 58
      super-ego, 53–55, 59
   influence and peers
      Althusser, 284
      contemporary, 70
      Jung, 56–57
      Lacan, 65
      Róheim, 67
   patients
      Anna O., 47
      Dora, 50–52
      Irma, 49
   psychoanalysis
      birth of, 47–52
   publications
      Beyond the Pleasure Principle, 53
      Ego and the Id, The, 53, 59
      Fragments of an Analysis of a Case of Hysteria, 50–52
      History of the Psychoanalytic Movement, The, 55–56
      Interpretation of Dreams, The, 48
      Jokes and their Relation to the Unconscious, 49
      Leonardo da Vinci, 68
      Moses of Michelangelo, The, 68
      New Introductory Lectures, 53
      Psychopathology of Everyday Life, The, 49
      Studies on Hysteria, 46, 47
      Three Essays on the Theory of Sexuality, 52
Friedan, Betty, 69, 151, 231
Friedman, Milton, 226, 364, 384
Friedman, Thomas, 564
Frisby, David, 30, 43
Fromm, Erich, 68, 216
Fromm-Reichmann, Frieda, 68
F-scale, 275
Fuchs, Eduard, 282
Fukuyama, Francis, 566

Galton, Francis, 215
Gandhi, Mohandas K., 11, 290, 291, 296–299, 302
   anti-imperialism, 299–308
   civil disobedience / satyagraha, 300, 303, 304
   Hind Swaraj, 301–302
   international influence, 308–309
   labor activism, 303–304
Garvey, Amy Ashwood, 440, 452
Garvey, Marcus, 309
Geddes, Patrick, 217
Gehlen, Arnold, 171
Genet, Jean, 230
Gentile, Giovanni, 7, 210, 234, 418, 420, 422

Index

George Circle, 10
George, Henry, 225
George, Stefan, 23
Giddings, Franklin, 218
Girard, René, 496
globalization, 541–544, 563
Glover, Edward, 62
Gödel, Kurt, 190
Goldmann, Lucien, 262
Goldstein, Kurt, 173
Goldwater, Barry, 226
Göttingen Munich invasion, 104
Gouges, Olympe de, 207, 313
Gramsci, Antonio, 8, 262–263, 268–270, 282, 289, 518, 540
gravitational waves, 77
Greimas, Julien, 470
Griesinger, Wilhelm, 45
Groddeck, Georg, 58
Grupo Lacaniano de Buenos Aires, 66
Guha, Ramachandra, 300
Guillaumin, Colette, 322–324
Gurian, Waldemar, 422
Guyau, Jean-Marie, 158
Guzzo, Augusto, 139

Habermas, Jürgen, 15, 20, 42, 262, 279–280, 284–286, 514, 517. *See also* critical theory
 public sphere
  mature theory, 527–530
  reappraisal, 520–522
  structural transformation, 522–527
Haeckel, Ernst, 161, 162–164, 165, 167–168, 169, 171
Hahn, Hans, 190
Haiti, 292, 296, 439–446, 457
Hall, Stanley, 56, 215
Harlem Renaissance, 228
Harrington, Michael, 231
Hartmann, Eduard von, 61, 158, 161, 164
Hartmann, Heinz, 60
Havel, Václav, 545
Hayek, Friedrich von, 402
Hegel, G. W. F, 24–25, 179, 266, 268, 286, 397, 403, 480, 525
 dialectics, 261
Heidegger, Martin, 4, 94–96, 98, 249, 338, 354, 493, 495, 498
 ideas
  anti-subjectivism, 117
  anxiety, 132, 250
  authenticity, 249–252
  Dasein, 116–117, 118, 120, 123, 131–134, 136, 250–252
  existentialism and, 131–136
  Existenz, 132
  lifeworld, 120
  Nazism, 9, 134, 172, 236, 252, 254
  philosophy of science, 96, 97–98, 119
 other thinkers and
  Derrida, 14
  Husserl and Merleau-Ponty, 115–123
  Sartre, 140–141
 publications
  Basic Problems of Phenomenology, 118
  Being and Time, 95, 115, 116, 118, 123, 131, 133–134, 148, 251–252
Heisenberg, Werner, 74–75, 97
Henry, Michel, 126
heroism, 19, 21–36, 39
 comic attitude, 23–24, 25, 38, 41, 43
 romantic attitude, 23–25
 sociological indifference to, 27
Hess, Moses, 410, 413
Hilbert, David, 78
Himes, Chester, 229
Historians' Controversy, 15
historicism, 386, 402–403
historicity, 134
Hitler, Adolf, 253–255, 403, 407, 419, 421, 431
Hitschmann, Eduard, 58
Hjelmslev, Louis, 469
Hobbes, Thomas, 484
Hobson, John, 293–294, 310
Honneth, Axel, 213
hooks, bell, 230, 335
Horkheimer, Max, 8, 97, 272–273, 274–275, 393
Horney, Karen, 12
Huizinga, Johan, 364
human rights, 11
humanism, 13
Husserl, Edmund, 2, 4, 93, 95, 102
 ideas
  anti-psychologism, 105
  correlationism, 106–110
  epoché, 107, 108–109
  intersubjectivity, 112–113
  spatial objects and extension, 111
  static phenomenology, 114
  temporality, 111–112
  transcendental reduction, 108
 other thinkers and, 105–106, 123
  Brentano, 104
  Heidegger and Merleau-Ponty, 115–123
 publications

Cartesian Meditations, 110
Crisis, 109, 110
Ideas I, 105–107
Lectures on the Phenomenology of the Consciousness of Internal Time, 111
Lectures on Thing and Space, 111
Logical Investigations, 103–107
relativity theory and, 93
hypnosis, 48
Hyppolite, Jean, 496
hysteria
Freud on, sexuality and, 46, 52–55

id, 53–55, 58–59, 67
imperialism, 290
meaning and connotations, 290
India, 291, 296, 300–305, 306–309, 450
communism, 305
nationalism, 303
Indian Uprising (1857), 296
intentionality, 103, 106, 110, 114
International African Friends of Abyssinia (IAFA), 440, 441
International African Service Bureau for the Defence of Africans and People of African Descent (IASB), 441
International Psychoanalytic Association, 56–59, 64, 66, 481, 482–483
interregnum, 289
intersubjectivity, 114
Iqbal, Muhammad, 302, 310
Isaac, Jules, 347
Islam
discrimination against Muslims, 16, 558, 562
theology, 348–349

Jackson, George, 230
Jacob, François, 174–175
Jacobinism *See also Black Jacobins*, 204
Jakobson, Roman, 468–469
James, C. L. R., 439–446, 449
James, Henry, Sr., 209
James, William, 208, 209–211
Jankélévitch, Vladimir, 172
Jaspers, Karl, 11, 135–137, 139–140, 171
Jay, Martin, 266
Jeanson, Francis, 147, 149, 460
Jefferson, Thomas, 204–205, 206–207
Jesus Christ, 341, 346, 347, 357, 358–359

Jews and Judaism, 91, 148–151, 234, 319, 323, 347, 410–411, 424–425. *See also* anti-Semitism; Zionism
theology, 341–343
Jones, Ernest, 44, 59, 61–62
Joyce, James, 337
Judt, Tony, 144
Jung, Carl
Freud and, 56–57
Jünger, Ernst, 9, 244–249, 253–256

Kahane, Max, 57
Kandel, Eric, 70
Kant, Immanuel, 19, 114–115, 156, 163, 167, 176–177, 508, 524, 538. *See also* Neo-Kantianism
analytic philosophy and, 177, 179–181, 185
Critique of Judgment, 156, 157
Husserl and, 110, 114–115
Kautsky, Karl, 263
Kay, Ellen, 314
Keats, John, 443
Kedourie, Elie, 396
Keynes, John Maynard, 6, 361, 366, 369, 373, 374, 375, 378
Khilafat/Non-Cooperation movement, 305–306, 308
Khrushchev, Nikita, 430, 485–486
Kierkegaard, Søren, 5, 130–132, 135, 342, 351, 353
existentialism and, 130–131
King, Martin Luther, Jr., 230
Kirk, Russell, 227, 395
Kisiel, Theodore, 131
Klein, Melanie, 61–64
Kloppenberg, James T., 200
Kluckhohn, Clyde, 221
Klug, Sam, 200
Knight, Frank, 226, 364, 383
Koebner, Richard, 290
Koffka, Kurt, 211
Kofman, Sarah, 332–333
Köhler, Wolfgang, 211
Kohut, Heinz, 61
Kojève, Alexandre, 148, 411
Korsch, Karl, 270–271
Koselleck, Reinhart, 19
Koyré, Alexander, 100
Kreis, George, 36
Krieck, Ernst, 254
Kripke, Saul, 199
Kris, Ernst, 59
Kristeva, Julia, 12, 501–506

Kroeber, Alfred, 221
Krug, Wilhelm Traugott, 159
Kuhn, Thomas, 100, 219
Kulpe, Oswald, 163

Lacan, Jacques, 64–67, 68, 479, 484, 487, 493, 494–495, 497, 504
   influence, 326
   structuralism and, 469, 479–484
Lacanism, 64–67
Lachelier, Jules, 157
Lakatos, Imre, 402
Lamarck, Jean-Baptiste de, 155
Lamming, Georges, 149
Landauer, Karl, 68
Langevin, Paul, 82
LaPorte, Paul M., 72
Laroui, Fouad, 349
Laski, Harold, 393
Latour, Bruno, 20
law, international, 542–544
Lawrence, D. H., 23
Le Play, Frédéric, 217
Le Roy, Édouard, 83
Le Senne, René, 138–139
Le Verrier, Urbain, 79
League for the Protection of Mothers, 314
League of Jewish Women, 315
League of Nations, 90
Lebensphilosophie, 4, 153, 154
   bio-politics and, 169–172
   Darwinism and, 160
   epistemological borders, 165–167
   life as concept, 155–158
   neo-Kantianism and, 161–165
   nineteenth century, 158–165
   phenomenology and, 167–169
   post-structuralism as, 172–175
Lefebvre, Henri, 145
Lefort, Claude, 417–418, 420, 429–436
Leiris, Michel, 460
Lenard, Philipp, 90, 91
Lenin, Vladimir, 6, 36, 270, 295–296, 306, 310, 440
Leoni, Bruno, 364
Lerner, Gerda, 231
Les Temps Modernes, 11
Levellers, 204
Lévinas, Emmanuel, 148, 343
Lévi-Strauss, Claude, 13, 469
Lévy, Benny, 484

Lévy, Bernard-Henri, 15
Lévy-Bruhl, Lucien, 93
Lewis, David, 199, 214
liberalism, 35, 227, 380, 382, 539
   conservatism and, 397–408
   neoliberal economics and, 361, 365, 370, 383
   totalitarianism and, 240–242, 253, 258, 379, 381, 423, 428, 526
liberty, 9, 397–408
libido, 3, 52–53, 59, 280, 512
Lieber, Francis, 201
Liebersohn, Harry, 35, 36, 37, 42
life sciences, 163
Lincoln, Abraham, 207
linguistics, 465–468
   structuralist, 13, 27, 484, 495
Lippmann, Walter, 210, 224–225, 364–365, 380–382, 387
Lipps, Theodor, 104
Lloyd George, David, 368
Locke, John, 204, 394, 397, 484
Loewenstein, Rudolph, 59, 64
logic, 177
   Fregean predicate, 182–186
   Husserl on, 104
   principles of, 182, 187
Lorentz, Hendrik, 75, 76, 84–87, 91, 93
Lotze, Hermann, 157
Lowie, Robert, 473
Lubac, Henri de, 344–345
Luckmann, Thomas, 125–126
Luhmann, Niklas, 535–538
Lukács, Georg, 8, 262, 264–268, 270–271, 274, 279, 283
Lunbeck, Elizabeth, 61
Luther, Martin, 131
Lynd, Robert and Helen, 218

Maastricht Treaty, 545
Macdonald, Dwight, 219
Mach, Ernst, 87–88, 90, 190
Macherey, Pierre, 484–485
Macksey, Richard, 496
macroeconomics, 373, 374–375
Madagascar, 454
Madison, James, 115, 206
Madrid, train bombings, 16
Makari, George, 57
Malcolm X, 229–230
Mandela, Nelson, 309
Manent, Pierre, 414–415
Manjapra, Kris, 222
Mann, Heinrich, 8

Index

Mann, Thomas, 8, 237
Mannheim, Karl, 37
Marcel, Gabriel, 5, 129, 136–138, 352, 353, 354
Marcus, George, 223
Marcuse, Herbert, 8, 68, 174, 201, 280–281
Marion, Jean-Luc, 16, 355
Maritain, Jacques, 11, 344, 559
Marjolin, Robert, 364, 367, 372, 376–377, 387
Marlio, Louis, 364
Marshall Plan, 372
Martineau, Harriet, 205
Martyr, Peter, 202
Marx, Karl, 267, 427, 429, 493–494
Marxism, 174, 264
    feminism and, 322
    Indian, 306
    structuralism and, 484–487
    Western, 259–264
        as German concept, 283–284
        dialectical method, 261, 266
        Soviet Communism and, 260–261
masculinity, 246–247
Maslow, Abraham, 216
Masotta, Oscar, 66–67
mass communication and media, 532–535
mathematics, foundations of, 177, 181, 188, 191
Mathieu, Nicole-Claude, 322, 324–325
Maurras, Charles, 234
Mauss, Marcel, 4, 221, 472
McNamara, Kathleen, 550
Mead, George Herbert, 213–214, 215, 216, 227
Mead, Margaret, 216, 221
Memmi, Albert, 149
Mercury, 80
Merleau-Ponty, Maurice, 98, 114, 123, 143–145, 150, 173, 405, 429, 431–432
    ideas
        correlationism, 118
        subjectivity, 120–121
    other thinkers and
        Einstein, 98
        Heidegger and Husserl, 115–123
    publications
        Phenomenology of Perception, 118
        Structure of Behavior, The, 122
Merton, Robert K., 101, 218–219
Meyer, Frank, 227
Meynert, Theodor, 45–47
Michelson–Morley experiment, 81, 84, 94
Mill, John Stuart, 179, 185, 207, 219, 400
Mill, Taylor, 207
Miller, Jacques-Alain, 484
Millett, Kate, 69

Mills, C. Wright, 219
Minkowski, Hermann, 74
Minogue, Kenneth, 397
Miró, Joan, 68
Mitzman, Arthur, 32, 36
modernity, 20, 21
    as heroization of the present, 18–20, 22–43
    comic attitude, 23–24, 25, 38, 41, 43
    Foucault on, 21
    heroism and, 27
    ironic approach to self-understanding, 20
    progress and, 26
    romantic attitude, 23–25
    sociology and, 25
Moltmann, Jürgen, 356–357, 358
Mommsen, Wolfgang, 35
Monism, 163
Monod, Jacques, 174, 175
Mont Pèlerin Society, 225, 370–372
Montaigne, Michel de, 203, 396
Montanton, Georges, 472
Moore, G. E., 176, 179–180, 189, 196
Morant Bay Uprising, 296
Moravcsik, Andrew, 564
More, Thomas, 202
Morgan, Lewis Henry, 223
Moritz, Karl Philipp, 159
Morocco, 556
Morrison, Toni, 230
Moscow Linguistic Circle, 468
Mouffe, Chantal, 539–541
Movement, Non-Aligned, 289
Moyn, Samuel, 70
Müller-Armack, Alfred, 364, 366, 370, 383
Münsterberg, Hugo, 215
Murad, Shaykh Abdal Hakim, 349
Murdock, George, 222
Murray, John Courtney, 231
Musil, Robert, 237
Muslims, 16
Mussolini, Benito, 3, 210, 420, 422, 431, 440

Napoleon III, 21
Nardal, Paulette and Jane, 228
nationalism, 10, 234
    India, 303
Naturphilosophie, 156
Naville, Pierre, 446, 455–456
Nazism, 9, 91, 134, 235–236, 253–256, 275
    Husserl and, 113
    Lebensphilosophie and, 154
    postwar assessment of, 14
Negri, Antonio, 553

négritude, 228
Neo-Kantianism, 2, 153, 161, 163, 164, 166–167, 168, 170
neoliberal economics, 226, 361–377
　Christianity and, 383–384
　early transnationalism, 366–367
　fascism and, 378–379, 388
　Keynesianism and, 375–376
　macroeconomics and, 373, 374–375
　Mont Pèlerin Society, 225, 370–372
　price mechanism, 363, 384, 385, 387
　social welfare and, 368–370
　societal and state concepts, 380–383
　values and concepts, 376–388
　Walter Lippmann Colloquium, 364–366
Neptune, 79–80
Neurath, Otto, 190
New Republic, The, 224
New York Times, 79, 81–82, 101, 200, 564
Niemöller, Martin, 340
Nietzsche, Friedrich, 13, 32–33, 40, 136
　other thinkers and, 158
　　Deleuze, 173
　vitalism and, 165–166
Nkrumah, Kwame, 229, 309–310, 446, 452, 462
Non-Cooperation movement, 305–306, 308
Norway, 546

Oakeshott, Michael, 392–396, 400–402, 404
Obama, Barack, 230
objectivity, 1
objects, spatial, 111
Ogburn, William, 218
Ogden, C. K., 189
Oppenheimer, Robert, 97
ordoliberalism, 370, 382, 387
Ortigues, Marie-Cécile and Edmund, 67
Orwell, George, 11
othering, 148–151, 229, 321, 343, 482

Padmore, George, 229, 440–442, 449–450, 452
Paine, Thomas, 204–205, 444
Pan-African Congresses, 452
Pan-Africanism, 309, 441, 452
Pankhurst, Emmeline, 314
Papini, Giovanni, 210
Pappenheim, Bertha, 47, 315
Pareyson, Luigi, 139
Paris Noir, 150
Park, Robert, 217
Parsons, Talcott, 27, 33, 35, 218–219, 221–222, 535

Pasteur, Louis, 73
Payne, Sylvia, 62
Peano, Giuseppe, 178, 181, 188
Péguy, Charles, 415–416
Peirce, Charles Sanders, 208–209, 211, 213–215
Periyar, 306
Pfänder, Alexander, 104
phenomenology, 4, 103, 210
　definitions, 103
　existence and non-existence, 110
　generative, 114
　genetic, 114
　historical overview, 102
　Husserl
　　spatio-temporal issues, 110–112
　influence and importance, 102
　Lebensphilosophie and, 168–169
　ontological content, 119–120
　post-Husserl, 115–123
　science and, 93
　sociology, 123–126
　static, 114
　subjectivity and, 117, 120–121
　vitalism and, 167–169
philosophy, 513
　American pragmatism, 208–214
　analytic, 7, 89, 176–178
　　decompositional analysis, 178
　　interwar, 186–189
　　logical positivism/empiricism, 88–89, 191–194, 195
　　ordinary language philosophy, 195–199
　　propositional analysis, 192–194
　Continental, 89, 102, 214
　　post-structuralist, 511–513
　Enlightenment, 155
　of life *See Lebensphilosophie*.
　religious, 349–355
　science and, 157
　transcendental, 105
　transcendental idealism, 105, 110
physics
　See also relativity: quantum mechanics, 93
　anti-Semitism and, 90–92
　Continental philosophy and, 92–93
　pre-modern crisis, 75–77
　technologies derived from, 73
Piaget, Jean, 284
Picasso, Pablo, 72, 211, 231
Pinel, Philippe, 480
Pinsker, Leo, 413
Planck, Max, 75, 84

Poincaré, Henri, 75–77, 80, 83–84, 86, 87, 93, 100
   St. Louis World's Fair presentation, 77
Poincaré, Raymond, 76
Polanyi, Michael, 225
political science, 227–228
   US and European mutual influence, 228
Politzer, Georges, 173
Popper, Karl, 89, 364, 385–387, 412, 423, 428
   conservatism and, 402–404
positivism, 2, 386
postcolonial theory, 287
postmodernism, 20, 29, 464, 491
post-structuralism, 14, 172, 175, 223, 488–489, 490–494, 513, 516
   core characteristics, 491–492
   historical analysis, 506–511
   intellectual antecedents, 493
   key figures
      Baudrillard, 490
      Derrida, 490, 497–501
      Foucault, 490, 506–511
      Kristeva, 501–506
   Lebensphilosophie and, 172–175
   structuralism and, 493–501
Prague Linguistic Circle, 469
Prezzolini, Giuseppe, 210
price mechanism, 363
prisons, 229–230, 509
psychoanalysis, 44, 47–48, 49–50, 55–57, 58–60, 63–69, 332–334, 479–482, 484–485
   as global movement, 55–61
   as science, 2, 55
   contemporary status, 69–70
   feminism and, 325–329
   history, 45, 56
   intellectual influence, 68–69
   Kleinianism, 61–64
   Lacanism, 64–67
   orthodoxy, 58–59
   professional associations, 57
   structuralism and, 479–484
psychologism, 2, 104–105, 169, 177, 180
psychology, 215–217
   US and European, 217
public intellectuals, 10
public sphere, 73, 517–544
   Arendt on, 538–539, 541
   globalization and, 541–544
   Habermas on, 520–522, 527–530
   Luhmann on, 535–538
   mass media and, 532–535
   Mouffe on, 539–541

Puccini, Giacomo, 10
Putnam, Hilary, 212, 214

quantum mechanics, 96–97
   concepts and interpretation
   Copenhagen interpretation, 75
   non-locality, 74
   quantum jumps, 74
   uncertainty relation, 74
   relativity theory and, 97
   technological influence, 73
   wave–particle duality, 74
Quetelet, Adolphe, 217
Quine, Willard Van Orman, 100, 195, 198, 214

race and racism, 297–299, 323, 471–472
Rahner, Karl, 345–346, 355
Ramadan, Tariq, 349
Ramsey, Frank, 189
Rancière, Jacques, 484
Rand, Ayn, 226
Rassemblement Démocratique Révolutionnaire, 144
Ratzinger, Joseph, 347
Rauschenbusch, Walter, 231
Ravaisson, Félix, 156–157
Rawls, John, 197, 227, 540
Raynal, Abbé Guillaume Thomas, 204, 444–445
Reagan, Ronald, 226
realism, spiritual, 157
Reich, Wilhelm, 58, 174, 255–256
Reichenbach, Hans, 88–89
Reinach, Adolf, 104–105
Reitler, Rudolf, 57
relativity theory
   conceptual innovations, 74
   general, 6, 78, 86
      experimental confirmation, 78–81
   philosophical critiques, 93–96
   popularization, 81–82
   quantum mechanics and, 97
   relativity principle, 78, 85
   special, 6, 81
   technology derived from, 73
religion. *See* theology
Renan, Ernest, 75
Rescher, Nicholas, 214
Rich, Adrienne, 231
Rickert, Heinrich, 31, 153, 163–165, 167
Ricœur, Paul, 137, 353–354
Right-wing politics, 233–236, 256–258
Riviere, Joan, 12

Robbins, Lionel, 364
Robeson, Paul, 441
Rodrik, Dani, 563
Rogers, Carl, 216
Róheim, Géza, 67
Roland, Pauline, 207
romantic, 23
Romanticism, 153, 159, 162, 409
Röntgen, Wilhelm, 84
Roosevelt, Franklin D., 200, 411, 438, 449, 451
Roosevelt, Theodore, 210
Rorty, Richard, 212, 214, 227
Rosaldo, Michelle Zimbalist, 223
Rosaldo, Renato, 223
Rosanvallon, Pierre, 553
Rosenberg, Alfred, 171
Rosenzweig, Franz, 5, 342
Ross, Edward A., 218
Rougier, Louis, 364
Rousseau, Jean-Jacques, 204–205, 400–401, 445, 484, 524
Rousset, David, 144
Roy, M. N., 306
Russell, Bertrand, 7, 11, 172, 176–177, 179–181, 184, 185–189, 190–192, 195
Russia, Bolshevik Revolution, 5
Rüstow, Alexander, 364, 377, 381, 387
Ruyer, Raymond, 173
Ryle, Gilbert, 195, 198

Said, Edward, 223
Saint-Domingue, 314, 440, 442
Samuelson, Paul, 226
Sandel, Michael, 227
Sarraute, Nathalie, 460
Sartre, Jean-Paul, 11–13, 140–143, 146–147, 148–151, 257, 318–319, 430, 455, 459–461
  early life, 140
  ideas
    American culture, 200–201
    being-in-itself, 140–141
    communism, 143–145
    transcendence and nothingness, 141
  other thinkers and
    Camus, 147–148
    influences, 140
    Merleau-Ponty, 144
  publications
    Anti-Semite and Jew, 148–151
    Being and Nothingness, 128, 140, 143, 148
    Critique of Dialectical Reason, 143
    Dirty Hands, 145
    Existentialism Is a Humanism, 143

Saussure, Ferdinand de, 208, 464–468, 495, 512
Scaff, Lawrence A., 31, 36, 37
Scharpf, Fritz, 563
Scheler, Max, 4, 105, 160, 167–171, 172–173, 354
Schelling, Friedrich, 89, 156, 174, 342
Schiller, F. C. S., 210
Schlick, Moritz, 190–193, 194–196
Schmitt, Carl, 7, 35, 235–236, 257–258, 422, 540
  influence, 367, 517, 526, 539
  liberalism and, 379, 381, 391, 422, 525, 539
  Nazism and, 254, 255–256
  total state, 7, 240–244, 422
Schoenberg, Arnold, 8
Schopenhauer, Arthur, 37, 160, 161, 165–167
Schrödinger, Erwin, 75, 96
Schroeder, Ralph, 31
Schumpeter, Joseph, 294–295, 310, 372
Schüssler-Fiorenza, Elisabeth, 358
Schutz, Alfred, 123–125, 211
schwarze Korps, Das, 255
science, 2
  analytic philosophy and, 177
  philosophy and theories of
    conventionalist, 83, 87
    falsificationism, 89, 403
    Frankfurt School, 97
    Kuhn, 219
    logical positivism, 88, 90, 95, 102, 174, 208
    relativity, 93–96
scientism, 119, 385
Scott, David, 445
Seigel, Jerrold, 10
semiology, 465, 467, 470, 471
Senghor, Léopold, 228, 309
sensation, 193
Shestov, Lev, 139, 351
Shusterman, Richard, 214
Sidgwick, Henry, 179, 210
Siewert, Charles, 103
Simmel, Georg, 26, 30–31, 37–43, 166–167, 172, 264
Simons, Henry, 364, 382
Simpson, George, 27, 28
skepticism, 108, 192
slavery, 206–207, 323–324, 331, 445
Smith, Adam, 205
Smuts, Jan, 452
Social Democratic Party (Germany), 522
Social Studies of Knowledge (SSK), 101
sociogenic principle, 297
sociology
  French, 30
  phenomenological, 123–126

Index

systems theory, 517, 535–538, 542
    US and European, 217–220
Solms, Mark, 70
Solzhenitsyn, Aleksandr, 15
Sombart, Werner, 26
Sorel, Georges, 3, 234
Soros, George, 403
South Africa, 300–301, 303, 304
Soviet Union, 6, 260, 420
    collapse, 16
space, relativistic conception, 74
Sparks, Jared, 206
Spencer, Herbert, 26, 27, 39, 217
Spengler, Oswald, 3, 23, 130, 170, 235, 236–240, 241, 253–256, 258
Spiegelberg, Herbert, 134
Spock, Benjamin, 70, 217
St. Gaudens, Augustus, 210
Stalin, Josef, 144, 419, 421, 428, 430, 433, 439–440, 485
Stark, Johannes, 90–91
state, absolutist, 7
Stebbing, Susan, 196
Stein, Edith, 354
Stein, Gertrude, 201, 210
Stekel, Wilhelm, 57
Stöcker, Helene, 314
Stovall, Tyler, 150
Strauss, Leo, 9, 201, 227, 411–414, 416
Strawson, Peter, 193
structuralism, 13, 464–465
    anthropology, 471–479
    linguistics, 13, 27, 465–468, 484, 495
    literary fiction and criticism, 468–471
    major figures
        Althusser, 484–487
        Barthes, 469–471
        Jakobson, 468–469
        Lacan, 479–484
        Lévi-Strauss, 469, 471–479, 494
        Saussure, 465–468
    post-structuralism, 488–489, 493–501
    post-structuralism and, 479–484
    psychoanalysis, 476–477, 479–484
subject, laboring, 304
subjectivity
    Heidegger and, 117
    Merleau-Ponty on, 120–121
swaraj, 300
systems theory, 517, 535–538, 542

Taine, Hippolyte, 75
Talmon, Jacob, 418, 428, 432, 433–434

Tarski, Alfred, 192
Thatcher, Margaret, 15, 226, 397
theology, 4–5, 11, 336–337, 338–339, 346, 354, 356, 360, 412
    Barth, 338–341
    Catholic, 343–348, 355, 357–358
    Christology, 358–359
    Islamic, 348–349
    Jewish, 341–343
    Protestant, 338–341, 356–357
Thieme, Karl, 347
Third International, 260
Third Reich, 154. *See also* Nazism
Third World, 458–460, 485–486
Thomism, 5, 138, 343
Thoreau, Henry David, 206, 302
Tillich, Paul, 5, 130, 352–353
time, 95, 102, 111–114, 133, 311, 316, 492, 494, 501
    Heidegger on, 94
    Husserl on, 111–112
    relativistic conception, 74, 93
Times, The, 79
Titchener, Edward, 216
Tolstoy, Leo, 302
Tönnies, Ferdinand, 31
totalitarianism, 9, 417–420, 436–437
    antitotalitarianism, 421–423, 427–428, 429, 435
    theorists
        Arendt, 423–429
        Gurian, 422–423
        Lefort, 429–436
    total state, 242, 243, 244, 256, 420–423
Toussaint L'Ouverture, François-Dominique, 443–446
Toynbee, Arnold, 256
transcendental reduction, 108
Treviranus, Gottfried Reinhold, 155
Troeltsch, Ernst, 339
Trotsky, Leon, 428, 431, 440
Trouillot, Michel-Rolph, 444
Trubetzkoy, Nikolai, 469, 479
Turkey, 348, 558
    EU membership, 558
Turner, Stephen, 35
twin paradox, 82

Uexküll, Jakob Johann von, 167
United Nations, 11, 344, 408, 450, 451–452, 517
United States, 201–204, 205, 228–230, 287, 353, 428–429, 449, 496, 515
    Declaration of Independence, 205
    discovery and colonization of America, 202–204

United States (cont.)
   émigrés, 201
   European influence on and from
      African Americans, 228–230
      American pragmatism, 208–214
      anthropology, 220–224
      artists and critics, 231
      economics, 224–227
      image of US, 206
      nineteenth century, 206–208
      political thought, 204–205, 228
      psychology, 217
      sociology, 217–220
   Sartre on, 200–201

Vatican II, 344, 345, 346, 347, 348, 357
Vespucci, Amerigo, 202
Vidal-Naquet, Pierre, 460
Vienna Circle, 6, 87, 88, 89, 90, 190–191, 193–195, 198
Vienna Psychoanalytic Society, 56
Vietnam, 451
vitalism. *See* Lebensphilosophie
vogue nègre, 228
Völkisch movement, 154

Wagner, Richard, 23
Wahl, Jean, 139–140
Waismann, Friedrich, 190
Walter Lippmann Colloquium, 364–366
Walzer, Michael, 227
war, 246
Watkins, Susan, 565
Watson, John B., 216
Webb, Beatrice and Sidney, 218
Weber, Max, 1, 30–39, 43, 123, 217–218, 264–265, 278, 518–520
Wednesday Psychological Society, 57
Weil, Felix, 271
Weimar Republic, 169

Weiß, Johannes, 338
Weizmann, Chaim, 410
welfare state, 368, 370, 427, 436, 525–526, 527, 542, 552
Wells, Ida B., 230
Wertheimer, Max, 211
Wertphilosophie, 164
Western Marxism *See* Marxism, Western
Whimster, Sam, 31, 32, 33, 35
Whitehead, Alfred North, 7, 186, 198
Wiener, Norbert, 231
Wilder, Gary, 445
Williams, Raymond, 290
Wilson, E. O., 223, 224
Wilson, Woodrow, 224
Winch, Peter, 197
Windelband, Wilhelm, 164
Wing, Betsy, 30
Winter, Timothy John, 349
Wisdom, John, 196
Wittgenstein, Ludwig, 7, 187–189, 190–199
Wittgenstein, Paul, 188
Wittig, Monique, 321
Wolf, Christa, 312
Wolff, Kurt H., 30, 159
Wollstonecraft, Mary, 207, 313
women's suffrage movement, 314
Woolf, Virginia, 6, 316
Wordsworth, William, 441, 443
World War I, 169
Wright, Richard, 129, 150–151, 201
Wynter, Sylvia, 291, 297

Yeats, William Butler, 3

Zeman, Miloš, 558
Zetkin, Clara, 315
Zilsel, Edgar, 172
Zionism, 90, 410–411, 413
Zola, Émile, 10